THE BEST OF Sunset

Over 500 All-time Favorite Recipes from the Magazine of Western Living

Layered Cheese Torta with Pesto (recipe, page 17)

By the Editors of Sunset Books
and Sunset Magazine

Sunset Publishing Corporation ■ Menlo Park, California

Giant Flour Tortilla Taco (page 95) demonstrates the bold spirit of Western cuisine: grand scale, Mexican influence, colorful fresh ingredients, and easy informality.

BOOK EDITORS
**Jerry Anne Di Vecchio
Home Economics Editor,
Sunset Magazine**

**Elizabeth L. Hogan
Managing Editor,
Sunset Books**

CONTRIBUTING EDITORS
Susan Warton

Rebecca LaBrum

Barbara J. Braasch

COORDINATING EDITOR
Linda J. Selden

DESIGN
Williams & Ziller Design

ABOUT THE BEST OF SUNSET

The more than 500 recipes in this book represent the best of *Sunset*'s collection over half a century—and the best of the West's exciting panorama of regional foods.

Throughout this book, you'll occasionally see recipes flagged as **"WESTERN CLASSICS."** These dishes are part of the West's history, were created here in the West, and often showcase ingredients indigenous to this region. Many also have an informal spirit typical of our Western life style.

For almost every recipe, we provide a **NUTRITIONAL ANALYSIS** prepared by Hill Nutrition Associates, Inc., of New York, stating calorie count; grams of protein, carbohydrate, and total fat; and milligrams of cholesterol and sodium. Nutritional information is usually stated for a single serving, based on the largest number of servings listed for each recipe (for example, if a recipe yields 6 to 8 servings, figures are given for ⅛ of the recipe). In some cases, though, you'll notice that the analysis applies to a different unit of measurement—"per tablespoon" for sauces, "per cooky" for cookies, and so forth.

The nutritional analysis does not include optional ingredients or those for which no specific amount is stated (salt to be added to taste, for example). If an ingredient is listed with an option— "butter or margarine," "plain yogurt or sour cream"—the information was calculated using the *first* choice. Likewise, if a range is given for the amount of an ingredient ("½ to 1 cup butter"), values were figured based on the first, lower amount.

Also given for most recipes, **PREPARATION AND COOKING TIMES** are based on having all ingredients at hand and ready to go. Unless otherwise specified, times were reckoned on the basis of slower preparation methods—chopping by hand rather than with a food processor, for example. We suggest you use our preparation times as a general guide only, since every cook works differently—and may prepare a particular dish more quickly or more slowly than we've indicated, based on kitchen organization, familiarity and any number of other factors.

Great adventures await you, your family, and your guests as you sample the *Best of Sunset*. We hope it gives you as savory an experience in the using as it has given us in its preparation.

PHOTOGRAPHERS: **Victor Budnik,** 130, 278; **Glenn Christiansen,** 2, 6 left, 9, 22, 57, 73, 88, 138, 143, 153, 156, 167, 170, 202, 230, 237, 243, 260, 270; **Norman A. Plate,** 1, 65, 76, 101, 112, 145, 191, 196, 218; **Teri Sandison,** 128; **David Stubbs,** 28, 277; **Michael Thompson,** 8 top; **Darrow M. Watt,** 4, 6 right, 7, 8 bottom, 10, 15, 19, 27, 33, 36, 44, 60, 68, 84, 104, 114, 117, 119, 122, 148, 160, 178, 193, 205, 215, 226, 246, 254, 259, 262, 267, 275; **Tom Wyatt,** 52, 75, 93, 96, 109, 140, 165, 183, 194, 208, 216, 223, 235, 238, 244, 251; **Nikolay Zurek,** 41, 49, 81, 127, 135, 173, 176, 186, 201, 213.

Front cover: Cracked Crab Feast, page 14. Design: Williams & Ziller Design. Photograph by Darrow M. Watt.

Back cover: Fruit-filled Cooky Baskets, page 256. Photograph by Darrow M. Watt.

Editor, Sunset Magazine: William Marken
Editor, Sunset Books: Elizabeth L. Hogan

Fifth printing January 1992

CONTENTS

Special Features

Nearly 60 Years of Western Publishing

People who live or travel in the West—along with many who stay east of the Rockies—know *Sunset* well as both the "Magazine of Western Living" and a series of popular softcover books on cooking, travel, gardening, and home improvement. For almost six decades, Lane Publishing Company of Menlo Park, California has reported in *Sunset* on the West's unique lifestyle, shaped by history, climate, and geography.

Today's *Sunset* hardly resembles the promotional vehicle created by the Southern Pacific Railroad in 1898, though its name derives from the *Sunset Limited*, a crack train that ran from Los Angeles to New Orleans. The original magazine simply promoted travel to the West Coast; some years later, in 1914, it was sold to a group of its staff members and became, for a short time, a literary periodical. Then, in September of 1928, Laurence W. Lane bought the magazine and launched the publication on its present course.

As sales manager for Meredith Publishing Company (publisher of *Better Homes & Gardens*), Kansas-born Lane came to know the West well. He recognized the need for a regional magazine that served Westerners in specialized ways no national publication could provide. A full-page announcement in the January, 1929, *Sunset* gave readers a preview of what was coming under Lane ownership: "The new *Sunset* will cover the whole range of home-life and family interests with timely and practical suggestions on gardening, building, home-decorating and furnishings, cooking and home management, traveling, enjoying outdoor life, and a host of other subjects of equal interest to men and women."

In the half century since that pronouncement, despite a few changes in style, *Sunset* has essentially kept to Lane's original plan for a regional family magazine. Still owned by the Lane family, today's magazine and books emphasize gardening, cooking, home improvement, and travel. The magazine focuses on regional interests of the 13 Western states (covering the area from the Rocky Mountains to the Pacific Ocean, and including Alaska and Hawaii). Today, zoned editions—Northwest, Southern California, Central West, and Desert—give more localized information to portions of the West.

The first issue of Sunset *under L. W. Lane's ownership appeared in February of 1929, with a Maurice Logan cover.*

Early *Sunset* covers were illustrated by artwork (including some by celebrated Western painters). In 1936, the first photograph appeared on a cover, and before long, photographed covers were the rule. At the same time, magazine photographs—valued for their greater realism—began to replace artwork. Color photography wasn't seen in the magazine until the 1954 Christmas issue, which boasted five colorful pages of baking and decorating ideas.

Since the late 1930s, *Sunset* has been completely staff-written. The masthead, which lists editors and their fields of responsibility, includes the name *The Pacific Monthly*—a subtitle dating from 1912, when *Sunset* consolidated with a Northwestern magazine of that name.

Originally based in San Francisco, *Sunset* relocated its headquarters in 1951, moving down

This panel from the late 1930s, early 1940s shows how greatly Kitchen Cabinet has changed over the years —in both its design and recipe style.

the Peninsula to new residential-style offices on a portion of an historic Spanish land grant in Menlo Park. Designed by architectural designer Cliff May, the handsome adobe building looks out on a sweeping garden that features native Western plants. In 1965, a second May-designed building was added for the growing *Sunset* Book Division. Along with our recent new building, Willow West, which opened in 1984, *Sunset*'s headquarters have become known to visitors as the "Laboratory of Western Living." Tours are available daily during office hours of *Sunset*'s test kitchens, photography studios, workshops, gardens, and editorial offices.

Kitchen Cabinet

Reader participation in *Sunset*'s adventures with food has been valued from the start. Our ever-popular Kitchen Cabinet feature appeared in Lane's first issue in February 1929, with this caption: "Our heroine discovers a new recipe department...a recipe exchange." Then as now, this monthly collection of reader-submitted recipes helped us keep up with Western trends in food, letting us know what readers liked and what they were cooking at home.

The feature occupied two pages, running step-by-step illustrations down the outside margins, as shown at left. Artists, art styles, and formats have changed over the years. Ruth Taylor White illustrated the first Kitchen Cabinet (hers is the example shown here); Antonio Sotomayor took over in the 1940s, Frank Stauffacher in the 1950s, and Jack Fagan in the 1960s. Our present artist is Alice Harth.

Chefs of the West

"Some men have learned to cook through necessity, others by accident (masters of one dish), a few because they have found in cooking a challenge to their creative skill, many because they like to eat. To the expert of the campfire and barbecue, to the one-dish chef and to masters of the culinary art, we dedicate this page." These words introduced an exciting new column "by men...for men"—

Harry Diamond illustrated Chefs of the West for more than 30 years with humorous art spots.

Chefs of the West—in March 1940. Like Kitchen Cabinet, Chefs of the West included recipes submitted by readers— but only male readers. Such men had already described their cooking adventures in Kitchen Rangers, a column that appeared briefly in 1933.

Humorous illustration has always added greatly to the appeal of Chefs of the West. Harry O. Diamond, whose work is shown above, produced a parade of fanciful drawings from 1952 until 1983. Recently, Dave Broad has enhanced the recipes with his own brand of mischief.

Testing, Tasting...then Publishing

Careful testing has been a cardinal rule at *Sunset* from its earliest days, when Mrs. L.W. Lane tried out every reader-submitted recipe in her own kitchen. An avid gardener, she also tested ideas for growing fruits and vegetables.

In both its gardens and its kitchens, *Sunset* has continued the testing-and-retesting tradition established by Ruth Lane. The first in-house test kitchens came with the move to Menlo Park; over time, they've been expanded and remodeled to keep up to date. Today's staff of food editors are all home economists, bringing creativity as well as technical knowledge to recipe development. And as we refine our recipes, we always keep our audience in mind, using tools and equipment our readers have at home.

Just how does a recipe reach the pages of *Sunset?* The first step, of course, is selection. Some recipes are taken from reader contributions or from interviews with good cooks, either home or professional. Others are developed by our staff to address particular foods or specific needs—we may want recipes using Asian pears, for example, or unusual make-ahead main dishes for parties. Once a recipe has been chosen, it's prepared by a food editor and submitted to a taste panel (drawn from the magazine staff) for a candid rating. Ballots are gathered and evaluated—and dishes that make the grade are refined to ensure that the preparation is as simple as possible, the results reliable, and the taste sensational. The food must look

Recipes don't reach publication in Sunset Magazine *until thoroughly tested for method, reliability, and great taste.*

A favorite stop for tours of Sunset's South Willow *building is the magazine editorial test kitchen, where visitors can see staff home economists developing, testing, and tasting recipes before publication.*

appetizing, too—and in the studio next door to the kitchens, photographers can immediately capture on film either finished dishes or those in states of preparation.

Finally, when the editor in charge has polished the recipe and written it in a form she feels is easy to follow, a retester (not a home economist, but simply someone who enjoys cooking) prepares the dish in our kitchens exactly as it's written.

Wining & Dining with Sunset

In 1973, *Sunset* celebrated its 75th anniversary with the opening of a spacious new expansion of its entertaining wing. The indoor-outdoor dining area, conference room, large kitchen, and wine cellar are all in frequent use for lunches, dinners, conferences, and seminars.

From the entertainment kitchen, commercially equipped to deal with cooking for large crowds, come dishes selected from the pages of *Sunset* Magazine and *Sunset* Books.

Our Book Business

Beginning in December, 1931, with a compilation of recipes from our Kitchen Cabinet feature, *Sunset* Books has grown up alongside *Sunset* Magazine. Early cook books merely brought together and reprinted recipe collections from the magazine, and *Sunset* Magazine continues to be a source of recipe material. But for many of our books, additional recipes are also developed to give more depth to certain subjects. And book editors and photographers have worked together in recent years to show food preparation, step by step, for particular recipes. One such sequence, illustrating the steps in making stew, is shown at left.

Today's *Sunset* cook books belong to a long, colorful series covering everything from cookies to pasta, Chinese food to homemade soups. Nearly 40 popular titles are currently in print.

Shown in step-by-step photos, the how-to's of a number of culinary techniques are presented in many recent Sunset *books.*

Three best sellers from Sunset *Books give a glimpse of the wide subject range covered by the cook book series—which includes many other tantalizing titles.*

Our Kind of Western Style

Over the years, *Sunset* Magazine & Books have developed a distinctive style, obvious at a glance to our readers—and much appreciated as a guide, whether in traveling to the Sierra or staying home to entertain with soup from the garden.

Though familiar to *Sunset*'s widespread Western "family" of readers, our kind of Western style is difficult to pinpoint. But here are some of its essential features...

Fresh & Easy

"Fresh" is a byword in the West. From fruits and vegetables to seafood and cheeses, Westerners revel in an extraordinary year-round supply of fresh foods. And long before fresh became fashionable, *Sunset* emphasized fresh ingredients for their quality, good flavor, and nutritional benefits. At the same time, though, we've always realized that not all our readers have access to the fresh foods we enjoy—and we're careful to suggest frozen, canned, or dried alternatives in many of our recipes.

"Easy" is another word we like at *Sunset*. "Easy" can mean you don't even have to cook— just let us help you choose a ripe melon or avocado for a simple first course, or follow our directions to wash and crisp greens for a perfect salad. "Easy" also describes dishes you can bake slowly in the oven or leave to simmer unattended on the range.

Rosy 'Bartlett' from Hood River, Oregon, is one of the earliest red pears to appear in Western markets. When these rosy fruits first became available, Sunset welcomed them with a detailed essay and appealing recipes.

Discovery

For years, *Sunset* editors have traveled around the world, gathering ideas to share with our readers. In a Mexican straw hut, we learned how to grind masa on a metate to make tortillas; in a Turkish kitchen, we cooked an authentic pilaf. We've shared Christmas with Swedish families; selected cheeses and vegetables at market with French housewives; baked bread in stone ovens in Italy; nibbled grilled chicken from a street stall in Thailand.

By learning "on location" how to use the ingredients and seasonings that give native dishes their character, we're better able to recommend substitutes—and we're more aware of the frequent links between cuisines. Southeast Asian cooking seems much more accessible and familiar, for example, when you realize that many of its typical seasonings are also Mexican favorites—cilantro, chiles, lime, mint, coconut, tamarind.

Discover that a crisp, fresh salad isn't always green. Discover that watermelon— which you thought was a dessert— makes a refreshing foil for chicken. And discover watermelon "seeds" that taste like black beans—in Watermelon & Smoked Chicken Salad, page 85.

Western Living

All along, *Sunset* has based its reporting on the premise that we live differently in the West. We enjoy the outdoors, whatever the weather. In some areas of the West, balmy days are the rule every month of the year; but even if the ground is snow covered, we prefer *al fresco* activity. Even holiday meals can be enjoyed out in the open.

Westerners are informal. We don't mind putting our guests to work. They might cook their own meals right at the table, Japanese style; or make a dinner out of appetizers at a walk-around party; or tend their own servings on the barbecue. We like to leave decisions up to the individual—providing a basic soup, salad, or dessert with an assortment of condiments or toppings. Guests choose just what to add—and get just what they want.

We're experimental. We've crossed gelato and tofu to produce tofulato, a frozen dessert that may sound odd but tastes marvelous. We make ravioli with egg roll skins, tortellini with potsticker wrappers. We cook our vegetables on the grill; we bake chicken in a clay jacket. And we pass all our successful innovations on to you.

Western living also means having fun. As one example of this, we've raised picnicking to an art form, publishing recipes and ideas for exciting menus to be enjoyed in any season and weather, and almost any location. These have included ideas for bike trips, for jaunts on horseback, for San Francisco Bay sailing excursions. Even snow won't daunt us, as you can see from the January picnic shown below.

Fine, fresh food, beautifully prepared and served in an easygoing, informal, outdoor setting—all this describes Western Living. We like to enjoy ourselves and do it best in a relaxed manner, making the most of our climate and regional foods.

For a taste of Western Living, look further into this book.

Neither snow nor ice will keep Westerners from a picnic based on a Sunset *menu— and this one takes place on a clear, sunny day at Lake Tahoe. Hot chicken soup warms up the January menu, to be cooled off afterwards by hot fudge sundaes. (See Winter Warm-up Picnic, page 20.)*

The Best of
Sunset
MENUS

An innovative menu, often an outdoor setting, a mood both festive and casual—all these are characteristic of Sunset's *distinctive entertaining style.*

For more than three decades, Sunset *has set the stage for Western entertaining. At our headquarters in Menlo Park, California, we've hosted both business guests and staff members at large-scale to intimate parties, always placing an exciting menu at the center of each event.*

We now invite you to sample several of our most prized menus. The Thanksgiving Fiesta celebrates the West's Mexican heritage in every dish, down to the cranberry salsa. At a sushi party, everyone gets involved, assembling their own hand-held servings. Simpler but no less inventive is the Almost All-Potato Buffet, presenting lots of small baked potatoes and nearly a dozen toppings. These—and all our other menus—will promise you lively gatherings and exciting eating.

Southwestern Buffet (page 12) is a hearty, festive menu
with two entrées: Santa Fe beef chili and pink beans, plus
roasted chicken legs with onion-seasoned rice. Salsa goes
with avocados—and everything else.

SOUTHWESTERN BUFFET
FOR 12
(Pictured on page 10)

Avocados with Fresh Salsa

Santa Fe Chili with Meat

Pink Beans   Chicken with Rice

Warm Corn Tortillas

Powdered Sugar Pound Cake

Tropical Fruit

Barbera or Cabernet Sauvignon

On Southwestern deserts, baking hot days cool off with nightfall. The same dramatic shift of temperature mirrors the desert background of this menu, which has received rave reviews from both our guests and readers.

Pueblo Indian cuisine, a strong influence in the Southwest, is also reflected in this Santa Fe dinner—in the mellow beef chili and chicken with rice.

Because so much can be completed ahead, this menu is especially easy to manage. You can make the salsa, chili, and beans 2 to 3 days in advance. You can also bake the Powdered Sugar Pound Cake (a great, all-occasion favorite, by the way) a day ahead of the event.

To accompany the meal, select a wine that can stand up to the rich flavors of the meat and chicken dishes; a hearty Barbera or Cabernet Sauvignon is a good choice.

Avocados with Fresh Salsa

PREPARATION TIME: 10 to 15 minutes
PER SERVING: 153 calories, 2 grams protein, 7 grams carbohydrate, 14 grams total fat, 0 milligram cholesterol, 11 milligrams sodium

> 3 small fresh jalapeño or serrano chiles, stemmed and finely chopped
> 1 tablespoon chopped fresh cilantro (coriander)
> 12 green onions (including tops), chopped
> 3 large firm-ripe tomatoes, peeled, cored, seeded, and chopped
> ¼ cup *each* salad oil and red wine vinegar
> 6 small ripe avocados
> Lemon juice

In a small bowl, combine chiles, cilantro, onions, tomatoes, oil, and vinegar. If made ahead, cover and refrigerate until next day.

Pit, peel, and quarter avocados; drizzle all over with lemon juice. Set bowl of salsa in center of a large platter and arrange avocado wedges around it. To eat, top avocados with salsa.

(Or halve and pit unpeeled avocados; brush cut surfaces with lemon juice. Spoon some of the salsa in each avocado cavity; eat avocados with knife and fork, offering extra salsa to spoon on top.)

Santa Fe Chili with Meat

PREPARATION TIME: 10 to 15 minutes
COOKING TIME: About 40 minutes for Red Chile Sauce; about 6½ hours for chili
PER SERVING: 650 calories, 37 grams protein, 15 grams carbohydrate, 49 grams total fat, 131 milligrams cholesterol, 329 milligrams sodium

> ½ cup olive oil or salad oil
> 2 large onions, chopped
> 3 cloves garlic, minced or pressed
> 5 pounds boneless beef chuck, cut into 1½-inch cubes
> ½ cup all-purpose flour
> Red Chile Sauce (recipe follows)
> 1 tablespoon minced fresh cilantro (coriander)
> 2 teaspoons *each* ground cumin, ground cloves, and dry oregano leaves
> 1½ teaspoons *each* dry rosemary and dry tarragon
> 2 large cans (28 oz. *each*) tomatoes
> 2 cups Homemade Chicken Broth (page 58) or 1 can (14½ oz.) regular-strength chicken or beef broth

Pour oil into a 6- to 8-quart pan over medium heat. Add onions and garlic; cook, stirring often, until onions are soft, about 10 minutes. Sprinkle meat with flour and mix together. Add meat and chile sauce to pan; cook, stirring, for about 5 minutes. Add cilantro, cumin, cloves, oregano, rosemary, tarragon, tomatoes and their liquid, and broth. Reduce heat and simmer gently, uncovered, until meat is very tender when pierced, about 6 hours; stir often. If made ahead, cover and refrigerate for up to 2 days; reheat to serve.

RED CHILE SAUCE. Stem and seed 4 ounces **dried New Mexico, California (Anaheim), or pasilla chiles** (12 to 15 chiles). Combine chiles with 3 cups **water** in a 2½- to 3-quart pan. Cover and simmer over medium-low heat until chiles are very soft, about 30 minutes. Lift out chiles, saving cooking water. Whirl chiles in a blender, adding cooking water as needed, until very smoothly puréed; rub firmly through a fine strainer and discard residue. Return purée to pan; boil over high heat, uncovered, until reduced to 1 cup. Stir often; add water if sauce reduces too much. Use hot or cold. To store, cover and refrigerate for up to 1 week. Makes 1 cup.

Pink Beans

PREPARATION TIME: 5 to 10 minutes
COOKING TIME: About 2½ hours
PER SERVING: 209 calories, 14 grams protein, 36 grams carbohydrate, 1 gram total fat, 4 milligrams cholesterol, 102 milligrams sodium

Sort 4 cups **dried pink or small red beans** (about 1½ lbs.) and remove any debris. Rinse and drain beans. In a 5- to 6-quart pan, combine beans, 12 cups **water,** and 2 small **meaty ham hocks** (about ½ lb. *each*). Bring to a boil; reduce heat, cover, and simmer until beans are tender to bite, 2 to 2½ hours. Lift out ham hocks. When cool enough to handle, discard skin, bones, and fat; tear meat into chunks and return to pan. Season to taste with **salt.** If made ahead, cover and refrigerate for up to 3 days.

To serve, bring to a simmer over medium heat, stirring. Garnish with **fresh cilantro (coriander) sprigs.**

Chicken with Rice

PREPARATION TIME: 5 to 10 minutes for chicken; about 5 minutes for rice
COOKING TIME: About 45 minutes to bake chicken; about 35 minutes to cook rice
PER SERVING: 209 calories, 17 grams protein, 4 grams carbohydrate, 13 grams total fat, 64 milligrams cholesterol, 87 milligrams sodium

   3 tablespoons butter or margarine
   3 tablespoons salad oil
      About ½ cup all-purpose flour
   1 teaspoon *each* chili powder and paprika
   ½ teaspoon pepper
 12 chicken drumsticks (about 3 lbs. *total*)
      Onion Rice (recipe follows)
      Chopped parsley

Combine butter and oil in a 10- by 15-inch rimmed baking pan. Set in a 400° oven until butter is melted. Meanwhile, in a small bag, combine flour, chili powder, paprika, and pepper. Rinse drumsticks and pat dry; then shake, a few at a time, in flour mixture. Arrange in pan, turning to coat with fat. Bake, uncovered, in a 400° oven until chicken is no longer pink at bone (cut to test), about 45 minutes.

Arrange chicken and rice on a large platter; sprinkle with parsley. (If desired, pile Santa Fe Chili with Meat on other side of platter.)

ONION RICE. In a 10- to 12-inch frying pan over medium heat, cook 3 slices **bacon,** diced, until fat melts. Add 1 small **onion,** chopped, and 1 cup **long-grain white rice;** cook, stirring, until rice is pale gold, about 10 minutes. Add 1 cup **Homemade Chicken Broth** (page 58) or canned regular-strength chicken broth; then stir in 1 cup **water.** Bring to a boil; reduce heat, cover, and simmer until rice is tender to bite and liquid is absorbed, about 20 minutes.

Warm Corn Tortillas

PREPARATION & HEATING TIME: 15 to 20 minutes
PER TORTILLA: 42 calories, 1 gram protein, 9 grams carbohydrate, .40 gram total fat, 0 milligram cholesterol, 22 milligrams sodium

Unwrap 36 **corn tortillas** (7- to 8-inch diameter) and stack in 2 equal piles. Wrap each pile airtight in foil. Place in a 400° oven until heated through, 15 to 20 minutes. Wrap in a towel to keep warm and serve from a basket. Offer **butter** or margarine to spread on warm tortillas.

Powdered Sugar Pound Cake

PREPARATION TIME: 15 to 20 minutes
BAKING TIME: About 1½ hours
PER SERVING: 470 calories, 5 grams protein, 56 grams carbohydrate, 26 grams total fat, 199 milligrams cholesterol, 270 milligrams sodium *

 1½ cups (¾ lb.) butter or margarine,
     at room temperature
   1 pound (3½ cups) unsifted powdered sugar
   6 large eggs
   1 teaspoon vanilla
 2¾ cups sifted cake flour
   ¼ cup sliced almonds (optional)

In a large bowl, beat butter with an electric mixer until creamy. Sift powdered sugar; gradually add to butter, beating until mixture is light and fluffy. Beat in eggs, 1 at a time, beating well after each addition. Beat in vanilla. Gradually beat flour into creamed mixture.

Heavily butter a 10-inch (12-cup) plain or decorative tube pan; add sliced almonds (if used), then tilt pan to coat inside surfaces with nuts. Or butter pan and dust with flour. Scrape batter into pan and smooth top surface.

Bake in a 300° oven until a slender wooden pick inserted in center comes out clean, about 1½ hours. Let cool in pan on a rack for 5 minutes; run a knife around edges of tube to loosen center of cake, then turn out onto rack to cool. Serve warm or cool, cut into thin slices. If made ahead, store airtight for up to 2 days.

WINE-MAKING in the West began with the founding of California's missions. Centuries later, during Prohibition, the industry was kept alive by producing wine for religious use. Immediately after repeal, Sunset responded with "now we can use wine again" recipes —and we've continued to cook with wine and to feature Western wines, wineries, and wine country touring in our pages.

CRACKED CRAB FEAST
FOR 4 TO 6

Cracked Crab

Herbed Artichokes

Melted Butter

Lemon Mayonnaise

Bread Sticks or
Sourdough French Bread

Lemon-glazed Butter Cake

Dry Sauvignon Blanc or Chardonnay

There are few simpler ways to feast than on cracked crab—one of the West's tastiest traditions. But there's no neat and tidy way to proceed; the only practical approach is to get involved with both hands. Artichokes, another Western classic that's eaten with the fingers, make a delectable partner for the sweet, moist crab.

To serve the meal, mound crab and artichokes on a large platter in the center of the table, within easy reach of all; present dipping sauce and/or mayonnaise in individual bowls. Then let guests select portions at their own speed.

Except for the timid, this feast requires almost no flatware, but be sure to provide big napkins or bibs. To refresh hands, offer finger bowls, small damp towels, or disposable hand wipes.

Buy the crab cleaned and cracked. Cook the artichokes shortly before the party to serve warm; or cook them the day before, when you bake the cake, and serve cold. Offer a crisp wine, such as dry Sauvignon Blanc or a lightly oaked Chardonnay.

Cracked Crab

PREPARATION TIME: About 10 minutes
PER SERVING OF CRAB WITHOUT SAUCE: 108 calories, 20 grams protein, .58 gram carbohydrate, 2 grams total fat, 116 milligrams cholesterol, 244 milligrams sodium

---

Select 4 to 6 small **cooked Dungeness crabs** in the shell (about 1½ lbs. *each*). Have crab cleaned and cracked at the market; if you wish, ask your meatman to spoon the **crab butter and fat** into a carton.

At home, rinse crab under cool running water to remove loose bits of shell. Pile crab onto a large platter; rinse crab backs and lay on top as garnish. Serve, or cover and refrigerate for up to 6 hours.

Melt ¼ to ⅓ cup **butter** or margarine for each serving; you'll need 1 to 2 cups (½ to 1 lb.) *total*. To make **crab butter sauce,** whirl melted butter with reserved crab butter and fat (if used) in a blender. As you shell crab to eat, dip meat into crab butter sauce, warm melted butter, or Lemon Mayonnaise.

Herbed Artichokes

PREPARATION TIME: 5 to 10 minutes
COOKING TIME: About 45 minutes
PER SERVING: 111 calories, 5 grams protein, 21 grams carbohydrate, 3 grams total fat, 0 milligram cholesterol, 140 milligrams sodium

---

Select 4 to 6 very large **artichokes** (4½ to 5-inch diameter). Break off small outer leaves (bracts), then cut off thorny tip of each artichoke with a knife. Use scissors to snip thorns from remaining outer leaves. Cut off stem and peel stem end.

While you trim artichokes, bring to a boil in a 6- to 8-quart pan: 12 cups **water,** 3 tablespoons **olive oil,** 2 tablespoons **vinegar,** ½ teaspoon *each* **dry thyme leaves** and **dry rosemary,** 1 teaspoon **mustard seeds,** 2 **bay leaves,** ½ teaspoon **whole black peppercorns,** 8 **whole allspice,** and 6 **whole cloves.**

Add artichokes and return liquid to a boil over high heat; then reduce heat, cover, and simmer until artichoke bottoms are just tender when pierced, about 45 minutes. Lift from water. Serve hot, at room temperature, or cold. Dip leaves and bottom into melted butter or Lemon Mayonnaise served with crab.

Lemon Mayonnaise

PREPARATION TIME: About 5 minutes
PER TABLESPOON: 85 calories, .25 gram protein, .20 gram carbohydrate, 9 grams total fat, 11 milligrams cholesterol, 16 milligrams sodium

---

In a blender or food processor, combine 1 **large egg,** 2 teaspoons **Dijon mustard,** 1 clove **garlic,** and 2 tablespoons **lemon juice.** Whirl until blended. With motor running, gradually add 1 cup **salad oil** in a thin, steady stream, processing until fully incorporated. If made ahead, cover and refrigerate for up to 2 days. Makes 1½ cups.

For quick lemon mayonnaise, flavor purchased mayonnaise to taste with lemon juice and Dijon mustard.

Lemon-glazed Butter Cake

PREPARATION TIME: 15 to 20 minutes
BAKING TIME: About 1 hour
COOLING TIME: At least 6 hours
PER SERVING: 512 calories, 6 grams protein, 84 grams carbohydrate, 18 grams total fat, 113 milligrams cholesterol, 259 milligrams sodium

---

1 cup (½ lb.) butter or margarine, at room temperature

1¼ cups sugar

3 large eggs

2 teaspoons *each* baking powder and grated lemon peel

¾ teaspoon almond extract

3 cups all-purpose flour

1 cup milk

Lemon Glaze (recipe follows)

Lemon slices

Grapes (optional)

In a bowl, combine butter and sugar; beat with an electric mixer on high speed until fluffy, about 5 minutes. Beat in eggs, 1 at a time, then mix in baking powder, lemon peel, and almond extract. With mixer on low speed, add flour and milk alternately, beating well after each addition.

With a flexible spatula, scrape batter into a heavily buttered and flour-dusted 10-cup plain or decorative tube pan. Tap pan smartly on counter several times to level batter and get rid of any air pockets.

Bake on center rack of a 325° oven until cake begins to pull from pan sides, about 1 hour. Set pan on a rack and let cool for 5 minutes. Run a sharp knife around edge of tube to loosen center of cake from pan. Place rack on top of pan and invert gently to release cake from pan. Invert again to return cake to pan.

With a thin wooden skewer, pierce through cake at 1-inch intervals. Pour all but ½ cup of Lemon Glaze over hot cake. Let cool completely on rack, at least 6 hours, then invert cake onto a serving plate and remove pan. Stir reserved glaze and spoon evenly over top of cake. Serve, or cover airtight and let stand until next day.

Garnish with lemon slices and grapes (if desired); cut into thin slices. Makes 10 to 12 servings.

LEMON GLAZE. In a large bowl, smoothly blend ¾ cup **lemon juice** into 1 pound (3½ cups) **unsifted powdered sugar.**

Glories of the Pacific coastline: crab from the sea, artichokes from the fields make up this marvelously easy menu. Crab and artichokes share butter, lemon mayonnaise. Tart lemon cake and fresh grapes end the meal.

WALK-AROUND RECEPTION
FOR 40

Pop-open Barbecue Clams

Sausages with Mustard Cream

Smoked Salmon with Endive

Crudités with
Green Goddess Dressing

Melted Brie in a Crust

Layered Cheese Torta with Pesto

Sparkling Water with Citrus Twists

Dry Rosé

Dry White Wines made from
Red Wine Grapes

Big or small parties, sit-down or walk-around—at Sunset, we've tried them all. This very manageable reception for 40 is one of our most successful and easily managed menus.

Stressing self-service and guest participation, this menu is designed to be easy on the hosts. Let guests cook their own clams on the barbecue—or, if you prefer, appoint a chef to grill both clams and sausage. Arrange the crudités, smoked salmon, and other appetizers (all help-yourself) at separate tables to avoid bottlenecks and encourage guests to move about. Offer several wines on ice for self-service; select dry rosés (also called blush wines) or crisp, dry white wines made from red wine grapes, such as Zinfandel or Pinot Noir Blancs.

Pop-open Barbecue Clams

PREPARATION TIME: 30 to 40 minutes to ignite charcoal; about 15 minutes to scrub clams
GRILLING TIME: About 3 minutes for each batch of clams (grill 10 to 15 at a time)
PER 1 CLAM: 14 calories, 2 grams protein, 1 gram carbohydrate, .15 gram total fat, 9 milligrams cholesterol, 36 milligrams sodium
PER TEASPOON BUTTER: 34 calories, .04 gram protein, 0 gram carbohydrate, 4 grams total fat, 10 milligrams cholesterol, 39 milligrams sodium

About 80 clams in shell, suitable for steaming, scrubbed (be sure clams are big enough not to fall through barbecue grill)
1 cup (½ lb.) **butter or margarine**
French bread, cut into bite-size chunks

Place clams in a bowl next to barbecue. Set grill 4 to 6 inches above a solid bed of hot coals (you should be able to hold your hand at grill level for no more than 2 to 3 seconds). Place butter in a 1- to 1½-quart pan—at edge of grill, so butter melts without burning.

Set clams on grill. When they just begin to open, about 3 minutes, turn and continue cooking until they pop wide open. Protecting your fingers with a napkin, hold clams over butter and drain juices into butter. To eat, spear clams with fork and dip in butter mixture; also dunk bread into butter. Makes 40 servings (2 clams per serving).

Sausages with Mustard Cream

PREPARATION TIME: 30 to 40 minutes to ignite charcoal; 20 to 25 minutes to cook and cool Mustard Cream
GRILLING TIME: About 10 minutes to heat sausages (grill half at a time)
PER OUNCE OF SAUSAGE: 87 calories, 3 grams protein, .49 gram carbohydrate, 8 grams total fat, 16 milligrams cholesterol, 287 milligrams sodium
PER TABLESPOON OF SAUCE: 25 calories, .29 gram protein, .98 gram carbohydrate, 2 grams total fat, 25 milligrams cholesterol, 71 milligrams sodium

4 **pounds cooked sausages such as knockwurst or kielbasa (Polish sausage)**
Mustard Cream (recipe follows)

Heat sausages on a grill 4 to 6 inches above a solid bed of hot coals (you should be able to hold your hand at grill level for no more than 2 to 3 seconds); turn until browned and hot, about 10 minutes. Cut sausages into bite-size pieces (40 to 80 *total*). Dip into Mustard Cream. Makes 40 servings (1 or 2 pieces per serving).

MUSTARD CREAM. In the top of a double boiler, beat together 4 **large egg yolks,** 2 tablespoons **sugar,** ½ cup **Dijon mustard,** ¼ cup **white wine vinegar,** 1 tablespoon **water,** 3 tablespoons **prepared horseradish,** and 2 tablespoons **butter** or margarine. Place over simmering water and stir until mixture thickens, 5 to 8 minutes. Set pan in **ice water** and stir often to cool quickly and thoroughly.

Beat 1 cup **whipping cream** until it holds stiff peaks. Fold mustard mixture into cream until completely blended. If made ahead, cover and refrigerate for up to 1 week. To serve, spoon into a bowl. Makes 3½ cups.

Smoked Salmon with Endive

PREPARATION TIME: 5 to 10 minutes to make sauce; 1½ to 2½ hours to smoke salmon (if homemade); about 10 minutes to wash greens and at least 30 minutes to chill and crisp them
PER PORTION WITH 1 BELGIAN ENDIVE LEAF: 89 calories, 5 grams protein, 8 grams carbohydrate, 4 grams total fat, 13 milligrams cholesterol, 1078 milligrams sodium

2 **large packages (8 oz. *each*) cream cheese, at room temperature**
½ cup **sour cream**
2 tablespoons **lemon juice**
3 tablespoons **minced shallots**
¼ cup **minced fresh dill or 1½ teaspoons dry dill weed**
1 **smoked salmon fillet (2½ to 3 lbs.), purchased or smoked as directed on page 144**
About 1 pound Belgian endive, separated into spears; or small inner leaves from 6 heads romaine lettuce; or some of each, washed and crisped
36 to 40 small (2-inch-diameter) **bagels, split**

Beat cream cheese until creamy. Add sour cream, lemon juice, shallots, and dill; beat until blended. If made ahead, cover and refrigerate until next day.

Set salmon on a platter or board. Set cheese mixture, endive, and bagels alongside. Cut fish into thin slanting slices, cutting flesh away from skin. To eat, place salmon on endive or bagels; top with a dollop of cheese mixture. Makes 72 to 80 portions.

Crudités with Green Goddess Dressing

PREPARATION TIME: About 30 minutes to rinse vegetables; at least 30 minutes to crisp lettuce; about 5 minutes to make dressing
PER 2 OUNCES OF VEGETABLES: 24 calories, 3 grams protein, 4 grams carbohydrate, .31 gram total fat, 0 milligram cholesterol, 4 milligrams sodium
PER TABLESPOON OF DRESSING: 114 calories, .90 gram protein, .42 gram carbohydrate, 12 grams total fat, 35 milligrams cholesterol, 22 milligrams sodium

    2 to 3 pounds small (1- to 1½-inch-diameter) button mushroom caps, rinsed and drained

    2 to 3 pounds asparagus (tough ends removed), broccoli (cut into small flowerets), small carrots (peeled), or edible-pod peas (strings removed); or some of each

  40 to 50 small inner leaves from 3 or 4 heads romaine lettuce, washed and crisped

    Green Goddess Dressing (recipe follows)

Arrange mushrooms, asparagus, and romaine in a basket. Serve dressing in a bowl and dip vegetables into it. Allow 2 or 3 pieces for a serving (presented alone, this makes 15 to 20 appetizer servings).

GREEN GODDESS DRESSING. In a blender, combine 3 **large egg yolks,** 3 tablespoons **white wine vinegar,** ⅔ cup chopped **parsley,** 1 can (2 oz.) **anchovy fillets** and oil, 6 **green onions** (including tops), chopped, and 1½ teaspoons **dry tarragon,** crumbled.

Whirl until smoothly puréed. With motor running, gradually add 1¼ cups **salad oil.** Increase flow of oil as mixture thickens; turn off and on to blend. Serve; or cover and refrigerate for up to a week. Makes 1½ cups.

Melted Brie in a Crust

PREPARATION TIME: 5 to 10 minutes
BAKING TIME: About 20 minutes
PER SERVING: 96 calories, 4 grams protein, 6 grams carbohydrate, 6 grams total fat, 15 milligrams cholesterol, 155 milligrams sodium

    1 round or oval loaf (about 1 lb.) day-old French bread

    ⅓ cup olive oil (or melted butter or margarine)

    2 cloves garlic, minced or pressed

    1 to 1½ pounds Brie, Camembert, or St. André cheese

With a serrated knife, cut down through top of bread to leave a shell about ½ inch thick on sides; do not cut through bottom crust. Slide your fingers down alongside center of loaf and pull free in a single piece, leaving a ½-inch-thick base in shell. Around rim of shell, make cuts 1½ inches deep and 1½ inches apart. Cut bread from center of loaf into ½-inch-thick slices.

Mix oil and garlic. Brush inside of shell with about 3 tablespoons of the oil; brush bread slices with remaining oil. Place cheese with rind (or trim off rind, if desired) in bread shell, trimming to fit.

Place filled shell and bread slices in a single layer in a 10- by 15-inch rimmed baking pan. Bake in a 350° oven until bread slices are toasted, about 10 minutes. Remove slices to a rack to cool. Continue baking filled shell until cut edge of bread is golden and cheese is melted, about 10 more minutes.

Place filled shell on a board; surround with toasted bread slices to dip into melted cheese. When all bread slices have been eaten, snap off crisp pieces from edge of shell for dippers. Makes about 40 portions (10 to 12 appetizer servings if presented alone).

Layered Cheese Torta with Pesto

Pictured on page 1

PREPARATION TIME: About 30 minutes
CHILLING TIME: About 1 hour (no longer than 1½ hours in mold)
PER 1-OUNCE SERVING: 302 calories, 2 grams protein, .76 gram carbohydrate, 33 grams total fat, 93 milligrams cholesterol, 87 milligrams sodium

    2 large packages (8 oz. *each*) cream cheese, at room temperature

    2 cups (1 lb.) unsalted butter or margarine, at room temperature

    Pesto (recipe follows)

    Fresh basil sprigs

    Thinly sliced baguettes

    Crisp raw vegetables (optional)

Using an electric mixer, beat cream cheese and butter until smoothly blended.

Cut two 18-inch squares of cheesecloth (or an 18-inch square of muslin); moisten with water, wring dry, and lay out flat, 1 on top of the other. Use cloth to smoothly line a 5- to 6-cup straight-sided plain mold such as a tall brioche or charlotte pan, or a loaf pan; drape excess cloth over rim of mold.

With your fingers or a rubber spatula, spread ⅙ of the cheese mixture in prepared mold. Cover with ⅕ of the pesto, extending it evenly to sides of mold. Repeat until mold is filled, finishing with cheese.

Fold ends of cloth over top and press down lightly with your hands to compact. Refrigerate until torta feels firm when pressed, 1 to 1½ hours; then unfold cloth from top, invert torta onto a serving dish, and gently pull off cloth (if torta is allowed to stand longer than 1½ hours, cloth will act as a wick and cause filling color to bleed onto cheese). If made ahead, cover and refrigerate for up to 5 days.

Garnish with basil sprigs. Spread on bread and vegetables (if used). Makes 16 servings.

PESTO. In a blender or food processor, whirl to a paste 2½ cups lightly packed **fresh basil leaves,** 1 cup (about 5 oz.) freshly grated **Parmesan or Romano cheese,** and ⅓ cup **olive oil.** Stir in ¼ cup **pine nuts** and season to taste with **salt** and **pepper.**

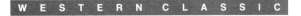

HAND-ROLLED SUSHI PARTY
FOR 6

Sushi Toppings Tray   Sushi Rice

Nori Squares   Soy Sauce

Wasabi Paste

Pickled Ginger

Pickled or Fresh Daikon Radish

Sesame Sauce

Toasted Sesame Seeds

Hot Miso Soup

Hot or Chilled Sake, or Tea or Beer

Sliced Tangelos & Kiwis

Japan's answer to our sandwich, sushi has made a hit in the West. Tabletop sushi (simple to assemble) is a hit with guests, as well. The make-your-own approach offers choices for both the timid and the brave.

To serve, present the tray of sushi toppings, with separate containers of nori (the seaweed wrapper for the sushi), sushi rice, toasted sesame seeds, and mayonnaise-based sesame sauce alongside. At each place setting, arrange small individual dishes of soy sauce, wasabi (extra-hot Japanese horseradish), thinly sliced pickled ginger, and sliced pickled or finely shredded raw daikon to nibble as a palate refresher. Also serve each guest a bowl of broth, such as miso soup made from a mix.

To assemble hand-rolled sushi, first lay a piece of nori in the palm of your hand. Spoon a small amount of sushi rice into the center; top with one or more foods from the sushi toppings tray, plus wasabi and sesame seeds or sauce. Wrap nori around filling; then dip, bite by bite, in soy sauce (flavored with wasabi, if desired).

You may need to shop at an Asian market for some of the sushi ingredients—nori, wasabi, pickles, soup stock mix. Buy fish that's very fresh, with firm flesh and a clean sea smell.

Sushi Toppings Tray

PREPARATION TIME: 45 minutes to 1 hour
COOKING TIME: 2 to 3 minutes
PER SERVING: 323 calories, 36 grams protein, 15 grams carbohydrate, 14 grams total fat, 160 milligrams cholesterol, 1595 milligrams sodium

- ⅓ cup seasoned rice vinegar for sushi; or 4 teaspoons sugar dissolved in ⅓ cup rice vinegar, distilled white vinegar, or white wine vinegar
- 2 medium-size carrots, peeled and cut into 3- to 4-inch pieces, then cut lengthwise into thin julienne strips
- About 1 pound spinach (stems and any yellow or wilted leaves discarded), washed
- 2 small ripe avocados
- ½ cup lemon juice
- 1 bag (3½ oz.) enoki mushrooms
- ½ English cucumber, cut into thin 3- to 4-inch julienne strips
- ½ pound cooked, shelled crab
- ½ pound cooked, shelled, deveined medium-size shrimp (about 45 per lb.) or tiny cooked, shelled shrimp
- ½ pound boned, skinned, thinly sliced yellowfin tuna, seabass, halibut, or rockfish
- ¼ pound thinly sliced smoked salmon
- ¼ cup (2 oz.) salmon caviar

In a 2- to 3-quart pan, bring vinegar to a boil. Add carrots; cook and stir just until tender-crisp to bite, about 30 seconds. Drain and set aside.

Rinse pan. Add 1 inch water and bring to a boil. Gently push spinach down into water. Cook and stir just until limp, about 1 minute; drain and set aside.

Halve, pit, and peel avocados. Slice lengthwise into strips about ⅛ inch thick. Place in a bowl with lemon juice; moisten each slice to prevent browning. Set aside. Trim and discard brown, woody ends from mushrooms.

On a large tray, separately arrange carrots, spinach, avocados, mushrooms, cucumber, crab, shrimp, tuna, salmon, and caviar. If made ahead, cover and refrigerate for up to 5 hours. Serve slightly cool.

Sushi Rice

PREPARATION TIME: 5 to 10 minutes
COOKING TIME: About 20 minutes
COOLING TIME: 5 to 10 minutes to fan; at least 20 more minutes to cool
PER SERVING: 376 calories, 7 grams protein, 84 grams carbohydrate, .40 gram total fat, 0 milligram cholesterol, 7 milligrams sodium

---

In a 3- to 4-quart pan, cover 3 cups **short-grain rice** (such as pearl) with **water** and stir; drain. Repeat until water is clear; drain.

Add 3½ cups **water** to rice. Cover and bring to a boil over high heat. Reduce heat to low and cook without stirring until all water is absorbed, about 15 minutes. Stir in ⅓ cup **seasoned rice vinegar for sushi** or 4 teaspoons sugar dissolved in ⅓ cup rice vinegar, distilled white vinegar, or white wine vinegar. Spread rice equally in two 10- by 15-inch rimmed baking pans. Stirring, cool quickly until no longer steaming, fanning with a piece of cardboard, a fan, or a hand-held hair dryer on cool setting. Then let stand until cooled to room temperature. If made ahead, cover tightly and hold at room temperature for up to 6 hours. Spoon sushi rice into a serving bowl.

Mosaic of sushi makings to tackle on your own: fill crisp nori with sushi rice, then top from a colorful selection within easy reach of each guest. Toppings are "safe" (cooked shrimp) to daring (raw tuna).

Nori Squares

PREPARATION TIME: 2 to 3 minutes to toast; 2 to 3 minutes to cut
PER SERVING: 17 calories, 2 grams protein, 3 grams carbohydrate, .07 gram total fat, 0 milligram cholesterol, 92 milligrams sodium

Buy 1½ ounces **roasted or unroasted nori** (dark green, paper-thin sheets). Roasting (more accurately, toasting) brings out the green color and makes nori crisper. To toast your own, draw a sheet of nori back and forth over a low gas flame or electric burner set on low until nori becomes quite crisp. With scissors, cut nori into 4- to 5-inch squares. If made ahead, let cool, then package airtight and hold at room temperature for several hours.

Stack nori on a plate or in a basket.

Wasabi Paste

PREPARATION TIME: 3 to 5 minutes

Stir 3 tablespoons **wasabi powder** (Japanese hot horseradish) with 3½ teaspoons **water** until smooth. Divide into 6 equal portions. Pinch into small cones and place 1 cone on each serving plate.

Sesame Sauce

PREPARATION TIME: 2 to 3 minutes
PER TABLESPOON: 108 calories, .26 gram protein, 2 grams carbohydrate, 11 grams total fat, 8 milligrams cholesterol, 78 milligrams sodium

Stir together 1 cup **mayonnaise,** 4 teaspoons *each* **honey** and **toasted sesame seeds** (directions follow), and 1½ teaspoons **Oriental sesame oil.** Spoon into 1 or 2 small serving bowls. Makes about 1 cup sauce.

Toasted Sesame Seeds

PREPARATION TIME: About 2 minutes
PER TEASPOON: 15 calories, .45 gram protein, .69 gram carbohydrate, 1 gram total fat, 0 milligram cholesterol, 1 milligram sodium

Toast ¼ cup **sesame seeds** in an 8- to 10-inch frying pan over medium heat until golden, about 2 minutes, shaking pan frequently. Spoon into 1 or 2 small serving bowls.

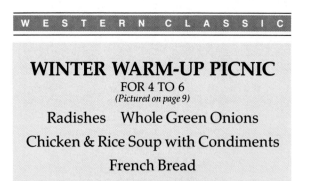

WINTER WARM-UP PICNIC
FOR 4 TO 6
(Pictured on page 9)

Radishes   Whole Green Onions

Chicken & Rice Soup with Condiments

French Bread

Hot Fudge Sundaes

White Chocolate Chip Cookies
(page 257), optional

Dry Chenin Blanc

Assorted Juices

Picnic season never ends in the West, where the outdoors offers as much fun in January as in July. Sunset food editors designed this alfresco menu especially for a snow-country outing. The meal features a warming chicken soup, made hearty with black beans and as fiery as you like with pepper sauce. To sip alongside, offer a dry Chenin Blanc that's only slightly fruity. The finale is both hot and cold—ice cream with hot fudge sauce.

Chicken & Rice Soup with Condiments

PREPARATION TIME: 5 to 10 minutes to start soup; about 30 minutes to cool and bone chicken and strain broth
COOKING TIME: About 2¾ hours for black beans; about 1 hour and 20 minutes for soup
PER SERVING OF SOUP: 347 calories, 29 grams protein, 34 grams carbohydrate, 10 grams total fat, 78 milligrams cholesterol, 198 milligrams sodium

    1 **broiler-fryer chicken (3 to 3½ lbs.), cut up**
  10 **cups Homemade Chicken Broth (page 58) or canned regular-strength chicken broth**
    2 **medium-size onions, quartered**
    1 **cup chopped parsley**
    5 **tablespoons canned tomato paste**
   ½ **cup long-grain white rice**
      Salt and pepper
      Black Beans (recipe follows)
      Pepper Sauce (recipe follows)
      Cilantro Butter (recipe follows)

Rinse chicken pieces and pat dry; pull off and discard lumps of fat. In an 8- to 10-quart pan, combine broth, chicken, onions, parsley, and tomato paste; cover and simmer until meat at thighbone is no longer pink (cut to test), 30 to 40 minutes.

Remove from heat. Lift out chicken and let cool; discard skin and bones. Tear meat into bite-size pieces and set aside.

Strain broth; discard onions and parsley. Bring broth to a boil and add rice. Reduce heat, cover, and simmer until rice is tender to bite, 20 to 25 minutes.

Skim and discard fat from broth. Add chicken; simmer until chicken is hot, about 5 minutes. Season to taste with salt and pepper. To hold for up to 3 hours, pour into a 3½-quart preheated thermos.

To serve, ladle soup into mugs or bowls; add beans, Pepper Sauce, and Cilantro Butter to taste.

BLACK BEANS. Sort ½ pound **dried black beans** (1¼ cups); remove debris. Rinse and drain beans.

In a 12- to 14-inch frying pan over medium heat, cook ½ pound **bacon** (diced) until crisp, stirring occasionally. Pour off and discard all but ¼ cup of the drippings. Add 1 medium-size **onion**, chopped, and 3 tablespoons minced **fresh ginger;** stir often until onion is soft, about 5 minutes. Stir in beans and 4 cups **Homemade Chicken Broth** (page 58) or 2 cans (14½ oz. *each*) regular-strength chicken broth. Bring to a boil; reduce heat, cover, and simmer until beans are tender to bite, 2 to 2½ hours. Stir occasionally and add more water as needed. If made ahead, let cool; then cover and refrigerate. Reheat, stirring, over low heat. To hold for up to 3 hours, put into a 3- to 4-cup preheated thermos.
PER ½ CUP: 298 calories, 13 grams protein, 31 grams carbohydrate, 14 grams total fat, 15 milligrams cholesterol, 226 milligrams sodium.

PEPPER SAUCE. Mix 2 tablespoons **salad oil** with 1 tablespoon **white wine vinegar.** Stir in ¾ cup minced **green bell pepper** and ¼ cup minced seeded **small fresh hot chiles.** If made ahead, cover and refrigerate until next day. Makes 1 cup.
PER TABLESPOON: 17 calories, .07 gram protein, .49 gram carbohydrate, 2 grams total fat, 0 milligram cholesterol, .45 milligram sodium.

CILANTRO BUTTER. Mix ½ cup (¼ lb.) **butter** or margarine (at room temperature), ½ cup firmly packed chopped **fresh cilantro (coriander) leaves,** and 2 cloves **garlic,** minced or pressed. Makes ⅔ cup.
PER TABLESPOON: 83 calories, .16 gram protein, .29 gram carbohydrate, 9 grams total fat, 25 milligrams cholesterol, 94 milligrams sodium.

Hot Fudge Sundaes

PREPARATION TIME: 2 to 3 minutes for sauce; 2 to 3 minutes to assemble
COOKING TIME (SAUCE): About 5 minutes
PER ½ CUP ICE CREAM: 244 calories, 4 grams protein, 18 grams carbohydrate, 18 grams total fat, 44 milligrams cholesterol, 55 milligrams sodium
PER TABLESPOON SAUCE: 55 calories, .43 gram protein, 4 grams carbohydrate, 5 grams total fat, 7 milligrams cholesterol, 2 milligrams sodium

In a 1- to 2-quart pan, stir 6 ounces **semisweet chocolate pieces** and ⅔ cup **whipping cream** over low heat until chocolate is melted. Remove from heat and stir in 2 tablespoons **coffee liqueur** (optional). If made ahead, let cool, then cover and refrigerate for up to 1 week; stir over low heat to reheat. To hold for up to 3 hours, pour into a preheated 1½- to 2-cup thermos.

To serve, pour fudge sauce over scoops of **vanilla or coffee ice cream,** 1 to 2 pints *total* (pack in dry ice or bury in snow to keep firm). Top with **sliced toasted almonds** (about ½ cup *total*).

TURKEY LOCO THANKSGIVING FIESTA
FOR 16

Antojitos Tray   Spanish Peanuts

Turkey Loco   Cranberry Salsa

Stuffed Chiles

Sweet Potatoes with Tequila & Lime

Roasted Onions   Buttered Hominy

Warm Corn Tortillas (page 13)

Pumpkin Crème Brûlée

Chardonnay   Cabernet Sauvignon

Fresh Limeade

In its native New England, a Thanksgiving turkey usually appears in the same formal attire every year. But out West, we often roast the bird informally on the patio barbecue, freeing up the kitchen for other dishes. Occasionally, as illustrated here, we completely reinvent the Thanksgiving tradition. Though we've included every essential holiday favorite in this menu—from turkey and stuffing to cranberries and pumpkin—each dish celebrates the West's appetizing Mexican heritage.

Turkey Loco takes its cooking technique from a popular Mexican style of barbecuing chicken. Split and butterflied, the bird cooks faster; lime juice adds tart flavor to its crisp, burnished skin. The stuffing goes into mild chiles, rather than inside the turkey; cranberry sauce shows up as a piquant salsa. Quickly sautéed sweet potato shreds are brightened with lime and a touch of tequila. And the pumpkin dessert that ends the feast is crustless, with a crispy broiled brown-sugar topping.

Antojitos Tray

PREPARATION TIME: About 10 minutes
PER SERVING WITHOUT SALT: 63 calories, 1 gram protein, 15 grams carbohydrate, .4 gram total fat, 0 milligram cholesterol, 4 milligrams sodium
PER ¼-TEASPOON SALT MIXTURE: .39 calorie, .01 gram protein, .07 gram carbohydrate, .01 gram total fat, 0 milligram cholesterol, 412 milligrams sodium

Cut 3 large unpeeled **oranges** into 8 wedges each. Cut 1 medium-size unpeeled ripe **pineapple** (about 4 lbs.) crosswise into ½-inch slices; remove core and cut each slice into quarters. Scrub, peel, and rinse 1½ pounds **jicama;** cut into ¼- by ¼- by 3-inch sticks. Coat fruit and jicama with about ½ cup **lime juice.**

Mix ¼ cup **salt,** 1 tablespoon **paprika,** and 1 teaspoon **cayenne** or chili powder. Arrange fruit, jicama, and seasoned salt (in a small dish) on a tray. If made ahead, cover with plastic wrap and refrigerate for up to 1 day.

To eat, dip foods in salt; offer **lime wedges** to squeeze over foods, if desired.

Turkey Loco

PREPARATION TIME: 30 to 40 minutes to ignite charcoal; 5 to 15 minutes to prepare turkey
GRILLING TIME: 1½ to 2 hours
PER SERVING: 261 calories, 45 grams protein, .93 gram carbohydrate, 7 grams total fat, 118 milligrams cholesterol, 114 milligrams sodium

> 1 turkey (10 to 12 lbs.), thawed if frozen
> About 4 limes, cut into halves
> About 4 teaspoons dry oregano leaves
> Salt and pepper

Have your meatman saw through length of turkey's backbone. Or, at home, use spring-loaded poultry shears to cut through length of backbone.

Lay turkey on its breast; pull open from back, pressing to flatten (some ribs will crack). Pull off and discard lumps of fat. Rinse turkey; pat dry. (At this point, you may cover and refrigerate until next day.)

Ignite 50 charcoal briquets on the fire grate of a barbecue (at least 21-inch diameter) with lid. When coals are just covered with gray ash, push half the coals to each side of the grate and set a 9- by 13-inch drip pan in center. Position barbecue grill 4 to 6 inches above fire grate. Lay spread-open bird, breast up, on grill over drip pan. Squeeze and rub 1 or 2 lime halves over turkey; sprinkle with oregano, then sprinkle lightly with salt and pepper.

Cover barbecue and open dampers. Every 30 minutes, squeeze and rub 1 or 2 more lime halves onto turkey and add 5 or 6 briquets to *each* side of coals to maintain a constant temperature. Cook turkey until a meat thermometer inserted in thickest part of breast (not touching bone) registers 170°F, 1½ to 2 hours. Transfer turkey to a platter. To carve, cut off wings and slice breast. Cut off legs and slice meat from thighs.

Cranberry Salsa

PREPARATION TIME: 5 to 10 minutes
PER TABLESPOON: 15 calories, .11 gram protein, 2 grams carbohydrate, 1 gram total fat, 0 milligram cholesterol, .22 milligram sodium

> 2 large oranges
> 2 cups cranberries
> ¼ cup *each* minced onion and salad oil
> 1 tablespoon *each* minced fresh cilantro (coriander) and minced fresh ginger
> 1 small fresh green jalapeño or serrano chile, stemmed, seeded, and minced
> Salt

Grate 4 teaspoons orange peel from oranges; place in a bowl. Using a sharp knife, cut remaining peel and all white membrane from oranges; coarsely chop oranges and place in a colander to drain.

Whirl cranberries in a food processor or blender until chopped; place in bowl with peel. Add drained chopped oranges, onion, oil, cilantro, ginger, and chile. Stir to blend; season to taste with salt.

Serve, or cover and refrigerate until next day. Makes about 3 cups.

Continued on next page

GOLD AND SILVER lured people Westward. Traces of "color" found by John Marshall at Sutter's Mill on the American River unleashed the stampede of 1849, one of the biggest gold rushes in history. Later discoveries attracted fortune hunters to Nevada, Montana, Colorado, and Alaska. Gold-seekers were nicknamed "sourdoughs," for the sour-smelling starter they carried with them to make bread.

Crazy turkey? Turkey loco is the highlight of this adventurous yet tradition-tied Thanksgiving dinner. Cranberries go into salsa, stuffing into chiles; sweet potatoes tingle with tequila and lime.

Stuffed Chiles

PREPARATION TIME: About 45 minutes
BAKING TIME: About 25 minutes
PER SERVING: 174 calories, 7 grams protein, 11 grams carbohydrate, 12 grams total fat, 37 milligrams cholesterol, 240 milligrams sodium

> **16 fresh green or red California (Anaheim) or ancho (poblano) chiles (2 to 2¼ lbs. *total*); or 16 small fresh pimentos or small green, red, or yellow bell peppers**
> **Chorizo Stuffing (recipe follows)**

Leave stems on chiles, pimentos, or peppers; slit each lengthwise. Pull out and discard seeds and ribs. Fill chiles equally with Chorizo Stuffing; place, side by side and stuffed side up, in a 10- by 15-inch rimmed baking pan. (At this point, you may cover and refrigerate until next day.)

Bake, uncovered, in upper third of a 400° oven until chiles are soft and light brown, about 25 minutes. Transfer to a platter, using a wide spatula.

CHORIZO STUFFING. Remove casings from ¾ pound **chorizo sausage,** purchased or homemade (page 110); or use ¾ pound bulk pork sausage. Put meat in a 12- to 14-inch frying pan over medium-high heat with 1 large clove **garlic,** minced; ¾ teaspoon **ground cumin;** and ½ teaspoon **dry oregano leaves.**

Crumble meat; stir often until browned, about 10 minutes.

Discard coarse stems and any yellow or wilted leaves from 2 pounds **spinach;** wash, drain, and coarsely chop remaining leaves. Finely chop ½ pound **button mushrooms.** Add spinach and mushrooms to meat and stir often over high heat until liquid has evaporated, about 10 minutes. Remove from heat and stir in 2 cups **soft bread crumbs,** ¾ cup shredded **jack cheese,** and 1 **large egg.** Mix well; add **salt** to taste. If made ahead, cover and refrigerate until next day before stuffing chiles.

Sweet Potatoes with Tequila & Lime

PREPARATION TIME: 10 to 25 minutes
COOKING TIME: About 20 minutes
PER SERVING: 251 calories, 2 grams protein, 23 grams carbohydrate, 18 grams total fat, 47 milligrams cholesterol, 187 milligrams sodium

> **1½ cups (¾ lb.) butter or margarine**
> **4 pounds sweet potatoes or yams**
> **¼ cup sugar**
> **¼ cup tequila (optional)**
> **2 tablespoons lime juice**
> **Salt and pepper**
> **Lime wedges or halves**

Put a rimmed metal baking pan (about 12 by 17 inches) on 2 burners over medium heat; add butter and stir until melted. Set aside.

Peel potatoes; then shred, using a food processor or coarse holes of a grater. At once, mix with butter in pan, then sprinkle with sugar. Cook over medium heat on the 2 burners, uncovered, until potatoes begin to caramelize and look slightly translucent, about 15 minutes. Turn occasionally with a wide spatula, taking care not to mash or break up shreds.

Stir in tequila (if used) and lime juice. Cook, stirring, for about 3 more minutes. Season to taste with salt and pepper. If made ahead, cover and refrigerate until next day; 15 minutes before serving, return covered pan to 2 burners over medium-low heat to warm. Stir occasionally.

Pour sweet potatoes into a bowl; garnish with lime wedges.

Roasted Onions

PREPARATION TIME: About 5 minutes
BAKING TIME: 1 to 1¼ hours
PER SERVING: 26 calories, .66 gram protein, 6 grams carbohydrate, .14 gram total fat, 0 milligram cholesterol, 72 milligrams sodium

    1½ cups water
     1 cup balsamic or red wine vinegar
     4 teaspoons firmly packed brown sugar
     ¼ teaspoon pepper
       About ½ teaspoon salt
     8 medium-size onions

Blend water, vinegar, and sugar; add pepper and ½ teaspoon of the salt. Pour equally into two 9- by 13-inch baking pans. Cut unpeeled onions in half lengthwise; place, cut side down, in vinegar mixture. (At this point, you may cover and refrigerate until next day.)

Bake, uncovered, in lower third of a 400° oven until onions give readily when gently squeezed, almost all liquid has evaporated, and cut sides of onions are glazed, 1 to 1¼ hours. Arrange, cut side up, on a platter. Season to taste with salt.

Buttered Hominy

PREPARATION TIME: 2 to 3 minutes
COOKING TIME: About 5 minutes
PER SERVING: 122 calories, 1 gram protein, 16 grams carbohydrate, 6 grams total fat, 16 milligrams cholesterol, 418 milligrams sodium

    ½ cup (¼ lb.) butter or margarine
     5 cans (14½ oz. *each*) yellow and/or white hominy, drained
       Salt and pepper

In a 12- to 14-inch frying pan, melt butter over high heat. Add hominy and stir, uncovered, until hot, about 5 minutes. Remove from heat; season to taste with salt and pepper. Pour into a bowl.

Pumpkin Crème Brûlée

PREPARATION TIME: 5 to 10 minutes for pumpkin custard; about 5 minutes for sugar crust
COOKING TIME: About 45 minutes to bake custard; 2 to 5 minutes to broil sugar crust
COOLING TIME: At least 3 hours for custard; about 15 minutes for sugar crust
PER SERVING: 285 calories, 4 grams protein, 18 grams carbohydrate, 23 grams total fat, 271 milligrams cholesterol, 30 milligrams sodium

    12 large egg yolks
    ⅔ cup granulated sugar
     1 can (1 lb.) pumpkin
     4 cups whipping cream (or 2 cups whipping cream and 2 cups half-and-half or light cream)
     2 teaspoons vanilla
       Boiling water
       Brown-sugar Brûlée Crust (directions follow)

In a large bowl, beat egg yolks and granulated sugar until thoroughly blended. Stir in pumpkin, cream, and vanilla.

Pour mixture into a 2- to 2½-quart shallow baking dish. Set dish in a larger pan and put in a 350° oven; at once pour boiling water into pan halfway up outside of dish. Bake until custard appears softly set when dish is gently shaken, 40 to 45 minutes. The surface should undulate a little but feel slightly firm when lightly touched in center.

Remove custard from oven and immediately lift from water. Let cool, then cover and refrigerate until cold, about 3 hours (or for up to 2 days).

To serve, carefully lay brown-sugar crust over custard. If you want to return dessert to refrigerator, crust will stay crisp for several hours, then gradually soften and melt. Spoon dessert into bowls in about ⅓- to ½-cup portions.

BROWN-SUGAR BRÛLÉE CRUST. Place your custard baking dish in center of a piece of heavy foil on a rimless baking sheet. With a pencil, trace around container, taking care not to tear foil. If container has a wide rim, make an inner line for actual top opening.

Heavily coat the outlined area with very soft **butter** or margarine.

Push **brown sugar** through a wire strainer to cover buttered area; allow 1 to 1½ tablespoons for each 3 square inches (Pumpkin Crème Brûlée requires 5 to 7 tablespoons).

Broil sugar about 6 inches below heat until it begins to melt, 2 to 5 minutes. Watch carefully, turning baking sheet as necessary to melt surface of the sugar evenly without scorching. Let stand until cool and hard, about 15 minutes. Ease crust free with a long spatula and use at once; or leave flat, wrap airtight, and use within 24 hours.

Lift fragile crust carefully, using a spatula to help. If crust cracks, fit pieces together on top of dessert.

ALMOST ALL-POTATO BUFFET
FOR 10 TO 12

Red, White & Brown
Baked Potatoes

Hot & Crisp Sausage

Golden Onions

Zucchini Provençal

A Trio of Sautéed Mushrooms

Tricolor Caviars

Black Beans with Blue Cheese

Sour Cream   Fresh Chives

Thousand Island Dressing

Sesame-Yogurt Topping

Shredded Jack & Cheddar Cheeses

Butter Lettuce Salad (page 70)

Ice Cream Sandwiches

Pears & Apples

Dry French Colombard   Merlot

Fruit Juices   Mineral Water

One potato, two potato, three potato, four—guests at this potato party may find themselves sampling that many baked potatoes just to savor all the tempting toppings included in the buffet.

Inspired by the potato bars in popular Western restaurants, this make-ahead menu is easy, inexpensive, and appealing to a broad range of tastes. Guests choose from nearly a dozen plain to adventurous toppings to embellish small red, white, and brown potatoes. To accompany the meal, choose a tart French Colombard and a mellow Merlot.

Look for the dried porcini and chanterelle mushrooms in the gourmet section of your supermarket; Asian markets carry the fermented salted black beans.

Red, White & Brown Baked Potatoes

PREPARATION TIME: 10 to 15 minutes
BAKING TIME: About 1 hour
PER 8 OUNCE POTATO: 175 calories, 5 grams protein, 40 grams carbohydrate, .22 gram total fat, 0 milligram cholesterol, 15 milligrams sodium

---

Scrub 3 to 4 pounds *each* (at least 9 lbs. *total*) **small red thin-skinned potatoes, white thin-skinned potatoes,** and **russet potatoes,** each 2½ to 3½ inches in diameter. Wipe potatoes dry, then rub skin with **butter,** margarine, or solid vegetable shortening (in all, you'll need about ⅓ cup). Pierce each potato in several places with a fork to let steam escape during baking.

Arrange potatoes in two or three 10- by 15-inch rimmed baking pans; keep larger potatoes together in 1 pan.

Bake potatoes, uncovered, in a 400° oven until they give readily to gentle pressure, about 1 hour for larger potatoes, 45 minutes for smaller ones. (Put larger potatoes in to bake first; add smaller ones after 15 minutes.)

Serve, or keep hot for up to 2 hours in a turned-off (but still warm) oven or in an insulated picnic chest.

To serve, pile hot potatoes in a basket or on a platter; place tongs alongside.

Hot & Crisp Sausage

PREPARATION TIME: 2 to 3 minutes
COOKING TIME: About 40 minutes
PER SERVING: 268 calories, 17 grams protein, 1 gram carbohydrate, 21 grams total fat, 65 milligrams cholesterol, 765 milligrams sodium

---

Remove casings from 1½ pounds *each* (3 lbs. *total*) **hot** and **mild Italian sausage;** coarsely chop sausage. Place in a 12- to 14-inch frying pan. Cook, uncovered, over medium-high heat, stirring frequently, until brown and crisp, about 40 minutes; discard fat. Season to taste with **salt** and **pepper.**

If made ahead, cover sausage and refrigerate for up to 2 days. Reheat before serving, stirring occasionally.

Spoon hot sausage into a bowl, then keep hot on a warming tray. Makes about 4 cups; allow ⅓ cup for a serving.

Golden Onions

PREPARATION TIME: 10 to 15 minutes
COOKING TIME: About 50 minutes
PER SERVING: 96 calories, 2 grams protein, 10 grams carbohydrate, 6 grams total fat, 16 milligrams cholesterol, 61 milligrams sodium

---

Thinly slice 7 large **onions** (about 3½ lbs. *total*). Melt 6 tablespoons **butter** or margarine in a 12- to 14-inch frying pan over medium heat. Add onions, cover, and cook until soft, about 15 minutes, stirring often. Remove cover and continue cooking, stirring often, until onions are very soft and pale gold, about 35 more minutes. Season to taste with **salt** and **pepper.**

If made ahead, cover and refrigerate for up to 2 days. Reheat over low heat before serving, stirring occasionally.

Spoon hot onions into a bowl, then keep hot on a warming tray. Makes about 3 cups; allow ¼ cup for a serving.

Zucchini Provençal

PREPARATION TIME: About 5 minutes
COOKING TIME: About 30 minutes
PER SERVING: 53 calories, 1 gram protein, 6 grams carbohydrate, 3 grams total fat, 0 milligram cholesterol, 143 milligrams sodium

Cut off and discard ends from 2 pounds **zucchini** (6 to 8 medium-size), then cut zucchini into ⅛-inch-thick slices. In a 12- to 14-inch frying pan over medium heat, cook zucchini in 2 tablespoons **olive oil** or salad oil, stirring constantly, until lightly browned, about 15 minutes. Stir in 1 can (about 1 lb.) **stewed tomatoes** and ½ teaspoon *each* **dry basil** and **dry oregano leaves.** Boil, uncovered, until liquid has evaporated, about 15 minutes, stirring gently.

If made ahead, let cool, then cover and refrigerate for up to 2 days. Reheat over medium heat before serving, stirring occasionally.

Pour hot zucchini into a bowl, then keep hot on a warming tray. Makes about 4 cups; allow ⅓ cup for a serving.

A Trio of Sautéed Mushrooms

PREPARATION TIME: 10 to 20 minutes
COOKING TIME: 20 to 30 minutes
PER SERVING: 78 calories, 2 grams protein, 6 grams carbohydrate, 6 grams total fat, 16 milligrams cholesterol, 63 milligrams sodium

Immerse 1 ounce *each* **dried porcini mushrooms** (cèpes or boletes) and **dried chanterelle mushrooms** (or 2 oz. *total* of either mushroom) in hottest tap water and let stand for 10 minutes; drain. Rinse several times with cool water; drain. Set aside.

In a 10- to 12-inch frying pan, melt 3 tablespoons **butter** or margarine. Add 1½ pounds **button mushrooms,** sliced. Cook, uncovered, stirring often, until liquid has evaporated, about 15 minutes. Add 2 more tablespoons **butter** or margarine to pan and, when melted, stir in cèpes, chanterelles, and ¼ teaspoon **dry thyme leaves.** Cook, stirring, until mushrooms are lightly browned. Season to taste with **salt** and **pepper.**

If made ahead, cover and refrigerate for up to 2 days. Reheat mushrooms over medium heat before serving, stirring; if mixture seems dry, add about 1 tablespoon **butter** or margarine.

Pour hot mushrooms into a bowl, then keep hot on a warming tray. Makes about 3 cups; allow ¼ cup for a serving.

Tricolor Caviars

PREPARATION TIME: 3 to 4 minutes
PER TABLESPOON: 45 calories, 5 grams protein, .69 gram carbohydrate, 2 grams total fat, 54 milligrams cholesterol, 312 milligrams sodium

You'll need 2 ounces (¼ cup) *each* chilled **black lumpfish caviar, red salmon caviar,** and **golden whitefish caviar.** (If using pasteurized caviars, pour them individually into a fine strainer and rinse under cool running **water** to remove excess salt and dye; drain well.) Just before serving, spoon caviars into small individual dishes and nestle in a larger rimmed container filled with small **ice cubes.** Allow 1 tablespoon caviar for a serving.

Black Beans with Blue Cheese

PREPARATION TIME: 5 to 10 minutes
STANDING TIME: At least 4 hours
PER SERVING: 136 calories, 5 grams protein, 2 grams carbohydrate, 12 grams total fat, 26 milligrams cholesterol, 984 milligrams sodium

Thoroughly rinse 1⅔ cups (8½ oz.) **fermented salted black beans.** Drain; set aside.

Stir together ¼ cup **white wine vinegar,** 1 large **egg yolk,** and 1 large clove **garlic** (minced or pressed). Whisk in ½ cup **salad oil** and ⅛ teaspoon **pepper.** Stir in beans. Cover and let stand for at least 4 hours (or refrigerate for up to 2 days, then bring to room temperature before serving). Stir in ½ cup chopped **parsley** and spoon into a serving bowl. Top with 1 cup (4 oz.) crumbled **blue-veined cheese.** Makes about 3 cups; allow about ¼ cup for a serving.

Sesame-Yogurt Topping

PREPARATION TIME: 3 to 5 minutes
STANDING TIME: At least 2 hours
PER TABLESPOON: 25 calories, .94 gram protein, 1 gram carbohydrate, 2 grams total fat, 1 milligram cholesterol, 7 milligrams sodium

Stir together ¼ cup **canned tahini** (sesame-seed paste); 1 cup **plain yogurt;** 2 **green onions** (including tops), finely chopped; and 2 cloves **garlic,** minced or pressed. Season to taste with **salt** and **pepper.** Cover and let stand for at least 2 hours. If made ahead, cover and refrigerate for up to 3 days. Makes about 1⅓ cups; allow 1 to 2 tablespoons for a serving.

LIKE AVOCADOS and chiles, potatoes are native to the Western Hemisphere. Spanish explorers discovered them centuries ago—and soon introduced them to Europe. Today's Western russets, also known as Idahos, grow not only in Idaho but also in Washington, Oregon, and California. Our red thin-skinned potatoes come from California and Colorado, white ones from California.

MALIHINI LUAU PARTY
FOR 8

Pupus of Your Choice

Hawaiian-style Curry:
Skewered Grilled Chicken Legs &
Shrimp with Curried Coconut
Cream Sauce

Hot Cooked Rice

Pineapple Wheels

Pickled Pink Onions

Condiments

Tropical Fruit Spritzers

Sliced Papayas with Lime Sherbet

In Hawaiian, malihini means "newcomer"—a term which also aptly describes key ingredients in this luau menu. Pungent curry spices from India and Southeast Asia—newcomers to island cuisine—blend deliciously with local foods.

Serve this Hawaiian-style curry directly from the barbecue. Skewered chicken and shrimp marinate in a thick, golden curry sauce before grilling. More sauce goes over the accompanying rice and pineapple. Island specialties, from macadamia nuts to mango chutney, make a tempting array of curry condiments.

To begin the meal, offer pupus (Hawaiian for "appetizers") such as crack seed (sweet and sour dried fruits), taro or coconut chips, Oriental pickled onions, sashimi, and sliced Chinese sausages. To make the Tropical Fruit Spritzers, let guests mix equal parts of dry white wine, sparkling mineral water, and a tropical fruit juice such as guava, papaya, or passion fruit.

Hawaiian-style Curry

PREPARATION TIME: 45 to 55 minutes to make coconut sauce; 5 to 10 minutes to make pink onions; about 5 minutes to cut up pineapple; 5 to 10 minutes to assemble condiments; about 15 minutes to skewer foods; 30 to 40 minutes to ignite charcoal; about 25 minutes to cook rice

MARINATING TIME: At least 4 hours

GRILLING TIME: 40 to 45 minutes

PER SERVING OF CHICKEN, SHRIMP, AND SAUCE: 1090 calories, 53 grams protein, 83 grams carbohydrate, 61 grams total fat, 199 milligrams cholesterol, 288 milligrams sodium

PER SERVING OF ONIONS: 36 calories, .53 gram protein, 9 grams carbohydrate, .11 gram total fat, 0 milligram cholesterol, 331 milligrams sodium

Curried Coconut Cream Sauce
(recipe follows)
16 chicken drumsticks (4 to 6 oz. *each*)
40 large shrimp (about 1¼ lbs. *total*), shelled
and deveined
15 green onions (including tops), cut into
2-inch lengths

8 to 10 cups hot cooked rice
1 large ripe pineapple (about 5 lbs.), peeled
and cut crosswise into 8 slices
Pickled Pink Onions (recipe follows)
Condiments (suggestions follow)

Pour 1 cup of the Curried Coconut Cream Sauce into a large heavy plastic bag set in a large pan. Rinse chicken and pat dry, then add to sauce in bag; mix to coat. Seal bag securely. In another heavy plastic bag, combine shrimp and ½ cup of the sauce; mix to coat, then seal bag and set beside chicken. Refrigerate for at least 4 hours or until next day, turning bags over occasionally. Also cover and refrigerate remaining sauce.

If using bamboo skewers, soak about 24 skewers in hot water to cover for 30 minutes. On a pair of parallel bamboo or metal skewers, thread 3 or 4 drumsticks alternately with onion pieces. Repeat with remaining chicken, using 3 or 4 more pairs of skewers. Thread 5 shrimp on a pair of parallel skewers, alternating with onion pieces; repeat with remaining shrimp, using 7 more pairs of skewers.

Place chicken skewers on a lightly greased grill 4 to 6 inches above a solid bed of medium coals (you should be able to hold your hand at grill level for 4 to 5 seconds). Cook, turning frequently, until chicken is no longer pink at bone (cut to test), 35 to 40 minutes. Set shrimp skewers on grill next to chicken. Cook, turning occasionally, until shrimp turn pink, 3 to 6 minutes.

Meanwhile, place remaining Curried Coconut Cream Sauce in a 3- to 4-quart pan and stir frequently over medium heat until hot, about 15 minutes. Pour sauce into a 1½-quart serving bowl.

Spoon rice over half of a large platter; arrange pineapple slices over other half. Present grilled chicken and shrimp skewers on top of fruit and rice.

To serve, place about 1 cup rice and 1 pineapple slice on each individual plate; slide chicken and shrimp from skewers onto plates. Top foods with sauce, then spoon Pickled Pink Onions and condiments alongside.

CURRIED COCONUT CREAM SAUCE. Melt 6 tablespoons **butter** or margarine in a 12- to 14-inch frying pan over medium-high heat. Add 3 large **onions,** chopped; 3 cloves **garlic,** minced or pressed; and 2 tablespoons minced **fresh ginger.** Cook, stirring occasionally, until onions are soft, about 15 minutes. Stir in ¼ cup **all-purpose flour,** 3 tablespoons **curry powder,** 1 tablespoon **sugar,** and ½ teaspoon **crushed dried hot red chiles.** Cook, stirring occasionally, until hot and bubbly. Remove from heat and smoothly blend in 4 cans (12 to 14 oz. *each*) **coconut milk,** thawed if frozen. (As an alternative to coconut milk, you may use 6 cups half-and-half or light cream mixed with 1 tablespoon *each* sugar and imitation coconut extract.)

Bring sauce to a boil over medium heat, stirring frequently. Continue to cook, uncovered, stirring frequently, until sauce is reduced to about 6 cups, 15 to 20 minutes. Season to taste with **salt.**

PICKLED PINK ONIONS. Thinly slice 2 large **mild red onions** and separate into rings. Place in a bowl and mix in 1½ tablespoons **salt.** Knead onions with your hands until limp. Place onions in a colander and rinse thoroughly with **cold water;** drain, place in a bowl, and add ¼ cup *each* **sugar** and **white wine vinegar.** Mix gently but thoroughly. If made ahead,

cover and let stand at room temperature until next day.

CONDIMENTS. Arrange in separate small containers: 1 cup **unsweetened flaked coconut;** 1 cup coarsely chopped **mango chutney;** 3 medium-size **ripe bananas,** sliced and coated with 1 tablespoon **lemon juice;** 1 cup **salted macadamia nuts** or peanuts, coarsely chopped; 2 **limes,** cut into wedges; ¾ cup lightly packed **fresh cilantro (coriander) leaves;** and about 2 tablespoons **crushed dried hot red chiles** (use cautiously).

Dust off the ukulele and bring on the leis—Hawaii's own way with curry makes a lavish spectacle. Grilled shrimp and chicken go with rice, pineapple, golden curry-coconut sauce and Island condiments.

The Best of Sunset

APPETIZERS

Fresh, exuberantly flavored, visually exciting—that's the nature of the varied and imaginative appetizers in this chapter.

With the zest of an artist facing a blank canvas, Sunset *creates hors d'oeuvres and snacks that showcase the West's vegetables, fruits, and other natural splendor—as simply as in Peas in the Pod or as elegantly as in Asparagus in Belgian Endive or Chèvre & Green Grapes.*

Let the dozens of appetizers in these pages—hot and cold, light and hearty—enrich your entertaining repertoire. And look for other appetizer and first-course ideas throughout the book; you'll find still more suggestions in our Salads chapter and in our Walk-around Reception for 40, for example.

At your next social event—whether for a few or for a multitude—this chapter will help you give your guests a fresh and exuberant Western welcome.

What's crackly, cheesy, and flamboyant with
Southwestern flavors? One taste, and you'll never forget
the name—Arizona Cheese Crisps (recipe on page 38).

Japanese Rumaki

PREPARATION TIME: About 30 minutes
MARINATING TIME: At least 2 hours
BROILING TIME: 5 to 8 minutes
PER APPETIZER: 53 calories, 5 grams protein, 3 grams carbohydrate, 3 grams total fat, 86 milligrams cholesterol, 367 milligrams sodium

Easy to make and a guaranteed favorite with guests, rumaki have been a busy hostess's standby for more than four decades. Years ago, these appetizers were considered rather exotic and unusual; today, we enjoy them simply for their great flavor.

Makes about 1½ dozen appetizers

¾ **pound chicken livers**
½ **pound sliced bacon**
1 **can (about 8 oz.) whole water chestnuts, drained**
½ **cup soy sauce**
1 **small clove garlic, pressed or minced**
½ **teaspoon crushed dried hot red chiles**
6 **thin, quarter-size slices fresh ginger**
Hot Chinese mustard (optional)

Rinse livers and pat dry, then cut each in half. Cut each bacon slice in half. Fold each piece of liver around a water chestnut, then wrap with a half-slice of bacon and carefully fasten with small, slender wooden picks.

In a bowl, combine soy, garlic, chiles, and ginger. Add chicken liver bundles, cover, and refrigerate for at least 2 or up to 8 hours, turning occasionally. Then place bundles on a rack in a 10- by 15-inch broiler pan; broil about 6 inches below heat, turning once or twice, until bacon is crisp, 5 to 8 minutes. Serve hot, with hot Chinese mustard, if desired.

Korean Beef Tartare

PREPARATION TIME: About 25 minutes
CHILLING TIME: At least 1 hour for beef tartare; at least 30 minutes to crisp lettuce
PER SERVING: 130 calories, 14 grams protein, 11 grams carbohydrate, 3 grams total fat, 32 milligrams cholesterol, 483 milligrams sodium

In this Far Eastern version of steak tartare, slivers of vividly seasoned raw beef surround a gleaming egg yolk. Add matchstick lengths of sweet pear and shredded cabbage and carrot for an adventurous first course.

Makes 4 servings

1½ **teaspoons sesame seeds**
½ **pound lean, tender boneless beef (such as sirloin or top round), trimmed of fat**
4 **teaspoons soy sauce**
2 **teaspoons sugar**
1 **teaspoon minced fresh ginger**
2 **tablespoons thinly sliced green onion (including top)**

⅛ to ¼ **teaspoon Korean ground hot red pepper or cayenne**
1 **small Asian pear or firm-ripe European pear**
Lemon juice
Red leaf or butter lettuce leaves, washed and crisped
4 **small egg yolks**
¾ **cup** *each* **finely shredded carrot and green cabbage**
Korean hot red pepper paste (optional)

Toast sesame seeds in a 6- to 7-inch frying pan over medium heat until golden, about 2 minutes, shaking pan frequently. Crush with a mortar and pestle (or whirl briefly in a blender); set aside.

Cut beef across the grain into ¼-inch slices; then cut slices into matchstick slivers. Combine sesame seeds, soy, sugar, ginger, onion, and red pepper; mix with meat. Cover and refrigerate for at least 1 hour or up to 4 hours.

Peel and core pear; cut into matchstick slivers and moisten with lemon juice. Line 4 plates with lettuce. Mound ¼ of the meat mixture on each plate, make a well in the center, and slip in an egg yolk. Arrange pear, carrot, cabbage, and a dab of pepper paste (if used) around meat.

To eat, mix egg yolk with meat; accompany with vegetables and pear.

Onion Knots with Ground Nut Sauce

PREPARATION TIME: 25 to 30 minutes
PER APPETIZER: 21 calories, .81 gram protein, 3 grams carbohydrate, .93 gram total fat, 0 milligram cholesterol, 46 milligrams sodium

When blanched, green onions lose their sassy bite, becoming sweetly mild—and flexible enough to tie in graceful loops. Dipped into our hot-sweet peanut sauce, they make a terrific appetizer.

Makes 2 to 3 dozen appetizers

Rinse 24 to 36 **green onions** and cut off roots. Immerse onions, a few at a time, in **boiling water** just until green ends begin to get limp, about 20 seconds. Lift out and at once immerse in **ice water;** when cool, lay out straight on muslin or paper towels to drain.

Pull tough outside layer (or layers) off each onion. Tie each onion in a loose knot so that white end protrudes about 1 inch; trim off green end about 1 inch from knot. Arrange onions on a tray. If made ahead, cover and refrigerate for up to 6 hours.

To prepare sauce, blend ¼ cup *each* **chunk-style peanut butter** and **plum jam** with 1 tablespoon **soy sauce.** Season to taste with **liquid hot pepper seasoning.** Spoon into a small bowl.

Place sauce on tray with onions. Dip white ends into sauce to eat.

Thai Leaf Wrap Appetizer

PREPARATION TIME: About 30 minutes
CHILLING TIME: At least 30 minutes to crisp lettuce
PER SERVING: 135 calories, 7 grams protein, 7 grams carbohydrate, 10 grams total fat, 18 milligrams cholesterol, 74 milligrams sodium

A snack sold in the open-air markets of Bangkok inspired this appealing appetizer of lettuce leaves filled with shrimp, peanuts, chiles, and other savory tidbits. Each bite is sweet, sour, hot, salty—and incredibly good.

Makes 5 or 6 servings

> 1 large head butter lettuce (about ⅓ lb.)
> ½ cup unsweetened shredded coconut
>   Coconut Syrup (recipe follows)
> ½ lime
> ½ cup tiny cooked, shelled shrimp
> ¼ cup thinly sliced shallots or red onion
> 3 tablespoons slivered fresh ginger
> ½ cup roasted salted peanuts
> ¼ to ½ cup chopped fresh or canned hot chiles, such as jalapeño

Rinse lettuce leaves and pat dry. Wrap in paper towels, enclose in plastic bags, and refrigerate for at least 30 minutes or up to 2 days.

Meanwhile, toast coconut in a 10- to 12-inch frying pan over medium-low heat until golden, 5 to 8 minutes, stirring frequently. Use ¼ cup to prepare Coconut Syrup; set remainder aside.

Tear or cut large lettuce leaves in half to make smaller cups. Thinly slice lime, then cut each slice into quarters.

On a serving tray, arrange lettuce, lime, shrimp, shallots, ginger, peanuts, chiles, reserved ¼ cup toasted coconut, and Coconut Syrup. To eat, spoon a bit of each condiment inside a lettuce leaf, drizzle lightly with syrup, wrap up, and eat.

COCONUT SYRUP. In a 1- to 1½-quart pan, stir together ½ cup *each* **sugar** and **water.** Bring to a boil over high heat; boil, uncovered, until syrup is reduced to about ½ cup, 3 to 5 minutes. Let cool. If made ahead, cover and refrigerate (syrup keeps indefinitely).

Shortly before serving, stir in 2 teaspoons minced **fresh ginger,** 2 tablespoons finely chopped **roasted salted peanuts,** and ¼ cup **toasted coconut.**
PER TABLESPOON: 50 calories, .48 gram protein, 9 grams carbohydrate, 1 gram total fat, 0 milligram cholesterol, 7 milligrams sodium.

Broiled Figs

PREPARATION TIME: About 15 minutes
BROILING TIME: 5 to 8 minutes
PER APPETIZER: 38 calories, 1 gram protein, 5 grams carbohydrate, 2 grams total fat, 3 milligrams cholesterol, 73 milligrams sodium

Fig trees flourish in the West, producing staggering crops that keep both home gardeners and Sunset home economics editors busy inventing ways to use the sweet, plump fruit. (Way back in 1929, we offered a $5 prize to the reader who submitted the best fresh fig recipe.) These hot bacon-wrapped appetizers are a simple variation on classic rumaki (page 30), with halved fresh figs taking the place of the typical chicken livers and water chestnuts.

Makes 20 appetizers

Cut 10 medium-size ripe **fresh figs** in half. Cut 10 slices **bacon** in half; wrap each fig half in a half-slice of bacon and secure with a small, slender wooden pick. Dip wrapped figs into **soy sauce,** then sprinkle lightly with **sugar.**

Arrange figs on a rack in a broiler pan. Broil about 6 inches below heat, turning once or twice, until bacon is crisp, 5 to 8 minutes.

Asparagus in Belgian Endive

PREPARATION TIME: About 30 minutes
CHILLING TIME: At least 30 minutes to crisp endive
COOKING TIME: About 3 minutes
PER APPETIZER: 25 calories, .51 gram protein, .86 gram carbohydrate, 2 grams total fat, 0 milligram cholesterol, 13 milligrams sodium

Looking as fresh and tender as they taste, leaves of Belgian endive cradle barely cooked asparagus tips in this elegant-looking appetizer. Dip endive and asparagus together into the accompanying tart mustard sauce.

Makes 2 dozen appetizers

> 24 asparagus spears
> 24 large outer leaves Belgian endive or small inner romaine lettuce leaves
> 2 teaspoons Dijon mustard
> 2 tablespoons white wine vinegar
> ¼ cup olive oil or salad oil

Cut asparagus tips to about the same length as endive leaves; if desired, peel stalks with a vegetable peeler. (Reserve remaining tender sections of asparagus for other uses, if desired.)

Rinse endive in cool water and pat dry. Wrap in paper towels, enclose in plastic bags, and refrigerate for at least 30 minutes or up to 2 days.

Meanwhile, prepare mustard sauce: in a small bowl, whisk together mustard, vinegar, and oil. Set aside.

In a 5- to 6-quart pan, bring 12 cups water to a boil over high heat. Add asparagus tips, pushing them down below water. Cook, uncovered, until bright green and barely tender when pierced, about 3 minutes. Immediately drain and immerse in ice water to cool quickly; lift out and drain.

Arrange Belgian endive leaves on a tray with an asparagus tip in each. If done ahead, cover and refrigerate for up to 6 hours.

To serve, place bowl of sauce on tray; pick up leaf and asparagus tip together and dip into sauce.

"IT'S A GOOD IDEA to use the tender leaves of young red cabbage, with its beautifully curled edges, to make attractive salad cups. They make an especially interesting base for fruit salads using grapes and other late-season fruits," suggested L.M. of Los Angeles, in an early 1940s example of Sunset's involvement with readers' contributions. Such "good idea" tidbits ran at the top of early Kitchen Cabinet columns for a period of time.

Chèvre & Green Grapes

PREPARATION TIME: 15 to 20 minutes
CHILLING TIME: About 2 hours
PER APPETIZER: 9 calories, .33 gram protein, .63 gram carbohydrate, .60 gram total fat, .05 milligram cholesterol, 14 milligrams sodium

Besides flavor and aroma, an attractive design is part of any appetizer's appeal. Sweet green grapes thinly coated with tangy goat cheese and crusted in minced pistachios are winners on all counts.

Makes 40 appetizers

Using an electric mixer, beat ¼ cup (2 oz.) **unripened unflavored chèvre** (such as Montrachet) until smooth, adding ¼ to ½ teaspoon **whipping cream** or milk, if needed. Pat ½ teaspoon chèvre around each of 20 large **seedless green grapes.** Place on a plate in a single layer; cover and refrigerate until firm, about 2 hours.

Roll grapes to coat in 2½ tablespoons minced **roasted pistachios.** With a sharp knife, gently cut grapes in half lengthwise, taking care not to crumble cheese. Place cut side up on a tray. Serve; or cover and refrigerate for up to 3 hours.

Cheese-stuffed Kumquats

PREPARATION TIME: About 30 minutes
COOKING TIME: About 35 minutes
PER PIECE: 46 calories, .53 gram protein, 8 grams carbohydrate, 2 grams total fat, 5 milligrams cholesterol, 15 milligrams sodium

Stuffed kumquats are equally good as an hors d'oeuvre or as a relish with roasted or barbecued meat or poultry. The cream cheese filling offers cool contrast to the fruit's tart-sweet flavor.

Makes about 48 pieces

> 2 **cups kumquats**
> ½ **cup refrigerated or canned pineapple juice**
> 1 **cup sugar**
> 1 **large package (8 oz.) cream cheese, at room temperature**

Place kumquats in a 2- to 3-quart pan and cover with warm water; bring to a boil, then drain. Repeat 3 more times. Then cover kumquats with warm water 1 more time and bring to a boil. Reduce heat to medium, cover, and simmer until fruit is tender when pierced, about 10 minutes. Drain, reserving ½ cup of the cooking water.

In pan, combine reserved ½ cup cooking water, pineapple juice, and sugar. Stir over low heat until sugar is dissolved. Add kumquats and boil for 5 minutes. Drain kumquats; let cool.

Split kumquats on 1 side, remove seeds, and stuff generously with cream cheese. If made ahead, cover and refrigerate until next day.

Jack Cheese Wafers

PREPARATION TIME: About 5 minutes
COOKING TIME: About 7 minutes
PER WAFER: 4 calories, .22 gram protein, 0 gram carbohydrate, .30 gram total fat, .78 milligram cholesterol, 5 milligrams sodium

Cooks who prefer fuss-free appetizers can rely on these cheese wafers, which practically make themselves. You just melt cheese cubes flat in the oven; upon cooling, they turn into crackling-crisp wafers. Simple, indeed— and intriguing to eat.

Makes about 10½ dozen wafers

Cut 4 ounces **jack cheese** into ¼-inch-thick slices; cut slices into ½-inch squares. Generously coat a 12- by 17-inch baking sheet (preferably one with a nonstick finish) with **nonstick cooking spray;** arrange cheese squares at least 2 inches apart on baking sheet.

Bake in a 350° oven until bubbly, 5 to 7 minutes. Let cool just until set, then lift off baking sheet. Serve; or store airtight for up to 3 days.

Peas in the Pod

W E S T E R N   C L A S S I C

PREPARATION TIME: 5 minutes
PER SERVING: 30 calories, 2 grams protein, 5 grams carbohydrate, .14 gram total fat, 0 milligram cholesterol, 3 milligrams sodium

Served with chilled white wine, fresh peas to pop from the pod make an appetizer that literally couldn't be simpler to prepare. The flavors of light, fruity wine and sweet green peas complement each other beautifully.

Allow 8 to 10 pods for a serving

Select **pea pods** with small peas (or unblemished sugar snap peas); rinse and drain. Serve with a chilled **fruity white wine** such as Chenin Blanc, Gewürztraminer, or Fumé Blanc. Shell peas to eat.

Peter Rabbit's Delight

PREPARATION TIME: 5 to 10 seconds to peel each carrot
PER SERVING: 39 calories, .93 gram protein, 9 grams carbohydrate, .17 gram total fat, 0 milligram cholesterol, 32 milligrams sodium

Tiny carrots tantalize with their utterly fresh flavor. You can use tender, bite-size thinnings from your own garden, or purchase the baby vegetables (with their feathery tops) from a produce market.

Allow 2 to 4 carrots per serving

Select tiny **carrots,** such as those pulled for thinning, and carefully peel. Rinse carrots and tops in cold water; pluck off any coarse leaves. Serve; or wrap damp carrots and tops in paper or muslin towels, enclose in plastic bags, and refrigerate until next day.

Bartletts with Ham & Cheese

W E S T E R N   C L A S S I C

PREPARATION TIME: About 10 minutes

PER SERVING: 149 calories, 7 grams protein, 25 grams carbohydrate, 3 grams total fat, 17 milligrams cholesterol, 426 milligrams sodium

Sweetest, juiciest, most aromatic and delicate of Western pears, Bartletts are also the earliest to appear, arriving in markets in late summer. It doesn't take much to turn them into a showpiece first course.

Makes 4 servings

Peel 4 small ripe **Bartlett pears,** leaving stems in place. Brush pears all over with **lemon juice** to prevent darkening. Set each pear upright on an individual plate; accompany each pear with 2 or 3 thin slices cold **baked ham** (rolled up) and 3 or 4 thin slivers **Leyden cheese.** Eat with knife and fork.

Watermelon-Lime Appetizers

Pictured at right

W E S T E R N   C L A S S I C

PREPARATION TIME: About 10 minutes

PER SERVING: 66 calories, 1 gram protein, 15 grams carbohydrate, .87 gram total fat, 0 milligram cholesterol, 75 milligrams sodium

Bright, bold, and super simple, these crisp bites will take your palate by surprise. Sweet melon, tart lime, salt, and hot pepper seasoning combine for a very refreshing study in contrasting flavors.

Makes about 16 servings

> 1 small watermelon (12 to 15 lbs.)
> ¾ cup lime juice
> Salt
> About ½ teaspoon liquid hot pepper seasoning

Split watermelon in half crosswise, then cut half the melon into 1-inch-thick slices. Cut slices into wedges, with rind side about 2 inches wide. Set unsliced half of watermelon on a platter; mound wedges alongside.

Rub rim of a shallow 1-cup glass or bowl with some of the lime juice. Dip rim in salt to coat. Pour remaining lime juice into glass and mix with ½ teaspoon *each* salt and hot pepper seasoning. Dip a wedge of watermelon into lime mixture and taste; add more salt and hot pepper seasoning, if desired. To eat, dip wedges into lime juice mixture; have a knife at hand to cut remaining melon.

Long a summertime favorite with children, watermelon also pleases a grown-up's palate. To enjoy the sophisticated refreshment of Watermelon-Lime Appetizers (recipe at left), dip bite-size wedges into lime juice seasoned with hot pepper seasoning and salt.

Munching without Guilt

At work, at play, in afternoon, evening, or midmorning—in today's world, just about any time is right for munching. There's a problem with all this snacking, though; crackers, chips, nuts, and other favorites don't always fit a healthful diet. *Sunset* solves the problem with these alternatives to popular snack fare. They provide the crisp, crackly, crunchy munching we all love—but they're also light, nourishing, and easy on the waistline.

All of these snacks are significant to excellent sources of B vitamins, calcium, fiber, iron, phosphorus, and potassium. They're also significantly lower in fat than most purchased chips and nuts.

Water-crisped Tortilla Chips

> 12 corn tortillas (7- to 8-inch diameter) or 10 flour or whole wheat tortillas (about 8-inch diameter)
>
> Salt (optional)

Immerse tortillas 1 at a time in water. Let drain briefly, then lay flat. Cut each tortilla into 6 or 8 wedges.

Fill a 10- by 15-inch rimmed baking pan with a single layer of tortilla wedges; arrange wedges close together but not overlapping. If desired, sprinkle lightly with salt. Bake in a 500° oven for 4 minutes. Turn with a wide spatula; continue to bake until golden brown and crisp—about 3 more minutes for corn tortillas, about 1 more minute for flour tortillas. Pour chips out of pan and fill again; repeat until all are baked.

Serve chips warm or cool. Store cooled chips airtight for up to 2 weeks. Makes about 2 quarts corn chips, about 3½ quarts flour tortilla chips.

Oven-baked Vinegar Chips

> 4 large russet potatoes (about 2 lbs. *total*), scrubbed
> ½ cup malt vinegar
> Nonstick cooking spray
> Salt (optional)

Fit thin slicing blade onto an Oriental shredder, or insert thin slicing blade (about 1 millimeter) in a food processor. Evenly cut potatoes into paper-thin slices. Meanwhile, bring 3 inches of water to a boil in a 3- to 4-quart pan over high heat. Drop ¼ of the slices into boiling water; cook, uncovered, until potatoes look slightly translucent, 1 to 2 minutes. Lift potatoes from water with a slotted spoon, drain briefly, and put in a large, shallow bowl. Add vinegar and mix very gently; lift potatoes out and set aside. Repeat with remaining potatoes.

Cover bottoms of 10- by 15-inch rimmed baking pans with wire racks (racks needn't fit exactly). You need about 4 pans; if you have fewer pans and racks, cook potatoes in batches. Coat racks with nonstick cooking spray.

Lay potato slices on racks, close together but not overlapping. Sprinkle lightly with salt, if desired. Bake, uncovered, in a 225° oven for 45 minutes. Turn potato slices over; continue to bake until chips feel dry and crisp and are a light golden brown, 45 to 60 more minutes. If using 1 oven, bake 2 pans of potatoes at a time, alternating pan positions after the first 45 minutes.

With a spatula, carefully ease potato slices from racks. Serve hot or cooled. If made ahead, let cool, then store airtight for up to 1 month. Makes about 2 quarts.

Legume Crisps

> 1 cup dried garbanzo beans, brown or red (decorticated, sometimes called Persian) lentils, or green or yellow split peas
>
> 3 tablespoons salad oil
>
> Coarse salt, Cumin Salt, Curry Salt, or Red Spices Salt (at right), optional

Sort legumes and remove any debris. In a 2- to 3-quart pan, bring 4 cups water and any one of the legumes (except red lentils) to a boil over high heat. Cover and remove from heat; let stand until grains are just tender enough to chew. Allow about 15 minutes for garbanzo beans or brown lentils, about 10 minutes for green or yellow split peas.

To prepare red lentils, put in a bowl and cover with about 4 cups hottest tap water; let stand until lentils are just tender to bite, about 10 minutes.

Drain legumes. Dry, fry, season, serve, and store as directed for Whole-grain Crisps (at right). Makes about 1 cup.

Whole-grain Crisps

> 1 cup whole-grain oats, rye, triticale, wheat, or long-grain brown or white rice
>
> 3 tablespoons salad oil
>
> Coarse salt, Cumin Salt, Curry Salt, or Red Spices Salt (recipes follow), optional

In a 2- to 3-quart pan, combine any one of the grains (except white rice) with 4 cups water and bring to a boil over high heat. Cover, remove from heat, and let stand until grains are tender enough to chew, but not soft—about 1 hour for grains, 15 to 20 minutes for brown rice. Drain.

To prepare white rice, put in a strainer and rinse vigorously under cool running water until water runs clear. In a 2- to 3-quart pan, bring 4 cups water to a boil; add rice, cover, and remove from heat. Let stand until rice is just tender enough to chew, about 20 minutes. Pour rice into strainer to drain, then rinse with cold running water until cool; drain again.

For each grain, line a 10- by 15-inch rimmed baking pan with several layers of paper towels. Spread drained grain out in pan and let dry for about 1 hour; blot occasionally with more paper towels.

In a 10- to 12-inch frying pan, stir grain and oil over medium-high heat until grains smell toasted and become crisp and dry to bite, 5 to 10 minutes (white rice will turn golden). Spread grains out on paper towels to drain; blot off excess oil with more towels.

Pour each grain into a serving bowl. Flavor with salt or seasoned salt, if desired; serve immediately or store airtight for up to 2 weeks. Makes about 1½ cups.

CUMIN SALT. Combine ½ teaspoon **coarse salt**, ¼ teaspoon *each* **ground cumin** and **celery salt**, and ⅛ teaspoon *each* **cayenne** and **garlic powder.**

CURRY SALT. Combine 1 teaspoon **coarse salt**, ¾ teaspoon **curry powder**, and ½ teaspoon **dry mustard.**

RED SPICES SALT. Combine ¾ teaspoon **coarse salt**, ½ teaspoon *each* **chili powder** and **paprika**, and ½ teaspoon **cayenne.**

Red & Green Chile Cream Cheese Spread

W E S T E R N   C L A S S I C

PREPARATION TIME: About 5 minutes
PER TABLESPOON: 59 calories, 1 gram protein, 3 grams carbohydrate, 5 grams total fat, 16 milligrams cholesterol, 43 milligrams sodium

Here's a colorful and casual appetizer—a very classy take-off on cream cheese and jelly sandwiches. You can put it together in about five minutes, when unexpected guests appear at the door.

Makes about 2 cups

Unwrap 2 large packages (8 oz. *each*) **cream cheese** and place slightly apart on a serving plate. Top one with **red jalapeño jelly**, the other with **green jalapeño jelly**, using about 3 tablespoons for each. Surround with **thin wheat crackers.**

Sour Cream Caviar Mold

PREPARATION TIME: About 20 minutes
CHILLING TIME: At least 4 hours
PER SERVING: 217 calories, 12 grams protein, 4 grams carbohydrate, 17 grams total fat, 134 milligrams cholesterol, 655 milligrams sodium

This delicately molded and festively garnished cream makes a dramatic appetizer. We shaped it in a shallow mold, then decorated the wide top surface with bright beads of red and black caviar.

Makes 8 servings

> 1 envelope unflavored gelatin
> ¼ cup cold water
> 1 tablespoon distilled white or white wine vinegar
> 2 cups sour cream
> 2 jars (4 oz. *each*) red or black salmon, lumpfish, or other inexpensive caviar (or 1 jar of each)
> 3 or 4 green onions (including tops), thinly sliced
> Melba toast rounds or unsalted wheat or rye crackers

In a 1- to 1½-quart pan, sprinkle gelatin over cold water; let stand for 5 minutes to soften. Heat, stirring, until gelatin is dissolved. Add vinegar and sour cream and stir until thoroughly blended and smooth. Pour into a shallow, flat-bottomed 3- to 4-cup mold; cover and refrigerate until firm, at least 4 hours or until next day.

To unmold, immerse mold up to rim in hot tap water for about 5 seconds (mold should just begin to liquefy right at edge). Immediately remove from water and slip tip of a blunt knife down side of mold in a few places. Invert mold onto a serving plate; lift off mold. Keep cold.

Pour caviar into a fine strainer (if using 2 colors of caviar, drain each separately); rinse gently with a stream of cool water to remove excess salt and dye. Drain well, tapping strainer against a towel.

Garnish top of mold with caviar and onions, keeping each of the elements separate. Spoon small portions onto toast rounds or crackers.

Zucchini Dip

PREPARATION TIME: 5 to 10 minutes
CHILLING TIME: At least 1 hour
PER TABLESPOON: 4 calories, .29 gram protein, .59 gram carbohydrate, .06 gram total fat, .21 milligram cholesterol, 3 milligrams sodium

Serving crisp vegetables as appetizers is a popular practice. This light but bold-flavored dip for raw vegetables offers yet another way to enjoy zucchini.

Makes about 1 cup

Finely shred enough **zucchini** to make 1 cup, firmly packed. Place zucchini in a strainer and press out excess moisture. Blend zucchini with ¼ cup **plain yogurt**, 2 cloves **garlic** (minced or pressed), and **salt** to taste. Cover and refrigerate for at least 1 hour to blend flavors. Stir before serving.

Cucumber Chile Dip

PREPARATION TIME: 5 to 10 minutes
CHILLING TIME: At least 1 hour
PER TABLESPOON: 25 calories, .55 gram protein, .81 gram carbohydrate, 2 grams total fat, 7 milligrams cholesterol, 92 milligrams sodium

Transform cool, crunchy cucumbers and smooth cream cheese into a refreshing dip with the addition of green chiles. Like Zucchini Dip (above), this one is good with raw vegetables.

Makes about 1 cup

Peel and mince 1 large **cucumber**; mix in ½ teaspoon **salt** and refrigerate for at least 1 hour to release liquid.

Smoothly blend 1 small package (3 oz.) **cream cheese** (at room temperature) with 2 tablespoons **sour cream**. Drain cucumber well and blend with cream cheese mixture. Stir in 2 tablespoons **canned diced green chiles** and **salt** to taste.

Purple Bells with Peppercorn Dip

Pictured below

PREPARATION TIME: About 15 minutes
PER SERVING: 92 calories, .57 gram protein, 3 grams carbohydrate, 9 grams total fat, 6 milligrams cholesterol, 64 milligrams sodium

Not so long ago, green bell peppers were just about the only type sold in most produce departments—though in autumn, you might have found a few markets offering sweet red bell peppers (really just ripe green bells). Sunset campaigned in a number of articles for increased availability of the mature peppers, reader demand advanced the colorful revolution—and today, red, yellow, and even purple and brown bell peppers dazzle a shopper's eye. Here's an easy way to show off these brilliant newcomers.

Makes 10 servings

In a blender, combine ½ cup **mayonnaise**, 1 clove **garlic**, ¼ cup sliced **green onions** (including tops), and 1 tablespoon *each* **whole green peppercorns** (dry or drained canned) and **white wine vinegar**. Whirl until smooth. If made ahead, cover and refrigerate until next day.

Cut out stem end of 2 medium-size (about 2½-inch-tall) purple or any other color **bell peppers**. Remove seeds; reserve caps. Trim bottoms slightly, if needed, so peppers can stand (be careful not to cut holes in bottoms of peppers). Fill peppers with sauce; replace caps, if desired. Remove stems and seeds from 3 or 4 medium-size purple or any other color **bell peppers** and cut into ¼-inch strips. Serve strips alongside filled peppers to dip into dressing.

Why not a purple pepper—or yellow, or red? Today's peppers offer colorful choices for creative cooks, and here's one appetizing creation of our own: Purple Bells with Peppercorn Dip (recipe above).

Potted Pork

PREPARATION TIME: About 20 minutes (10 minutes before baking, 10 minutes after)
BAKING TIME: About 4½ hours
CHILLING TIME: About 2 hours
PER TABLESPOON: 26 calories, 3 grams protein, .05 gram carbohydrate, 1 gram total fat, 11 milligrams cholesterol, 54 milligrams sodium

This excellent potted pork comes from a Sunset article featuring foods we sampled in England's pubs. It's an enticing spread for toast, crackers, sandwiches, or raw vegetables such as bell peppers, turnips, or zucchini.

Makes 4 to 5 cups

> 3 **pounds lean boneless pork shoulder, butt, or loin end, trimmed of fat and cut into 2-inch chunks**
> 1½ **teaspoons salt**
> 1 **teaspoon pepper**
> 1 **clove garlic, minced or pressed**
> ½ **teaspoon dry thyme leaves**
> 3 or 4 **bay leaves**
> 1 **cup water**
> 5 or 6 **whole black peppercorns**
> **Toast, crackers, or crisp raw vegetables such as green bell pepper strips, turnip slices, or zucchini slices**

Place pork in a deep 2- to 2½-quart casserole. Mix in salt, pepper, garlic, thyme, and 1 bay leaf. Pour in water. Cover and bake in a 250° oven until meat falls apart in shreds when prodded with a fork, 3½ to 4½ hours.

Discard bay leaf; skim and discard fat from meat mixture. Pull meat into shreds, using 2 forks. Blend meat well with juices, then pack into a 5- to 6-cup serving container. Arrange remaining bay leaves on top as garnish; scatter with peppercorns. Cover and refrigerate until cooled to room temperature, about 2 hours (or for up to 1 week; serve at room temperature).

To serve, spread on toast, crackers, or vegetables; or use as a sandwich filling.

Bagna Cauda

PREPARATION TIME: 30 to 40 minutes for vegetables; about 10 minutes for sauce
HEATING TIME: About 5 minutes
PER SERVING: 141 calories, 1 gram protein, .53 gram carbohydrate, 15 grams total fat, 28 milligrams cholesterol, 141 milligrams sodium

The ancient custom of eating from the same dish to signify the spirit of good fellowship is deliciously represented in bagna cauda *(Italian for "hot bath"). It's simply fresh vegetables, dipped—but not cooked—in a shared bowl of bubbly butter and olive oil, bold with garlic and anchovies. Swirl the vegetable in the sauce; then eat, holding a slice of bread beneath to catch drips.*

Makes 16 to 20 servings

> 1 **cup (½ lb.) butter or margarine**
> ½ **cup olive oil**
> 5 **large cloves garlic, minced or pressed**

2 tablespoons lemon juice
1½ teaspoons pepper
2 cans (2 oz. *each*) anchovy fillets
Fresh vegetables (suggestions follow)
Thinly sliced French bread or sliced crusty rolls

In a 3- to 4-cup heatproof container, combine butter, oil, garlic, lemon juice, and pepper. Drain oil from anchovies into butter, then finely chop anchovies and add to container. Place over medium heat until butter is melted. Keep hot over a candle or alcohol flame, or reheat periodically in the kitchen. Sauce may brown lightly; check occasionally to be sure butter doesn't burn.

Present vegetables alongside; break off pieces to eat, or have a knife at hand if pieces need to be cut.

To eat, swirl a piece of vegetable through hot sauce; hold a slice of bread under each portion to catch any drips as you eat. Dip bread in sauce, too.

FRESH VEGETABLES. You'll need 1 to 2 cups vegetable pieces for each person (5 to 10 quarts for 16 to 20 servings), but you'll have to estimate quantities if you want to present vegetables whole and natural looking. Choose a colorful assortment, such as white or purple **cauliflower;** green or golden **zucchini;** red, yellow, or green **bell peppers; cherry tomatoes** or yellow pear tomatoes; **green onions;** and **edible-pod peas.** Rinse well, drain, and arrange attractively. If assembled ahead, cover with damp paper towels, then with plastic wrap, and refrigerate for up to 6 hours.

Chicken Liver Pâté

PREPARATION TIME: About 20 minutes (10 minutes before cooking, 10 minutes after)
COOKING TIME: 5 to 10 minutes
CHILLING TIME: At least 4 hours
PER SERVING: 191 calories, 5 grams protein, 2 grams carbohydrate, 18 grams total fat, 171 milligrams cholesterol, 199 milligrams sodium

Though Sunset *focuses on the Western United States, we have long explored the cuisines of other countries in our pages. We came across this simple and delectable pâté in a French country kitchen.*

Makes 12 to 16 servings

1 pound chicken livers
1½ cups (¾ lb.) butter or margarine
¼ cup chopped parsley
¼ cup chopped shallots or green onions (including tops)
½ teaspoon dry thyme leaves
2 tablespoons brandy or Madeira
½ cup dry red wine
Salt
Cornichons
Crusty bread or toast

Rinse chicken livers and pat dry; cut each in half. Melt ½ cup of the butter in a 10- to 12-inch frying pan over medium heat; add livers, parsley, shallots, and thyme. Cook, stirring often, until livers are firm but still slightly pink in center (cut to test).

In a 2- to 3-cup pan, heat brandy until bubbly; carefully ignite with a match (not beneath a vent, fan, or flammable items). Pour over livers and shake pan until flame dies. Add wine and bring to a simmer; remove from heat and let cool to room temperature.

Pour liver mixture into a blender or food processor; whirl until smoothly puréed. Cut remaining 1 cup butter into chunks. With motor running, add butter chunks, a few at a time, whirling until smooth and well blended. Season to taste with salt.

Pour liver mixture into a deep rectangular 4- to 5-cup dish or pan. Cover and refrigerate until firm, at least 4 hours (or for up to 1 week). Freeze for longer storage; thaw in refrigerator before serving.

To serve, cut pâté into slices, using a wide spatula to lift them out (first slice is hard to remove neatly). Present on a plate; accompany with cornichons and spread on bread.

Chile con Queso

W E S T E R N   C L A S S I C

PREPARATION TIME: About 15 minutes
COOKING TIME: About 10 minutes
PER APPETIZER SERVING: 138 calories, 7 grams protein, 4 grams carbohydrate, 11 grams total fat, 31 milligrams cholesterol, 536 milligrams sodium

Mexico's answer to fondue, chile con queso *is simply melted cheese with chiles, perfect for scooping onto tortilla chips and bell pepper chunks. Processed cheese gives the mixture extra smoothness.*

Makes 12 to 16 appetizer servings, 6 to 8 entrée servings

2 tablespoons butter or margarine
1 large onion, chopped
1 cup prepared hot chile salsa
1 pound processed American cheese, shredded
½ cup buttermilk or plain yogurt
6 to 8 medium-size bell peppers (red, green, yellow, or a combination), stemmed, seeded, and cut into 1-inch-wide strips
Tortilla chips

Melt butter in a 2- to 3-quart pan (one suitable to serve from, if desired) over medium-high heat. Add onion and stir often until soft, 7 to 10 minutes. Add salsa and bring to a boil. Remove from heat, add cheese, and stir until melted. Add buttermilk and stir over low heat until hot but not bubbling.

For an appetizer, keep sauce warm over a candle or on a warming tray. For an entrée, pour equal portions into small bowls. If you like, sliver several bell pepper strips to garnish servings. Present pepper strips and chips to dip into sauce.

Arizona Cheese Crisps

Pictured on page 28

PREPARATION TIME: 3 to 4 minutes to assemble each crisp (allow an additional 30 minutes if you make your own tortillas)

COOKING TIME: About 5 minutes to fry each tortilla; about 7 minutes to bake

PER APPETIZER SERVING: 265 calories, 13 grams protein, 15 grams carbohydrate, 17 grams total fat, 41 milligrams cholesterol, 554 milligrams sodium

What's a cheese crisp? It's Arizona's name for the tostada de harina, a local snack that's also popular in neighboring Sonora, Mexico. To make it, you layer cheeses, chiles, and chorizo on platter-size tortillas. (For a really authentic flavor, fry the tortillas in lard.)

Makes 12 to 16 appetizer servings,
6 to 8 entrée servings

> Lard or salad oil
> Flour tortillas (directions follow)
> 4 cups (1 lb.) shredded asadero (Mexican-style string cheese), Cheddar, or jack cheese
> 1 cup (about 4 oz.) coarsely crumbled cotija (Mexican-style dry white cheese) or 1 cup (about 5 oz.) freshly shredded Parmesan cheese
> 1 can (7 oz.) whole green chiles, cut into long, thin strips
> Fried chorizo (directions follow), optional
> Fresh cilantro (coriander) sprigs
> 1 pickled pepper or chile (optional)

In a 12- to 14-inch frying pan, melt enough lard so fat is ¼ to ½ inch deep (or pour in oil to this depth). Over high heat, bring to 375°F on a deep-frying thermometer; to check, tilt pan so fat is deep enough for thermometer to register.

Slide 1 tortilla into pan (largest ones will curve up pan sides), coating top with fat. While tortilla is still pliable, form a rim on it. If using a square pan, use 2 sets of tongs to push tortilla into a corner, guiding the edge up 1 to 3 inches against adjacent 2 sides of pan; then lift opposite rims of tortilla up 1 to 3 inches, creating a squarish bowl. If using a round pan, use pan to support 1 edge of tortilla and tongs to support 2 edges, forming a triangular bowl.

When tortilla is crisp and golden on bottom and sides are slightly rigid, 2 to 3 minutes, gently tilt it with tongs to cook each rim in fat until pale gold.

With tongs, carefully transfer tortilla to paper towels and let drain, cupped side down. Repeat to cook remaining tortillas, adding fat to maintain its depth; return temperature to 375°F before each addition.

If you fry shells ahead, let cool, then individually wrap airtight in plastic wrap (be careful—they're fragile). Store at room temperature for up to 2 days.

To make cheese crisps, sprinkle cheeses evenly inside shells. Distribute green chiles and chorizo (if used) over cheese. Put shells on a slightly larger baking pan. Bake, uncovered, in a 350° oven just until asadero, Cheddar, or jack cheese is melted, 5 to 7 minutes. Slide tortilla onto a platter; garnish with cilantro and pickled pepper (if used). While 1 tortilla is being eaten, bake another.

FLOUR TORTILLAS. Make your own tortillas as directed below, or use purchased tortillas. You need 4 tortillas 12 inches wide, 3 tortillas 15 inches wide, or 2 tortillas 18 inches wide.

In a food processor, place 2 cups **all-purpose flour;** or use 1¼ cups all-purpose flour and ⅔ cup dehydrated masa flour (corn tortilla flour). Add ¼ cup **lard** or solid vegetable shortening and 1 teaspoon **salt.** Whirl until mixture forms fine crumbs. Add ½ cup **lukewarm water,** ¼ cup at a time, and whirl until dough holds together. (Or use your fingers and rub flour, lard, and salt together until mixture forms fine crumbs; stir in water with a fork.)

Pat dough into a ball. Sprinkle a board with about ¼ cup more **all-purpose flour.** Place dough on board and knead until smooth, about 1 minute. Divide dough into quarters, thirds, or halves; to prevent drying, keep dough covered with plastic wrap at all times.

On a lightly floured board, roll dough quarters into 12-inch rounds, dough thirds into 15-inch rounds, or dough halves into 18-inch rounds; turn often and add **all-purpose flour** as needed to prevent sticking.

On an ungreased griddle, 12- by 17-inch baking sheet, or 14-inch pizza pan, cook each tortilla over medium heat until dry looking and speckled with brown on each side. (If tortilla overlaps pan, use tongs or your fingers to slide it around and to hold it away from burner.) Stack tortillas as you cook them. Use for cheese crisps; or serve hot with **butter** or margarine. If made ahead, let cool, wrap airtight, and refrigerate for up to 2 days. Makes four 12-inch tortillas, three 15-inch tortillas, or two 18-inch tortillas.

FRIED CHORIZO. Remove casings from ½ pound **chorizo sausages.** Crumble or thinly slice meat. Cook in a 10- to 12-inch frying pan over medium-high heat, stirring, until browned. Drain and discard fat. Use meat hot or cold.

Pecan-crowned Baked Brie

PREPARATION TIME: About 10 minutes

BAKING TIME: About 15 minutes

PER SERVING: 165 calories, 8 grams protein, .99 gram carbohydrate, 14 grams total fat, 40 milligrams cholesterol, 248 milligrams sodium

Soft, flowing Brie—you can wait for it to ripen to this state, but it may take a while. Or you can apply the less orthodox method used here—bake the cheese. Serve the exquisite fondue-like result with fruit wedges and bread sticks for dipping.

Makes 24 servings

Place a 2-pound whole, firm **Brie cheese** in a 10- to 11-inch round rimmed baking dish. Brush with 2 tablespoons melted **butter** or margarine. Arrange 1 cup **pecan or walnut halves** on top. Bake, uncovered, in a 350° oven just until cheese begins to melt, 15 to 20 minutes. Scoop up with **apple or pear wedges** or bread sticks. Keep hot on a warming tray.

FREEZING FOOD was a topic of much fascination during Sunset's early years. Stories in 1936 and 1940 detailed how to freeze foods, but it wasn't until after World War II that we broadened the topic and told readers how to choose a food freezer. Today, of course, freezers are standard in Western homes and commonly used to preserve foods, as well as to simplify meal and party preparations.

Oven-roasted Potato Skins

PREPARATION TIME: About 10 minutes
BAKING TIME: At least 1 hour for whole potatoes; about 12 minutes for skins
PER SERVING: 128 calories, 1 gram protein, 9 grams carbohydrate, 10 grams total fat, 27 milligrams cholesterol, 107 milligrams sodium

Mothers and food scientists know that potato skins, often tossed unappreciatively aside, are noteworthy repositories of nutrients. Hot, salted, and crusty, they're also sure to please hungry guests. Dunk the skins in prepared salsa for a spunky variation.

Makes 4 to 6 servings

> **5 large russet potatoes (2½ to 3 lbs. *total*)**
> **About ⅓ cup butter or margarine, melted**
> **Salt (optional)**

Scrub potatoes and pierce each with a fork. Place directly on oven racks. Bake, uncovered, in a 400° oven until potatoes feel soft when squeezed, about 1 hour.

Let potatoes cool until you can handle them. Cut each in half lengthwise; cut each half in half crosswise. Scoop flesh from skins with a spoon, leaving a ⅛-inch-thick shell; reserve flesh for other uses. (At this point, you may hold skins at room temperature, uncovered, for up to 6 hours.)

Brush potato skins inside and out with butter. Arrange, cut side up and side by side, on a 12- by 15-inch baking sheet. Bake, uncovered, in a 500° oven until crisp, about 12 minutes. Serve hot; sprinkle with salt, if desired.

If made ahead, let cool, then cover and refrigerate until next day. To reheat, arrange on a 12- by 15-inch baking sheet; bake, uncovered, in a 400° oven until crisp, about 8 minutes.

Grilled Italian Sausage & Cheese

PREPARATION TIME: 30 to 40 minutes to ignite charcoal; about 15 minutes to cook sausage; 5 minutes to arrange cheese
GRILLING TIME: 10 to 15 minutes
PER SERVING: 260 calories, 13 grams protein, 22 grams carbohydrate, 13 grams total fat, 36 milligrams cholesterol, 616 milligrams sodium

The barbecue is the cook for these hearty appetizers, keeping the cheese and sausages at the proper temperatures while guests assemble their own portions at their own pace.

Makes 8 to 10 servings

> **About 1 pound mild Italian sausages**
> **About 1¼ pounds teleme or jack cheese, thickly sliced**
> **1 cup (4 oz.) shredded mozzarella cheese**
> **1 loaf (about 1 lb.) sourdough or French bread**

Prick sausages in several places; then place in a 10- to 12-inch frying pan and add enough water to cover. Bring to a boil over high heat; reduce heat to low, cover, and simmer for 10 minutes. Drain and set aside. If cooked ahead, cover and refrigerate until next day.

Arrange teleme cheese slices in a rimmed metal platter (about 10 by 15 inches), such as a steak platter that can go onto the barbecue grill. Sprinkle teleme evenly with mozzarella cheese.

Place sausages on grill 4 to 6 inches above a solid bed of hot coals (you should be able to hold your hand at grill level for no more than 2 to 3 seconds). Cook sausages, turning as needed, until lightly browned and hot through (cut to test), 8 to 10 minutes. Push to a cool area of grill.

Place pan of cheese directly over coals; place bread (unwrapped) in a cooler area. Cover barbecue (or drape loosely with foil). When cheese is melted, push pan away from direct heat; slice a few sausages onto 1 end of pan.

Let guests make small open-faced sandwiches on chunks or slices of bread, using a spoonful of cheese and a piece of sausage for each. Slice more sausages as needed.

Hasty Hots

WESTERN CLASSIC

PREPARATION TIME: About 10 minutes
BROILING TIME: About 5 minutes
PER APPETIZER: 50 calories, 1 gram protein, 4 grams carbohydrate, 3 grams total fat, 3 milligrams cholesterol, 90 milligrams sodium

A standard in Sunset's hors d'oeuvre repertoire since the early years, Hasty Hots are enduring favorites for some very sound reasons: they're good tasting, easy to assemble, and made from ingredients regularly on hand in most kitchens.

Makes about 2 dozen appetizers

> **4 green onions (including tops), finely minced**
> **½ cup freshly grated Parmesan cheese**
> **About 6 tablespoons mayonnaise**
> **About 24 slices cocktail-size rye bread or ¼-inch-thick baguette slices**

Stir together onions, cheese, and 6 tablespoons of the mayonnaise until well blended; add more mayonnaise, if necessary, to give mixture a spreading consistency. Arrange bread slices side by side in a 10- by 15-inch rimmed baking pan. Broil about 6 inches below heat until bread is toasted. Turn slices over and spread cheese mixture on untoasted side. Broil about 6 inches below heat until bubbly and lightly browned, about 3 minutes.

Happy Hour Mushrooms

WESTERN CLASSIC

PREPARATION TIME: About 15 minutes
BROILING TIME: About 3 minutes
PER APPETIZER: 86 calories, 1 gram protein, 3 grams carbohydrate, 8 grams total fat,
20 milligrams cholesterol, 152 milligrams sodium

An old favorite among Sunset's tried-and-true hors d'oeuvres, these baked stuffed mushrooms rarely last longer than the first few minutes of happy hour.

Makes 10 appetizers

   10 **medium-size (1¼- to 1½-inch-diameter)
       button mushrooms (about ½ lb. *total*)**
    6 **tablespoons butter or margarine,
       at room temperature**
    1 **clove garlic, minced or pressed**
    3 **tablespoons shredded jack cheese**
    2 **tablespoons dry white or red wine**
    1 **teaspoon soy sauce**
    ⅓ **cup fine cracker crumbs**

Remove stems from mushrooms and reserve for other uses. Melt 2 tablespoons of the butter and mix well with mushroom caps. Thoroughly blend remaining 4 tablespoons butter, garlic, cheese, wine, soy, and cracker crumbs.

   Place mushrooms, cavity side up, in an 8- or 9-inch-wide baking pan. Evenly mound filling in each mushroom, pressing it in lightly. (At this point, you may cover and refrigerate for up to 6 hours.) Broil about 6 inches below heat until bubbly and lightly browned, about 3 minutes.

Artichoke Nibbles

WESTERN CLASSIC

PREPARATION TIME: 15 to 20 minutes
BAKING TIME: About 30 minutes, plus about 15 minutes to cool
PER APPETIZER: 27 calories, 1 gram protein, .68 gram carbohydrate, 2 grams total fat,
19 milligrams cholesterol, 28 milligrams sodium

Spicy cheese custard studded with marinated artichoke hearts is high on the list of Sunset's most requested appetizers. Cut into squares and serve warm, at room temperature, or cold.

Makes about 6 dozen appetizers

    2 **jars (6 oz. *each*) marinated
       artichoke hearts**
    1 **small onion, finely chopped**
    1 **clove garlic, minced or pressed**
    4 **large eggs**
    ¼ **cup fine dry bread crumbs**
    ⅛ **teaspoon *each* pepper, dry oregano leaves,
       and liquid hot pepper seasoning**
    2 **cups (8 oz.) shredded sharp
       Cheddar cheese**
    2 **tablespoons minced parsley**

Drain marinade from 1 jar of artichokes into a 10- to 12-inch frying pan. Drain remaining jar; reserve marinade for other uses. Chop all artichokes and set aside. Heat marinade in frying pan over medium heat; add onion and garlic and cook, stirring, until onion is soft.

   In a bowl, beat eggs with a fork. Stir in bread crumbs, pepper, oregano, and hot pepper seasoning. Then stir in cheese, parsley, artichokes, and onion mixture. Pour into a greased 7- by 11-inch baking pan; bake, uncovered, in a 325° oven until custard feels set when lightly touched, about 30 minutes. Let stand in pan until warm, about 15 minutes; or let cool completely. Cut into 1-inch squares.

   Serve; or cover and refrigerate, then serve cold. To reheat, bake, uncovered, in a 325° oven until hot, 10 to 12 minutes.

Crisp Artichoke Appetizers

WESTERN CLASSIC

PREPARATION TIME: 15 to 20 minutes
DEEP-FRYING TIME: About 10 minutes (includes time to heat oil)
PER APPETIZER: 27 calories, .80 gram protein, 3 grams carbohydrate, 1 gram total fat,
8 milligrams cholesterol, 57 milligrams sodium

A big, broad thistle plant, the artichoke thrives along the cool, misty California coastline between San Francisco and Monterey. These fried artichokes are a specialty of Castroville, the self-proclaimed Artichoke Capital of the World.

Makes 2½ to 3 dozen appetizers

    1 **large egg**
    ¼ **cup water**
    ½ **teaspoon salt**
    ¼ **teaspoon pepper**
    5 **medium-size artichokes**
      Salad oil
      Fine dry bread crumbs

In a bowl, beat together egg, water, salt, and pepper. Set aside.

   Cut off top half of each artichoke and trim stem to 1 inch. Snap off tough outer leaves down to pale green inner leaves; trim base to make smooth. Cut each artichoke in half lengthwise and remove fuzzy choke. Then, holding each artichoke half steady with your hand, cut lengthwise into ¼-inch-thick slices (cut end pieces in half). Add to egg mixture and stir to coat.

   In a deep 3- to 4-quart pan, heat 1 to 1½ inches oil to 375°F on a deep-frying thermometer. Lift artichoke pieces, 1 at a time, from egg mixture; drain, coat with bread crumbs, and shake off excess. Add to oil (do not crowd pan); cook, turning once, until golden brown, about 1 minute. Remove with a slotted spoon and drain well on paper towels.

   Serve as cooked, or arrange in a single layer on baking sheets and keep warm in a 150° oven until all are cooked.

Golden, light, and parchment-thin, Won Ton Crispies (recipe below) intrigue guests with the appetizing appeal of a Western Classic.

Fila Cheese Onion Rolls

PREPARATION TIME: About 20 minutes to cook onions; about 25 minutes to fill and shape
BAKING TIME: 12 to 17 minutes
PER APPETIZER: 50 calories, 2 grams protein, 3 grams carbohydrate, 3 grams total fat, 10 milligrams cholesterol, 34 milligrams sodium

Some cooks think of fila pastry as a sort of kitchen miracle worker; you can use the tissue-thin sheets to produce wonderfully impressive treats, both savory and sweet, in very little time. Here, crackly layers of fila enclose a mellow cheese and onion filling.

Makes about 5 dozen appetizers

- ½ **cup (¼ lb.) butter or margarine**
- 3 **large onions, thinly sliced**
- 2 **small packages (3 oz. *each*) cream cheese, at room temperature**
- 1½ **cups (6 oz.) shredded Gruyère, Samsoe, or Swiss cheese**
- ½ **teaspoon caraway seeds (optional)**
- 9 **to 12 sheets fila, *each* about 16 by 24 inches (about ½ lb. *total*), thawed if frozen**

Melt 3 tablespoons of the butter in a 10- to 12-inch frying pan over medium heat. Add onions; cook, stirring frequently, until soft and pale gold but not browned, about 20 minutes. Remove from heat and let stand until lukewarm; then mix in cream cheese, Gruyère, and caraway seeds (if used). Set aside.

Melt remaining 5 tablespoons butter. To make each cheese roll, stack 3 or 4 fila sheets, brushing very lightly between layers with some of the butter (just streak in a few places; don't coat the whole sheet). Along widest edge of top sheet of fila, spoon ⅓ of the cheese-onion mixture in an even band. Roll to enclose. Cut roll in half crosswise. Place halves, seam side down and a few inches apart, in a buttered 10- by 15-inch rimmed baking pan; brush entire surface of rolls well with butter to prevent drying.

Repeat with remaining fila and cheese filling to make 2 more large rolls. (At this point, you may cover with plastic wrap and refrigerate until next day.)

Cut rolls in pans into 1-inch lengths, leaving in place. Bake, uncovered, in a 400° oven until very well browned, about 12 minutes (about 17 minutes if refrigerated). Let cool slightly, then serve. Bake rolls in sequence if you want a continuous supply of hot appetizers; or keep warm on a warming tray.

Won Ton Crispies

Pictured above

W E S T E R N   C L A S S I C

PREPARATION TIME: 5 to 10 minutes
BAKING TIME: About 6 minutes to bake each panful
PER APPETIZER: 27 calories, .82 gram protein, 2 grams carbohydrate, 2 grams total fat, 7 milligrams cholesterol, 31 milligrams sodium

You'd guess they were deep-fried, but no—these light, cracker-crisp bites are just brushed with melted butter, sprinkled with Parmesan cheese, and quickly baked.

Makes 40 appetizers

- ¼ **cup (⅛ lb.) butter or margarine, melted**
- 20 **thin won ton skins or 5 egg roll skins**
- ½ **cup freshly grated Parmesan cheese**
  Instant minced onion; or any dry herb or herb blend (optional)

Brush some of the butter in a 10- by 15-inch rimmed baking pan. Cut each won ton skin in half to make rectangles (or cut each egg roll skin into quarters, then cut each quarter in half to make 8 small rectangles *total*). Arrange close together, without overlapping, in baking pan; brush tops with butter. Sprinkle with cheese, then with onion, if desired.

Bake, uncovered, in a 375° oven until golden, 5 to 6 minutes. Repeat until all are baked.

Chili Chicken Chunks

PREPARATION TIME: About 20 minutes for chicken; 5 to 10 minutes for each dip
DEEP-FRYING TIME: 20 to 25 minutes (includes time to heat oil)
PER APPETIZER SERVING: 197 calories, 22 grams protein, 11 grams carbohydrate, 7 grams total fat, 51 milligrams cholesterol, 174 milligrams sodium

Bite-size chunks of crisp, crusty, boneless chicken—currently jockeying for position as the American alternative to hamburgers—take on a Western character when liberally seasoned with chili powder and herbs.

Makes 8 to 10 appetizer servings,
4 or 5 entrée servings

>   3 **whole chicken breasts (about 1 lb.** *each***), split; 3 pounds chicken thighs (10 to 12); or half of each**
> ¾ **cup all-purpose flour**
> ¼ **cup yellow cornmeal**
>   2 **teaspoons chili powder**
> ½ **teaspoon** *each* **paprika and salt**
> ¼ **teaspoon** *each* **ground cumin and dry oregano leaves**
> ⅛ **teaspoon pepper**
> ¾ **cup beer**
>   **Salad oil**
>   **Dips (recipes follow)**

Skin and bone chicken. Rinse meat and pat dry, then cut into bite-size chunks (1- to 1½-inch squares or rectangles) and set aside. In a bowl, mix flour, cornmeal, chili powder, paprika, salt, cumin, oregano, and pepper. Add beer and stir until batter is smooth.

Add chicken pieces to batter; if making a combination batch, keep light and dark meat separate and add an equal amount of batter to each. Stir chicken to coat evenly.

In a deep 3- to 4-quart pan, heat 1 to 1½ inches oil to 350°F on a deep-frying thermometer. Lift chicken from batter, 1 piece at a time, and add to hot oil. Fill pan with a single layer of chicken (do not crowd); stir occasionally to separate pieces that stick together. Cook until chicken is richly browned and no longer pink in center (cut to test), about 2 minutes for breast pieces, 3 minutes for thigh pieces. Lift from oil with a slotted spoon and drain briefly.

Place cooked chicken in a single layer in a 10- by 15-inch rimmed baking pan lined with several thicknesses of paper towels; keep warm while you cook remaining chicken. If made ahead, let cool, then cover and refrigerate until next day. To reheat, place towel-lined pan of chicken in a 350° oven until hot, about 15 minutes.

Mound chicken in a napkin-lined basket. Pick up pieces and dunk, bite by bite, into dips.

DIPS. You'll need 1½ to 2 cups. Use 1 dip or, for variety, make up several half-recipes. (All 3 dips can be made ahead and refrigerated for up to 1 day; stir well before serving.) If you like, include purchased sauces, such as a barbecue sauce or seafood cocktail sauce.

Guacamole Dip. Pit, peel, and mash 2 medium-size ripe **avocados**. Blend avocados with ¼ cup **sour cream** or plain yogurt, 2 tablespoons **lime or lemon juice**, 2 tablespoons chopped **fresh cilantro (coriander)**, ½ teaspoon **ground cumin**, and 2 to 4 tablespoons **canned diced green chiles**. Season to taste with **salt** and **liquid hot pepper seasoning**. Makes about 2 cups.
PER TABLESPOON: 22 calories, .33 gram protein, 1 gram carbohydrate, 2 grams total fat, .10 milligram cholesterol, 8 milligrams sodium.

Dijon Dip. Blend 1 cup **mayonnaise** or sour cream with 8 to 10 tablespoons **Dijon mustard**, 2 teaspoons **lemon juice**, and ¼ teaspoon **pepper**. Makes about 1½ cups.
PER TABLESPOON: 73 calories, .10 gram protein, 1 gram carbohydrate, 8 grams total fat, 5 milligrams cholesterol, 219 milligrams sodium.

Horseradish Dip. Blend 1 cup **mayonnaise** or sour cream with 8 to 10 tablespoons **prepared horseradish** and 4 teaspoons **lemon juice**. Makes about 1½ cups.
PER TABLESPOON: 68 calories, .17 gram protein, .83 gram carbohydrate, 7 grams total fat, 5 milligrams cholesterol, 58 milligrams sodium.

Garlic Pork Nuggets

PREPARATION TIME: 15 to 20 minutes
BAKING TIME: About 1 hour
PER SERVING: 66 calories, 6 grams protein, .05 gram carbohydrate, 4 grams total fat, 25 milligrams cholesterol, 19 milligrams sodium

For an appetizer buffet that's substantial enough to serve as a light meal, include at least a few hearty snacks—such as these garlicky baked pork nuggets, originally published as part of a New Year's Eve party menu. Serve the rich, crisp chunks of meat with wooden picks for spearing and a bowl of chile salsa for dipping.

Makes about 50 servings

>   5 **pounds lean boneless pork butt or shoulder, trimmed of fat and cut into 1-inch cubes**
>   3 **cloves garlic, pressed**
>   **Freshly ground black pepper**
>   **Salt**
>   **Prepared red or green chile salsa (optional)**

Thoroughly mix pork and garlic. Sprinkle generously with pepper and lightly with salt. Spread meat mixture in a single, solid layer in 10- by 15-inch rimmed baking pans. Bake, uncovered, in a 350° oven until meat is crisp and well browned, about 1 hour; stir occasionally. Drain off fat. (If made ahead, let cool, then cover and refrigerate until next day. To serve, reheat in a 350° oven until sizzling, about 10 minutes.) Serve in a shallow container on a warming tray, or in a chafing dish in a hot water jacket over a flame. Spear cubes of meat with wooden picks; offer salsa in a small bowl for dipping, if desired.

Punches, Spritzers, Coolers & Cordials

It will come as no surprise that entertaining at *Sunset* is generally attended by fine West Coast wines. But guests who prefer nonalcoholic or lightly alcoholic drinks always find plenty of choices—such as the popular recipes here. Many begin with fruit, and several display the flavors of faraway cuisines.

Ginger Punch

- **1 small pineapple (3 to 3½ lbs.), peeled, halved, and cored; or 4 cups refrigerated or canned pineapple juice**
- **4 cups water**
- **¼ pound fresh ginger, scrubbed and cut into 1-inch chunks**
- **½ cup lemon juice**
- **About ¾ cup sugar**

Cut pineapple into 1-inch chunks and whirl, a portion at a time, in a blender with 2 cups of the water. Pour purée through a fine strainer into a large bowl, squeezing pulp to remove all juice; discard pulp. (If using pineapple juice, mix it with the 2 cups water in the bowl.) Whirl ginger in blender with remaining 2 cups water. Pour through strainer into pineapple juice, squeezing liquid from pulp; discard pulp. Stir in lemon juice, then add sugar to taste.

Pour into a pitcher, cover, and refrigerate for about 2 hours or until next day. Stir and pour over ice to serve. Makes 7 to 8 cups, about 10 servings.

Praline Eggnog

- **1¼ cups sugar**
- **3 to 6 cups milk**
- **3 cinnamon sticks (*each* about 3 inches long)**
- **1 vanilla bean (about 7 inches long), cut in half lengthwise**
- **2 cups whipping cream**
- **12 large eggs**
- **Freshly grated or ground nutmeg**

Pour half the sugar into a 3- to 4-quart pan over high heat. Shake pan frequently as sugar begins to melt, then tilt pan constantly to keep well mixed as liquid turns pale amber. Watch closely to prevent scorching. Remove from heat; at once add 3 cups of the milk, cinnamon sticks, and vanilla bean. Mixture will sputter.

Return pan to medium heat and stir until caramelized sugar is dissolved. Cover and refrigerate until cold, at least 3 hours or until next day. Remove cinnamon sticks and vanilla bean; rinse vanilla bean, let dry, and reserve for other uses.

Whip cream until it holds soft peaks. Set aside. Whip eggs with remaining sugar until about tripled in volume; then whisk egg mixture and half the cream into milk mixture. For a less rich eggnog, add remaining 3 cups milk. Pour into a 4- to 5-quart punch bowl, top with remaining whipped cream, and sprinkle with nutmeg.

If preparing ahead, whip only 1 cup of the cream; whisk into milk mixture along with eggs. Cover and refrigerate for up to 2 days. To serve, whip remaining 1 cup cream until it holds soft peaks. Whisk eggnog gently to blend, then top with whipped cream and nutmeg. Dip down into punch as you serve. Makes 12 to 16 cups, 16 to 20 servings.

Citrus Spritzer

- **4 or 5 large oranges**
- **2 or 3 large limes**
- **1 bottle (24 oz.) or 3 cups white grape juice**
- **About 3 cups sparkling water**

With a vegetable peeler, cut 3 strips of peel (*each* ½ by 3 inches, orange part only) from 1 orange; cut 2 strips (*each* ½ by 3 inches, green part only) from 1 lime. Place peel in a pitcher; bruise with a heavy spoon.

Squeeze oranges to make 2 cups juice. From 1 lime, cut 5 thin center slices; cut slices in half and reserve. Squeeze remaining limes to make ¼ cup juice. Add orange juice, lime juice, and grape juice to pitcher; mix. Serve, or cover and refrigerate until next day.

Offer citrus blend with sparkling water, reserved lime slices, and ice. For each serving, fill glass with ice, juice, and water, using about 2 parts juice to 1 part water; garnish with a lime slice. Makes about 8 cups, about 10 servings.

Dried Fruit Cordials

- **1 pound dried apricots, prunes with pits, pears, or peaches**
- **1 bottle (750 ml.) or 3⅓ cups dry white wine**
- **1 cup brandy**
- **2 cups sugar**

In a glass, ceramic, or stainless steel container, combine dried fruit, wine, brandy, and sugar. Stir well. Cover tightly and set aside at room temperature for at least a week to allow flavors to develop. Stir occasionally for the first few days until sugar is dissolved.

After 1 week, apricots, prunes, and pears will have the texture of poached fruit and be ready to eat; peaches will be comparatively firmer. The fruit taste in the wine reaches maximum intensity in 3 to 4 weeks. After about 6 weeks, the fruit may become softer than you like and, if so, should be removed and served; the wine keeps indefinitely.

To serve, offer a piece of fruit in a glass with some of the wine; sip wine and eat fruit. Or serve wine and fruit separately.

To give these fruit cordials as gifts, you can repack in small containers with tight-fitting lids. Makes about 1½ quarts (yield varies because some fruits absorb more liquid than others).

Sangría de Guadalajara

In a glass that will hold at least 1½ cups, blend 2 tablespoons **Simple Syrup** (recipe follows), 1½ tablespoons **lime juice,** and ⅓ cup chilled **sparkling water**. Drop in 4 or 5 **ice cubes,** then *carefully* pour ½ cup chilled **dry red wine** onto ice; wine will float in a distinct layer on sparkling water base.

Insert drinking straws and serve; you can sip from each layer or swirl to blend. Makes 1 serving.

SIMPLE SYRUP. Combine ½ cup *each* **sugar** and **water** in a 1- to 1½-quart pan and bring to a boil, stirring; boil until syrup is clear and sugar is completely dissolved. Cover and refrigerate until cold (syrup will keep indefinitely). Makes about ⅔ cup.

The Best of Sunset

SOUPS

Pozole, yosenabe, *or* minestrone—*the names of popular Western soups read like a roll call of nationalities that have settled here. Those who came often brought along cherished family recipes for soup. A comfort to sip, soup is also a masterpiece of economy to make, which explains why people everywhere have relied on it. The pot makes thrifty use of fuel, while working wonders with limited yet various ingredients.*

As Sunset *has demonstrated for more than 50 years, many of these classics taste even better when recrafted to display the West's bounty of fresh ingredients. The Western presentation can be imaginative, too, when it comes to serving soup—participation is often as much of the party as conversation. Guests individualize their own portions with a wide choice of garnishes, or even share in the cooking. Soup still reflects Old World tradition—but in the West, it also promises flavorful innovation.*

Six onions show their colors in A Quartet of Colorful Onion Soups (recipes on page 62). Reds make a sweet-sour borscht; whites yield a creamy bisque; yellows form a golden soup; and leeks, green onions, and chives combine in a lemon-tart green chowder.

Gazpacho

PREPARATION TIME: 1½ hours to cook Soup Broth; about 4 hours to chill Soup Broth; 20 minutes to assemble soup

CHILLING TIME: At least 30 minutes

PER SERVING: 91 calories, 2 grams protein, 12 grams carbohydrate, 4 grams total fat, 0 milligrams cholesterol, 12 milligrams sodium

This chunky, chilled, fresh tomato soup from Mexico offers guests the opportunity to season their own servings with an array of condiments presented buffet style: green onions, salted almonds, watercress, diced avocado, and lime. Each bowl of soup is equivalent to a vegetable salad.

Our gazpacho begins with a homemade broth based on chicken and ham hocks; if you'd like to save time, use canned regular-strength chicken broth instead.

Makes 8 to 10 servings

> 6 medium-size ripe tomatoes
> Soup Broth (recipe follows); or 10 cups canned regular-strength chicken broth and 1 teaspoon dry oregano leaves
> ½ teaspoon dry oregano leaves
> 1 tablespoon wine vinegar
> 1½ tablespoons olive oil
> Salt
> Condiments (suggestions follow)

Peel, core, and chop tomatoes. In a serving bowl, combine tomatoes, Soup Broth, oregano, vinegar, and oil. Season to taste with salt. Cover and refrigerate for at least 30 minutes or up to 24 hours. Offer condiments to add to each serving.

SOUP BROTH. In a 5- to 6-quart pan, combine 12 cups **Homemade Chicken Broth** (page 58) or 2 large cans (49½ oz. *each*) regular-strength chicken broth; 1 pound **meaty ham hocks,** cut into 1-inch-thick slices; 1 pound **bony chicken pieces** (wings, backs, necks); 1 teaspoon **dry oregano leaves;** and 2 medium-size **onions,** cut into chunks. Cover and bring to a boil, then reduce heat and simmer for 1½ hours.

Pour broth through a strainer into a bowl. If desired, let ham hocks cool, then discard skin, bones, and fat; reserve lean meat for other uses. Discard remaining residue from broth. Cover broth and refrigerate until fat is solidified, about 4 hours (or for up to 2 days); lift off and discard fat. Measure broth; you should have 10 cups. If necessary, add **water** to make this amount.

CONDIMENTS. Arrange in separate bowls: 1 to 1½ cups *each* chopped **green onions** (including tops), **salted almonds** (optional), and **watercress;** 2 medium-size ripe **avocados,** pitted, peeled, diced, and sprinkled with **lime juice** to prevent darkening; and 3 **limes,** cut into wedges.

ALMONDS...APRICOTS ...artichokes... avocados...these choice crops of Western soil head the long, proud alphabetical list of our regional produce that supplies much of the nation. Given Sunset's longstanding appreciation of all the West's crops and the immense spectrum grown on Western farmlands, it's hardly surprising that we're always delighted to embrace such newcomers to the produce market as jicama, kiwi, radicchio, or arugula.

Chilled Avocado Soup

W E S T E R N   C L A S S I C

PREPARATION TIME: About 5 minutes

PER SERVING: 106 calories, 2 grams protein, 6 grams carbohydrate, 9 grams total fat, 7 milligrams cholesterol, 14 milligrams sodium

The avocado has been popular with Westerners for a long time—this velvety, pale green classic appeared in Sunset's Kitchen Cabinet in 1957. Sprinkle the soup with chopped chives, or slip a spoonful of sour cream into each bowl.

Makes 4 to 6 servings

> 1 large ripe avocado
> ½ cup half-and-half, light cream, or whipping cream
> 1½ cups chilled Homemade Chicken Broth (page 58) or canned regular-strength chicken broth
> 1 tablespoon lemon juice
> Salt
> Chopped chives

Halve, pit, and peel avocado. Place avocado halves, half-and-half, broth, and lemon juice in a blender; whirl until smooth. Season to taste with salt. If made ahead, cover and refrigerate for up to 24 hours. Sprinkle each serving with chives.

Chilled Melon Soup

PREPARATION TIME: About 10 minutes

CHILLING TIME: At least 2 hours

PER SERVING: 100 calories, 1 gram protein, 24 grams carbohydrate, 1 gram total fat, 0 milligram cholesterol, 23 milligrams sodium

If you make this soup with a large melon, use the shell to create a dramatic serving bowl. First set the melon on a countertop to see which side it rests most steadily on; then slice off the top third and scoop out the flesh. Cover and chill the melon shell until serving time (or for up to 2 days); fill with soup just before serving.

Makes 6 to 8 servings

> 2 teaspoons salad oil
> 2 fresh serrano or jalapeño chiles, stemmed, seeded, and minced; or ¼ teaspoon liquid hot pepper seasoning
> ½ cup fruity white wine, such as Gewürztraminer or Chenin Blanc
> 6 to 8½ pounds green or orange honeydew, Crenshaw, Persian, casaba, or cantaloupe melon
> ⅔ cup lime juice or lemon juice
> 2 tablespoons honey
> ¼ teaspoon white pepper
> 2 or 3 strawberries, thinly sliced

Pour oil into a 1- to 2-quart pan over medium-high heat. Add chiles; cook, stirring, until soft, about 3 minutes. Add wine and bring to a boil, uncovered. (Or bring wine to a boil in pan and add hot pepper seasoning.) Remove from heat.

Cut open melon or melons. Scoop out and discard seeds. With a spoon, scoop flesh from melon shell; you need 8 to 10 cups melon.

In a food processor or blender, whirl melon pieces, wine mixture, lime juice, honey, and white pepper, a portion at a time, until puréed. Pour into a bowl; cover and refrigerate until cold, about 2 hours (or for up to 2 days).

Garnish each serving with strawberry slices.

Home-style Menudo

PREPARATION TIME: 20 to 25 minutes
COOKING TIME: About 8 hours
PER SERVING: 327 calories, 36 grams protein, 29 grams carbohydrate, 7 grams total fat, 107 milligrams cholesterol, 697 milligrams sodium

"Good for what ails you"—that's menudo's claim to fame. Thought to soothe the overindulgent after a wild night out, it's a Sunday specialty in Mexican restaurants as well as a popular family dish. Made with less-prized cuts of beef (tripe and shanks), mild chiles, and hominy, menudo is served with a variety of condiments—diners embellish their bowlfuls with cilantro, lime wedges, and more.

Makes 5 to 6 quarts, 10 to 12 servings

> 3½ pounds regular or honeycomb beef tripe, rinsed very well and cut into 1-inch squares
> 3 to 3½ pounds meaty beef shanks
> 2 medium-size onions, chopped
> 10 cloves garlic, minced or pressed
> 2 teaspoons ground cumin
> 10 cups water
> Red Chile Purée (recipe follows)
> 3 large cans (29 oz. *each*) white or yellow hominy, drained
> Salt
> Condiments (suggestions follow)

In an 8- to 10-quart pan, combine tripe, beef shanks, onions, garlic, cumin, and water. Bring to a boil over high heat. Reduce heat to low, cover, and simmer until tripe is very tender to bite, 6 to 7 hours.

Skim off and discard fat from liquid. Lift beef shanks from pan; discard bones and fat. Cut meat into chunks and return to pan along with chile purée and hominy. Season menudo to taste with salt. Bring to a boil and simmer, covered, for about 30 minutes to blend flavors. If made ahead, let cool, then cover and refrigerate for up to 2 days. Reheat to simmering before serving.

Ladle hot menudo into bowls; offer condiments to add to individual portions.

RED CHILE PURÉE. Discard stems and seeds from 9 large (5- to 6-inch) **dried California (Anaheim) or**

New Mexico chiles. Place chiles in a bowl with 3¼ cups **warm water.** Let stand until softened, 20 to 30 minutes. Discard all but 1¼ cups liquid. In a blender or food processor, whirl chiles with liquid until smooth; scrape sides of container once or twice.

CONDIMENTS. Arrange in separate bowls: 3 **limes** or lemons, cut into wedges; ½ cup **dry oregano leaves;** 1 cup **fresh cilantro (coriander) sprigs** or coarsely chopped fresh mint leaves; and 1 medium-size **onion,** chopped.

Also offer ¼ cup **crushed dried hot red chiles** or 5 **fresh serrano or jalapeño chiles,** stemmed and thinly sliced; use sparingly.

Thai Beef & Romaine Soup

PREPARATION TIME: About 10 minutes
COOKING TIME: About 4½ hours if tendon is used; about 30 minutes if tendon is not used
PER SERVING: 328 calories, 23 grams protein, 22 grams carbohydrate, 16 grams total fat, 161 milligrams cholesterol, 182 milligrams sodium

A refreshingly light party entrée, this broth-based soup from Thailand gains rich flavor from beef tendon slowly simmered to succulence. To add substance, offer a side dish of hot rice or thin noodles. (You can order beef tendon from your butcher or buy it at a Chinese meat market.)

Makes 6 to 8 servings

> 1 **pound beef tendon or ligament (optional)**
> 4½ **quarts Homemade Chicken Broth (page 58) or canned regular-strength chicken or beef broth**
> 4 **cups water**
> **Seasoned Beef (recipe follows)**
> 2 **pounds romaine lettuce, rinsed well**
> 2 **cups celery leaves**

If using beef tendon, place in a 10- to 12-quart pan and add broth and water. Simmer, covered, until tendon is very tender when pierced, 3½ to 4 hours. Lift out. When cool enough to handle, remove and discard fat. Cut tendon into about 1-inch chunks. Return to broth. (At this point, you may cover and refrigerate for up to 2 days. Lift off fat before continuing.)

Bring broth to a gentle boil. Form Seasoned Beef into about 1-inch balls and drop into broth as formed. After all beef is added, cover and simmer until meatballs are no longer pink in center (cut to test), 7 to 10 minutes. Skim and discard fat. Cut romaine crosswise into 1-inch strips. Stir in romaine, then immediately remove soup from heat. Transfer to a serving container; sprinkle with celery leaves.

SEASONED BEEF. Mix 1½ pounds **ground lean beef,** ¾ teaspoon **pepper,** 8 cloves **garlic** (minced or pressed), 3 large **eggs,** ⅓ cup minced **green onions** (including tops), ¼ cup minced **fresh cilantro (coriander),** and 1 tablespoon **fish sauce** (*nam pla*) or soy sauce.

Beef Soup with Shining Noodles

PREPARATION TIME: About 15 minutes
COOKING TIME: About 10 minutes for soup; 45 minutes for sauce
PER SERVING: 384 calories, 23 grams protein, 31 grams carbohydrate, 18 grams total fat, 51 milligrams cholesterol, 2353 milligrams sodium

Hot, peppery dishes from Hunan province in south-central China quickly gained an enthusiastic audience when introduced to the West in the '70s. This richly flavored soup is one example of Hunan cuisine. We've adjusted the amount of chiles to produce a moderately hot flavor; if you like your soup really fiery, use additional chiles or generously add our hot pepper sauce.

The soup is very simple to make. You simply bring water to a boil with bouillon cubes and bean threads, then add thinly sliced beef and heat through. (Asian markets carry bean threads and fermented black beans.)

Makes 4 servings

- 4 ounces bean threads (also called long rice or cellophane noodles)
- ¾ pound lean boneless beef (sirloin or top round)
- 2 teaspoons *each* cornstarch, dry sherry, and salad oil
- 2 tablespoons salad oil
- 3 tablespoons fermented salted black beans, rinsed and patted dry
- 3 to 6 small dried hot red chiles
- 1 tablespoon finely chopped garlic
- 6 cups water
- 6 chicken bouillon cubes
- 1 tablespoon soy sauce
- 1½ teaspoons sugar
- 3 green onions (including tops), cut into 3-inch lengths
- 1 teaspoon Oriental sesame oil (optional)
  Hunan Hot Pepper & Black Bean Sauce (recipe follows)

Soak bean threads in warm water to cover until soft and pliable, about 15 minutes. Drain, cut into 6-inch lengths, and set aside.

Cut beef into matchstick strips; mix with cornstarch, sherry, and the 2 teaspoons salad oil. Set aside.

Pour the 2 tablespoons salad oil into a 3- to 4-quart pan over high heat. Add black beans, chiles, and garlic. Cook, stirring, until chiles begin to brown, 1 to 2 minutes. Add water, bouillon cubes, soy, sugar, and bean threads. Bring to a boil; stir in beef mixture and onions. Cook, stirring occasionally, just until meat is no longer pink, about 3 minutes. Stir in sesame oil, if desired. Offer Hunan Hot Pepper & Black Bean Sauce to add to individual servings.

HUNAN HOT PEPPER & BLACK BEAN SAUCE. In a jar or bowl, mix 5 tablespoons **salad oil**, 3 tablespoons **crushed dried hot red chiles**, 1½ tablespoons **fermented salted black beans** (rinsed and drained well), 1½ tablespoons finely chopped **garlic**, 2 teaspoons **dry sherry**, and 2 teaspoons **Oriental sesame oil** (optional). Cover tightly and place on a rack over simmering water; cover and steam for 45 minutes. Let cool. Serve at room temperature. To store, cover and refrigerate for up to 6 months. Makes 1 cup.

PER TABLESPOON: 50 calories, .35 gram protein, 1 gram carbohydrate, 5 grams total fat, 0 milligram cholesterol, 133 milligrams sodium.

Korean Whole Meal Rib Soup

Pictured on facing page

PREPARATION TIME: 25 to 30 minutes
COOKING TIME: 3½ to 4 hours
PER SERVING: 761 calories, 33 grams protein, 22 grams carbohydrate, 60 grams total fat, 346 milligrams cholesterol, 1894 milligrams sodium

Beef short ribs are exceptionally popular with Koreans, and one of their favorite rib recipes is this sweet-hot soup—a dish Westerners began to enjoy in the '60s. Soy, sugar, garlic, ginger, toasted sesame seeds, and green onions create the flavor base.

In cities with large Korean populations, you can buy pre-cut ribs in supermarkets; you can also have them cut for you at your meat market. We give instructions for toasting your own sesame seeds, but you may be able to find the toasted seeds in an Oriental market.

Makes 4 servings

- 2 tablespoons sesame seeds
- 2 pounds lean beef short ribs, cut into 2- to 3-inch lengths
- 3 cups Homemade Chicken Broth (page 58) or canned regular-strength chicken or beef broth
- 6 cups water
- ⅓ cup soy sauce
- 3 tablespoons sugar
- 2 teaspoons minced or pressed garlic
- 3 thin, quarter-size slices fresh ginger
- ½ to ¾ teaspoon cayenne
- 4 green onions, root ends trimmed off
- ¼ pound daikon or turnips, peeled and thinly sliced
- 1 tablespoon Oriental sesame oil
- 4 large eggs
  Thinly sliced green onions (including tops)

A robust dish, Korean Whole Meal Rib Soup (recipe begins on facing page) combines softly cooked eggs, sliced daikon, and succulent beef short ribs to create a tasty one-dish meal. A traditional sweet-hot seasoning flavors the rich broth.

Toast sesame seeds in a 6- to 7-inch frying pan over medium heat until golden, about 2 minutes, shaking pan frequently. Reserve 1 teaspoon of the seeds; transfer remaining seeds to a mortar or blender. Coarsely crush with pestle, or whirl very briefly in blender. Place in a 5- to 6-quart pan and add ribs, broth, water, soy, sugar, garlic, ginger, cayenne, and whole onions. Bring to a boil over medium heat; reduce heat, cover, and simmer until beef is tender when pierced, 2½ to 3 hours.

With a slotted spoon, lift out ribs; let cool. Lift out and discard ginger and onions. Skim and discard fat from broth. When ribs are cool, discard bones and fat; shred meat with your fingers. Return meat to broth. (At this point, you may cover and refrigerate for up to 2 days.)

Bring soup to a boil over medium-high heat; add daikon. Reduce heat, cover, and simmer until daikon is tender to bite, 10 to 15 minutes. Add oil. Gently break eggs, 1 at a time, into barely simmering broth; cover and cook just until eggs are softly set, about 2 minutes.

Ladle soup and eggs into bowls; sprinkle sliced onions and reserved sesame seeds into soup.

Corned Beef Brisket, Sour Cream Spinach Soup

PREPARATION TIME: About 30 minutes if brisket is used; about 5 minutes if brisket is not used

COOKING TIME: About 4¼ hours if brisket is used; about 10 minutes if brisket is not used

PER SERVING OF SOUP: 157 calories, 5 grams protein, 8 grams carbohydrate, 12 grams total fat, 25 milligrams cholesterol, 481 milligrams sodium

PER SERVING OF CORNED BEEF: 402 calories, 29 grams protein, .75 grams carbohydrate, 30 grams total fat, 157 milligrams cholesterol, 1815 milligrams sodium

The first version of our enduringly popular puréed spinach soup was published in July 1955. It's still as tasty as ever—and with blenders and food processors in today's kitchens, it's also exceptionally easy to make. This version starts with boiled beef brisket; the brisket broth makes the soup base, while the sliced meat makes sandwiches to round out a classic meal. (For a shortcut, purchase the brisket cooked and use regular-strength chicken broth to make soup.)

Makes 6 to 8 servings

>   4 pounds corned beef brisket (preferably center-cut)
>   1 bay leaf
>   1 cinnamon stick (3 to 4 inches long)
>   1 small dried hot red chile
>   ½ teaspoon *each* whole coriander, whole allspice, and mustard seeds
>   1 large onion, sliced
>   2 packages (10 oz. *each*) frozen chopped spinach
>   2 cups sour cream or plain yogurt; or 1 cup *each* sour cream and yogurt

Wash corned beef well under cold running water, then place meat in a 6- to 8-quart pan. Cover with 8 cups water and bring to a boil; drain and cover again with 8 cups water. Bring to a boil, then reduce heat and add bay leaf, cinnamon stick, chile, coriander, allspice, mustard seeds, and onion. Cover and simmer gently until meat is very tender when pierced, about 4 hours. Skim and discard fat from broth.

Dip out 4 cups of the cooking broth and pour through a wire strainer; discard residue. Taste broth. If it is quite salty (as occasionally happens if the corned beef has been prepared in a particularly strong brine), discard it; instead, use 4 cups Homemade Chicken Broth (page 58) or 2 cans (14½ oz. *each*) regular-strength chicken broth.

Keep brisket hot; or let cool, then cover and refrigerate.

Combine the 4 cups broth with spinach in a 3- to 4-quart pan and bring to a boil, breaking spinach apart as quickly as possible. Whirl spinach mixture, a portion at a time, in a blender until puréed. While blending, add sour cream to 1 portion of the spinach mixture.

Return all soup to pan and stir well; then serve (reheat, if needed—do not boil). Or refrigerate and serve cold. Strain remaining brisket broth and reserve to thin chilled soup if you prefer a thinner consistency; or use for making other soups.

Serve brisket hot or cold to slice for sandwiches.

Cabbage Patch Soup

PREPARATION TIME: About 10 minutes

COOKING TIME: About 25 minutes

PER SERVING: 330 calories, 19 grams protein, 18 grams carbohydrate, 20 grams total fat, 67 milligrams cholesterol, 482 milligrams sodium

Simple, homey, and quick, this vegetable-filled ground beef soup is a sure pleaser for cool-weather family suppers. Tomatoes, red kidney beans, green cabbage, and celery add touches of color.

Makes 4 to 6 servings

>   2 tablespoons butter or margarine
>   1 pound ground lean beef
>   1 medium-size onion, thinly sliced
>   ½ cup thinly sliced celery
>   1 can (about 1 lb.) tomatoes
>   2 cups water
>   1 can (about 1 lb.) red kidney beans
>   1 teaspoon chili powder
>   ⅛ teaspoon pepper
>   2 cups finely shredded green cabbage
>   Salt

Melt butter in a 10- to 12-inch frying pan or a 5- to 6-quart pan over medium heat. Add beef; cook, stirring, until browned and crumbly. Add onion and celery and stir often for about 5 minutes.

Stir in tomatoes (break up with a spoon) and their liquid, water, beans, chili powder, and pepper. Bring to a boil; add cabbage, reduce heat, cover, and simmer until cabbage is tender, about 5 minutes. Season to taste with salt.

Lamb & Sausage Soup

PREPARATION TIME: 10 minutes; 30 minutes if meat is boned

COOKING TIME: About 3 hours

PER SERVING: 508 calories, 31 grams protein, 33 grams carbohydrate, 28 grams total fat, 87 milligrams cholesterol, 566 milligrams sodium

For comfortable, casual entertaining, few dishes can surpass a substantial soup. Only the simplest accompaniments are needed—a green salad, good bread, and perhaps a dessert. This hearty soup of lentils, lamb shanks, and plump garlic sausages is served in wide bowls, to be eaten with knife and fork as well as soup spoon.

Makes 6 to 8 servings

>   1 package (12 oz.) lentils (1¾ cups)
>   2 medium-size carrots, coarsely chopped
>   2 medium-size onions, chopped
>   9 cups water
>   4 lamb shanks
>   ¾ pound meaty ham hocks
>   About 1½ cups dry red wine
>   6 to 8 garlic sausages
>   Salt

Sort lentils and remove any debris. Rinse and drain lentils; place in an 8- to 10-quart pan and add carrots, onions, and water. Bring to a boil, then add lamb shanks, ham hocks, and 1 cup of the wine. Reduce heat, cover, and simmer gently until meats are very tender when pierced, about 2½ hours. If you wish, lift out meats; when cool enough to handle, remove skin, bones and fat. Tear meat into bite-size pieces and return to soup. (At this point, you may cover and refrigerate for up to 2 days.)

Skim (or lift off) and discard fat from soup. Bring soup to a simmer. Add sausages (whole or thickly sliced) and simmer for about 20 more minutes. Ladle soup into large soup bowls and add about 1 tablespoon wine to each serving, if desired. (A small decanter for the wine makes it easier to serve.) Season to taste with salt.

Escarole & Lamb Soup

PREPARATION TIME: About 15 minutes
COOKING TIME: About 2½ hours
PER SERVING: 606 calories, 28 grams protein, 33 grams carbohydrate, 40 grams total fat, 107 milligrams cholesterol, 323 milligrams sodium

Brimming with cubes of tender lamb, this slowly simmered meat-and-vegetable soup is an ideal and economical entrée. Delicate, leafy escarole joins the pot just before serving, adding a fresh and colorful accent.

Makes 5 or 6 servings

   1 tablespoon salad oil
   2 pounds boneless lamb stew meat, cut into 1-inch cubes
   1 medium-size onion, chopped
   1 clove garlic, minced or pressed
   1 large can (28 oz.) pear-shaped tomatoes
   4 cups Homemade Chicken Broth (page 58) or 2 cans (14½ oz. *each*) regular-strength chicken or beef broth
   1 bay leaf
   4 medium-size thin-skinned potatoes, peeled and diced
   1 medium-size head escarole
   Salt and pepper

Heat oil in a 5- to 6-quart pan over medium-high heat. Add lamb and brown well on all sides; push to side of pan. Add onion and garlic; cook, stirring often, until soft. Stir in tomatoes (break up with a spoon) and their liquid, broth, and bay leaf. Cover and simmer until meat is tender when pierced, about 1½ hours. (At this point, you may let cool, then cover and refrigerate for up to 2 days.)

Skim (or lift off) and discard fat from soup. Bring soup to a simmer. Add potatoes; cover and simmer until tender when pierced, 10 to 15 minutes. Meanwhile, wash and drain escarole; cut into thin strips. Add to soup, cover, and simmer just until escarole is tender to bite, 3 to 5 minutes. Season to taste with salt and pepper.

Sopa de Guadalajara

PREPARATION TIME: About 45 minutes
COOKING TIME: 2¾ to 3 hours
PER SERVING: 493 calories, 40 grams protein, 36 grams carbohydrate, 21 grams total fat, 115 milligrams cholesterol, 157 milligrams sodium

Inspired by the sopa de frijoles *served in a tiny restaurant in the working man's district of Guadalajara, this robust pork and bean soup goes well with hot, soft tortillas, guacamole, and beer. Add a chilled caramel flan or fresh pineapple for dessert.*

Makes 6 to 8 servings

   1 cup dried small red beans
   2 tablespoons salad oil
   3½ to 4 pounds boneless pork butt or shoulder, trimmed of fat and cut into 1½-inch cubes
   2 medium-size onions, chopped
   2 cloves garlic, minced or pressed
   2 teaspoons chili powder
   1 teaspoon *each* dry oregano leaves and cumin seeds
   7 cups water
   4 cups Homemade Chicken Broth (page 58) or 2 cans (14½ oz. *each*) regular-strength chicken or beef broth
   4 cups thinly sliced carrots
   1 can (about 8 oz.) baby corn, drained; or 1 package (10 oz.) frozen baby corn, thawed
   Salt and pepper
   Condiments (suggestions follow)

Sort beans and remove any debris; rinse beans well, drain, and set aside.

Heat oil in a 6- to 8-quart pan over medium-high heat. Add pork, about ¼ at a time, and brown well on all sides. Lift out and set aside.

Add onions and garlic to drippings in pan and cook, stirring occasionally, until onions are soft, about 10 minutes. Return pork and any accumulated juices to pan; stir in chili powder, oregano, cumin seeds, water, broth, and beans.

Bring to a boil over high heat; reduce heat, cover, and simmer until meat and beans are tender when pierced, about 1½ hours. (At this point, you may let cool, then cover and refrigerate until next day.)

Skim (or lift off) and discard fat from soup. Bring soup to a boil over high heat, stirring frequently. Add carrots; reduce heat, cover, and simmer until carrots are tender to bite, 10 to 15 minutes. Add corn and heat until steaming. Season to taste with salt and pepper.

Present condiments to add to individual servings.

CONDIMENTS. Arrange in separate bowls: 1½ to 2 cups **cherry tomatoes,** stemmed and halved; 1 cup chopped **fresh cilantro (coriander);** 1 cup **sour cream;** ½ to ¾ cup thinly sliced **green onions** (including tops); 2 or 3 **limes,** cut into wedges; and **bottled jalapeño sauce.**

DINING DISCOVERIES along the Pacific Coast, reported by Sunset *in the summer of 1930, included fried abalone in Monterey, pickled peaches at the Mission Inn of Riverside, and seafood cocktail (for 15¢) at San Francisco's Fisherman's Wharf. Up in the Northwest, there was frozen frango at Frederick & Nelson's tea room in Seattle, as well as Olympia oysters, kippered salmon, reindeer and venison. Still scarce, lamented the article, were good Mexican restaurants.*

Italy's minestrone is served up in dozens of regional interpretations. Minestrone, Genoa Style (recipe at right) presents bright green, tender-crisp vegetables, looking and tasting as fresh as springtime. A spoonful of Genoa's famous pesto sauce traditionally tops each serving.

Minestrone, Genoa Style

Pictured at left

PREPARATION TIME: 30 to 40 minutes

COOKING TIME: About 2½ hours

PER SERVING: 193 calories, 7 grams protein, 21 grams carbohydrate, 10 grams total fat, 4 milligrams cholesterol, 1530 milligrams sodium

Minestrone—Italy's hearty, everyday vegetable-and-bean soup—came West with immigrating Italian families. This all-fresh Genoese version, served with a touch of that region's distinctive pesto sauce, is one classic variation of the dish. Its refreshing character suits it perfectly to spring and summer meals.

Makes 6 to 7 quarts, 10 to 12 servings

- 4 **quarts water**
- 1 **pound ham**
- 1 **pound bony chicken pieces (wings, backs, necks)**
- ¼ **pound sliced prosciutto or bacon**
- 2 **cups diced potatoes**
- 2 **cups sliced celery**
- 4 **small zucchini, ends trimmed, cut into ½-inch slices**
  About 1½ cups sliced leeks
- 1 **pound Italian green beans, stem ends snapped off, cut into 2- to 3-inch lengths**
- ½ **cup dry salad macaroni (ditalini)**
  About 1 cup shelled fresh peas
- 3 **to 4 cups shredded green cabbage**
  Salt
- 1 **cup Basic Pesto Sauce (page 221)**

In a 6- to 8-quart pan, combine water, ham, chicken, and prosciutto. Bring to a boil; then reduce heat, cover, and simmer for 2 hours. Pour broth through a strainer, discarding meat and bones. (At this point, you may let cool, then cover and refrigerate for up to 2 days.)

Skim (or lift off) and discard fat from broth. Bring to a boil. Add potatoes; reduce heat, cover, and simmer for 10 minutes. Add celery, zucchini, leeks, beans, and macaroni; simmer until potatoes are tender to bite, about 5 more minutes. Stir in peas and cabbage and simmer until cabbage is limp but still bright green, 4 to 5 more minutes. Season to taste with salt. Immediately ladle soup into bowls; offer pesto to spoon into soup.

Pellegrini's Minestrone

PREPARATION TIME: About 45 minutes

COOKING TIME: About 1 hour to soak beans; about 2¼ hours to make soup

PER SERVING: 689 calories, 31 grams protein, 52 grams carbohydrate, 41 grams total fat, 67 milligrams cholesterol, 1051 milligrams sodium

A long-time Sunset *contributor, Dr. Angelo Pellegrini submitted his first Chefs of the West recipe in February 1949. Every vegetable included in his minestrone (a*

1984 contribution) grows in his Seattle garden; as the seasons change, so does the makeup of this satisfying soup.

Makes about 4 quarts, 8 servings

Soaked Beans (directions follow)
1 coteghino sausage (about 1 lb.) or 1 pound mild Italian sausages
8 cups water
2 tablespoons olive oil or salad oil
¼ pound pancetta (Italian-style bacon) or salt pork, minced
1 large onion, minced
3 cloves garlic, minced or pressed
¼ cup minced celery leaves
¼ cup minced Italian or regular parsley
1 can (about 14 oz.) pear-shaped tomatoes, cut into pieces; or ⅓ cup canned tomato paste; or 2 large tomatoes (peeled, cored, and chopped) and 1 cup water
4 cups Homemade Chicken Broth (page 58) or 2 cans (14½ oz. *each*) regular-strength chicken broth
1 large carrot, peeled and diced
3 large stalks celery, thinly sliced
1 large (about 3-inch-diameter) thin-skinned potato, peeled and diced
1 large zucchini, ends trimmed, thinly sliced
4 cups coarsely chopped, lightly packed greens, such as green cabbage, kale, or Swiss chard
1 cup lightly packed fresh basil leaves (optional)
Salt and pepper
1 cup (about 5 oz.) freshly grated Parmesan cheese

Soak beans as directed.

Pierce sausage casing with a fork; put sausage in pan with beans and 8 cups water. Bring to a boil; then reduce heat, cover, and simmer until beans mash readily, about 1¼ hours. Lift out sausage and set aside. (If using Italian sausages, cook for only 20 minutes, then lift out.)

Ladle beans and 1 cup cooking water into a food processor; whirl until beans are coarsely puréed (or mash beans in a food mill or with a potato masher). Return purée to pan; set aside.

In a 6- to 8-quart pan, combine oil, pancetta, onion, garlic, celery leaves, and parsley; cook over medium heat, stirring frequently, until onion is soft, about 15 minutes. Add beans and liquid, tomatoes and their liquid, broth, carrot, celery, and potato. Bring to a boil; reduce heat, cover, and simmer for 15 minutes. Add zucchini and greens; simmer, uncovered, until vegetables are tender to bite, about 8 more minutes. Add basil (if used); season to taste with salt and pepper. Slice sausage, add to soup, and simmer until hot. Ladle soup into bowls; offer cheese to add to taste.

SOAKED BEANS. Sort 2 cups **dried Great Northern beans** and remove any debris. Rinse beans, drain, and combine with 5 cups **water** in a 4- to 5-quart pan. Bring to a boil; boil for 1 to 2 minutes. Cover and let stand for 1 hour. Drain beans and use.

Pozole

PREPARATION TIME: About 40 minutes
COOKING TIME: About 2½ hours
PER SERVING: 151 calories, 6 grams protein, 21 grams carbohydrate, 5 grams total fat, 13 milligrams cholesterol, 536 milligrams sodium

From the Mexican state of Jalisco comes this regional specialty, a hot soup laden with ham and hominy. Crisp lettuce, crunchy tortilla strips, and chunks of cream cheese are just a few of the condiments added to each bowl.

Makes 8 to 10 servings

12 cups Homemade Chicken Broth (page 58) or 2 large cans (49½ oz. *each*) regular-strength chicken broth
3 pounds meaty ham hocks, cut into 1-inch-thick slices
1 pound bony chicken pieces (wings, backs, necks)
1 teaspoon dry oregano leaves
½ teaspoon cumin seeds
2 large onions, cut into chunks
1 large can (29 oz.) yellow hominy, drained
Condiments (suggestions follow)
Fresh Tomato Salsa (recipe follows)
½ recipe Tortilla Strips (page 163)

In a 6- to 8-quart pan, combine broth, ham hocks, chicken, oregano, cumin seeds, and onions. Bring to a boil; then reduce heat, cover, and simmer gently until meat is tender when pierced, about 2 hours. Pour broth through a wire strainer and return to pan; reserve ham hocks and discard chicken and onions. When ham hocks are cool enough to handle, discard skin, bones, and fat; tear meat into chunks and return to broth. (At this point, you may cover and refrigerate for up to 2 days.)

Skim (or lift off) and discard fat from broth; bring broth to a simmer. Stir in hominy, cover, and simmer gently for 30 minutes. Serve hot; offer condiments, salsa, and Tortilla Strips to add to each serving.

CONDIMENTS. Arrange in separate bowls: 2 or 3 **limes,** cut into wedges; 2 small packages (3 oz. *each*) **cream cheese,** diced; 1 jar (about 7 oz.) **roasted red peppers,** drained and diced (or 1 to 1½ cups diced red bell pepper); 2 cups shredded **iceberg lettuce;** and 1 to 1½ cups thinly sliced **green onions** (including tops).

FRESH TOMATO SALSA. Peel, core, and finely chop 2 medium-size firm-ripe **tomatoes.** Stir in ¼ cup **canned diced green chiles** and ½ cup chopped **onion.** Makes about 2 cups.
PER TABLESPOON: 3 calories, .08 gram protein, .57 gram carbohydrate, 0 milligram cholesterol, 7 milligrams sodium.

Swedish Pea Soup with Ham

PREPARATION TIME: About 12 hours for soaking Swedish peas; about 30 minutes to prepare soup

COOKING TIME: About 3½ hours; about 45 minutes to reheat

PER SERVING: 450 calories, 35 grams protein, 50 grams carbohydrate, 12 grams total fat, 61 milligrams cholesterol, 1447 milligrams sodium

In Sweden, Thursday's main meal traditionally features a hearty yellow pea soup. To make it, use Swedish whole dried yellow peas, sold in delicatessens or fancy food sections of supermarkets; or substitute yellow or green split peas. This comforting classic of Scandinavia came to Sunset by way of Huntington Beach, California, which proves that it pleases in both chilly and balmy climates. We discovered it as a thrifty and informal party entrée, served buffet style.

Makes 12 to 14 servings

> 2 **pounds Swedish whole dried yellow peas or 2 pounds yellow or green split peas**
> 3½ **quarts water**
> 3 **large onions, finely chopped**
> 4 **large carrots, finely chopped**
> 1 **teaspoon cumin seeds**
> 1 **shank-end, bone-in section fully cooked ham (5 to 6 lbs.)**
> **Mustard and prepared horseradish**
> **Buttered rye bread**
> **Salt**

Sort Swedish peas and discard any debris. Rinse and drain, then place in a 10- to 12-quart pan and add water. Bring to a boil; remove from heat, cover, and let stand until next day. (If using split peas, omit this boiling and soaking step.)

Add onions, carrots, and cumin seeds; bring to a boil. Reduce heat, cover, and simmer for 1 hour. Add ham. Cover and simmer until Swedish peas mash easily, about 2 more hours (split peas will have fallen apart). Stir occasionally to prevent sticking.

If made ahead, remove ham from soup and let meat and soup cool; then cover and refrigerate until next day. Reheat together until ham and soup are hot, about 45 minutes.

To serve, transfer ham to a platter, scrape surface clean of soup, and cut into slices. Accompany ham with mustard, horseradish, and bread. Season soup to taste with salt; serve in bowls.

Self-styled Black Bean Soup

W E S T E R N   C L A S S I C

PREPARATION TIME: 40 to 50 minutes

COOKING TIME: About 4 hours

PER SERVING: 340 calories, 13 grams protein, 38 grams carbohydrate, 16 grams total fat, 12 milligrams cholesterol, 269 milligrams sodium

Made ahead of time, this thick, smooth black bean soup is a perfect single-dish supper for casual entertaining. Guests embellish their own servings, choosing from an array of condiments.

Makes 20 to 24 servings

> ½ **cup olive oil**
> ½ **pound salt pork or bacon, diced**
> ½ **pound Westphalian ham, Black Forest ham, or prosciutto, diced; or 1 pound meaty ham hocks, cut into 2-inch-thick slices**
> 8 **large onions (about 4 lbs. *total*), chopped**
> 8 **cloves garlic, minced or pressed**
> 6 **large stalks celery (including leaves, if any), chopped**
> 2 **pounds dried black beans (about 5 cups)**
> ½ **teaspoon cayenne**
> 4 **teaspoons ground cumin**
> 6 **quarts Homemade Chicken Broth (page 58) or 4 large cans (49½ oz. *each*) regular-strength chicken broth**
> ¼ **cup wine vinegar**
> 1 **cup dry sherry**
> **Condiments (suggestions follow)**

In a 10- to 12-quart pan over medium-high heat, combine oil, salt pork, ham, onions, garlic, and celery. Cook, stirring occasionally, until vegetables are soft and lightly browned and all liquid has evaporated, about 40 minutes.

Sort beans and remove any debris; rinse beans well, drain, and add to pan along with cayenne, cumin, and broth. Bring to a boil over high heat; reduce heat, cover, and simmer until beans mash easily, 2½ to 3 hours. (If using ham hocks, lift out and let cool. Discard skin, bones, and fat; tear meat into bite-size pieces and return to pan.) Skim and discard fat.

Whirl bean mixture, a portion at a time, in a food processor or blender until smooth. If made ahead, let cool; cover and refrigerate for up to 2 days.

Return soup to pan and heat until steaming, stirring often. Blend in vinegar and sherry. Offer condiments to add to individual servings.

CONDIMENTS. Arrange in separate bowls: 3 pounds warm **kielbasa** (Polish sausage), cut into ½-inch-thick slices; 4 to 6 cups **hot cooked rice;** 2 cups finely chopped **mild red onions;** 8 **hard-cooked large eggs,** chopped; 4 **lemons,** cut into paper-thin slices; 1½ cups **sweet pickle relish;** and 2 cans (7 oz. *each*) **diced green chiles.**

Harvest Soup

PREPARATION TIME: About 45 minutes

COOKING TIME: About 2½ hours to make broth; about 30 minutes to cook vegetables

PER SERVING: 201 calories, 11 grams protein, 27 grams carbohydrate, 6 grams total fat, 19 milligrams cholesterol, 262 milligrams sodium

If an overabundant zucchini crop is causing groans at your family table or Swiss chard is losing its charm, even out the bounty by swapping with other vegetable gardeners—and then turn the swap into a harvest soup party. Into a flavorful, bubbling broth goes a sampling of fresh produce from all who appear. What you get— quickly—is a soup that's individual to the occasion and no-fail in its fresh appeal.

Home-grown strawberries, plums, or peaches might be the basis of a dessert—such as shortcake or pie.

Makes about 10 quarts, 12 to 14 servings

> 4½ **quarts Homemade Chicken Broth (page 58) or 3 large cans (49½ oz. *each*) regular-strength chicken broth**
>
> 3 **pounds meaty ham hocks, cut into 1-inch-thick slices**
>
> **About 2 pounds meaty beef shanks, cut into 1½-inch-thick slices**
>
> 2 **large onions, chopped**
>
> 4 **to 5 quarts vegetables (suggestions follow), peeled and seeded as necessary, cut into bite-size pieces**
>
> **Salt**
>
> **Sour cream**
>
> **Freshly grated Parmesan cheese**
>
> **Lemon wedges**

In a 12- to 14-quart pan, combine broth, ham hocks, beef shanks, and onions. Bring to a boil; reduce heat, cover, and simmer until meats are very tender when pierced, about 2 hours. Lift out meats; when cool enough to handle, remove and discard skin, bones, and fat. Cut meat into bite-size pieces and return to broth. (At this point, you may cover and refrigerate for up to 2 days.)

Skim (or lift off) and discard fat from broth. Return broth to a boil. To retain freshness and color, add vegetables to broth in sequence according to their cooking times—those which require 30 minutes first, then those requiring 15 minutes, then those requiring 5 minutes. After 30 minutes total cooking time, test longest-cooking vegetables for doneness; they should be tender when pierced. Season soup to taste with salt; offer sour cream, cheese, and lemon wedges to add to individual servings.

VEGETABLES. Choose any number and combination of these vegetables. (You may add tomatoes at any time; they contribute flavor all along.)

Vegetables requiring 30 minutes cooking time: beets (if used in quantity, they'll tint the soup and other vegetables red), carrots, eggplant, onions, parsnips, potatoes, rutabagas, winter squash, turnips.

Vegetables requiring 15 minutes cooking time: green beans, wax beans, bok choy, Brussels sprouts, cauliflower, celery, mild chiles, fennel, kohlrabi, Jerusalem artichokes (sunchokes), okra, bell peppers, stems of Swiss chard.

Vegetables requiring 5 minutes cooking time: Italian green beans, broccoli, cabbage, corn (cut off the cob, or cut through cob into 1-inch lengths), leafy greens, summer squash.

Creamed Barley-Prosciutto Soup

PREPARATION TIME: 5 to 10 minutes

COOKING TIME: About 40 minutes

PER SERVING: 404 calories, 15 grams protein, 32 grams carbohydrate, 25 grams total fat, 71 milligrams cholesterol, 634 milligrams sodium

Chewy, broth-plumped barley contrasts with petite green peas in this robust soup. Because barley only takes about half an hour to cook, the soup goes together in a short time. Top with grated cheese and nutmeg.

Makes 6 to 8 servings

> ¼ **cup (⅛ lb.) butter or margarine**
>
> ¼ **cup finely chopped shallots**
>
> 1 **cup pearl barley, rinsed**
>
> 6 **cups Homemade Chicken Broth (page 58) or 1 large can (49½ oz.) regular-strength chicken broth**
>
> ¼ **pound prosciutto or other dry-cured ham, cut into thin strips**
>
> ¼ **teaspoon pepper**
>
> 1 **cup whipping cream**
>
> 1 **package (10 oz.) frozen tiny peas, thawed**
>
> 1 **cup (about 5 oz.) freshly grated Parmesan cheese**
>
> **Freshly grated or ground nutmeg**

Melt butter in a 5- to 6-quart pan over medium heat. Add shallots; cook, stirring, until soft. Add barley; stir until it turns light golden. Stir in broth, prosciutto, and pepper. Bring to a boil; reduce heat, cover, and simmer until barley is tender, about 30 minutes. Add cream and peas; cook just until heated through. Offer cheese and nutmeg to sprinkle on inidividual servings.

MORE WOMEN WORKING, more men cooking—that's what we observe in today's Western home. For years, Sunset has shown that food and entertaining can be twice as exciting when everyone gets into the act, even guests. Cooks become more daring and adventurous as they pool their efforts—in a small way on a weeknight, or with a complex menu for a special party.

Lemon Chicken Soup

PREPARATION TIME: 20 to 30 minutes
COOKING TIME: About 1¾ hours
PER SERVING: 662 calories, 49 grams protein, 10 grams carbohydrate, 47 grams total fat, 276 milligrams cholesterol, 280 milligrams sodium

Lemon accents the light, rich quality of this chicken soup, a delicious version of a classic Belgian dish called waterzooi. *Serve with whole wheat bread and a watercress salad.*

Makes 6 to 8 servings

> 5 tablespoons butter or margarine
> 2 cups diced celery (use tender inner stalks)
> ¾ cup sliced leeks (white part only)
> 1 large onion, chopped
> 8 cups water
> 2 parsley sprigs
> 1 bay leaf
> 1 fresh thyme sprig (3 to 4 inches long) or ½ teaspoon dry thyme leaves
> 6 whole black peppercorns
> 2 broiler-fryer chickens (3 to 3½ lbs. *each*), cut up
> 6 tablespoons all-purpose flour
> 2 large egg yolks
> About 3 tablespoons lemon juice
> Salt
> Thin lemon slices
> Minced parsley
> Coarsely ground black pepper

Melt 1 tablespoon of the butter in a 6- to 8-quart pan over medium heat. Add celery, leeks, and onion; cook, stirring often, until soft but not browned, about 15 minutes. Add water, parsley sprigs, bay leaf, thyme, and peppercorns. Bring to a boil over high heat; reduce heat, cover, and simmer for 30 minutes.

Rinse chicken and pat dry. Pull off and discard lumps of fat. Set breast pieces aside; add remaining chicken to pan, cover, and simmer for 20 minutes. Add breast pieces. Cover and simmer until meat at thighbone is no longer pink (cut to test), about 20 more minutes.

Transfer chicken pieces to a large tureen and keep warm. Discard bay leaf and parsley sprigs; skim and discard fat from broth. Bring broth to a simmer. Melt remaining 4 tablespoons butter in a 2- to 3-quart pan and blend in flour. Gradually mix in about 4 cups of the broth. Bring to a boil over high heat, stirring until thickened. Return thickened mixture to simmering broth.

In a bowl, beat egg yolks lightly with 3 tablespoons of the lemon juice; mix in some of the hot broth, then return to pan. Immediately remove from heat. Season to taste with salt and additional lemon juice; pour over chicken.

Serve soup in large, wide soup bowls. Garnish each serving with lemon slices, minced parsley, and a little pepper.

Chicken & Vegetable Soup

W E S T E R N   C L A S S I C

PREPARATION TIME: About 30 minutes
COOKING TIME: About 1½ hours
PER SERVING: 122 calories, 20 grams protein, 2 grams carbohydrate, 3 grams total fat, 95 milligrams cholesterol, 75 milligrams sodium

Recalling the days when California belonged to Mexico, this soup takes its spirited flavor from chipotle chiles and fresh cilantro. The serving style is typically Western: guests spoon on toppings from a vivid assortment.

Makes 8 to 10 servings

> 1 broiler-fryer chicken (3½ to 4 lbs.)
> 12 cups water
> 8 cloves garlic
> 10 whole black peppercorns
> ½ can (7-oz. size) chipotle chiles in adobo sauce; or 6 dried California (Anaheim) or New Mexico chiles, stemmed and seeded
> Salt
> Toppings (suggestions follow)

Remove chicken neck and giblets; rinse. Reserve neck and liver for other uses; place remaining giblets in a 6- to 8-quart pan. Pull off and discard lumps of fat from chicken; rinse chicken and add to pan. Add water, garlic, peppercorns, and chiles. Bring to a boil over high heat; reduce heat, cover, and simmer until meat at thighbone is no longer pink (cut to test), about 1 hour.

Remove chicken from heat and let cool in broth. Discard skin and bones; tear meat into shreds and return to broth. If made ahead, cover and refrigerate for up to 2 days.

Skim (or lift off) and discard fat from soup. Bring soup to a simmer; season to taste with salt. Offer toppings to add to individual servings.

TOPPINGS. Arrange in separate bowls: ½ can (7-oz. size; leftover from soup) chopped **chipotle chiles in adobo sauce;** 1 can (about 1 lb.) **garbanzo beans,** drained; 1 large firm-ripe **avocado,** pitted, peeled, thinly sliced, and sprinkled with **lime juice** to prevent darkening; 1 cup **fresh cilantro (coriander) leaves;** and 4 or 5 **limes,** cut into quarters.

Colombian Chicken & Potato Soup

Pictured on facing page

PREPARATION TIME: About 30 minutes
COOKING TIME: About 1 hour
PER SERVING: 594 calories, 41 grams protein, 60 grams carbohydrate, 21 grams total fat, 110 milligrams cholesterol, 144 milligrams sodium

Chicken simmered in broth is the base for this colorful knife-and-fork soup from Colombia. Punctuated with a variety of vegetables and accented with fresh lime and avocado, it makes a substantial one-bowl entrée for a festive dinner.

Makes 4 to 6 servings.

- **1 broiler-fryer chicken (3½ to 4 lbs.), cut up**
- **12 cups Homemade Chicken Broth (page 58) or 2 large cans (49½ oz. *each*) regular-strength chicken broth**
- **2 large russet potatoes (about 1 lb. *total*), peeled and cut into 1-inch chunks**
- **2 large onions, finely chopped**
- **2 cloves garlic, minced or pressed**
- **½ teaspoon dry thyme leaves**
- **¾ teaspoon ground cumin**
- **1 pound small (1½-inch-diameter) red thin-skinned potatoes, scrubbed**
- **3 large carrots, cut into ¼-inch-thick slices**
- **1 bay leaf**
- **3 ears corn, husked and cut into 1-inch slices**
- **Condiments (suggestions follow)**

Rinse chicken and pat dry; pull off and discard lumps of fat. Set breast pieces aside; place remaining chicken in an 8- to 10-quart pan and add broth, russet potatoes, onions, garlic, thyme, and cumin. Bring to a boil over high heat; reduce heat, cover, and simmer for 20 minutes. Add breast pieces, thin-skinned potatoes, carrots, and bay leaf. Cover and simmer until meat at thighbone is no longer pink, 20 to 25 more minutes. (At this point, you may let cool, then cover and refrigerate until next day.)

Skim (or lift off) and discard fat from soup. Bring to a boil over high heat; add corn. Reduce heat, cover, and simmer until corn is hot, about 5 minutes.

Offer condiments to add to individual servings.

CONDIMENTS. Arrange in separate bowls: 1 cup chopped **fresh cilantro (coriander);** 2 large firm-ripe **avocados,** pitted, peeled, sliced, and sprinkled with **lime juice** to prevent darkening; ½ cup thinly sliced **green onions** (including tops); ⅓ cup drained **capers;** 1 cup **whipping cream** (optional); and 2 or 3 **limes,** cut into wedges.

Pour cream into Colombian Chicken & Potato Soup (recipe begins on facing page) to enrich the light broth. Corn, red potatoes, and condiments add splashes of color.

Aztec Soup

W E S T E R N   C L A S S I C

PREPARATION TIME: About 40 minutes
COOKING TIME: About 35 minutes
PER SERVING: 378 calories, 12 grams protein, 34 grams carbohydrate, 24 grams total fat, 24 milligrams cholesterol, 179 milligrams sodium

For autumn parties, try our version of this native American soup. If you like, serve it in a big, golden pumpkin, hollowed out to make a tureen. (You'll need a pumpkin shell with an 8-quart capacity; cut off the top and scrape the inside clean, then heat the shell as directed for Autumn Squash Soup, page 64. Allow about 30 minutes to clean and heat the pumpkin shell.)

Makes 10 to 12 servings

> 3 tablespoons butter or margarine
> ⅔ cup pine nuts
> ¾ cup walnut halves
> 1 large onion, chopped
> 2 cloves garlic, minced or pressed
> 12 cups Homemade Chicken Broth (recipe follows) or 2 large cans (49½ oz. *each*) regular-strength chicken broth
> 4 cups peeled chunks of pumpkin, acorn squash, or Hubbard squash (cut ½ inch thick, then cut into 1-inch squares)
> 3 cups fresh corn kernels; or 2 packages (10 oz. *each*) frozen corn kernels
> ¾ cup salted shelled pumpkin seeds
> 2 cups (8 oz.) shredded jack cheese
> ½ recipe Tortilla Strips (page 163)
> 1 large firm-ripe avocado, pitted, peeled, and diced (optional)

Melt 1 tablespoon of the butter in a 6- to 8-quart pan over medium heat. Add pine nuts and walnuts; cook, stirring, until golden brown, about 2 minutes. Remove from pan and set aside. Melt remaining 2 tablespoons butter in pan, add onion and garlic, and cook, stirring often, until golden, about 10 minutes. Pour in broth; bring to a boil. Stir in pumpkin and cook until tender when pierced, 5 to 10 minutes. Add corn; cook for 5 more minutes. Sprinkle with pumpkin seeds just before serving. Offer nuts, cheese, Tortilla Strips, and avocado (if used) to top soup.

HOMEMADE CHICKEN BROTH. Rinse 5 pounds **bony chicken pieces** (wings, backs, necks, carcasses) and place in a 6- to 8-quart pan. Add 2 large **onions,** cut into chunks; 2 large **carrots,** cut into chunks; 6 to 8 **parsley sprigs;** ½ teaspoon **whole black peppercorns;** and 3½ quarts **water.** Bring to a boil over high heat; then reduce heat, cover, and simmer for 3 hours. Let stand until cool.

Pour broth through a fine strainer into a bowl. Discard scraps. Cover broth and refrigerate until fat is hard, at least 4 hours (or for up to 2 days). Lift off and discard fat. To store, freeze in 1-cup to 1-quart portions. Makes about 10 cups.

Note: This unsalted broth is good in soups, sauces, and any other recipe calling for chicken broth. Let diners add salt to taste at the table. (If desired, you may boil the broth down for a richer flavor.)

Malaysian Chicken & Rice Soup

PREPARATION TIME: About 15 to 20 minutes for soup; about 2 hours for rice (cooling); about 10 minutes for onions; about 10 minutes for meatballs; about 5 minutes for sauce; about 10 minutes for condiments
COOKING TIME: About 50 minutes for soup; about 25 minutes for rice; about 20 minutes for onions; about 20 minutes for meatballs
PER SERVING OF SOUP: 272 calories, 24 grams protein, 12 grams carbohydrate, 14 grams total fat, 71 milligrams cholesterol, 68 milligrams sodium

A popular noontime meal throughout Malaysia is soto, a spicy chicken and rice soup with as many different variations as there are cooks.

Makes 8 servings

> 1 broiler-fryer chicken (3 to 3½ lbs.), cut up
> 1 teaspoon minced fresh ginger
> 1 large onion, chopped
> 2 teaspoons ground coriander
> 1 cinnamon stick (about 3 inches long)
> 4 cloves garlic, minced or pressed
> 10 cups Homemade Chicken Broth (this page) or canned regular-strength chicken broth
> Rice Cubes (recipe follows)
> Fried Onions (recipe follows)
> Beef & Potato Meatballs (recipe follows)
> Chile-Soy Sauce (recipe follows)
> ½ pound bean sprouts
> 1 cup chopped celery leaves
> 1 cup thinly sliced radishes

Rinse chicken and pat dry; pull off and discard lumps of fat. Set breast pieces aside; place remaining chicken in a 6- to 8-quart pan and add ginger, onion, coriander, cinnamon stick, garlic, and broth. Bring to a boil; reduce heat, cover, and simmer for 20 minutes.

Add chicken breast pieces. Cover and simmer until meat at thighbone is no longer pink, 20 to 25 more minutes. Lift out chicken and let cool. Discard skin and bones; cut meat into bite-size pieces.

Skim and discard fat from broth. Heat broth until steaming. Meanwhile, wrap chicken in foil; set in a 350° oven until heated through, about 20 minutes.

In separate dishes, arrange chicken, Rice Cubes, Fried Onions, meatballs, sauce, bean sprouts, celery, and radishes to add to individual servings.

RICE CUBES. In a 2- to 3-quart pan, combine 1½ cups **short-grain rice** (such as pearl) and 2½ cups **water.** Bring to a boil over high heat; reduce heat, cover, and simmer until water is absorbed, about 20 minutes. Pour hot rice into a 9-inch square pan; with the back of a spoon, press firmly into an even layer. Let cool. Run a knife around edge of pan; turn rice out onto a board. With a wet knife, cut into 1-inch squares. Serve at room temperature.
PER SERVING: 136 calories, 3 grams protein, 30 grams carbohydrate, .15 gram total fat, 0 milligram cholesterol, 2 milligrams sodium.

FRIED ONIONS. Thinly slice 3 large **onions.** In a 10- to 12-inch frying pan, heat ½ inch **salad oil** to 350°F on a deep-frying thermometer. Cook ⅓ of the onions at a time until golden, about 5 minutes; turn often. Lift out; drain.

Per Serving: 59 calories, 1 gram protein, 6 grams carbohydrate, 4 grams total fat, 0 milligram cholesterol, 2 milligrams sodium.

BEEF & POTATO MEATBALLS. Combine 1 pound **ground lean beef**; 1 cup peeled, shredded raw **potato**; 1 **large egg**, beaten; 1½ teaspoons **curry powder**; ½ teaspoon **salt**; and ¼ teaspoon **pepper**. Mix until well blended. Shape into 1-inch balls. Pour **salad oil** into pan used for onions until oil reaches a depth of 1 inch; heat to 350°F on a deep-frying thermometer. Beat 1 **large egg** with 2 tablespoons **water**.

Dip meatballs, a few at a time, into egg mixture; drain briefly, then lower into oil. Cook, turning, until browned on all sides, about 3 minutes. Lift out and drain.

Per Serving: 171 calories, 13 grams protein, 4 grams carbohydrate, 11 grams total fat, 108 milligrams cholesterol, 182 milligrams sodium.

CHILE-SOY SAUCE. Stir together ⅓ cup **soy sauce**, 2 tablespoons **white wine vinegar**, and 1 can (4 oz.) **diced green chiles**.

Per Serving: 12 calories, .78 gram protein, 2 grams carbohydrate, .16 gram total fat, 0 milligram cholesterol, 963 milligrams sodium.

Lemon Shrimp Soup

PREPARATION TIME: About 20 minutes
COOKING TIME: About 30 minutes
PER SERVING: 70 calories, 12 grams protein, 4 grams carbohydrate, .64 gram total fat, 92 milligrams cholesterol, 1050 milligrams sodium

Lemon grass, a citrus-scented herb from Southeast Asia, lends its appealing fragrance and flavor to this spicy Thai soup.

Makes 6 servings

  8 cups water
  6 chicken bouillon cubes
  3 to 5 small dried hot red chiles
  1 stalk fresh lemon grass (about 12 inches long), tough outer layers peeled off; or 1½ tablespoons crushed dry lemon grass
  1 pound medium-size shrimp (about 45 per lb.), shelled and deveined
  ⅓ cup lemon juice
  3 green onions (including tops), cut into 2-inch lengths
  ¼ cup coarsely chopped fresh cilantro (coriander)

In a 3- to 4-quart pan, combine water, bouillon cubes, and chiles. Slice fresh lemon grass and tie loosely in a piece of moistened cheesecloth; or place dry lemon grass in a teaball or wrap in cheesecloth. Add to pan. Bring to a boil; reduce heat, cover, and simmer for 20 minutes. Add shrimp; cover and simmer until shrimp turn pink, 6 more minutes. Stir in lemon juice, onions, and cilantro. Remove lemon grass; serve soup.

Yosenabe

PREPARATION TIME: About 45 minutes
COOKING TIME: About 20 minutes
PER SERVING: 293 calories, 18 grams protein, 40 grams carbohydrate, 7 grams total fat, 70 milligrams cholesterol, 1201 milligrams sodium

Yosenabe (*yo-suh*-nah-*beh*), loosely translated as "a bit of everything," names a flavorful Japanese dish that gathers an assortment of shellfish and vegetables in chicken broth.

In the kitchen, you cook ingredients one at a time in the broth, then arrange in a preheated casserole. To serve, pour broth over seafood and vegetables and ladle into individual serving bowls.

Makes 4 to 6 servings

  4 ounces bean threads (also called long rice or cellophane noodles)
  8 to 10 clams in shell, suitable for steaming
  8 to 10 large shrimp (about 30 per lb.)
  1 cooked large Dungeness crab (2 to 2½ lbs.)
  ½ small head (1½-lb. size) napa cabbage
  ½ pound tofu
  12 cups Homemade Chicken Broth (page 58) or 2 large cans (49½ oz. *each*) regular-strength chicken broth
  2 tablespoons Dijon mustard
  ¼ cup soy sauce
  ½ cup dry sherry
  4 teaspoons grated or minced fresh ginger
  About 2 cups watercress sprigs

Soak bean threads in warm water to cover until soft and pliable, about 15 minutes. Meanwhile, scrub clams well with a brush. Shell and devein shrimp. Pull off and discard back shell from crab. Break off legs and crack. Break belly flap off body; rinse loose material and gills from body. Cut body into 4 sections. Core cabbage and separate leaves. Drain tofu, then cut into 1-inch cubes.

Combine broth, mustard, soy, sherry, and ginger in a 5- to 6-quart pan. Bring to a boil over high heat; reduce heat, cover, and keep broth at a simmer.

Rinse a 4- to 5-quart covered casserole with hot water to heat; drain. Drain bean threads, cut into 5- to 6-inch lengths, and place in warmed casserole; cover and keep warm.

Add clams to broth; cover and simmer for 5 minutes. Add shrimp and crab; cook until clams open, about 3 more minutes. Lift seafood from broth and arrange in casserole. Re-cover; keep warm.

Add cabbage leaves to broth and cook just until wilted, about 3 minutes; lift out with tongs and arrange in casserole. Re-cover casserole and keep warm. Reduce heat under pan so broth steams but no bubbles break the surface. Carefully add tofu and cook for 5 minutes; transfer to casserole. Garnish with watercress. Pour steaming broth into casserole up to level of vegetables and seafood; pour remaining broth into a pitcher. Ladle a selection of foods with broth into 4 to 6 wide soup plates. Eat foods with forks and spoons or with chopsticks; sip extra broth or add to bowls.

ASIAN INFLUENCE on Western cooking began long ago—spicing life during the Gold Rush days and railroad construction of the late 19th century. In the 1930s, Sunset was already touting the nutritive virtue of tofu, also pointing out the growing popularity of Chinese dishes across much of the U.S. Later on, we showed readers how to use chopsticks, hot-pot cookers, and woks. In the 1950s, we introduced our readers to stir-frying, then to a parade of new ingredients and classic preparations from the Orient.

Tart with limes, hot with chiles, fragrant with lemon grass— Thai Seafood Firepot (recipe below) features bold flavor contrasts. Serve this shellfish-laden soup in wide bowls, with additional lime wedges.

Thai Seafood Firepot

Pictured above

PREPARATION TIME: 15 to 20 minutes

COOKING TIME: About 55 minutes

PER SERVING: 258 calories, 29 grams protein, 22 grams carbohydrate, 6 grams total fat, 191 milligrams cholesterol, 349 milligrams sodium

Aromatic lemon grass holds its own in this light, hot-tart seafood soup. If you can't find fresh lemon grass, substitute the dried and crushed version.

You might start the meal with potstickers or fried wonton; for dessert, serve fresh strawberries or pineapple spears on a bed of cracked ice.

Makes 4 to 6 servings

- 12 **cups Homemade Chicken Broth (page 58) or 2 large cans (49½ oz. *each*) regular-strength chicken broth**
- 3 **cups water**
- 1 **stalk fresh lemon grass (about 12 inches long), ¼ cup crushed dry lemon grass, or yellow part of peel only pared from 1 lemon**
- 1 **or 2 fresh or canned jalapeño chiles, stemmed and thinly sliced**
- 1 **strip (about 8 inches long) green part of peel only pared from 1 lime**
- 18 **clams in shell, suitable for steaming, scrubbed**
- 1½ **pounds large shrimp (about 30 per lb.), shelled and deveined**

   About 2 pounds cooked whole crab (such as Dungeness or blue), cleaned and cracked
- ⅔ **cup lime juice**
- ½ **cup fresh cilantro (coriander) sprigs**
- 3 **green onions (including tops), cut into 1-inch lengths**

   Lime wedges

In an 8- to 10-quart pan, combine broth and water. Slice lemon grass. Loosely tie lemon grass, chiles, and lime peel in a piece of moistened cheesecloth; add to pan. Bring to a boil over high heat; reduce heat, cover, and simmer for 45 minutes. Discard seasonings.

Add clams, shrimp, and crab to pan. Cover and simmer until clams open and shrimp turn pink, about 7 minutes. Stir in lime juice. Lift out seafood and place in a large serving bowl; pour in broth. Garnish with cilantro and onions. Serve with lime wedges.

Chowder at the Beach

PREPARATION TIME: About 10 minutes if fish are cleaned
COOKING TIME: 35 to 45 minutes
PER SERVING: 439 calories, 41 grams protein, 14 grams carbohydrate, 24 grams total fat, 229 milligrams cholesterol, 354 milligrams sodium

All along the Pacific Coast, a multitude of delightful beaches invite picnicking. In times past, part of the adventure was collecting ingredients on the spot for a cook-at-the-beach chowder. Nowadays, regulations have curtailed this free-wheeling approach, except at specific locations during certain seasons. But you can still enjoy chowder at the beach—just bring the foods from the market (and a portable stove).

Makes 10 to 12 servings

  4 large onions (about 2 lbs. *total*), chopped
  2 or 3 stalks celery, sliced
  2 bay leaves
  ½ cup (¼ lb.) butter or margarine
  8 cups Homemade Chicken Broth (page 58) or canned regular-strength chicken broth
  About 1½ cups dry white wine
  2 cups whipping cream
  2 or 3 spiny lobsters (live, cooked, or thawed frozen), split and cleaned
  2 Dungeness crabs (1½ to 2 lbs. *each*), live, cooked, or thawed frozen, cleaned and cracked
  2 pounds boned, skinned rockfish or giant seabass, cut into large chunks
  1 pound large shrimp (about 30 per lb.), deveined
  6 to 8 medium-size sole fillets (1¼ to 1½ lbs. *total*)
  4 slices fresh or thawed frozen abalone (about ½ lb. *total*), cut into chunks (optional)

In a deep 12- to 14-quart pan, combine onions, celery, bay leaves, and butter. Place over a hot fire (flames should dance against bottom of pan) or over high heat. Cook, stirring, until butter is melted; then cover and cook until vegetables are soft, stirring occasionally. Add broth, wine, and cream; stir well, cover, and bring to a boil.

If lobster and crab are live or uncooked, add to pan, cover, and cook for 10 minutes. If they're cooked (or cooked, frozen, and thawed), add to pan along with rockfish, shrimp, and sole. Push fish well down into soup. Cover and cook until liquid returns to a boil, 5 to 8 minutes. Stir in abalone (if used) and

remove pan from fire. Cover and let stand for 2 to 3 minutes.

To serve seafood, lift it from chowder with a slotted spoon or ladle. Strip meat from lobster shells; divide into serving-size pieces. Make sure each diner gets a sampling of all the seafood. After fish has been served, ladle broth into cups for sipping.

Mussel Chowder

PREPARATION TIME: About 10 minutes
COOKING TIME: About 40 minutes
PER SERVING: 252 calories, 13 grams protein, 12 grams carbohydrate, 17 grams total fat, 77 milligrams cholesterol, 307 milligrams sodium

Not so long ago, you could gather your own mussels from the blue-black clusters that cover rocks and pilings along the Pacific shore. Though dangerous during the red tides of summer, the shellfish were otherwise safe, free, and delicious. Today, governmental restrictions limit what you can harvest yourself, but commercial farms in the Northwest and Maine provide markets with a steady supply of mussels.

In this simple chowder, chicken broth enriched with half-and-half provides a creamy background for the buttery, succulent shellfish.

Makes 4 to 6 servings

  2 quarts Steamed Mussels (page 152) and their liquid
  ¼ cup (⅛ lb.) butter or margarine
  1 large onion, chopped
  1 stalk celery, thinly sliced
  ½ pound button mushrooms, sliced
  1 bay leaf
  ½ teaspoon paprika
  2 cups Homemade Chicken Broth (page 58) or 1 can (14½ oz.) regular-strength chicken broth
  1½ cups half-and-half or light cream

Remove mussels from shells; discard shells. Line a colander with moistened cheesecloth; pour mussel liquid through cloth. Measure liquid; you need 1½ cups (add water, if necessary). Set aside.

Melt butter in a 3- to 4-quart pan; add onion, celery, and mushrooms. Cook, stirring occasionally, until mushrooms are soft and lightly browned, 15 to 20 minutes. Add bay leaf, paprika, broth, and mussel liquid. Bring to a boil, then reduce heat, cover, and simmer for 15 minutes. Remove bay leaf. Stir in half-and-half and mussels, then cover and place over low heat just until hot; do not boil.

A Quartet of Colorful Onion Soups

Pictured on page 44

Warm to cool in hue, these four soups display the delicate palette of different onion varieties. Slow cooking brings out the natural sweetness of each type; additional ingredients reinforce color and enhance flavor. Red onions, fortified with shredded beet, make a borscht. Pale white onions are enriched with cream, topped with a sprinkle of nutmeg, then garnished with cheese-topped toast rounds. Traditional yellow onions are in a broth laced with sherry, flavored with turmeric and coriander, and crowned with Parmesan and homemade croutons. Sautéed leeks and green onions are the base for a delicate, lemon-fragrant chowder that's embellished with chives, lemon slices, and whipped cream.

Red Onion Borscht

    ¼ cup (⅛ lb.) butter or margarine
    4 large red onions (3 to 3½ lbs. *total*), thinly sliced
    ½ cup red wine vinegar
    ½ pound beets, peeled and shredded
    2½ tablespoons all-purpose flour
    6 cups Homemade Chicken Broth (page 58) or 1 large can (49½ oz.) regular-strength chicken broth
    ⅓ cup port (optional)
    Sour cream

Melt butter in a 5- to 6-quart pan over medium heat. Reserve ⅓ cup of the onions for garnish; add remaining onions, vinegar, and beets to pan. Cook, stirring often, until onions are very soft, 25 to 30 minutes. Stir in flour. Add broth. (At this point, you may let cool, then cover and refrigerate for up to 2 days.)

Bring soup to a boil; add port, if desired. Ladle into 4 to 8 bowls and garnish each with a spoonful of sour cream and a few slices of reserved onion. Makes 4 to 6 entrée servings, 8 first-course servings.

Golden Onion Soup

    ¼ cup (⅛ lb.) butter or margarine
    6 large yellow onions (3 to 3½ lbs. *total*), thinly sliced
    1 clove garlic, minced or pressed
    ¾ teaspoon ground coriander
    ⅛ teaspoon ground turmeric
    2½ tablespoons all-purpose flour
    5 cups Homemade Chicken Broth (page 58) or canned regular-strength chicken broth
    ⅓ cup dry sherry (optional)
    ½ cup freshly grated Parmesan cheese
    Croutons (recipe follows)

Melt butter in a 5- to 6-quart pan over medium heat. Add onions and garlic; cook, stirring often, for 20 minutes. Add coriander and turmeric and cook over low heat, stirring, until onions are very soft, 5 to 10 more minutes. Stir in flour. Add broth. (At this point, you may let cool, then cover and refrigerate for up to 2 days.)

Bring to a boil, stirring occasionally; add sherry, if desired. Ladle into 4 to 8 bowls. Garnish each serving with cheese and croutons. Makes 4 to 6 entrée servings, 8 first-course servings.

CROUTONS. Cut about ¼ pound **French bread** into ½-inch cubes to make 2½ cups; place in a 10- by 15-inch baking pan. Bake in a 325° oven until toasted, about 25 minutes. If made ahead, let cool; then store for up to 2 days. Before serving, mix with ½ cup (¼ lb.) melted **butter** or margarine.

Creamy White Onion Bisque

    ¼ cup (⅛ lb.) butter or margarine
    6 large white onions (3 to 3½ lbs. *total*), thinly sliced
    2 tablespoons all-purpose flour
    5 cups Homemade Chicken Broth (page 58) or canned regular-strength chicken broth
    1 cup whipping cream
    ⅛ teaspoon white pepper
    Toast Rounds (recipe follows)
    Freshly grated or ground nutmeg

Melt butter in a 5- to 6-quart pan over medium heat. Add onions; cook, stirring often, until onions are very soft, 25 to 30 minutes. Stir in flour. Add broth, cream, and pepper. (At

this point, you may let cool, then cover and refrigerate for up to 2 days.)

Bring to a boil, stirring occasionally. Ladle into 4 to 8 bowls; lay Toast Rounds atop each bowl of soup. Sprinkle with nutmeg. Makes 4 to 6 entrée servings, 8 first-course servings.

TOAST ROUNDS. Place 10 to 16 **baguette slices,** each about ½ inch thick, in a single layer in a 10- by 15-inch baking pan. Bake in a 325° oven until toasted, about 25 minutes. If made ahead, let cool, then wrap airtight and store for up to 2 days.

Shortly before serving, brush toast with ¼ cup (⅛ lb.) melted **butter** or margarine; then sprinkle with ½ cup shredded **Swiss cheese.** Broil in pan about 4 inches below heat until cheese is melted, about 1 minute. Use hot.

Triple Green Onion Chowder

    6 large leeks (about 3 lbs. *total*)
    ¼ cup (⅛ lb.) butter or margarine
    2½ tablespoons all-purpose flour
    6 cups Homemade Chicken Broth (page 58) or 1 large can (49½ oz.) regular-strength chicken broth
    ½ teaspoon dry thyme leaves
    ⅛ teaspoon white pepper
    3 cups thinly sliced green onions (including tops)
    ¾ teaspoon grated lemon peel
    2 tablespoons lemon juice
    ½ cup whipping cream, whipped
    Whole chives
    Thin lemon slices

Trim and discard ends and tops of leeks, leaving about 3 inches of green leaves. Discard tough outer leaves. Split leeks lengthwise; rinse well, then thinly slice crosswise.

Melt butter in a 5- to 6-quart pan over medium heat. Add leeks and cook, stirring often, until very soft, about 20 minutes. Stir in flour. Add broth, thyme, and white pepper. (At this point, you may let cool, then cover and refrigerate for up to 2 days.)

Bring to a boil, stirring occasionally; add onions and cook just until they turn bright green. Stir in lemon peel and lemon juice. Ladle into 4 to 8 bowls. Garnish with whipped cream, chives, and lemon slices. Makes 4 to 6 entrée servings, 8 first-course servings.

Browny's Clam Chowder

PREPARATION TIME: 20 to 30 minutes
COOKING TIME: About 40 minutes
PER SERVING: 470 calories, 18 grams protein, 23 grams carbohydrate, 35 grams total fat, 162 milligrams cholesterol, 1154 milligrams sodium

This chowder is a specialty of Browny's Seafood Broiler in Richmond Beach, just north of Seattle. Michael Brown, owner and chef, often serves it as a starter for a meal featuring mesquite-grilled fish. While Browny admits that the chowder recipe originally came from Sunset, *he explains that he has done some restyling. He feels that letting the chowder sit overnight improves it; the clam flavor soaks into the vegetables.*

Makes about 4 quarts, 10 to 12 entrée servings

   6 slices bacon, chopped
   2 medium-size carrots, thinly sliced
   2 stalks celery, thinly sliced
   1 small onion, chopped
   ½ small green bell pepper, stemmed, seeded, and chopped
   1 clove garlic, minced or pressed
   1½ pounds red thin-skinned potatoes, scrubbed
   2 bottles (8 oz. *each*) clam juice
   8 cans (6½ oz. *each*) chopped clams
   1 bay leaf
   ½ teaspoon liquid hot pepper seasoning
   ¼ teaspoon pepper
   1½ teaspoons Worcestershire
   ¾ teaspoon dry thyme leaves
   4 cups whipping cream
     Salt

Place bacon in an 8- to 10-quart pan; cook over medium heat, stirring occasionally, until crisp. With a slotted spoon, lift out bacon and drain on paper towels; discard all but 2 tablespoons of the drippings. Add carrots, celery, onion, bell pepper, and garlic to pan; cook, stirring often, until onion is soft.

Cut potatoes into ½-inch cubes. Add potatoes and clam juice to carrot mixture; bring to a boil, reduce heat to low, cover, and cook until potatoes are tender when pierced, about 15 minutes. Stir in clams and their liquid, bay leaf, hot pepper seasoning, pepper, Worcestershire, thyme, cream, and bacon. Season to taste with salt. Heat until steaming, then serve. If made ahead, let cool, then cover and refrigerate for up to 24 hours; reheat just before serving.

Newport Red Pepper Chowder

PREPARATION TIME: 10 to 15 minutes
COOKING TIME: About 35 minutes
PER SERVING: 318 calories, 25 grams protein, 23 grams carbohydrate, 14 grams total fat, 78 milligrams cholesterol, 140 milligrams sodium

Almost any white-fleshed fish can be used in this red and white chowder; choose the type that's most economical when you shop. If you like, prepare the dish a day ahead, then reheat. To use the chowder as an easy party entrée, simply add an appetizer, salad, crusty bread and dessert.

Makes 6 to 8 servings

   ¼ cup (⅛ lb.) butter or margarine; or ¼ cup salad oil
   2 medium-size onions, chopped
   ½ pound button mushrooms, sliced (optional)
   1 tablespoon lemon juice
   2 large red bell peppers, stemmed, seeded, and cut into thin strips
   4 cups Homemade Chicken Broth (page 58) or 2 cans (14½ oz. *each*) regular-strength chicken broth
   1 pound thin-skinned potatoes, scrubbed and sliced
   2 tablespoons *each* cornstarch and water, stirred together
   1 cup sour cream
   1½ to 2 pounds boned, skinned white fish, such as halibut, rockfish, or sole
   ¼ cup minced parsley
     Salt and pepper
     Lemon wedges

Melt butter in a 4- to 5-quart pan over medium-high heat. Add onions, mushrooms (if used), lemon juice, and bell peppers; cook, stirring, until vegetables are barely soft, about 10 minutes. Add broth and potatoes. Bring to a boil over high heat; then reduce heat, cover, and simmer until potatoes are tender when pierced, about 15 minutes.

Stir together cornstarch-water mixture and sour cream. Gradually stir in some of the soup liquid; then, stirring constantly, pour back into pan and bring to a boil over high heat.

Meanwhile, rinse fish, pat dry, and cut into bite-size chunks. Add fish and parsley to soup. Return to a boil; reduce heat, cover, and simmer until fish flakes readily when prodded with a fork, about 2 minutes. If made ahead, let cool, then cover and refrigerate until next day. Reheat until steaming before serving.

To serve, season soup to taste with salt and pepper; offer lemon wedges to squeeze into soup.

Puget Sound Oyster Stew

WESTERN CLASSIC

PREPARATION TIME: 10 to 15 minutes
COOKING TIME: About 30 minutes
PER SERVING: 281 calories, 10 grams protein, 15 grams carbohydrate, 20 grams total fat, 105 milligrams cholesterol, 173 milligrams sodium

Fresh shucked oysters from the shores of Puget Sound— or from Tomales Bay at Point Reyes, or from your fish market—are the starting point for a delicately seasoned whole-meal soup.

Makes 4 to 6 servings

¼ **cup (⅛ lb.) butter or margarine**
1 **large onion, chopped**
½ **cup chopped parsley or 2 tablespoons parsley flakes**
1 **large green bell pepper, stemmed, seeded, and chopped**
4 **cups Homemade Chicken Broth (page 58) or 2 cans (14½ oz. *each*) regular-strength chicken broth**
1 **cup dry white wine**
1 **pound potatoes, peeled and cut into ¼-inch cubes (optional)**
½ **to 1 cup whipping cream**
2 **to 3 cups shucked raw oysters and juices (cut large oysters in bite-size pieces)**
 Salt and pepper

Melt butter in a 4- to 5-quart pan over medium-high heat. Add onion, parsley, and bell pepper. Cook, stirring often, until onion is soft, about 10 minutes. Stir in broth and wine, cover, and bring to a boil.

If using potatoes, add to boiling broth; reduce heat, cover, and simmer until potatoes mash easily, 10 to 15 minutes.

Add cream and oysters; simmer just until oysters are heated through, 1 to 2 minutes. Season to taste with salt and pepper.

Venetian Rice & Peas in Broth

PREPARATION TIME: About 5 minutes
COOKING TIME: About 20 minutes
PER SERVING: 139 calories, 4 grams protein, 26 grams carbohydrate, 2 grams total fat, 0 milligram cholesterol, 70 milligrams sodium

This light soup is attractive and good tasting—and almost ridiculously simple to make. In Venice, it typically precedes sautéed liver or fish.

Makes 6 servings

6 **cups Homemade Chicken Broth (page 58) or 1 large can (49½ oz.) regular-strength chicken broth**
½ **cup long-grain white rice**
1 **package (10 oz.) frozen tiny peas**
 Freshly grated Parmesan cheese (optional)

In a 3- to 4-quart pan, bring broth to a boil. Add rice; reduce heat, cover, and simmer until rice is tender, about 15 minutes. (At this point, you may cool, cover, and refrigerate until serving time.)

Return broth-rice mixture to a boil; stir in peas (first bang package sharply against a hard surface to separate peas). Simmer gently for 5 minutes. If desired, offer cheese to add to individual servings.

Autumn Squash Soup

Pictured on facing page

PREPARATION TIME: About 30 minutes to start soup; about 10 minutes to purée soup; about 30 minutes to clean and heat pumpkin shell
COOKING TIME: About 2½ hours
PER SERVING: 217 calories, 4 grams protein, 41 grams carbohydrate, 5 grams total fat, 0 milligram cholesterol, 20 milligrams sodium

Hard-shelled winter squash displays surprising variety in shape, size, color, and texture. When cooked, the flesh has differing degrees of sweetness, with flavors ranging from very mild to distinctly nutty. Use your favorite squash for this smooth, thick soup; for an especially handsome presentation, serve it in a natural tureen made from a hollowed-out pumpkin.

Makes 12 to 16 servings

¼ **cup salad oil**
4 **medium-size onions, chopped**
2 **teaspoons dry thyme leaves**
 About ½ teaspoon ground nutmeg
1 **pound rutabagas, peeled and diced**
2 **pounds thin-skinned potatoes, peeled and cubed**
7 **to 8 pounds squash (banana, butternut, Hubbard, pumpkin, or acorn), peeled and cubed (16 cups)**
3½ **quarts Homemade Chicken Broth (page 58) or canned regular-strength chicken broth**
1 **large pumpkin shell (about 6-qt. capacity), top cut off and inside scraped clean (optional)**

In an 8- to 10-quart pan, combine oil, onions, thyme, and ½ teaspoon of the nutmeg; cook over medium-high heat, stirring often, until onions are soft, about 15 minutes.

Add rutabagas, potatoes, and squash; cook over medium heat, stirring occasionally, for about 30 minutes. Pour in broth and bring to a boil over high heat. Reduce heat, cover, and simmer until squash mashes easily, about 1½ hours.

Heat pumpkin shell, if used: fill with boiling water and let stand until shell feels warm, about 20 minutes. Drain off water.

While shell is heating, whirl squash mixture, a portion at a time, in a food processor or blender until smooth. Return to pan and bring to a boil over medium-high heat, stirring often.

Pour soup into shell, then ladle into cups or mugs; sprinkle individual servings with nutmeg.

Hollowed-out pumpkin creates both a handsome harvest-season centerpiece and a natural tureen to hold smooth, thick and hearty Autumn Squash Soup (recipe on facing page).

Mustard Greens & Millet Soup

PREPARATION TIME: 10 to 15 minutes

COOKING TIME: 25 to 30 minutes; 30 to 35 minutes if eggs are used

PER SERVING: 147 calories, 4 grams protein, 26 grams carbohydrate, 4 grams total fat, 0 milligram cholesterol, 23 milligrams sodium

Mustard greens add a pleasant nip to this lean, light millet soup. (For a heartier dish, poach eggs in the soup and top each serving with cheese.) You'll find millet in most well-stocked supermarkets and health food stores; the pale-colored grain has an interesting waxy-creamy texture.

Makes 4 to 6 servings

  10 cups Homemade Chicken Broth (page 58)
      or canned regular-strength chicken broth

   2 cloves garlic, minced or pressed

  ½ cup millet

  ¾ pound mustard greens, tough stems
      trimmed off

  4 to 6 large eggs (optional)

  1 cup (4 oz.) shredded jack cheese
      (optional)

In a 5- to 6-quart pan, bring broth, garlic, and millet to a boil over high heat. Reduce heat, cover, and simmer until millet is tender to bite, about 20 minutes.

Meanwhile, wash mustard greens well and pat dry. Stack leaves and cut crosswise into ½-inch strips. Stir mustard greens into broth; simmer, covered, for 5 minutes. Serve, or add eggs.

To add eggs, crack each egg into a bowl, then slide into soup; space eggs apart. Reduce heat slightly so soup does not bubble. Cover pan and cook until whites are set and yolks are soft or firm, as desired, 3 to 6 minutes.

Gently transfer eggs from pan to a tureen or individual bowls; ladle soup over eggs. Offer cheese to add to individual portions, if desired.

Corn Chowder with Cheese

PREPARATION TIME: 10 to 15 minutes
COOKING TIME: About 35 minutes
PER SERVING: 459 calories, 16 grams protein, 44 grams carbohydrate, 26 grams total fat, 79 milligrams cholesterol, 302 milligrams sodium

This vegetable chowder is wholesome and easy to prepare —and all the ingredients are old favorites. Serve with sourdough rye for a comforting lunch or supper.

Makes 4 to 6 servings

> 3 tablespoons butter or margarine
>
> 1 clove garlic, minced or pressed
>
> 2 large onions, chopped
>
> 4 cups Homemade Chicken Broth (page 58) or 2 cans (14½ oz. *each*) regular-strength chicken broth
>
> ½ teaspoon dry thyme leaves
>
> 1 bay leaf
>
> 1 pound thin-skinned potatoes, scrubbed and cut into ½-inch cubes
>
> 3 cups fresh corn kernels or 2 packages (10 oz. *each*) frozen corn kernels
>
> 2 cups milk
>
> ½ cup whipping cream
>
> Salt and pepper
>
> 1½ cups (6 oz.) shredded sharp Cheddar cheese

Melt butter in a 5- to 6-quart pan over medium-high heat. Add garlic and onions; cook, stirring often, until onions are soft, about 10 minutes. Add broth, thyme, and bay leaf; bring to a boil. Add potatoes; reduce heat, cover, and simmer until potatoes are tender enough to mash easily, 10 to 15 minutes.

Add corn, milk, and cream. Stir soup over low heat until hot (do not boil). Pour into a tureen, then ladle into bowls. Season to taste with salt and pepper. Offer cheese to add to individual servings.

Lentil Cream Soup

PREPARATION TIME: 10 to 15 minutes
COOKING TIME: 30 minutes to 1½ hours, depending on type of lentil
PER SERVING: 277 calories, 5 grams protein, 18 grams carbohydrate, 21 grams total fat, 66 milligrams cholesterol, 33 milligrams sodium

Lentils are rustic and old fashioned, but they can still deal out a few surprises—as in this creamy soup with sherry.

Unlike dried beans, lentils require no soaking; they also cook more quickly. Unskinned lentils simmer to tenderness in an hour or less; if the skin is removed, cooking time is only about 15 minutes. Skinned—or

decorticated—lentils are flat on one side; skin-on lentils are rounded on both sides.

Makes 6 to 8 servings

> ½ cup lentils
>
> 4 cups Homemade Chicken Broth (page 58) or 2 cans (14½ oz. *each*) regular-strength chicken or beef broth
>
> 1 medium-size carrot, peeled
>
> 8 to 10 parsley sprigs
>
> ¼ teaspoon whole cloves
>
> 1 tablespoon olive oil or salad oil
>
> ½ cup chopped shallots or red onion
>
> 1 cup dry sherry
>
> 2 tablespoons lemon juice
>
> 2 cups whipping cream
>
> ½ teaspoon pepper
>
> Edible flowers such as pansies or rose petals, rinsed (optional)
>
> Whole chives (optional)

Sort lentils and remove any debris. Rinse lentils, drain, and place in a 2- to 3-quart pan; add broth, carrot, parsley sprigs, and cloves. Bring to a boil; reduce heat, cover, and simmer until lentils are very tender to bite—about 15 minutes for decorticated lentils, up to 1 hour for unskinned lentils. Discard carrot, parsley, and as many cloves as you can find.

Heat oil in a 5- to 6-quart pan over medium heat. Add shallots; cook until soft, stirring occasionally. Add sherry and lemon juice and boil over high heat, uncovered, until reduced to about ¼ cup. Stir in lentils and their cooking liquid, cream, and pepper. Heat to simmering, then pour into a tureen or bowls. Garnish with flowers and chives, if desired.

Maritata

PREPARATION TIME: 5 to 10 minutes
COOKING TIME: About 10 minutes
PER SERVING: 485 calories, 15 grams protein, 16 grams carbohydrate, 40 grams total fat, 286 milligrams cholesterol, 466 milligrams sodium

This version of rich, creamy maritata *(mar-ee-tah-tah) was created by a Genoese chef. The velvety soup "marries" broth with butter, cheese, egg yolks, and whipping cream. It is rich—but worth it.*

Makes 4 to 6 servings

> 6 cups Homemade Chicken Broth (page 58) or 1 large can (49½ oz.) regular-strength chicken broth
>
> ⅓ cup dry tiny pasta shapes (pastina); or 2 ounces dry vermicelli, broken into short lengths
>
> ½ cup (¼ lb.) unsalted butter, at room temperature
>
> 1 cup (about 5 oz.) freshly grated Parmesan cheese
>
> 4 large egg yolks
>
> 1 cup whipping cream
>
> Freshly grated or ground nutmeg (optional)

In a 4- to 5-quart pan, bring broth to a boil over high heat. Add pasta to boiling broth. Reduce heat to medium and simmer, uncovered, until pasta is tender to bite, 3 to 5 minutes.

Meanwhile, in a food processor (or a bowl), whirl (or beat) butter, cheese, and egg yolks until well blended; beat in cream. Slowly pour about 1 cup of the broth into egg mixture, beating constantly; then pour all into pan, beating constantly. Ladle into individual bowls; dust each serving with nutmeg, if desired.

Caldo Xochilt

PREPARATION TIME: 15 to 20 minutes
COOKING TIME: About 20 minutes
PER SERVING: 171 calories, 3 grams protein, 22 grams carbohydrate, 9 grams total fat, 0 milligram cholesterol, 80 milligrams sodium

This chile-seasoned soup (pronounced call-doh-soh-chilt) hails from Guadalajara. Add your choice of a simple tomato salsa, chopped onion, and avocado; then add a squeeze of lime. (The mild dried chile that flavors the broth is available in Mexican markets and well-stocked supermarkets.)

Makes 4 or 5 servings

> 1 dried ancho (poblano), California (Anaheim), or New Mexico chile, stemmed and seeded
> 6 cups Homemade Chicken Broth (page 58) or 1 large can (49½ oz.) regular-strength chicken broth
> 2 tablespoons long-grain white rice
> ⅓ cup drained canned garbanzo beans
> 1 medium-size onion, chopped
> 2 tablespoons canned diced green chiles
> 1 medium-size firm-ripe tomato, peeled, cored, and chopped
> 1 medium-size firm-ripe avocado
> 2 limes, cut into wedges
> ½ cup chopped fresh cilantro (coriander)
> Salt

Cover dried chile with boiling water and let stand for 10 minutes. Drain chile, then cut into large pieces.

In a 2- to 3-quart pan, bring broth to a boil; add chile pieces, rice, and garbanzos. Reduce heat, cover, and simmer until rice is tender to bite, about 15 minutes.

Meanwhile, in a small bowl, combine ¼ cup of the chopped onion with green chiles and tomato; set aside. Place remaining onion in another bowl. Pit, peel, and dice avocado; place in a third bowl. Squeeze some lime juice over avocado to prevent darkening.

Remove soup from heat and stir in cilantro. Season to taste with salt. Offer tomato mixture, chopped onion, avocado, and lime wedges to add to individual servings.

Cream of Pistachio Soup

W E S T E R N   C L A S S I C

PREPARATION TIME: About 35 minutes if you shell nuts; about 15 minutes if nuts are purchased shelled
COOKING TIME: About 50 minutes
PER SERVING: 456 calories, 9 grams protein, 24 grams carbohydrate, 38 grams total fat, 66 milligrams cholesterol, 112 milligrams sodium

A major Western nut crop, pistachios add mellow flavor to this hot soup, both as an ingredient and as a crunchy garnish. Serve small portions for a first course; offer heartier servings as a luncheon entrée, along with a crisp salad.

Makes 6½ cups, 4 to 6 servings

> 1½ cups shelled (3 cups or ¾ lb. in shell) natural, roasted, or roasted salted pistachios
> ¼ cup (⅛ lb.) butter or margarine
> 1 small onion, finely chopped
> ½ cup chopped celery
> 1 clove garlic, minced or pressed
> 2 tablespoons dry sherry
> 6 cups Homemade Chicken Broth (page 58) or 1 large can (49½ oz.) regular-strength chicken broth
> ¼ cup long-grain white rice
> 2 parsley sprigs
> 1 small bay leaf
> 1 cup whipping cream
> Whole chives

Rub pistachios in a clean towel to remove as much of skins (and salt) as possible; then set aside.

In a 4- to 5-quart pan, melt butter over medium heat. Add onion, celery, and garlic; cook, stirring often, until onion is very soft but not browned, about 15 minutes. Add sherry, broth, rice, parsley, bay leaf, and ¾ cup of the pistachios. Bring to a boil over high heat; reduce heat, cover, and simmer until rice is very tender to bite, about 25 minutes. Discard bay leaf.

Whirl pistachio mixture, a portion at a time, in a food processor or blender until very smooth; pour through a wire strainer and discard residue. Return soup to pan. Stir in cream and heat until steaming.

Garnish individual servings with chives and sprinkle with remaining ¾ cup pistachios.

INTERNATIONAL themes for dinner parties came into vogue in the 1950s— a direct result of the post-war travel boom that sent many Westerners abroad for the first time. As tourists, they discovered fascinating new foods and seasonings. As cooks, back at home again, they sought recipes and kitchen tools that were "authentic" to some faraway land.

The Best of Sunset

SALADS

California's Salinas Valley calls itself the "Salad Bowl of the World" with justified pride. In fact, fertile fields and orchards in many parts of the West now provide the fine, fresh ingredients that turn salad-making into an ongoing adventure.

For salads, anything goes, as you'll see in the recipes ahead. From Sunset's inventive point of view, salads can involve leafy greens, vegetables, fish, poultry, meat, vegetables, fruits, or nuts—raw or cooked, hot or cold, exotic or homegrown.

One practical note: Ultra-clean, crisp greens make the best salads. Wash leaves well in cool water; drain, then pat, shake or spin to remove excess moisture. If greens are slightly limp, crisp them: wrap the damp leaves in paper towels, enclose in a plastic bag, and refrigerate until cool and crisp—usually 30 minutes to 1 hour, depending on quantity. Thus refreshed, most greens keep well for several days in the refrigerator.

Seasonal fruits and greens add festive color to a
winter menu in this Mixed Winter Fruit Salad
(recipe on page 82). Serve as a first course before a
beef or poultry entrée.

Caesar Salad

WESTERN CLASSIC

PREPARATION TIME: About 30 minutes
CHILLING TIME: At least 30 minutes if lettuce is chilled to crisp
STANDING TIME: At least 1 hour to flavor oil with garlic
PER SERVING: 171 calories, 4 grams protein, 4 grams carbohydrate, 16 grams total fat,
50 milligrams cholesterol, 125 milligrams sodium

Nobody knows whether this Western classic was created by, or for, a Caesar. We published our first version in 1945, presenting the salad as it was made in a Coronado, California, restaurant. But our research indicates that the dish probably originated in nearby Tijuana, during its heyday in the '20s and '30s.

This later version of Caesar salad contains all the classic ingredients: crisp romaine, anchovies, croutons, Parmesan cheese—and barely warm eggs to make the dressing cling to the leaves.

Makes 10 to 12 servings

**2 large heads romaine lettuce
(about 1 lb. *each*)
1 clove garlic
¾ cup olive oil or salad oil
2 cups ¾-inch cubes day-old French bread
2 large eggs
Freshly ground black pepper
3 tablespoons lemon juice
6 to 8 canned anchovy fillets, chopped
½ cup freshly grated Parmesan cheese**

WESTERN CLASSICS have sometimes been discovered by chance. In 1935, we received a garlic bread recipe from a reader who mentioned in her letter that it was served in a Coronado, California, café with a "romaine lettuce salad"—none other than today's popular Caesar Salad.

Discard coarse romaine leaves. Break remaining leaves from head; rinse well and drain. If greens are not as crisp as you like, wrap in paper towels, enclose in plastic bags, and refrigerate for at least 30 minutes or until next day.

Crush garlic in a small bowl, pour oil over it, and let stand for at least 1 hour or up to 8 hours.

Heat ¼ cup of the garlic oil in a 10- to 12-inch frying pan over medium heat. Add bread cubes and stir often until browned on all sides. (Or coat bread cubes with ¼ cup garlic oil, spread in a 10- by 15-inch rimmed baking pan, and toast in a 325° oven until browned; stir occasionally.)

Immerse eggs in boiling water to cover for exactly 1 minute; lift out with a slotted spoon. Use warm or cool.

Tear romaine leaves into bite-size pieces and place in a large salad bowl; sprinkle generously with pepper. Pour remaining ½ cup garlic oil over lettuce; mix until leaves are coated.

Break eggs over salad, sprinkle with lemon juice, and lift with a salad fork and spoon to mix well. Add anchovies and cheese; mix again. Add croutons and mix gently. Serve at once.

Butter Lettuce Salad

WESTERN CLASSIC

PREPARATION TIME: 10 to 15 minutes
CHILLING TIME: At least 1 hour to crisp lettuce
PER SERVING: 68 calories, .56 gram protein, 1 gram carbohydrate, 7 grams total fat,
0 milligram cholesterol, 40 milligrams sodium

Salad in the typical Western home is apt to be this basic, uncomplicated, and enduring composition of tender butter lettuce leaves dressed with oil, vinegar, mustard, and garlic. To serve just four diners, use one head of lettuce and a third of the dressing.

Makes 12 servings

**3 large heads butter lettuce
(1 to 1¼ lbs. *total*)
1 tablespoon Dijon mustard
1 clove garlic, minced or pressed
3 tablespoons white wine vinegar
6 tablespoons olive oil, preferably
extra-virgin
Salt and pepper**

Rinse butter lettuce heads well in cool water. Shake to remove excess moisture; discard bruised leaves. To crisp and dry, wrap heads in paper towels, enclose in plastic bags, and refrigerate for at least 1 hour or up to 2 days.

Gently separate leaves. If desired, arrange leaves in a large shallow bowl to resemble 1 head, with large green leaves on the outside and smaller, paler leaves in the center. (At this point, you may cover and refrigerate for up to 4 hours.)

Whisk together mustard, garlic, vinegar, and oil. If made ahead, cover and let stand for up to 4 hours; stir to reblend before using.

Pour dressing over lettuce; mix, then season to taste with salt and pepper. Serve at once.

Radicchio with Butter Lettuce

PREPARATION TIME: 20 to 25 minutes
CHILLING TIME: At least 30 minutes to crisp lettuce and radicchio
PER SERVING: 133 calories, 3 grams protein, 7 grams carbohydrate, 11 grams total fat,
9 milligrams cholesterol, 133 milligrams sodium

Though it looks like a small, loose-leafed red cabbage, radicchio is actually a kind of chicory related to Belgian endive—and like Belgian endive, it has a delicately bitter flavor. Some radicchio is imported from Italy, some grown locally; it's all rather pricy, but a small amount goes a long way.

Makes 4 servings

**3 slices bacon
Salad oil (if needed)
1 tablespoon *each* red wine vinegar and
minced shallot
½ teaspoon Dijon mustard**

1 medium-size orange

2 cups lightly packed butter lettuce leaves, washed and crisped

3 cups lightly packed radicchio leaves, washed and crisped

Whole chives or long slivers of green onion tops (optional)

Salt and pepper

In a 10- to 12-inch frying pan, cook bacon over medium heat until crisp, about 10 minutes. Lift out and drain on paper towels; break into pieces.

Measure drippings; add oil, if necessary, to make 3 tablespoons. Return to pan with bacon, vinegar, shallot, and mustard. (At this point, you may cover and refrigerate until next day.)

Using a sharp knife, cut peel and all white membrane from orange. Cut between sections; lift out sections and place in a large bowl. Add lettuce and radicchio; mix. Heat bacon mixture to simmering and pour over salad. Mix quickly, then arrange on a platter; if desired, garnish with a spray of chives. Season to taste with salt and pepper.

Sesame Shiitake Salad

PREPARATION TIME: 15 to 20 minutes

CHILLING TIME: At least 30 minutes if lettuce is chilled to crisp

PER SERVING: 119 calories, 1 gram protein, 6 grams carbohydrate, 11 grams total fat, 0 milligram cholesterol, 223 milligrams sodium

In Japan, shiitake mushrooms were once called an "elixir of life" and believed to keep people young and vigorous. They're still cherished today for their rich, meaty taste. Long available dry, the mushrooms are now widely cultivated in the United States; fresh shiitake are more delicate in flavor than the dried type.

Makes 4 to 6 servings

2 medium-size heads butter lettuce (about ¼ lb. *each*)

¼ cup salad oil

2 tablespoons sesame seeds

2½ tablespoons distilled white or white wine vinegar

1½ tablespoons sugar

1 tablespoon soy sauce

¼ pound fresh shiitake mushrooms

⅓ cup thinly sliced green onions (including tops)

Discard coarse or bruised lettuce leaves. Rinse tender leaves in cool water; drain. If leaves need crisping, wrap in paper towels, enclose in plastic bags, and refrigerate for at least 30 minutes or up to 2 days.

In a 6- to 7-inch frying pan, combine oil and sesame seeds. Cook over medium-low heat, stirring often, until seeds begin to turn golden, 3 to 4 minutes. Remove from heat and let cool. Mix in vinegar, sugar, and soy; set aside.

Rinse mushrooms and pat dry. Cut off and discard stems; cut caps into ¼-inch strips. Tear lettuce into bite-size pieces. Add mushrooms, sesame dressing, and onions; mix and serve.

Red Lettuce Spears with Beans & Tangerine Mayonnaise

PREPARATION TIME: About 15 minutes

CHILLING TIME: At least 30 minutes to crisp lettuce

PER SERVING: 132 calories, 1 gram protein, 7 grams carbohydrate, 11 grams total fat, 8 milligrams cholesterol, 84 milligrams sodium

A fan of lightly cooked green beans, a spear of red leaf lettuce, a spoonful of tangerine mayonnaise, and a few thin strips of red or yellow bell pepper add up to a handsome, easily assembled salad. You'll find fresh tangerines in autumn and winter; at other times of year, you can make the salad with oranges.

Makes 8 servings

1 head red leaf lettuce (½ to ¾ lb.)

¾ pound green beans, stem ends snapped off

½ teaspoon olive oil or salad oil

1 to 2 tablespoons tangerine or orange juice

Tangerine Mayonnaise (recipe follows)

1 small red or yellow bell pepper, stemmed, seeded, and cut vertically into 16 strips

2 medium-size tangerines or small oranges, *each* cut into 8 wedges

Cut lettuce vertically into eighths through core and leaves. Trim away most of core, but keep leaves attached. Rinse lettuce and discard any bruised leaves; drain. Wrap in paper towels, place in a plastic bag, and refrigerate for at least 30 minutes or until next day.

In a 4- to 5-quart pan, bring 3 inches of water to a boil over high heat. Add beans; cook, uncovered, until barely tender when pierced, 2 to 3 minutes. Drain beans well, then immediately immerse in cold water until cool; drain again. (At this point, you may cover and refrigerate until next day.)

Mix beans with oil. On each of 8 salad plates, lay a section of lettuce and a cluster of beans. Sprinkle lettuce evenly with tangerine juice. Spoon ⅛ of the Tangerine Mayonnaise at base of each cluster of beans; garnish mayonnaise with bell pepper strips. Offer tangerine wedges to squeeze onto salads.

TANGERINE MAYONNAISE. Mix ½ cup **mayonnaise**, 1 teaspoon thawed **frozen tangerine juice concentrate**, 1 small clove **garlic** (minced or pressed), ¼ teaspoon grated **tangerine peel** or orange peel, and ⅛ teaspoon **white pepper**. Cover and refrigerate for at least 30 minutes or up to 2 days to blend flavors.

Oriental Endive Salad

PREPARATION TIME: About 15 minutes
CHILLING TIME: At least 1 hour to crisp endive
PER SERVING: 307 calories, 5 grams protein, 14 grams carbohydrate, 27 grams total fat, 0 milligram cholesterol, 522 milligrams sodium

The pleasantly bitter bite of Belgian endive stands out amid the other emphatic flavors in this Oriental-style salad. You use the large, pale outer endive leaves to create a bold sunburst on each salad plate; mounded in the sunburst's center is a mixture of chopped inner endive leaves, green onions, mushrooms, and toasted almonds.

Makes 4 servings

> **3 heads Belgian endive (about ¼ lb. *each*)**
> **⅓ cup slivered almonds**
> **1 cup lightly packed fresh cilantro (coriander) leaves**
> **¼ pound button mushrooms, thinly sliced**
> **¼ cup thinly sliced green onions (including tops)**
> **Sesame Dressing (recipe follows)**
> **1 small red bell pepper, stemmed, seeded, and slivered**

To crisp Belgian endive, rinse heads in cold water, wrap in paper towels, place in a plastic bag, and refrigerate for at least 1 hour or up to 2 days.

Spread almonds in a 9- or 10-inch-wide baking pan and toast in a 350° oven until golden, about 8 minutes. Set aside.

Thinly slice off discolored base of each endive head, then break off 24 of the largest leaves. Arrange 6 leaves in each of 4 salad bowls or plates, positioning leaves in a sunburst shape with tips pointing toward rim of bowl or plate. Chop remaining endive.

In each bowl, equally mound chopped endive, cilantro, mushrooms, onions, and almonds in center of "sunburst." (At this point, you may cover and refrigerate for up to 4 hours.)

To serve, pour ¼ of the dressing over each salad; garnish equally with bell pepper.

SESAME DRESSING. Whisk together 3 tablespoons *each* **Oriental sesame oil, salad oil,** and **white wine vinegar;** 1½ tablespoons *each* **soy sauce, dry sherry,** and **sugar;** and ¼ teaspoon **ground ginger.**

Spinach & Enoki Salad

PREPARATION TIME: 20 to 30 minutes
CHILLING TIME: At least 30 minutes to crisp spinach
PER SERVING: 88 calories, 3 grams protein, 12 grams carbohydrate, 4 grams total fat, 0 milligram cholesterol, 74 milligrams sodium

Captivating in appearance and delicate in flavor, dainty white enoki mushrooms have a pleasant tender-crisp texture that makes them a perfect addition to salads. Here, the slender mushrooms join dark spinach leaves, cherry tomatoes, and thin slices of carrot.

Makes 6 to 8 servings

> **About 1½ pounds spinach**
> **1 or 2 bags (3½ oz. *each*) enoki mushrooms**
> **1 cup cherry tomatoes, stemmed and halved**
> **1 carrot, thinly sliced**
> **2 green onions (including tops), thinly sliced**
> **¼ cup sugar**
> **⅓ cup white wine vinegar**
> **2 tablespoons salad oil**
> **Salt**

Discard stems and any yellow or wilted leaves from spinach. Wash spinach and pat dry. Wrap in paper towels, enclose in plastic bags, and refrigerate for at least 30 minutes or up to 2 days.

Tear spinach into bite-size pieces (you should have about 4 quarts). Trim and discard brown, woody ends from mushrooms; rinse mushrooms, then shake off excess water.

In a large serving bowl, combine spinach, mushrooms, tomatoes, carrot, and onions. In a small bowl, stir together sugar, vinegar, and oil until sugar is dissolved. Pour over spinach mixture, mix to coat, and season to taste with salt.

Spinach Salad with Crisp Red Chiles

Pictured on facing page

W E S T E R N   C L A S S I C

PREPARATION TIME: 40 to 50 minutes if using fresh cactus; 25 to 35 minutes if using canned nopalitos
CHILLING TIME: At least 30 minutes to crisp greens
PER SERVING: 362 calories, 15 grams protein, 14 grams carbohydrate, 29 grams total fat, 44 milligrams cholesterol, 439 milligrams sodium

The bold flavor and color of red chiles contrast brightly with cool cactus and spinach leaves in this Latin salad. The cactus tastes something like cucumber; you'll find it, fresh or canned, in Mexican markets and in supermarkets well stocked with Mexican foods.

Makes 6 to 8 servings

> **1 pound spinach**
> **¼ pound watercress**
> **6 large dried California (Anaheim) chiles**
> **¼ cup olive oil or salad oil**

Red-hued chile oil blended with vinegar dresses chilled spinach leaves, cubes of lightly cooked cactus, queso asadero *(a mozzarella-like cheese), and crisp-fried strips of mild chiles. The recipe for festive Spinach Salad with Crisp Red Chiles begins on the facing page.*

1 **pound fresh whole or diced cactus (nopales) or 1 jar (15 oz.) nopalitos, drained and rinsed**

1 **large red onion, thinly sliced**

1 **cup sliced radishes**

1 **pound queso asadero or mozzarella cheese, cut into ½-inch cubes**

2 **large ripe avocados**

   Cider Dressing (recipe follows)

Discard spinach stems and any yellow or wilted leaves; wash spinach and pat dry. Wrap in paper towels, enclose in plastic bags, and refrigerate for at least 30 minutes or up to 2 days. Also discard tough watercress stems and yellow leaves; wash and crisp watercress as for spinach.

With scissors, cut chiles crosswise into thin strips; discard seeds and stems. In a 10- to 12-inch frying pan, stir oil and chiles over low heat until chiles are crisp, 2 to 3 minutes (watch closely to avoid burning). Lift chiles from oil; set aside. Save oil for dressing.

If whole cactus pad has thorns or prickly hairs, hold pad with tongs and use a knife to scrape off thorns or hairs (wear gloves). Trim around edge of pad to remove skin and any thorns, then peel remaining pad if skin is tough. Cut into about ½-inch squares. In a 3- to 4-quart pan, bring about 8 cups water to a boil. Add fresh cactus, reduce heat, and simmer, uncovered, until cactus is barely tender when pierced, about 5 minutes. Drain and rinse well with water. (Cactus is mucilaginous, much like okra.) If using canned cactus, omit cooking.

Tear spinach into bite-size pieces; you should have 3 to 4 quarts. Place half the spinach in a large salad bowl. Top with half *each* of the watercress, onion, radishes, cactus, and cheese. Repeat layers. (At this point, you may cover and refrigerate for up to 4 hours.)

To serve, pit, peel, and slice avocados. Arrange avocados and chiles over salad. Spoon dressing over salad and mix.

CIDER DRESSING. Whisk together **oil from chiles,** ⅔ cup **cider vinegar,** 1 clove **garlic** (pressed or minced), 1 tablespoon **soy sauce,** and ¼ teaspoon **pepper.**

Corn Salad with Three-Herb Dressing

PREPARATION TIME: 30 to 35 minutes if using fresh corn; 15 to 20 minutes if using frozen corn

PER SERVING: 498 calories, 5 grams protein, 27 grams carbohydrate, 44 grams total fat, 0 milligram cholesterol, 125 milligrams sodium

Native American corn reaches its peak under the hot midsummer sun—but frozen corn kernels, available all year, make this a recipe for all seasons. It's a simple vinaigrette-dressed salad featuring fresh or frozen corn seasoned with mint, cilantro, and dill.

Makes 6 servings

> 1 cup salad oil
> 4 cups fresh corn kernels (5 or 6 medium-size ears, about 5 lbs. in husks); or 4 cups frozen corn kernels
> ½ cup white wine vinegar
> 4 teaspoons Dijon mustard
> 2 teaspoons sugar
> ½ cup *each* finely chopped fresh mint and fresh cilantro (coriander)
> ¼ cup finely chopped fresh dill
> Salt and pepper
> 1 large ripe avocado
> 1 large firm-ripe tomato

Warm ⅓ cup of the oil in a 10- to 12-inch frying pan over medium-high heat. Add corn and cook, stirring, until corn is hot and a darker golden yellow, about 2 minutes. Transfer corn to a large bowl.

To make dressing, whisk together remaining ⅔ cup oil, vinegar, mustard, and sugar. Combine dressing with corn, mint, cilantro, and dill. Mix gently to coat corn with dressing. Season to taste with salt and pepper.

Pit and peel avocado; cut into 12 to 18 slices. Core tomato and cut into 12 wedges. On each of 6 salad plates, alternate 2 or 3 avocado slices with 2 tomato wedges. Lift corn salad from bowl with a slotted spoon; mound equal portions on each plate. Drizzle any remaining dressing over tomato and avocados.

Tomato & Avocado Salad with Mogul Dressing

PREPARATION TIME: 15 to 20 minutes

STANDING TIME: At least 2 hours to allow dressing flavors to blend

CHILLING TIME: At least 30 minutes to crisp lettuce, if used

PER SERVING OF SALAD (WITHOUT DRESSING): 149 calories, 2 grams protein, 9 grams carbohydrate, 13 grams total fat, 0 milligram cholesterol, 14 milligrams sodium

This recipe was given to us by an Indian living in San Francisco; its distinctive flavor comes from the Chinese five-spice blend used in the dressing. At the time of publication, the beefsteak-type tomatoes used in the salad were more likely to come from a home garden than a supermarket; today, though, these big, meaty tomatoes are widely grown commercially.

Makes 4 to 6 servings

> 2 large ripe tomatoes, peeled, cored, and thinly sliced
> 2 large ripe avocados, pitted, peeled, and sliced
> 12 to 18 thin cucumber slices (optional)
> 12 to 18 small inner romaine lettuce leaves, washed and crisped (optional)
> Mogul Dressing (recipe follows)
> Salt

Arrange tomatoes and avocados on a platter. Garnish with cucumber and romaine, if desired. Offer Mogul Dressing and salt to add to salads.

MOGUL DRESSING. Whisk together ½ cup **salad oil**, 2 tablespoons **tarragon wine vinegar**, 1 teaspoon *each* **dry basil** and **Chinese five-spice**, ½ teaspoon **lemon juice**, 1 small clove **garlic** (minced or pressed), and ⅛ teaspoon *each* **dry mustard** and **pepper**. Cover and let stand for at least 2 hours or up to 2 days before using. Makes about ⅔ cup.

PER TABLESPOON: 98 calories, .04 gram protein, .37 gram carbohydrate, 11 grams total fat, 0 milligram cholesterol, .20 milligram sodium.

Tomatoes & Gorgonzola with Black Beans

PREPARATION TIME: About 10 minutes

PER SERVING WITHOUT DRESSING: 70 calories, 4 grams protein, 6 grams carbohydrate, 4 grams total fat, 8 milligrams cholesterol, 395 milligrams sodium

A surprising salad idea, this bold-flavored arrangement results from Sunset's bent toward using exotic ingredients in everyday dishes. Here, the focus is on fermented black beans, sold in Asian markets and in well-stocked supermarkets.

Makes 6 servings

> 3 large ripe tomatoes, cored and sliced
> 1 tablespoon minced shallot or onion
> ⅛ teaspoon freshly ground black pepper
> ½ cup crumbled Gorgonzola cheese
> 2 tablespoons fermented salted black beans, rinsed and patted dry
> Watercress sprigs
> Olive oil or salad oil
> Red wine vinegar

Overlap tomato slices at 1 end of a platter. Sprinkle with shallot and pepper. Mound cheese alongside; mound beans next to cheese. Garnish with watercress.

Offer oil and vinegar in cruets. Let each diner spoon a portion of each ingredient onto an individual plate and dress to taste with oil and vinegar.

Beautiful Bottle-mates...Flavored Vinegars

Among the most beautiful and special gifts to emerge from the kitchen, these vinegars, aromatic with fresh herbs and whole spices, are both easy and inexpensive to make.

Use your imagination in creating flavorings for wine vinegars; we suggest a few seasoning combinations in the recipes that follow. For best results, start with the best ingredients—top-quality vinegars and the freshest herbs.

Be sure to begin the vinegars well in advance, since you'll need to let them stand for a while to absorb the flavors.

Give the vinegars in decorative bottles (3- to 3½-cup size). Any bottle you choose should have a tight-fitting screw top, stopper, or cork. Put the flavoring of your choice in the clean bottle and fill it with plain wine vinegar. Leave an inch free at the top if you need to insert a cork or glass stopper.

Let the bottle stand undisturbed in a cool, dark place for at least 3 weeks so flavors can develop. The vinegars keep well for about 4 months.

To speed up the process, heat the vinegar to lukewarm; then pour it into a bottle over herbs that have been crushed or coarsely chopped. Let the bottle stand in a warm, dark place, shaking it gently each day. When the flavor suits you (check after about 10 days), strain the vinegar, discarding the seasonings. Return the vinegar to the rinsed bottle; add a fresh herb sprig, if desired.

Before giving, identify the vinegar's flavor by writing it on a decorative tag or label. You may want to indicate the bottling date, too.

Aromatic fresh herb sprigs, a dash of spice, hot chiles, a spear of garlic cloves—these simple ingredients turn ordinary wine vinegar into unique culinary gifts. Present in decorative glass bottles sealed with corks.

Herb-flavored vinegars

Each of our recipes makes about 3½ cups vinegar.

GARLIC VINEGAR. Peel 6 large cloves **garlic** and impale them on a thin bamboo skewer (or put 3 garlic cloves on each of 2 skewers). Insert in a bottle and fill with **red wine vinegar**.

TARRAGON OR DILL VINEGAR. Poke 4 **fresh tarragon or dill sprigs** (*each* about 5 inches long) into a bottle. Fill with **red or white wine vinegar**.

ROSEMARY-PEPPERCORN VINEGAR. Put into a bottle 4 **fresh rosemary sprigs** (*each* about 5 inches long) and, if desired, 2 **fresh lemon thyme sprigs**. Add 1 teaspoon **whole black peppercorns** and fill with **white wine vinegar**.

BASIL-OREGANO-PEPPERCORN VINEGAR. Put into a bottle 2 **fresh basil sprigs** and 4 **fresh oregano sprigs** (*each* about 5 inches long). Add 6 **whole black peppercorns** and fill with **red wine vinegar**.

GARLIC-GREEN ONION VINEGAR. Put into a bottle 4 cloves **garlic** (peeled) and 2 **green onions** (*each* about 6 inches long). Fill with **white wine vinegar**.

SPICY CHILE VINEGAR. Poke into a bottle 4 **bay leaves**, 6 **small dried hot red chiles**, and 4 large cloves **garlic** (peeled). Fill with **red or white wine vinegar**.

GARLIC-LEMON-MINT VINEGAR. Put into a bottle 4 large cloves **garlic** (peeled) and 4 **fresh mint sprigs** (*each* about 5 inches long). Add ¼-inch-wide strip **lemon peel** (cut in a continuous spiral). Fill with **white wine vinegar**.

Fragrant fresh basil—a favorite herb of Western cooks—combines with pine nuts and ripe tomatoes in colorful Tomato-Basil Mignonette (recipe below).

Tomato-Basil Mignonette

Pictured above

PREPARATION TIME: 10 to 15 minutes

PER SERVING OF SALAD: 72 calories, 3 grams protein, 12 grams carbohydrate, 3 grams total fat, 0 milligram cholesterol, 19 milligrams sodium

The basil family is quite extensive, and each type has its own character. In this salad, you can use sweet, lemon, cinnamon, 'Piccolo Verde Fino,' or 'Dark Opal' basil.

Makes 4 servings

- **2 tablespoons pine nuts**
- **4 large ripe tomatoes**
- **24 to 36 medium-size to large fresh basil leaves; or ½ cup small leaves or tiny sprigs**
  Mignonette Dressing (recipe follows)
  Salt

In a 6- to 8-inch frying pan over medium heat, stir pine nuts until lightly browned, about 5 minutes.

Core tomatoes and cut crosswise into ¼-inch-thick slices. Arrange tomato slices and basil leaves equally on each of 4 salad plates. Spoon Mignonette Dressing over tomatoes and basil and garnish with pine nuts; season to taste with salt.

MIGNONETTE DRESSING. Whisk together ¼ cup **dry white wine;** 2 tablespoons *each* minced **shallot,** chopped **fresh basil leaves,** and **lemon juice;** and ¼ teaspoon **freshly ground black pepper.**

PER TABLESPOON: 10 calories, .13 gram protein, 1 gram carbohydrate, .02 gram total fat, 0 milligram cholesterol, 2 milligrams sodium.

Tomatillo, Jicama & Apple Salad

PREPARATION TIME: 20 to 25 minutes

PER SERVING: 52 calories, 2 grams protein, 11 grams carbohydrate, .48 gram total fat, 0 milligram cholesterol, 3 milligrams sodium

Cool, crisp wedges of apple and jicama contrast with tangy tomatillos and cilantro in this refreshing layered salad. Serve as an appetizer or to accompany the main course.

Makes 8 to 10 servings

- **2 medium-size, tart green-skinned apples**
  About 2 tablespoons lime juice
  About 1 pound jicama (½ medium-size), scrubbed
- **7 medium-size (1½- to 1¾-inch-diameter) tomatillos**
  Fresh cilantro (coriander) leaves
  Coarse salt

Core apples and cut each into 15 or 16 thin wedges. Dip into lime juice to coat.

Peel jicama; cut in half, then cut into 30 or 32 thin wedges. Remove and discard stems and husks from tomatillos; rinse tomatillos and pat dry, then cut to make 30 or 32 thin slices.

On each slice of jicama, stack a piece of apple, a tomatillo slice, and a cilantro leaf. Arrange, overlapping, on a platter. (At this point, you may cover and refrigerate for up to 2 hours.) To serve, drizzle with remaining lime juice and sprinkle with salt.

Cilantro Slaw

PREPARATION TIME: 15 to 20 minutes
PER SERVING: 147 calories, 1 gram protein, 6 grams carbohydrate, 14 grams total fat, 0 milligram cholesterol, 13 milligrams sodium

Cilantro and a touch of lime juice give this crisp slaw its special sophistication. Offer it with enchiladas or chili, or use it in tacos in place of lettuce and tomatoes.

Makes 6 to 8 servings

> 1 small head green cabbage (about 1 lb.), finely shredded
> 1 small onion, minced
> 2 tablespoons minced fresh cilantro (coriander)
> 1 European cucumber (about 1 lb.)
> Lime & Garlic Dressing (recipe follows)
> Salt and pepper

Mix cabbage, onion, and cilantro. Peel and seed cucumber; cut into 3-inch-long sticks. (At this point, you may cover and refrigerate cabbage mixture and cucumber separately for up to 1 day.)

Stir dressing into cabbage mixture; pile into a bowl or onto a platter. Garnish with cucumber; season to taste with salt and pepper.

LIME & GARLIC DRESSING. Whisk together ½ cup **salad oil,** ⅓ cup **lime juice,** and 2 cloves **garlic,** minced or pressed. If made ahead, cover and refrigerate for up to 2 days; stir to reblend before using.

Poached Fennel Salad

PREPARATION TIME: About 25 minutes
COOKING TIME: 30 to 35 minutes
PER SERVING OF FENNEL: 41 calories, 2 grams protein, 7 grams carbohydrate, 1 gram total fat, 0 milligram cholesterol, 105 milligrams sodium

Fresh fennel—also called sweet anise or finocchio—is good raw, but poaching accentuates its mildly sweet, refreshing licorice flavor. The peppery mayonnaise adds an appealing accent.

Makes 4 servings

> 1 large head fennel (about 1 lb.), rinsed
> 2 cups Homemade Chicken Broth (page 58) or 1 can (14½ oz.) regular-strength chicken broth
> Pepper Mayonnaise (recipe follows)
> Pepper
> Salt

Cut fennel vertically into quarters. Cut off and discard woody stems; reserve feathery leaves.

In a 3- to 4-quart pan, bring broth to a boil. Add fennel; reduce heat, cover, and simmer until tender when pierced, about 30 minutes. Drain (reserve broth for soup, if desired). Let cool to room temperature,

then use (or wrap airtight and refrigerate for up to 1 day).

Place 1 fennel quarter on each of 4 salad plates (or arrange fennel on a platter). Spoon some of the Pepper Mayonnaise over fennel; garnish with reserved fennel leaves and sprinkle with pepper. Offer remaining Pepper Mayonnaise from a pitcher; season salads to taste with salt.

PEPPER MAYONNAISE. In a bowl or food processor, combine 2 **large egg yolks,** 2 teaspoons **lemon juice,** 1 teaspoon **canned tomato paste,** ½ teaspoon **Dijon mustard,** and ⅛ to ¼ teaspoon **cayenne.** Beat with a wire whisk (or whirl) until blended. Beating (or processing) constantly, add ½ cup **salad oil** in a slow, steady stream. If made ahead, cover and refrigerate for up to 2 days. Makes about ⅔ cup.
PER TABLESPOON: 183 calories, .96 gram protein, .40 gram carbohydrate, 20 grams total fat, 91 milligrams cholesterol, 23 milligrams sodium.

Red Potato Salad with Yogurt

PREPARATION TIME: About 20 minutes
COOKING TIME: About 30 minutes
PER SERVING: 273 calories, 4 grams protein, 31 grams carbohydrate, 15 grams total fat, 13 milligrams cholesterol, 133 milligrams sodium

Yogurt and mild, slightly sweet rice vinegar give this potato salad its refreshingly light and tangy flavor. Use homemade yogurt (page 175), if you like.

Makes 6 servings

> 2 pounds red thin-skinned potatoes (about 5 large potatoes)
> ½ cup *each* plain yogurt and mayonnaise
> 3 tablespoons rice vinegar; or 3 tablespoons white wine vinegar plus 1 teaspoon sugar
> 2 cloves garlic, pressed or minced
> 1 tablespoon minced fresh thyme leaves or dry thyme leaves
> ½ cup *each* thinly sliced green onions (including tops) and thinly sliced celery
> Salt and pepper

Scrub potatoes well. In a 5- to 6-quart pan, combine potatoes and about 8 cups water. Bring to a boil over high heat. Reduce heat, cover, and simmer until potatoes are tender when pierced, 20 to 25 minutes. Drain, then immerse in cold water to cool. When potatoes are cool, drain and cut into ¾-inch cubes.

In a large bowl, stir together yogurt, mayonnaise, vinegar, garlic, thyme, onions, and celery. Add potatoes and mix gently. Season to taste with salt and pepper. If made ahead, cover and refrigerate for up to 24 hours.

Rustic Roasted Vegetable Salad

PREPARATION TIME: 10 to 15 minutes
COOKING TIME: About 30 minutes to broil peppers; about 40 minutes to bake vegetables (if you have 2 ovens, broil and bake concurrently)
PER SERVING: 512 calories, 9 grams protein, 36 grams carbohydrate, 39 grams total fat, 5 milligrams cholesterol, 276 milligrams sodium

Roasting brings out sweet robust flavors in the vegetables that compose this salad—especially in the garlic and bell peppers. The oil that makes them glisten as they cook also serves as a mellow dressing.

Makes 4 to 6 servings

> 2 large heads garlic, cut crosswise about ⅓ of the way from root end
> 16 to 20 large (about 2-inch-diameter) button mushrooms, ends trimmed
> 3 medium-size zucchini (about ¾ lb. *total*), ends trimmed, cut into ½-inch-thick diagonal slices
> 1 cup olive oil
> 2 tablespoons lemon juice
> 12 thin baguette slices
> 4 roasted fresh bell peppers (directions follow) or 2 jars (about 7 oz. *each*) roasted red peppers
> Niçoise or black ripe olives
> 1 can (2 oz.) anchovy fillets, drained
> Salt and pepper

Place garlic, cut side down, in a 10- by 15-inch rimmed baking pan; arrange mushrooms and zucchini alongside in a single layer. Pour oil and lemon juice over vegetables. Roast in a 350° oven until garlic is golden on bottom, about 40 minutes.

Also place bread in a single layer on oven rack in same oven. Bake until dry, about 10 minutes; set aside.

You can serve these ingredients hot or at room temperature. If made ahead, let cool, then cover and refrigerate (with oil) until next day; bring to room temperature before serving.

Lift roasted vegetables from oil and arrange with bell peppers, bread, olives, and anchovies on 4 to 6 dinner plates. Drizzle with oil from pan. Season to taste with salt and pepper. To eat, pluck garlic out of skin with a fork and eat with other vegetables or spread on bread.

ROASTED FRESH BELL PEPPERS. Set 4 large **red, yellow, or green bell peppers** in a 9-inch square baking pan. Broil 1 inch below heat, turning as needed, until charred on all sides, about 30 minutes.

Cover pan and let peppers stand until cool. Pull off and discard skins along with stems and seeds. If made ahead, cover and refrigerate for up to 3 days.

Jicama with Oranges

PREPARATION TIME: About 15 minutes
CHILLING TIME: At least 30 minutes to crisp greens
PER SERVING: 82 calories, 2 grams protein, 19 grams carbohydrate, .35 gram total fat, 0 milligram cholesterol, 10 milligrams sodium

Brighten a meal with this simple salad of citrus and jicama. If you like, you can slice the oranges and jicama a day in advance.

Makes 4 servings

> 2 medium-size oranges
> ¾ pound jicama, scrubbed
> 4 to 8 large mustard green leaves (tough stems trimmed off) or butter lettuce leaves, washed and crisped
> ¼ cup orange juice
> 2 tablespoons lime juice
> 1 to 2 tablespoons fresh cilantro (coriander) leaves
> Salt

Using a sharp knife, cut peel and all white membrane from oranges; thinly slice oranges crosswise. Peel jicama and cut into ¼-inch-thick julienne strips. (At this point, you may cover oranges and jicama separately and refrigerate until next day.)

Line a shallow serving dish (or 4 individual salad plates) with mustard greens; arrange oranges and jicama on greens. Mix orange juice with lime juice and pour over salad, then sprinkle with cilantro. Season to taste with salt.

Soy-braised Onions with Daikon & Carrot

PREPARATION TIME: 25 to 30 minutes
COOKING TIME: About 30 minutes
PER SERVING: 292 calories, 5 grams protein, 48 grams carbohydrate, 11 grams total fat, 0 milligram cholesterol, 2700 milligrams sodium

Ginger-spiked, soy-braised onions nestle in strands of carrot and Oriental radish—resembling eggs in a nest. Serve as a first course or as an accompaniment to simply cooked meat or poultry.

Makes 4 servings

> 1 pound small (¾- to 1½-inch-diameter) white onions
> 3 tablespoons salad oil
> ½ cup *each* soy sauce and sugar
> ⅔ cup distilled white vinegar
> 1 teaspoon minced fresh ginger
> 1 piece daikon (6 inches long and 1½ inches thick), peeled, ends trimmed
> 2 medium-size carrots, peeled, ends trimmed
> About 2 teaspoons finely chopped parsley (optional)

Peel onions and arrange in a single layer in a 10- to 12-inch frying pan. Add oil and cook over medium heat, uncovered, until lightly browned, about 10 minutes; shake pan to turn onions. Add soy, sugar, vinegar, and ginger; bring to a boil. Then reduce heat, cover, and simmer small onions for 10 minutes, larger onions for 15 minutes. Uncover and continue to cook until sauce is reduced by about a quarter and onions are tender but still slightly crisp when pierced, about 5 more minutes. Set onions aside and let cool (or let stand, covered, for up to 24 hours).

Using a knife or an Oriental shredder, cut daikon and carrots into long, very thin slivers; to use shredder, draw vegetables their full length across the fine shredding blade. (At this point, you may cover daikon and carrots and refrigerate for up to 24 hours.)

To serve, make a wreath of daikon and carrots on a shallow serving plate (or make individual wreaths on 4 salad plates). Spoon onions into center. Sprinkle onions with parsley, if desired.

Beets & Pears with Dandelion Greens

PREPARATION TIME: 25 to 30 minutes
COOKING TIME: About 40 minutes
PER SERVING: 248 calories, 2 grams protein, 12 grams carbohydrate, 21 grams total fat, 0 milligram cholesterol, 136 milligrams sodium

Matchstick slivers of beet and pear, dressed with a light vinaigrette and spooned alongside shredded dandelion greens, make a bright, festive-looking salad that's ideal for a holiday menu.

Makes 4 servings

- 2 (about 2½-inch-diameter) beets
- 1 medium-size ripe pear
  Mustard Vinaigrette (recipe follows)
- 3 cups slivered dandelion greens
- 2 tablespoons finely chopped walnuts

Cut off and discard all but 1 inch of beet tops; do not trim roots. Scrub beets. In a 1½- to 2-quart pan, boil beets, covered, in enough water to cover until tender when pierced, about 35 minutes. Drain; let cool. Rub off skins; cut off ends and discard. Cut beets into ⅛-inch julienne strips; set aside. (At this point, you may cover and refrigerate until next day.)

Just before serving, peel and core pear; cut into ⅛-inch julienne strips and mix at once with vinaigrette to preserve color.

Arrange dandelion greens on 1 side of a shallow serving dish (or arrange equal portions on 4 salad plates). Alongside, make 2 or 3 alternating layers of beets and pears; drizzle with any remaining vinaigrette, then sprinkle with walnuts.

MUSTARD VINAIGRETTE. Whisk together 2 teaspoons *each* **Dijon mustard** and finely chopped **red onion,** 2 tablespoons **distilled white vinegar,** and ⅓ cup **salad oil.**

Celery Root with Green Beans

PREPARATION TIME: 25 to 30 minutes
COOKING TIME: 15 to 20 minutes
PER SERVING: 251 calories, 4 grams protein, 20 grams carbohydrate, 19 grams total fat, 3 milligrams cholesterol, 229 milligrams sodium

Rough diamond of the produce department, lumpy, bumpy celery root tastes much better in this salad than it looks au naturel. *Green beans, salami slices, and an anchovy dressing add appetizing polish.*

Makes 4 servings

- ¼ cup distilled white vinegar
- 1 celery root (1½ to 1¾ lbs.), scrubbed
- ¼ pound green beans, stem ends snapped off
  Anchovy Dressing (recipe follows)
- 12 thin slices dry salami (optional)

In a 3- to 4-quart pan, combine vinegar and 1 cup water. Peel celery root, cut into ½-inch cubes, and immediately drop into vinegar-water mixture. Bring to a boil over high heat; then reduce heat and simmer, uncovered, just until root is tender when pierced, about 10 minutes. Drain and set aside.

While celery root is cooking, cut beans lengthwise into thin strands with a knife or French bean cutter. Bring ½ cup water to a boil in pan used to cook celery root; add beans and cook, uncovered, until bright green and just tender to bite, about 4 minutes. Drain and immerse at once in ice water to preserve color; drain again. (At this point, you may cover celery root and beans separately and refrigerate for up to 24 hours.)

To serve, mix celery root and beans with Anchovy Dressing; mound on a shallow serving dish (or 4 salad plates). Arrange salami slices (if used) around salad.

ANCHOVY DRESSING. Whisk together ⅓ cup **salad oil,** 1½ tablespoons **white wine vinegar** or distilled white vinegar, 5 **canned anchovy fillets** (chopped), ¾ teaspoon **dry thyme leaves,** and ⅛ teaspoon **freshly ground black pepper.**

SALAD BARS, popular in many restaurants today, are really nothing new in the West. In 1940, one of our Chefs of the West wrote up the way he served salad—with each element presented separately, so guests could create their own combinations. Informal guest participation has long been a Sunset hallmark.

Avocados with Lime & Hazelnut Oil

Pictured on facing page

PREPARATION TIME: 20 to 25 minutes
PER SERVING: 422 calories, 5 grams protein, 13 grams carbohydrate, 42 grams total fat, 0 milligram cholesterol, 14 milligrams sodium

Even the simplest recipes can be spectacular, especially when such elegant ingredients as avocado, lime, and fragrant hazelnut oil join forces.

Makes 4 servings

24 to 30 whole hazelnuts
2 large ripe avocados
2 to 3 tablespoons hazelnut oil
1 to 2 tablespoons lime juice
Salt and pepper
Watercress sprigs
Lime wedges

Spread hazelnuts in a 9- or 10-inch-wide baking pan. Toast in a 350° oven until lightly browned beneath skins, about 15 minutes. Let cool slightly; pour onto a clean towel, fold towel to enclose nuts, and rub briskly between your hands to remove as much of skins as possible. Set nuts aside.

Halve and pit avocados. Place 1 half on each of 4 salad plates. Moisten avocados with oil, pouring some into cavity; sprinkle avocados with lime juice, then sprinkle lightly with salt and pepper. Garnish with toasted hazelnuts and watercress. Offer lime wedges to squeeze over avocados.

Orange & Avocado Salad with Cumin Vinaigrette

W E S T E R N   C L A S S I C

PREPARATION TIME: About 25 minutes
PER SERVING: 215 calories, 2 grams protein, 14 grams carbohydrate, 18 grams total fat, 0 milligram cholesterol, 7 milligrams sodium

Oranges and avocados are especially compatible fruits, and many salads pairing the two have graced the pages of Sunset. This cumin-dressed version is particularly appealing. As a classic variation, substitute grapefruit segments for the oranges.

Makes 6 to 8 servings

4 medium-size oranges
2 large ripe avocados
Cumin Dressing (recipe follows)
2 green onions (including tops), sliced
Salt and pepper

Using a sharp knife, cut peel and all white membrane from oranges. Cut oranges crosswise into ¼-inch-thick slices. Pit and peel avocados; cut lengthwise into ½-inch-thick wedges.

Arrange orange slices and avocado wedges on a platter. Pour dressing over them; sprinkle with onions. Serve, or let stand at room temperature for up to 1 hour. Season to taste with salt and pepper before serving.

CUMIN DRESSING. Whisk together 5 tablespoons **olive oil** or salad oil, 1 tablespoon *each* **red wine vinegar** and **orange juice,** 1 teaspoon **sugar,** ¼ teaspoon **ground cumin,** and 1 small clove **garlic,** minced or pressed. Cover and let stand for at least 1 hour to let flavors blend (or refrigerate for up to 2 days); stir to reblend before using.

Orange, Onion & Olive Salad

W E S T E R N   C L A S S I C

PREPARATION TIME: About 15 minutes
CHILLING TIME: At least 30 minutes to crisp lettuce
PER SERVING: 263 calories, 6 grams protein, 15 grams carbohydrate, 21 grams total fat, 17 milligrams cholesterol, 401 milligrams sodium

Commonplace today, oranges were once considered a luxury. In the late 1800s, an agricultural "gold rush" drew settlers to sunny Southern California to grow the juicy citrus. This colorful salad pays tribute to their golden groves.

Makes 6 servings

3 large oranges
1 medium-size mild white onion
12 to 18 pitted black ripe olives, sliced if desired
4 ounces Roquefort or other blue-veined cheese
1 clove garlic, minced or pressed
6 tablespoons olive oil or salad oil
3 tablespoons red wine vinegar
6 to 12 large butter lettuce leaves, washed and crisped
Salt and pepper

Using a sharp knife, cut peel and all white membrane from oranges; cut oranges crosswise into thin slices. Cut onion into very thin slices. In a large bowl, mix oranges, onion, and whole or sliced olives.

In a small bowl, mash cheese with a fork; stir in garlic, oil, and vinegar. Pour over orange mixture. Line 6 salad plates with lettuce; spoon salad atop lettuce. Season to taste with salt and pepper.

Mérida Salad

PREPARATION TIME: 15 to 20 minutes
PER SERVING: 81 calories, 1 gram protein, 21 grams carbohydrate, .35 gram total fat, 0 milligram cholesterol, 2 milligrams sodium

This salad is a popular first course in Mérida, capital city of Yucatán. In the traditional version, the fruit is cut into small chunks—but the salad is prettier with sliced fruit, as presented here.

Makes 8 servings

> 2 **large oranges**
> 2 **medium-size tangerines**
> **(or 1 more large orange)**
> 2 **large pink grapefruit**
> 2 **large, tart green-skinned apples**
> ¼ **cup lime juice**
> ½ **cup fresh cilantro (coriander) leaves**
> **Salt**

Using a sharp knife, cut peel and all white membrane from oranges, tangerines, and grapefruit; hold fruit over a bowl to catch any juices. Slice oranges and tangerines crosswise; cut between grapefruit sections, then lift sections out. Core and thinly slice apples.

In a shallow serving dish, attractively arrange apples, oranges, tangerines, and grapefruit. Sprinkle evenly with lime juice and any of the citrus juices. Garnish with cilantro. Season to taste with salt.

Prosciutto Pear Plate

PREPARATION TIME: 5 to 10 minutes
PER SERVING: 413 calories, 13 grams protein, 16 grams carbohydrate, 33 grams total fat, 45 milligrams cholesterol, 1056 milligrams sodium

Crisp as apples, Asian pears have won rave reviews in Western produce markets. Drizzled with shallot dressing and coarsely ground pepper, the sliced pears join paper-thin sheets of Italian prosciutto or salami in this simple knife-and-fork first course.

Makes 4 servings

> 2 **large or medium-size (3- to 3½-inch**
> **diameter) Asian pears, peeled if desired**
> 12 **thin slices prosciutto or dry salami**
> **Shallot Dressing (recipe follows)**
> **Coarsely ground black pepper**
> **Parsley sprigs**

Cut pears crosswise into thin slices. Arrange ¼ of the pear slices on 1 side of each of 4 salad plates. Arrange 3 prosciutto slices on other side of each plate. Spoon dressing over pears; sprinkle with pepper and garnish with parsley.

SHALLOT DRESSING. Whisk together ¼ cup **salad oil,** 1½ tablespoons **rice vinegar** (or white wine vinegar plus ½ teaspoon sugar), .and 2 tablespoons minced **shallot.**

As an elegant yet effortless first course, present Avocados with Lime & Hazelnut Oil (recipe on facing page). Garnish with watercress sprigs and a scatter of toasted hazelnuts; finish with a squeeze of lime.

Red Pear & Cheese Salad

PREPARATION TIME: 15 to 20 minutes
PER SERVING: 300 calories, 8 grams protein, 14 grams carbohydrate, 24 grams total fat, 15 milligrams cholesterol, 428 milligrams sodium

Red pears taste the same as non-red members of the same variety, but they deserve special recipes to showcase their glorious color. Here's a salad that's a good choice for an elegant first course.

Makes 6 servings

> 3 medium-size ripe red pears
> Lemon juice
> 4 ounces chèvre (such as Bûcheron or Montrachet), Parmesan cheese, or Romano cheese
> Dijon Vinaigrette (recipe follows)
> Freshly ground black pepper
> Fresh cilantro (coriander) sprigs
> Salt

Cut pears in half from stem through blossom end; core. Cut a wedge from blossom end, making a ¾-inch-wide cut. Eat wedges or discard. Brush cut surfaces with lemon juice. Place each pear half on a salad plate.

Cut cheese into 6 equal triangles and stuff into wedge-shaped space in pears. Drizzle pears with Dijon Vinaigrette; sprinkle with pepper and garnish with cilantro. Season to taste with salt.

DIJON VINAIGRETTE. Whisk together 6 tablespoons **olive oil** or salad oil, 3 tablespoons **lemon juice,** 1 tablespoon **Dijon mustard,** and 1 tablespoon finely chopped **shallot** or red onion.

Gingered Tropical Fruit Plate

PREPARATION TIME: About 20 minutes
PER SERVING OF FRUIT: 175 calories, 2 grams protein, 44 grams carbohydrate, .99 gram total fat, 0 milligram cholesterol, 8 milligrams sodium

For a light dessert, why not wind up with this colorful fruit salad? It combines tropical fruits with juicy citrus and a bold, gingery dressing. Garnish with fragrant orange blossoms, if available.

Makes 4 servings

> 3 medium-size ripe bananas
> Lemon juice
> ½ small pineapple (3-lb. size)
> 1 medium-size ripe papaya (about 1 lb.)
> 2 large oranges
> Fresh raspberries (optional)
> Citrus blossoms (optional)
> Honey Ginger Dressing (recipe follows)

Slice bananas and dip in lemon juice to prevent darkening. Peel pineapple; cut crosswise into ¼-inch-thick slices, then cut each slice in half. Peel, seed, and slice papaya. Cut peel and all white membrane from oranges; slice oranges crosswise.

Arrange fruit equally on 4 salad plates; garnish with raspberries and citrus blossoms, if desired. Offer dressing to spoon over fruit.

HONEY GINGER DRESSING. Stir together 1 cup **sour cream** and 1½ tablespoons *each* **honey** and chopped **crystallized ginger.**
PER TABLESPOON: 37 calories, .40 gram protein, 3 grams carbohydrate, 3 grams total fat, 6 milligrams cholesterol, 8 milligrams sodium.

Mixed Winter Fruit Salad

Pictured on page 68

W E S T E R N   C L A S S I C

PREPARATION TIME: About 1 hour
CHILLING TIME: At least 30 minutes to crisp greens
PER SERVING: 266 calories, 2 grams protein, 48 grams carbohydrate, 10 grams total fat, 0 milligram cholesterol, 60 milligrams sodium

In this seasonal showpiece, pomegranate seeds sparkle like rubies among wedges of crisp persimmon and segments of citrus.

Makes 12 servings

> 6 large (about 4-inch-diameter) firm-ripe crisp persimmons, such as Fuyu
> 6 large tight-skinned tangerines or mandarins
> 3 large pink grapefruit
> 1 medium-size (about 4-inch-diameter) pomegranate
> 1 medium-size head Belgian endive, washed and crisped
> 2 cups watercress sprigs, washed and crisped
> Honey Mustard Dressing (recipe follows)
> Salt and pepper

With a sharp knife, cut stems from persimmons and peel fruit. Hold persimmons over a bowl; cut into wedges, dropping fruit into bowl. Also cut peel and all white membrane from tangerines and grapefruit. Then, holding fruit over bowl with persimmons, cut between sections, lift sections out, and add to bowl.

To seed pomegranate, cut off crown end. Score peel, cutting lengthwise down sides of fruit to divide it into quarters. To prevent staining your hands and clothes, immerse fruit in a bowl of cool water; break pomegranate apart where scored. With fingers, loosen seeds from pulp and peel. Skim pulp and peel from water and discard. Drain seeds and set aside.

With a slotted spoon, lift persimmons, tangerines, and grapefruit from juice and put in a wide salad bowl (reserve juice for other uses). Add pomegranate seeds. Break endive leaves from head and add to salad along with watercress and dressing. Mix to blend; season to taste with salt and pepper.

HONEY MUSTARD DRESSING. Whisk together ¼ cup **salad oil,** 3 tablespoons **cider vinegar,** 1½ tablespoons **Dijon mustard,** 2 teaspoons **honey,** and ¼ teaspoon **dry tarragon.**

Spur-of-the-Moment Salad Suppers

One supermarket stop yields fixings for these lavish, quickly put together salad menus. You buy foods that don't require cooking, then just unpack and assemble, finishing each salad with a fresh, simple dressing or sauce. For the first salad, bring home a barbecued chicken from the supermarket's deli section; for the second, purchase large cooked shrimp.

Even if time is limited, you'll want to consider the easy, speedy desserts that complete these dinners. Try the crisp seasoned pocket bread, too; it heartily enhances both salads.

Sherry Coolers
Pistachios in the Shell
Crisp Radishes
Mediterranean Chicken Salad Platter
Chardonnay
Blackberry Macaroon Parfaits

While you assemble the salad platter, let guests make their own sherry coolers by pouring soda water or mineral water over dry sherry and ice. Offer nuts and whole radishes for nibbling.

Mediterranean Chicken Salad Platter

- 1 jar (6 oz.) marinated artichoke hearts
- ½ cup olive oil or salad oil
- ¼ cup red wine vinegar
- 1 clove garlic, minced or pressed
- ½ teaspoon *each* dry basil and dry tarragon
- 1 purchased barbecued chicken (about 2 lbs.), cut into serving-size pieces
- 1 cup pitted Spanish green olives
- 1 jar (about 7 oz.) roasted red peppers, drained
- ½ small red onion, thinly sliced
- 1 can (2 oz.) rolled anchovy fillets with capers
- About 3 cups watercress sprigs, rinsed
- 6 slices toasted French bread

Drain artichoke hearts, reserving marinade. Stir together marinade, oil, vinegar, garlic, basil, and tarragon; set aside.

On a large platter, attractively arrange chicken, olives, peppers, onion, artichoke hearts, and anchovies. Cluster watercress on 1 side and arrange toast on the other. Moisten all with dressing. Makes 3 servings.

Blackberry Macaroon Parfaits

Beat ½ cup **whipping cream** and ¼ teaspoon **vanilla** until cream holds soft peaks; sweeten with about 1 tablespoon **powdered sugar.** Coarsely crush 2 cups crisp **almond macaroon cookies;** spoon half the crumbs into 3 dessert dishes.

Divide 2 to 3 cups **blackberries** or boysenberries (fresh or thawed unsweetened frozen) among dishes and top with equal amounts of cream. Sprinkle remaining crumbs over each. Offer **orange or black raspberry liqueur** to splash over portions. Makes 3 servings.

String Cheese   Roasted Almonds
Shrimp, Endive & Avocado Salad
with Mustard Mayonnaise
Crisp Seasoned Pocket Bread Rounds
Gamay Rosé
Toasted Coconut Raisin Sundaes

Set out almonds and string cheese to eat while sipping a glass of wine; serve the same wine with dinner.

Shrimp, Endive & Avocado Salad with Mustard Mayonnaise

- ¾ cup mayonnaise
- 2 teaspoons mustard seeds
- ¼ teaspoon *each* ground cumin and curry powder
- 1 large ripe avocado
- 12 to 15 colossal-size cooked unshelled shrimp (about 1 lb. *total*); or ¾ pound tiny cooked, shelled shrimp
- 1 large head Belgian endive or 12 to 15 small inner romaine lettuce leaves, washed

Stir together mayonnaise, mustard seeds, cumin, and curry powder; set aside.

To assemble plates, spoon ⅓ of the mayonnaise directly in center of 3 dinner plates (or spoon into small bowls and set on plate). Pit, peel, and slice avocado. Arrange avocado, shrimp, and endive on each plate.

Let each person shell shrimp to dip in sauce and eat with endive and avocado. Makes 3 servings.

Crisp Seasoned Pocket Bread Rounds

Slit 2 or 3 small rounds (5- or 6-inch-diameter) of **pocket bread** and separate each into 2 thin rounds. Spread inside of each with about 2 teaspoons soft **butter** or margarine and sprinkle lightly with **Italian herb seasoning** and freshly grated **Parmesan cheese.** Place rounds, seasoned side up, in a 10- by 15-inch rimmed baking pan. Bake in a 350° oven until crisp, about 10 minutes; serve hot.

Toasted Coconut & Raisin Sundaes

In an 8- to 10-inch frying pan, combine ½ cup *each* **golden raisins** and **sweetened shredded coconut.** Place over medium-low heat and stir constantly until raisins are plumped and coconut is golden, 5 to 7 minutes. Remove from heat. If done ahead, reheat to serve.

Scoop **vanilla ice cream** (about 1 pint *total*) into 3 dessert dishes; top with equal portions of coconut and raisins. Makes 3 servings.

Sailing in a delicate pastry shell, a cargo of chicken salad with pea pods offers splashy refreshment as a supper Salad-in-a-Boat (recipe below).

Salad-in-a-Boat

Pictured above

W E S T E R N   C L A S S I C

PREPARATION TIME: 10 to 15 minutes to make pastry; less than 30 minutes to make any of the fillings

BAKING TIME: About 40 minutes; allow at least 1 hour to cool pastry

PER SERVING OF PASTRY: 175 calories, 5 grams protein, 11 grams carbohydrate, 12 grams total fat, 163 milligrams cholesterol, 132 milligrams sodium

Sunset loves to launch spectacular new ideas. This recipe made a big splash when it appeared on the magazine's cover in 1980. You simply bake a crisp boat of cream puff pastry, then fill it with your choice of cool, colorful summer salads. Serve as an easy, impressive patio main course.

Makes 4 to 6 servings

> ⅔ **cup water**
>
> 5 **tablespoons butter or margarine, cut into small chunks**
>
> ⅔ **cup all-purpose flour**
>
> 3 **large eggs**
>
> **Chicken or egg salad (recipes follow)**

In a 2- to 3-quart pan, combine water and butter. Bring to a full boil over high heat, stirring to melt butter. Add flour all at once and stir with a heavy spoon until dough forms a ball. Remove from heat. Add eggs, 1 at a time, beating after each addition until dough is smooth and glossy. Spoon dough into a greased 9-inch springform pan or cheesecake pan with a removable bottom; spread evenly over bottom and up sides.

Bake in a 400° oven until puffed and brown, about 40 minutes. Turn off oven. Prick pastry crust with a wooden pick in 10 to 12 places and leave in closed oven for about 10 minutes to dry, then remove pan from oven and let crust cool completely. Remove pan sides.

If made ahead, cover loosely with foil and store at room temperature for up to 1 day; freeze for longer storage. Recrisp before using: heat crust (thawed if frozen), uncovered, in a 400° oven for 10 minutes. Let cool.

To serve, spoon salad of your choice into crust and garnish as directed. Cut into thick wedges.

CHICKEN & PEA POD SALAD. Combine 3 cups **cooked chicken** (in bite-size pieces), 1 can (about 8 oz.) **water chestnuts** (drained and sliced), ½ cup thinly sliced **green onions** (including tops), and 2 **hard-cooked large eggs** (coarsely chopped). In a small bowl, stir together 1 cup **sour cream,** 1 teaspoon **lime juice,** 2 teaspoons *each* **sugar** and **curry powder,** and ½ teaspoon **ground ginger.** Pour dressing over chicken mixture and mix well. Season to taste with **salt** and **pepper.**

Remove ends and strings from ¼ pound **edible-pod peas.** Drop into a 2- to 3-quart pan filled with 2 inches of rapidly **boiling water;** boil for 1½ minutes. Drain and plunge into ice water; when cool, drain again. Assemble salad; or cover and refrigerate chicken mixture and peas separately for up to 24 hours.

To serve, arrange peas in bottom and up sides of crust. Pile chicken salad on top and garnish with **fresh cilantro (coriander)** or parsley.

Per Serving: 279 calories, 25 grams protein, 10 grams carbohydrate, 15 grams total fat, 170 milligrams cholesterol, 108 milligrams sodium.

EGG & SPINACH SALAD. Combine 12 **hard-cooked large eggs** (coarsely chopped); 3 **green onions** (including tops), thinly sliced; and 1 cup thinly sliced **celery.** In a small bowl, stir together ½ cup **mayonnaise,** 1 teaspoon *each* **Dijon mustard** and **mustard seeds,** and ¼ teaspoon **ground cumin.** Gently mix into egg mixture. Season to taste with **salt** and **pepper.** If made ahead, cover and refrigerate for up to 24 hours.

To serve, line crust with about 1½ cups washed and crisped small **spinach** leaves (or coarsely shredded large leaves). Pile egg salad over spinach and garnish with 8 to 10 **cherry tomatoes,** stemmed and halved.

Per Serving: 305 calories, 13 grams protein, 4 grams carbohydrate, 26 grams total fat, 559 milligrams cholesterol, 297 milligrams sodium.

Watermelon & Smoked Chicken Salad

Pictured on page 8

PREPARATION TIME: 35 to 40 minutes

COOKING TIME: At least 1 hour for pickles (at least 12 hours to cool); 1½ to 2 hours for beans (3 to 4 hours to cool); about 14 hours to brine and smoke chicken or turkey if you smoke your own

CHILLING TIME: At least 30 minutes to crisp lettuce

PER SERVING: 343 calories, 33 grams protein, 41 grams carbohydrate, 6 grams total fat, 50 milligrams cholesterol, 1860 milligrams sodium

There's a certain amount of trompe l'oeil *in this stunning main-dish salad—those "watermelon seeds" you see mingling with pink watermelon chunks, pale green fresh watermelon pickles, and strips of smoked chicken are really shiny black beans.*

It's easiest to make the salad in two stages. Cook the pickles and beans one day; prepare the dressing and assemble the salad the next.

Makes 6 servings

　　1 small smoked chicken (about 3 lbs.) or 1½
　　　　pounds boned smoked turkey (purchase
　　　　smoked poultry or smoke your own as
　　　　directed on page 136)

　　1 medium-size onion, chopped
　　4 chicken bouillon cubes (if using smoked
　　　　turkey)
　　½ pound dried black beans (about 1¼ cups)
　　1 piece watermelon (4 to 5 lbs.)
　　6 to 12 large romaine or iceberg lettuce
　　　　leaves, washed and crisped
　　8 cups shredded romaine or iceberg lettuce
　　　　Watermelon Rind Pickles and
　　　　Watermelon Pickle Dressing
　　　　(recipes follow)

Pull skin off chicken; pull meat off bones. Cut or tear meat into strips and place in a bowl. (At this point, you may cover and refrigerate until next day.) Place chicken skin and bones in center of a 2-foot-square piece of cheesecloth along with onion; tie to form a loose bag. Set bag in a 4- to 5-quart pan. (If using turkey, put any skin with onion and bouillon cubes in cheesecloth bag.)

Sort beans and remove any debris. Rinse beans and add to pan with 8 cups water. Bring to a boil; then reduce heat, cover, and simmer until beans are just tender to bite, 1½ to 2 hours. Discard bag. Drain beans and let cool; if made ahead, cover and refrigerate until next day.

Cut rind off watermelon; use to make pickles. Cut watermelon flesh into 1½- to 2-inch chunks; pick out and discard seeds.

Line 6 individual plates with lettuce leaves. Combine chicken, beans, watermelon, lettuce, and drained Watermelon Rind Pickles; mound on plates. Offer dressing to spoon over each portion.

WATERMELON RIND PICKLES. Cut rind from a 2- to 3-pound piece of **watermelon,** leaving about ¼ inch of pink flesh on the rind. (To use remaining flesh for salad, keep pieces large, wrap, and refrigerate until next day.)

With a vegetable peeler, pare thin, tough outer peel off rind and discard. Cut rind into ½-inch-square chunks; you should have 3 cups. Put chunks in a 3- to 4-quart pan; add 1 cup **distilled white vinegar** and ½ cup **sugar.** Bring to a boil over high heat; stir often. Reduce heat, cover, and simmer until rind is tender to bite, about 1 hour. Refrigerate pickles in syrup, covered, for at least 12 hours or up to 2 weeks.

WATERMELON PICKLE DRESSING. Drain ¾ cup of the **syrup from pickles** and put into a 3- to 4-quart pan. Boil over high heat, uncovered, until reduced to 6 tablespoons. Let cool. With a blender or electric mixer on high speed, beat 1 **large egg yolk.** Add syrup and ½ cup *each* **walnut oil** and **salad oil** (or all salad oil) in a slow, steady stream. If made ahead, cover and refrigerate for up to 1 week. Makes about 1½ cups.

Per Tablespoon: 92 calories, .11 gram protein, 2 grams carbohydrate, 9 grams total fat, 11 milligrams cholesterol, .41 milligram sodium.

Papaya & Avocado Chicken Salad

WESTERN CLASSIC

PREPARATION TIME: About 25 minutes
CHILLING TIME: At least 30 minutes to crisp lettuce
PER SERVING: 444 calories, 36 grams protein, 27 grams carbohydrate, 22 grams total fat, 101 milligrams cholesterol, 161 milligrams sodium

Hawaii provides the United States with a bountiful supply of papayas. In markets, you'll find both the familiar golden, pear-shaped fruit (Solo Kapoho) and the rosy-fleshed Solo Sunshine. Choose unbruised fruit; when ripe, it shows some yellow color and gives slightly when gently pressed.

Makes 4 servings

¼ cup sliced almonds
1 cup plain yogurt
¼ cup Major Grey chutney, finely chopped
1 tablespoon lemon juice
Dash of cayenne
3 cups shredded cooked chicken
4 to 8 large butter lettuce leaves, washed and crisped
1 medium-size papaya (about 1 lb.), peeled, seeded, and sliced
1 large firm-ripe avocado, pitted, peeled, and sliced

Spread almonds in a 9- or 10-inch-wide baking pan and toast in a 350° oven until golden, about 8 minutes. Let cool.

Combine yogurt, chutney, lemon juice, and cayenne. Mix ¾ cup of the yogurt dressing with chicken.

Line 4 salad plates with lettuce; mound ¼ of the chicken mixture on each plate. Equally arrange papaya and avocado slices over chicken salad; spoon remaining dressing over top. Garnish with almonds.

Shrimp Avocado Salad with Pistachio Nuts

WESTERN CLASSIC

PREPARATION TIME: 15 to 20 minutes
CHILLING TIME: At least 30 minutes to crisp lettuce
PER SERVING: 363 calories, 13 grams protein, 10 grams carbohydrate, 32 grams total fat, 85 milligrams cholesterol, 124 milligrams sodium

Three of the West's most delectable foods combine here in a first-course feast. Avocado shells hold avocado chunks and pink shrimp in a bold garlic marinade; a sprinkling of green pistachio nuts lends crunchy contrast.

Makes 4 servings

¼ cup *each* salad oil and white wine vinegar
4 large cloves garlic, minced or pressed
12 cold, cooked extra-jumbo shrimp (about 16 per lb.), shelled and deveined
2 medium-size avocados
4 to 8 large butter lettuce leaves, washed and crisped
2 tablespoons roasted salted pistachio nuts, coarsely chopped

In a small bowl, blend oil, vinegar, and garlic. Slice 4 shrimp in half lengthwise; cut remaining shrimp in ½-inch pieces. Add all shrimp to oil mixture; stir gently to coat. Set aside.

Cut avocados in half lengthwise and remove pits. With a spoon, carefully remove avocado from shells in bite-size chunks. Add avocado chunks to shrimp mixture and stir gently to coat well; reserve avocado shells. (At this point, you may cover salad mixture and shells separately and refrigerate for up to 6 hours; stir gently once or twice.)

To serve, line 4 salad plates with lettuce. Set aside shrimp halves and fill avocado shells with remaining salad mixture. Set a filled avocado shell on each plate; top each with 2 shrimp halves and sprinkle with pistachios.

Crab Louis

WESTERN CLASSIC

PREPARATION TIME: 15 to 20 minutes
CHILLING TIME: At least 30 minutes to crisp greens
PER SERVING: 719 calories, 29 grams protein, 30 grams carbohydrate, 57 grams total fat, 401 milligrams cholesterol, 669 milligrams sodium

Solari's Grill of San Francisco was one of the first restaurants to serve this salad, around the turn of the century. Today, the colorful specialty of fishermen's wharves from Monterey northward has become a Western classic, equally celebrated when made with shrimp.

Makes 4 servings

2 medium-size heads iceberg lettuce (about 1 lb. *each*)
¼ cup whipping cream
1 cup mayonnaise
¼ cup *each* tomato-based chili sauce, chopped green bell pepper, and chopped green onions (including tops)
Lemon juice
2 cooked large Dungeness crabs (2 to 2½ lbs. *each*), cleaned, cracked, and meat removed from shells
4 large firm-ripe tomatoes, cored, *each* cut into 6 wedges
4 hard-cooked large eggs, *each* cut into 6 wedges
Salt

Cut cores from lettuce and discard; break off and discard coarse outer leaves. Rinse lettuce (from core end) under cold running water; shake to remove excess water. Wrap lettuce in paper towels, enclose in plastic bags, and refrigerate for at least 30 minutes or up to 2 days.

Beat cream until it holds soft peaks; stir together whipped cream, mayonnaise, chili sauce, bell pepper, and onions. Season to taste with lemon juice.

Line 4 large plates with outer lettuce leaves; shred remaining lettuce and arrange equally atop leaves. Place body meat of crab on shredded lettuce. Arrange tomato and egg wedges equally around crab. Pour enough dressing over salads to cover crab; garnish with crab legs. Offer remaining dressing to spoon over salad; season salad to taste with salt.

Topopo

PREPARATION TIME: 30 to 35 minutes

PER SERVING: 757 calories, 29 grams protein, 46 grams carbohydrate, 54 grams total fat, 107 milligrams cholesterol, 626 milligrams sodium

Topopo is Mexico's counterpart to our hearty chef's salad, but it takes the much more dramatic shape of a mountain or volcano. Typical of the cuisine shared by the Mexican state of Sonora and nearby Arizona, the dish reflects tastes on both sides of the border.

Makes 4 servings

4 **fried corn tortillas (directions follow)**
About 1 cup canned **refried beans,** heated
Topopo Salad (recipe follows)

16 to 24 cold, cooked large **shrimp** (about 30 per lb.), shelled, deveined, and cut in half lengthwise; or about 2 cups cold, sliced cooked **chicken** or **turkey**

2 ripe **avocados,** pitted, peeled, sliced, and sprinkled with **lime juice** to prevent darkening

½ cup finely diced **Longhorn** or mild **Cheddar cheese**

¼ cup canned diced **green chiles**

½ cup shredded or freshly grated **Romano cheese**

4 **tomato** wedges or small canned whole **jalapeño chiles**

To prepare each salad, spread 1 tortilla with about ¼ cup hot beans, covering completely. Place tortilla on a dinner plate; mound ¼ of the Topopo Salad onto it, using your hands to create a mountain shape. Arrange 8 to 12 shrimp halves around sides of salad, then fill in with ¼ of the avocado slices. Sprinkle 2 tablespoons of the Longhorn cheese and 1 tablespoon of the diced chiles over salad; spoon 2 tablespoons of the Romano cheese over tip of salad and top with a tomato wedge or a chile.

FRIED CORN TORTILLAS. Heat ¼ inch **salad oil** in an 8- to 10-inch frying pan over medium-high heat. Add 1 **corn tortilla** (7- to 8-inch diameter); cook, turning several times, until crisp, 30 to 60 seconds. Drain on paper towels. Repeat to fry 3 more tortillas; use tortillas hot or warm.

TOPOPO SALAD. Combine 2 cups **frozen tiny peas,** thawed and drained; 2 teaspoons minced **fresh or canned jalapeño chile;** 1 cup chopped **green onions** (including tops); 8 to 10 cups finely shredded **iceberg lettuce;** ½ cup **salad oil;** and ¼ cup **vinegar.** Season to taste with **salt.**

Warm Chinese Sausage Salad

PREPARATION TIME: About 10 minutes if using fresh mushrooms; about 25 minutes if using dried mushrooms

COOKING TIME: About 40 minutes

PER SERVING: 387 calories, 11 grams protein, 7 grams carbohydrate, 35 grams total fat, 51 milligrams cholesterol, 718 milligrams sodium

In Sunset's parlance, taking the bitter with the sweet means adventuresome flavor. In this case, it's an East-West adventure—a salad of garland chrysanthemum leaves and shiitake mushrooms, served with Chinese link sausages. Shop for the ingredients at an Asian or specialty market (or use the readily available alternatives noted).

Makes 4 to 6 servings

¼ **pound fresh shiitake mushrooms; or 4 large dried shiitake mushrooms (½ oz. total)**
About ¼ pound **oyster** or **button mushrooms**

6 cups lightly packed washed **garland chrysanthemum** (*shungiku*), **mustard greens, arugula,** or **watercress**

1 pound **Chinese link sausages** (*lop cheong*)
Mustard Oil (recipe follows)

If using dried mushrooms, soak in warm water to cover until soft, about 15 minutes; then drain. Rinse all shiitake; cut off and discard stems, then cut caps into ⅛-inch-wide strips. Cut oyster mushrooms into bite-size clusters (slice button mushrooms). Set all mushrooms aside.

Trim and discard tough stems from greens; tear leaves into bite-size pieces and place in a bowl. Cover and refrigerate until ready to use.

Pierce each sausage in several places. In a 10- to 12-inch frying pan, cook sausages over medium heat until browned, turning often. Add 1 cup water; cover and simmer for 20 minutes. Uncover; boil until liquid has evaporated. Lift out sausages and set aside 8 to 12; reserve drippings. Cut remaining sausages diagonally into bite-size pieces.

Add Mustard Oil and mushrooms to drippings; cook and stir until mushrooms are slightly limp. Mix in sliced sausages. If using chrysanthemum or mustard greens, add to pan and stir until lightly wilted. Or pour hot mixture over arugula or watercress in bowl; mix.

Arrange salad on 4 to 6 dinner plates; place 2 whole sausages alongside each serving.

MUSTARD OIL. Blend 2 tablespoons *each* **salad oil, red wine vinegar,** and minced **onion;** 2 teaspoons *each* **Dijon mustard** and **soy sauce;** and ¼ teaspoon **pepper.**

WHAT DO WE CONSIDER Western foods? The list goes on and on, but starts off with vegetables and fruits that the West has long supplied to the rest of the country—artichokes, olives, avocados, citrus, persimmons, walnuts, almonds, grapes, melons, nectarines, pears, and apples—as well as salad greens.

The Best of Sunset

MEATS

Before irrigation brought orange groves and broccoli fields, the West belonged to cattle. And cattle, sheep, and pigs are still raised here, providing wonderful meats to enrich our tables. Sunset's best recipes for beef, lamb, pork, and more—gathered from nearly 60 years of culinary experience—are collected in this chapter.

Barbecuing is an art in the West, and meats are a favorite choice for cooking on the grill. But our focus isn't only on familiar chops and steaks; you'll also find chilis, stews, and other braised dishes, some with a foreign heritage.

There's something for everyone in these pages…for the daring and persevering, a spit-roasted pig; for the innovative host, communally cooked Mizutaki; and for the cook who likes to take it easy, simple Double Onion Roast Beef or London Broil.

Boned, butterflied, herbed, and barbecued, our Crossswords Butterflied Lamb (recipe on page 108) is easy to cook, carve, and enjoy.

Double Onion Roast Beef

PREPARATION TIME: About 5 minutes for roast; about 15 minutes for green onions; about 10 minutes for puffs

COOKING TIME: 2 to 3¼ hours for roast; 2 minutes for green onions; 1½ hours for puffs

PER SERVING: 554 calories, 34 grams protein, 5 grams carbohydrate, 44 grams total fat, 125 milligrams cholesterol, 98 milligrams sodium

If one is good, two is better. That isn't always true—but in this case, a double helping of onions makes roast beef doubly delicious. Colorful green onions echo the flavor of the crisp onion puffs served to soak up the good beef juices. (Suggested wine: mature Cabernet Sauvignon)

Makes 8 to 12 servings

> 1 beef standing rib roast (5 to 8 lbs.)
>
> 2 cups Homemade Chicken Broth (page 58) or 1 can (14½ oz.) regular-strength chicken or beef broth
>
> 2 *each* fresh rosemary and fresh thyme sprigs (*each* about 4 inches long)
>
> 36 to 60 green onions, root ends and part of green tops trimmed
>
> Onion Cheese Puffs (recipe follows)

Place roast directly in an 11- by 17-inch roasting pan; pour ½ cup of the broth over meat and lay herbs in pan. Roast, uncovered, in a 325° oven until a meat thermometer inserted in center (not touching bone) registers 135°F for rare. Allow about 25 minutes per pound—about 2 hours *total* for a 5-pound roast, 3¼ hours *total* for an 8-pound roast.

Set meat on a carving board. Cover lightly; let rest in a warm place for 15 minutes. Skim and discard fat from pan juices; discard herbs. Add remaining 1½ cups broth to pan; bring to a boil, stirring to scrape browned bits free. Pour into a serving bowl.

Meanwhile, in a 10- to 12-inch frying pan, bring about 1 inch water to a simmer. Lay half the onions in pan and cook just until tops are limp, about 30 seconds. Lift from water and arrange alongside meat. Repeat with remaining onions. Serve juices to spoon over Onion Cheese Puffs, onions, and sliced roast.

ONION CHEESE PUFFS. Melt ¼ cup (⅛ lb.) **butter** or margarine in an 8- to 10-inch frying pan over medium-low heat. Add 1 large **onion,** chopped; cook, stirring often, until onion is soft and deep golden in color, about 25 minutes. Let cool.

In a 2- to 3-quart pan over medium heat, bring 1 cup **milk** and ¼ cup (⅛ lb.) **butter** or margarine to a full boil. Add 1 cup **all-purpose flour** all at once; stir until mixture leaves sides of pan and forms a ball, about 2 minutes. Remove pan from heat and add 4 **large eggs,** 1 at a time, beating after each addition until mixture is smooth and well blended. Stir in sautéed onion and ½ cup shredded **Swiss cheese.**

Spoon 8 to 12 equal-size mounds of dough, 2 inches apart, onto a greased 12- by 15-inch baking sheet. Sprinkle with ½ cup shredded **Swiss cheese.**

Bake in center of a 375° oven until well browned and crisp, about 50 minutes. Serve hot. If made ahead, let cool on a rack. Reheat puffs on a baking sheet in a 325° oven until hot, 10 to 15 minutes.

PER PUFF: 189 calories, 7 grams protein, 11 grams carbohydrate, 13 grams total fat, 124 milligrams cholesterol, 139 milligrams sodium.

Smoky Brisket, Oven-style

PREPARATION TIME: About 25 minutes before baking; about 30 minutes to assemble for reheating

BAKING TIME: About 5 hours to cook; about 45 minutes to reheat

CHILLING TIME: At least 4 hours

PER SERVING: 354 calories, 41 grams protein, 13 grams carbohydrate, 15 grams total fat, 115 milligrams cholesterol, 758 milligrams sodium

Lean and relatively economical fresh beef brisket, flavored by a smoky onion sauce and baked slowly to tenderness, makes a practical and easy-to-manage entrée. Serve it to 8 to 12 guests, or use it for two 4- to 6-serving meals. (Suggested wine: full-bodied Barbera)

Makes 8 to 12 servings

> 4½ to 5½ pounds center-cut lean beef brisket
>
> 1½ teaspoons smoke-flavored salt
>
> 6 to 8 medium-size onions, thinly sliced and separated into rings
>
> 1 bottle (12 oz.) or 1 cup tomato-based chili sauce
>
> 1 tablespoon celery seeds
>
> 2 tablespoons mustard seeds
>
> ½ teaspoon pepper

Sprinkle brisket with smoke-flavored salt; then place meat in a 12- by 15-inch roasting pan. Bake, uncovered, in a 500° oven, turning once, until lightly browned on both sides, about 30 minutes.

Remove from oven. Lift meat from pan and set aside; with a spoon, stir pan juices to scrape browned bits free. Arrange half the onions in an even layer in pan bottom. Drizzle with half the chili sauce and sprinkle with half the celery seeds, mustard seeds, and pepper. Set meat (with any accumulated juices) on onions, then cover with remaining onions and top with remaining chili sauce, celery seeds, mustard seeds, and pepper.

Cover pan tightly with a close-fitting lid or with heavy foil, folding foil snugly around pan rim. Bake in a 275° oven until meat is tender when pierced, 4 to 4½ hours. (When uncovering meat to test, lift lid or foil away from you to avoid hot steam.) If pan is not tightly sealed, juices will evaporate and meat may scorch; if there is any indication that this is happening, add water to pan as needed to keep bottom slightly moist.

Cover pan loosely and refrigerate until meat is well chilled, about 4 hours (or until next day). Lift out meat and cut across the grain into ¼-inch-thick slices. Divide half the onions equally between two 9- by 13-inch or 10- by 15-inch baking pans or casseroles; spread onions evenly. Arrange half the meat slices over onions in each pan, overlapping meat to fit. Then, in each pan, make a band of half the remaining onions around edge of meat. Add half of any juices to each pan. (At this point, you may cover pans and refrigerate for up to 2 days or wrap airtight and freeze for up to 2 weeks. Let thaw for 12 to 24 hours in the refrigerator before reheating.) To reheat, cover pan tightly with a close-fitting lid or heavy foil and bake in a 375° oven until meat is hot throughout, 35 to 45 minutes.

London Broil

PREPARATION TIME: 30 to 40 minutes to ignite charcoal; about 5 minutes for meat
GRILLING TIME: 10 to 15 minutes
PER SERVING: 303 calories, 32 grams protein, 0 gram carbohydrate, 19 grams total fat, 87 milligrams cholesterol, 104 milligrams sodium

When Sunset *introduced this classic recipe 30 years ago, most Western cooks felt that flank steak had to be braised to be edible. We showed that grilling or broiling—just to the rare or medium-rare stage, to preserve flavor and tenderness—was a better method. The idea caught on fast, and soon meat markets were selling flank steak, then top round, as "London broil." (Suggested wine: dry red jug or Cabernet Sauvignon)*

Makes 4 servings

> 1 **flank steak (about 1½ lbs.), trimmed of fat**
> **Salt and pepper**
> **Butter or margarine (optional)**

Place steak on a grill 4 to 6 inches above a solid bed of hot coals (you should be able to hold your hand at grill level for no more than 2 to 3 seconds). Cook, turning once, until meat is done to your liking (cut to test)—about 10 minutes for rare, 15 minutes for medium-rare.

You may also broil meat. Place on a rack in a broiler pan (about 12 by 15 inches) and broil 4 to 5 inches below heat, turning once, just until meat is done to your liking (cut to test)—about 10 minutes for rare, 15 minutes for medium-rare.

Use a sharp knife to cut meat across the grain into thin, slanting slices. Season with salt and pepper; top each serving with a pat of butter, if desired.

Fajitas

PREPARATION TIME: 30 to 40 minutes to ignite charcoal; about 20 minutes for meat; about 15 minutes for beans; about 25 minutes for salsa
MARINATING TIME: At least 4 hours
GRILLING TIME: About 20 minutes
PER SERVING: 518 calories, 31 grams protein, 40 grams carbohydrate, 26 grams total fat, 70 milligrams cholesterol, 87 milligrams sodium

No one knows exactly how burrito-style fajitas evolved, but in the West it's become a catchall term for any grilled—or even stir-fried—meat wrapped in a tortilla to eat out of hand. (Suggested wine: fruity Zinfandel)

Makes 8 to 10 servings

> 3 **pounds skirt steak, trimmed of fat**
> ½ **cup lime juice**
> ⅓ **cup salad oil**
> ⅓ **cup tequila or lime juice**
> 4 **cloves garlic, minced or pressed**
> 1½ **teaspoons ground cumin**
> 1 **teaspoon dry oregano leaves**
> ½ **teaspoon pepper**
> 4 or 5 **small onions (unpeeled), cut in half lengthwise**
> 8 to 10 **green onions (including tops), rinsed well and drained**
> **Frijoles (recipe follows)**
> 16 to 20 **flour tortillas (8- to 10-inch diameter)**
> **Salsa Fresca (recipe follows)**
> **Guacamole, homemade (page 222) or purchased**
> **Sour cream**
> **Fresh cilantro (coriander) sprigs**

Cut steak crosswise into about 12-inch lengths, then place in a 9- by 13-inch dish. In a small bowl, stir together lime juice, oil, tequila, garlic, cumin, oregano, and pepper. Pour over meat; turn meat to coat. Place onion halves, cut side down, in marinade alongside meat. Cover and refrigerate for at least 4 hours or until next day, turning meat occasionally.

Tie green onions together with string about 3 inches from roots to form a brush.

Place onion halves on a grill 4 to 6 inches above a solid bed of hot coals (you should be able to hold your hand at grill level for no more than 2 to 3 seconds). Cook for about 7 minutes; turn over. Lift meat from marinade and drain briefly (reserve marinade). Place on grill. Baste meat and onion halves with marinade, using green onion roots as a brush. Continue to cook onion halves until browned and slightly soft when pressed, 5 to 9 more minutes. Cook meat, turning once, until browned and done to your liking (cut to test), about 6 minutes for rare. Place meat and onion halves on a carving board as cooked; cover loosely to keep warm.

As meat cooks, place Frijoles on grill away from main heat; stir often until hot. Roll onion brush in marinade and lay on grill. Turn brush often until tops are wilted, 3 to 5 minutes. Place brush on board; remove string. Thinly slice meat across the grain.

Let individuals heat their own tortillas on grill, turning often with tongs just until soft, 15 to 30 seconds. Place a few meat slices down center of each tortilla; top with some Frijoles, a few pieces from onion halves, salsa, guacamole, sour cream, and cilantro. Fold up bottom, then fold in sides to enclose. Eat grilled green onions alongside.

FRIJOLES. Cut 4 slices **bacon** into ½-inch pieces. Cook in a 2- to 3-quart pan over medium heat, stirring, until limp. Add 1 large **onion,** chopped, and 2 teaspoons **chili powder;** stir until onion is soft. Add 3 cans (about 1 lb. *each*) or 4½ cups cooked **pinto beans** (drained); add **salt** to taste. If made ahead, cover and refrigerate until next day. Makes 5 cups.
PER ½ CUP: 129 calories, 6 grams protein, 17 grams carbohydrate, 5 grams total fat, 5 milligrams cholesterol, 56 milligrams sodium.

SALSA FRESCA. Core and dice 2 large ripe **tomatoes;** remove husks and stems from 2 large **tomatillos,** then chop. (Or omit tomatillos and use 3 large ripe tomatoes.) Combine tomatoes, tomatillos, ½ cup chopped **fresh cilantro (coriander),** and 1 small **onion,** chopped. Add 5 to 7 tablespoons seeded, minced **fresh hot chiles;** 3 to 4 tablespoons **lime juice;** and **salt** to taste. If made ahead, let stand for up to 2 hours. Makes 4 cups.
PER TABLESPOON: 3 calories, .11 gram protein, .56 gram carbohydrate, .02 gram total fat, 0 milligram cholesterol, .66 milligram sodium.

SPHERE-SHAPED BARBECUES swept onto Western patios in the 1960s and quickly revolutionized the barbecue experience. By regulating dampers and fuel, you could control outdoor cooking with precision—and achieve splendidly predictable results. Soon appetizers, vegetables, and breads joined meats and fish on the grill.

Korean Barbecued Short Ribs

PREPARATION TIME: 30 to 40 minutes to ignite charcoal; about 30 minutes for meat

MARINATING TIME: At least 4 hours

GRILLING TIME: About 20 minutes

PER SERVING: 866 calories, 35 grams protein, 13 grams carbohydrate, 74 grams total fat, 142 milligrams cholesterol, 2437 milligrams sodium

At Korean markets, beef short ribs are sold cut into short lengths, ready to grill. You can ask your meatman to cut and score the ribs the same way. (Suggested wine: soft, rich Barbera or Zinfandel)

Makes 6 servings

⅓ cup sesame seeds

4 pounds lean beef short ribs, cut into 2½-inch lengths

1 cup soy sauce

⅓ cup sugar

2½ tablespoons *each* minced garlic and fresh ginger

⅓ cup Oriental sesame oil

⅔ cup thinly sliced green onions (including tops)

Toast sesame seeds in an 8- to 10-inch frying pan over medium heat until golden, about 2 minutes, shaking pan frequently. Crush coarsely with a mortar and pestle or whirl briefly in a blender. Set aside.

Place ribs, bone side down, on a cutting board. Make a series of parallel cuts ½ inch apart, cutting halfway to bone each time. Then make another series of parallel cuts at right angles to the first set; make cuts ½ inch apart and ½ inch deep. In a bowl, combine sesame seeds, soy, sugar, garlic, ginger, oil, and onions. Add meat; turn to coat. Cover and refrigerate for at least 4 hours or up to 8 hours.

Lift ribs from marinade, drain briefly, and place on a grill 4 to 6 inches above a solid bed of hot coals (you should be able to hold your hand at grill level for no more than 2 to 3 seconds). Cook until browned on all sides and done to your liking (cut to test), 15 to 20 minutes for medium-rare.

Pueblo-style Tostadas

WESTERN CLASSIC

PREPARATION TIME: About 25 minutes for meat; 30 to 35 minutes for bread

COOKING TIME: About 2 hours for meat; about 20 minutes for bread (includes time to heat oil)

PER SERVING: 766 calories, 38 grams protein, 46 grams carbohydrate, 47 grams total fat, 118 milligrams cholesterol, 1102 milligrams sodium

Puffy, fried rounds of baking powder dough are a popular Southwestern Indian bread, frequently sold by street vendors in New Mexico and Arizona. Topped with chile-seasoned beef stew, cheese, and lettuce, the golden fry breads make tasty Pueblo-style tostadas. (Suggested beverage: dry red jug wine; or beer)

Makes 6 servings

2 tablespoons salad oil

1½ pounds boneless beef round steak, trimmed of fat and cut into ½-inch cubes

1 tablespoon all-purpose flour

3 cups water

1 can (about 1 lb.) tomatoes

2 cloves garlic, minced or pressed

1 or 2 cans (7 oz. *each*) diced green chiles
Salt

1 large ripe avocado (optional)
Indian Fry Bread (recipe follows)

5 to 6 cups shredded lettuce

1½ cups (6 oz.) shredded Cheddar cheese
About ½ cup sour cream
About ½ cup thinly sliced green onions (including tops)

Pour oil into a 4- to 5-quart pan over high heat. When oil is hot, add meat; cook, stirring frequently, until lightly browned. Stir in flour. Add water, tomatoes (break up with a spoon) and their liquid, and garlic. Bring to a boil; then reduce heat, cover, and simmer, stirring occasionally, until meat is tender when pierced, about 1½ hours.

Add chiles, season to taste with salt, cover, and simmer for 30 more minutes. If stew is too juicy, boil, uncovered, until almost all juices have evaporated. If made ahead, let cool, then cover and refrigerate until next day. Reheat over low heat, stirring occasionally.

If using avocado, pit, peel, and slice. Place fry bread (whole or cut into quarters) on individual plates. Offer avocado, lettuce, hot stew, cheese, sour cream, and onions to top fry bread.

INDIAN FRY BREAD. Mix 2 cups **all-purpose flour,** ½ cup **instant nonfat dry milk,** 1 tablespoon **baking powder,** and ½ teaspoon **salt.** Add 2 tablespoons **lard** or solid vegetable shortening. With your fingers, rub in fat until mixture resembles fine crumbs. Using a fork, stir in ¾ cup **water** and mix until dough clings together.

Turn dough out onto a floured board and knead until smooth and velvety, about 5 minutes. Divide into 6 equal portions; shape each into a ball, then press with your hands on a floured board to form a 6- to 7-inch round. Keep rounds lightly covered with plastic wrap until all are shaped.

In a 10- to 12-inch frying pan, heat about 1 inch **salad oil** to 375°F on a deep-frying thermometer. Add 1 dough round; cook, turning once or twice, until puffy and golden, about 2 minutes. Drain on paper towels and keep warm. Repeat to cook remaining 5 dough rounds.

If made ahead, let cool completely; wrap airtight and store at room temperature for up to 1 day (freeze for longer storage). To reheat, arrange breads (thawed if frozen) in a single layer on 12- by 15-inch baking sheets; heat, uncovered, in a 375° oven until warm, 5 to 10 minutes.

Mexican-seasoned Platter Burger

Pictured below

PREPARATION TIME: 30 to 40 minutes to ignite charcoal; about 45 minutes for meat and toppings
GRILLING TIME: 15 to 20 minutes
PER SERVING: 599 calories, 34 grams protein, 42 grams carbohydrate, 32 grams total fat, 129 milligrams cholesterol, 727 milligrams sodium

Grill a platter-size meat patty, serve it on a round of French bread with a crown of cheese, chiles, tomatoes, avocado, and olives, and you've turned the everyday hamburger into a showstopper. Two baking sheets help the chef flip the patty. (Suggested wine: dry red jug or proprietor-labeled dry red wine)

Makes 8 to 10 servings

- 1 round loaf (1½ lbs.) French bread (about 11-inch diameter)
- ½ cup (¼ lb.) butter or margarine, at room temperature
- 1 tablespoon chili powder
- ¼ cup prepared taco sauce
- 3 tablespoons instant minced onion
- 2 cloves garlic, minced or pressed
- 2 teaspoons *each* chili powder and dry oregano leaves
- 1 teaspoon ground cumin
- 2½ pounds ground lean beef
- 8 ounces thinly sliced Cheddar cheese
  Toppings (directions follow)
  Salt

Using a long serrated knife, cut bread in half horizontally. In a small bowl, beat butter and the 1 tablespoon chili powder until blended; spread evenly over cut sides of bread. Set bread aside.

In a large bowl, combine taco sauce, onion, garlic, the 2 teaspoons chili powder, oregano, cumin, and beef; mix well. Scoop meat mixture onto a 12- by 17-inch baking sheet lined with wax paper; pat into a round patty 1 inch wider than bread (meat patty will be approximately 12 inches in diameter).

Holding both ends of baking sheet, invert meat patty onto a lightly greased grill 4 to 6 inches above a solid bed of medium coals (you should be able to hold your hand at grill level for 4 to 5 seconds). Lift off wax paper. Cook for about 7 minutes. Then turn, using 2 rimless baking sheets: with 1 baking sheet, push patty onto second sheet. Then hold patty between baking sheets; invert sheets to flip patty. Slide patty back onto grill, cooked side up; overlap cheese slices on top. Continue to cook until done to your liking (cut to test), about 7 more minutes for medium-rare.

Slide cooked burger back onto 1 baking sheet; keep warm. Place bread halves on grill, cut side down, and heat until lightly toasted. Cut top half of bread into wedges; keep warm. Slide burger onto bottom half of bread. Arrange toppings over burger. Cut into serving-size wedges; accompany with bread wedges. Season to taste with salt.

TOPPINGS. Halve and pit 2 medium-size ripe **avocados**; scoop flesh into a bowl and mash with a fork. Stir in 3 tablespoons **lemon juice** and season to taste with **garlic salt** and **liquid hot pepper seasoning.** Have ready 2 cans (4 oz. *each*) **whole green chiles,** split open; 2 medium-size ripe **tomatoes,** cored and sliced; and 3 large **pitted black ripe olives,** sliced.

Garnished with chiles, tomatoes, avocado, and olives, super-size Mexican-seasoned Platter Burger (recipe above) fits onto a toasted round of French bread. Accompany the burger with toasted wedges cut from the top half of the bread.

Involve Your Guests with Mizutaki

Mizutaki is a Japanese dish that's perfectly suited to a casual dinner party. In Japan, a restaurant hostess would oversee the cooking; but for at home entertaining in the United States, you can put your guests to work, letting them cook their own servings right at the table.

Mizutaki is a showy meal to present whether you use Asian or Western cooking and serving pieces. An authentic mizutaki cooker (Mongolian hotpot) makes the greatest visual impact, but a pan on a portable burner works just as well. You set the cooker in the center of the table and fill it with boiling broth; trays of colorful, attractively arranged vegetables and meats —all cut into bite-size, ready-to-cook pieces—go alongside the cooker. (One cooker can handle a maximum of six diners; for larger dinner parties, duplicate the set-up at another table.) Guests choose the tidbits they like, drop them into the simmering broth, then fish them out when cooked (in just a few minutes). The steaming foods are dipped into a luxurious sauce, then eaten with rice.

You don't need a starter course for this complete meal, but a simple dessert is welcome; try fresh fruit or fruit ice with ginger rice cookies. Tea is the perfect beverage throughout.

1½ pounds boned beef sirloin, trimmed of fat, cut 1½ to 2 inches thick; or 1½ pounds pork tenderloin, trimmed of fat

6 chicken thighs (about 2 lbs. *total*) or 3 whole chicken breasts (about 3 lbs. *total*)

6 slender carrots

½ head (1½-lb. size) cauliflower or ½ pound edible-pod peas

6 to 8 green onions

½ pound fresh shiitake or button mushrooms

1 pound spinach or watercress

½ pound medium or firm tofu

8 cups Homemade Chicken Broth (page 58) or canned regular-strength chicken or beef broth

Mizutaki Sauce (recipe follows)

6 to 8 cups hot cooked rice

Cut beef or pork across the grain into ⅛- to ¼-inch-thick slices. Skin and bone chicken; cut meat across the grain into ⅛- to ¼-inch-thick slices. Wrap beef and chicken separately and refrigerate.

Scrub or peel carrots and thinly slice diagonally.

Separate cauliflower into flowerets; break flowerets into small bite-size pieces or slice lengthwise. (Or, if using peas, remove ends and strings.)

Trim root ends from onions; then cut onions, including tops, into 2-inch lengths.

Rinse mushrooms and pat dry. Cut off and discard tough shiitake stems. Slice mushrooms about ¼ inch thick.

Discard tough spinach (or watercress) stems and any yellow or wilted leaves. Wash remaining leaves well; drain.

Arrange vegetables on a large tray, grouping each kind separately. (Or assemble 2 trays, arranging half of each vegetable on each tray.) Cover with damp paper towels, then with plastic wrap; refrigerate for up to 8 hours.

To set up the dinner table, place cooker in center of table within easy reach of all diners. If you use a mizutaki cooker, be sure it's designed for cooking, not decoration. Also called Mongolian hotpot, the cooker has a ring-shaped moat with a lid, mounted on a small, chimney-vented charcoal brazier. If you don't have a mizutaki cooker, use an electric wok, electric frying pan, or 4- to 5-quart pan on a portable electric or butane burner.

Drain tofu and cut into ½-inch cubes. Arrange beef, chicken, and tofu on a tray. Place trays of prepared foods, uncovered, on table beside cooker.

At each place, have a small plate, a small bowl about ⅓ full of Mizutaki Sauce (pour remaining sauce into a small pitcher and set on the table); a small covered bowl for hot rice; and chopsticks, tongs, or individual strainer ladles.

Mizutaki cookers are charcoal-fueled, so if you use one, the room must be *very well ventilated;* be sure there are at least several open windows. To protect table from heat, set cooker in a wide, shallow dish (such as a clay flowerpot saucer) filled with at least 1 inch water. Heat broth to boiling in the kitchen; fill moat about ⅔ full of broth. Then place 6 to 8 ignited charcoal briquets on fire grate in chimney and top with 2 or 3 more unlit briquets (if moat is empty, pan can be damaged by heat).

To use other pans, fill ⅔ full (or with 2 to 3 inches) of broth. Keep broth boiling. Fill bowls with hot rice.

The host or hostess can begin the first round of cooking, filling pan with some of each food, starting with the slower cooking carrots and cauliflower and ending with meat. Cover pan and let cook until chicken is no longer pink in center, 3 to 5 minutes. Remove lid; let guests fish out portions, a bite at a time. Dip each bite in Mizutaki Sauce, then eat with rice. As the pan is emptied, guests choose and add more foods and cook them to taste. (Be prepared for territorial debates, as foods tend to float about.) Add hot broth to pan as needed to maintain liquid level. Offer extra Mizutaki Sauce to replenish servings.

When appetites are satisfied, turn off heat (cover chimney of mizutaki cooker to snuff, but be sure some liquid remains in moat as long as coals are hot). Ladle the enriched broth into sauce cups, adding more sauce as desired, and sip as a delectable conclusion to the main course. Makes 6 servings.

MIZUTAKI SAUCE. In a blender or food processor, combine 1 **large egg,** 2 tablespoons **rice vinegar** or white wine vinegar, and ¼ teaspoon **dry mustard;** whirl until blended. With motor running, pour in 1 cup **salad oil** in a slow, steady stream. Pour mixture into a bowl; stir in ½ cup **sour cream,** 2 tablespoons **soy sauce,** 2 tablespoons **mirin** (sweet sake) or dry sherry, and ⅓ cup **Homemade Chicken Broth** (page 58) or canned regular-strength chicken or beef broth. If made ahead, cover and refrigerate until next day. Makes about 2 cups.

Layered Chili

PREPARATION TIME: About 30 minutes for chili; about 15 minutes for onions; 30 to 40 minutes for relishes
COOKING TIME: About 1 hour
PER SERVING: 775 calories, 40 grams protein, 69 grams carbohydrate, 40 grams total fat, 85 milligrams cholesterol, 1319 milligrams sodium

Hot chili topped with pickled pink onions and your choice of nearly a dozen relishes makes a complete main course, good for at-home dining as well as picnicking (the chili travels well in an insulated container). Accompany with warm tortillas; offer fruit for dessert. (Suggested wine: dry Zinfandel Blanc)

Makes 6 servings

    4 large onions (about 2 lbs. *total*), chopped
    6 tablespoons salad oil
    1 tablespoon mustard seeds
    1½ pounds ground lean beef
    1 tablespoon chili powder
    1 teaspoon cumin seeds
    ¼ teaspoon *each* ground cardamom and cinnamon
    1 can (about 1 lb.) tomatoes
    1 can (6 oz.) tomato paste
    1 cup water
    3 cans (about 1 lb. *each*) kidney beans
    Pink Onions (recipe follows)
    Relishes (suggestions follow)
    3 or 4 limes or lemons, cut into wedges

In an 8- to 10-quart pan, combine onions and oil. Stir often over medium-high heat until onions are soft and slightly golden, 15 to 20 minutes. Add mustard seeds and stir for about 1 minute. Add beef; crumble apart with a spoon and cook, stirring occasionally, until lightly browned. Add chili powder, cumin seeds, cardamom, cinnamon, tomatoes (break up with a spoon) and their liquid, and tomato paste. Add water and undrained beans. Simmer rapidly, uncovered, until chili is thickened and almost all liquid has evaporated, about 40 minutes. Stir frequently to prevent scorching.

Ladle chili into wide-rimmed plates or bowls and top with Pink Onions and relishes as desired. Squeeze on lime juice to taste.

PINK ONIONS. In a 2- to 3-quart pan, bring 4 cups **water** and 3 tablespoons **vinegar** to a boil over high heat. Add 2 large **red onions,** thinly sliced, and push down into liquid (you may also use white onions, but they won't turn pink). Return to a boil and cook, uncovered, for 2 to 3 minutes. Drain onions well and let cool. Blend with onions 1 tablespoon **vinegar,** 2 tablespoons **salad oil,** 1 teaspoon **mustard seeds,** ½ teaspoon **cumin seeds,** and **salt** to taste. Serve at room temperature. If made ahead, cover and refrigerate for up to 2 days. Makes about 2 cups.
Per ⅓ Cup: 70 calories, 1 gram protein, 6 grams carbohydrate, 5 grams total fat, 0 milligram cholesterol, 2 milligrams sodium.

RELISHES. Choose at least 5 of the following: 3 medium-size **tomatoes,** cored and chopped; 1 can (7 oz.) **diced green chiles;** 1 medium-size **cucumber,** chopped; 1 cup sliced **green onions** (including tops) or diced onion; 2 cups **sour cream;** 2 cups (8 oz.) shredded **jack or Cheddar cheese;** 2 green bell peppers, stemmed, seeded, and diced; 2 to 3 cups shredded **iceberg lettuce;** 2 medium-size ripe **avocados,** pitted, peeled, diced, and mixed with 3 tablespoons **lemon juice;** and **prepared red or green chile salsa.**

Giant Flour Tortilla Tacos
Pictured on page 2

PREPARATION TIME: About 10 minutes for tortillas and filling; 30 to 40 minutes for lettuce and relishes
COOKING TIME: About 20 minutes for tortillas (includes time to heat oil); about 30 minutes for filling
PER SERVING: 422 calories, 32 grams protein, 12 grams carbohydrate, 27 grams total fat, 103 milligrams cholesterol, 456 milligrams sodium

Here's a dramatic entrée for a Mexican-style dinner: giant tacos made with plate-size flour tortillas that are crisply fried and gently curved into half-open shells. (Suggested wine: dry red jug or full-bodied Zinfandel)

Makes 6 to 8 servings

    Salad oil
    6 to 8 large flour tortillas (10- to 12-inch diameter)
    6 to 8 cups shredded iceberg lettuce
    Beef Filling (recipe follows)
    Garnishes (suggestions follow)

In a 12- to 14-inch frying pan, heat ½ inch oil over medium to medium-high heat to 375°F on a deep-frying thermometer. Add 1 tortilla; cook, turning quickly and carefully with 2 wide spatulas, until bubbly and just golden but still flexible, about 30 seconds. Bend tortilla in half at about a 45° angle as you lift it from oil with spatulas. Let drain on a thick layer of paper towels. Lean tortilla against something sturdy (such as a 28-oz. can) so it holds its shape as it cools. Repeat to fry and shape remaining tortillas, cooking them 1 at a time.

To assemble each taco, place a fried tortilla on a plate; cover bottom with 1 cup lettuce. Spoon on about 1 cup Beef Filling, then add relishes as desired. Serve with knife and fork to eat like a salad; break off top section of tortilla and eat it like bread.

BEEF FILLING. In a 10- to 12-inch frying pan, cook 3 pounds **ground lean beef** over medium-high heat until browned, stirring often. Pour off fat. Add 2 large **onions,** chopped; stir until soft. Stir in 4 teaspoons **chili powder,** 1½ teaspoons *each* **dry oregano leaves** and **paprika,** ¾ teaspoon *each* **ground cumin** and **pepper,** 1 tablespoon **Worcestershire,** and 1 can (15 oz.) **tomato sauce.** Simmer, uncovered, until hot; stir often. Season to taste with **garlic salt.**

GARNISHES. Arrange in separate containers: 2 or 3 small **tomatoes,** cored and sliced; 1 or 2 **avocados,** pitted, peeled, sliced, and sprinkled with **lemon or lime juice** to prevent darkening; jumbo **pitted ripe olives;** large **radishes; sour cream;** and **fresh cilantro (coriander) sprigs.**

Dishes combining meat and fruit have long been popular in Europe, where they're often accompanied with sturdy whole-grain bread. Sample this traditional flavor combination in Veal Scallops with Pears (recipe on facing page), an elegant entrée featuring tender veal slices, sweet baked pear halves, and crisp triangles of rye toast.

Mrs. Morier's Roast Veal

PREPARATION TIME: About 10 minutes

ROASTING TIME: About 2½ hours

PER SERVING: 351 calories, 42 grams protein, 4 grams carbohydrate, 17 grams total fat, 151 milligrams cholesterol, 148 milligrams sodium

In travels abroad, Sunset *editors have been welcomed into the homes and kitchens of many superb cooks—and we've collected dozens of delightful family-style recipes. During one trip to France, we met Mrs. Morier, who shared with us her excellent, no-nonsense way with roast veal. (Suggested wine: mature, oaky Chardonnay)*

Makes about 8 servings

- 1 boned, rolled, and tied veal shoulder or leg roast (3½ to 4 lbs.)
- ½ teaspoon dry thyme leaves
- ¼ teaspoon rubbed sage
- 1 medium-size onion, finely chopped
- 1½ cups Homemade Chicken Broth (page 58) or canned regular-strength chicken or beef broth
- ¼ cup Madeira
- 1 tablespoon *each* cornstarch and water, stirred together
- Salt

Rub veal with thyme and sage. Place in a 10-inch square or 9- by 13-inch baking pan; distribute onion around meat. Add ¼ cup of the broth.

Roast, uncovered, in a 325° oven for 1 hour; pour remaining 1¼ cups broth into pan and stir to scrape any browned bits free. Continue to roast, uncovered, until a meat thermometer inserted in thickest part of meat registers 170°F, about 1 more hour; baste meat once or twice with pan juices.

Remove meat from oven. Pour Madeira into a 2- to 4-cup pan; warm over medium heat until bubbly, then carefully ignite with a match (not beneath a vent, fan, or flammable items). Pour over meat and let flames die down. Transfer meat to a platter and keep warm.

Skim and discard fat from pan juices. Bring juices to a boil over high heat, stirring; stir in cornstarch-water mixture until thickened. Offer sauce to spoon over sliced meat. Season to taste with salt.

Veal Scallops with Pears

Pictured on facing page

PREPARATION TIME: About 40 minutes

COOKING TIME: About 30 minutes

PER SERVING: 764 calories, 30 grams protein, 30 grams carbohydrate, 59 grams total fat, 224 milligrams cholesterol, 406 milligrams sodium

Pounded to ensure marvelous tenderness, veal slices cook in just a few minutes. Juicy baked pear halves and crisp, garlic-buttered rye toast nicely complement the meat. Because this entrée lends itself well to advance preparation, it's a good choice for fuss-free entertaining. But if you're a cook who enjoys company in the kitchen, you may not want to bother with make-ahead steps; you can just enlist the aid of your guests in preparing the main course. (Suggested wine: spicy Gewürztraminer)

Makes 6 servings

> 1¾ pounds boneless veal, cut ½ inch thick, trimmed of tough membrane and fat
> ¾ teaspoon ground sage
> ¼ cup all-purpose flour
> About ½ cup (¼ lb.) butter or margarine
> About 3 tablespoons salad oil
> 2 cups whipping cream
> ⅔ cup dry white wine
> ⅓ cup pear liqueur or rum (optional)
> ¾ teaspoon Dijon mustard
> Salt
> 1 clove garlic, minced or pressed
> 6 slices dark rye bread, crusts trimmed off and bread cut in half diagonally
> 1 tablespoon lemon juice
> 3 small firm-ripe pears
> 1 tablespoon red currant jelly (optional)
> Parsley sprigs

Place pieces of veal well apart on plastic wrap; sprinkle with sage. Cover with another sheet of plastic wrap, then pound with a flat-surfaced mallet until 1/16 inch thick; veal pieces will approximately triple in size. Coat veal with flour and shake off excess.

Melt 1 tablespoon of the butter in 1 tablespoon of the oil in a 10- to 12-inch frying pan over medium-high heat. When butter begins to brown slightly, add veal, without crowding; cook, turning as needed, until browned on both sides, 2 to 4 minutes. Scrape pan as necessary. Lift out meat and lay pieces side by side in a 10- by 15-inch rimmed baking pan. Add remaining veal to pan as space permits; add more butter and oil, 1 tablespoon at a time, as needed.

Drain any juices that have accumulated with cooked veal into frying pan; stir to scrape browned bits free. Stir in cream, wine, liqueur (if used), and mustard; boil over high heat, uncovered, stirring often, until reduced to 1½ cups. Season to taste with salt. (At this point, you may cover meat and sauce separately and hold at room temperature for up to 3 hours or refrigerate until next day.)

Blend 3 tablespoons of the butter with garlic; spread on 1 side of each piece of bread. Place bread, buttered side down, in a 9- by 13-inch baking pan. If made ahead, cover and let stand until next day.

Melt 2 more tablespoons butter with lemon juice in a 9-inch square baking pan. Peel, halve, and core pears; put in pan. Turn to coat with butter. Put pears, veal, and bread, all uncovered, in a 450° oven. Bake until pears are warm, veal hot, and bread sizzling, about 10 minutes. Also bring sauce to a boil over medium heat, stirring often.

On a platter, overlap veal slices; arrange toast triangles along 1 side of meat, pears along other side. Fill each pear cavity with ½ teaspoon jelly, if desired.

Spoon a little sauce over meat; offer remaining sauce to add to taste. Garnish with parsley.

Venetian Liver with Onions

PREPARATION TIME: About 20 minutes

COOKING TIME: About 20 minutes

PER SERVING: 442 calories, 31 grams protein, 21 grams carbohydrate, 26 grams total fat, 454 milligrams cholesterol, 114 milligrams sodium

In Venice, lemon peel often adds a fresh accent to liver and onions. Try preceding this simple entrée with Venetian Rice & Peas in Broth (page 64). (Suggested wine: mellow Barbera)

Makes 5 or 6 servings

> 4 large onions (about 2 lbs. *total*)
> ½ cup olive oil
> ½ teaspoon grated lemon peel
> 2 pounds calf's liver or baby beef liver, cut into ½-inch-thick slices
> All-purpose flour
> Salt and pepper

Cut onions into quarters, then separate into layers. In a 10- to 12-inch frying pan, combine onions and oil; stir over medium-high heat until onions are soft and slightly golden, about 10 minutes. Stir in lemon peel. Lift onions from pan with a slotted spoon, leaving oil in pan; set onions aside. (At this point, you may cover onions and let stand at room temperature for up to 4 hours or refrigerate until next day.)

Trim any tough membrane from liver slices; rinse liver and pat dry. Coat liver with flour and shake off excess. As pieces are floured, arrange them side by side on wax paper.

Return frying pan with oil to medium-heat. When oil is hot, add as many liver slices as will fit without crowding; cook, turning as needed, until browned on both sides and just barely pink in center (cut to test), about 5 minutes. Transfer to a warm platter and keep warm. Repeat to cook remaining liver.

Return onions to pan; stir until heated through, then pour over liver. Season to taste with salt and pepper. If made ahead, cover and keep warm in a 150° oven or on a warming tray for up to 30 minutes.

Beefsteak, Kidney & Oyster Pie

PREPARATION TIME: 1 to 1½ hours

BAKING TIME: About 2½ hours

PER SERVING: 537 calories, 30 grams protein, 29 grams carbohydrate, 33 grams total fat, 224 milligrams cholesterol, 352 milligrams sodium

This very English steak pie is actually made with practical beef chuck. Like a casserole, it can be put together in advance, then baked to serve. Its crust is made from an easy-to-handle cream cheese pastry; the full-flavored sauce starts with a canned product. (Suggested wine: mellow Merlot)

Makes 10 to 12 servings

> 2 **pounds lean boneless beef chuck,** **trimmed of fat and cut into thin slices**
>
> **About ¼ cup all-purpose flour**
>
> **About ¼ cup (⅛ lb.) butter or margarine;** **or ¼ cup salad oil**
>
> 3 **veal kidneys (¼ lb.** *each***) or ¾ pound lamb** **kidneys, trimmed of white membranes** **and fat**
>
> 1 **jar (10 oz.) shucked raw oysters**
>
> **Cream Cheese Pastry (recipe follows)**
>
> ½ **pound small button mushrooms, cut into** **quarters**
>
> 1 **cup chopped onion**
>
> ½ **cup minced parsley**
>
> 1 **teaspoon dry thyme leaves**
>
> **Pepper**
>
> 2 **cans (10 oz.** *each***) brown gravy sauce**

Coat beef with flour; shake off excess. Melt ¼ cup of the butter in a 10- to 12-inch frying pan over medium-high heat. Add beef and cook, stirring often, until lightly browned; add more butter as needed. Remove from heat.

Thinly slice kidneys and set aside. Drain oysters, reserving liquid; cut oysters into bite-size pieces. Set aside.

On a floured board, roll out half the pastry and fit into a shallow 3½- to 4-quart casserole, covering bottom and sides. Place beef in pastry-lined dish; scatter kidneys and oysters over beef, then sprinkle with oyster liquid. Mix mushrooms, onion, parsley, and thyme; sprinkle over meats. Sprinkle lightly with pepper. Pour brown gravy sauce evenly over all.

Roll out remaining pastry to cover pie; set in place atop filling. Pinch edges of top and bottom crusts together to seal. Cut a 1-inch hole in center of top crust to allow steam to escape. Roll out any pastry scraps and cut into decorative shapes; moisten shapes on 1 side with water and set in place on top crust, moistened side down. (At this point, you may cover and refrigerate for up to 6 hours.)

Bake, uncovered, in a 350° oven until crust is deep golden brown, about 2½ hours. If edges of crust begin to turn dark before center is browned, cover dark areas loosely with foil. Serve hot or warm; to serve, dish out portions with a large spoon.

FROM CAMPFIRES to portable barbecues —cooking outdoors has enjoyed a long history in the West. In the July 1929 issue of Sunset Magazine, *we told how to build an outdoor fireplace, including a cooking grill.*

CREAM CHEESE PASTRY. Place 2½ cups **all-purpose flour** in a food processor or a large bowl. Add 1 large package (8 oz.) **cream cheese,** cut into chunks; ⅔ cup (⅓ lb.) **butter** or margarine, cut into chunks; and ⅓ cup **solid vegetable shortening,** cut into chunks. Whirl (or rub with your fingers) until mixture is crumbly. Sprinkle with 3 tablespoons **water.** Whirl (or mix with a fork) just until dough holds together. Gather into a ball with your hands. If made ahead, wrap airtight and refrigerate for up to 2 days. Bring to room temperature to use.

Salt-cured Rabbit

PREPARATION TIME: About 20 minutes

CHILLING TIME: At least 10 hours

COOKING TIME: About 50 minutes

PER SERVING: 387 calories, 48 grams protein, .93 gram carbohydrate, 20 grams total fat, 148 milligrams cholesterol, 1392 milligrams sodium

If you've shied away from rabbit because you think it tastes dry, try salt-curing the meat. This simple, old-fashioned technique helps keep the delicate rabbit juicy; the salt alters the texture of the meat, so it holds its moisture when cooked. (Suggested wine: fruity Zinfandel)

Makes 3 or 4 servings

> 1 **fryer rabbit (about 2½ lbs.), cut into** **pieces**
>
> 2 **teaspoons salt**
>
> ½ **teaspoon** *each* **ground allspice, cayenne,** **and black pepper**
>
> 1 **teaspoon** *each* **crushed bay leaves and dry** **thyme leaves; or 2 teaspoons fresh thyme** **leaves**
>
> 1 **tablespoon olive oil or salad oil**
>
> 1 **can (about 6 oz. drained weight) pitted** **green ripe olives, drained**

Rinse rabbit and pat dry. Combine salt, allspice, cayenne, black pepper, bay leaves, and thyme. In a glass, ceramic, or stainless steel bowl, coat rabbit with blended seasonings; cover and refrigerate for 10 to 12 hours. Thoroughly rinse rabbit under cold running water, rubbing lightly to release as much salt as possible; drain rabbit and pat dry. (At this point, you may cover and refrigerate for up to 8 hours.)

Pour oil into a 12- to 14-inch frying pan (with a tight-fitting lid) over medium-high heat. Add rabbit and olives. Cook, uncovered, turning rabbit pieces as needed, until well browned on all sides, about 15 minutes. Then reduce heat to medium-low, cover, and cook until meat is tender when pierced, about 30 minutes; turn rabbit pieces occasionally. With a slotted spoon, transfer rabbit and olives to a platter; keep warm.

Measure pan drippings and add water to make ¾ cup. Pour liquid into pan, stirring to scrape browned bits free. Bring to a boil over high heat. Pour juices into a sauce boat. Spoon rabbit and olives onto dinner plates and offer juices to pour onto individual portions.

Venison Saddle with Port Sauce

PREPARATION TIME: About 40 minutes for meat; about 10 minutes for sauce
ROASTING TIME: About 45 minutes plus 15 minutes to rest, carve, and reassemble
PER SERVING: 384 calories, 24 grams protein, 31 grams carbohydrate, 18 grams total fat, 90 milligrams cholesterol, 253 milligrams sodium

Hunting isn't the only way to satisfy a taste for game. Today, much game is commercially raised; if you want to dine on venison, for example, you can purchase meat exported from ranches in New Zealand. (Suggested wine: mature Cabernet Sauvignon)

Makes 12 to 16 servings

> 1 **bone-in venison saddle roast, rack or loin section (6 to 8 lbs.), thawed if frozen**
> **About 10 slices bacon**
> ½ **cup (¼ lb.) butter or margarine, melted**
> **About 3 pounds yams or sweet potatoes, scrubbed and cut into 2-inch lengths**
> 5 **or 6 medium-size red apples**
> 2 **tablespoons lemon juice**
> **Port Sauce (recipe follows)**

Trim all fibrous sinew off venison; rinse meat and pat dry. Make 1-inch-long, ½-inch-deep slits between rib bones on each side of saddle. Cut 5 of the bacon slices into 1-inch pieces; insert a piece of bacon into each slit. Drape 5 more bacon slices across saddle.

Brush a 12- by 17-inch roasting pan with ¼ cup of the butter. Set venison saddle in pan with bones down; arrange yam pieces around saddle. Brush venison and yams with remaining ¼ cup butter.

Roast, uncovered, in a 425° oven for 20 minutes. Halve and core apples; dip cut surfaces in lemon juice. Add apples to pan. Baste apples, yams, and venison with pan juices. Continue to roast until a meat thermometer inserted in center of venison (not touching bone) registers 135°F, 15 to 25 more minutes.

Lift saddle to a platter; remove and reserve large pieces of bacon. Let venison stand for 5 minutes, then carve. To carve, cut along both sides of backbone down to ribs. On each side, turn knife sideways; slice along ribs toward backbone to free loin. Lift loin off bones; place on a board and cut crosswise into 1-inch-thick slices. Reassemble loin atop rib bones. Place roast on a platter and top with reserved bacon; accompany with yams and apples. Keep warm while you prepare sauce. To serve, offer sauce to spoon over meat.

PORT SAUCE. Skim and discard fat from **venison drippings** in roasting pan. To pan, add ⅓ cup minced **shallots**, 3 cups **port**, and 1½ cups **Homemade Chicken Broth** (page 58) or canned regular-strength chicken or beef broth; stir. Boil over high heat, uncovered, until reduced to 1½ cups. Reduce heat to low. Add 1 cup (½ lb.) **butter** or margarine in 1 or 2 chunks; stir until blended.

PER TABLESPOON: 48 calories, .18 gram protein, 2 grams carbohydrate, 5 grams total fat, 12 milligrams cholesterol, 77 milligrams sodium.

Seed-crusted Buffalo Rib Roast

PREPARATION TIME: 40 to 45 minutes
ROASTING TIME: 1¾ to 2½ hours, plus 15 minutes to rest
PER SERVING: 175 calories, 43 grams protein, 1 gram carbohydrate, 2 grams total fat, 49 milligrams cholesterol, 45 milligrams sodium

You won't find buffalo for the table roaming the Western ranges these days; they're now ranch-raised, too. Though the meat is leaner than beef, it looks about the same. Our simple presentation with aromatic seeds makes the most of the roast's special, mild flavor. (Suggested wine: mature Cabernet Sauvignon or young, fresh Zinfandel)

Makes 15 to 18 servings

> 1 **center-cut buffalo rib roast (7 to 9 lbs.)**
> 2 **teaspoons** *each* **anise seeds, coriander seeds, fennel seeds, and mustard seeds**
> 1 **teaspoon celery seeds**
> 1½ **cups dry red wine**
> 1 **cup regular-strength beef broth**

Rinse roast and pat dry. Neatly trim any excess fat from roast. Then remove heavy silver-colored membrane (if present) that covers meat: slip a thin, sharp knife under membrane at 1 end of roast to free a portion, then use this flap to hold membrane taut as you slide knife under it. If desired, also cut cartilage from between rib bones down to meat to give roast a decorative look (trimmings have a little coarse-textured meat you can use for stock).

To keep roast compact as it cooks, tie it snugly with cotton string between each rib. Set roast, meat side up, on a rack in a 10- by 15-inch rimmed baking pan.

Using a mortar and pestle, coarsely crush anise, coriander, fennel, mustard, and celery seeds. (Or whirl seeds in a blender until crushed.) Pat crushed seeds onto roast.

Roast, uncovered, in a 450° oven for 15 minutes. Reduce oven temperature to 300° and continue to roast until a meat thermometer inserted in thickest part of meat (not touching bone) registers 130°F for rare; do not overcook. Allow about 16 minutes per pound (untrimmed weight), or about 2 hours *total* for a 7½-pound roast.

Transfer roast to a platter and let rest in a warm place for 15 minutes, then snip strings free and remove them.

Meanwhile, skim and discard any fat from drippings. Add wine and broth to pan and bring to a boil, stirring to scrape browned bits free. Boil over high heat, uncovered, until reduced to 1¼ cups; stir often. Pour into a small bowl.

To serve, cut parallel to side of each rib; there is a portion-size slice of meat between ribs. Or slice roast free by cutting next to all bones at once, then cutting across the grain to make thick or thin pieces. Accompany with pan juices.

Pork Leg with Orange-Lemon Glaze

PREPARATION TIME: About 45 minutes

ROASTING TIME: About 5 hours, plus 20 minutes to rest

PER SERVING: 940 calories, 62 grams protein, 61 grams carbohydrate, 49 grams total fat, 216 milligrams cholesterol, 205 milligrams sodium

Fresh citrus juices, boiled down to intensify their flavor, make a gleaming, tart-sweet glaze for leg of pork. The glaze is brushed on shortly before the meat is done; if added earlier, it's inclined to scorch. (Suggested wine: Grignolino Rosé or Zinfandel Blanc)

Makes 14 to 16 servings

    3½ cups orange juice
    ½ cup lemon juice
    1 bone-in pork hind leg (14 to 16 lbs.)
    14 to 16 small (5- to 6-inch-long) yams or sweet potatoes, scrubbed
    6 pounds tiny (about 4-inch-long) carrots, peeled
    Orange halves and fresh rosemary sprigs or citrus leaves (optional)

In an 8- to 10-inch frying pan over high heat, boil orange and lemon juices, uncovered, until reduced to about ⅔ cup; stir often to prevent scorching. Set glaze aside.

If desired, score skin of pork leg with a sharp knife to make a 1-inch diamond pattern. Set meat, hip joint down, directly in a roasting pan (at least 12 by 17 inches). Roast, uncovered, on lowest rack of a 400° oven for 30 minutes, then reduce oven temperature to 325°. Continue to roast until a meat thermometer inserted in thickest part (not touching bone) registers 165° to 170°F. Allow about 20 minutes per pound, or about 5 hours *total* for a 15-pound leg. Siphon off and discard fat occasionally.

About 1½ hours before pork is done, arrange some of the yams and carrots around roast; put remaining vegetables in a 9- by 13-inch baking pan and bake alongside meat. Baste vegetables occasionally with pork juices.

About 10 minutes before leg is done, brush evenly with half the glaze.

Lift cooked roast from pan (use potholders to protect hands) and transfer to a platter; surround with vegetables. Let roast stand in a warm place for about 20 minutes before carving.

Meanwhile, skim and discard fat from pan juices; stir in remaining glaze. Bring to a boil over medium-high heat, scraping pan to loosen crusty bits; pour into a serving dish. Garnish roast with orange halves and rosemary, if desired. Cut skin from roast and snip into small pieces with scissors. Carve meat. Offer sauce to spoon over individual portions of meat, vegetables, and crisp skin.

Swedish-cured Barbecued Pork Loin

Pictured on facing page

PREPARATION TIME: 30 to 40 minutes to ignite charcoal; about 20 minutes for meat

CHILLING TIME: At least 24 hours

GRILLING TIME: About 1 hour, plus 10 to 20 minutes to rest

PER SERVING: 380 calories, 31 grams protein, 2 grams carbohydrate, 27 grams total fat, 111 milligrams cholesterol, 737 milligrams sodium

This pork roast gets its succulence from a Swedish-style treatment with sugar and salt. (Suggested wine: dry Sauvignon Blanc)

Makes 8 to 10 servings

    1 boned, rolled, and tied pork loin (3½ to 4 lbs.), rinsed and patted dry
    3 tablespoons sugar
    2 tablespoons salt
    1 teaspoon cumin seeds (optional)
    ½ teaspoon ground cardamom (optional)

Place meat in a close-fitting glass dish. Mix sugar, salt, cumin seeds (if used), and cardamom (if used); rub onto meat. Cover; refrigerate for 24 to 36 hours. Discard juices; rinse meat well under cool running water, rubbing to release salt. Pat dry.

To set up barbecue (use a covered one): on fire grate with lid off and with drafts open, ignite 50 to 60 charcoal briquets. When briquets are covered with ash, 30 to 40 minutes, bank half of them on each side of grate; place a drip pan in center. Add 5 or 6 fresh briquets to each side of coals; also add 5 or 6 more briquets to each side of coals every 30 minutes throughout cooking.

Set grill in place 4 to 6 inches above coals; set meat on grill above pan. Cover barbecue; open drafts. Cook until a meat thermometer inserted in thickest part of roast registers 150°F, about 1 hour. Meat should no longer be pink in center; cut to test.

Let roast rest on a platter for 10 to 20 minutes; then slice, discarding strings.

Yucatecan Steamed Pork in Banana Leaves

PREPARATION TIME: About 30 minutes for meat and achiote paste; about 20 minutes for salsa

STANDING TIME: At least 12 hours for achiote paste; at least 8 hours to chill meat

BAKING TIME: About 3½ hours

PER SERVING: 581 calories, 31 grams protein, 36 grams carbohydrate, 34 grams total fat, 116 milligrams cholesterol, 81 milligrams sodium

Baked over water in a covered pan, this leaf-wrapped pork successfully duplicates the Yucatecan original. (Suggested beverage: Sangría de Guadalajara, page 43)

Makes 8 to 10 servings

    1 boned pork butt or shoulder (3½ to 4 lbs.)
    Banana leaves (directions follow) or foil

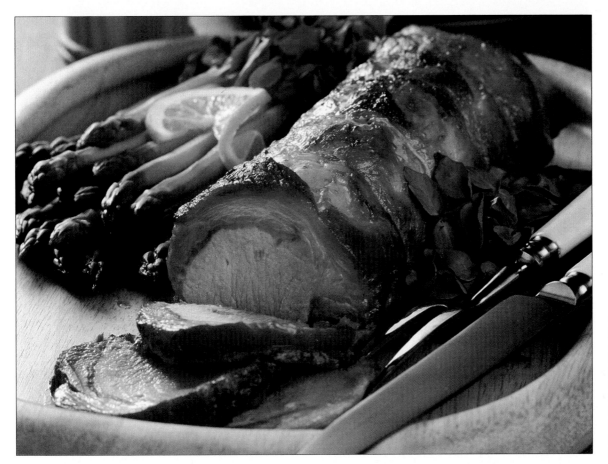

Accompany tender, juicy Swedish-cured Barbecued Pork Loin (recipe on facing page) with steamed asparagus. Grill pork in a covered barbecue and cook just until meat is no longer pink in center for best flavor and texture.

⅔ **cup purchased achiote condiment or Achiote Paste (recipe follows)**

16 to 20 flour tortillas (about 8-inch diameter)

Salsa (recipe follows)

Score fat side of pork in a diamond pattern, making ½-inch-deep cuts. Position meat in center of banana leaf rectangle or a 12- by 20-inch piece of foil. Spread achiote condiment (available in some Mexican markets) or paste all over roast, rubbing it into cuts. Fold leaf or foil around roast like an envelope to enclose; tie with string to make a secure bundle. Refrigerate for at least 8 hours or until next day.

To cook, place a rack in bottom of a deep oven-proof 6- to 8-quart pan; pour in 1½ cups water and set wrapped roast on rack. Cover and bake in a 350° oven until roast is very tender when pierced through leaves, 3 to 3½ hours; check pan occasionally and add more hot water as needed.

About 30 minutes before roast is done, stack tortillas and wrap in foil; heat in oven alongside pork until warm, 20 to 25 minutes.

To present, place roast on a platter. Slit packet open lengthwise on top with a sharp knife or scissors; peel back leaf. Pour pan juices over meat (if you used foil, the juices will not be flavored by drippings, so discard them). Let guests pull off pieces of pork to pile on warm tortillas and top with Salsa.

BANANA LEAVES. Buy 1 package (usually about 1 lb.) **refrigerated or frozen banana leaves;** thaw if frozen (you can refreeze extra leaves).

Thoroughly rinse several leaves and pat dry. Glide flat surface of leaves across gas flame (on high) or electric element (on high) of your range; in just a few seconds, leaves will become shiny and more flexible. Cut 1 leaf to make a 12- by 20-inch rectangle (or, if necessary, overlap several leaves to make this size rectangle, then cut). Set aside until ready to use.

ACHIOTE PASTE. Place 2 ounces (⅓ cup) **achiote (annatto) seeds** (available in Mexican markets) in a small bowl with **boiling water** to cover; cover tightly and let stand for at least 12 hours to soften.

Drain seeds and discard liquid. Combine seeds in a blender with 1 tablespoon **ground cumin,** 1 teaspoon **coarsely ground black pepper,** 2 teaspoons **ground allspice,** 2 tablespoons chopped **garlic,** 2 small **dried hot red chiles** (broken into pieces), ½ teaspoon **salt,** and 6 tablespoons *each* **orange juice** and **white wine vinegar.**

Whirl until smooth (takes several minutes). If made ahead, cover and refrigerate for up to 10 days; freeze for longer storage. Makes about 1 cup.

SALSA. Stir together 2 cups chopped ripe **tomatoes;** 2 **fresh or canned jalapeño chiles,** stemmed, seeded and chopped; 1 large **red onion,** chopped; 1 cup chopped **fresh cilantro (coriander);** and ⅓ cup *each* **orange juice** and **white wine vinegar.** Makes 4 cups.

PER TABLESPOON: 3 calories, .10 gram protein, .70 gram carbohydrate, .01 gram total fat, 0 milligram cholesterol, 5 milligrams sodium.

Vietnamese Skewered Pork & Onion

PREPARATION TIME: 30 to 40 minutes to ignite charcoal; about 1 hour for meat, marinade, and sauce
MARINATING TIME: At least 4 hours
GRILLING TIME: About 10 minutes
PER SERVING: 372 calories, 29 grams protein, 6 grams carbohydrate, 25 grams total fat, 102 milligrams cholesterol, 160 milligrams sodium

Bright, fresh flavors and a light hand with oil characterize Vietnamese cuisine. Here, squares of lean pork are dipped in a fragrant lemon grass marinade, then wrapped around onion pieces, skewered, and grilled. (Suggested wine: dry Sauvignon Blanc or fruity Zinfandel)

Makes 6 to 8 servings

> 2½ to 3 pounds boneless pork loin or leg
>   Lemon Grass Marinade (recipe follows)
> 1 large onion
>   Seasoning Sauce (recipe follows)

If using bamboo skewers, soak 16 to 20 skewers in hot water to cover for 30 minutes.

Cut pork across the grain into ¼-inch thick slices; cut each slice into 2-inch squares. Dip pork squares into marinade to coat.

Cut onion into 1-inch chunks; separate each chunk into layers. Place an onion piece in center of each meat square. Wrap meat around onion to enclose, then insert a bamboo or metal skewer through meat and onion to hold onion in place. Repeat with remaining onion and meat, threading 4 to 6 bundles on each skewer. Also roll up any meat pieces too small to wrap around onion; thread on skewers. Arrange skewers in a rimmed pan. Cover and refrigerate for at least 4 hours or until next day.

Place skewers on a grill 4 to 6 inches above a solid bed of hot coals (you should be able to hold your hand at grill level for no more than 2 to 3 seconds). Cook, turning frequently, until meat is browned on all sides and no longer pink in center (cut to test), 7 to 10 minutes. Serve with Seasoning Sauce.

LEMON GRASS MARINADE. Thinly slice enough **fresh lemon grass** to make 3 tablespoons. (Or use 3 tablespoons sliced dry lemon grass, soaked in hot water for 30 minutes; or use 1 teaspoon grated lemon peel.) In a food processor, combine lemon grass or lemon peel; 1 medium-size **onion**, cut into chunks; 3 or 4 cloves **garlic**; 3 tablespoons **sugar**; 2 tablespoons **roasted salted peanuts**; 1 tablespoon **fish sauce** *(nuoc mam or nam pla)* or soy sauce; 1½ teaspoons **pepper**; and 1 teaspoon **Chinese five-spice** (or ¼ teaspoon *each* ground cinnamon, allspice, cloves, ginger, and crushed anise seeds). Whirl until smooth.

SEASONING SAUCE. In a bowl, stir together 2 tablespoons **fish sauce** *(nuoc mam or nam pla)* or soy sauce, 1 tablespoon **lime juice**, 2 cloves **garlic** (minced or pressed), 2 tablespoons **sugar**, ¼ cup **water**, and 2 tablespoons finely shredded **carrot**.
Per Tablespoon: 12 calories, .20 gram protein, 3 grams carbohydrate, .03 gram total fat, 0 milligram cholesterol, 222 milligrams sodium.

Pork Stew with Purslane

W E S T E R N   C L A S S I C

PREPARATION TIME: About 1 hour for meat and sauce
COOKING TIME: About 3 hours for stew (includes about 1 hour for sauce)
PER SERVING: 361 calories, 36 grams protein, 10 grams carbohydrate, 19 grams total fat, 119 milligrams cholesterol, 211 milligrams sodium

Purslane, a sprawling weed common in Western gardens in late spring and summer, adds slightly crisp texture and mildly tart flavor to pork stew. The dish harks back to hacienda days, when foraging for edible wild plants brought variety to the table. When purslane isn't in season (it's sold as verdolaga *in some Mexican markets), you can make the stew with spinach. (Suggested beverage: dry red jug wine; or beer)*

Makes 8 to 10 servings

> 4½ to 5 pounds boneless pork shoulder or
>   butt
> 4 cloves garlic
> 2 cups water
>   Tomatillo Sauce (recipe follows)
>   Salt
> 8 to 10 cups purslane (verdolaga) sprigs
>   (about 1½ lbs.), coarse stems discarded; or
>   14 cups lightly packed spinach leaves (1 to
>   1½ lbs.)

Trim fat from pork; reserve for Tomatillo Sauce. Cut meat into 1½-inch cubes; place in a 5- to 6-quart ovenproof pan with garlic and 2 cups water. Cover and bring to a boil; then reduce heat and simmer for 45 minutes.

Remove pan from heat and ladle out 2 cups broth; skim and discard fat, then reserve broth for sauce. Bake meat in pan, uncovered, in a 425° oven until well browned, about 1 hour. Stir often.

Return pan to direct heat; add Tomatillo Sauce and season to taste with salt. Stir to scrape browned bits free. Simmer, covered, until meat is very tender when pierced, about 1 hour; stir occasionally. (At this point, you may let cool, then cover and refrigerate for up to 3 days; reheat before continuing.)

Rinse purslane (or spinach) well; drain in a colander. Pour 2 to 4 quarts boiling water over greens to wilt them. Pour stew into a serving bowl; top with wilted greens.

TOMATILLO SAUCE. Remove papery husks from 2 pounds **tomatillos** (about 8 cups); rinse tomatillos and put them in a 10- by 15-inch rimmed baking pan. Bake in a 500° oven until tinged with brown, about 15 minutes. (Or, instead of roasted fresh tomatillos, use three 13-oz. cans tomatillos and their liquid.) In a blender or food processor, whirl tomatillos and 4 stemmed and seeded **fresh or canned jalapeño chiles** until puréed. Set aside.

In a 12- to 14-inch frying pan over medium heat, render ¼ cup **reserved pork fat**; discard any remaining fat. Add 4 large **onions** (about 2 lbs. *total*), sliced, and 3 cloves **garlic**, minced or pressed. Stir often until onions are golden. Add reserved 2 cups **broth**; boil, uncovered, until almost all liquid has evaporated. Pour in tomatillos. Use hot or cold. If made ahead, cover and refrigerate for up to 3 days.

The Ultimate Barbecue: Spit-roasted Pig

You need time, friends, and funds to spit-roast a pig. But the golden brown, succulent results of your efforts make a memorable show and a grand feast for a crowd.

Briefly, here's what you have to do. Find a source and order the pig. Rent a spit (check the Yellow Pages). Select and prepare the cooking area (you need to use the spit to set up the firebed, so prepare the firebed *after* you've picked up the spit—and before you pick up the pig). Secure the pig on the spit and keep it cool until time to cook (for up to 14 hours). Cooking time is about 12 hours.

THE PIG. Order a pig weighing 100 pounds *or less*. A meat market or supermarket that cuts up carcasses can usually make the arrangements, but you may have to wait for up to a month to get the size pig you want. Check prices when you order; if possible, shop around for the best value.

If the pig arrives a day or so ahead, have it held for you in the market's refrigerator. After spitting the pig, you can keep it cold for up to 14 hours. Place pig on a plastic sheet in a cool place; drape it with sealed plastic bags filled with ice. Cover with another sheet of plastic; protect from animals and insects. Replace ice as it melts.

PREPARING THE FIREBED. For the cooking site, choose a spot protected from wind and rain.

You'll need this equipment: a shovel, the spit-roasting equipment, 20 pounds of sand, 14 concrete blocks (6- by 6- by 12-inch size), about 120 pounds of long-burning charcoal briquets, fire starter and matches, a garden rake, long-handled tongs, potholder mitts, and a large box of baking soda.

Clear a level 3- by 5-foot area down to the soil. Down the center, spread sand in a 1½- by 3-foot rectangle.

Set spit supports at 3-foot ends of rectangle and put spit in position. Adjust supports so that spit is 20 to 24 inches above ground and centered over rectangle. Line perimeter of the 3- by 5-foot area with concrete blocks (open sides up) to make a solid wall.

SPIT-ROASTING EQUIPMENT. You need a spit that's at least 7 feet long, spit forks to keep the pig from slipping on the spit, spit supports to hold the spitted pig over the heat, and a means to turn the spit (manual or motorized).

You can rent a spit at some shops that sell barbecue equipment. Reserve it well ahead; before leaving the shop, make sure you have all the parts and check them for defects.

SPITTING & TYING THE PIG: A TEAM OPERATION. Allow at least 2 hours for spitting and tying. First, insert spit through mouth and out tail of pig; one person pushes spit, the other guides it along backbone. Spit should not pierce any bone or meat. Make sure pig is centered on length of spit.

Next, wire spine to spit. You'll need three 24-inch lengths of heavy wire (such as baling wire), an ice pick, and pliers.

At mid-back, make a hole on each side of spine with an ice pick, poking from rib side out through skin. Working from skin side, force the 2 ends of 1 wire through holes into pig cavity. With pliers, twist wire ends together over spit, securely uniting spit and spine (spine curves and may not actually touch spit). Position remaining 2 wires about 12 inches away from center wire on either side.

Force metal spit forks firmly and securely into thickest parts of hind and shoulder ends; clamp or wire spit forks tightly to secure to spit.

Use double strands of heavy cotton string to tie front and rear legs to spit. Because legs are stiff, this task may require a little brute strength.

To hold skin in place as it cooks, make a string net over rib loin sections. Suspend spit between 2 counters or set it on spit supports so you can pass string under and around pig. First tie string tightly at 3-inch intervals around body between front and rear legs. Then wrap strings at right angles to make 3-inch squares.

Once pig is spitted and tied, position it on spit supports and rotate it to make sure that equipment works and that pig is balanced. (Adjust spit forks or tighten netting if necessary.) A well-balanced pig that doesn't shift its weight on the spit is essential if equipment is motor-operated.

Remove pig and keep cool while you start the fire.

ROASTING THE PIG. Pile 10 pounds of charcoal briquets at each end of firebed and ignite. When coals are ash-covered and glowing hot (about 1 hour), set spitted pig on supports. Rake coals into an even layer underneath pig. Begin rotating motor-operated spit, or manually rotate pig a quarter-turn every 5 to 10 minutes. Continue rotating throughout cooking.

After about 1 hour, when fat begins to drip, rake briquets from directly beneath pig to expose sand. (Sand catches grease and reduces flare-ups.) Arrange coals so most are underneath thickest parts of pig, with a 6- to 8-inch-wide band of coals along sides of pig.

To keep skin from charring, sprinkle any grease fires with baking soda to smother flames.

About every 30 minutes, rake briquets to knock off ash. Add 10 pounds of briquets about every hour to maintain heat; make a single row along sides and distribute balance at each end.

After about 10 hours, fat will cease dripping excessively; at this point, rake hot coals back beneath pig, concentrating heat under thighs and shoulders. Internal temperature in thickest part of animal at bone (inside thigh or neck section of shoulder) should be 140°F on a meat thermometer; use a rapid-reading thermometer to check temperature in several places.

A spit-cooked pig exposed to the air often reaches only 140° to 150°, but if cooking continues at this temperature for at least 1 hour, the meat is both safe and very palatable to eat. (The organism responsible for trichinosis is destroyed when the internal temperature exceeds 137°F and is held there for a few minutes.)

Cooking typically takes 10 to 12 hours, though breezy or cool weather will slow it down.

If the pig is ready before the rest of the meal, rake coals from beneath pig so it will cease cooking but stay hot; keep hot on spit for up to 1 hour.

To serve, transfer spitted pig to a table topped with a pig-size tray of heavy foil; pull out spit and cut off strings. Garnish pig with parsley. Pull off skin; tear or carve meat from bones. Season to taste with salt and pepper.

A 100-pound pig makes 100 servings.

Barbecued on a skewer with red pepper strips, juicy Italian sausages line up in this handsome whole-meal sandwich. The recipe for Red Bell Pepper & Sausage Loaf is on the facing page.

Chinese-style Mo Shu Pork

PREPARATION TIME: About 45 minutes to soak and marinate filling ingredients; about 1 hour to assemble filling; about 1½ hours to make pancakes

COOKING TIME: About 10 minutes for filling; about 5 minutes to reheat pancakes

PER SERVING: 218 calories, 12 grams protein, 6 grams carbohydrate, 16 grams total fat, 208 milligrams cholesterol, 702 milligrams sodium

To make the most authentic version of these egg- and pork-filled pancakes, you'll need to shop in an Asian market. We include the recipe for the thin pancakes; you can also substitute frozen ready-made wrappers which are labeled Peking doilies or Filipino lumpia wrappers. To use purchased wrappers, thaw and separate; then restack, wrap in foil, and steam until hot. (Suggested beverage: dry Emerald Riesling or beer)

Makes 4 to 6 servings

 ⅓ **cup dried tiger lily buds**
 4 **dried black fungus (also called cloud or tree ears)**
 1 **teaspoon cornstarch**
 1 **tablespoon** *each* **soy sauce and dry sherry**
 ½ **pound lean boneless pork shoulder or butt, trimmed of fat and cut into matchstick pieces**
 3½ **tablespoons salad oil**
 5 **green onions (including tops)**
 4 **large eggs**
 ¼ **teaspoon salt**
 ½ **teaspoon minced fresh ginger**
 ½ **cup sliced bamboo shoots, cut into matchstick pieces**
 1 **small carrot, shredded**
 2 **cups shredded iceberg lettuce**
 Cooking Sauce (recipe follows)
 About 18 Mandarin Pancakes (recipe follows)
 Canned hoisin sauce
 Green onion brushes (directions follow)

Soak lily buds and fungus in warm water to cover for 30 minutes; drain. Pinch off and discard hard tips of lily buds; cut buds in half lengthwise. Pinch out and discard hard, knobby centers of fungus; thinly slice remaining fungus. Set aside.

In a bowl, combine cornstarch, soy, and sherry. Add pork and stir to coat. Stir in 1½ teaspoons of the oil. Let marinate for 15 minutes.

Cut onions into 1½-inch lengths; then cut lengthwise into shreds. Reserve half the onion shreds for cooking; set other half aside to offer at the table.

In a bowl, lightly beat eggs with salt. Heat a wok or 10- to 12-inch frying pan over medium-high heat. When pan is hot, add 1 tablespoon of the oil. When oil is hot, add eggs and cook, stirring, until softly set; then slide out of pan.

Pour remaining 2 tablespoons oil into pan and increase heat to high. When oil is hot, add ginger and stir once. Add pork mixture and stir until lightly browned, about 4 minutes. Add lily buds and fungus and stir for 1 minute, adding a few drops of water if pan appears dry. Add bamboo shoots, carrot, lettuce, reserved onion shreds, and Cooking Sauce; cook, stirring, just until lettuce is wilted, about 2 minutes. Stir in eggs, breaking them into bite-size pieces. When eggs are hot, pour mixture into a serving dish and serve at once.

Have on the table Mandarin Pancakes, hoisin, onion shreds, and onion brushes. To eat, paint a little hoisin on a pancake with an onion brush, spoon on some of the meat mixture, and garnish with onion shreds. Wrap to enclose filling; eat out of hand.

COOKING SAUCE. In a bowl, combine 1 tablespoon *each* **soy sauce, dry sherry,** and **water;** 1 teaspoon *each* **sugar, cornstarch,** and **Oriental sesame oil;** and ¼ teaspoon **salt.**

MANDARIN PANCAKES. Place 2 cups **all-purpose flour** in a bowl. With a fork or chopsticks, mix in ¾ cup **boiling water.** Stir dough until it holds together; then turn out onto a lightly floured board and knead until smooth and satiny, about 10 minutes. Cover with plastic wrap and let rest at room temperature for 30 minutes. Roll dough into a 12-inch-long log. Cut into 12 equal pieces and keep covered.

Cut 1 piece of dough exactly in half; roll each half into a ball and flatten slightly. On a lightly floured board, roll out each ball into a 3-inch-diameter round. Brush top of 1 round lightly with **Oriental sesame oil** or salad oil (you'll need about 2 tablespoons *total*). Cover oil-coated round with the other round. Press the 2 rounds lightly but firmly together. Place double round on a lightly floured board and roll out from center to edges until 7 to 8 inches in diameter. Turn frequently; brush board lightly with flour as necessary. Repeat to shape 1 or 2 more pieces of dough, making 1 or 2 more double pancakes; cook these before rolling more.

Heat an ungreased 10- to 12-inch frying pan over medium heat; place one 2-layer pancake in pan. Turn pancake about every 15 seconds until it's blistered by air pockets, turns parchment color, and feels dry. Pancake should not be brown, but a few golden spots won't hurt. (Pancake becomes brittle if overcooked.) Remove from pan. Carefully pull the 2 halves apart. Stack on a plate and keep covered with plastic wrap. Cook remaining 2-layer cakes, pull apart, and add to stack.

Repeat rolling, cooking, and stacking until all pancakes have been prepared. Serve warm. Or let cool, wrap airtight, and refrigerate for up to 3 days (freeze for longer storage).

To reheat, thaw if frozen. Line a rack in a steamer with a towel dipped in water and wrung dry; let towel hang over edge of steamer. Stack pancakes on rack and fold towel over them. Cover and steam over boiling water for 5 minutes. Fold hot pancakes in half, then in half again. Since they dry out quickly, serve just a few at a time and keep remainder covered in steamer over low heat. Makes 2 dozen.

Per Pancake: 48 calories, 1 gram protein, 8 grams carbohydrate, 1 gram total fat, 0 milligram cholesterol, .20 milligram sodium.

GREEN ONION BRUSHES. Cut the white part of 3 **green onions** into 1½-inch lengths. Using scissors or a sharp knife, slash each end of onion pieces lengthwise 3 or 4 times, ½ inch into onion. Cover with **ice water;** refrigerate until ends curl (about 1 hour).

Red Bell Pepper & Sausage Loaf

Pictured on facing page

PREPARATION TIME: 30 to 40 minutes to ignite charcoal; about 25 minutes to assemble ingredients and precook meat
GRILLING TIME: 8 to 10 minutes
PER SERVING: 625 calories, 28 grams protein, 46 grams carbohydrate, 36 grams total fat, 105 milligrams cholesterol, 1331 milligrams sodium

It takes time for green bell peppers to turn red and ripe— but the mellow flavor and brilliant hue are well worth waiting for. Here, sliced red bell peppers brighten a grilled sandwich supper. (Suggested wine: mature Zinfandel)

Makes 6 servings

> 6 mild Italian sausages (1¼ to 1½ lbs. *total*)
> ¼ cup (⅛ lb.) butter or margarine
> 1 clove garlic, minced or pressed
> 1 long loaf (1 lb.) French bread, cut in half horizontally
> 2 large red bell peppers, stemmed, seeded, and cut into 1½-inch strips
> 6 ounces sliced mozzarella, provolone, or jack cheese
> Prepared mustard

Prick sausages in several places; then place in a 10- to 12-inch frying pan and add enough water to cover. Bring to a boil over high heat; reduce heat to low, cover, and simmer for 5 minutes. Drain sausages and set aside.

Melt butter in a 2- to 4-cup pan over medium heat; stir in garlic. Brush garlic butter evenly over cut side of each bread half; set aside.

On a sturdy metal skewer at least 12 inches long, thread sausages alternately with bell pepper strips, running skewer through center of and perpendicular to each sausage and pepper strip.

Place skewer on a grill 4 to 6 inches above a solid bed of hot coals (you should be able to hold your hand at grill level for no more than 2 to 3 seconds). Cook, turning occasionally, until sausages are well browned on outside and hot throughout (cut to test), 5 to 8 minutes. Near end of cooking time, set bread halves, cut side down, on grill. Cook, watching carefully, just until bread is streaked with brown, 1 to 2 minutes.

To serve, overlap cheese slices on 1 hot bread half. Top with skewered sausages and peppers. Set top of bread in place; pull out skewer. Cut loaf into 6 equal portions; offer mustard to add to sandwiches.

Chimichanga Platter

PREPARATION TIME: About 25 minutes

COOKING TIME: About 1¾ hours for filling; about 15 minutes to bake chimichangas and heat fruit

PER SERVING: 717 calories, 38 grams protein, 38 grams carbohydrate, 47 grams total fat, 166 milligrams cholesterol, 496 milligrams sodium

Chimichangas—filled flour tortillas—are usually deep-fried to make them flaky and crisp. But you can oven-fry them with equally delicious results (and less mess). For a complete entrée, serve these pork-filled chimichangas with shredded lettuce and sautéed fruit; top with salsa and sour cream. (Suggested wine: young Ruby Cabernet)

Makes 2 to 4 servings

¼ cup (⅛ lb.) butter or margarine

4 medium-size (about 8-inch-diameter) or 2 large (10- to 12-inch-diameter) flour tortillas

Shredded Pork Filling (recipe follows)

4 round slices fresh pineapple, *each* ¼ inch thick, peel removed

2 medium-size firm-ripe bananas, peeled

3 to 4 cups finely shredded romaine lettuce

Sliced radishes (optional)

1½ cups (6 oz.) shredded jack cheese

Blender Salsa (recipe follows)

¾ cup sour cream

Melt butter in a 10- to 12-inch frying pan; brush some of the butter over both sides of each tortilla. Spoon filling equally in a band across center of tortillas. To enclose, lap ends of each tortilla over filling; then fold sides to center to make a packet. Place tortillas, seam side down, in a 9- by 13-inch baking pan. Bake in a 500° oven until golden, 8 to 10 minutes.

Meanwhile, add pineapple to pan with butter. Cook over medium-high heat until hot, turning once. Remove from pan and keep warm. Cut bananas into 1-inch chunks. Add bananas to pan and cook until hot, turning once. Add to pineapple.

Set each chimichanga on a plate and arrange equal portions of fruit and romaine alongside; garnish with radishes, if desired. Sprinkle chimichangas with cheese and offer salsa and sour cream as toppings.

SHREDDED PORK FILLING. Trim and discard excess fat from 1 pound **lean boneless pork butt** or shoulder; cut meat into 1½-inch pieces. Put in a 2- to 3-quart pan. Cover and cook over medium heat to draw out juices, about 10 minutes. Uncover and cook over high heat, stirring often, until liquid has evaporated and meat is well browned.

Add 2 cups **water**; stir to scrape browned bits free from pan. Bring to a boil; then reduce heat, cover, and simmer until meat is very tender when pierced, 1 to 1¼ hours. Uncover; boil over high heat until all liquid has evaporated. Reduce heat to low.

Add 2 tablespoons **distilled white vinegar;** 3 tablespoons **canned diced green chiles;** 1 clove **garlic,** minced or pressed; and ¼ teaspoon *each* **ground oregano** and **ground cumin.** Stir to scrape browned bits free; remove from heat.

Shred meat, using 2 forks (or let cool, then pull apart with your fingers). Season to taste with **salt.** If made ahead, cover and refrigerate for up to 3 days; warm before using.

BLENDER SALSA. In a blender or food processor, combine 2 medium-size ripe **tomatoes,** cored and quartered; ½ small **onion;** 3 tablespoons **canned diced green chiles;** 4 teaspoons **distilled white vinegar;** and 1 tablespoon chopped **fresh cilantro (coriander).** Whirl until puréed; season to taste with **salt.** If made ahead, cover and refrigerate until next day. Makes about 1 cup.

PER TABLESPOON: *5 calories, .19 gram protein, 1 gram carbohydrate, .04 gram total fat, 0 milligram cholesterol, 11 milligrams sodium.*

Shanghai Spareribs

PREPARATION TIME: About 25 minutes

MARINATING TIME: At least 12 hours

BAKING TIME: About 1 hour (includes time to cut apart ribs and finish sauce)

PER SERVING: 655 calories, 43 grams protein, 22 grams carbohydrate, 44 grams total fat, 171 milligrams cholesterol, 1300 milligrams sodium

The ultimate in sweet-tart succulence, these juicy, easy-to-make roasted ribs definitely qualify for a "finger-lickin' good" rating. (Suggested wine: young Barbera)

Makes 4 to 5 servings

¼ cup *each* honey and soy sauce

1 cup Homemade Chicken Broth (page 58) or canned regular-strength chicken broth

4 cloves garlic, minced or pressed

1 teaspoon dry mustard

¼ cup canned tomato paste

4 pounds pork spareribs, trimmed of fat

1 tablespoon cornstarch and 2 tablespoons water, stirred together

In a bowl, stir together honey, soy, broth, garlic, mustard, and tomato paste. Place ribs in a 12- by 17-inch roasting or broiler pan; pour honey mixture over meat. Cover and refrigerate for 12 to 24 hours, turning ribs several times.

Pour off excess sauce; set aside. Cover ribs with foil and bake in a 350° oven for 45 minutes. Uncover; drain juices from pan and reserve. Continue to bake, uncovered, basting frequently with reserved sauce (using all), until ribs are tender when pierced, about 1 more hour. Cut between bones to separate individual ribs. Arrange ribs on a platter and keep warm.

Skim and discard fat from reserved pan juices, then measure juices; if necessary, add water to make 1 cup *total*. Return juices to pan, stirring to scrape browned bits free.

Stir cornstarch-water mixture into pan. Bring to a boil over high heat, stirring constantly. Pour sauce into a small bowl and offer to spoon onto individual servings.

Tuscan Pigs' Feet Stew

PREPARATION TIME: About 30 minutes
COOKING TIME: About 4¼ hours
PER SERVING: 447 calories, 20 grams protein, 38 grams carbohydrate, 24 grams total fat, 76 milligrams cholesterol, 229 milligrams sodium

Even if you're dubious about pigs' feet, the tempting aroma of this Northern Italian dish will whet your appetite. With long, gentle simmering, the bony meat becomes meltingly tender; cubed potatoes crumble and thicken the broth. (Suggested wine: mature Barbera)

Makes 6 to 8 servings

>   3 pounds (about 4) pigs' feet, sawed into
>   2-inch pieces
>   2 large onions, chopped
>   ⅓ cup olive or salad oil
>   5 cups Homemade Chicken Broth (page 58)
>   or canned regular-strength chicken broth
>   1 can (8 oz.) tomato sauce
>   3 pounds russet potatoes, peeled and cut
>   into 1-inch cubes
>   Parsley sprigs

Rinse and drain pigs' feet; set aside. In a 6- to 8-quart pan over medium-high heat, combine onions and oil; cook, uncovered, stirring occasionally, until onions are pale gold, about 10 minutes.

Add pigs' feet, broth, and tomato sauce. Bring to a boil; then reduce heat, cover, and simmer for 2 hours. Add potatoes and continue to simmer, covered, until pigs' feet are very tender when pierced and fall apart when prodded, 1½ to 2 more hours; stir occasionally. If made ahead, let cool, then cover and refrigerate for up to 3 days; reheat to serve.

Ladle stew into bowls; allow 2 to 3 cups for a serving because the feet are so bony. Top with parsley.

Sugared Bacon

PREPARATION TIME: About 15 minutes
BAKING TIME: About 25 minutes, plus 5 minutes to cool
PER SERVING: 111 calories, 4 grams protein, 10 grams carbohydrate, 6 grams total fat, 11 milligrams cholesterol, 205 milligrams sodium

Brown sugar makes a sweet glaze for bacon in this simple breakfast treat. If you wish, partially cook the bacon the day before and drain off the fat; bake and serve the next morning.

Makes 4 servings

>   8 to 12 slices bacon
>   3 tablespoons firmly packed brown sugar

Line a 10- by 15-inch rimmed baking pan with foil. Lay bacon slices side by side on foil. Bake, uncovered, in a 350° oven for 10 minutes. Remove pan from oven; drain off and discard fat.

Evenly sprinkle bacon with sugar, then smooth sugar with the back of a spoon to make an even layer on bacon. (At this point, you may let cool, then cover and refrigerate until next day. Uncover before baking.)

Bake bacon in a 350° oven until golden brown, about 15 more minutes. Lift bacon from pan with tongs or a wide spatula and arrange, sugared side up, in a single layer on a rack set over paper towels. Serve bacon when cooled and crisp.

Crisp & Tender Pork

PREPARATION TIME: 10 to 15 minutes
COOKING TIME: 2 to 3 hours
PER SERVING: 689 calories, 46 grams protein, 2 grams carbohydrate, 54 grams total fat, 200 milligrams cholesterol, 143 milligrams sodium

This simple entrée is a good choice for a cook-ahead picnic. Pork knuckles or shoulder are simmered in a well-seasoned broth until tender, then baked until crisp. Eat the meat with your fingers, dipping each bite into a Filipino-inspired vinegar-garlic sauce. (Suggested wine: dry Chenin Blanc)

Makes 4 servings

>   4 pork knuckles (about 2 lbs. *each*); or
>   2½ pounds boneless pork shoulder or
>   butt, cut into 4 equal pieces
>   3 to 6 cups Homemade Chicken Broth (page
>   58) or canned regular-strength chicken
>   broth
>   1 lemon, cut in half crosswise
>   2 bay leaves
>   1 tablespoon dry thyme leaves
>   ¼ teaspoon *each* whole cloves and whole
>   black peppercorns
>   Vinegar-Garlic Dipping Sauce
>   (recipe follows)

If cooking knuckles, use 6 cups broth and an 8- to 10-quart pan; for shoulder, use a 3- to 4-quart pan and 3 cups broth. Bring broth, lemon, bay leaves, thyme, cloves, and peppercorns to a boil. Add pork, then reduce heat, cover, and simmer until pork pulls apart easily—about 2½ hours for knuckles, about 2 hours for shoulder. Lift pork from broth; drain. To save broth to use in other dishes, pour through a strainer; discard seasonings. (At this point, you may let pork cool, then cover and refrigerate until next day.)

Place knuckles in an ungreased 10- by 15-inch rimmed baking pan; put shoulder in a greased 9- or 10-inch square baking pan. Bake in a 500° oven, uncovered, until skin on knuckles is crisp, about 30 minutes, or until shoulder is browned, about 10 minutes. Serve warm or at room temperature. To eat, tear meat in shreds and dip into sauce.

VINEGAR-GARLIC DIPPING SAUCE. In a 1- to 2-quart pan, combine 1 cup **distilled white vinegar**, 1 tablespoon **soy sauce**, and ½ teaspoon **crushed dried hot red chiles.** Bring to a rolling boil over high heat, uncovered. Let cool, then stir in 5 cloves **garlic,** minced or pressed. Serve, or cover and refrigerate for up to 1 week. Makes 1 cup.
PER TABLESPOON: 4 calories, .11 gram protein, 1 gram carbohydrate, .02 gram total fat, 0 milligram cholesterol, 84 milligrams sodium.

THE OREGON TRAIL, mapped by Lewis and Clark early in the 1800s, opened the way for the first pioneer families to reach Oregon's fertile Willamette Valley. Starting from Omaha, Independence, or Kansas City, they made the journey in ox-drawn wagons—crossing half a continent at an estimated average of 12 miles per day. In December 1929, Sunset recounted early Christmas memories from three such homesteading families.

Rosemary Lamb Chops

Pictured on facing page

PREPARATION TIME: 30 to 40 minutes to ignite charcoal; 5 to 10 minutes for chops
GRILLING TIME: 10 to 12 minutes
PER SERVING: 349 calories, 14 grams protein, 1 gram carbohydrate, 32 grams total fat, 87 milligrams cholesterol, 116 milligrams sodium

Rosemary, prized for both its form and fragrance, grows in gardens all over the West. Here, it adds its distinctive flavor to the basting sauce for lamb chops. (Suggested wine: fresh, light Cabernet Sauvignon)

Makes 3 to 6 servings

¼ cup (⅛ lb.) butter or margarine, melted
3 tablespoons lemon juice
4 cloves garlic, minced or pressed
½ teaspoon chopped fresh rosemary
6 lamb rib or loin chops, cut about 1 inch thick
Fresh rosemary sprigs

In a small bowl, stir together butter, lemon juice, garlic, and chopped rosemary. Place lamb chops on a grill 4 to 6 inches above a solid bed of hot coals (you should be able to hold your hand at grill level for no more than 2 to 3 seconds). Cook, turning once and basting often with butter mixture, until chops are done to your liking (cut to test), 10 to 12 minutes for medium-rare. Garnish with rosemary sprigs.

Lamb Shanks, Thompson Style

W E S T E R N   C L A S S I C

PREPARATION TIME: About 10 minutes
COOKING TIME: 2 to 2½ hours to bake shanks; about 25 minutes to cook rice and grapes
PER SERVING: 662 calories, 26 grams protein, 78 grams carbohydrate, 26 grams total fat, 96 milligrams cholesterol, 138 milligrams sodium

Years ago, a horticulturist came across a seedless green grape—a naturally occurring mutation—on a Mr. Thompson's ranch in California's Central Valley. The immensely popular Thompson seedless, and many more seedless types as well, were developed from that strain. Here, green grapes provide a crisp, sparkling accent for tender oven-braised lamb shanks and rice. (Suggested wine: mature Barbera)

Makes 4 servings

4 meaty lamb shanks, cracked
3 cups Homemade Chicken Broth (page 58) or canned regular-strength chicken broth
2 tablespoons butter or margarine
1½ cups long-grain white rice
2 cups seedless green grapes

Place lamb shanks in a deep 3-quart casserole. Pour in broth, cover, and bake in a 375° oven until meat is very tender when pierced, 2 to 2½ hours. Drain broth

from casserole and reserve; cover lamb, return to oven, and turn off heat.

Melt 1 tablespoon of the butter in a 3- to 4-quart pan over medium-high heat. Add rice; cook, stirring, until lightly browned. Skim and discard fat from lamb broth; pour 3 cups broth into pan with rice. Bring to a boil; then reduce heat, cover, and simmer until rice is tender, about 20 minutes. Arrange rice in a serving dish and place lamb on top.

Immediately melt remaining 1 tablespoon butter in a 10- to 12-inch frying pan over high heat. Add grapes; turn in butter just until shiny and hot. Spoon over lamb and rice.

Miche's Leg of Lamb

PREPARATION TIME: About 15 minutes
ROASTING TIME: 1½ to 2 hours
PER SERVING OF LAMB: 316 calories, 44 grams protein, .41 gram carbohydrate, 14 grams total fat, 165 milligrams cholesterol, 143 milligrams sodium

This leg of lamb is memorable both for its simplicity and its flavor. Before roasting the leg, you trim off all the surface fat, stud the meat with garlic for mellow pungency, and rub it all over with butter to promote browning. (Suggested wine: full-bodied Cabernet Sauvignon)

Makes 7 or 8 servings

Trim almost all skin and surface fat from 1 **leg of lamb** (5 to 6 lbs.). Cut 3 or 4 cloves **garlic** into slivers; make small gashes in lamb and insert a garlic sliver in each gash. Rub lamb with 2 to 3 tablespoons soft **butter** or margarine. Place in a 10- by 15-inch roasting pan.

Roast, uncovered, in a 325° oven until a meat thermometer inserted in thickest part of roast (not touching bone) registers 145°F for rare, 1½ to 2 hours. Transfer meat to a platter; keep warm.

Pour 1 cup **Homemade Chicken Broth** (page 58) or canned regular-strength chicken broth into roasting pan. Place over medium-high heat and bring to a boil, stirring to scrape browned bits free. Skim and discard fat; pour sauce into a small bowl.

To serve lamb, grasp narrow end of leg (protect your hands) and slice meat, cutting parallel to bone. Serve with sauce; season to taste with **salt** and **pepper.**

Cross-swords Butterflied Lamb

Pictured on page 88

PREPARATION TIME: 30 to 40 minutes to ignite charcoal; 10 to 15 minutes for lamb
MARINATING TIME: At least 2 hours
GRILLING TIME: About 1¼ hours
PER SERVING: 322 calories, 44 grams protein, 2 grams carbohydrate, 14 grams total fat, 156 milligrams cholesterol, 107 milligrams sodium

Boned, butterflied leg of lamb has long been a favorite of Western barbecue chefs. It cooks faster than bone-in meat and, when grilled on a covered barbecue, requires little attention as it browns. Crossed skewers support the lamb as you move it on and off the grill. (Suggested wine: full-bodied Merlot)

Makes 6 to 8 servings

- **1 leg of lamb (5 to 6 lbs.), boned, surface fat trimmed off**
- **½ cup medium-dry sherry**
- **2 tablespoons olive oil**
- **1 medium-size onion**
- **8 to 10 fresh rosemary sprigs (*each* 3 to 4 inches long), optional**
- **Salt and pepper**

Lay lamb flat in a close-fitting pan. Mix sherry and oil; rub over lamb. Cover and refrigerate for at least 2 hours or until next day, turning meat over occasionally. Lift from pan, reserving marinade; place leg boned side up. At 2- to 3-inch intervals, cut about ⅔ of the way through thickest parts of leg.

Cut onion into ½-inch-thick slices, then cut each slice in half crosswise. Fit slices, rounded edge up, into meat slashes.

Thread a long, sturdy metal skewer into meat about 2 inches in from edge and parallel to longest side, securing onions. Insert another skewer through the opposite side so skewers cross near tips.

Set up barbecue as directed for Swedish-cured Barbecued Pork Loin, page 100. Place meat on grill above drip pan, onion side up. Cover barbecue and open drafts. Cook until a meat thermometer inserted in thickest part of lamb (not touching skewer) registers 140°F, about 1¼ hours; baste several times with reserved marinade. Because of the uneven thickness, you will have both rare and well-done meat. About 5 to 10 minutes before roast is done, tuck sprigs of rosemary (if used) into slashes in lamb.

Using skewers to lift, transfer lamb to a platter and let stand for 5 to 10 minutes. Pull out skewers and slice meat. Season to taste with salt and pepper.

Western-style mixed grill features tempting Rosemary Lamb Chops (recipe on facing page) surrounded by colorful peppers and squash.

Homemade Sausage...Salami, Chorizo, Italian

The flavor is great. Preparation is easy. And the cost is low—a third reason to try our homemade sausages. If you make your own, it's also easier to get exactly what you want; you can vary the amounts of seasonings and salt (and even fat) to suit your taste.

Choose from picnic salami, baked in easy-to-slice rolls, and two different bulk-style sausages—Mexican chorizo and mild Italian sausage.

PICNIC SALAMI. Our picnic salami isn't like dry Italian salami, but more like the cured luncheon meat you can buy. You start with the least expensive ground beef, then mix in various seasonings and chill the mixture overnight. Next day, roll the portions in nylon net (it acts like a casing) and bake to cook and firm the meat and get rid of excess fat. You'll be left with lean, easy-to-slice meat rolls that keep in the refrigerator for up to 3 weeks, in the freezer for up to 2 months.

The only special ingredient you'll need is the prepared curing salt that gives the salami its appetizing reddish pink color. You can buy the curing salt from some butcher's equipment and supply companies and from many feed stores, especially in rural areas.

The nylon net is sold by the yard in fabric stores. Purchase the least expensive net with the largest holes.

Smoky Beef Salami

In a large bowl, *thoroughly* mix 4 pounds **ground beef (maximum fat content about 25 percent),** ¼ cup **curing salt,** 2 tablespoons **liquid smoke,** 1½ teaspoons **garlic powder,** and 1½ teaspoons **pepper** (or 2 teaspoons whole black peppercorns). Cover and refrigerate for 24 hours.

Divide mixture into fourths. Shape each into a compact 8-inch log and place each on a 12- by 18-inch piece of nylon net. Roll up tightly; tie ends with string. Place logs on a rack in a 10- by 15-inch rimmed baking pan and bake in a 225° oven for 4 hours.

Remove from oven and take off net. Pat rolls well with paper towels to absorb excess fat. Let cool, then serve. Or, to store, wrap in foil and refrigerate for up to 3 weeks or freeze for up to 2 months. Cut into slices to serve. Makes 4 salami, about 3 pounds *total.*

Spicy Beef Salami

Follow directions for **Smoky Beef Salami,** but make these changes. Omit liquid smoke and add 3 tablespoons **dry white wine.** Reduce garlic powder to 1 teaspoon and omit pepper. Instead, add 2 tablespoon **chili powder, 2 teaspoons crushed dried hot red chiles,** and 1 teaspoon **ground cumin.**

Herb Beef Salami

Follow directions for **Smoky Beef Salami,** but make these changes. Omit liquid smoke and add 3 tablespoons **dry red wine.** Reduce garlic powder to 1 teaspoon and omit pepper. Instead add 2 tablespoons **mustard seeds,** 1 tablespoon *each* **dry basil** and **dry oregano leaves,** 1 teaspoon **onion powder,** and ⅔ cup freshly grated **Parmesan cheese.**

CHORIZO & ITALIAN SAUSAGE. These two sausages are great on their own, fried in juicy patties, but they're also important starting points for spaghetti sauces, casseroles, and more. Because they're made in bulk, they're extra quick to prepare; you don't have to bother with stuffing the meat into casings.

Mexican Chorizo

- 2 **pounds ground lean pork**
- 1 **clove garlic, minced or pressed**
- ¼ **cup red wine vinegar**
- 1 **teaspoon salt**
- 2 **tablespoons chili powder**
- 1 **tablespoon paprika**
- 2 **teaspoons dry oregano leaves**
- ½ **teaspoon ground cumin**
- ½ to ¾ **pound ground pork fat (firm fat trimmed from meat surface), optional**
- **Salad oil**

In a large bowl, thoroughly mix pork, garlic, vinegar, salt, chili powder, paprika, oregano, and cumin. If you prefer a fattier sausage (like commercial chorizo), add pork fat and mix well.

To pan-fry, shape sausage into ½-inch-thick patties or 1-inch-diameter logs. Coat a 10- to 12-inch frying pan lightly with salad oil and place over medium heat. Add as many patties or logs as will fit without crowding; cook, uncovered, turning as needed, until

meat is well browned on all sides and no longer pink in center (cut to test). Remove from pan as cooked; keep warm while you cook remaining sausage.

To broil, shape as for pan-fried chorizo. Arrange patties or logs on a rack in a 12- by 15-inch broiler pan. Broil about 3 inches below heat until well browned, 4 to 5 minutes on each side.

Makes about 2 pounds (4 cups) sausage, 6 to 8 servings.

Mild Italian Sausage

- 2½ **pounds boneless pork butt or shoulder, cut into 1-inch cubes**
- 1½ **teaspoons** *each* **coriander seeds and parsley flakes**
- 1 **tablespoon fennel seeds**
- 1 **large clove garlic, minced or pressed**
- ¾ **teaspoon** *each* **salt and coarsely ground black pepper**
- **Butter, salad oil, or olive oil**

Put pork cubes twice through a food chopper fitted with a coarse blade, or coarsely chop in a food processor. (If using a processor, first place meat in a single layer on a baking sheet and freeze until firm but not hard, about 20 minutes. This allows the processor blade to make cleaner cuts.)

Finely crush together coriander seeds, parsley flakes, and fennel seeds with a mortar and pestle (or whirl briefly in a blender). Add to chopped pork. Add garlic, salt, and pepper. Mix well with your hands to distribute seasonings. Cover and refrigerate for at least 8 hours to blend flavors.

To pan-fry, shape sausage into 10 to 12 patties, each ½ inch thick. (At this point, you may stack patties, separating them with double thicknesses of wax paper, wrap airtight, and refrigerate for up to 2 days or freeze for up to 3 months. Thaw frozen patties before cooking.)

Place as many patties as will fit without crowding in a 10- to 12-inch frying pan lightly coated with butter or oil. Cook over medium heat, turning once, until browned and no longer pink in center (cut to test). Remove from pan as cooked; keep warm while you cook remaining sausage.

Makes 2½ pounds (about 6 cups), 10 to 12 servings.

Mansef

PREPARATION TIME: About 20 minutes
COOKING TIME: About 2¼ hours for lamb (sauce, tortillas, rice, and nuts are cooked during this time)
PER SERVING: 1081 calories, 70 grams protein, 85 grams carbohydrate, 51 grams total fat, 391 milligrams cholesterol, 362 milligrams sodium

Nomadic tribes of Northern Africa feast on mansef—a spiced lamb stew traditionally served communally, with the braised meat and rice mounded on a single, shared platter. Authentic mansef is made with mare's milk; we approximate its unique slightly tart flavor by adding cream cheese to the cooking broth. (Suggested wine: young Gamay)

Makes 6 to 8 servings

    1 leg of lamb (5 to 6 lbs.)
    4½ quarts water
    2 cinnamon sticks (*each* 3 to 4 inches long)
    10 whole cloves
    2 large packages (8 oz. *each*) cream cheese, at room temperature
    5 tablespoons lemon juice
    Salt
    16 flour tortillas (about 8-inch diameter)
    ¼ cup (⅛ lb.) butter or margarine
    2 cups long-grain white rice
    1 cup pine nuts
    Fresh mint sprigs and lemon wedges

Have your meatman bone lamb, but save bones. Trim and discard excess fat from meat; cut meat into 1- to 1½-inch chunks. Put meat and bones in an 8- to 10-quart pan with 6 cups of the water, cinnamon sticks, and cloves. Bring to a boil; then reduce heat, cover, and simmer for 1 hour.

Skim and discard fat from cooking broth. Ladle out 3 cups broth. Using an electric mixer, beat cream cheese until smooth, gradually adding the 3 cups broth. (Or whirl cream cheese in a blender; slowly add broth with motor running.) Return cream cheese mixture to pan. Add lemon juice, cover, and continue to simmer until meat is very tender when pierced, about 1 more hour. Remove and discard bones, cinnamon sticks, and as many cloves as you can find. Season to taste with salt. (At this point, you may let cool, then cover and refrigerate until next day. Reheat before continuing.)

About 30 minutes before meat is done, dot tortillas with 2 tablespoons of the butter; stack, wrap in foil, and heat in a 350° oven until warm, 20 to 25 minutes. Also bring remaining 12 cups water to a boil in a 5- to 6-quart pan; add rice. Reduce heat, cover, and simmer until rice is tender to bite, about 20 minutes. Drain well and season to taste with salt.

Melt remaining 2 tablespoons butter in a 10- to 12-inch frying pan over medium heat. Add pine nuts; stir until lightly browned, being careful not to scorch. Mix most of nuts with rice and pile on a large rimmed platter. Lift meat from juices with a slotted spoon and distribute through rice. Sprinkle remaining nuts over all.

Fold tortillas in quarters and arrange around mansef. Garnish liberally with mint sprigs and lemon wedges.

Keep meat juices very hot; just as you serve, pour several ladlefuls of juices over mansef. Keep mansef hot by spooning on steaming juices as needed. To eat, spoon a little of the meat-rice mixture onto a half or quarter of a tortilla; fold up and eat with your fingers. Or eat with a fork from a plate.

Lamb with Fruit & Honey

PREPARATION TIME: About 30 minutes
COOKING TIME: About 1½ hours
PER SERVING: 344 calories, 29 grams protein, 25 grams carbohydrate, 15 grams total fat, 106 milligrams cholesterol, 380 milligrams sodium

In Morocco, this delicious lamb dish and the covered pot it's traditionally cooked in are both called tajine *(tahdjeen). You can serve it with rice or couscous—tiny pasta-like pellets, sold in many Western supermarkets. (Suggested wine: dry Pinot Noir Blanc)*

Makes 5 or 6 servings

    1 tablespoon sesame seeds
    1 tablespoon salad oil
    2 pounds lean boneless lamb, trimmed of fat and cut into 2-inch cubes
    1 medium-size onion, finely chopped
    1 teaspoon ground coriander
    1 cinnamon stick (about 3 inches long)
    ½ teaspoon pepper
    ¼ teaspoon ground ginger
    2 cups water
    2 beef bouillon cubes
    1 pound apples or 1 cup dried apricots
    ½ lemon, thinly sliced
    ¼ cup honey

Toast sesame seeds in a 5- to 6-quart pan over medium heat until golden, about 2 minutes, shaking pan frequently. Pour seeds out of pan; set aside.

Pour oil into pan. Add lamb, onion, coriander, cinnamon stick, pepper, ginger, water, and bouillon cubes. Bring to a boil; then reduce heat, cover, and simmer for 45 minutes. Uncover and continue to cook until meat is tender when pierced, about 30 more minutes.

Peel and core apples, then cut each into 8 wedges. Add apples, lemon, and honey to lamb mixture; stir gently and cook until fruit is tender when pierced but still holds its shape, about 15 minutes.

With a slotted spoon, lift out meat and fruit and arrange in a serving container. Keep warm in a 150° oven. Boil cooking juices over high heat until slightly thickened. Pour over meat and fruit; top with sesame seeds.

You eat this Armenian open-face sandwich, Lahmejun (recipe on facing page), like a taco. Add your favorite coleslaw, tomatoes, cheese, onions, and other toppings, then fold up and eat out of hand.

Buffet Stew

W E S T E R N   C L A S S I C

PREPARATION TIME: About 45 minutes for stew; up to 45 minutes for additional vegetables

COOKING TIME: About 2½ hours for stew; ½ to 1 hour for additional vegetables

PER SERVING WITHOUT ADDITIONAL VEGETABLES: 750 calories, 30 grams protein, 43 grams carbohydrate, 51 grams total fat, 152 milligrams cholesterol, 569 milligrams sodium

To make this stew, you "sweat" lamb, pork, or veal in its own juices to bring out its flavor, then simmer the meat in a wine and herb broth with potatoes, turnips, and carrots. Other vegetables are cooked separately, then presented alongside. (Suggested wine: any well-aged, mellow, dry red wine)

Makes 8 to 10 servings

> **3 to 4 pounds boneless lamb, pork, or veal stew meat, cut into 1- to 2-inch chunks**
> **2 tablespoons soy sauce**
> **½ cup Madeira or port**
> **4 teaspoons mustard seeds**
> **¾ teaspoon dry thyme leaves**
> **¼ teaspoon *each* dry tarragon and whole black peppercorns**
> **2 or 3 bay leaves**

> **1½ cups Homemade Chicken Broth (page 58) or canned regular-strength chicken broth**
> **1 cup dry red or white wine**
> **2 to 2½ pounds small (2-inch-diameter) thin-skinned potatoes, scrubbed and cut in halves**
> **20 to 24 slender carrots, peeled**
> **6 to 8 small turnips, peeled and cut in halves**
> **Cooked vegetables (directions follow)**
> **1 cup whipping cream**
> **1 tablespoon Dijon mustard**
> **¼ cup (⅛ lb.) butter or margarine**
> **Watercress sprigs**

Place meat in a 12- to 14-inch frying pan and add soy. Cover tightly with a dome lid and bring to a boil over medium heat; let meat simmer in its own accumulating juices for 30 minutes. Uncover; boil over high heat until juices have evaporated. When meat starts to sizzle, stir often until richly browned. Add Madeira and stir well; then add mustard seeds, thyme, tarragon, peppercorns, bay leaves, broth, and wine.

Lay potatoes, carrots, and turnips on meat. Bring to a boil, then reduce heat, cover pan as snugly as possible, and simmer until meat and vegetables are tender when pierced, about 1 hour.

With a slotted spoon, lift vegetables and meat from broth and mound individually on a large platter. Arrange separately cooked vegetables (except green vegetables; cook these at the last minute) with stew, mounding each individually. Cover with foil and keep hot in a 150° oven for up to 30 minutes.

Add cream and mustard to pan juices. Boil over highest heat until reduced to 1¾ cups. Reduce heat to medium and add butter in 1 chunk, stirring constantly until blended into sauce. Pour sauce into a serving dish. Garnish stew with watercress.

Let guests serve themselves, spooning sauce onto individual portions.

COOKED VEGETABLES. Choose from the following, selecting at least 3 or 4 different vegetables.

Baked eggplant. Cut 4 medium-size **Japanese or slender French eggplants** (about ¾ lb. *total*) into 1-inch slices. Pour ⅓ cup **olive oil** into a 10- by 15-inch rimmed baking pan and turn eggplant slices in oil; place slices side by side. Bake in a 450° oven until eggplant is well browned and feels very soft when pressed, 30 to 40 minutes. Turn off heat; leave eggplant in oven with door ajar until ready to use.

Braised onions. Peel 24 small (1- to 1½-inch-diameter) **white onions.** Put 3 tablespoons **butter** or margarine in a 10- to 12-inch frying pan and add 1 teaspoon **soy sauce** and onions. Cover and cook over medium heat just until onions are tender when pierced but still hold their shape, about 30 minutes; turn onions occasionally when they begin to brown. Keep warm until serving; stir drippings into stew sauce.

Green vegetables. Select at least 1 or 2 kinds; you'll need ½ to ¾ pound of each. In a 5- to 6-quart pan, bring 3 inches of water to a boil over high heat. Add vegetables in sequence (by cooking time) to rapidly boiling water; boil, uncovered, until tender when pierced. **Green beans** or *haricots verts*, slender **broccoli** spears (cut large pieces lengthwise), and small **zucchini** (split lengthwise) or pattypan squash (split crosswise) all take 5 to 8 minutes. **Asparagus** (peeled) and **edible-pod peas** (including sugar snap peas) take 3 to 5 minutes. Drain vegetables and serve them at once with stew.

Lahmejun, Baked & Raw

Pictured on facing page

PREPARATION TIME: About 2½ hours for meat and condiments
BAKING TIME: About 1¼ hours
PER SERVING: 565 calories, 43 grams protein, 57 grams carbohydrate, 19 grams total fat, 127 milligrams cholesterol, 404 milligrams sodium

This Armenian open-face lamb sandwich is the Middle East's answer to pizza or tacos. You spread some of the well-seasoned lamb mixture on flour tortillas (instead of traditional rounds of yeast dough) to bake; some you spread on crispbread to eat raw. (Suggested beverage: sparkling water with dry red wine and lemon)

Makes 10 servings

> 4 medium-size green bell peppers
> 2 pounds ripe pear-shaped, Roma-type tomatoes

> 4 pounds ground lean lamb
> 3½ cups lightly packed minced parsley
> 3 cloves garlic, minced or pressed
> 1 can (12 oz.) tomato paste
> 4 teaspoons *each* ground allspice, pepper, and paprika
> Salt
> 24 flour tortillas (about 8-inch diameter)
> Condiments (suggestions follow)
> Armenian cracker bread

Stem and seed bell peppers and finely chop. Core tomatoes and finely chop. Put vegetables in a 5- to 6-quart pan over medium heat; stir often until vegetables are juicy. Increase heat to high and stir frequently until almost all liquid has evaporated; when you draw spoon across pan bottom, there should be no liquid. Take care not to scorch. Set aside until cool.

In a large bowl, thoroughly mix cooked vegetables, lamb, parsley, garlic, tomato paste, allspice, pepper, and paprika. Season to taste with salt.

For raw lahmejun, set aside 1½ cups of the lamb mixture; cover and refrigerate for up to 12 hours.

Fill 1 or 2 lightly greased 12- by 15-inch rimmed baking pans with a single layer of tortillas. Spoon ½ cup of the meat mixture onto each tortilla; with your fingers or a fork, evenly pat or spread meat in thin coating over tortilla, leaving a ½-inch rim all around.

Bake in a 500° oven, 1 or 2 pans of lahmejun at a time, until tortilla rims are well browned and meat looks dry, 8 to 10 minutes; alternate pan positions halfway through baking. Slide a spatula under hot lahmejun to make sure they are not stuck to pan, then let cool for several minutes for bottoms to firm. Transfer with a wide spatula to a flat surface; reuse pans until all lahmejun are cooked.

While filled pans are in oven, pat lamb on more tortillas, making enough to refill pans. Put in oven and start another batch. You may need to wash, dry, and grease pans occasionally. The cooking process goes much faster if you have more than 1 oven.

Serve lahmejun as baked, at room temperature, or reheated. To store, stack lahmejun, filled sides facing; wrap airtight and refrigerate for up to 2 days or freeze for up to 1 month. To reheat, place single or stacked lahmejun pairs side by side on baking sheets. Bake, uncovered, in a 500° oven until hot, about 6 minutes; eat stacked lahmejun in pairs, or carefully separate.

To serve, offer condiments to top baked lahmejun; fold lahmejun around condiments and eat like a taco. Also offer cracker bread to spread with raw lahmejun (allow about 2 tablespoons per serving).

CONDIMENTS. Arrange in separate containers: At least 20 stalks **celery,** with tops; 2 to 3 cups **salt-cured olives;** 3 or 4 large **cucumbers,** sliced; about 1½ pounds **pear-shaped Roma-type tomatoes,** cored and cut into wedges; at least 20 **green onions** (including tops), ends trimmed; 2 or 3 cans (7 oz. *each*) **whole green chiles;** about 2 cups mildly hot **pickled peppers;** 1 pound **string cheese,** torn into thin strings; 1 pound **feta cheese,** sliced.

The Best of Sunset

POULTRY

Stir-fried, steeped, baked in clay, or set aflame ... with grapes, pears, or jalapeño jelly ... for a picnic or a black-tie dinner ... served hot or cold ... in broth or over lettuce ... to eat with forks, fingers, or chopsticks ... all these are among poultry's possibilities, as you'll discover from the recipes featured in this chapter.

Poultry has been popular with Sunset readers since our early issues in the 1930s, when chicken and turkey were costly, while game birds were free for the hunting. Today, circumstances are reversed: plentiful chicken and turkey are now best buys, and game birds, mostly farm raised, are expensive and usually reserved for festive occasions.

In the next pages, we celebrate chicken, duck, squab, and more in a tribute to poultry's great flavors, moist tenderness, and versatility of cooking style. From Chicken Laurel to Pheasant with Jeweled Fruits, you're in for adventures beyond the ordinary.

Hickory-smoked turkey from your barbecue, served with assorted fresh and pickled fruits, is a splendid centerpiece for a holiday picnic. Instructions for smoke-cooking are on page 136.

Chicken Laurel

PREPARATION TIME: 25 to 30 minutes
ROASTING TIME: 2½ to 3 hours (includes finishing sauce)
PER SERVING: 621 calories, 54 grams protein, 24 grams carbohydrate, 33 grams total fat, 183 milligrams cholesterol, 234 milligrams sodium

When you dine in Rome, roast chicken may arrive aflame at your table, wreathed in laurel leaves. With native bay laurel trees scenting the air throughout much of the West, this festive recipe was sure to spark Sunset's interest. Ours is a simplified version of the Italian classic, garnished with peas, orange slices, and fresh bay leaves. (Suggested wine: fruity Chardonnay)

Makes 5 or 6 servings

> 1 roasting chicken (5 to 6 lbs.)
> 2 or 3 large oranges
> 1 medium-size onion, sliced
> 6 fresh bay leaves or 3 or 4 dry bay leaves
> ¼ cup (⅛ lb.) butter or margarine
> ½ teaspoon grated orange peel
> ½ cup orange juice
> ¼ cup orange liqueur
> 2 to 3 cups hot cooked fresh peas or hot cooked frozen tiny peas, drained
> Small cluster of fresh bay leaves (optional)

Remove chicken neck and giblets; reserve for other uses. Pull off and discard lumps of fat. Rinse chicken inside and out; pat dry. Cut 1 unpeeled orange into chunks; fill neck cavity and body cavity of chicken with orange chunks, onion, and the 6 bay leaves.

Place chicken, breast down, on a rack in a 12- by 15-inch roasting pan. Roast, uncovered, in a 350° oven for 30 minutes. Rub skin with 1 tablespoon of the butter. Roast for 30 more minutes, then turn chicken over and rub with 1 more tablespoon butter. Continue to roast until a meat thermometer inserted in thickest part of thigh (not touching bone) registers 185°F or until meat at thighbone is no longer pink (cut to test), 1 to 1¼ more hours.

Remove and discard orange chunks, onion, and bay leaves from chicken cavities. Protecting your hands, tip chicken to drain juices from body into roasting pan; transfer chicken to a platter and keep warm.

Using a sharp knife, cut peel and all white membrane from remaining oranges; slice oranges crosswise and set aside. Skim and discard fat from pan drippings. Add orange peel and orange juice; bring to a boil over high heat, stirring to scrape browned bits free. Add remaining 2 tablespoons butter and stir until blended into sauce. Pour liqueur into a 2- to 4-cup pan; warm over medium heat until bubbly, then carefully ignite with a match (not beneath a vent, fan, or flammable items). Stir into sauce. Pour sauce into a serving bowl.

Arrange peas on platter around chicken; garnish with orange slices and a cluster of bay leaves. Offer sauce to spoon over meat.

Harvest Chicken with Vegetables & Roasted Potatoes

WESTERN CLASSIC

PREPARATION TIME: 20 to 30 minutes
ROASTING TIME: 1 to 1¼ hours
PER SERVING: 697 calories, 49 grams protein, 38 grams carbohydrate, 36 grams total fat, 174 milligrams cholesterol, 195 milligrams sodium

Celebrating the fresh vegetable bounty for which the West is famed, this roasted chicken shares the pan with colorful tomatoes, squash, carrots, peppers, potatoes, onions, and sprigs of fragrant rosemary. (Suggested wine: dry Sauvignon Blanc or Nouveau Beaujolais)

Makes 4 or 5 servings

> 4 or 5 red thin-skinned potatoes, *each* 2 to 3 inches in diameter, scrubbed
> 1 broiler-fryer chicken (3½ to 4 lbs.)
> 3 large carrots, cut into 1½-inch chunks
> 4 or 5 small pattypan squash
> 3 medium-size crookneck squash, cut into 1½-inch chunks
> 2 large red or green bell peppers, stemmed, seeded, and cut into eighths
> 2 cloves garlic, quartered
> 1 large onion, quartered
> 10 to 12 fresh rosemary sprigs (*each* about 6 inches long) or 1 teaspoon dry rosemary
> 8 to 12 cherry tomatoes, stemmed

Pierce potatoes in several places and set on rack in oven as it preheats to 375°.

Remove chicken neck and giblets; reserve for other uses. Pull off and discard lumps of fat. Rinse chicken inside and out, then pat dry. Place, breast up, in a 12- by 15-inch roasting pan (not on a rack). Arrange carrots, pattypan squash, crookneck squash, bell peppers, garlic, and onion around chicken. Lay 4 or 5 of the rosemary sprigs on vegetables (or sprinkle with all the dry rosemary).

Roast chicken and vegetables, uncovered, in oven with potatoes until a meat thermometer inserted in thickest part of chicken thigh (not touching bone) registers 185°F or until meat at thighbone is no longer pink (cut to test), 1 to 1¼ hours. Add tomatoes during last 10 minutes of cooking. Stir vegetables around chicken several times to moisten with pan drippings.

Transfer chicken to a large platter; carefully lift vegetables from pan with a slotted spoon and mound alongside chicken. Place potatoes on platter. Garnish with remaining rosemary sprigs. Skim and discard fat from pan juices; spoon juices over vegetables.

Beggar's Chicken

A showy entrée served in Chinese restaurants around the world, Beggar's Chicken steam-bakes inside its own custom clay "pot." When it's done, your guests will enjoy watching you crack open the clay shell—but they'll enjoy the fragrant, moist bird inside even more.

According to Chinese fable, this dish earned its name from a pauper who was so hungry he couldn't wait to pluck a bird before cooking it. Lacking tools—and even a pot—he wrapped it in mud, feathers and all, and threw it into his campfire. The heat sealed the mud, and the chicken steamed to succulence. With refinements, the technique was passed on to the chefs of royalty.

We use this method, only slightly modified, to produce a whole-meal dish of herb-scented chicken with carrots and potatoes. To preserve the juices, the ingredients are first wrapped in baking parchment or foil.

You don't need to be an artist to produce the dramatic clay overcoat. Simply shape a sheet of low-fire white ceramic clay, available at ceramic and art supply stores, around the parchment. The shape of the food suggests the form. You'll use most of the clay to wrap the food; use the trimmings to decorate the clay package, creating a rustic chicken.

You can wrap the bird in clay a day ahead, then cover with wet towels and plastic wrap and refrigerate until baking.

- 1 **broiler-fryer or roasting chicken (4½ to 5 lbs.)**
  Olive oil or salad oil
  Salt and pepper
- 3 **cloves garlic, slivered**
- 20 **to 25 pounds low-fire white ceramic clay**
- 6 **green onions, ends trimmed**
- 4 **or 5 small (2-inch-diameter) red thin-skinned potatoes, scrubbed and halved**
- 1 **pound carrots, peeled and cut into 1-inch pieces**
- 3 **slices partially cooked bacon**
- 4 **to 6 fresh rosemary sprigs** (*each about 6 inches long*)

Remove chicken neck and giblets and reserve for other uses. Pull off and discard lumps of fat. Rinse chicken inside and out and pat dry. Rub all over with oil; sprinkle with salt and pepper. Make about 20 small ½-inch-deep slits in chicken breast and insert a sliver of garlic into each. Keep chicken cold.

Cut clay into ½-inch-thick slices. Arrange slices with edges touching on a pastry cloth, muslin towel, or parchment paper that measures at least 15 by 30 inches. With a rolling pin, roll clay into a 15- by 25-inch rectangle about ⅜ inch thick. Lay a 15- by 30-inch piece of baking parchment or foil on clay. Set chicken in center of parchment.

Arrange onions next to chicken; surround with potatoes and carrots. Drape bacon over breast, then fill chicken cavity with half the rosemary; set remaining rosemary on top. Bring sides of parchment together and fold over to seal, then fold ends to seal in bird.

Shape clay around package by bringing opposite sides to center; dampen with water where edges overlap, then pinch clay snugly against chicken to seal. Pinch open ends together. Cut off excess clay, leaving a 1-inch edge on top and ends.

Lift clay bundle (it's quite heavy) from cloth and transfer to baking sheet (at least 12 by 17 inches). If desired, use trimmings to shape a chicken's head and tail on bundle. Smooth clay with wet hands. Pierce clay in several places to allow steam to escape, if you wish, to minimize the cracking that occurs as the bird bakes. (At this point, you may cover clay-wrapped bird with wet towels, then wrap in plastic wrap and refrigerate until next day.)

Bake in a 375° oven for 2 hours (2 hours and 15 minutes if refrigerated); expect clay to crack slightly. Let stand for 10 to 20 minutes.

Transfer clay bird to a board or tray and invite guests to watch as you gently crack clay with a mallet or hammer. Pull off major clay pieces. Unfold parchment; you may prefer to take chicken back to kitchen and put it and vegetables on a platter and juices in a bowl. Carve bird to serve with vegetables and juices. Makes 4 or 5 servings.

1. Enclose rosemary-seasoned chicken and vegetables in baking parchment.

2. Bring 1 side of clay over chicken; dampen edge, then fold over other side and press to seal.

3. Crack open baked clay wrapping with a mallet or hammer. Pull off large clay pieces.

4. Unfold parchment to reveal steaming, succulent Beggar's Chicken.

Cheese-crusted Chicken with Cream

PREPARATION TIME: About 10 minutes
COOKING TIME: About 1¼ hours
PER SERVING: 755 calories, 63 grams protein, 2 grams carbohydrate, 54 grams total fat, 261 milligrams cholesterol, 428 milligrams sodium

In their travels abroad, Sunset editors have always sought out the finest examples of simple and enduring family-style dishes. One of our favorite country French classics is this exquisite baked chicken. As its ingredients of cheese and cream suggest, it comes from the Jura Mountains southeast of Dijon.

Serve with crusty French—or San Francisco sourdough—bread, and follow with a simple mixed green salad. (Suggested wine: dry White Riesling)

Makes 4 servings

> 1 broiler-fryer chicken (3½ to 4 lbs.)
> About 1 tablespoon butter or margarine, melted
> 1¼ cups (5 oz.) shredded Gruyère or Swiss cheese
> 1 tablespoon Dijon mustard
> About ¾ cup whipping cream
> Watercress sprigs

Remove chicken neck and giblets; reserve for other uses. Pull off and discard lumps of fat. Rinse chicken inside and out, then pat dry. Brush skin with butter. Place chicken, breast up, on a rack in a 12- by 15-inch roasting pan. Roast, uncovered, in a 375° oven until a meat thermometer inserted in thickest part of thigh (not touching bone) registers 185°F, or until meat at thighbone is no longer pink (cut to test), about 1 hour.

Using poultry shears or a knife, cut chicken into quarters. Arrange pieces, skin side up and slightly apart, in a shallow ovenproof serving dish (use a 9- by 13-inch rectangular or 12- to 15-inch oval dish). Sprinkle with ¾ cup of the cheese. Return to oven and turn off heat.

Skim and discard fat from pan drippings. Stir in mustard and ¾ cup of the cream; bring to a boil over high heat and boil, stirring, until shiny bubbles form, 3 to 4 minutes. Remove from heat, add remaining ½ cup cheese, and stir until cheese is melted and sauce is smooth (if necessary, thin sauce with a little more cream). Keep sauce warm.

Broil chicken 4 to 5 inches below heat until cheese is bubbly, about 1 minute. Pour sauce around chicken; garnish with watercress.

Barbecued Herb-Mustard Chicken

W E S T E R N   C L A S S I C

PREPARATION TIME: 30 to 45 minutes to ignite charcoal; about 10 minutes to prepare chicken
MARINATING TIME: At least 4 hours
GRILLING TIME: About 50 minutes
PER SERVING: 576 calories, 45 grams protein, 4 grams carbohydrate, 41 grams total fat, 143 milligrams cholesterol, 293 milligrams sodium

This simple, herb-flavored chicken is a long-time favorite with Sunset's guests. For variety, try different mustards in the spicy marinade—Dijon, tarragon, green peppercorn, hot English-style, and German coarse-grained mustards are all possibilities. (Suggested wine: dry French Colombard or light Merlot)

Makes 4 servings

> 1 broiler-fryer chicken (3 to 3½ lbs.), cut into quarters
> ½ cup dry white wine
> ⅔ cup salad oil
> 6 tablespoons wine vinegar
> 2 tablespoons finely chopped onion
> 1 teaspoon Italian herb seasoning or dry thyme leaves
> 2 cloves garlic, minced or pressed
> ½ teaspoon pepper
> ¼ cup spicy brown mustard
> Salt

Rinse chicken and pat dry. Pull off and discard lumps of fat. In a bowl, combine wine, oil, vinegar, onion, herb seasoning, garlic, pepper, and mustard. Turn chicken in marinade to coat. Cover and refrigerate for at least 4 hours or until next day, turning occasionally.

Lift chicken from marinade and drain briefly; reserve marinade. Place chicken, skin side up, on a grill 4 to 6 inches above a solid bed of medium coals (you should be able to hold your hand at grill level for no more than 4 to 5 seconds). Cook, turning and basting frequently with marinade, until meat at thighbone is no longer pink (cut to test), 40 to 50 minutes. Season to taste with salt.

Chicken with Port Cream, French Style

Pictured on facing page

PREPARATION TIME: 5 to 10 minutes
COOKING TIME: About 30 minutes to brown chicken; about 40 minutes to simmer chicken; 7 to 10 minutes to make sauce
PER SERVING: 705 calories, 42 grams protein, 4 grams carbohydrate, 57 grams total fat, 368 milligrams cholesterol, 257 milligrams sodium

A glistening glaze of port, cream, and egg yolks cloaks this elegantly braised chicken. The influence is French, but the simplicity has made it a favorite of Sunset *readers for over 20 years. (Suggested wine: soft Zinfandel)*

Makes 4 servings.

   1 **broiler-fryer chicken (3 to 3½ lbs.), cut up**
   3 **tablespoons butter or margarine**
   ½ **cup port**
   ¾ **cup whipping cream**
   2 **large egg yolks**
      Chopped parsley
      Salt

Rinse chicken and pat dry. Pull off and discard lumps of fat. Melt butter in a 10- to 12-inch frying pan over medium heat; add chicken, a portion at a time, with-out crowding, and brown on all sides. Return chicken (except breast pieces) to pan; add port and cream. Reduce heat, cover, and simmer for 20 minutes. Add breast pieces; continue to simmer, covered, until meat at thighbone is no longer pink (cut to test), about 20 more minutes. (At this point, you may let cool, then cover and refrigerate. Reheat before continuing.)

Transfer chicken to a serving dish and keep warm. Boil pan juices over high heat until reduced to about 1⅓ cups. In a small bowl, lightly beat egg yolks; beat in a little of the hot sauce, then return yolk mixture to pan. Cook over low heat, stirring constantly, just until sauce is thickened, 7 to 10 minutes; do not boil. Pour sauce over chicken and sprinkle with parsley. Season to taste with salt.

An example of simple and unpretentious French cuisine, Chicken with Port Cream, French Style (recipe begins on facing page) has been a much-requested Sunset *classic for years.*

Chicken with Sweet Onions

PREPARATION TIME: About 25 minutes, plus 30 minutes to cook onions as chicken bakes
BAKING TIME: About 1 hour
PER SERVING: 657 calories, 49 grams protein, 27 grams carbohydrate, 39 grams total fat, 175 milligrams cholesterol, 263 milligrams sodium

Popular everywhere, mild-mannered chicken takes on different flavor accents in each region of the world. In this Moroccan-style recipe, tender chicken pieces are cloaked with mellow, slowly cooked onions, sweetened by brown sugar and cinnamon. (Suggested wine: dry Sauvignon Blanc)

Makes 4 servings

¼ **cup slivered almonds**
1 **broiler-fryer chicken (3 to 3½ lbs.), cut up**
Pepper and paprika
¼ **cup (⅛ lb.) butter or margarine**
4 or 5 **large onions (2 to 2½ lbs. *total*), thinly sliced and separated into rings**
2 **tablespoons firmly packed brown sugar**
½ **teaspoon ground cinnamon**
Lemon wedges
Salt

Spread almonds in a 9- or 10-inch-wide baking pan. Toast nuts in a 350° oven until golden, about 8 minutes, stirring frequently. Set aside. Increase oven temperature to 400°.

Rinse chicken and pat dry. Pull off and discard lumps of fat. Sprinkle with pepper and paprika. Arrange, skin side down, in a greased 10- by 15-inch shallow baking pan. Bake, uncovered, in a 400° oven for 30 minutes. Turn skin side up; continue to bake, uncovered, until skin is browned and meat at thighbone is no longer pink (cut to test), 15 to 20 more minutes.

Meanwhile, melt butter in a 10- to 12-inch frying pan over medium heat. Add onions and cook, stirring often, until sweet tasting and golden, about 30 minutes. Onions should not show signs of browning during the first 15 minutes; if they do, reduce heat. Sprinkle in sugar and cinnamon and stir to blend.

Place chicken pieces on a platter and cover with onions. Sprinkle with toasted almonds. Offer lemon wedges to squeeze over onions and chicken; season to taste with salt.

North Indian Chicken Curry

PREPARATION TIME: 20 to 25 minutes
COOKING TIME: About 1¼ hours
PER SERVING: 281 calories, 26 grams protein, 4 grams carbohydrate, 17 grams total fat, 88 milligrams cholesterol, 128 milligrams sodium

Northern India's climate is moderate; its curries are likewise mild—like this one—and rich with sweet spices. Farther south, where the weather is hotter, flavors tend to be much more fiery. Regardless of their origins, though, all kinds of curries have found ready reception in the West. (Suggested wine: tart Chenin Blanc)

Makes 8 servings

2 **medium-size onions, cut into chunks**
2 **cloves garlic**
1 to 2 **teaspoons minced fresh or canned jalapeño chile (seed before mincing for a milder curry)**
3 **tablespoons coarsely chopped fresh ginger**
About ¼ cup water
⅓ **cup salad oil**
2 **tablespoons canned tomato paste**
1 **teaspoon ground turmeric**
¼ to ½ **teaspoon cayenne**
½ **cup plain yogurt**
8 **whole chicken legs, thighs attached (about 4 lbs. *total*)**
Salt
Fresh cilantro (coriander) sprigs
Garam Masala (recipe follows)

In a blender or food processor, whirl onions, garlic, chile, ginger, and ¼ cup of the water until puréed. Pour into a 10- to 12-inch frying pan and cook over medium heat, stirring occasionally, until dry and thick, 15 to 20 minutes. Reduce heat to medium-low; stir in oil, tomato paste, turmeric, cayenne, and yogurt. Cook, uncovered, stirring occasionally, until thickened, 5 to 10 minutes.

Meanwhile, pull skin off chicken; discard. Cut drumsticks and thighs apart; rinse meat and pat dry. Add to sauce and turn to coat. Cover and simmer, turning once, until meat at thighbone is no longer pink (cut to test), 40 to 45 minutes. Add about 1 tablespoon more water if sauce begins to stick to pan. Transfer chicken to a serving dish. Skim and discard fat from sauce, then season to taste with salt. Spoon sauce over chicken. Garnish with cilantro. Offer Garam Masala to sprinkle over each serving.

GARAM MASALA. In a 6- to 7-inch frying pan, cook 3 tablespoons **coriander seeds** and 2 teaspoons **cumin seeds** over medium-low heat until lightly browned, about 4 minutes, shaking pan often. Place in a blender, then add 8 **whole cloves;** 1 **cinnamon stick** (about 2 inches long), broken in half; ½ teaspoon **whole black peppercorns;** and 4 **bay leaves.** Whirl until finely ground. Use, or store airtight for up to 2 months. Makes about ¼ cup.
PER TEASPOON: 6 calories, .22 gram protein, 1 gram carbohydrate, .31 gram total fat, 0 milligram cholesterol, 1 milligram sodium.

Chicken with Oranges & Wild Rice

W E S T E R N   C L A S S I C

PREPARATION TIME: About 15 minutes to organize chicken; about 30 minutes to prepare onion-rice mixture

BAKING TIME: About 20 minutes to cook onions; about 50 minutes to cook rice; about 50 minutes to cook chicken

PER SERVING: 491 calories, 26 grams protein, 49 grams carbohydrate, 22 grams total fat, 87 milligrams cholesterol, 112 milligrams sodium

From the marmalade glaze to the squeeze of fresh juice just before serving, oranges enrich chicken's delicacy with a tart-sweet flavor. Wild rice with cinnamon-spiked onions completes an elegant dinner. (Suggested wine: dry Sauvignon Blanc)

Makes 4 to 6 servings

> 6 chicken thighs (about 2 lbs. *total*)
> 1 tablespoon orange marmalade
> Wild Rice with Cinnamon Onions (recipe follows)
> 3 or 4 medium-size oranges
> Salt and pepper
> Parsley sprigs (optional)

Arrange chicken thighs side by side, skin side up, in a 9- by 13-inch baking pan or dish. Bake, uncovered, in a 375° oven until skin is browned and meat is no longer pink at bone (cut to test), about 40 minutes. Remove from oven and tilt pan to drain off juices; discard all but 2 tablespoons of the drippings. Blend reserved drippings with marmalade, brush mixture over chicken, and bake, uncovered, for 10 more minutes.

If you wish, prepare rice while chicken bakes. Or, if you've prepared rice ahead, cover baking dish tightly with foil and set in oven with chicken after chicken has cooked for 30 minutes. Bake until hot in center, about 20 minutes.

Meanwhile, using a sharp knife, cut peel and all white membrane from all but 1 of the oranges. Thinly slice peeled oranges crosswise. Remove chicken and rice from oven and lay chicken pieces on top of heated rice; pour any pan juices over chicken. Season to taste with salt and pepper; arrange sliced oranges around chicken. Garnish with parsley, if desired.

Cut remaining unpeeled orange in half. Squeeze juice of orange halves over chicken and serve.

WILD RICE WITH CINNAMON ONIONS. Rinse 1⅓ cups **wild rice** with **cold water**; drain, place in a 4- to 5-quart pan, and add 3 cups **Homemade Chicken Broth** (page 58) or canned regular-strength chicken broth and 2 teaspoons grated **orange peel**. Bring to a boil; then reduce heat, cover, and simmer until rice is tender to bite, about 50 minutes. Drain well.

While rice cooks, melt 2 tablespoons **butter** or margarine in a 12- to 14-inch frying pan over medium heat. Thinly slice 4 medium-size **onions** and add to butter along with 1 teaspoon **ground cinnamon**. Cook, stirring often, until onions are soft and flavor is sweet, 25 to 30 minutes. Add to drained wild rice and mix gently. Pour rice mixture into a 9- by 13-inch or 10- by 12-inch casserole.

Lemon Chicken with Fermented Black Beans

PREPARATION TIME: 10 to 15 minutes

STEAMING TIME: About 30 minutes

PER SERVING: 420 calories, 40 grams protein, 12 grams carbohydrate, 23 grams total fat, 130 milligrams cholesterol, 1805 milligrams sodium

The Chinese technique of steaming is particularly effective in blending the flavors of this lemony chicken dish. The recipe contains only 2 teaspoons of fat (the aromatic Oriental sesame oil), and you can even omit that if you'd like to make the Western-style variation. (Suggested wine: dry blend white with Sauvignon Blanc)

Makes 4 servings

> 2 teaspoons sugar
> ¼ cup cornstarch
> 2 teaspoons Oriental sesame oil
> 3 tablespoons soy sauce
> 2 tablespoons dry sherry
> ¼ cup fermented salted black beans, rinsed and patted dry
> 1 clove garlic
> About 2½ pounds chicken thighs and legs
> 1 lemon

In a large bowl, smoothly blend sugar, cornstarch, oil, soy, and sherry. In a small bowl, mash black beans with garlic and add to cornstarch paste. Rinse chicken and pat dry. With a heavy cleaver or knife, cut through bones into 1- to 1½-inch lengths. Add chicken to cornstarch mixture; stir to coat well. (At this point, you may cover and refrigerate for up to 4 hours. Stir well before continuing.)

Arrange chicken evenly in a 10- to 11-inch-wide rimmed heatproof serving dish that will fit inside a steamer or large pan. Roll lemon under your palm to soften, then cut in half and squeeze juice over chicken. Cut juiced lemon into eighths and distribute over chicken.

Cover top of dish completely with wax paper. Support dish on a rack or stand above 1 to 2 inches of boiling water. Cover pan and simmer rapidly for 30 minutes. Remove from heat and test chicken; meat at bone should no longer be pink (cut to test). If necessary, cover and continue to steam for a few more minutes.

To serve, discard wax paper; lift dish from rack and dry base with a towel.

WESTERN-STYLE LEMON CHICKEN

Follow directions for **Lemon Chicken with Fermented Black Beans,** but omit Oriental sesame oil and fermented salted black beans. Press garlic and mix with chicken pieces. Garnish the finished dish with 1 small firm-ripe **avocado,** pitted, peeled, and sliced.

Named for the hometown of the Sunset *reader who sent us this tasty idea, Sacramento Wings (recipe at right) are baked, then dipped, in your choice of tempting sauces.*

Sacramento Wings

Pictured at left

PREPARATION TIME: About 40 minutes for wings; 5 to 10 minutes for each of the sauces
BAKING TIME: About 50 minutes
PER ENTRÉE SERVING: See individual baking sauces that follow

Named for a Sacramento reader who shared with us her variation upon New York's popular "Buffalo chicken wings," these are served with celery and a dip—as is their prototype. But you can use a lower-calorie yogurt dip in place of New York's blue cheese, and your choice of baking sauces adds lively new flavor to the chicken. (Suggested wine: dry white wine with sparkling water)

Makes 4 to 6 entrée servings, 12 appetizer servings

> **4 pounds chicken wings**
> **Baking Sauces (recipes follow)**
> **2 bunches celery (about 2 lbs. *total*)**
> **Salt**
> **Dipping Sauces (recipes follow)**

Rinse chicken wings and pat dry. Cut apart at joints; reserve wingtips for other uses.

Line each of two 10- by 15-inch baking pans with a single piece of 12-inch-wide heavy foil, pinching a ridge of foil about ¾ inch high across the middle of each pan if you want to flavor the wings with 4 different baking sauces (omit ridge if using only 1 or 2 sauces). Arrange about 1 pound wings in each half of each pan.

Bake wings, uncovered, in a 400° oven until golden brown, 30 to 35 minutes. Remove pans from oven and pour baking sauce of your choice over each 1-pound portion of wings, turning wings to coat well.

Return wings to oven and bake until sauce is bubbling and edges of wings are crisp, about 15 more minutes; turn wings once or twice.

Meanwhile, break celery stalks from bunch, rinse well. Arrange hot or room-temperature wings and celery in a basket or on a tray; salt chicken and celery to taste. Spoon 1 or 2 dipping sauces into small bowls. Serve wings and celery to swish through dipping sauces.

BAKING SAUCES. Choose from the following; each is enough to season 1 pound of wings. You can double, triple, or quadruple each recipe. If made ahead, cover and refrigerate for up to 1 week.

Red Hot Sauce. Stir together 2 tablespoons *each* **vinegar** and **water,** 1 tablespoon **canned tomato paste,** 1 teaspoon **sugar,** 1 to 3 teaspoons **liquid hot pepper seasoning** (less for mild heat), and ¼ to 1 teaspoon **cayenne** (less for mild heat).
PER SERVING: 335 calories, 24 grams protein, 15 grams carbohydrate, 20 grams total fat, 94 milligrams cholesterol, 615 milligrams sodium.

Ginger Sauce. In a food processor or blender, whirl 2 tablespoons chopped **fresh ginger,** 2 tablespoons *each* **honey** and thawed **frozen pineapple juice concentrate,** and 1 tablespoon **vinegar** until smoothly puréed.
PER SERVING: 500 calories, 24 grams protein, 59 grams carbohydrate, 20 grams total fat, 94 milligrams cholesterol, 228 milligrams sodium.

Garlic Sauce. In a 6- to 8-inch frying pan, combine ¼ cup minced or pressed **garlic** and 1 tablespoon **olive oil;** stir over medium heat until garlic is light gold. Pour into a blender or food processor and add 2 tablespoons **dry sherry;** 2 teaspoons *each* **lemon juice, vinegar,** and minced **fresh or dry rosemary;** and ½ teaspoon drained **capers.** Whirl until smoothly puréed.

Per Serving: 496 calories, 26 grams protein, 24 grams carbohydrate, 34 grams total fat, 94 milligrams cholesterol, 270 milligrams sodium.

Mustard Sauce. Mix 2 tablespoons *each* **corn syrup** and **Dijon mustard,** 1 tablespoon **vinegar,** and 1 teaspoon **pepper.**

Per Serving: 459 calories, 24 grams protein, 43 grams carbohydrate, 22 grams total fat, 94 milligrams cholesterol, 1142 milligrams sodium.

DIPPING SAUCES. A full recipe of either of these sauces is enough to accompany 4 pounds of chicken wings. If you want to serve both, divide each recipe in half. If made ahead, cover and refrigerate for up to 3 days.

Yogurt Dip. Stir together 2 cups **plain yogurt,** ¼ cup minced **green onions** (including tops), and 1 teaspoon *each* **mustard seeds** and **cumin seeds.** Makes 2⅓ cups.

Per Tablespoon: 8 calories, .45 gram protein, .65 gram carbohydrate, .42 gram total fat, 2 milligrams cholesterol, 6 milligrams sodium.

Blue Cheese Dip. Coarsely mash ¼ pound **blue-veined cheese** with a fork. Stir in 1 cup **sour cream** and add 1 teaspoon minced **garlic,** ½ teaspoon **dry mustard,** and ⅛ teaspoon **pepper.** Makes 1⅓ cups.

Per Tablespoon: 43 calories, 2 grams protein, .63 gram carbohydrate, 4 grams total fat, 9 milligrams cholesterol, 81 milligrams sodium.

Pollo Toscana

PREPARATION TIME: About 30 minutes for chicken; about 30 minutes for mushrooms

COOKING TIME: About 30 minutes to brown chicken and mushrooms; about 30 minutes to bake; 10 to 15 minutes to heat water and cook pasta

PER SERVING OF CHICKEN AND PASTA: 679 calories, 57 grams protein, 37 grams carbohydrate; 32 grams total fat, 199 milligrams cholesterol, 303 milligrams sodium

PER SERVING OF MUSHROOMS: 104 calories, 7 grams protein, 2 grams carbohydrate, 8 grams total fat, 80 milligrams cholesterol, 172 milligrams sodium

A magnificent Italian meal of chicken in tomato sauce with vermicelli and stuffed mushrooms, this marvelous entrée is undeniably time-consuming to prepare—but well worth your while. And because you can make the dish ahead, it can be company fare for week nights as well as weekends. As a variation, try serving the stuffed mushrooms on their own as a light main dish. (Suggested wine: slightly oaked Chardonnay)

Makes 4 or 5 servings

 1 broiler-fryer chicken with giblets
   (3 to 3½ lbs.), cut up
 1 whole chicken breast (about 1 lb.)
 2 tablespoons butter or margarine
 2 tablespoons olive oil
   Stuffed Mushrooms (recipe follows)

 ¼ cup chopped onion
 1 large firm-ripe tomato, peeled, cored,
   seeded, and diced
 ½ teaspoon dry basil
 ⅛ teaspoon dry rosemary
 ¼ cup *each* dry white wine and water
 ¼ cup minced prosciutto or cooked ham
 8 ounces dry vermicelli or capellini
   Minced parsley
   Salt

Bone chicken breasts and thighs; cut meat into large pieces. Reserve bones, neck, and back of chicken for broth, if desired. Rinse giblets and all chicken pieces and pat dry.

Melt butter in oil in a 10- to 12-inch frying pan over medium-high heat. Add wings, drumsticks, thigh meat, gizzard, and heart; brown on all sides, then push to side of pan to continue cooking. Add liver and breast pieces without crowding; cook until lightly browned but still pink in center (cut to test). Remove breast and liver from pan as cooked. Then remove all chicken from pan; set aside.

Add mushrooms to pan, stuffed side up, and cook until lightly browned on bottom. Remove from pan and set aside.

To pan drippings, add onion, tomato, basil, and rosemary; cook, stirring, until onion is soft. Add wine and water and boil rapidly until reduced by about half. Return chicken and any accumulated juices to pan, stir in prosciutto, and simmer for 10 minutes.

Pour chicken and sauce into a shallow 2- to 3-quart casserole. Top with mushrooms. (At this point, you may cover and refrigerate until next day.) Bake, uncovered, in a 375° oven just until breast pieces are no longer pink in center (cut to test), about 30 minutes (40 minutes if refrigerated).

Meanwhile, bring 3 to 4 quarts water to a boil in a 5- to 6-quart pan over high heat. Add pasta; cook, uncovered, until tender to bite, 3 to 9 minutes. Drain well; keep hot.

To serve, set mushrooms around edge of a platter; swirl hot pasta in center, top with chicken, and pour sauce over all. Sprinkle with parsley; season to taste with salt.

STUFFED MUSHROOMS. Rinse 8 large (about 2-inch-diameter) **button mushrooms** and pat dry. Gently remove stems and scoop out centers slightly. Mince scraps and stems; set aside. Melt 1 tablespoon **butter** or margarine in a 6- to 7-inch frying pan over medium-high heat. Add minced mushrooms and ¼ cup minced **onion;** cook, stirring often, until vegetables are lightly browned, about 10 minutes. Remove from heat.

In a 2- to 3-quart pan, cook ½ pound **sweetbreads** in **boiling water** to cover for 10 minutes. Drain; peel off membranes. Whirl sweetbreads in a food processor until finely ground (or put sweetbreads through a food chopper fitted with a fine blade).

Stir together sweetbreads, onion mixture, ⅓ cup freshly grated **Parmesan cheese,** and ¼ cup chopped **prosciutto** or cooked ham; season to taste with **salt.** Pack filling equally into mushroom caps.

Yakitori

PREPARATION TIME: 30 to 40 minutes to ignite charcoal; 45 minutes to 1 hour to skewer chicken and vegetables

GRILLING TIME: 5 to 15 minutes, depending on part of chicken

PER SERVING: 683 calories, 71 grams protein, 19 grams carbohydrate, 34 grams total fat, 271 milligrams cholesterol, 1145 milligrams sodium

At the end of a day, Tokyo office workers sometimes stop at a street stall for beer, gossip, and the grilled chicken tidbits called yakitori. The same tasty morsels lend themselves readily to a garden party menu. Present the skewers on a tray and let guests cook their own selections on a hibachi.

Serve yakitori with rice, Japanese pickled vegetables, clear dashi soup (from a mix), and—for dessert—strawberries with sliced oranges and plum wine. (Suggested wine: dry Pinot Noir Blanc)

Makes 4 to 6 servings

> **2 broiler-fryer chickens with giblets (3 to 4 lbs. *each*), cut up**
>
> **Chicken Balls (recipe follows)**
>
> **5 to 7 green onions**
>
> **½ small green or red bell pepper, stemmed and seeded**
>
> **4 to 6 large (3½-inch caps) or 8 to 16 small (1½-inch caps) fresh or dried shiitake mushrooms**
>
> **1 can (about 6 oz.) ginkgo nuts**
>
> **Yakitori Glaze (recipe follows) or purchased teriyaki baste and glaze**
>
> **Sansho pepper, salt, and soy sauce**

Lay about 10 dozen slender 8- to 9-inch bamboo skewers in a rimmed pan. Pour water over skewers to cover and let stand for at least 30 minutes.

Rinse chicken and giblets and pat dry. Pull off all skin; cut skin into 1- by 3-inch strips. Thread each strip lengthwise on a skewer. Set aside.

Bone breasts, thighs, and drumsticks; cut meat into ¾- to 1-inch cubes. If necessary, cut thin pieces larger and fold to make this size; keep light and dark meat separate. Reserve odd-shaped scraps to make Chicken Balls. Trim any large bits of meat from breast and back bones and add to scraps; if needed, add thigh and breast meat to make ¾ pound. Reserve bones for broth, if desired.

Prepare Chicken Balls; push 1 or 2 balls onto each skewer. Set aside.

Cut wings apart at joints. Cut livers and gizzards apart where a natural separation occurs. Skewer each section of wing, running skewer alongside bone. Thread livers, gizzards, and hearts onto skewers, using 2 or 3 pieces per skewer.

Cut off and discard onion ends. Cut white portion into ¾- to 1-inch lengths. Thread chicken breast meat and onion pieces alternately on skewers, using 3 meat pieces and 2 onion pieces per skewer; position onion perpendicular to skewer.

Cut bell pepper into strips ¼ inch wide and ¾ to 1 inch long. Thread dark meat and pepper strips alternately on skewers, using 3 meat pieces and 2 pepper strips per skewer; position pepper strips perpendicular to skewer.

Arrange chicken on a tray, grouping by kinds. Place skewered skin on tray with chicken.

Soak dried mushrooms in hot water to cover until soft, about 15 minutes. Rinse soaked or fresh mushrooms and gently squeeze water from dried mushrooms; trim off stems and discard. Thread a skewer horizontally through 1 or 2 mushroom caps. Place on tray with chicken.

Drain ginkgo nuts; rinse. Thread nuts onto skewers, using 4 or 5 nuts per skewer. Place on tray with chicken. (At this point, you may cover all skewered foods and refrigerate until next day.)

To cook yakitori, pour glaze into a narrow glass or jar. Dip skewered foods into glaze; lift out, draining briefly. Lay skewered foods on a hibachi (or other small barbecue) grill 2 to 4 inches above a solid, 2-layer-deep bed of very hot coals (you should be able to hold your hand at grill level for no more than 1 to 2 seconds). To maintain heat, add 8 to 10 ignited briquets to hibachi every 20 to 30 minutes. Turn foods to cook evenly; dip into glaze as many times as desired.

Cooked skin should be slightly crisp and browned; white and dark meat and Chicken Balls should no longer be pink in center, and giblets should look moist in center (cut to test). Mushrooms and ginkgo nuts should be very hot and well glazed. Total cooking time for foods ranges from 5 to 15 minutes. Season foods to taste with sansho pepper, salt, and soy.

CHICKEN BALLS. Finely chop ¾ pound **reserved chicken scraps** in a food processor, or chop small portions at a time in a blender; you should have 1½ cups. Mix with 3 tablespoons **soy sauce,** 2 tablespoons **sake,** 1 tablespoon minced **fresh ginger,** and ¼ teaspoon **salt.** Shape chicken into 1-inch balls; roll each to coat in ¾ cup **panko** (Japanese-style bread crumbs) or fine dry bread crumbs.

YAKITORI GLAZE. In a 2- to 3-quart pan, combine 1¼ cups **sake,** ⅔ cup **mirin** (sweet sake), ¾ cup **sugar,** and ⅓ cup **soy sauce.** Boil, uncovered, until reduced to 1½ cups. If made ahead, cover and refrigerate until next day.

PER TABLESPOON: 46 calories, .27 gram protein, 10 grams carbohydrate, .05 gram total fat, 0 milligram cholesterol, 293 milligrams sodium.

Chicken Schnitzel

PREPARATION TIME: About 10 minutes to bone chicken (or purchase boned); about 5 minutes to pound
COOKING TIME: 5 to 8 minutes
PER SERVING: 239 calories, 34 grams protein, 0 gram carbohydrate, 10 grams total fat, 109 milligrams cholesterol, 184 milligrams sodium

Boned and skinned, then pounded thin—like veal for German schnitzel—chicken thighs or breasts cook in just a few minutes. The results are meltingly tender. If you like, you can pound the chicken a day ahead and refrigerate it, ready to use in this recipe or any number of other delectable dishes (such as Chicken Scaloppine with Brandy Cream, below). (Suggested wine: soft Pinot Blanc)

Makes 3 or 4 servings

> 2 whole chicken breasts (about 1 lb. *each*), split; or 8 chicken thighs (2 to 2½ lbs. *total*); or half of each
> Dry basil, dill weed, rubbed dry sage, dry oregano leaves, dry marjoram leaves, or seasoned pepper
> 2 to 4 tablespoons butter or margarine
> Lemon wedges
> Salt

Skin and bone chicken; discard skin and bones, then rinse meat and pat dry. Place chicken pieces 5 to 6 inches apart on a sheet of plastic wrap; tuck any scraps of meat under larger pieces. Cover with another sheet of plastic wrap. Pound meat firmly with a flat-surfaced mallet (do not hit hard enough to break meat apart) until each piece is evenly ³⁄₁₆ to ¼ inch thick. (At this point, you may fold up meat in plastic wrap, enclose in a plastic bag, and refrigerate until next day.)

Sprinkle chicken lightly with herbs or pepper. In a 10- to 12-inch frying pan, melt just enough butter to coat bottom of pan over high heat. Add chicken, a portion at a time, without crowding; cook just until lightly browned, 1 to 1½ minutes on each side. Add more butter to pan as needed. Lift meat from pan as cooked; keep warm. Offer lemon wedges to squeeze over meat; season to taste with salt.

Chicken Scaloppine with Brandy Cream

PREPARATION TIME: About 10 minutes to bone chicken (or purchase boned); about 5 minutes to pound
COOKING TIME: 5 to 8 minutes for chicken, 2 to 4 minutes for sauce
PER SERVING: 282 calories, 34 grams protein, .44 gram carbohydrate, 15 grams total fat, 125 milligrams cholesterol, 189 milligrams sodium

Both Sunset Magazine and Sunset Books have devoted many pages to demonstrating how a single technique can be used in a number of different dishes. Like Chicken Schnitzel (above), our chicken scaloppine begins with skinned, boned, and pounded chicken pieces—but it finishes quite differently, with a rich, creamy sauce flavored with brandy. (Suggested wine: dry blend white with Sauvignon Blanc)

Makes 3 or 4 servings

> 2 whole chicken breasts (about 1 lb. *each*), split; or 8 chicken thighs (2 to 2½ lbs. *total*); or half of each
> 2 to 4 tablespoons butter or margarine
> 2 tablespoons brandy
> ¼ cup whipping cream
> Salt

Skin, bone, pound, and cook chicken (using 2 to 4 tablespoons butter) as directed for Chicken Schnitzel (at left). When all meat has been cooked, return it to frying pan and add brandy; carefully ignite with a match (be sure pan is not beneath a vent, fan, or flammable items). Shake pan until flames die.

Remove pan from heat; quickly lift meat from juices and keep warm in a serving dish. Return pan to high heat and add cream. Stir to scrape browned bits free; boil until large, shiny bubbles form, 2 to 3 minutes. Drain any accumulated juices from chicken into sauce; stir to blend, then pour over chicken. Season to taste with salt.

CHICKEN WITH LEMON MUSTARD SAUCE

Follow directions for **Chicken Scaloppine with Brandy Cream,** but use 2 tablespoons **lemon juice** instead of brandy. Add 2 teaspoons **Dijon mustard** along with the cream.

DUTCH CHICKEN

Follow directions for **Chicken Scaloppine with Brandy Cream,** but use 2 tablespoons **gin** (flame as directed) instead of brandy. Add ½ cup sautéed sliced **button mushrooms** (optional) along with the cream.

SCOTCH BIRDS

Follow directions for **Chicken Scaloppine with Brandy Cream,** but use 2 tablespoons **Scotch whiskey** (flame as directed) instead of brandy. Add 2 tablespoons minced **shallots** or onion along with the cream.

CHICKEN SAUTÉ WITH MADEIRA

Follow directions for **Chicken Scaloppine with Brandy Cream,** but use 3 tablespoons **Madeira,** port, or dry sherry instead of brandy (these liquors may not flame).

CHICKEN PIQUANT

Follow directions for **Chicken Scaloppine with Brandy Cream,** but use 2 tablespoons **lemon juice** instead of brandy. Omit cream. Place chicken and pan juices in a serving dish and garnish with 6 to 8 **canned rolled anchovy fillets with capers.**

Mexican-style Baked Chicken

Pictured on facing page

PREPARATION TIME: About 15 minutes
BAKING TIME: About 35 minutes for breasts; about 45 minutes for thighs
PER SERVING: 508 calories, 43 grams protein, 31 grams carbohydrate, 24 grams total fat, 211 milligrams cholesterol, 538 milligrams sodium

Westerners have long taken inspiration from the bold and colorful cuisine of neighboring Mexico. Sometimes cross-cultural recipes result, such as this baked chicken that's lavished with the trimmings of a tostada. (Suggested wine: dry Gewürztraminer or dry mellow Barbera)

Makes 6 servings

> 3 **whole chicken breasts (about 1 lb. *each*), skinned, boned, and split; or 12 chicken thighs (3 to 3½ lbs. *total*), skinned**
> 2 **large eggs**
> 1 **clove garlic, minced or pressed**
> **Purchased green chile salsa or taco sauce**
> 1½ **cups fine dry bread crumbs**
> 2 **teaspoons *each* chili powder and ground cumin**
> ½ **teaspoon ground oregano**
> 6 **tablespoons butter or margarine**
> 1 **large ripe avocado**
> 4 **to 6 cups shredded iceberg lettuce**
> **About 1 cup plain yogurt or sour cream**
> **About 6 tablespoons thinly sliced green onions (including tops)**
> 12 **to 18 cherry tomatoes**
> 1 **or 2 limes, cut into wedges**
> **Salt**

Rinse chicken and pat dry. Set aside.

In a shallow bowl, beat together eggs, garlic, and ¼ cup salsa. In another shallow bowl, combine bread crumbs, chili powder, cumin, and oregano. Dip 1 chicken piece in egg mixture to coat; drain briefly, then coat in crumb mixture. Shake off excess. Repeat with remaining chicken pieces.

Melt butter in a 10- by 15-inch rimmed baking pan in a 375° oven. Add chicken; turn to coat with butter. Bake, uncovered, until meat in thickest part is no longer pink (cut to test)—30 to 35 minutes for breasts, about 45 minutes for thighs.

Pit, peel, and slice avocado. Arrange chicken on a bed of shredded lettuce and top each piece with a dollop of yogurt or sour cream. Garnish with green onions, tomatoes, and lime wedges. Offer additional yogurt and salsa. Season chicken to taste with salt.

Chicken Breasts in Chutney Cream

PREPARATION TIME: About 10 minutes to pound breasts and organize; about 5 minutes to start rice
COOKING TIME: About 25 minutes for chicken; 30 to 35 minutes for rice
PER SERVING OF CHICKEN: 428 calories, 36 grams protein, 16 grams carbohydrate, 23 grams total fat, 150 milligrams cholesterol, 244 milligrams sodium
PER SERVING OF RICE: 182 calories, 2 grams protein, 28 grams carbohydrate, 6 grams total fat, 16 milligrams cholesterol, 62 milligrams sodium

The assertive flavors of ginger (both fresh and crystallized) and Major Grey chutney enliven these pounded, sautéed chicken breasts. Curry-seasoned rice makes a superb accompaniment; if you include it, start it cooking before you brown the chicken. (Suggested wine: dry Sauvignon Blanc or Fumé Blanc)

Makes 4 to 6 servings

> 3 **whole chicken breasts (about 1 lb. *each*), skinned, boned, and split**
> **About ¼ cup all-purpose flour**
> **About 6 tablespoons butter or margarine**
> 2 **green onions (including tops), finely chopped**
> ½ **teaspoon minced fresh ginger**
> 3 **tablespoons Major Grey chutney**
> ⅓ **cup Madeira**
> ¾ **cup Homemade Chicken Broth (page 58) or canned regular-strength chicken broth**
> ¾ **cup whipping cream**
> 2 **tablespoons chopped crystallized ginger**
> **Curried Rice (recipe follows)**
> **Parsley sprigs**
> **Salt**

Rinse chicken and pat dry. Place each breast half between pieces of plastic wrap and pound with a flat-surfaced mallet until about ¼ inch thick. Dust chicken pieces lightly with flour; shake off excess.

In a 10- to 12-inch frying pan, melt 3 tablespoons of the butter over medium-high heat. Add chicken, a portion at a time, without crowding. Cook, turning, until browned on both sides, 4 to 6 minutes. As chicken is cooked, lift from pan and arrange on a warm platter. Add more butter to pan as needed.

To pan, add onions, fresh ginger, chutney, Madeira, and broth. Boil over high heat, stirring, until reduced by half, about 5 minutes. Add cream and boil, stirring, until reduced to about 1¼ cups. Pour sauce over chicken and sprinkle with crystallized ginger. Spoon Curried Rice alongside chicken. Garnish with parsley; season to taste with salt.

CURRIED RICE. In a 10- to 12-inch frying pan or 2- to 3-quart pan, melt 3 tablespoons **butter** or margarine over medium heat. Add 1 small **onion,** chopped; cook, stirring, until onion is soft, about 5 minutes. Stir in 1 teaspoon **curry powder** and 1 cup **long-grain white rice.** Cook, stirring, until rice turns opaque, about 7 minutes. Add 1¼ cups **Homemade Chicken Broth** (page 58) or canned regular-strength chicken broth and 1¼ cups **water.** Bring to a boil; then reduce heat, cover, and simmer until rice is tender to bite and liquid is absorbed, about 20 minutes.

Mexican-style Baked Chicken (recipe on facing page) bakes in a crunchy, cumin-chili coating and arrives at the table decked out in colorful condiments: yogurt or sour cream, avocado, cherry tomatoes, lime wedges, and green onions. Pass the salsa and a basket of hot, crusty popovers to round out a festive Western meal.

Chicken Breasts Véronique

W E S T E R N   C L A S S I C

PREPARATION TIME: About 5 minutes to organize

COOKING TIME: About 25 minutes

PER SERVING: 357 calories, 46 grams protein, 13 grams carbohydrate, 13 grams total fat, 147 milligrams cholesterol, 176 milligrams sodium

---

To the French, Véronique *promises the exquisite addition of grapes, as in this elegant dish. But here—despite the classic name and ingredients—the technique is decidedly Western, a faster, fresher treatment than in the traditional recipe. The chicken is lightly browned, then briefly simmered; the grapes are quickly turned in the pan juices just until heated and glazed, then arranged—like glistening jewels—around the meat. (Suggested wine: mature, slightly oaked Chardonnay)*

Makes 4 to 6 servings

> **4 whole chicken breasts (about 1 lb.** *each***) skinned, boned, and split**
>
> **About 2 tablespoons butter or margarine**

1½ tablespoons orange marmalade

½ teaspoon dry tarragon

½ cup dry white wine

½ cup whipping cream

2 teaspoons *each* **cornstarch and water, stirred together**

1½ cups seedless green grapes

Salt

Rinse chicken and pat dry. Melt 2 tablespoons of the butter in a 10- to 12-inch frying pan over medium heat. Add chicken, a portion at a time, without crowding. Cook, turning as needed, until lightly browned on both sides, about 5 minutes. Add more butter to pan as needed.

Return all chicken to pan. Stir in marmalade, tarragon, and wine. Cover and simmer very gently until meat in thickest part is no longer pink (cut to test), 15 to 20 minutes. Transfer chicken to a serving dish; keep warm.

Stir cream into pan juices; bring to a rolling boil. Stir in cornstarch-water mixture; return to a boil, stirring. Mix in grapes, return to a boil, and immediately pour over chicken. Season to taste with salt.

Tamale Pie

When we ran our earliest recipe for tamale pie in 1929, the dish was already a household favorite. Over the years we've published many more recipes for this homey classic, almost all based—loosely—on the tamale. Our various tamale pies were usually casseroles lined (and sometimes topped) with cornmeal mush, polenta, or ground hominy and filled with ground beef, chicken, or leftover cooked meat. (In the 1930s, canned tamales baked with beans and sprinkled with cheese enjoyed great popularity.) Tamale pie, thus defined, was definitely not like anything one was apt to encounter in Mexico—or so we thought.

But on a recent trip to Yucatán, *Sunset* editors discovered a bona fide tamale pie. To speed up production of her chicken tamales (*mucbil-pollo*), the chef of the Hotel Hacienda Uxmal chose not to shape them individually. Instead, she lined a big pan with banana leaves, then added masa dough and filling to create a casserole. It's a guaranteed winner, even if you use foil instead of banana leaves.

Achiote, a condiment available in Mexican markets, adds mild flavor and deep red color to the pie. However, we've included some easy-to-make alternates if you can't find it.

Since 1929, Sunset has published 36 versions of tamale pie. It's a timeless Western classic. Even Mexico has used the idea, converting mucbil-pollo (chicken tamales) to this big casserole.

Mucbil-Pollo

4 ounces (½ cup) purchased achiote condiment or achiote paste (page 101); or achiote substitute (directions follow)

5 cups water

4 chicken bouillon cubes

⅛ teaspoon anise seeds

½ teaspoon dry mint

1 broiler-fryer chicken (4 lbs.), cut up

2 large firm-ripe tomatoes

2 medium-size onions, quartered

1 tablespoon dehydrated masa flour (corn tortilla flour) mixed with 3 tablespoons water (if using achiote substitute)

Double recipe Masa Dough (page 172)

4 hard-cooked large eggs, halved lengthwise

About 24 *each* radishes and green onions, ends trimmed

Put achiote condiment or paste in a 6- to 8-quart pan. Use a heavy spoon to work condiment into a smooth paste, gradually adding a little of the water and mixing until well blended. Add remaining water and bouillon cubes and bring to a boil. Reduce heat and simmer, uncovered, for about 10 minutes, then pour liquid through a fine wire strainer and return to pan; discard residue in strainer. (If you are using achiote substitute, it is not necessary to strain the broth.)

To broth, add anise seeds, mint, and chicken, placing chicken on top. Bring to a boil, reduce heat, cover, and simmer for 45 minutes; do not stir.

Core tomatoes and cut each into 6 wedges. After chicken has cooked for 25 minutes, add onions. After 10 more minutes, add tomatoes alongside onions.

At end of cooking time, remove pan from heat. Gently lift out vegetables and chicken, letting broth drain back into pan. When chicken is cool to touch, remove and discard skin and bones. Tear meat into bite-size pieces.

Boil broth over highest heat, uncovered, until reduced to 2 cups; stir to prevent sticking. (If using achiote substitute, add masa flour–water mixture and return to a boil, stirring.) Remove from heat.

Grease a 3-quart shallow casserole; evenly spread about half the Masa Dough (you need 5 cups dough *total*) over bottom and sides of casserole, flush with rim. Add chicken, tomatoes, onions, and eggs, distributing evenly, then cover with broth. Shake dish gently to level filling.

Gently spoon dollops of remaining dough on top, then spread carefully to enclose filling; don't worry if a few thin areas develop and bits of filling show. Cover tightly with foil. Bake on lowest rack of a 425° oven for 30 minutes; remove foil and continue to bake until top is golden brown, about 1 more hour.

Remove from oven and let stand for at least 10 minutes before serving. Accompany with radishes and green onions. Makes 8 servings.

ACHIOTE SUBSTITUTE. Mix 2 tablespoons **vinegar**, 3 tablespoons **paprika**, 1½ teaspoons **dry oregano leaves**, 3 cloves **garlic** (pressed), and ½ teaspoon **ground cumin.**

Hot & Sour Chicken

PREPARATION TIME: 5 to 10 minutes
COOKING TIME: 8 to 10 minutes
PER SERVING: 432 calories, 34 grams protein, 13 grams carbohydrate, 27 grams total fat, 79 milligrams cholesterol, 336 milligrams sodium

In China's Hunan province, people like their food peppery hot. In this lively dish, shared with us by the owners of San Francisco's Hunan Restaurant, we have moderated the amount of red chile. (Suggested wine: dry Sauvignon Blanc)

Makes 2 or 3 servings

- 1¼ to 1½ **pounds chicken breasts, skinned and boned**
- 2 teaspoons *each* **cornstarch, dry sherry, and salad oil**
- ¼ teaspoon **pepper**
- 4 to 5 tablespoons **salad oil**
- 1 tablespoon finely chopped **garlic**
- 2 teaspoons finely chopped **fresh ginger**
- 1 tablespoon **fermented salted black beans, rinsed and patted dry**
- 1 small **green bell pepper, stemmed, seeded, and cut into 1-inch squares**
- 1 medium-size **carrot, thinly sliced**
- 1 can (about 8 oz.) sliced **bamboo shoots, drained**
- **Cooking Sauce** (recipe follows)

Rinse chicken, pat dry, and cut into ¾-inch cubes. Mix chicken with cornstarch, sherry, the 2 teaspoons salad oil, and pepper.

Pour 4 tablespoons salad oil into a wok or 10- to 12-inch frying pan over high heat. When oil is hot, add chicken mixture; cook, stirring, for 2 minutes. Add 1 more tablespoon oil, if needed; then add garlic, ginger, and black beans. Cook, stirring constantly, until chicken is lightly browned, about 2 more minutes. Then add bell pepper, carrot, and bamboo shoots; cook, stirring, for 2 minutes. Stir in sauce. Cook, stirring, until sauce boils and thickens.

COOKING SAUCE. Stir together 2 teaspoons **cornstarch**, ½ teaspoon **crushed dried hot red chiles**, 2 tablespoons **soy sauce**, 2½ tablespoons **white wine vinegar**, and ½ cup **Homemade Chicken Broth** (page 58) or canned regular-strength chicken broth.

Burmese Chicken Curry

PREPARATION TIME: About 30 minutes
COOKING TIME: About 1 hour
PER SERVING: 734 calories, 49 grams protein, 75 grams carbohydrate, 25 grams total fat, 86 milligrams cholesterol, 115 milligrams sodium

Curries are featured in every cuisine of Southeast Asia. Some reflect India's influence; others, like this one from Burma, have a definite character of their own. Let guests assemble their own servings, tailoring the curry to taste with crushed red chiles, hard-cooked eggs, fresh cilantro, green onions, lemon wedges, and crisp noodles. An exciting mix of flavors and textures is part of the curry experience. (Suggested wine: dry Gewürztraminer or Chenin Blanc)

Makes 10 to 12 servings

- ¾ **cup yellow split peas**
- 1½ **cups water**
- ½ **cup salad oil**
- ¼ teaspoon **ground turmeric**
- 3 large **onions, chopped**
- 3 or 4 cloves **garlic, minced or pressed**
- 2 tablespoons finely chopped or crushed **fresh ginger**
- 1 teaspoon **cayenne**
- 2 tablespoons **curry powder**
- ½ teaspoon **ground cumin**
- 6 whole **chicken breasts** (about 1 lb. *each*), skinned, boned, and cut into ½-inch-thick, 3-inch-long strips
- 1 **bay leaf**
- 1 **cinnamon stick** (2 inches long)
- 8 cups **Homemade Chicken Broth** (page 58) or canned regular-strength chicken broth
- 1½ cups **coconut milk, homemade** (page 209), canned, or thawed frozen
- **Fish sauce** *(nam pla)* or salt
- **Boiled noodles** (directions follow)
- **Crushed dried hot red chiles** (optional)
- **Condiments** (suggestions follow)

In a blender, whirl split peas until finely ground. Mix with water. Set aside.

Pour oil into an 8- to 10-quart pan over low heat. When oil is warm, stir in turmeric and cook, stirring, for about 1 minute (do not allow to burn). Add onions; cook, stirring occasionally, until very soft but not browned, about 20 minutes. Add garlic, ginger, cayenne, curry powder, and cumin; cook, stirring, for about 1 minute. Stir in chicken, bay leaf, and cinnamon stick.

Add broth, then stir in split pea mixture and coconut milk. Bring to a boil; reduce heat, cover, and simmer, stirring often, until broth thickens, about 30 minutes. Add fish sauce to taste. If made ahead, let cool, then cover and refrigerate for up to 1 day; reheat, covered, over low heat. Let guests spoon curry over noodles, then top with chiles (if desired) and condiments.

BOILED NOODLES. In an 8- to 10-quart pan, bring 4 to 5 quarts **water** to boil. Add 2 pounds **dry Chinese noodles** or dry vermicelli; cook until tender to bite, 6 to 9 minutes. Drain. Rinse with **warm water**, drain, and mix with ¼ cup **salad oil**. Serve at room temperature. If made ahead, cover and let stand for up to 2 hours. Mound in a bowl to serve.

CONDIMENTS. Arrange in separate bowls: about 2 cups **fresh cilantro (coriander) leaves**; 2 cups thinly sliced **green onions** (including tops); 6 **hard-cooked large eggs**, thinly sliced; 2 to 3 cups **canned crisp-fried chow mein noodles**; and 2 **lemons**, cut into small wedges.

A cool choice for a summer meal, Steeped Chicken with Basil Dressing (recipe on facing page) is a colorful salad of moist and tender white meat and sliced tomatoes. A bright basil vinaigrette and sprigs of cilantro provide finishing touches of flavor.

Chicken & Vegetable One-pot Meal

W E S T E R N   C L A S S I C

PREPARATION TIME: About 1 hour
COOKING TIME: At the table
PER SERVING: 297 calories, 34 grams protein, 30 grams carbohydrate, 6 grams total fat, 61 milligrams cholesterol, 211 milligrams sodium

Gathered round this communal pot of simmering broth, your guests select and cook their own dinner. When the food is cooked, in at most a minute or two, they fish it out, a bite at a time, and dip it into a simple peanut sauce. (Suggested wine: soft Sauvignon Blanc)

Makes 4 to 6 servings

- 1½ **to 2 pounds skinned, boned chicken breasts**
- 1½ **to 2 pounds mustard greens, washed, tough stems trimmed off, and leaves chilled**
- **Mushroom Bundles (directions follow) or ½ pound small (about 1-inch-diameter) button mushrooms, stems trimmed**
- **Carrot Bundles (directions follow)**
- **Spinach Rolls (directions follow)**
- 12 **cups Homemade Chicken Broth (page 58) or 2 large cans (49½ oz. *each*) regular-strength chicken broth**
- ½ **cup finely chopped green onions (white part only)**
- 2 **limes, *each* cut into 4 wedges**
- 1 **tablespoon crushed dried hot red chiles**
- **Peanut Sauce (recipe follows)**

Rinse chicken, pat dry, and cut into 1- by 2-inch strips no thicker than 1 inch. Arrange separately on a large tray (or 2 small ones) the chicken, mustard greens, Mushroom Bundles, Carrot Bundles, and Spinach Rolls. (At this point, you may cover and refrigerate until next day. If using regular mushrooms, rinse and add to platter just before serving.)

Place a 5- to 6-quart pan with a heat source in the center of a table within easy reach of all. You may use an electric wok or deep electric frying pan, an electric hot plate, or a butane-fueled tabletop burner. (With an independent heat source, you will also need a table-presentable pan.) In the kitchen, bring broth to a boil. Add to serving pan on the table; adjust heat to keep broth simmering. Place tray of foods alongside. Place onions, limes, and chiles in separate containers alongside tray. Invite guests to add foods to broth. Lift out vegetables when hot, about 1 minute. Lift out chicken when it turns white and is firm when pressed, about 2 minutes.

Flavor Peanut Sauce to taste with onions, a squeeze of lime, and chiles. Dip vegetables and chicken into sauce to eat. When guests have eaten all they want, turn off heat under broth. Ladle hot broth into cups, add Peanut Sauce to taste, and sip broth.

MUSHROOM BUNDLES. Divide 2 bags (3½ oz. *each*) **enoki mushrooms** into 6 equal portions, laying mushrooms parallel.

Cut 6 **green stems** (tops) from about 2 **green onions;** reserve white part to chop (see preceding recipe). Immerse stems until limp in **boiling water,** about 30 seconds; drain and let cool. Tie each portion of mushrooms with an onion stem. Cut off and discard brown, woody ends of mushrooms.

CARROT BUNDLES. Peel and trim ends from 2 medium-size **carrots.** Cut each carrot crosswise into thirds; cut each third into thin sticks. Divide into 12 equal portions and lay sticks parallel. Cut 12 **green stems** (tops) from about 4 **green onions;** reserve white part to chop (see preceding recipe). Immerse stems in **boiling water** until limp, about 30 seconds; drain and let cool. Tie each portion of carrots with an onion stem.

SPINACH ROLLS. Wash 2 pounds **spinach;** discard stems and wilted leaves. Set spinach aside.

In a 5- to 6-quart pan, bring about 3 inches water to a boil. Cut 4 large outer **napa cabbage** leaves, 9 to 10 inches each, free at base (save remainder of head for other uses). Immerse leaves in **boiling water** until limp, about 2 minutes. Lift cabbage from water; drain, lay flat, and pat dry. Trim thick part of rib from center of each leaf, making a V-shaped cut.

Add spinach to boiling water and cook until limp, about 2 minutes; drain. Let cool; firmly squeeze out moisture with your hands.

On a muslin towel, lay 2 cabbage leaves side by side (stems in opposite directions), with edges overlapping several inches. Lay half the spinach in an even row along outer edge of cabbage leaves. Form a compact roll by lifting cloth with one hand (from spinach side); smooth roll with other hand. Make roll tight so it will hold its shape when heated in broth. Form another roll with remaining cabbage and spinach. Cut rolls crosswise into 1½-inch slices.

PEANUT SAUCE. Smoothly blend ⅔ cup **cream-style peanut butter,** 2 tablespoons **soy sauce,** 4 teaspoons **distilled white vinegar,** and 2 teaspoons **sugar.** Slowly whisk in 1 cup **Homemade Chicken Broth** (page 58) or canned regular-strength chicken broth. Serve sauce in a pitcher. Makes 1¾ cups.

Per Tablespoon: 40 calories, 2 grams protein, 2 grams carbohydrate, 3 grams total fat, 0 milligram cholesterol, 124 milligrams sodium.

Steeped Chicken with Basil Dressing

Pictured on facing page

PREPARATION TIME: 10 to 15 minutes to make salad; 5 to 10 minutes to make dressing
CHILLING TIME: At least 30 minutes to crisp lettuce
STEEPING TIME: About 20 minutes
PER SERVING: 181 calories, 35 grams protein, 4 grams carbohydrate, 2 grams total fat, 86 milligrams cholesterol, 103 milligrams sodium

Gentler than poaching, steeping is a classic Chinese method of cooking in hot water without direct heat. A cool, light, and appetizing entrée, this chicken salad with fresh basil shows off the moist, smooth-textured results of cooking poultry by this technique. (Suggested wine: Grignolino Rosé or dry Zinfandel Blanc)

Makes 4 servings

> 2 **whole chicken breasts (about 1 lb.** *each*), **split**
> 2 **thin slices** *each* **lemon and onion**
> 1 **thin, quarter-size slice fresh ginger**
> 3 **parsley or fresh thyme sprigs**
> **Lettuce leaves, washed and crisped**
> 3 **large ripe tomatoes, cored and thinly sliced**
> **Fresh basil or cilantro (coriander) leaves**
> **Basil Dressing (recipe follows)**

Rinse chicken and pat dry. Place in a 4- to 5-quart pan; pour in enough water to cover chicken by 1 to 2 inches. Lift out chicken; add lemon, onion, ginger, and parsley to water.

Cover pan and bring water to a rolling boil over high heat. Remove from heat and immediately immerse chicken in water. Cover pan tightly and let stand for 18 to 20 minutes. Remove lid and quickly check doneness by cutting to center of thickest part of chicken; meat should no longer be pink. If chicken is not done, return to hot water, cover, and let steep for a few more minutes.

Drain chicken; plunge into ice water to cool quickly. When cool, gently peel off skin and remove meat from bones, keeping chicken pieces whole. Discard skin and bones. (At this point, you may cover and refrigerate chicken until next day.)

Line ends of a platter with lettuce; arrange tomato slices on top. Slice chicken across the grain about ½ inch thick; arrange in center of platter. Garnish with basil leaves. Drizzle chicken and tomatoes with a little Basil Dressing. Offer remaining dressing to add to individual servings.

BASIL DRESSING. In a blender or food processor, combine 1 cup lightly packed **fresh basil leaves** (or 3 tablespoons dry basil and ¼ cup chopped parsley), 2 cloves **garlic,** ¼ cup **white wine vinegar,** ½ cup **olive oil** or salad oil, 2 tablespoons freshly grated **Parmesan cheese,** and ⅛ teaspoon **pepper.** Whirl until puréed. Makes about 1 cup.

Per Tablespoon: 65 calories, .37 gram protein, .72 gram carbohydrate, 7 grams total fat, .49 milligram cholesterol, 12 milligrams sodium.

Chicken & Asian Pear Salad with Mint

PREPARATION TIME: About 10 minutes

CHILLING TIME: At least 30 minutes to crisp lettuce

STEEPING TIME: About 20 minutes

PER SERVING: 436 calories, 36 grams protein, 38 grams carbohydrate, 16 grams total fat, 87 milligram cholesterol, 130 milligrams sodium

Crisp, juicy Asian pears are just one of the many ethnic foods Sunset has helped guide into the market mainstream. First, we offered tips for finding these delightful "pear-apples" in Asian markets; when the first major domestic crop was harvested in 1984, we ran a big feature article on the fruit (and even presented it on our cover). Today, you'll find Asian pears in more and more Western supermarkets. (Suggested wine: brut or extra-dry Champagne)

Makes 2 servings

> 1 whole chicken breast (about 1 lb.), split
> ½ cup rice vinegar or white wine vinegar
> 1½ tablespoons sugar (¼ cup if using wine vinegar)
> 3 tablespoons chopped fresh mint
> Lettuce leaves, washed and crisped
> 2 medium-size (2½- to 3-inch-diameter) Asian pears, peeled if desired and thinly sliced crosswise through core
> Fresh mint sprigs

Rinse chicken and pat dry. Steep, cool, bone, and skin as directed for Steeped Chicken with Basil Dressing (page 131), using a 3- to 4-quart pan. Cut meat diagonally into thin slices. (At this point, you may cover and refrigerate until next day.)

Mix vinegar, sugar, and chopped mint until sugar is dissolved. Line 2 dinner plates with lettuce; arrange pear slices and chicken on lettuce. Pour mint dressing over, then garnish with mint sprigs.

Vietnamese Chicken Salad

PREPARATION TIME: About 5 minutes to make dressing; about 10 minutes to cut up ingredients; about 10 minutes to fry shrimp chips

CHILLING TIME: At least 30 minutes

PER SERVING WITHOUT SHRIMP CHIPS: 156 calories, 15 grams protein, 16 grams carbohydrate, 4 grams total fat, 42 milligrams cholesterol, 506 milligrams sodium

A fairly recent arrival to the U.S., Vietnamese cuisine is light, fresh, delicately flavored—and popular with Westerners (some call it the nouvelle cuisine of Southeast Asia). This minted chicken salad is a fine example of the country's refreshing cookery. (Suggested wine: dry white wine with sparkling water)

Makes 4 to 6 servings

> 1 medium-size onion, thinly sliced
> 3 tablespoons *each* sugar and distilled white vinegar
> ¼ teaspoon pepper
> Salad oil
> About 36 small (2-inch) oval shrimp chips or prawn crackers
> 2 tablespoons lime juice
> 2 tablespoons fish sauce (*nuoc mam* or *nam pla*) or soy sauce
> 1 clove garlic, minced or pressed
> 4 cups finely shredded green cabbage
> 2 cups *each* shredded carrots and shredded cooked chicken
> ⅓ cup thinly slivered fresh mint

In a bowl, mix onion, sugar, vinegar, and pepper. Cover and refrigerate for at least 30 minutes or until next day.

Meanwhile, in a deep 3- to 4-quart pan, heat about 1 inch of oil to 350°F on a deep-frying thermometer. Add 3 or 4 shrimp chips at a time and cook just until puffy, only a few seconds. Remove chips and drain on paper towels. If made ahead, store airtight for up to 1 day.

Stir lime juice, fish sauce, garlic, and ¼ cup salad oil into marinated onion; then stir in cabbage, carrots, and chicken. Spoon into a serving dish and sprinkle with mint; offer shrimp chips as an accompaniment.

Sesame Chicken Salad

PREPARATION TIME: 20 to 25 minutes

STEEPING TIME: About 20 minutes

PER SERVING: 416 calories, 35 grams protein, 23 grams carbohydrate, 21 grams total fat, 94 milligrams cholesterol, 1175 milligrams sodium

This Oriental-style main-dish salad combines shredded chicken, toasted sesame seeds, and colorful, crisp vegetables. A soy-ginger dressing adds zest. (Suggested wine: dry white wine with sparkling water)

Makes 4 servings

> 2 whole chicken breasts (about 1 lb. *each*), split
> 3 tablespoons sesame seeds
> 2 green onions (including tops)
> 6 large stalks celery, cut into thin diagonal slices (about 3 cups)
> 3 medium-size red bell peppers, stemmed, seeded, and cut into thin strips about 3 inches long
> Soy Dressing (recipe follows)
> 4 small celery stalks with leaves

Rinse chicken and pat dry. Steep, cool, bone, and skin chicken as directed for Steeped Chicken with Basil Dressing (page 131). Tear meat into shreds. (At this point, you may cover and refrigerate until next day.)

Toast sesame seeds in a 6- to 7-inch frying pan over medium heat until golden, about 2 minutes, shaking pan frequently. Set aside. Trim off and discard ends of onions, then cut onions into 3-inch pieces; cut each piece lengthwise into thin shreds. Set aside.

Mix chicken with sliced celery, bell peppers, and dressing. Mound equal portions of chicken mixture on 4 dinner plates. Sprinkle with onion shreds and sesame seeds. Garnish with small celery stalks.

SOY DRESSING. Stir together 6 tablespoons **rice vinegar** (or 6 tablespoons white wine vinegar mixed with 1½ tablespoons sugar), 3 tablespoons **soy sauce,** 2 tablespoons **sugar,** 1 tablespoon **Oriental sesame oil** (optional), 1½ tablespoons minced **fresh ginger,** and 1 clove **garlic,** pressed or minced.

Turkey Tonnato

PREPARATION TIME: About 5 minutes to make breast oven-ready
BAKING TIME: 1½ to 2 hours
CHILLING TIME: At least 4 hours to chill turkey; at least 4 hours to chill sauce
PER SERVING: 476 calories, 61 grams protein, 4 grams carbohydrate, 23 grams total fat, 297 milligrams cholesterol, 348 milligrams sodium

In this imaginative, simplified variation on Italy's classic vitello tonnato, *economical turkey breast replaces veal— and the breast is baked, not poached. To make the traditional tuna sauce lighter, simply omit the mayonnaise. (Suggested wine: Fumé Blanc)*

Makes 6 to 8 servings

> 1 boned, rolled, and tied turkey breast (3½ to 5 lbs.)
> 1 small onion, finely chopped
> ½ cup dry white wine
> 2 tablespoons butter or margarine, melted
> 1 can (7 oz.) water- or oil-packed tuna, drained
> 2 tablespoons *each* drained capers and lemon juice
> 1 clove garlic
> ½ cup mayonnaise (optional)
> 3 or 4 hard-cooked large eggs, halved
> 3 medium-size firm-ripe tomatoes, cored and cut into wedges
> Watercress sprigs

Place turkey, skin up, in a 9- by 13-inch baking pan (not on a rack). Mix onion, wine, and butter; pour over meat.

Bake, uncovered, in a 325° oven until a meat thermometer inserted in center registers 165°F. Allow 20 to 25 minutes per pound—about 1½ hours *total* for a 3½-pound breast, 2½ hours *total* for a 5-pound

breast. Baste several times with pan drippings. Remove turkey from oven, let cool, and wrap airtight. Refrigerate for at least 4 hours or up to 2 days.

Skim and discard fat from pan juices. Scrape free browned bits on pan bottom, then pour juices into a measuring cup. Add water if needed to make ½ cup. In a blender or food processor, purée tuna, capers, lemon juice, and garlic. Add a little of the pan juices to keep mixture moving, then add any remaining juices when puréed. Pour into a serving dish and stir in mayonnaise (if used), then cover and refrigerate for at least 4 hours or up to 2 days.

Discard strings and skin from turkey roast; thinly slice meat and arrange on a platter. Surround with eggs, tomatoes, and watercress. Offer tuna sauce to spoon over individual portions.

Barbecued Turkey Breast Steaks

W E S T E R N   C L A S S I C

PREPARATION TIME: 30 to 40 minutes to ignite charcoal; about 10 minutes to make sauces
GRILLING TIME: 5 to 8 minutes
PER SERVING: 256 calories, 47 grams protein, 0 gram carbohydrate, 6 grams total fat, 123 milligrams cholesterol, 133 milligrams sodium

Lean, tender, and thrifty, turkey is a family favorite too good to limit to holiday menus. Convenient turkey breast steaks are ideal for the barbecue; quickly grilled, they turn out moist and delicious. Serve the steaks plain, or accent them with fresh tomato salsa and creamy garbanzo-bean dressing. (Suggested wine: dry Sauvignon Blanc or dry Zinfandel Blanc)

Makes 3 or 4 servings

> 1½ to 2 pounds boned and skinned turkey breast, cut into ½- to ¾-inch-thick steaks
> Olive oil or salad oil
> Salt and pepper
> Lemon wedges
> Garbanzo Dressing (page 212)
> Fresh Tomato Salsa (recipe follows)

Brush turkey with oil. Arrange on a grill 4 to 6 inches above a solid bed of hot coals (you should be able to hold your hand at grill level for no more than 2 to 3 seconds). Cook, turning as needed, until lightly browned on both sides and no longer pink in center (cut to test), 5 to 8 minutes. Season to taste with salt, pepper, and lemon. Serve with Garbanzo Dressing and salsa.

FRESH TOMATO SALSA. In a bowl, combine 1 large firm-ripe **tomato,** cored and chopped (including juice); ¼ cup chopped **fresh green California (Anaheim) chile;** 3 tablespoons *each* minced **green onions** (including tops), **salad oil,** and **red wine vinegar;** and 1 tablespoon chopped **fresh cilantro (coriander).** Season to taste with **salt** and **pepper.** If made ahead, cover and refrigerate for up to 1 day. Makes 1½ cups.
PER ¼ CUP: 72 calories, .50 gram protein, 3 grams carbohydrate, 7 grams total fat, 0 milligram cholesterol, 5 milligrams sodium.

Turkey & Green Chile Tumble

PREPARATION TIME: 20 to 25 minutes
CHILLING TIME: At least 30 minutes to crisp lettuce
COOKING TIME: 5 to 8 minutes
PER APPETIZER SERVING: 156 calories, 12 grams protein, 5 grams carbohydrate, 10 grams total fat, 38 milligrams cholesterol, 330 milligrams sodium

When ground turkey became widely available in supermarkets, Westerners were quick to use this leaner, lighter product in dishes traditionally made with ground beef or pork. In this recipe, turkey joins a hot and lively Chinese stir-fry, which is spooned onto chilled lettuce leaves, rolled, and eaten out of hand. (Suggested wine: crisp, dry Sauvignon Blanc)

Makes 4 to 6 appetizer servings or 2 entrée servings

- ¾ **pound ground turkey**
- 1 **large egg white**
- 2 **tablespoons dry sherry**
- 1 **teaspoon** *each* **sugar, cornstarch, and soy sauce**
- 1 **clove garlic, minced or pressed**
- 2 **tablespoons salad oil**
- 4 to 6 **tablespoons canned diced green chiles**
- 1 **tablespoon grated fresh ginger**
  Cooking Sauce (recipe follows)
- 4 **green onions (including tops), thinly sliced**
  Salt
  About 36 small butter lettuce or romaine leaves, washed and crisped
- 1 **cup lightly packed fresh cilantro (coriander) sprigs (optional)**

Mix turkey with egg white, sherry, sugar, cornstarch, soy, and garlic.

Pour oil into a 10- to 12-inch frying pan or wok over high heat. When oil is hot, add turkey mixture, chiles, and ginger; cook, stirring, until meat is no longer pink, 3 to 4 minutes. Add Cooking Sauce and onions; cook, stirring, until sauce thickens and boils, about 1 minute. Season to taste with salt.

Pour meat mixture into a serving dish and accompany with lettuce and cilantro, if desired. To eat, wrap hot turkey mixture and cilantro in lettuce.

COOKING SAUCE. Stir together 1 teaspoon **cornstarch**, 1 tablespoon *each* **water** and **dry sherry**, and 2 teaspoons **soy sauce.**

Tea-smoked Duck

Pictured on facing page

PREPARATION TIME: 20 to 25 minutes
SMOKING TIME: About 40 minutes
ROASTING TIME: About 2½ hours
PER SERVING: 832 calories, 47 grams protein, 2 grams carbohydrate, 69 grams total fat, 205 milligrams cholesterol, 879 milligrams sodium

All of China loves duck and prepares it in ways that are deservedly celebrated the world around. Szechwan cooks smoke duck over tea leaves, then steam and deep-fry it. We've shortened and simplified the procedure—you roast the duck after smoking it, achieving the same crisp succulence with a subtle, fruity smokiness. Look for hoisin sauce, Szechwan peppercorns, and dried tangerine peel in Asian markets; many large supermarkets also carry these items. (Suggested wine: full-bodied Merlot)

Makes 2 or 3 servings

- 1 **duck (about 4 lbs.), thawed if frozen**
- 1 **teaspoon salt**
- 1 **tablespoon Szechwan peppercorns**
- 2 **tablespoons dry sherry**
- ¼ **cup** *each* **rice, firmly packed brown sugar, and black tea leaves**
- 2 **tablespoons coarsely chopped orange peel or 2 tablespoons dried tangerine peel**
- 6 **thin, quarter-size slices fresh ginger, crushed**
- 5 **green onions (including tops)**
  Brown-and-serve rolls or steamed buns
  Hoisin sauce
  Fresh cilantro (coriander) sprigs

Remove duck neck and giblets; reserve for other uses. Rinse duck inside and out and pat dry. Trim off and discard excess neck skin; also discard lumps of fat. With a fork, pierce skin all over duck.

In a 6- to 7-inch frying pan over medium-low heat, cook salt and peppercorns, shaking pan often, until salt begins to brown and peppercorns become fragrant, about 10 minutes. Let cool, then coarsely crush with a mortar and pestle or a rolling pin. Combine mixture with sherry; rub over duck, inside and out.

To smoke duck, you'll need a wok at least 14 inches in diameter (*do not* use an electric wok with a nonstick finish). Line wok with heavy foil. Add rice, sugar, tea leaves, and orange peel; stir together. Position a round cake rack or steamer rack (about 9-inch diameter) in bottom of wok, at least 1 inch above tea mixture. Set duck on rack; place wok over high heat.

When mixture begins to smoke, cover pan tightly and smoke for 5 minutes. Reduce heat to medium and continue to smoke, without uncovering wok, for 15 minutes. Turn off heat and leave covered until smoke subsides, about 15 more minutes. Remove duck; discard tea mixture. (At this point, you may cover and refrigerate until next day.) Place ginger and 2 of the onions inside body cavity; fasten opening shut with a small skewer, if necessary. Place duck, breast down, on a rack in a 12- by 15-inch roasting pan. Roast, uncovered, in a 350° oven for 1½ hours. Drain and discard fat from pan and turn bird over;

China's celebrated Tea-smoked Duck (recipe on facing page) is traditionally enjoyed as an extraordinarily succulent sandwich. Use steamed buns —or brown-and-serve rolls.

continue to roast until thigh feels soft when pressed, 45 to 60 more minutes. Drain and discard all fat from pan. Increase oven temperature to 450°; return duck to oven and roast just until skin is crisp, about 5 more minutes.

Meanwhile, place rolls slightly apart in a pan on a rack set inside a wok over simmering water. Cover and steam until hot, 5 to 10 minutes.

Slice duck meat from bones; cut remaining 3 onions into thin slivers. Place duck slices in a warm roll; top with onions, hoisin, and cilantro, then close and eat out of hand.

Duck with Green Olives

PREPARATION TIME: About 15 minutes
COOKING TIME: About 2 hours
PER SERVING: 852 calories, 42 grams protein, 10 grams carbohydrate, 71 grams total fat, 172 milligrams cholesterol, 1139 milligrams sodium

From our appetizing research for Sunset's *first French cook book—which involved months of gathering simple, wonderful recipes from skilled home cooks—comes this tender braised duck bedecked with olives. (Suggested wine: young Barbera or Zinfandel)*

Makes 3 or 4 servings

1 duck (4½ to 5 lbs.), thawed if frozen
1 medium-size onion, finely chopped

2 large cloves garlic, minced or pressed
½ cup canned tomato sauce
2½ cups water or regular-strength beef broth
1 can (6 oz. drained weight) pitted green ripe olives, drained
1 jar (3 oz. drained weight) Spanish-style pitted green olives (with or without pimentos), drained
Salt

Remove duck neck and giblets. Reserve duck neck for other uses; rinse giblets and set aside. Cut duck into serving-size pieces; pull off and discard lumps of fat. Rinse duck pieces; pat dry.

Place all duck pieces (including giblets) in a 12- to 14-inch frying pan over medium-low heat. Cook, uncovered, turning pieces as needed, until well browned, about 45 minutes. Remove duck from pan and set aside. Pour off and discard all but ¼ cup of the drippings.

To drippings in pan, add onion and garlic; cook, stirring, until onion is soft. Add tomato sauce, water, and all olives; stir well. Return duck to pan, reduce heat to low, cover, and simmer until meat is tender when pierced, about 1 hour. Skim and discard fat; season to taste with salt.

Smoke-cooking in Your Covered Barbecue

If you have a covered barbecue, you can produce moist, succulent smoked poultry and fish that taste just as rich and delicious as costly commercial products. The technique is simple. You begin by soaking foods in a spicy-sweet brine to promote a moist texture and sweeten the smoky flavor. (If unbrined, smoked food may have an acrid taste.) When you're ready to cook, you ignite the coals and arrange them so they are not directly under the food, then top with wet wood chips. The wood's fragrant smoke flavors the food as it cooks.

Serve the food hot from the smoker, or prepare it in advance to enjoy cool or chilled. When you plan your cooking schedule, keep in mind that larger foods (such as turkey and other poultry) require 10 to 20 hours of brining.

BASIC EQUIPMENT AND FUEL. Only a few pieces of equipment are required: a barbecue with a lid and air vents to help regulate heat, an oven thermometer, tongs, and a metal pan (or another barbecue). You'll also need wet wood chips and 2-inch-size charcoal briquets.

Mesquite charcoal (not to be confused with mesquite wood or mesquite chips for smoking) doesn't work well for smoking foods, since you need at least 5 pounds (7¼ quarts) to get an even heat pattern—and this provides too much heat for smoking. But either fuel is fine for regular barbecue cooking; use an equal volume of mesquite or regular briquets (not weight, as mesquite is lighter) to get equal heat.

THE WOOD. Your choice of wood depends on the flavor you prefer; hickory, alder, mesquite, cherry, and apple wood are all popular. Hickory and alder add a delicate, sweet flavor; mesquite has a woodsy character; and the fruit woods really do lend fruity overtones.

Buy wood chips, small bits, or shavings. Check the instructions for individual foods to find out what quantity you need, then soak the wood before using: place the chips in a container, add warm water to cover, and let stand for at least 20 minutes. (Chips will float, so stir occasionally.) Drain before using.

THE BASIC TECHNIQUE. Begin with a specific number of briquets.

The exact amount depends on the size of your barbecue. Use 20 briquets for a 26-inch round or 19- by 33-inch rectangular barbecue; 16 briquets for a 22-inch round barbecue; and 14 briquets for an 18-inch round barbecue.

Open the barbecue's air vents and ignite the briquets on the fire grate. When they're covered with gray ash (in 30 to 40 minutes), use tongs to transfer 4 of them to a metal pan (or another barbecue). Push half the remaining coals to each side of the grate; add 2 or 3 fresh briquets to each mound of coals. Set a drip pan in the center of the grate, if required (see instructions for specific foods).

Set the barbecue grill about 6 inches above the fire grate. Place your choice of foods in the center of the grill; no part of the food should extend over the coals. Put an oven thermometer in the center of the grill (*not* over coals). Place the designated amount of wet wood chips on each pile of coals, then set the barbecue lid in place. Partially close the air vents. (When the vents are wide open, the fuel burns hottest; when they're closed, it's extinguished.)

After 20 minutes, check the temperature; adjust the heat as necessary to keep the temperature at the correct level (see instructions for specific foods). If the barbecue is too cool, add 2 to 4 of the reserved ignited briquets and open the vents. If it's too hot, remove 2 to 4 hot coals and reserve.

Continue to check and adjust the temperature every 30 minutes. To keep the temperature constant, also add 2 or 3 fresh briquets to each pile of coals every 30 minutes, along with more wet wood chips as directed. Quickly recover barbecue to minimize heat loss.

THE BRINE. Both poultry and fish are soaked in the same brine. To make it, you need an 8- to 10-quart (or larger) noncorrodible container (glass or stainless steel); or use any suitably large pan, lined with an 8- to 13-gallon plastic bag.

In container, combine 12 cups **cool water,** 2 cups firmly packed **brown sugar,** 1½ cups **salt,** 2 teaspoons **whole black peppercorns,** and 4 **bay leaves.** Stir briskly until salt and sugar are dissolved. Add foods, making sure they are submerged. Cover and refrigerate for the designated time (see instructions for specific foods).

Lift food from brine and rinse thoroughly under a slow stream of **cool water,** rubbing gently to release salt. Pat food dry; set on a rack over pan and let dry until surface feels tacky. (At this point, you may cover and refrigerate brined food until next day.)

Food choices

Turkey and chicken are ideal candidates for this method of smoking. So is firm-fleshed fish (see Smoked Salmon, page 144).

SMOKED TURKEY. Select a 12- to 16-pound **turkey,** thawed if frozen. Remove neck and giblets; reserve for other uses. Pull off and discard lumps of fat. Rinse bird inside and out; pat dry.

Prepare a double recipe of **brine;** brine bird for 18 to 20 hours. Rinse and let dry as directed.

To smoke, place a drip pan on fire grate between mounds of ignited coals. Set turkey over pan; set thermometer on or beside turkey. Adjust barbecue to keep temperature at 180° to 200°F. You'll need 4 cups **soaked hickory wood chips** *total.* Begin by scattering 1 cup wet chips evenly over coals; add about 1 cup more wet chips to coals every 30 minutes until all are used. Smoke until a meat thermometer inserted in thickest part of breast (not touching bone) registers 170°F, 5 to 7 hours.

Serve turkey warm, cool, or chilled. To store, wrap airtight and refrigerate for up to 2 weeks, or freeze for up to 6 months (thaw to serve). Makes 16 to 24 main-dish servings.

SMOKED CHICKEN. Use 2 **broiler-fryer chickens** (3½ to 4 lbs. *each*). Remove necks and giblets; reserve for other uses. Pull off and discard lumps of fat. Rinse birds inside and out; pat dry. Prepare **brine** and brine birds for 10 to 12 hours. Rinse and let dry as directed.

To smoke, prepare barbecue and add wood chips as directed for **smoked turkey.** Smoke chicken until a meat thermometer inserted in thickest part of breast (not touching bone) registers 160°F, 4 to 5 hours. Serve or store as directed for turkey. Makes 8 main-dish servings.

Hot Duck on Rye

PREPARATION TIME: About 20 minutes to bone duck, peel oranges, and assemble sandwiches

CHILLING TIME: About 30 minutes to crisp watercress

COOKING TIME: About 15 minutes

PER SERVING: 640 calories, 69 grams protein, 14 grams carbohydrate, 32 grams total fat, 253 milligrams cholesterol, 333 milligrams sodium

Rows of gleaming brown barbecued ducks are a familiar sight in Chinatown markets of San Francisco and Los Angeles. In smaller communities, these same ducks are often sold frozen in Chinese grocery stores. Such ready-cooked birds are usually an excellent value, especially when you consider the price of fresh duck and the effort typically involved in cooking it. Here, barbecued duck goes into a Western-style sandwich—the meat is shredded and served open-faced on rye bread, topped with juicy fresh oranges. (Suggested wine: soft Merlot)

Makes 4 servings

> 2 **large oranges**
> 1 **Chinese barbecued duck (about 2½ lbs.) with accompanying juices; or use ½ cup Homemade Chicken Broth (page 58) or canned regular-strength chicken broth in place of juices**
> 4 **slices rye bread, toasted**
>   **Mayonnaise**
>   **Mustard**
> 2 **cups lightly packed watercress sprigs, washed and crisped**

Using a sharp knife, cut peel and all white membrane from oranges; set oranges aside.

Drain any juices from inside duck and combine with juices that come separately; set aside.

Pull meat from duck (reserve carcass for making broth, if desired). Pull duck skin and fat from meat; coarsely shred meat and set aside. With a sharp knife, cut skin into thin strips. Place in a 10- to 12-inch frying pan and cook over medium heat, stirring, until crisp, 7 to 10 minutes. Remove skin from pan and drain; discard fat in pan.

Add reserved juices to frying pan and bring to a boil over high heat. Reduce heat to low and add duck meat; cover and warm duck until heated through, 3 to 5 minutes.

Meanwhile, spread each slice of toasted bread with mayonnaise and mustard; top with watercress. Thinly slice oranges crosswise to make 12 pieces. Lift duck from juices and place equal portions on each bed of watercress. Top each sandwich with 3 slices of orange, then sprinkle with crisp duck skin. Pour hot juices into a small bowl and offer to spoon over each sandwich.

Skewered Birds, Thai-style

PREPARATION TIME: 30 to 40 minutes to ignite charcoal; 30 to 40 minutes to skewer birds

GRILLING TIME: About 8 minutes for quail, 12 for squab, 25 for game hens

PER SERVING: 621 calories, 69 grams protein, 6 grams carbohydrate, 34 grams total fat, 220 milligrams cholesterol, 208 milligrams sodium

Street vendors in Bangkok grill small poultry in multiples over hot coals. The birds are butterflied for quick cooking, then laced onto long skewers for ease of handling—ideas worth borrowing for a Western barbecue. We've also replicated the Thais' distinctive dipping sauce to accompany the birds. (Suggested wine: dry white blend with Sauvignon Blanc)

Makes 8 servings

> 8 **Rock Cornish game hens (1 to 1½ lbs. *each*), 8 squab (1 lb. *each*), or 16 to 24 quail (3 to 4 oz. *each*); thaw birds if frozen**
> ½ **cup minced fresh cilantro (coriander)**
> ⅓ **cup freshly ground black pepper**
> 24 **cloves garlic, minced or pressed**
>   **Thai Sauce (recipe follows)**

Remove poultry necks and giblets; reserve for other uses. With poultry or kitchen shears, cut birds lengthwise through breastbone and cartilage. Place birds, skin side up, on a flat surface. Press firmly, cracking bones slightly so birds lie reasonably flat. Rinse and pat dry.

Using long skewers (about 18 inches or longer), thread birds by forcing 1 skewer into drumstick, through thigh, under backbone, through second thigh, and out through second drumstick. Run a second skewer parallel to the first, going through breast, middle section of wing, over backbone, through middle section of the second wing, and out through other side of breast. Skewers 18 inches long will hold 2 or 3 game hens or squab, or up to 6 quail.

Mash together cilantro, pepper, and garlic. Rub mixture evenly over birds. Place birds on a grill 4 to 6 inches above a solid bed of hot coals (you should be able to hold your hand at grill level for no more than 2 to 3 seconds). Cook, turning as needed for even browning. For rare quail, allow 8 to 10 minutes; for rare squab, allow 12 to 15 minutes; for well-done game hens (meat at thighbone is no longer pink when cut), allow 25 to 30 minutes. Remove from skewers and serve with Thai Sauce.

THAI SAUCE. In a blender or food processor, whirl 1 can (8 oz.) **tomato sauce**, 3 tablespoons firmly packed **brown sugar**, 6 cloves **garlic**, ⅛ to ½ teaspoon **cayenne**, and ¼ cup **vinegar** until blended. Add 1¼ cups **golden raisins** and ⅓ cup **water**; whirl until raisins are coarsely chopped. In a 2- to 3-quart pan, boil sauce, stirring, until reduced to 1½ cups. Let cool, then cover and refrigerate until cold. Season to taste with **salt**; serve cold.

PER TABLESPOON: 34 calories, .41 gram protein, 9 grams carbohydrate, .04 gram total fat, 0 milligram cholesterol, 59 milligrams sodium.

Savor the Southwest in the peppery succulence of Grilled Birds with Jalapeño Jelly Glaze (recipe below) served on a bed of crisp Cilantro Slaw (page 77) and garnished with cucumber sticks and cilantro.

Grilled Birds with Jalapeño Jelly Glaze

Pictured above

W E S T E R N   C L A S S I C

PREPARATION TIME: 30 to 40 minutes to ignite charcoal; 15 to 20 minutes to prepare birds

GRILLING TIME: About 8 minutes for quail; about 40 minutes for game hens

PER SERVING: 785 calories, 75 grams protein, 19 grams carbohydrate, 43 grams total fat, 259 milligrams cholesterol, 292 milligrams sodium

In choosing birds to grill and baste, a Southwestern cook's first choice of poultry would be quail; Rock Cornish game hens are a more widely available alternative. Farm-raised quail can be ordered through meat markets; they may come fresh or frozen. (Suggested wine: soft Cabernet Sauvignon)

Makes 6 to 8 servings

    6 **to 8 Rock Cornish game hens (1¼ to 1½ lbs.** *each***) or 12 to 24 quail (3 to 4 oz.** *each***); thaw birds if frozen**

¼ **cup (⅛ lb.) butter or margarine**

1 **jar (about 7½ oz.) jalapeño jelly**

2 **tablespoons lime juice**

    Salt and pepper

Remove poultry necks and giblets; reserve for other uses. With poultry or kitchen shears, cut hens in half; or split quail through backbone and pull open to flatten. Rinse birds and pat dry.

Combine butter and jelly in a 1- to 2-quart pan; stir over medium-high heat until melted (or stir on the barbecue over hot coals). Stir in lime juice; set aside.

Sprinkle birds lightly with salt and pepper. Place birds, skin side up (quail laid out flat), on a grill 4 to 6 inches above a solid bed of coals—medium-hot for quail (you should be able to hold your hand at grill level for no more than 3 to 4 seconds), low for game hens (you should be able to hold your hand at grill level for no more than 6 to 7 seconds).

Cook hens, turning several times, until skin is browned and breast is no longer pink at bone (cut to test), 30 to 40 minutes. Baste with jelly mixture during last 15 minutes of cooking, using all.

Cook quail, turning several times, until skin is browned and breast is light pink at bone (cut to test), 7 to 8 minutes. Baste often with jelly mixture during last 5 minutes of cooking, using all (be careful, since drips may cause flare-ups).

Squab with Pears & Red Wine Sauce

PREPARATION TIME: 10 to 15 minutes to poach pears; 10 to 15 minutes to brown birds; 5 to 10 minutes to make sauce

ROASTING TIME: 15 to 25 minutes

PER SERVING: 1181 calories, 57 grams protein, 26 grams carbohydrate, 94 grams total fat, 55 milligrams cholesterol, 211 milligrams sodium

For a festive display, arrange squab (or chukar or quail) and pears around a mound of hot wild rice. To keep the delicate birds moist and succulent, take special care not to overcook. The birds' roasting-pan juices combine with butter and wine to make a magnificent, though very rich, sauce. (Suggested wine: mature Cabernet Sauvignon)

Makes 6 servings

- 1½ cups dry red wine
- ¼ cup sugar
- ¾ teaspoon whole black peppercorns
- 3 medium-size firm-ripe Bosc or Comice pears
- 6 squab or chukar (¾ to 1 lb. *each*) or 12 to 18 quail (3 to 4 oz. *each*); thaw birds if frozen
- ⅔ cup (⅓ lb.) butter or margarine
- ⅓ cup minced shallots or mild red onion
- ¾ cup Homemade Chicken Broth (page 58) or canned regular-strength chicken or beef broth
- Hot cooked wild rice (optional)

In a 4- to 5-quart pan, combine wine, sugar, and peppercorns. Peel pears, cut in half lengthwise, and core; add to wine mixture. Bring to a boil over high heat; then reduce heat, cover, and simmer, turning several times, until pears are tender when pierced, about 7 minutes. Set aside; keep warm.

Remove necks and giblets from birds; reserve for other uses. Rinse birds inside and out and pat dry. Melt 2 tablespoons of the butter in a 10- to 12-inch frying pan over medium-high heat. Add birds, a portion at a time, without crowding. Cook, turning, until browned on all sides; if necessary, add 1 more tablespoon butter to prevent sticking.

Place birds, breast up, on a rack in a 12- by 17-inch roasting pan. Roast, uncovered, in a 400° oven until breast meat near bone is still moist but not wet-looking (make a slash in breast just above wing joint to test); squab and quail should still be red, and chukar should be white with a little pink at the bone. Allow 12 to 15 minutes for quail, 20 to 25 minutes for squab or chukar.

Drain juices from birds into roasting pan. Transfer birds to a large platter; lift pears from poaching liquid and arrange alongside birds. Keep warm.

Pour roasting pan drippings into frying pan, add shallots, and stir over high heat for 1 minute. Add broth and ¾ cup of the pear poaching liquid (discard any remaining poaching liquid). Boil rapidly until sauce is reduced to ⅔ cup. Reduce heat to low and add remaining butter all in 1 chunk; stir constantly until butter melts and blends into sauce. Pour sauce through a fine strainer into a small bowl; offer to spoon over individual portions. Accompany birds with wild rice, if desired.

Pheasant with Jeweled Fruits

PREPARATION TIME: About 20 minutes to organize; 5 minutes to prepare birds; 20 minutes to prepare fruit and onion sauce

ROASTING TIME: 20 to 25 minutes

PER SERVING: 913 calories, 77 grams protein, 32 grams carbohydrate, 53 grams total fat, 54 milligrams cholesterol, 317 milligrams sodium

Green grapes, golden onions, and tart pomegranate seeds make an opulent garnish for roast pheasant. Try spinach as a quiet, fresh-tasting accompaniment for the fruited and brandy-sauced holiday bird. (Order the pheasant or guinea fowl—farm-raised and usually sold frozen—through your meat market.) (Suggested wine: mature, full-bodied Chardonnay)

Makes 2 or 3 servings

- 1 pheasant (about 2½ lbs.) or 1 guinea fowl (1¾ to 2½ lbs.); thaw birds if frozen
- ¼ cup (⅛ lb.) butter or margarine
- 10 to 15 small (about 1½-inch-diameter) white onions, peeled
- 1½ to 2 cups seedless green grapes
- ½ to 1 cup pomegranate seeds
- ⅓ cup sour cream
- ½ teaspoon cornstarch
- ½ cup Homemade Chicken Broth (page 58) or canned regular-strength chicken or beef broth
- 2 tablespoons brandy
- ⅛ teaspoon dry tarragon

Remove pheasant or guinea fowl neck and giblets; reserve for other uses. Rinse bird inside and out and pat dry.

Melt 2 tablespoons of the butter in a 10- to 12-inch frying pan over medium-high heat. Add pheasant or guinea fowl; cook, turning, until browned on all sides, about 3 minutes.

Arrange bird, breast up, on a rack in an 11- by 14-inch roasting pan. Roast, uncovered, in a 450° oven until breast meat at bone is white with a touch of pink; meat should look moist but not soft and wet (to test, make a slash to breastbone parallel to wing joint). Allow about 20 minutes for a 1¾-pound bird, 25 minutes for a 2½-pound bird.

While bird roasts, melt remaining 2 tablespoons butter in frying pan over medium heat. Add onions; cook, turning frequently, until golden. Add ½ cup water, cover, and cook until onions are just tender when pierced and liquid has evaporated, about 20 minutes. Before serving, add grapes and pomegranate seeds and stir until warmed.

Set roasted bird on a platter with onions and fruit alongside; keep warm. Mix sour cream with cornstarch and add to roasting pan with broth, brandy, and tarragon. Boil over high heat, whisking constantly, until reduced to ½ cup.

Carve bird and offer sour cream sauce to spoon over individual portions.

The Best of Sunset

FISH & SHELLFISH

The Pacific Ocean—its waves crashing along the coastline from Alaska to Mexico and beyond—favors the West with an abundance of fish and shellfish. Sweet Dungeness crab is one locally celebrated variety, harvested in the cooler waters north of Santa Barbara and up as far as Alaska. Also much esteemed are the magnificent salmon that return from the Pacific each year to spawn in the fresh waters of coastal rivers and streams.

More varieties of fish come from inland waters or, frozen, from seaports all over the world. Aquatic farming supplies mussels and oysters and more to Western markets. And since its earliest issues, Sunset has shown Westerners how to enjoy the succulence of all this fish and shellfish splendor.

When you try the recipes in this chapter, you'll savor Sunset's expertise in such varied and tempting fare as Hangtown Fry, Braised Black Cod, Shrimp & Jicama with Chile Vinegar, and two local versions of Cioppino, the West's celebrated fisherman's stew.

Provide thick-sliced French bread and big napkins—and enjoy the messy goodness of San Francisco-style Cioppino (recipe on page 158). A local creation of Italian-American fishermen, the seafood soup has at least as many versions as the West has seaports.

Baked Salmon with Fish Mousse

PREPARATION TIME: 25 to 30 minutes for fish; about 10 minutes for sauce
BAKING TIME: 40 to 45 minutes
COOLING AND CHILLING TIME: At least 3 hours
PER SERVING OF FISH: 343 calories, 30 grams protein, 2 grams carbohydrate, 23 grams total fat, 87 milligrams cholesterol, 117 milligrams sodium

A festive choice for a buffet luncheon, this make-ahead entrée features baked salmon fillets topped with a chive-flecked fish mousse. Accompany with a thick fresh-basil mayonnaise. (Suggested wine: a very crisp, lightly oaked Chardonnay)

Makes 25 servings

> 1 **whole salmon, 8 to 10 pounds (6 to 8 lbs. without head and tail), cleaned and filleted, skin left on**
>
> 1¾ **pounds firm, boneless white-fleshed fish such as sole, lingcod, or rockfish**
>
> 3 **cups whipping cream**
>
> 3 **large egg whites**
>
> ½ **cup minced chives or green onions (including tops)**
>
> ½ **teaspoon white pepper**
>
> **Salt**
>
> 3 **cups dry white wine**
>
> **Basil Mayonnaise (recipe follows)**

Rinse salmon and white-fleshed fish; pat dry. Cut white-fleshed fish into 1-inch chunks and whirl in a food processor until finely ground. Add cream and egg whites; whirl until very smooth and well blended. Add chives and white pepper. Whirl until combined; season to taste with salt, then cover and refrigerate.

Cut 2 pieces of heavy foil several inches longer and wider than salmon fillets. Place each piece of foil in a 12- by 17-inch pan at least 1 inch deep. Place a salmon fillet, skin side down, on foil in each pan.

Spoon half the puréed fish mousse mixture into a large pastry bag fitted with a ¾-inch star (or plain) tip. Pipe fish in a decorative layer down center of 1 salmon fillet, leaving edge of salmon exposed. Repeat with remaining mousse mixture to coat remaining salmon fillet.

Pour 1½ cups of the wine into each pan. Bake salmon, uncovered, in a 350° oven for 10 minutes. Loosely tent pans with foil, without touching topping, and continue to bake until mousse feels firm when gently touched and salmon is opaque in thickest part (cut to test), 25 to 30 minutes. Remove fish from oven and let cool, then cover lightly and refrigerate until cold, at least 2 hours or up to 24 hours.

Tilting pans carefully, pour out wine. With a sharp knife or scissors, trim foil flush with salmon edges. Using foil to help support salmon, lift it with your hands and move to a platter.

If desired, divide into equal serving portions: cut salmon lengthwise down center, then crosswise into 2- to 3-inch slices. Lift pieces from foil with a spatula (skin will stick to foil). Top portions with Basil Mayonnaise.

BASIL MAYONNAISE. In a blender or food processor, combine 6 **large egg yolks,** 6 tablespoons **white wine vinegar,** ½ cup chopped **green onions** (including tops), and 3½ cups lightly packed **fresh basil leaves;** whirl until smoothly puréed.

With motor running, slowly add 2 cups **salad oil** in a thin stream to form a thick mayonnaise. Season to taste with **salt.** If made ahead, cover and refrigerate for up to 2 days; stir before using. Makes about 3 cups.

PER TABLESPOON: 92 calories, .53 gram protein, .91 gram carbohydrate, 10 grams total fat, 34 milligrams cholesterol, 2 milligrams sodium.

Barbecued Salmon

W E S T E R N C L A S S I C

PREPARATION TIME: 30 to 40 minutes to ignite charcoal; 15 to 30 minutes to butterfly fish (or purchase butterflied); about 10 minutes to prepare fish for grilling
GRILLING TIME: 30 to 35 minutes
PER SERVING OF FISH: 339 calories, 39 grams protein, 0 gram carbohydrate, 26 grams total fat, 75 milligrams cholesterol, 157 milligrams sodium

In the Northwest, salmon replaces steak as the most popular candidate for the barbecue. And it's no wonder —the fish is wonderfully easy to manage when cooked as a big, beautiful double fillet. (Suggested wine: a well-developed, crisp but mature Chardonnay)

Makes 10 to 12 servings

> 1 **whole salmon 6 to 8 lbs. (4 to 6 lbs. without head and tail)**
>
> 3 **tablespoons butter or margarine, melted**
>
> **Soy Butter Sauce (recipe follows)**

At the fish market, have your fishman remove salmon head, tail, and back fin, then butterfly salmon from stomach side (do not separate fillets along back) and bone it, leaving skin intact. At home, trim any white membrane from belly area of fish. Rinse fish and pat dry. Lay salmon out, skin side down, on heavy foil. Cut foil to follow outline of fish.

Place salmon on foil on a grill 4 to 6 inches above a solid bed of hot coals (you should be able to hold your hand at grill level for no more than 2 to 3 seconds). Brush fish with melted butter, then cover lightly with a sheet of foil, forming a small dome.

Cook for 30 minutes, then check doneness; when done, fish should flake readily when prodded with a fork in thickest part. If necessary, continue to cook, checking doneness about every 5 minutes.

Supporting fish with foil, slip onto a large platter. To serve, lift pieces of salmon from foil with a wide spatula (skin will stick to foil). Accompany with Soy Butter Sauce (add pungent sauce sparingly).

SOY BUTTER SAUCE. Melt ¾ cup (⅜ lb.) **butter** or margarine in a 1- to 2-quart pan. Stir in 2 cloves **garlic,** minced or pressed; 1½ tablespoons *each* **soy sauce** and **dry mustard;** ⅓ cup **dry sherry** or regular-strength chicken broth; and 3 tablespoons **catsup.** Keep warm on barbecue. Makes 1½ cups.

PER TABLESPOON: 23 calories, .22 gram protein, 1 gram carbohydrate, 2 grams total fat, 5 milligrams cholesterol, 125 milligrams sodium.

Indian-style Salmon Bake

One of the Northwest's grand traditions has been handed down to us by the region's coastal Indians. It's their method of baking salmon—butterflied, woven on wood, and cooked over an outdoor fire. *Sunset* has used this technique many times over the years, since we first mentioned it in an eyewitness report in April, 1933.

Indians traditionally use three-legged frames of alder to hold the salmon. If you do not have access to green alder (or fruit wood branches), use milled lumber (any nonresinous wood). We've modified the design of the frame to a two-piece central stake. The butterflied fish is "woven" against the main stake with smaller strips of wood. Pounded into sand or soft soil, the stake holds the salmon fillet upright and flat so it will cook evenly, at about 2 feet above the fire.

Indian-style baked salmon makes a dramatic focus for a picnic, and it suits perfectly the informality of outdoor dining—to serve, you just let guests pull chunks of cooked salmon from the frame onto individual plates. Push small foil-wrapped potatoes down into coals to roast as the salmon cooks; serve a green or cabbage salad with the fish and potatoes.

Each salmon makes 10 to 12 servings.

1 or 2 whole salmon (6 to 8 lbs. each), butterflied as directed for Barbecued Salmon, page 142

Light brine (¼ cup salt to each 4 quarts water)

Frame (directions follow)

¼ cup (⅛ lb.) butter or margarine, melted

2 tablespoons lemon juice

Place fish in a deep pan or a heavy plastic bag set in a pan. Cover completely with brine; let stand for 45 minutes to 1½ hours. (Brining firms the fish and gives it a moister, more succulent texture when cooked.)

Lay one 6-foot section of frame flat. Wrap a piece of foil slightly longer than fish smoothly around center of stake. Position 3 of the 18-inch frame pieces at right angles to stake, centering pieces and spacing evenly apart.

Staked at an angle over a hot fire, Indian-style Salmon Bake requires only a simple wood frame at beach or creekside.

Lift fish from brine; rinse and pat dry. Align center of fish with long stake; lay fish on top of 18-inch frame pieces (wide end of fish should be pointed toward sharpened end of stake). Adjust position of 18-inch pieces so entire edge of fish overlaps them by 2 to 3 inches at top and bottom.

On top of salmon, place remaining two 18-inch frame pieces, centered between and parallel to frame pieces beneath fish—in effect, you're weaving the fish in place.

Foil-wrap the second 6-foot stake as you did the first. Lay second stake directly over first, sharpened ends together, with fish and short frame pieces sandwiched between. Tightly wrap wire around the 2 long stakes above and below fish to hold stakes together securely.

If cooking a second fish, repeat framing steps.

As you are framing salmon, start fire in a location sheltered from wind. The ideal fire for baking the salmon is a driftwood fire built against the base of a large rock or rocky cliff (the rock helps cook fish by reflecting heat). The firebed should be at least twice as long as width of fish when fish are placed side by side. Burn fire until you have a solid bed of glowing coals—this takes at least 30 minutes. Add more wood to keep a gentle blaze going while fish is cooking. Push fire around beneath fish to control heat, particularly if there's a breeze.

Face fish toward heat. With a hammer, pound sharpened ends of double stakes into sand (or soft soil) at least 12 inches from firebed until bottom edge of fish is about 2 feet above fire. If fire is against a rock, angle stake at about a 60° angle over fire. If fire is in the open, angle stake at a 45° angle over fire. (You can control angle of stakes by wedging a rock between base of stakes and sand.)

Cook fish for 25 minutes; mix butter with lemon juice and baste fish several times as it cooks. Then carefully pull out stakes, rotate fish so back is toward the fire, and cook until it flakes readily when prodded in thickest part with a fork, about 25 more minutes; baste several times.

Push fire away or move fish back from heat. Pull chunks from frame to eat.

FRAME. *For each frame,* you'll need nonresinous milled lumber: two 6-foot-long pieces, ¾- by ¾-inch stock; five 18-inch-long pieces, ¼- by ¾-inch stock; and 2 feet of 22-gauge or heavier wire. Sharpen 1 end of each of the 6-foot stakes.

Soak wood in water overnight so it won't burn; wrap 18-inch pieces smoothly with foil.

Salmon in Crisp Tortilla Baskets

PREPARATION & COOKING TIME: 25 to 30 minutes
PER SERVING: 325 calories, 25 grams protein, 14 grams carbohydrate, 19 grams total fat, 39 milligrams cholesterol, 99 milligrams sodium

For lunch, consider a salmon salad dressed with nippy chile mayonnaise and nested in a crisp tortilla basket. The golden baskets can be made ahead, then reheated in the oven. (Suggested beverage: a very dry Sauvignon Blanc, or beer)

Makes 6 servings

> 1 can (8¾ oz.) corn kernels, drained
> 4 cups lightly packed shredded romaine lettuce
> 2½ to 3 cups cooked salmon, broken into large pieces (about 1½ lbs. steaks, with bones and skin removed)
> 6 hot Tortilla Baskets (page 163)
> Chile Mayonnaise (recipe follows)

In a bowl, lightly mix corn, romaine, and salmon; spoon into hot Tortilla Baskets. Add Chile Mayonnaise to taste.

CHILE MAYONNAISE. In a food processor or blender, whirl 1½ cups **mayonnaise** with 1 can (4 oz.) **diced green chiles** until smooth. Stir in **cayenne** to taste. If made ahead, cover and refrigerate for up to 1 day. Makes 1¾ cups.
Per Tablespoon: 85 calories, .15 gram protein, .55 gram carbohydrate, 9 grams total fat, 7 milligrams cholesterol, 92 milligrams sodium.

Lomi Salmon-stuffed Tomatoes

W E S T E R N   C L A S S I C

PREPARATION TIME: 25 to 30 minutes
MARINATING TIME: At least 12 hours; plus 2 hours to rinse
PER SERVING: 107 calories, 10 grams protein, 6 grams carbohydrate, 5 grams total fat, 15 milligrams cholesterol, 1685 milligrams sodium

If you're planning a traditional Hawaiian luau, you'll want to include lomi salmon. This salted salmon is sold ready to use in the Islands; it's also easy to make at home, though you'll need to start the day before the party. (Suggested beverage: at a luau, beer or dry white wine with sparkling water and lime)

Makes 12 servings

> 1 pound boned, skinned salmon fillets
> ½ cup rock salt
> 3 tablespoons lemon juice
> 12 medium-size firm-ripe tomatoes
> ½ cup chopped green onions (including tops)

Rinse salmon and pat dry. Cut into ½-inch cubes and place in a bowl. Cover with rock salt; then sprinkle with lemon juice and mix gently. Cover and refrigerate for at least 12 hours or up to 24 hours, stirring occasionally. Fish will become very firm and salty.

Rinse fish well to remove salt, then soak in cold water for 2 hours, changing water several times. Pat fish dry and shred with your fingers.

Cut a thin slice from top of each tomato, then scoop out pulp with a spoon. Chop tomato pulp; mix with fish and onions and spoon into tomato shells.

Smoked Salmon

PREPARATION TIME: 6 hours to brine; at least 1 hour to dry; 30 to 40 minutes to ignite charcoal
SMOKING TIME: Up to 2½ hours
PER SERVING: 380 calories, 34 grams protein, 13 grams carbohydrate, 20 grams total fat, 59 milligrams cholesterol, 917 milligrams sodium

Making your own succulent smoked salmon is easier than you might think. You just need a covered barbecue, a few other pieces of equipment, and wet wood chips; the simple procedure is described in detail on page 136. (Suggested wine: full-bodied dry, fruity Zinfandel)

Allow at least ⅓ pound boned fish per serving

> 1- to 1½-inch-thick salmon steaks or fillets with skin on
> Brine (page 136)
> 4 cups hickory wood chips
> Smoked Salmon Baste (recipe follows)

Rinse fish and pat dry. Prepare Brine; brine fish for 6 hours. Rinse and let dry as directed. Cover wood chips with warm water and let stand for at least 20 minutes; drain.

To smoke, ignite charcoal briquets and set up barbecue as directed on page 136. Adjust barbecue to maintain a temperature of 160° to 180°F. Scatter 1 cup of the wet wood chips evenly over coals; add 1 cup wet chips to coals every 30 minutes until all are used. Each time you add chips, blot fish dry with paper towels and baste with Smoked Salmon Baste.

Smoke fish until it flakes readily when prodded with a fork in thickest part—1½ to 2½ hours for 1- to 1½-inch-thick pieces. Loosen fish from grill and lift off with a spatula; for a large fillet, slide from grill onto a rimless baking sheet. Serve hot, warm, or cool. To store, wrap airtight and refrigerate for up to 2 weeks or freeze for up to 6 months (thaw to serve).

SMOKED SALMON BASTE. Mix ⅓ cup **maple syrup** or maple-flavored syrup, 1½ tablespoons **soy sauce**, and ¼ teaspoon **ground ginger.**

SMOKED ALBACORE, SWORDFISH, BLACK COD (BUTTERFISH), OR STURGEON
Use 1- to 1½-inch-thick steaks or fillets with skin on. Follow directions for **Smoked Salmon.**

Cured with salt, sugar, and dill, salmon becomes the Scandinavian delicacy Gravlax Plus (recipe below). Carve it in paper-thin, slanting slices and offer with lemon, sour cream, tart-sweet Mustard Sauce, and thin-sliced bread.

Gravlax Plus

Pictured above

PREPARATION TIME: 10 to 15 minutes
CHILLING TIME: 24 hours
PER SERVING OF FISH: 234 calories, 18 grams protein, 7 grams carbohydrate, 15 grams total fat, 30 milligrams cholesterol, 2960 milligrams sodium

The Swedes cure salmon in salt and sugar, with plenty of fresh dill, for an elegant appetizer called gravlax. *You can do the same with more economical lingcod, halibut, trout, or tuna. The cured fish keeps in the refrigerator for several days. (Suggested beverage: full-bodied Chardonnay, beer, or aquavit)*

Makes 10 to 12 servings

> 1 boned, unskinned salmon, lingcod, or halibut fillet (about 2 lbs.); 1 skinned tuna (including albacore) loin (about 2 lbs.); 2 pounds tuna steaks, cut 1½ inches thick; or 2 pounds boned, unskinned trout fillets
>
> ¼ cup salad oil
>
> ⅓ cup *each* sugar and salt
>
> 1½ tablespoons whole white peppercorns, coarsely crushed
>
> ¼ cup cognac (optional)
>
> 1 small red onion, thinly sliced
>
> 2 to 3 cups lightly packed fresh dill sprigs
>
> Lemon wedges and sour cream
>
> Mustard Sauce (recipe follows)

If you're using fresh salmon, freeze for at least 7 days at 0°F before curing to destroy any dangerous parasites. If you buy frozen (or frozen and thawed) salmon, this step isn't necessary.

Rinse fish, pat dry, and rub with oil. Mix sugar, salt, and crushed peppercorns; lightly rub some of the mixture over all sides of fish. Choose a glass baking dish that's just big enough to hold fish (fish should almost fill dish). Place fish, skin side down, in dish. Pat remaining salt mixture on top of fish; spoon cognac (if used) over it. If using tuna, coat completely with salt mixture to keep fish from turning a very dark (harmless) color.

Lay onion and 1 to 2 cups of the dill on fish. Cover dish tightly with plastic wrap. Refrigerate for 12 hours; baste fish with accumulating juices 3 or 4 times. Turn fish over, with dill and onion under it. Cover and refrigerate for 12 more hours; baste 3 or 4 times with juices.

After 24 hours, fish is ready to serve, though you may leave it in brine for another 24 hours. To keep for 2 additional days, remove fish from brine (it will grow increasingly salty otherwise), pat dry, enclose in a plastic bag, and refrigerate.

Place fish, skin side down, on a serving board; discard dill and onion. Garnish fish with remaining dill. With a sharp knife, cut fish in paper-thin slanting slices; you can offer the whole fish on a buffet to cut and serve.

Eat fish with a squeeze of lemon, a dot of sour cream or Mustard Sauce, and a garnish of dill.

MUSTARD SAUCE. In a bowl, stir together ⅔ cup **Dijon mustard,** ½ cup **salad oil,** 1½ tablespoons **white wine vinegar,** and 1 tablespoon **sugar.** Just before using, stir in ¼ cup chopped **fresh dill** and season to taste with **pepper.** Makes about 1¼ cups.
PER TABLESPOON: 61 calories, .03 gram protein, 2 grams carbohydrate, 6 grams total fat, 0 milligram cholesterol, 239 milligrams sodium.

Barbecued Albacore Loin with Basil & Cucumbers

PREPARATION TIME: 30 to 40 minutes to ignite charcoal; about 15 minutes to assemble
MARINATING TIME: At least 3 hours
GRILLING TIME: About 15 minutes
PER SERVING: 514 calories, 40 grams protein, 4 grams carbohydrate, 37 grams total fat, 86 milligrams cholesterol, 129 milligrams sodium

Fragile-fleshed, delicate-flavored albacore has always been caught along Western shores. It's only recently, though, that it has become readily available fresh; in the past, most of the catch was canned. (Today, most canned tuna, including albacore, is imported.) Here, albacore loin is cooked rare—like steak—with amazingly tender, moist, and meatlike results. The fish is also excellent raw, as sashimi or with sushi. (Suggested wine: a fresh, crisp Cabernet Sauvignon Blanc or mellow Merlot)

Makes 5 or 6 servings

> ¾ cup lightly packed fresh basil leaves; or 3 tablespoons dry basil and ¼ cup lightly packed parsley sprigs
> ⅔ cup salad oil
> ½ cup white wine vinegar
> ¼ cup freshly grated Parmesan cheese
> 3 cloves garlic
> ¼ teaspoon pepper
> 1 boned, skinned or unskinned albacore loin (about 2 lbs.)
> 1 medium-size cucumber, peeled
> Salt

In a food processor or blender, whirl basil, oil, vinegar, cheese, garlic, and pepper until puréed; set aside.

Rinse fish and pat dry. Fit 1 large plastic bag (big enough to hold fish flat) inside another. Place fish in double bag and top with ⅔ of the basil mixture. Press out air, close bag with a twist-tie, and roll bag to coat fish with mixture. Refrigerate for 3 to 6 hours, turning bag occasionally.

Meanwhile, cut cucumber in half lengthwise. Scoop out and discard seeds. Cut cucumber into ¼-inch-thick slices. Mix with remaining ⅓ of basil mixture; refrigerate for 3 to 6 hours to blend flavors.

Carefully lift fish from marinade (reserve marinade) and place on a grill 4 to 6 inches above a solid bed of hot coals (you should be able to hold your hand at grill level for no more than 2 to 3 seconds). Cook until fish is firm on surface but still translucent and moist about ½ inch below surface (cut to test), about 15 minutes. Baste often with marinade and turn with a wide spatula as needed to brown all sides; extinguish any flare-ups with a spray of water.

Lift fish from grill and place on a platter. Arrange cucumber mixture alongside. Cut fish crosswise into 1-inch-thick slices. Season to taste with salt.

Steamed Lingcod

PREPARATION TIME: About 15 minutes to soak mushrooms; about 5 minutes to assemble
STEAMING TIME: About 15 minutes
PER SERVING: 250 calories, 51 grams protein, 4 grams carbohydrate, 2 grams total fat, 154 milligrams cholesterol, 166 milligrams sodium

Chinese steam cooking offers several advantages—flavors mingle more completely, very little (if any) fat is used, and you can serve right from the cooking dish. This delicate steamed lingcod is lightly seasoned with fresh ginger and decorative dried mushrooms. (Suggested wine: dry, tart Chenin Blanc)

Makes 4 or 5 servings

> 6 to 8 (about 2-inch-diameter) dried shiitake mushrooms
> 3 to 4 pounds lingcod steaks, cut about 2 inches thick
> 2 quarter-size slices fresh ginger (*each* about ¼ inch thick), cut into slivers
> 1 tablespoon soy sauce (optional)

Soak mushrooms in warm water to cover until soft, about 15 minutes. Drain. Cut off and discard stems; squeeze caps dry. Rinse fish steaks and pat dry. Arrange close together in a 10- or 11-inch rimmed heatproof serving dish that will fit inside a steamer. Decorate fish with ginger and soaked mushrooms.

Cover dish completely with wax paper; support dish on a rack or stand in steamer above 1 to 2 inches of boiling water. Cover pan and cook until fish flakes readily when prodded with a fork in thickest part, 12 to 15 minutes. To test, remove pan from heat, lift lid, and fold back a corner of paper; cover fish and pan for any additional cooking.

Remove pan from heat and uncover. Discard wax paper, and lift out dish. Pour soy over fish, if desired; serve.

Steeped Fish with Watercress Cream

PREPARATION TIME: 2 to 3 minutes for fish; 5 to 6 minutes for sauce
STEEPING TIME: About 8 minutes
PER SERVING OF FISH: 433 calories, 45 grams protein, 0 gram carbohydrate, 27 grams total fat, 78 milligrams cholesterol, 148 milligrams sodium

Delicate-textured fish takes especially well to steeping in hot-off-the-fire water. Surprisingly, cooking fish by this Chinese method is just as fast as poaching over direct heat—but steeping is gentler, so the flesh firms more smoothly and has a moister texture. Accompany the hot fish with a cold, creamy watercress dressing. (Suggested wine: a dry Pinot Blanc)

Makes 4 servings

> 4 fish steaks, such as lingcod or salmon (about ½ lb. *each*), cut about 1 inch thick
> Watercress sprigs
> Watercress Cream (recipe follows)

Rinse fish steaks, then place in a deep 12-inch frying pan, 5- to 6-quart pan, or other pan that will allow you to cover steaks with at least 1 inch of water. Steaks may overlap, but water needs to flow between them. Cover fish with 1 to 2 inches of water. Lift out fish; leave water in pan.

Cover pan and bring water to a rolling boil. Remove from heat; quickly immerse fish in boiling water. Cover pan tightly and let stand, covered, for 6 to 8 minutes. Then check doneness by cutting a small slit in thickest part of fish; it should look just opaque throughout. If fish is not done, return it to hot water, cover, and let steep for a few more minutes.

Drain fish and arrange on 4 dinner plates. Garnish with watercress sprigs; offer Watercress Cream to spoon over fish.

WATERCRESS CREAM. In a blender or food processor, combine ½ cup lightly packed **watercress sprigs**, 2 tablespoons coarsely chopped **green onion** (including top), 1 teaspoon **anchovy paste**, 1 tablespoon **lemon juice**, ¼ teaspoon **dry tarragon**, and 2 tablespoons **whipping cream**; whirl until puréed. Beat 6 tablespoons **whipping cream** until stiff. Fold into watercress mixture to blend. Makes about 1 cup.

Per Tablespoon: 23 calories, .26 gram protein, .34 gram carbohydrate, 2 grams total fat, 8 milligrams cholesterol, 6 milligrams sodium.

Monkfish Scaloppine

PREPARATION TIME: 15 to 20 minutes
COOKING TIME: 5 to 6 minutes
PER SERVING: 211 calories, 22 grams protein, 3 grams carbohydrate, 12 grams total fat, 61 milligrams cholesterol, 299 milligrams sodium

Sometimes called "poor man's lobster," monkfish acquired its nickname not just from its delicate flavor and lobster-like texture, but from its shape when filleted. The fillets resemble giant lobster tails—one end is thick and rounded, the other flat and tapering. (Suggested wine: a fresh, young Chardonnay)

Makes 4 servings

> 1 large monkfish fillet (1 to 1½ lbs.)
> All-purpose flour
> 1 to 2 tablespoons butter or margarine
> 1 to 2 tablespoons salad oil
> Salt and white pepper
> Lemon wedges

Rinse fish and pat dry. If fillet is encased in a tough membrane, pull and cut off membrane from 1 side of fillet. Then lay fillet on a board, membrane side down. With a sharp knife, starting 3 to 4 inches from tapered end of fillet, cut toward tapered end at about a 45° angle to form ¼- to ⅜-inch-thick slices. As you come to base of fillet, angle knife to slice flesh free of membrane on bottom. Slice fillet until you reach thick end and pieces become too short for large slices. Cut remaining triangular chunk from membrane; discard membrane. Cut almost through thickest part of chunk; open at cut to flatten.

Place fish slices between sheets of plastic wrap. With a flat-surfaced mallet, gently and evenly pound slices until about ⅛ inch thick. Coat fish with flour; lay pieces in a single layer on wax paper.

Place a 10- to 12-inch frying pan over medium-high heat. Add about 1 tablespoon *each* of the butter and oil. When butter is melted, place as many fish pieces in pan as will fit without crowding. Cook, turning once, until fish is opaque in center (cut to test), 1½ to 2 minutes. Keep warm. Cook remaining fish, adding more butter and oil as needed. Sprinkle with salt and white pepper; serve with lemon wedges.

Oven-fried Sizzling Sole

W E S T E R N   C L A S S I C

PREPARATION TIME: 4 to 5 minutes
BAKING TIME: 8 to 10 minutes
PER SERVING: 339 calories, 26 grams protein, 3 grams carbohydrate, 24 grams total fat, 139 milligrams cholesterol, 355 milligrams sodium

On the West Coast, most sole are marketed as boneless fillets. But if you order ahead, you can get some types whole—English, Dover, rex, sanddab, and petrale. These are just the right size to bake on sizzling-hot individual platters in a hot oven, then serve dramatically "on the bone." (Suggested wine: a crisp, mature Chardonnay)

Makes 4 servings

> 4 whole sole (1 to 1¼ lbs. *each*), cleaned, heads removed
> Pepper
> All-purpose flour
> ½ cup (¼ lb.) butter or margarine (or use half butter, half olive oil)
> Salt

Rinse fish and pat dry. Have ready 4 metal or heat-proof ceramic platters, each large enough to hold 1 fish flat; or 1 or 2 platters large enough to hold fish flat and slightly apart. Place in oven; preheat oven to 500° if using metal, 450° if using ceramic.

Meanwhile, sprinkle fish lightly on both sides with pepper, then coat with flour; shake off excess.

Remove hot platters from oven; add 2 tablespoons of the butter (or 1 tablespoon *each* butter and oil) to platter for each fish that's to be placed on it. Quickly slide butter around until melted; add fish and turn to coat. Return to oven. Bake, uncovered, until fish is browned and flakes readily when prodded with a fork in thickest part, 8 to 10 minutes.

Serve hot platters at the table on heavy mats or wooden liners. For each diner, have ready a plate for bones. The host or hostess can bone all the fish or guide guests through the simple process.

To bone fish, cut around edge of fish where row of fine lateral fin bones meets body; lift off and discard these bony edges. With a dinner knife, cut to bone along center crease of fish (center crease marks vertebral column). Push the 2 fillets on top of fish aside. With serving tools or fingers, firmly grasp exposed bone at end of fish; lift off and discard. Season fish to taste with salt.

LEWIS AND CLARK, during their exploration of the Northwest, came across Indian salmon bakes similar to the kind described, years later, in Sunset's Kitchen Rangers *column. From our story, readers learned how Skokomish Indians wove salmon onto a wooden web, then drove part of the frame into the ground to support the fish beside the fire. (To try this technique yourself, see page 143.)*

Sweet & Sour Deep-fried Fish

Pictured below

PREPARATION TIME: About 15 minutes

DEEP-FRYING TIME: About 10 minutes (includes time to heat oil)

PER SERVING OF FISH: 241 calories, 19 grams protein, 16 grams carbohydrate, 11 grams total fat, 52 milligrams cholesterol, 61 milligrams sodium

Crisp deep-fried whole fish with bright red sweet-sour sauce is a traditional dish for a Chinese New Year's banquet. You can prepare the sauce ahead of time; frying the fish takes only a few minutes. (Suggested beverage: a crisp, tart Chenin Blanc, or beer)

Makes 2 or 3 servings

> 1 **whole red rockfish or rock cod (2 to 2½ lbs.), cleaned and scaled (leave on head and tail)**
> ¼ **cup dry sherry**
> **About ½ cup cornstarch**
> **Salad oil**
> **Red Sweet & Sour Sauce (recipe follows)**
> 1 **small green bell pepper, stemmed, seeded, and slivered**
> 1 **small firm-ripe tomato, cored and cut into 6 wedges**
> **Fresh cilantro (coriander) sprigs**

Rinse fish and pat dry. With a sharp knife, make about six ½-inch-deep diagonal slashes across each side of fish. Rub fish all over with sherry; then coat with cornstarch, patting it on.

Half-fill a wok or deep 12- to 14-inch frying pan with oil and heat to 375°F on a deep-frying thermometer. Slowly slide fish into oil. Cook fish until golden brown, about 5 minutes; if fish isn't completely submerged, gently spoon hot oil over fish as it cooks.

With a large wire skimmer or 2 wide slotted spatulas, carefully lift fish from oil. Drain briefly, then place on a heatproof rimmed platter; serve, or keep warm in a 150° oven for up to 15 minutes.

Heat Red Sweet & Sour Sauce until bubbly. Stir in bell pepper and tomato. Pour sauce around (not over) fish on platter. Garnish with cilantro. Lift portions of fish onto plates; spoon sauce over top.

RED SWEET & SOUR SAUCE. Heat 2 tablespoons **salad oil** in a 2- to 3-quart pan over medium-high heat. Add 1 small **onion,** sliced and separated into rings; cook, stirring, for 1 minute. Stir in ½ cup *each* **catsup, red wine vinegar,** and **unsweetened pineapple juice;** then add ¾ cup **sugar,** ½ teaspoon **Worcestershire,** and ⅛ teaspoon **liquid hot pepper seasoning.** Combine 2 tablespoons *each* **cornstarch** and **water** and stir in. Cook, stirring, until sauce boils and thickens, about 2 minutes. Makes 2 cups.

PER TABLESPOON: 35 calories, .10 gram protein, 7 grams carbohydrate, .86 gram total fat, 0 milligram cholesterol, 46 milligrams sodium.

Customarily featured at Chinese New Year banquets, Sweet & Sour Deep-fried Fish (recipe above) is served whole, garnished with vegetables and cilantro, and bathed in a hot, fruited sauce.

Pine Cone Fish

PREPARATION TIME: 15 to 20 minutes for fish; 5 to 6 minutes for sauce
DEEP-FRYING TIME: About 10 minutes (includes time to heat oil)
PER SERVING OF FISH: 273 calories, 26 grams protein, 12 grams carbohydrate, 14 grams total fat, 70 milligrams cholesterol, 79 milligrams sodium

This intriguing entrée gets its name from its appearance: First you almost fillet a whole fish, leaving the fillets attached just at the tail—then you score the flesh deeply on both sides. When deep-fried, the fish looks like a prickly pine cone. A light sweet and sour sauce laced with diced carrots is spooned atop the fish; toasted pine nuts add crunch. (Suggested beverage: a crisp, tart Chenin Blanc, or beer)

Makes 4 servings

> ¼ cup **pine nuts** or **slivered almonds**
>
> 1 whole **red rockfish** or other **rockfish** (about 4 lbs.), cleaned and scaled (leave on head and tail)
>
> About 2 tablespoons **dry sherry**
>
> **White pepper**
>
> About ½ cup **cornstarch**
>
> **Salad oil**
>
> **Sweet & Sour Sauce** (recipe follows)
>
> 1 cup lightly packed fresh **cilantro (coriander) sprigs**

Place pine nuts in a 9- or 10-inch-wide baking pan and toast in a 350° oven until golden, about 6 minutes; shake pan several times. Set aside.

Rinse fish and pat dry. Cut behind fish collarbone down to backbone. Turn knife parallel to backbone; with your other hand, grasp fish (as cut free) at collarbone. Cut closely along backbone, just to 3 inches above tail; as you cut, pull fish back to provide tension. Repeat on other side of fish. Fold both fillets back from backbone; tap knife with a mallet to cut through backbone 3 inches above tail. Discard head and backbone section. You will now have 2 fillets connected at tail.

Lay fillets, skin side down, on a board. Score flesh in a crisscross pattern, cutting just to skin and forming ½-inch diamonds. Sprinkle with sherry, rubbing it into crevices; sprinkle lightly with white pepper. Coat scored flesh with cornstarch, patting and rubbing it into crevices. Shake off excess.

Half-fill a wok or deep 12- to 14-inch frying pan with oil and heat to 375°F on a deep-frying thermometer. Turn fish inside out, so skin sides touch. Grasp ends of fillets with 1 hand, tail with the other. Slowly immerse fish in hot oil. Cook until richly browned, about 5 minutes; if fish is not completely submerged, gently spoon oil over fish as it cooks.

With a large wire skimmer or 2 wide slotted spatulas, lift fish from oil, drain briefly, and place on a heatproof rimmed platter. Serve, or keep warm in a 150° oven for up to 15 minutes.

Heat sauce to boiling; pour over fish. Sprinkle with nuts and garnish with cilantro. Cut into chunks to serve; spoon sauce over each serving.

SWEET & SOUR SAUCE. Heat ¼ cup **salad oil** in a 2- to 3-quart pan over medium-high heat. Add ⅓ cup *each* diced **carrot** and thinly sliced **green onions** (including tops) and 3 cloves **garlic** (minced or pressed). Cook, stirring, for 1 minute. Add 1¼ cups **Homemade Chicken Broth** (page 58) or canned regular-strength chicken broth; 6 tablespoons *each* **soy sauce, red wine vinegar,** and **sugar;** and 2½ tablespoons **cornstarch** mixed with 2½ tablespoons **water.** Cook, stirring, until sauce boils and thickens. If made ahead, cover and let stand at room temperature for up to 4 hours. Makes 2¾ cups.

PER TABLESPOON: 23 calories, .18 gram protein, 3 grams carbohydrate, 1 gram total fat, 0 milligram cholesterol, 182 milligrams sodium.

Braised Black Cod

W E S T E R N   C L A S S I C

PREPARATION TIME: About 10 minutes
MARINATING TIME: At least 1 hour
COOKING TIME: About 10 minutes
PER SERVING: 260 calories, 42 grams protein, 5 grams carbohydrate, 7 grams total fat, 114 milligrams cholesterol, 1931 milligrams sodium

A common sight in Western fish markets, black cod goes by several different names; you may find it labeled as butterfish or sablefish. It's a mild, soft-textured fish that benefits from bold seasonings—as in this recipe, where soy, sherry, ginger, and garlic complement its delicate flavor.

Black cod is also a good choice for smoking (see page 144); the commercially smoked type is sold as Alaskan cod. (Suggested wine: a dry, fresh Zinfandel Blanc)

Makes 3 servings

> 1½ pounds **black cod fillets;** or **black cod steaks,** cut about ¾ inch thick
>
> ½ cup minced **green onions** (including tops)
>
> ¼ cup *each* **soy sauce** and **dry sherry**
>
> 1 large clove **garlic,** minced or pressed
>
> ½ teaspoon grated **fresh ginger**
>
> 1 tablespoon **salad oil**
>
> 1 teaspoon **Oriental sesame oil**
>
> **Hot boiled small potatoes**

Rinse fish, pat dry, and set aside.

In a bowl, mix onions, soy, sherry, garlic, and ginger. Add fish, turning to coat all sides. Cover and refrigerate for at least 1 hour or up to 1½ hours, turning occasionally.

Place a 10- to 12-inch frying pan over high heat. When pan is hot, add salad oil. Lift fish from marinade and drain briefly (reserve marinade). Add fish to hot pan and cook, uncovered, turning once, until browned on both sides, about 5 minutes. Use a wide spatula to turn fish carefully—it falls apart easily. Add sesame oil to reserved marinade and pour over browned fish. Cook over high heat, uncovered, until marinade has almost evaporated. Carefully lift fish from pan and serve with pan juices and potatoes.

Macadamia Parmesan Sole

PREPARATION TIME: About 10 minutes
BAKING TIME: 10 to 15 minutes
PER SERVING: 518 calories, 35 grams protein, 6 grams carbohydrate, 40 grams total fat, 243 milligrams cholesterol, 925 milligrams sodium

Nuts add flavor and a little glamour to many fish recipes. A Western favorite, the buttery macadamia nut, combines with grated Parmesan to turn oven-fried sole fillets into a luxurious entrée for a special occasion.

Sent to Hawaii from Australia in the late 1800s, macadamia trees were first grown in the Islands as ornamentals. Today, though, they're cultivated (both in Hawaii and Southern California) for their rich, creamy-textured nuts. (Suggested wine: full-bodied, fruity Fumé Blanc)

Makes 4 servings

> 2 large eggs
> ¾ cup freshly grated Parmesan cheese
> 2 tablespoons all-purpose flour
> 4 sole fillets (4 to 6 oz. *each*)
> 3 tablespoons salad oil
> 3 tablespoons butter or margarine
> ½ cup finely chopped roasted salted macadamia nuts
> Watercress or parsley sprigs
> Lemon halves

Put a 10- by 15-inch rimmed baking pan in oven as it preheats to 425°.

In a 9- or 10-inch-wide pan, beat eggs to blend. On a piece of wax paper, mix cheese and flour. Rinse fish and pat dry. Dip in egg to coat; drain off excess, then coat fish in cheese mixture. Set fish in a single layer on wax paper.

Remove heated pan from oven; add oil and butter and swirl until butter is melted. Lay a piece of fish in pan; turn to coat with butter. Repeat with remaining fish, arranging pieces slightly apart in pan. Sprinkle fish evenly with nuts.

Bake, uncovered, in a 425° oven until fish is just opaque in thickest part (cut to test), 7 to 10 minutes. With a wide spatula, transfer fish to a platter. Garnish with watercress and lemon halves.

ADVERTISEMENTS to come West, placed in European newspapers by American railroad companies, encouraged waves of immigration—and led to the foreign character of a number of Western communities. Enticed by rich prospects in lumber, fishing, and farming, many Scandinavians settled in the Northwest.

Oven-poached Fish with Horseradish Cream Sauce

PREPARATION TIME: About 10 minutes for fish; 5 to 6 minutes for sauce
COOKING TIME: 10 to 22 minutes for fish; 10 to 12 minutes to heat fish and sauce
COOLING & CHILLING TIME: About 3 hours to chill fish after baking; about 1 hour to cool sauce
PER SERVING: 233 calories, 29 grams protein, 4 grams carbohydrate, 10 grams total fat, 112 milligrams cholesterol, 175 milligrams sodium

Oven-poaching is a simple way to manage this distinguished fish entrée in convenient make-ahead steps. You cook and chill the fish in advance, then top with a creamy, piquant horseradish sauce and reheat briefly to serve. (Suggested wine: dry Sauvignon Blanc)

Makes 4 or 5 servings

> 1½ to 2 pounds boned, skinned lingcod, Greenland turbot, halibut, giant seabass, rockfish, or sole fillets (no more than 1 inch thick) or steaks (cut about 1 inch thick)
> About ½ cup Homemade Chicken Broth (page 58) or canned regular-strength chicken broth
> 1 tablespoon lemon juice
> Salt (optional)
> Horseradish Cream Sauce (recipe follows)
> Minced parsley or green onions (including tops)

Rinse fish and pat dry. Arrange fillets side by side in a shallow, close-fitting baking dish or pan. If any fillets are thinner than ½ inch, fold them in half. Pour ½ cup of the broth over fish; sprinkle with lemon juice, then sprinkle lightly with salt, if desired. Cover and bake in a 400° oven until fish flakes readily when prodded with a fork in thickest part, 10 to 22 minutes. Let cool slightly.

Holding fish in place with a wide spatula, drain juices into a measuring cup; you should have about 1 cup liquid. If necessary, boil to reduce to 1 cup or add additional broth to make 1 cup. Cover fish and refrigerate until cold, about 3 hours.

Prepare Horseradish Cream Sauce and let cool; spoon over cold fish, covering completely. (At this point, you may cover and refrigerate until next day.)

Bake fish, uncovered, in a 400° oven until sauce is bubbly around edges and fish is hot, 10 to 12 minutes. Garnish with parsley.

HORSERADISH CREAM SAUCE. Melt 3 tablespoons **butter** or margarine in a 1- to 1½-quart pan over medium heat. Blend in 2 tablespoons **all-purpose flour;** stir until bubbly. Remove from heat; gradually add 1 cup **fish oven-poaching liquid,** ⅓ cup **half-and-half** or light cream, and 1 tablespoon **prepared horseradish,** stirring constantly. Return to heat and boil until thickened, 1 to 2 minutes. Remove from heat and let cool for about 1 hour.

Oven-fried Orange Roughy with Sesame

PREPARATION TIME: About 5 minutes

BAKING TIME: 10 to 15 minutes

PER SERVING: 283 calories, 32 grams protein, 3 grams carbohydrate, 13 grams total fat, 0 milligram cholesterol, 14 milligrams sodium

A golden crust of sesame seeds coats these lean, oven-browned fillets. Orange roughy, imported from New Zealand, is widely available in fish markets and super-markets; it's sold either frozen or thawed. (Suggested wine: dry Sylvaner or Fumé Blanc)

Makes 4 servings

- **1 large egg white**
- **⅓ cup sesame seeds**
- **4 boned, skinned orange roughy (New Zealand perch) fillets (6 to 8 oz. *each*), thawed if frozen**
- **2 tablespoons salad oil**
  Lemon wedges
  Soy sauce

Put egg white in a shallow 9- or 10-inch-wide pan and beat with a fork until slightly frothy. Put sesame seeds in another shallow 9- or 10-inch-wide pan.

Rinse fish and pat dry. Dip fillets on 1 side only in egg white, lift out, and let drain briefly. Then lay egg-moistened side in sesame seeds, coating heavily and equally. Lay fillets, seeds up, side by side on a sheet of wax paper.

Place a 10- by 15-inch rimmed baking pan in a 500° oven and heat for about 5 minutes. Swirl oil in pan; then lay fish, seeds down, in pan. Bake on lowest oven rack, uncovered, until fish flakes readily when prodded with a fork in thickest part and seeds on bottom are lightly browned, about 8 minutes. Transfer fillets, seed side up, onto 4 dinner plates. Offer lemon wedges and soy to add to taste.

Honfleur Fish Stew

PREPARATION TIME: About 10 minutes

COOKING TIME: About 40 minutes

PER SERVING: 267 calories, 22 grams protein, 25 grams carbohydrate, 9 grams total fat, 72 milligrams cholesterol, 160 milligrams sodium

Like many of the country dishes we've discovered on our scouting trips abroad, this French fish stew is simple, delicious, and easy to duplicate. (Suggested wine: Pinot Blanc)

Makes 3 or 4 servings

- **2 tablespoons butter or margarine**
- **1 medium-size onion, chopped**
- **4 cups Homemade Chicken Broth (page 58) or 2 cans (14½ oz. *each*) regular-strength chicken broth**
- **1 cup dry white wine**
- **2 medium-size russet potatoes, peeled and cut into 1-inch chunks**

- **1 bay leaf**
- **½ teaspoon fennel seeds**
- **1 pound boned, skinned sole, halibut, or rockfish**
  Salt and pepper

Melt butter in a 3- to 4-quart pan over medium-high heat. Add onion; cook, stirring, until soft. Add broth, wine, potatoes, bay leaf, and fennel seeds. Bring to a boil; then reduce heat, cover, and simmer until potatoes are tender when pierced, about 20 minutes.

Rinse fish, pat dry, and cut into chunks. Add to stew, cover, and simmer until fish flakes readily when prodded with a fork, about 3 minutes. Season to taste with salt and pepper.

Fish & Potato Selyanka

PREPARATION TIME: About 15 minutes

COOKING TIME: About 20 minutes, plus 20 minutes to rest

PER SERVING (WITHOUT BUTTER): 239 calories, 28 grams protein, 22 grams carbohydrate, 3 grams total fat, 61 milligrams cholesterol, 77 milligrams sodium

Russian heritage and definite Finnish personality come together in selyanka—*a name given to a number of Finnish dishes that combine meat or fish with vegetables. This one is a dill-seasoned halibut and potato soup. (Suggested wine: very dry Sauvignon Blanc)*

Makes 5 or 6 servings

- **2 pounds halibut steaks or Greenland turbot fillets**
- **6 cups Homemade Chicken Broth (page 58) or 1 large can (49½ oz.) regular-strength chicken broth**
- **1 pound thin-skinned potatoes, peeled and cut into ½-inch cubes**
- **1 large onion, finely chopped**
  About 1 teaspoon dry dill weed
- **1 medium-size mild red or white onion, chopped**
- **6 tablespoons butter or margarine, melted**
  Salt and pepper

Rinse fish, pat dry, and place in a 4- to 5-quart pan. Add broth. Cover and bring to a boil over medium heat; then reduce heat and simmer until fish flakes readily when prodded with a fork in thickest part, 2 to 4 minutes.

Set aside for at least 20 minutes; or let cool completely, then cover and refrigerate fish in broth to intensify the fish flavor. Lift out fish with a slotted spoon. Remove and discard skin and bones; cut fish into bite-size chunks.

Return pan with broth to high heat. Add potatoes, the large chopped onion, and 1 teaspoon of the dill weed. Boil, covered, until potatoes mash easily, about 15 minutes. Add fish and heat through.

Ladle soup into bowls. Offer chopped red onion, melted butter, salt and pepper, and additional dill weed to add to individual servings.

Steamed Mussels

Pictured on facing page

PREPARATION TIME: 10 to 15 minutes to scrub mussels; about 10 minutes to make broth
STEAMING TIME: About 10 minutes
PER SERVING: 281 calories, 24 grams protein, 11 grams carbohydrate, 15 grams total fat, 114 milligrams cholesterol, 602 milligrams sodium

Now grown in underwater farms, mussels are available the year around. Inside their blue shells, the farm-grown shellfish are usually gray or pale orange; wild mussels, harvested during posted "safe seasons" along the Pacific coast, often have bright orange flesh. If you gather your own mussels, clean them by scraping off any barnacles; then scrub them with a stiff brush under running water. (Suggested wine: fruity, lightly oaked Chardonnay)

Makes 2 or 3 entrée servings, 8 to 12 first-course servings

> 3 tablespoons butter or margarine
> 1 clove garlic, minced or pressed
> 1 small onion, chopped
> 1 cup dry white wine; or 1 cup Homemade Chicken Broth (page 58) or canned regular-strength chicken broth
> ½ cup minced parsley
> ⅛ teaspoon pepper
> 2 to 3 quarts mussels in shells, scrubbed
> Melted butter or margarine

Melt the 3 tablespoons butter in a 5- to 6-quart pan. Add garlic and onion; cook over medium-high heat until soft, stirring occasionally. Add wine, parsley, and pepper; bring to a boil. Add mussels. Reduce heat, cover, and simmer gently until mussels have opened, 8 to 10 minutes; discard any that don't open.

With a slotted spoon, transfer mussels to individual bowls; ladle cooking broth evenly over servings or into small cups. To eat, pull each mussel from shell; pluck off and discard the coarse "beard," then dip mussel, if desired, in melted butter.

Steamed Fish & Clams in Black Bean Sauce

PREPARATION TIME: 10 to 15 minutes
STEAMING TIME: About 10 minutes
PER SERVING: 166 calories, 13 grams protein, 26 grams carbohydrate, 2 grams total fat, 35 milligrams cholesterol, 940 milligrams sodium

Pungent fermented black beans, used sparingly with garlic and ginger, make a flavorful sauce for seafood. (Suggested wine: dry, tart Chenin Blanc, or beer)

Makes 2 or 3 servings

> 1 rockfish or lingcod fillet (about 1 lb.), about 1 inch thick
> 1½ tablespoons fermented salted black beans, rinsed and patted dry
> 2 cloves garlic

> 1 tablespoon *each* soy sauce and dry sherry
> 2 green onions (including tops)
> 3 thin slices fresh ginger
> 12 clams in shell, suitable for steaming, scrubbed
> 2 tablespoons salad oil

Rinse fish and pat dry. Place in a heatproof dish at least 1 inch deep that will fit inside a steamer.

Mince or mash black beans and garlic; add soy and sherry. Drizzle over fish. Cut 1 onion into thirds; place cut onion and ginger on top of fish. Cut remaining onion into 2-inch lengths; cut lengths into thin shreds and set aside. Arrange clams around fish.

Cover dish completely with wax paper; then support dish on a stand or rack in steamer over 1 to 2 inches of boiling water. Cover pan and cook until fish flakes readily when prodded with a fork in thickest part, about 10 minutes. If clams open before fish is done, remove them and continue to cook fish for a few more minutes; then return clams to dish.

Lift dish from steamer; discard wax paper. Discard ginger and onion pieces from top of fish. Sprinkle onion slivers over fish. Heat oil in a small pan until it ripples when pan is tilted; pour over fish (oil will sizzle).

Shrimp & Jicama with Chile Vinegar

PREPARATION TIME: 10 to 15 minutes
PER SERVING: 359 calories, 31 grams protein, 55 grams carbohydrate, 13 grams total fat, 181 milligrams cholesterol, 195 milligrams sodium

Light and full of flavor, this refreshing salad boasts a leanness that would win approval from a health spa. (Suggested wine: dry white wine with sparkling water and lime)

Makes 4 servings

> Chile Vinegar (recipe follows)
> 2 cups shredded peeled jicama (about 9 oz.)
> 1 pound small cooked, shelled shrimp
> 4 large ripe tomatoes, cored and sliced
> 4 large (about 2-inch-diameter) tomatillos, husked and sliced
> Fresh cilantro (coriander) sprigs
> Salt

Mix ⅓ cup of the vinegar with jicama and ⅓ cup with shrimp; reserve remainder.

On 4 dinner plates, arrange tomatoes and tomatillos, overlapping slices slightly. Mound jicama alongside tomato slices. Place shrimp on top of jicama. Spoon remaining vinegar over tomatoes and tomatillos. Garnish with cilantro; add salt to taste.

CHILE VINEGAR. Stir together ⅔ cup **white wine vinegar**, ¼ cup **sugar**, 2 to 3 tablespoons seeded, minced **fresh hot chile** (such as jalapeño or serrano), and 3 to 4 tablespoons chopped **fresh cilantro (coriander)**. Makes 1 cup.

Skewered Shrimp with Garlic Butter

PREPARATION TIME: 30 to 40 minutes; 45 to 60 minutes including vegetables
BROILING TIME: About 6 minutes
PER SERVING OF SHRIMP WITH ARTICHOKE: 178 calories, 26 grams protein, 17 grams carbohydrate, 1 gram total fat, 184 milligrams cholesterol, 275 milligrams sodium

Many feel that shrimp taste sweetest if cooked in the shell. Others prefer to cook them shelled, since shelling the cooked shrimp can be a bit messy. It's simply a matter of taste, as our recipe is delicious both ways. (Suggested wine: mature, full-flavored Chardonnay with medium oak)

Makes 6 servings

> 2 **pounds large shrimp**
> **(about 30 per lb.)**
>
> **Garlic Butter (recipe follows)**
>
> 2 **tablespoons lemon juice**
>
> 6 **artichokes, cooked (see page 184), or**
> **2 pounds asparagus, cooked (see page**
> **190); use cooked vegetables hot or cool**

Shell shrimp, if desired; then devein. To devein unshelled shrimp, slide a thin skewer through back of each shrimp, guiding skewer under vein. Then pull skewer gently up through back, lifting and pulling out vein. Repeat along back in several spots to remove entire vein.

Rinse shrimp and pat dry; divide into 6 equal portions. Thread each portion of shrimp on 2 parallel thin skewers (at least 10 inches long). With 1 skewer, pierce shrimp through thick section of body, arranging shrimp atop each other with tails parallel. Run a second thin skewer parallel to the first, piercing through tail ends of shrimp.

Lay shrimp, side by side, on a rack in a broiler pan (about 12 by 15 inches). Brush with about 2 tablespoons of the Garlic Butter. Broil 4 inches below heat until shrimp turn bright pink, about 3 minutes. Turn shrimp; broil until bright pink on other side and opaque in thickest part (cut to test), about 3 more minutes.

Arrange shrimp on a tray or on 6 dinner plates. Immediately reheat Garlic Butter until bubbling; stir in lemon juice, then pour into 6 small bowls. Accompany shrimp with artichokes or asparagus; dip shrimp and vegetables into hot Garlic Butter.

GARLIC BUTTER. In a 1- to 1½-quart pan, combine ½ cup (¼ lb.) **butter** or margarine, ½ cup **olive oil,** 3 cloves **garlic,** minced or pressed, and 3 tablespoons minced **parsley.** Stir occasionally over medium-high heat until bubbling. Makes about 1 cup.
PER TABLESPOON: 112 calories, .10 gram protein, .22 gram carbohydrate, 12 grams total fat, 16 milligrams cholesterol, 59 milligrams sodium.

Blue-black mussels pop open when steamed, revealing brilliant-hued—and delicious—meat inside. Dip them in melted butter and eat; savor the wine and garlic cooking broth, too. The recipe for Steamed Mussels is on the facing page.

Microwave Meals for One—in 5 to 25 Minutes

These five cook-by-the-plate dinners from the microwave are perfect for those times when you need a one-serving meal. They're wholesome and attractive; there's little mess and no leftovers to contend with. You just add individual servings of foods to a single plate, microwaving them in sequence to assure even cooking. You can prepare each dinner in only 5 to 25 minutes.

Note: All foods are microwaved on **HIGH (100%)** throughout the cooking time.

Smoked Pork Chop Supper

      9 or 10 dried apricot halves
      Honey Mustard Sauce (recipe follows)
   1 smoked pork chop, about ¾ inch thick
   ¼ pound edible-pod peas, ends and strings removed
   1 to 2 teaspoons butter or margarine
   1 bran muffin, purchased or homemade

Put apricot halves in center of a nonmetal dinner plate and spoon sauce on top. Cover tightly with plastic wrap and microwave on **HIGH (100%)** until hot, about 1 minute.

Set pork chop on plate and spoon apricots and sauce over top. Cover and microwave until pork chop is heated through, 1½ to 2 more minutes.

Arrange peas on plate; cover and microwave until heated through, 30 to 40 seconds. Remove plate from oven and dot peas with butter. If desired, microwave muffin just to heat, 10 to 20 seconds, then set on plate.

HONEY MUSTARD SAUCE. Mix 1 tablespoon *each* **Dijon mustard** and **honey** with ⅛ teaspoon **ground ginger**.

Clam Paella

   ⅓ cup long-grain white rice
   ⅓ cup dry white wine
      About ½ cup water
   1 tablespoon finely chopped parsley
   1 small clove garlic, minced or pressed (optional)

      6 or 7 cherry tomatoes, stemmed and halved
   10 clams in shell, suitable for steaming, scrubbed

In a nonmetal soup plate or rimmed dinner plate, combine rice, wine, ⅓ cup of the water, parsley, garlic, and tomatoes. Cover loosely with plastic wrap and microwave on **HIGH (100%)**, stirring 3 or 4 times, until rice is tender to bite and liquid is absorbed, 15 to 18 minutes. If necessary, add more water to rice as it cooks to prevent it from getting dry.

Arrange clams around rim of plate. Cover loosely with a new piece of plastic wrap and microwave until clams pop open, 4 to 6 more minutes.

Yam & Chicken Dinner

   1 medium-size yam or sweet potato (about ½ lb.), scrubbed
   ½ chicken breast (about ½ lb.), skinned and boned
   6 to 8 large spinach leaves, washed
   1 to 3 teaspoons butter or margarine
   ½ lemon

Cut a lengthwise slit in yam almost through to each end and set on a nonmetal dinner plate. Cover tightly with plastic wrap and microwave on **HIGH (100%)** until yam is soft when pierced, 4 to 5 minutes.

Arrange chicken next to yam, cover, and microwave, turning chicken over once, until meat in thickest part is no longer pink (cut to test), 4 to 5 more minutes.

Slip spinach under chicken. Cover again and microwave just until spinach is wilted, about 30 seconds. Open slit in yam and tuck butter inside; serve with lemon half.

Pizza-topped Onion with Linguisa

   1 medium-size onion, peeled and cut in half lengthwise
      About ¼ pound green beans (9 or 10), stem ends snapped off
   1 linguisa sausage (about 5 oz.)
   2 tablespoons canned tomato paste
   2 slices mozzarella cheese

      About 2 tablespoons shredded or freshly grated Parmesan cheese
   ½ teaspoon dry oregano leaves

Put onion halves in center of a nonmetal dinner plate; cover tightly with plastic wrap and microwave on **HIGH (100%)** until tender when pierced, 5 to 6 minutes.

Arrange beans alongside, cover, and microwave until beans begin to turn bright green, about 2 more minutes.

Cut almost through sausage lengthwise and open out flat. Arrange on plate next to onion halves. Cover and microwave until sausage is heated through, about 1 minute.

Spread about 1 tablespoon of the tomato paste on top of each onion half. Top each with a slice of mozzarella cheese and about 1 tablespoon Parmesan cheese; then sprinkle each with ¼ teaspoon of the oregano leaves. Cover and microwave just long enough to melt cheese, 40 to 45 more seconds.

Salmon & Cucumber with Dilled Potatoes

   3 small (about 1½-inch-diameter) thin-skinned potatoes, scrubbed
   1 to 3 teaspoons butter or margarine
   1 salmon steak (about 10 oz.), rinsed and patted dry
   ½ teaspoon prepared horseradish
   ¼ to ½ cucumber, peeled and cut into julienne strips
      Dry dill weed

Pierce potatoes in several places or cut a strip of peel from around center to prevent bursting. Put potatoes on 1 side of a nonmetal dinner plate and dot with butter. Cover loosely with plastic wrap and microwave on **HIGH (100%)** until potatoes are soft when pierced, 4 to 6 minutes.

Set salmon next to potatoes; cover and microwave, rotating plate once, until fish is lighter pink almost to center (cut to test), 4 to 5 more minutes. Turn salmon over and top with horseradish; then arrange cucumber strips on plate, turning to coat with juices. Sprinkle potatoes lightly with dill weed. Cover and microwave just until cucumber is heated, 40 to 50 more seconds.

Grilled Scallops with Red Pepper Sauce

PREPARATION TIME: About 50 minutes to prepare peppers; about 2 minutes to make sauce; 30 to 40 minutes to ignite charcoal

GRILLING TIME: 5 to 8 minutes

PER SERVING: 272 calories, 18 grams protein, 6 grams carbohydrate, 19 grams total fat, 91 milligrams cholesterol, 485 milligrams sodium

Sweet, mellow red pepper purée, thickened with butter to make a velvety-smooth sauce, tops these quickly grilled scallops. You can make the sauce ahead and keep it warm for up to several hours; if reheated, it will separate. (Suggested wine: a fruity, dry Zinfandel or Zinfandel Blanc)

Makes 4 to 6 servings

>   2 small red bell peppers or ¾ cup canned roasted red peppers
> ½ cup Homemade Chicken Broth (page 58) or canned regular-strength chicken broth
> ¼ cup dry white wine
> ¼ teaspoon dry basil
> ½ cup (¼ lb.) butter or margarine
> 1½ pounds scallops, *each* 1 to 1½ inches in diameter
> Melted butter
> Salt and pepper

Place fresh bell peppers in a 9- or 10-inch-wide baking pan. Bake, uncovered, on lowest rack of a 450°oven, turning often, until skins blister and blacken, about 35 minutes. Cover pan and let peppers cool; peel off and discard skins along with stems and seeds.

Place fresh or canned roasted peppers, broth, and wine in a blender; whirl until smooth. Pour mixture into a 10- to 12-inch frying pan. Add basil. Boil, stirring, until reduced to about ¾ cup. (At this point, you may let cool, then cover and refrigerate for up to 2 days. Reheat to boiling before continuing.)

Reduce heat to medium. Add the ½ cup butter in 1 chunk; stir constantly until completely blended. Keep warm while you grill scallops. (To keep warm for up to 4 hours, pour into the top of a double boiler or a 2-cup measuring cup and set in hot-to-touch water. Stir occasionally and replace water as needed.)

Rinse scallops, pat dry, and thread through their diameters onto thin skewers (scallops should lie flat). Brush generously with melted butter. Place on a grill 2 to 4 inches above a solid bed of very hot coals (you should be able to hold your hand at grill level for no more than 1 to 2 seconds). Cook, turning once, until scallops are opaque in thickest part (cut to test), 5 to 8 minutes.

Pour sauce onto a warm platter or equally onto 4 to 6 warm dinner plates. Lay scallops in sauce. Season to taste with salt and pepper.

GRILLED SCALLOPS WITH GINGER-LIME SAUCE

In a 10- to 12-inch frying pan, combine ½ cup **dry white wine**, ½ cup **Homemade Chicken Broth (page 58)** or canned regular strength chicken broth, 2 tablespoons minced **shallot** or onion, 1 teaspoon grated **fresh ginger,** and ¼ teaspoon grated **lime peel.** Bring to a boil; boil, uncovered, until reduced by half. Add ½ cup **whipping cream;** boil, uncovered, until reduced to ¾ cup.

Reduce heat to medium. Add ¼ cup (⅛ lb.) **unsalted butter** in 1 chunk; stir constantly until butter is completely blended. Keep warm while you grill scallops.

Grill 1 pound **scallops** as directed for **Grilled Scallops with Red Pepper Sauce.** Pour ginger-lime sauce onto a warm serving platter or equally onto 4 warm dinner plates; lay scallops in sauce. Makes 4 servings.

Hangtown Fry

W E S T E R N   C L A S S I C

PREPARATION TIME: About 40 minutes (including 30 minutes to let oysters dry)

COOKING TIME: 5 to 8 minutes

PER SERVING: 488 calories, 22 grams protein, 14 grams carbohydrate, 38 grams total fat, 777 milligrams cholesterol, 466 milligrams sodium

This egg and oyster dish takes its name from California's Mother Lode town of Placerville—called Hangtown in its brawling youth. Supposedly, it's descended from a spur-of-the-moment supper created to satisfy a gold miner's extravagant tastes. (Suggested wine: a low-profile, dry Chardonnay)

Makes 2 servings

> 5 large eggs
> 2 tablespoons whipping cream
> ¼ pound shucked raw oysters (if large, cut into bite-size pieces)
> All-purpose flour
> 3 tablespoons cracker crumbs
> 3 tablespoons butter or margarine
> Salt and pepper

Beat eggs and cream together until blended; set aside. Coat oysters with flour; shake off excess. Dip oysters in beaten eggs, then roll in cracker crumbs; set slightly apart on a rack and let stand until surface is slightly dried, about 30 minutes.

Melt 2 tablespoons of the butter in a 10- to 12-inch frying pan over medium-high heat. When hot, place oysters slightly apart in pan. Cook, uncovered, until golden, about 1 minute on each side. Lift out with a spatula; drain on paper towels and keep warm.

Add remaining 1 tablespoon butter to pan; when melted, add remaining beaten eggs. As eggs begin to set on bottom, lift cooked portions to allow uncooked egg to flow underneath; cook until eggs are firm but still moist. Slide eggs out of pan onto a warm platter; top with oysters. Season to taste with salt and pepper.

For an elegant picnic, tumble a mound of bright scarlet crayfish, poached in wine and herbs, onto a platter. Then unpack crusty French bread, a bottle of wine, and a pot of mayonnaise for dipping. Recipe for Boiled Crayfish is on the facing page.

Oven-shucked Pacific Oysters

WESTERN CLASSIC

PREPARATION TIME: 3 to 4 minutes to scrub every 12 oysters
BAKING TIME: 20 to 30 minutes
PER SERVING OF 6 MEDIUM-SIZE OYSTERS WITH 2 TEASPOONS BUTTER: 124 calories, 7 grams protein, 3 grams carbohydrate, 9 grams total fat, 63 milligrams cholesterol, 140 milligrams sodium

Shucking oysters can be a real challenge, but here's a way to sidestep the problem: simply bake the oysters. Oven heat makes them open just far enough for you to slip in a knife and open the shells. This treatment is ideal for Giant Pacific oysters, a type that (despite the "giant") actually ranges in size from small to large. You'll find these oysters sold under different names, usually reflecting the location of origin—Willapa, Quilcene, and Hamma Hamma, for example. (Suggested wine: a dry, mature Chardonnay)

Allow 6 to 12 small or medium-size, well-scrubbed **Pacific oysters** per serving. Fill a 12- by 15-inch baking pan with about ¼ inch **water;** lay oysters in pan, cupped side down, arranging close together in 1 or 2 layers. Prepare 2 pans for the same oven if you want to cook large quantities, or cook oysters in sequence for a hot batch as desired.

Bake in a 400° oven for 20 to 30 minutes. If you can pry the oysters open after 20 minutes, they will be just nicely heated and very juicy; after 30 minutes they will definitely have a cooked appearance, but the shells will gape slightly and be easier to open.

To open oysters, place oyster, cupped side of shell down, on your plate. Protect your fingers with a potholder if shell is still hot. With an oyster knife or a blunt table knife, pry shell open at wide end, slipping in knife to cut adductor muscle that holds shell closed, then pull off top shell; preserve juices. The tricky part is seeing where these wildly voluted shells come together and deciding where to pry.

Drizzle melted **butter** or margarine over oyster; sprinkle with **freshly ground black pepper.**

Spectacular, Easy, Delicious: Dutch Baby

Whether for brunch, lunch, or sit-down dinner, you'll steal the show when you present our spectacular, golden Dutch Baby. Beyond its magnificent size, it's really just a glorified, bowl-shaped Yorkshire pudding.

The light, fluffy Dutch Baby presented here was made famous in the first half of this century at Manca's, a family-run restaurant that was practically an institution in Seattle. Victor Manca baked miniatures of a giant German oven pancake; his children dubbed the delectable result "Dutch Babies." The name stuck—and the Dutch Baby now comes in all sizes.

This pancake is so spectacular when it first comes from the oven that you'll want to have everyone seated before you bring it to the table. On cooling, the pancake will settle noticeably, though it won't sink as much as a soufflé. Serve it with powdered sugar or a fruit topping, either spooned over or served alongside; round out your menu with browned sausages, crisp bacon, or pan-fried ham slices.

The batter we use here is full of eggs and puffs up dramatically in the oven. The results are even more stunning when the batter is baked in a big container such as a paella pan. If you don't have a paella pan, you can use a big iron frying pan or a large baking dish. Any shape will do, but the container must not be much more than 3 inches deep.

Once you decide on a pan, measure its total volume by pouring in quarts of water. When you've determined the pan's volume, select the recipe proportions you need from the chart below.

Pan size	Butter or margarine	Large eggs	Milk & flour
2–3 qt.	¼ cup	3	¾ cup *each*
3–4 qt.	⅓ cup	4	1 cup *each*
4–4½ qt.	½ cup	5	1¼ cups *each*
4½–5 qt.	½ cup	6	1½ cups *each*

Place butter in pan and set in a 425° oven. While butter melts, mix batter quickly. Put eggs in a blender or food processor and whirl on high speed for 1 minute. With motor running, gradually pour in milk, then slowly add flour; continue whirling for 30 seconds. (Or, in a bowl, beat eggs until blended; gradually beat in milk, then flour.)

Remove pan from oven and pour in batter. Return pan to oven and bake until pancake is puffy and well browned, 20 to 25 minutes, depending on pan size.

Dust pancake with **ground nutmeg**, if you wish. Cut into wedges and serve at once with any of the following toppings. Makes 3 to 6 servings.

POWDERED SUGAR CLASSIC. Have a shaker or bowl of **powdered sugar** and thick wedges of **lemon** at the table. Sprinkle sugar on hot pancake, then squeeze on lemon juice.

FRUIT. Use sliced **strawberries** or peaches, sweetened to taste; or any fruits in season, cut and sweetened.

HOT FRUIT. Sautéed **apples,** pears, or bananas make a good topping; offer with **sour cream** or plain or fruit-flavored yogurt.

SYRUPS. Pour warm or cold **honey,** maple syrup, or fruit syrup over hot pancake.

Pique-nique Quiches

PREPARATION TIME: About 25 minutes
BAKING TIME: About 40 minutes
PER SERVING: 283 calories, 8 grams protein, 16 grams carbohydrate, 21 grams total fat, 137 milligrams cholesterol, 182 milligrams sodium

Anyone who knows Sunset *knows that we love to picnic—anywhere, in any weather, at any season. Of all our farflung suggestions on the subject, this* pique-nique *tart is one of the most appealing. The French savory travels deliciously to boats, beaches, mountain slopes, and beyond.*

Makes 8 to 10 servings

> **Pastry Dough (recipe follows)**
> **About 1 cup (4 oz.) shredded Swiss or Gruyère cheese**
> **2 large eggs**
> **1½ cups half-and-half or light cream**
> **⅛ teaspoon pepper**

Prepare Pastry Dough. Divide into 8 or 10 equal portions; press evenly over bottom and up sides of about eight 1- by 4-inch or about ten 1- by 3-inch tart pans, making dough flush with pan rim. Set pans on a 12- by 15-inch baking sheet; evenly sprinkle cheese in pastry-lined pans.

In a bowl, beat eggs, half-and-half, and pepper until blended. Pour evenly into pastry shells; don't let filling overflow or pastry will stick to pans. Set baking sheet on lowest rack of a 350° oven. Bake until filling puffs and tops are lightly browned, 35 to 40 minutes.

Let quiches cool for about 10 minutes (filling will settle); then, protecting your hands, tip quiches out of pans into your hand. Place right side up on a serving plate and serve hot; or place on a rack and let cool to room temperature, then serve. If made ahead, cover cooled quiches and refrigerate until next day. To reheat, place on a baking sheet and bake, uncovered, in a 350° oven for about 10 minutes.

To eat, use a knife and fork; or eat cooled quiches out of hand.

PASTRY DOUGH. In a food processor or a bowl, combine 1½ cups **all-purpose flour** and 10 tablespoons (¼ lb. plus 2 tablespoons) **butter** or margarine, cut into chunks. Whirl (or rub with your fingers) until crumbly. Add 1 **large egg** and whirl (or mix with a fork) until dough holds together. Shape into a smooth ball.

ONION-ZUCCHINI QUICHES

Prepare **Pastry Dough** and press into tart pans as directed for **Pique-nique Quiches**. Place pastry-lined pans on a 12- by 15-inch baking sheet.

For the filling, combine 1 cup lightly packed shredded **zucchini**, 1 cup (4 oz.) shredded **Swiss cheese**, and 1 tablespoon all-purpose **flour**; stir to blend, then distribute equally among pastry shells. Sprinkle evenly with ½ cup finely chopped **green onions** (including tops).

In a bowl, beat 3 **large eggs**, 1½ cups **half-and-half** or light cream, 1 clove **garlic** (minced or pressed), ¼ teaspoon **garlic salt,** and ⅛ teaspoon **pepper** until blended. Divide equally among pastry shells. Arrange 3 thin **zucchini** slices (*each* 1 to 1¼ inches in diameter), slightly overlapping, in center of each quiche. (You will need 1 or 2 small zucchini *total.*)

Bake and serve as directed for **Pique-nique Quiches.**

California Green Chile & Cheese Pie

W E S T E R N   C L A S S I C

PREPARATION TIME: About 15 minutes
BAKING TIME: About 1 hour
PER SERVING: 488 calories, 20 grams protein, 24 grams carbohydrate, 35 grams total fat, 273 milligrams cholesterol, 565 milligrams sodium

Our Spanish-Mexican heritage shows up in architecture, place names, and regional recipes of the West. One of our favorite ingredient combinations—mild green chiles cooled by creamy jack cheese—appears in a pie with the spirit of chiles rellenos.

Makes 6 servings

> **1¼ cups all-purpose flour**
> **6 tablespoons butter or margarine, cut into chunks**
> **4 large eggs**
> **1½ cups (6 oz.) shredded jack cheese**
> **1 cup (4 oz.) shredded mild Cheddar cheese**
> **1 can (4 oz.) diced green chiles, drained**
> **1 cup half-and-half or light cream**
> **⅛ teaspoon ground cumin (optional)**

In food processor or a bowl, combine flour and butter. Whirl (or rub with your fingers) until fine crumbs form. Add 1 egg to flour mixture and whirl (or mix with a fork) until dough holds together. Shape into a smooth ball.

On a lightly floured board, roll out dough and fit it into a 9- or 10-inch pie pan; pinch any tears together to rejoin. Flute edges; lightly prick bottom and sides of pastry shell all over with a fork. Bake in a 400° oven just until pale golden, about 12 minutes. Let cool slightly. Reduce oven temperature to 325°.

Sprinkle jack cheese and ½ cup of the Cheddar cheese over bottom of partially baked crust. Evenly distribute chiles over cheese.

In a medium-size bowl, beat half-and-half, remaining 3 eggs, and cumin (if used) until blended; pour over chiles. Sprinkle evenly with remaining ½ cup Cheddar cheese. Bake in a 325° oven until center of pie appears set when pan is gently shaken, about 40 minutes. Let stand for about 15 minutes before cutting; serve warm or at room temperature.

Savory Cheesecake

PREPARATION TIME: About 10 minutes
BAKING TIME: About 50 minutes
PER SERVING: 217 calories, 9 grams protein, 6 grams carbohydrate, 18 grams total fat, 116 milligrams cholesterol, 342 milligrams sodium

Unusual in that it isn't sweet, this cheesecake shows off the bold personality of Camembert, feta, or blue cheese. Its silky smooth texture and savory flavor go well with garnishes such as radishes, olives, or walnuts. Serve in thin wedges as an hors d'oeuvre.

Makes 12 to 16 servings

> 1 **pound Camembert, blue-veined, feta, or unflavored, unripened or ripened chèvre cheese, at room temperature**
> 1 **large package (8 oz.) cream cheese**
> 3 **large eggs**
> **Whole Wheat Press-in Crust (recipe follows)**
> **Garnishes (suggestions follow), optional**

Leave rind on Camembert cheese, but trim off and discard any hard rind on ripened chèvre. Cut all cheeses into about 1-inch chunks. In a large bowl, beat eggs with an electric mixer until well blended. Add Camembert and cream cheese pieces, a few at a time, beating until smooth and well blended. Spoon into baked crust. Bake in a 350° oven until center barely jiggles when pan is gently shaken, 25 to 30 minutes. Let cake cool to room temperature on a rack, then serve. Or, if made ahead, cover and refrigerate until next day; for best texture, bring to room temperature before serving (takes 2 to 3 hours).

To serve, remove pan sides. Garnish, if desired, and cut into thin wedges.

WHOLE WHEAT PRESS-IN CRUST. In a food processor or a bowl, combine 1 cup **whole wheat flour** and 6 tablespoons **butter** or margarine, cut into chunks. Whirl (or rub with your fingers) until coarse crumbs form. Add 1 **large egg;** whirl (or mix with a fork) until dough forms a ball. Press dough in a firm, even layer over bottom and about 1¾ inches up sides of a 9-inch springform pan or round cake pan with a removable bottom. Bake in a 350° oven until lightly browned, about 20 minutes. Use hot or cold.

GARNISHES. Top Camembert or blue cheesecake with **walnut or pecan halves** or toasted sliced almonds. Top feta cheesecake with whole **black salt- or brine-cured olives** or thinly sliced green onions. Arrange thinly sliced **radishes** or small watercress sprigs over top of chèvre cheesecake.

Cheese Knishes

PREPARATION TIME: About 1 hour
BAKING TIME: About 7 minutes; 15 minutes if frozen
PER SERVING: 339 calories, 14 grams protein, 28 grams carbohydrate, 21 grams total fat, 49 milligrams cholesterol, 254 milligrams sodium

Pronounce the "k" when you ask for another serving of this Jewish pastry. Our recipe turns out plump, strudel-like enclosures for smooth cream cheese and mild, squeaky-textured farmers cheese. Topped with cherry sauce and sour cream, the knishes make a satisfying dessert.

Makes about 4 dozen knishes, 12 to 16 servings

> 1 **large egg**
> ¼ **cup salad oil**
> ¾ **cup water**
> 1 **teaspoon vinegar**
> 2½ to 3 **cups all-purpose flour**
> **Cheese Filling (recipe follows)**
> **Sweet Cherry Sauce (recipe follows)**
> **Sour cream or plain yogurt**

In a bowl, beat egg, oil, water, vinegar, and 2½ cups of the flour with a dough hook in an electric mixer (or with a heavy spoon) until smooth. Then beat in about ½ cup more flour or enough to make a smooth, shiny dough. Cover dough and let stand for 15 minutes.

Divide dough in half. On a large floured board, roll out 1 portion as thinly as possible, making about a 20-inch-diameter circle. Spoon half the filling in a band around dough circle, about 1 inch in from edge. Spread or press filling to make thickness even. Roll edge of dough up over filling; then roll dough 4 to 6 turns toward center, encasing filling. Pull and stretch dough as you roll. Cut away dough center, freeing filled roll. Pull and stretch cut edge up over filled roll; press gently to seal. Turn roll seam side down; cut into 12-inch lengths. Pinch ends of each piece to seal.

Discard center scrap of dough. Roll out remaining dough and repeat steps to fill and shape, using remaining filling.

Arrange knishes about 1½ inches apart on well-oiled baking sheets. (At this point, you may freeze on baking sheets until solid, then transfer to plastic bags and return to freezer. To bake, unwrap frozen knishes, but do not thaw.)

Bake knishes in a 425° oven until hot and lightly browned, about 7 minutes (12 to 15 minutes if frozen). Cut into 2-inch lengths; serve hot, with cherry sauce and sour cream.

CHEESE FILLING. Follow directions for Cheese Filling (page 177), but use ¼ cup (⅛ lb.) **butter** or margarine, 2 large **onions,** 4 small packages (3 oz. *each*) **cream cheese,** and 2¼ pounds **farmers cheese.**

SWEET CHERRY SAUCE. Drain 1 can (1 lb.) **pitted dark sweet cherries,** reserving liquid. In a 1½- to 2-quart pan, combine cherry liquid and 1 tablespoon *each* **cornstarch** and **sugar.** Cook over high heat, stirring, until sauce boils and thickens. Remove from heat and let cool, then stir in cherries. If made ahead, cover and refrigerate for up to 24 hours.

PICNICKING, in Sunset's estimate, is nothing less than an art form, or perhaps a gourmet sport. We've advocated outings for every season and weather, headed to the beach, mountains, desert, country, city, or patio at home. In 1948, we coined the phrase "tailgate picnic." By the time we published "The Tailgate as Picnic Table" in 1954, this term had become part of the language.

Simpler than a soufflé, more delicate than an omelet, this lovely Orange Omelet-Soufflé with Warm Strawberries (recipe at right) captures the best of both. It's simply sweetened whipped egg whites and whipped yolks folded together and baked in a fresh orange sauce. Serve it hot and puffy from the oven, with warmed strawberries. Like a soufflé, it sinks quickly as it cools.

Orange Omelet-Soufflé with Warm Strawberries

Pictured at left

PREPARATION TIME: 10 to 15 minutes

COOKING TIME: 15 to 20 minutes

PER SERVING: 532 calories, 11 grams protein, 44 grams carbohydrates, 35 grams total fat, 488 milligrams cholesterol, 279 milligrams sodium

Airy as any soufflé but easier to make, this sweet froth of eggs bakes in a buttery citrus sauce. Served with warm berries and cool cream, it makes a showy brunch entrée that combines the best of both omelet and soufflé.

Makes 4 to 6 servings

    9 large eggs, separated
  ¾ cup sugar
    3 tablespoons all-purpose flour
  ¾ teaspoon grated orange peel
    6 tablespoons butter or margarine
  ½ cup orange juice
  ½ cup whipping cream
  ½ cup sour cream
    Warm Strawberries (recipe follows)

Using an electric mixer, beat egg whites on high speed until foamy, then gradually beat in 9 tablespoons of the sugar until whites just hold stiff, moist peaks. Do not overbeat or underbeat, or soufflé may separate and have a custard-like layer.

In a small mixing bowl (you don't need to rinse the beaters), beat egg yolks, gradually adding flour, until mixture is thick and light colored. Beat in ½ teaspoon of the orange peel. Gently and thoroughly fold yolk mixture into whites.

Melt butter over medium heat in a 10- to 12-inch ovenproof frying pan (the pan should be about the same diameter on top and bottom) or oval frying pan with about a 2-quart capacity. Stir in remaining 3 tablespoons sugar, orange juice, and remaining ¼ teaspoon orange peel. Cook until bubbling vigorously, then remove from heat. At once, gently slide large spoonfuls of egg mixture into hot sauce.

Bake in a 350° oven until omelet-soufflé is lightly browned on top, set around edge, and moist and slightly creamy in center (center will jiggle slightly when pan is gently shaken)—9 to 10 minutes for a 12-inch pan or oval pan, 13 to 15 minutes for a 10-inch pan. If you prefer a firmer texture, bake for 3 to 5 more minutes.

While omelet-soufflé bakes, beat whipping cream until stiff; fold into sour cream. Prepare strawberries. Serve omelet-soufflé at once; spoon portions into bowls or plates, spooning down to pan bottom to ladle out some of the orange sauce with each portion. Serve with strawberries and the whipped cream–sour cream topping.

WARM STRAWBERRIES. In a 10- to 12-inch frying pan, melt 2 tablespoons **butter** or margarine over medium heat. Stir in 2 tablespoons **sugar**, ½ teaspoon grated **orange peel,** and ½ cup **orange juice.** Heat until bubbling, then stir in 3 cups sliced **fresh strawberries** and remove from heat.

Spanish Omelet Picnic Loaf

PREPARATION TIME: About 15 minutes
COOKING TIME: About 25 minutes
PER SERVING: 360 calories, 14 grams protein, 29 grams carbohydrate, 21 grams total fat, 324 milligrams cholesterol, 518 milligrams sodium

Through the years, many good cooks have been invited to Sunset's test kitchens to share their talents with us—and our readers. One such visitor, a retired chef, produced this hearty entrée. It duplicates the omelet-filled loaf he fondly remembers accompanying family picnics and train trips during his boyhood in Spain.

Makes 6 to 8 servings

- 1 large (10- to 12-inch-diameter) round loaf sourdough French bread
- About 4 tablespoons olive oil
- About 10 ounces chorizo sausage
- 1 large thin-skinned potato, cooked, peeled, and thinly sliced
- 1 medium-size onion, finely chopped
- 1 clove garlic, minced or pressed
- 1 medium-size green bell pepper, stemmed, seeded, and chopped
- 1 medium-size red bell pepper, stemmed, seeded, and chopped
- 9 large eggs, lightly beaten
- Salt and pepper

With a long serrated knife, cut bread in half horizontally. Partially hollow centers of halves, leaving a 1-inch-thick shell. Brush cut surfaces with about 1 tablespoon of the oil. Reassemble loaf, wrap in foil, and keep warm in a 300° oven while preparing omelet.

Remove casings from chorizo and crumble meat into a nonstick 10- to 11-inch frying pan. Cook over medium-high heat, stirring, until lightly browned. Remove sausage with a slotted spoon; discard drippings. Heat 1 tablespoon of the oil in pan over medium-high heat; add potato, onion, and garlic and cook, turning often, until potato is nicely browned, about 3 minutes. Add green and red bell peppers and cook for 1 more minute; stir in chorizo.

Reduce heat to medium and push potato mixture to side of pan; drizzle 1 more tablespoon olive oil over pan bottom. Redistribute vegetables in pan and pour in eggs. As edges begin to set, push toward center and shake pan vigorously to allow uncooked egg to flow underneath.

Cook omelet until bottom is lightly browned and top is just set but appears moist, about 5 minutes. To turn omelet, run a wide spatula around edge and under it to loosen. Invert a plate or rimless baking sheet over omelet. With 1 hand on plate, the other gripping pan handle, quickly invert pan, turning omelet out onto plate. Add 1 more tablespoon oil to pan, return to medium heat, and gently slide omelet back into pan. Cook until lightly browned on bottom side, about 2 minutes. Remove from heat.

Remove bread from oven; unwrap. Invert bottom half of loaf over top of omelet, then quickly invert pan, turning omelet out into loaf. Sprinkle with salt and pepper. Replace top of loaf; serve. If made ahead, wrap in several thicknesses of foil to keep warm for up to 4 hours. Or refrigerate wrapped loaf until next day; reheat in a 400° oven until omelet is hot and steamy, 25 to 30 minutes. To serve, cut into wedges with a serrated knife.

Country Corn Omelet

PREPARATION TIME: About 10 minutes
COOKING TIME: About 20 minutes
PER SERVING: 552 calories, 21 grams protein, 18 grams carbohydrate, 45 grams total fat, 543 milligrams cholesterol, 500 milligrams sodium

Boldly contrasting flavors, textures, and colors have made this open-faced omelet a favorite with Sunset readers. Corn, kale, sour cream, bacon, and almonds dress up a busy cook's standby ingredient—eggs.

Makes 4 servings

- 4 slices bacon, diced
- ¼ cup sliced almonds
- 3 to 4 tablespoons butter or margarine
- 1 cup fresh or frozen corn kernels
- 1 small onion, diced
- 4 cups lightly packed coarsely shredded green or red kale or Swiss chard
- 6 to 8 large eggs
- ½ cup finely diced jack cheese
- ⅓ cup sour cream

In a 10- to 11-inch frying pan, cook bacon over medium heat until crisp. Lift out bacon; drain on paper towels and set aside.

Add almonds to pan drippings. Cook over medium heat, stirring gently, until lightly browned, 1 to 2 minutes. Lift out and set aside.

Pour pan drippings into a measuring cup; add butter, if needed, to make 4 tablespoons. Return drippings and butter to pan; add corn and onion and cook over medium heat, stirring often, until onion is soft, about 6 minutes. Remove corn and onion from pan; keep warm.

To pan, add 1 tablespoon butter; then add kale. Stir over medium heat until limp and tender to bite, about 2 minutes; remove from pan and keep warm.

Add 2 more tablespoons butter to pan and reduce heat to medium-low. In a bowl, beat eggs just until blended; pour into pan. When eggs begin to set, push cooked portion aside to allow uncooked portion to flow underneath. When eggs are set but top still looks moist and creamy, arrange kale on top in an even layer; spoon corn mixture over kale, then sprinkle evenly with cheese and bacon. Mound sour cream in center; garnish with almonds. Present omelet in pan; cut into wedges to serve.

Small Cheese Tamales

WESTERN CLASSIC

PREPARATION TIME: About 1½ hours to assemble; allow 2 hours to soak husks
STEAMING TIME: About 45 minutes
PER SERVING: 133 calories, 3 grams protein, 8 grams carbohydrate, 10 grams total fat, 14 milligrams cholesterol, 146 milligrams sodium

Tamales have been part of Western cuisine since hacienda days, when California was under Mexican rule. They vary in size and shape, but almost always include masa (a corn flour dough)—unless made with fresh corn—and a corn husk wrapper to enclose the filling. These miniatures, called tamalitos con queso *in Spanish, can be made a day in advance; they contribute spirit to a barbecue menu.*

Look for dried corn husks and epazote in Mexican markets and imported food sections of some supermarkets. The husks typically come in 8-ounce bags, enough for 75 small tamales; they'll keep indefinitely.

Makes 24 tamales, 8 to 10 servings

> **Soaked corn husks (directions follow)**
> **Masa Dough (recipe follows)**
> **8 ounces jack cheese, cut into 24 cubes**
> **2 tablespoons chili powder, 24 small fresh epazote leaves, or 1 tablespoon dried epazote**
> **1 jar (12 oz.) green chile salsa**

Sort through husks and select 24 that are at least 5 inches wide across base and free of holes or large tears.

Working with 1 husk at a time, spread it out flat and put a scant 2 tablespoons of masa in center. Push a cube of cheese and ¼ teaspoon chili powder (or 1 small epazote leaf or ⅛ teaspoon dried epazote) into masa.

With your fingers, pat masa up and around cheese and seasoning. Fold sides of husk over masa, then lift ends up over filling. With a thin strip of husk, tie tamale to hold shut. Repeat to make 23 more tamales. (At this point, you may cover and refrigerate until next day.)

Set tamales, tied ends up, stacked to permit air circulation, in a steamer on a rack over at least 1 inch of boiling water. Cover and set heat at medium so water will boil gently (add boiling water to pan as required). Cook until masa is firm to touch and does not stick to husk (open a tamale to test, then retie), about 45 minutes. Serve, or keep warm in steamer for up to an hour. If made ahead, let cool, then cover and refrigerate until next day; reheat by steaming as directed for about 20 minutes.

To serve, open husks and spoon salsa to taste onto tamales.

SOAKED CORN HUSKS. Sort through and select 30 to 36 nicely shaped **dried corn husks**, discarding bits of dried silk and other extraneous materials. Cover with **warm water** and let stand until pliable, about 2 hours or until next day. You should have ample husks for 24 small tamales and ties (made by tearing husks lengthwise in thin strips).

MASA DOUGH. Whip ⅔ cup (⅓ lb.) **lard,** butter, margarine, or solid vegetable shortening until fluffy, then stir in 2 cups **dehydrated masa flour** (corn tortilla flour) and 1⅓ cups **Homemade Chicken Broth** (page 58) or canned regular-strength chicken or beef broth. Stir until mixture holds together. If made ahead, cover and refrigerate for up to 3 days; bring to room temperature before using.

Crêpes Ravioli with Toasted Walnuts

PREPARATION TIME: About 25 minutes to make crêpes; about 10 minutes to assemble
BAKING TIME: 12 to 15 minutes
PER SERVING: 600 calories, 34 grams protein, 17 grams carbohydrate, 45 grams total fat, 258 milligrams cholesterol, 521 milligrams sodium

For a buffet breakfast, prepare these cheese-and-ham crêpes the night before, then heat them just before serving. The dish comes from Italy; because the crêpes enclose a filling, they're also often called ravioli.

Makes 6 servings

> **4 cups (1 lb.) shredded fontina or Swiss cheese**
> **6 ounces thinly sliced cooked ham, cut into julienne strips (about 1⅓ cups)**
> **12 Blender Crêpes (recipe follows)**
> **About 1 cup walnut halves**
> **1 tablespoon melted butter or margarine**

Mix cheese and ham. Distribute about ⅓ cup of the cheese mixture over half of each crêpe; fold other half over to cover cheese, then fold in half again to make triangles. Arrange slightly apart in an 18- to 20-inch shallow oval baking dish or two 9- by 13-inch baking dishes. (At this point, you may cover and refrigerate until next day.)

Bake, uncovered, in a 450° oven until hot, 8 to 10 minutes. Mix walnuts with butter and arrange on crêpes. Continue to bake until nuts are lightly toasted and cheese is melted, about 3 more minutes.

BLENDER CRÊPES. In a blender, whirl 3 **large eggs** and ⅔ cup **all-purpose flour** until smooth (or beat eggs and flour with a whisk). Add 1 cup **milk** and blend well. Heat a 6- to 7-inch crêpe pan or other flat-bottomed frying pan over medium heat. Add ¼ teaspoon **butter** or margarine and swirl to coat pan surface. Stir batter and pour 2 to 2½ tablespoons into pan, quickly tilting it so batter coats pan bottom.

Cook until surface of crêpe feels dry and edge is lightly browned. Turn with a spatula and brown other side. Turn out onto plate. Repeat with remaining batter, stacking crêpes as made. If made ahead, package airtight and refrigerate for up to 4 days; freeze for longer storage. Bring to room temperature before separating (if cold, crêpes will tear). Makes 12 to 14 crêpes.

Cheese Ramekins

Pictured below

PREPARATION TIME: 1¾ hours to dry toast; about 10 minutes to assemble
BAKING TIME: 5 to 7 minutes
PER SERVING: 337 calories, 14 grams protein, 9 grams carbohydrate, 28 grams total fat, 90 milligrams cholesterol, 194 milligrams sodium

Select Bonbel, fontina, provolone, teleme, jack, or other mild-flavored, smooth-melting cheese for this recipe. Present individual ramekins as a first course for a wine-and-cheese party, or serve two ramekins to each person for a satisfying light lunch or supper entrée.

Makes 6 to 8 appetizer servings

> **6 to 8 slices firm-textured white bread**
> **½ cup (¼ lb.) butter or margarine**
> **3 to 4 cups (¾ to 1 lb.) shredded Bonbel, fontina, provolone, teleme, or jack cheese**
> **2 tablespoons minced parsley**

Select 6 to 8 shallow ½- to ¾-cup casseroles. Cut bread to fit into bottom of each dish. Place bread directly on oven rack and bake in a 200° oven for 45 minutes; turn off heat and leave toast in closed oven for 1 hour.

Melt butter in a 10- to 12-inch frying pan over low heat. Add toast and cook until golden brown on both sides. Place a toast slice in each casserole. Distribute cheese evenly over top. (At this point, you may cover and refrigerate until next day.)

Sprinkle with parsley and bake, uncovered, in a 400° oven until cheese is bubbling, 5 to 7 minutes. Allow 2 ramekins for each entrée serving, 1 for each appetizer serving.

Bubbling hot cheese, flecked with parsley, blankets slices of crisp toast in these simple Cheese Ramekins (recipe above). For vivid contrast, serve with nippy radishes and green onions.

Mexican Grilled Cheese

PREPARATION TIME: 30 to 40 minutes to ignite charcoal; 5 to 15 minutes for toppings (depending on choice); about 5 minutes for cheese; about 15 minutes for Tostaditas
GRILLING TIME: About 5 minutes
PER SERVING: 212 calories, 14 grams protein, .38 gram carbohydrate, 17 grams total fat, 50 milligrams cholesterol, 304 milligrams sodium

Queso fundido and queso al horno *are Mexico's answer to Swiss fondue. You simply melt a dish of mild cheese, plain or with toppings, over hot coals. Invite guests to scoop up the soft cheese with tortilla chips.*

Makes 12 to 16 servings

> 2 pounds mild, smooth-melting cheese, such as jack, Münster, teleme, fontina, Edam, or Gouda
> Topping (suggestions follow)
> Tostaditas (recipe follows)

Trim any wax coating from cheese; cut cheese into ¼-inch-thick slices. Arrange in an 8- to 10-inch metal pan or heatproof ceramic dish at least 1½ inches deep, overlapping slices to cover pan bottom and extend up just to edges. (At this point, you may cover and let stand for up to 4 hours.)

Just before heating, add your choice of topping to cheese as directed below. Place pan on a grill 4 to 6 inches above a solid bed of medium coals (you should be able to hold your hand at grill level for 4 to 5 seconds). Keep a section of fire grate empty so there's a cool area on grill. Let cheese melt, checking frequently to be sure it isn't scorching on bottom by pushing down into center of dish with the tip of a knife. If cheese gets too hot, move it to cool area.

To eat, scoop melted cheese mixture onto Tostaditas.

TOPPINGS. Choose one of the following toppings.

Yucatecan Tomato & Shrimp Salsa. Heat 1½ tablespoons **olive oil** or salad oil in a 10- to 12-inch frying pan over medium-high heat. Add 1 large **onion,** chopped; stir often until soft, about 10 minutes. Add 2 large firm-ripe **tomatoes,** cored, seeded, and coarsely chopped, and ¼ teaspoon **ground cinnamon.** Stir over high heat for 1 minute. Stem, seed, and chop 4 to 6 **fresh or canned jalapeño chiles;** stir into tomato mixture. Season to taste with **salt.** If made ahead, cool, cover and refrigerate until next day.

Spoon salsa over cheese in a 6-inch circle, then heat cheese on grill. Top with 1 cup **tiny cooked, shelled shrimp** and 3 **fresh or canned jalapeño chiles.**
PER SERVING: 35 calories, 3 grams protein, 3 grams carbohydrate, 1 gram total fat, 13 milligrams cholesterol, 15 milligrams sodium.

Green chiles. Drain 3 cans (4 oz. *each*) **diced green chiles.** Sprinkle over cheese; heat cheese on grill.
PER SERVING: 5 calories, .19 gram protein, 1 gram carbohydrate, .02 gram total fat, 0 milligram cholesterol, 130 milligrams sodium.

TOSTADITAS. Cut 24 **corn tortillas** (7- to 8-inch diameter) into quarters. Pour 2 inches **salad oil** into a deep 2- to 3-quart pan over medium-high heat. Heat oil to 375°F on a deep-frying thermometer. Add tortilla pieces, 6 to 8 at a time, and cook until crisp and golden brown, about 1 minute. Lift out with a slotted spoon; drain on paper towels. If made ahead, let cool, then store airtight at room temperature for up to 2 days. To reheat, spread in a single layer in 10- by 15-inch baking pans. Bake in a 400° oven until crisp, about 5 minutes.
PER SERVING: 93 calories, 2 grams protein, 14 grams carbohydrate, 4 grams total fat, 0 milligram cholesterol, 33 milligrams sodium.

Raclette

PREPARATION TIME: About 25 minutes to cook potatoes, about 1 hour to marinate onions
COOKING TIME: 2 to 3 minutes per portion
PER SERVING: 630 calories, 35 grams protein, 38 grams carbohydrate, 38 grams total fat, 110 milligrams cholesterol, 1066 milligrams sodium

For a full appreciation of Swiss raclette, you have to experience it: let the faces of a chunk of cheese melt by the fire, then scrape off this flowing gold to crown a morsel of hot cooked potato. Accompany with crisp pickles and marinated onions.

Makes 6 to 9 servings

> 3 pounds very small (1- to 1½-inch-diameter) thin-skinned potatoes, scrubbed
> Marinated Onions (recipe follows)
> 2 cups cornichons or tiny sweet pickles
> 1 large chunk (2 to 3 lbs.) raclette, jack, fontina, Gruyère, Samsoe, or Swiss cheese

Place potatoes in a 3- to 4-quart pan; add water to cover and bring to a boil over high heat. Reduce heat, cover, and simmer until tender when pierced, about 20 minutes. Drain off most of water. Set potatoes, covered, next to fire or on a warming tray to keep warm. Arrange onions and pickles in separate dishes. Trim any wax coating from cheese.

To make raclette at a fireplace, place cheese chunk in a shallow pan somewhat larger than cheese. Make just 1 portion of raclette (or what you plan to eat at once) at a time. Set pan on hearth and push wide surface of cheese in close to fire. When surface of cheese begins to melt, scrape it off and spoon onto a bit of hot potato. Eat with onions and pickles. Pull cheese away from heat until you are ready for the next serving; diners can tend to their own needs.

To make raclette using a broiler, cut cheese into ½-inch-thick slices. Arrange slices, side by side, to cover bottom of a shallow pan such as a 9- or 10-inch pie pan. Broil about 4 inches below heat until cheese is melted and bubbling; serve at once. Have ready as many pans of cheese as you will need; broil as needed. Eat cheese with potatoes, onions, and pickles.

MARINATED ONIONS. Thinly slice 2 medium-size **mild white onions.** Place in a bowl and mix in ⅓ cup **white wine vinegar,** ½ teaspoon **salt,** and 1½ teaspoons **sugar.** Cover and refrigerate for at least 1 hour, stirring occasionally.

Our Own Fresh Yogurt

In 1980, *Sunset* set out to do the definitive study on homemade yogurt. This smooth, thick, fresh-tasting product was the delicious result—higher in protein than most commercial low-fat yogurts, with only half the fat. Here's how to make it—and how to convert it to a tangy low-calorie cheese.

To make our yogurt, you need only milk, a small amount of purchased yogurt to start the bacterial action, and a way to maintain a temperature of about 115°F. Temperatures above 120°F will kill the living organisms; below 105°F, their action is slowed considerably. You'll need an accurate thermometer that measures in the 100° to 120°F range, as do standard dairy thermometers.

Because it's made with a combination of fluid milk and nonfat dry milk, our yogurt has a thick, velvety-smooth texture without additives. Dry milk boosts the protein content.

If made with low-fat milk, our yogurt has 150 calories, 3 grams fat, and 13 grams protein per cup; made with nonfat milk, it has about 133 calories, .5 gram fat, and 13 grams protein per cup.

For your starter, buy a yogurt that you like. It must be fresh—not more than a week old—since the organisms become less active as yogurt ages. After making your first batch, you can use your own yogurt for a starter, but it, too, must be fresh. The dry milk should be almost odor-free; sniff it for freshness.

Make sure all the equipment you use is dishwasher-clean or scalded to prevent any bacterial growth that could interfere with the action of the starter.

Do not disturb the yogurt while it is setting. Too much motion can slow or even stop the action. Once the yogurt is softly set, it's safe to remove it from the heat source and chill it; it will thicken a bit more in the refrigerator.

Ways to Culture Yogurt

To culture yogurt, you need a way to keep the mixture of milk and starter at 115°F until the yogurt is thickened.

To make yogurt in a vacuum bottle, first check to make sure that the bottle will maintain the proper temperature. Fill a 1- to 2-quart wide-mouth vacuum bottle with water at 115°F. Close and leave undisturbed for 3 hours, then check temperature. If temperature is below 105°F, try again with the bottle wrapped in a warm blanket.

To make yogurt, first fill bottle with water at 115°F; cap it and let stand while you start the yogurt. Pour water out of the bottle and immediately replace it with the yogurt mixture at 115°F. Replace cap; leave undisturbed for about 4 hours. Check; if yogurt has not set, recap quickly and test again every ½ hour. When yogurt is set, remove lid, cover loosely, and refrigerate.

To use a yogurt-making appliance, follow the manufacturer's instructions for operating the unit. We recommend preheating the unit; it shortens the culturing time, often by several hours, and produces a yogurt that's less tart.

While starting yogurt, fill the container with warm water (about 115°F). Then turn on electric units or cover nonelectric ones. Pour out the water and immediately replace with the yogurt mixture at 115°F. Reset unit and leave undisturbed until yogurt is set, 3½ to 5 hours. Turn off or remove from heat and refrigerate.

Thick Yogurt

> ¼ cup fresh plain yogurt
> Water
>
> 2 cups fluid low-fat or nonfat milk
>
> ¾ cup noninstant nonfat dry milk or 1⅓ cups instant nonfat dry milk

Place yogurt in a small bowl and set it in a pan of warm water (about 115°F); stir occasionally. Meanwhile, set up your yogurt culture system.

Place fluid milk in a pan over medium heat and warm to 185°F. Or pour into a glass bowl and heat to 185°F in a microwave oven on HIGH (100%). Let cool slightly; discard scum from top of milk.

While milk cools, pour ½ cup hot water into a blender container. Add dry milk. Whirl on low speed, scraping sides of container often, just until smooth but not foamy. Measure; then add enough cold water to make 1¾ cups. Add mixture to milk, then check temperature.

When liquid has cooled to 115°F, add a few spoonfuls to warm yogurt starter and mix until smooth. Pour yogurt starter back into milk mixture; stir until smooth. Skim off and discard any foam with a slotted spoon. Pour milk mixture into preheated yogurt container. Keep warm to culture. When yogurt is set (usually in 3½ to 5 hours), cover and refrigerate until cold. Makes 1 quart.

FRESH STRAWBERRY YOGURT. In a bowl, stir together 1½ cups mashed **strawberries** and ¼ cup **sugar.** Let stand until you can spoon off ½ cup of the juice. In a 2- to 4-cup pan, sprinkle 1 envelope **unflavored gelatin** over the ½ cup juice. Let stand for about 5 minutes to soften; then stir over low heat until gelatin is completely dissolved. Stir gelatin mixture into strawberries, then whisk into 2 cups **Thick Yogurt** until well mixed. Sweeten with additional **sugar** or honey, if desired. Cover and refrigerate until firm, 2 to 3 hours, (or for up to 2 days).

FRESH ORANGE YOGURT. Follow directions for **Fresh Strawberry Yogurt,** but omit strawberries and the ¼ cup sugar. Instead, use 1 cup seeded, chopped **fresh orange pulp** (cut off peel and all white membrane, saving all juices) combined with ¼ teaspoon grated **orange peel** and 3 to 4 tablespoons **sugar.** Measure; add more orange juice, if needed, to make 1½ cups. Complete as directed for **Fresh Strawberry Yogurt.**

Yogurt Cheese

To make cheese, line a colander with a clean, wet muslin cloth. Pour cold **Thick Yogurt** into cloth. Tie cloth to enclose yogurt; hang over a container or the sink and allow whey to drain off for 4 to 6 hours. Place cloth-wrapped yogurt in colander, then set in a drip pan; cover entire unit with plastic wrap and refrigerate until next day.

Untie cloth and remove yogurt cheese; season to taste with **salt,** if desired. Serve. Or store airtight in the refrigerator for up to 1 week; or freeze for longer storage (thaw in the refrigerator before using). Each quart of yogurt makes about 1½ cups cheese.

Nothing is better than a breakfast of Cheese Blintzes (recipe below), unless it's brunch of the same—especially if they're Sunset's tender crêpe bundles of mild cheeses, lavished with cold sour cream and plump, sweet cherries.

Cheese Blintzes

Pictured above

PREPARATION TIME: About 50 minutes to make crêpes; about 20 minutes to make filling; about 10 minutes to assemble

COOKING TIME: About 10 minutes

PER SERVING: 669 calories, 26 grams protein, 38 grams carbohydrate, 50 grams total fat, 260 milligrams cholesterol, 570 milligrams sodium

Mellow cheese, sour cream, and glistening cherries promise a trio of mouthwatering flavors. But would you add onions, too? Surprisingly—yes. Slowly cooked to a sweet, caramelized condition, they bring a unique richness to these Russian-Jewish blintzes.

Makes 20 to 24 blintzes, 5 or 6 servings

> **4 large eggs**
> **¾ cup all-purpose flour**
> **2 cups water**
> **Butter or margarine**
> **Cheese Filling (recipe follows)**
> **Salad oil**
> **Sour cream**
> **Cherry Sauce (recipe follows), Sweet Cherry Sauce (page 169), or 1 can (21 oz.) cherry pie filling**

In a blender or food processor, whirl eggs and flour until smooth (or beat eggs and flour with a whisk). Add water and blend well.

Heat a 6- to 7-inch crêpe pan or other flat-bottomed frying pan over medium heat; add about ¼ teaspoon butter and swirl to coat pan surface. Stir batter, then pour 2 to 2½ tablespoons into pan, quickly tilting it so batter coats pan bottom. Cook until surface of crêpe feels dry and bottom is lightly browned. Turn out onto a plate. Repeat until all batter has been used, stacking crêpes as made. If made ahead, package airtight and refrigerate for up to 4 days; freeze for longer storage. Bring to room temperature before separating (if cold, crêpes will tear).

To make each blintz, place a rectangular mound of about 3 tablespoons filling in center of browned side of each crêpe. Fold crêpe over filling to enclose. Set filled crêpes seam side down.

Melt 3 tablespoons butter in about 3 tablespoons oil in a 10- to 12-inch frying pan over high heat. Add blintzes, seam side down, without crowding; cook until golden on both sides, about 2 minutes *total*. As blintzes are cooked, transfer to a platter and keep warm. Add more butter and oil to pan as needed.

Top blintzes with sour cream and Cherry Sauce.

CHEESE FILLING. Melt 2 tablespoons **butter** or margarine in a 10- to 12-inch frying pan over medium heat. Add 1 large **onion,** finely chopped; cook, stirring often, until soft and golden, about 20 minutes. Transfer to a bowl; add 1 large package (8 oz.) **cream cheese,** at room temperature, and 1½ pounds **farmers cheese.** Beat until smoothly blended. If made ahead, cover and refrigerate for up to 24 hours.

CHERRY SAUCE. Pit 2 to 3 cups **fresh sweet cherries** (Bing, if possible). In a 1½- to 2-quart pan, combine 2 teaspoons **cornstarch,** ¼ cup **sugar,** ½ cup **water,** and 2 teaspoons **lemon juice.** Stir in cherries. Bring to a boil over high heat, stirring constantly. Serve hot; or cover and refrigerate for up to 24 hours. To reheat, stir over medium heat until warmed through.

With 2 or 3 layers rinsed, wrung cheesecloth (or 1 layer muslin), line a 2- to 2½-quart paskha mold (a truncated pyramid with drain at base), a clean 2- to 2½-quart plastic or clay flowerpot (with drain at base), or a colander. Spoon cheese mixture into cloth; fold cloth over top. Set a plate on cloth, then set several heavy objects (such as canned goods) on plate. Place mold in a larger pan, elevating it so it can drain; cover entire unit with plastic wrap. Refrigerate for 12 to 24 hours.

Remove weights, fold back cloth, and invert cheese onto serving dish; discard whey. Cover cheese and refrigerate until ready to serve, or for up to 3 days. Freeze to store.

To present, decorate top with rosebuds and base with colored eggs. Serve in thick slices.

Paskha with Custom Base

PREPARATION TIME: About 1 hour to make and cool custard base; about 30 minutes to assemble
CHILLING TIME: At least 12 hours
PER SERVING: 357 calories, 12 grams protein, 13 grams carbohydrate, 29 grams total fat, 154 milligrams cholesterol, 24 milligrams sodium

Russians were among the West's early settlers, and some of their culinary traditions linger here. Among the finest of these is paskha, a sweet, delicate cheese which always appears at Russian Easter feasts.

For a really authentic-looking paskha, you'll need a special wooden mold with a flattened pyramid shape. But this recipe—given to Sunset by a Romanov who fled to California—tastes exquisite regardless of its shape. Order the uncreamed cottage cheese from your grocer or dairy.

Makes about 4½ pounds, 16 to 18 servings

> ¾ cup **whipping cream**
> 1 cup **sugar**
> 5 large **egg yolks**
> 1 **vanilla bean** (6 to 8 inches long)
> 2 cups (1 lb.) **unsalted butter,** at room temperature
> ¼ teaspoon **salt**
> 2½ pounds (about 5 cups, packed) **baker's uncreamed cottage cheese**
> 1 cup **sour cream**
> **Rosebuds and colored Easter eggs**

In the top of a double boiler, blend cream, sugar, and egg yolks. Cook over simmering water, stirring, until custard coats a metal spoon in a thick, shiny layer, 15 to 20 minutes. Remove from heat and let cool.

Split vanilla bean lengthwise with a sharp knife and scrape out seeds. Place butter and vanilla seeds in a large bowl (rinse vanilla bean; let dry and store in a jar of sugar to make vanilla sugar). Beat butter until fluffy; then add salt, cottage cheese and sour cream, blending thoroughly. Slowly add cooled custard, mixing constantly.

Ricotta Cheese Spread with Anise Sugar

PREPARATION TIME: 5 to 10 minutes
PER SERVING: 105 calories, 9 grams protein, 4 grams carbohydrate, 6 grams total fat, 23 milligrams cholesterol, 95 milligrams sodium

Some of our tidbit-size recipes, taking only an inch of a column and a few minutes to prepare, capture very exciting flavors. Here's an example that was tucked into a summer weekend breakfast menu. Spread this orange-scented ricotta cheese on crisp Twice-baked Ginger Toast, then top with anise-flavored sugar or honey. (Try the sugar or honey on fruit or in coffee, too.)

Makes 5 or 6 servings

> 1 pound **ricotta cheese**
> 1½ teaspoons **grated orange peel**
> **Twice-baked Ginger Toast (page 253), whole-grain toast, or rusks**
> **Anise Sugar or Anise Honey (recipes follow)**

Blend ricotta cheese and orange peel. Serve; or cover and refrigerate for up to 2 days. Use as a spread for toast; sprinkle with Anise Sugar (or drizzle with Anise Honey).

ANISE SUGAR OR ANISE HONEY. Lightly crush 2 teaspoons **anise seeds,** using a mortar and pestle (or crush under a flat-bottomed glass). Mix crushed seeds with ½ cup **sugar.** Or combine crushed seeds and ½ cup **honey** in a 2- to 4-cup pan; stir over low heat until honey is flavored, about 5 minutes. Serve honey warm or cooled. Both sugar and honey will keep indefinitely at room temperature.

PER TABLESPOON: 50 calories, .09 gram protein, 13 grams carbohydrate, .08 gram total fat, 0 milligram cholesterol, .20 milligram sodium.

The Best of Sunset
VEGETABLES

The sun smiles on fertile Western farmlands, which in turn produce a glorious bounty of vegetables to fill our gardens and our markets, then our tables.

Over the years, this grand range of choices has challenged both Sunset and Sunset readers to come up with new and better ways to cook—and grow—familiar as well as more exotic produce. Coverage in our pages has won increased appreciation (and heightened demand) for spaghetti squash, squash blossoms, ripe red bell peppers, and jicama, among others.

In this chapter, we invite you to enjoy vegetables, Western style. You'll learn about grilling and butter-steaming, two of our favorite vegetable cooking techniques. You'll find both rich and everyday fare, from luxurious Corn Risotto to simple Swiss Rosti. And you'll note the influence of Italian immigrants in many recipes—Marinated Artichoke Hearts, Florentine-style Swiss Chard, Italian Beans in a Mist, and more.

Streaked by the heat of the grill and glistening with an aromatic herb baste, golden bell peppers, broccoli, sweet potato wedges, and tiny squash make an appealing case for vegetables from the barbecue (see page 188).

Potato Risotto

PREPARATION TIME: About 20 minutes
COOKING TIME: 30 to 35 minutes
PER SERVING: 210 calories, 4 grams protein, 21 grams carbohydrate, 13 grams total fat, 35 milligrams cholesterol, 154 milligrams sodium

Simmered in a well-seasoned broth and finished with a touch of whipping cream and Parmesan cheese, shredded potatoes retain their texture surprisingly well, but also turn deliciously creamy—like risotto, the famous Italian rice dish.

Makes 4 to 6 servings

　　¼ **cup (⅛ lb.) butter or margarine**
　　1 **small onion, finely chopped**
　　1 **clove garlic, minced or pressed**
　　½ **teaspoon fresh thyme leaves or ¼ teaspoon dry thyme leaves**
　　1¾ **cups Homemade Chicken Broth (page 58) or 1 can (14½ oz.) regular-strength chicken broth**
　　3 **cups peeled, finely shredded thin-skinned potatoes (about 1¼ lbs.)**
　　¼ **cup** *each* **whipping cream and freshly grated Parmesan cheese**
　　　Salt
　　　Fresh thyme sprigs (optional)

Melt butter in a 2- to 3-quart pan over medium heat. Add onion, garlic, and thyme leaves; cook, stirring often, until onion is soft. Add broth; bring to a boil over high heat, then boil, uncovered, until mixture is reduced to 1½ cups. Add potatoes and cook over medium heat, uncovered, stirring often, until potatoes are tender to bite, about 25 minutes. Remove from heat and mix in cream and cheese. Season to taste with salt. Pour into a warm bowl and garnish with thyme sprigs, if desired.

Italian Oven-roasted Potatoes

PREPARATION TIME: 25 to 30 minutes
BAKING TIME: 2 to 2½ hours
PER SERVING: 229 calories, 3 grams protein, 25 grams carbohydrate, 14 grams total fat, 0 milligram cholesterol, 8 milligrams sodium

Cubed potatoes and onions roasted with olive oil make a golden vegetable dish with a delicious blend of flavors. The secret is the long, slow cooking time. If you like, set a 4- to 5-pound beef roast in the same oven; by the time the potatoes are done, the meat will be cooked rare.

Makes 6 to 8 servings

　　2 **pounds russet potatoes (about 4 large potatoes), peeled and cut into ½-inch cubes**
　　3 **large onions, coarsely chopped**
　　½ **cup olive oil**
　　　Salt and pepper

In a 10- by 15-inch rimmed baking pan, mix potatoes, onions, and oil. Season to taste with salt and pepper. Spread vegetables evenly in pan.

Bake, uncovered, in a 325° oven until vegetables are light golden and potatoes mash very easily, 2 to 2½ hours; stir occasionally.

Curried New Potatoes & Green Onions

W E S T E R N　　C L A S S I C

PREPARATION TIME: 20 to 25 minutes
COOKING TIME: About 30 minutes to boil potatoes; about 15 minutes to brown
PER SERVING: 301 calories, 4 grams protein, 33 grams carbohydrate, 18 grams total fat, 47 milligrams cholesterol, 190 milligrams sodium

Snap, crunch, freshness—that's what you get when you add curry powder, mustard seeds, and lots of green onions to little red boiled potatoes. This bright dish is a great partner for barbecued lamb or beef.

Makes 8 servings

　　3 **pounds small (about 1½-inch-diameter) red thin-skinned potatoes, scrubbed**
　　½ **to 1 cup (¼ to ½ lb.) butter or margarine**
　　2 **teaspoons** *each* **curry powder and mustard seeds**
　　2 **cups chopped green onions (including tops)**
　　　Salt

Into a 5- to 6-quart pan, pour enough water to cover potatoes. Bring water to a boil; add potatoes, reduce heat, cover, and simmer until potatoes are tender throughout when pierced, 20 to 30 minutes. Drain and let cool. (At this point, you may cover and refrigerate until next day.)

Coarsely chop unpeeled potatoes. Melt ½ cup of the butter in a 10- to 12-inch frying pan over medium-high heat. Add potatoes and cook, turning frequently with a wide spatula, for about 5 minutes; add more butter as needed to prevent sticking. Sprinkle curry powder and mustard seeds over potatoes and mix in; continue to cook, stirring often, until potatoes begin to brown lightly. Mix in onions and heat through; season to taste with salt.

Swiss Rosti

PREPARATION TIME: 25 to 30 minutes
BAKING TIME: About 45 minutes
PER SERVING: 217 calories, 3 grams protein, 26 grams carbohydrate, 12 grams total fat, 31 milligrams cholesterol, 125 milligrams sodium

Finely diced new potatoes and onions bake at high heat to make the nicely browned dish known as rosti. For a

HAS ANY JOURNAL in the U.S. even come close to Sunset's in-depth reporting on avocados, artichokes, eggplants, boysenberries and countless other kinds of Western produce? Keeping our readers abreast of the changing marketplace has been a Sunset trademark. We've shown how to recognize quality—and how to get it. Our 1985 essay on stone fruits advises, "Don't be afraid to nag the produce man," if that's what it takes to get the perfect peach.

quick meal, serve with Polish or garlic sausages and crisp cabbage salad.

Makes 6 servings

> **6 tablespoons butter or margarine**
> **1½ pounds thin-skinned potatoes, scrubbed and cut into ¼-inch cubes**
> **2 large onions, finely chopped**
> **Salt and pepper**

In an 8- by 12-inch oval baking pan (or other 2-quart shallow baking pan), melt butter over medium heat. Add potatoes and onions; mix to coat with butter, then season to taste with salt and pepper.

Spread vegetables evenly in pan. Cook over medium heat until vegetables begin to brown at pan edge, about 5 minutes. Then bake in a 450° oven until vegetables are well browned and potatoes are tender when pierced, about 45 minutes.

Sweet-Sour Onions

PREPARATION TIME: 15 to 20 minutes
BAKING TIME: About 45 minutes
COOLING TIME: At least 30 minutes
PER SERVING: 213 calories, 3 grams protein, 19 grams carbohydrate, 14 grams total fat, .62 milligram cholesterol, 95 milligrams sodium

Here's a pleasing Tuscan dish—sweet-sour baked onions, crusted with seasoned bread crumbs. Use fresh rosemary and sage from your garden, or substitute dry herbs. Because the onions are served at room temperature, they're a good choice when you need a vegetable dish that can wait.

Makes 8 servings

> **4 large (3- to 4-inch-diameter) onions (about 2 lbs. *total*)**
> **2 tablespoons vinegar**
> **2 teaspoons sugar**
> **1 cup fine dry bread crumbs**
> **½ cup olive oil**
> **½ teaspoon chopped fresh sage leaves or ¼ teaspoon ground sage**
> **1 teaspoon fresh or dry rosemary**
> **¼ cup minced parsley**
> **Salt and pepper**

Peel onions and cut in half horizontally. Set cut side up in a 9- by 13-inch baking pan. Mix vinegar and sugar; spoon onto cut surface of onions.

Mix bread crumbs, ¼ cup of the oil, sage, rosemary, and parsley; pat evenly on top of onions. Drizzle with remaining ¼ cup oil. Bake, uncovered, in a 375° oven until onions are tender when pierced, about 45 minutes.

Let cool to room temperature. If made ahead, cover and let stand until next day. Season to taste with salt and pepper.

Slow-cooked Onions

W E S T E R N   C L A S S I C

PREPARATION TIME: 15 to 20 minutes
COOKING TIME: 30 to 40 minutes
PER ¼ CUP: 102 calories, 2 grams protein, 11 grams carbohydrate, 6 grams total fat, 16 milligrams cholesterol, 62 milligrams sodium

Slow and gentle cooking gives any type of onion a rich, mellow sweetness. The soft, golden rings can be used in any number of ways—with meat, poultry, or fish; with other vegetables; or in omelets, soups, or hot sandwiches.

Makes about 1½ cups

Melt 3 tablespoons **butter** or margarine in a 10- to 12-inch frying pan over medium heat. Add 4 large **onions** (about 2 lbs. *total*), thinly sliced and separated into rings. Cook for about 30 minutes, stirring occasionally at first and more frequently as rings begin to develop a golden color and sweet flavor (taste to check). The onions should not show signs of browning for at least 15 minutes; if they do, reduce heat.

Serve hot. If made ahead, let cool, then cover and refrigerate for up to 4 days. To reheat, stir often over medium heat until hot.

Crisp-fried Onions

PREPARATION TIME: About 10 minutes
DEEP-FRYING TIME: About 20 minutes
PER ¼ CUP: 56 calories, .49 gram protein, 3 grams carbohydrate, 5 grams total fat, 0 milligram cholesterol, .42 milligrams sodium

These fragile, crisp-fried shreds bear almost no resemblance to the typical thick, batter-coated fried onion rings. You dust thin onion rings with flour, then sizzle in oil until much of the moisture has cooked away, leaving sweet-tasting, appealingly brown slivers to enjoy with soups, salads, sandwiches—or all alone.

Makes about 6 cups

> **2 large onions (about 1 lb. *total*)**
> **½ cup all-purpose flour**
> **Salad oil**
> **Salt**

Thinly slice onions and separate into rings. Place flour in a bag, add onions, and shake to coat evenly with flour.

In a deep 2½- to 3-quart pan over high heat, bring 1½ inches oil to 300°F on a deep-frying thermometer. Add onions, about ¼ at a time; cook, stirring often, until golden, about 5 minutes. Oil temperature will drop at first but rise again as onions brown; regulate heat accordingly.

With a slotted spoon, lift out onions and drain on paper towels (discard any scorched bits). Serve warm, piled in a napkin-lined basket or on a plate; sprinkle with salt. Or let cool completely, package airtight, and refrigerate for up to 3 days. To reheat, spread in a single layer in a 10- by 15-inch rimmed baking pan and heat in a 350° oven for 2 to 3 minutes.

Pressed Leek Terrine

Pictured on facing page

PREPARATION TIME: About 1 hour
COOKING TIME: About 15 minutes
CHILLING TIME: At least 8 hours
PER SERVING: 168 calories, 4 grams protein, 37 grams carbohydrate, 2 grams total fat, 0 milligram cholesterol, 49 milligrams sodium

It may look complicated, but this sophisticated terrine is actually quite simple to prepare. Just split and poach leeks, let them cool, and pull apart leaf by leaf; stack the layers flat in a terrine, then weight and chill to press layers together firmly. For a distinctive first course or salad, serve slices of terrine with a Dijon mustard dressing.

Makes 10 servings

> 5 pounds small to medium-size leeks
> 1 teaspoon dry tarragon
> 6 cups Homemade Chicken Broth (page 58) or 1 large can (49½ oz.) regular-strength chicken broth
> **Mustard-Lemon Dressing (recipe follows)**
> Salt

Trim root ends and tops from leeks, leaving only about 1 inch of dark green leaves; save 10 tender green inner leaves from leek tops. Cut leeks in half lengthwise; rinse under running water, gently separating layers to remove any dirt. Rinse reserved inner leaves.

In a 4- to 5-quart pan, bring tarragon and broth to a boil over high heat. Add all leeks, reduce heat, cover, and simmer until tender when pierced, about 15 minutes. Drain; save broth for other uses.

Oil the inside of a 5- by 9-inch loaf pan. Separate leeks into individual layers and set each piece flat in pan; distribute dark green tops equally throughout terrine. Cut long pieces to fit pan length; patch layers to use all leaves. Oil bottom of an identical pan and set on top of leeks; put about 4 pounds of canned goods or dried beans in top pan to weight leeks. Refrigerate for at least 8 hours or up to 2 days to firm; pour off any liquid that accumulates.

Remove weighted pan. With a very sharp knife, gently cut loaf crosswise into 10 slices. Using 2 spatulas, lift out slices to a platter or individual salad plates. Top with dressing and season to taste with salt. (Though more difficult to slice, the terrine is handsome inverted onto a platter. Cut carefully.)

MUSTARD-LEMON DRESSING. Blend ½ cup **olive oil** or salad oil, 3 tablespoons **lemon juice,** 1 tablespoon **Dijon mustard,** and ¼ teaspoon **pepper.** Makes ¾ cup.
PER TABLESPOON: 82 calories, .01 gram protein, .44 gram carbohydrate, 9 grams total fat, 0 milligram cholesterol, 38 milligrams sodium.

Jicama with Fried Potatoes

PREPARATION TIME: 25 to 30 minutes
COOKING TIME: About 30 minutes
PER SERVING: 239 calories, 4 grams protein, 26 grams carbohydrate, 14 grams total fat, 37 milligrams cholesterol, 152 milligrams sodium

Jicama (hee-cah-mah), a Mexican root vegetable that looks like a giant brown turnip, is now grown commercially in the West. It's delicious raw in salads and appetizers, and equally good when pan-fried—as in this recipe. The cooked root retains its crunchy texture, but takes on a sweeter, mellower flavor.

Makes 4 or 5 servings

> 6 tablespoons butter or margarine
> 2 large russet potatoes (about 1 lb. *total*), peeled and cut into ¼-inch-thick slices
> 1 large onion, thinly sliced and separated into rings
> About 1 pound jicama, scrubbed, peeled, and cut into ¼-inch-thick slices about 1½ inches square (about 3 cups slices)
> ½ cup minced green onions (including tops)
> Salt and pepper

Melt butter in a 10- to 12-inch frying pan over medium heat. Add potatoes, onion rings, and jicama. Cook, turning as needed with a wide spatula, until potatoes are lightly browned and tender when pierced, 25 to 30 minutes. Mix in green onions; season to taste with salt and pepper.

Roasted Jerusalem Artichokes

PREPARATION TIME: 5 to 10 minutes
BAKING TIME: About 50 minutes
PER SERVING: 188 calories, 4 grams protein, 32 grams carbohydrate, 6 grams total fat, 0 milligram cholesterol, .33 milligram sodium

Knobby Jerusalem artichokes, also called sunchokes, look like a cross between russet potatoes and fresh ginger. Scrubbed and sliced, the crunchy little tubers are good raw as appetizers or snacks. Cooked, they taste slightly smoky and retain a touch of crispness.

Makes 4 or 5 servings

> 2 pounds Jerusalem artichokes (sunchokes)
> 2 tablespoons olive oil or salad oil
> 2 tablespoons fresh rosemary leaves or 1 tablespoon dry rosemary
> Salt and pepper

Scrub Jerusalem artichokes with a brush under cool running water. Drain and pat dry; if large, cut in half.

In a 9- or 10-inch square baking pan, mix artichokes with oil and rosemary. Bake in a 375° oven until artichokes are tender when pierced, about 50 minutes; stir several times. Season to taste with salt and pepper.

Shadings of green flow through slices of Pressed Leek Terrine (recipe on facing page). Top with a tangy mustard dressing and garnish with slices of radish and lemon, if desired.

Italian Beans in a Mist

PREPARATION TIME: About 20 minutes
COOKING TIME: About 15 minutes
PER SERVING: 148 calories, 6 grams protein, 8 grams carbohydrate, 11 grams total fat,
11 milligrams cholesterol, 289 milligrams sodium

Throughout the Mediterranean area, long, slow steaming is a popular method of cooking vegetables. The results, though delicious, can be drab-looking where green vegetables are concerned. Here, we modify the technique, combining a slow-cooked seasoning mixture of onions, garlic, and minced ham with briefly boiled Italian green beans. The dish tastes as rich as its traditional counterpart—but it's lovely looking, too.

Makes 4 to 6 servings

¼ cup olive oil
1 large onion, minced
1 large clove garlic
¼ pound cooked ham, minced; or ¼ pound button mushrooms, thinly sliced
1 pound Italian green beans, stem ends snapped off
Salt

In a 10- to 12-inch frying pan over medium-low heat, combine oil, onion, garlic clove, and ham. Cook until onion is soft, stirring often. Remove from heat; cover.

In a 3- to 4-quart pan, bring 8 cups water to a boil over high heat. Add beans, pushing them down. Cook, uncovered, until beans are just tender when pierced, about 3 minutes after boil resumes. Drain beans and immediately immerse in ice water. When cool, drain.

Add 3 tablespoons water to onion mixture and bring to a simmer over medium heat. Add beans and stir gently until heated through. Season to taste with salt; discard garlic, if desired.

Savory Beans & Tomatoes

PREPARATION TIME: 25 to 30 minutes
BAKING TIME: 20 to 30 minutes
PER SERVING: 106 calories, 2 grams protein, 7 grams carbohydrate, 8 grams total fat,
21 milligrams cholesterol, 129 milligrams sodium

Thin, tender green or wax beans are dressed up with tomatoes, mushrooms, herbs, and buttery bread crumbs.

Makes 14 to 16 servings

½ cup (¼ lb.) plus 2 tablespoons butter or margarine
1 large onion, chopped
½ pound button mushrooms, sliced
3 cloves garlic, minced or pressed
1½ teaspoons *each* dry basil and dry oregano leaves
2½ pounds green or wax beans (stem ends snapped off), cut into 2-inch pieces, cooked, and cooled
4 tomatoes, cored and cut into thin wedges
Salt
1½ cups soft bread crumbs
⅓ cup freshly grated Parmesan cheese

Melt ¼ cup of the butter in a 10- to 12-inch frying pan over medium heat. Add onion, mushrooms, and ⅔ of the garlic. Cook, stirring, until onion is lightly browned. Stir in 1 teaspoon *each* of the basil and oregano. Combine mushroom mixture, beans, and tomatoes; season to taste with salt and pour into a shallow 3-quart baking dish.

Melt remaining 6 tablespoons butter and mix with remaining garlic, bread crumbs, cheese, and remaining ½ teaspoon *each* basil and oregano. Sprinkle crumb mixture over beans. Cover; bake in a 400° oven for 20 minutes. Uncover; bake until hot throughout, about 5 more minutes.

Boiled Artichokes

PREPARATION TIME: 35 to 40 minutes
COOKING TIME: About 40 minutes
PER SERVING OF ARTICHOKES: 93 calories, 4 grams protein, 20 grams carbohydrate, 1 gram total fat, 0 milligram cholesterol, 130 milligrams sodium

Prickly artichokes flourish in the cool, foggy fields along the West Coast–and Westerners often cite this rather intimidating vegetable as an example of a food unique to the region. Past the thorny exterior, there's some superb eating. Here, we enhance boiled artichokes with a trio of tasty sauces.

Makes 10 to 12 servings

⅓ **cup vinegar**
3 **bay leaves**
12 **whole black peppercorns**
3 **tablespoons olive oil**
10 **to 12 large (4- to 4½-inch-diameter) artichokes**
Tarragon Cream, Caper Mayonnaise, and/ or Mustard Vinaigrette (recipes follow)

In a 10- to 12-quart pan, combine 5 to 6 quarts water, vinegar, bay leaves, peppercorns, and oil. Bring to a boil over high heat.

Meanwhile, remove coarse outer leaves from artichokes and trim stems even with base. With a sharp knife, cut off top third of each artichoke. With scissors, trim thorns from tips of remaining leaves. Immerse artichokes in cool water and swish back and forth. Lift from water; hold with stem end up and shake out water. Place artichokes in the boiling water. Reduce heat, cover, and boil gently until artichoke bottoms are tender when pierced, 30 to 40 minutes. Drain. Serve hot; or let cool, cover, and refrigerate for up to 2 days to serve chilled. Offer 1 or more sauces to accompany artichokes.

TARRAGON CREAM. Stir together ¾ cup **sour cream,** ¼ cup **Dijon mustard,** and 1 teaspoon **dry tarragon.** Makes 1 cup.
PER TABLESPOON: 28 calories, .36 gram protein, 1 gram carbohydrate, 2 grams total fat, 5 milligrams cholesterol, 117 milligrams sodium.

CAPER MAYONNAISE. In a blender or food processor, combine 1 **large egg,** 1 tablespoon **drained capers,** 1 clove **garlic,** and 2 tablespoons **white wine vinegar.** Whirl until blended. With motor running, gradually add 1 cup **salad oil** in a thin, steady stream. Garnish with 1 teaspoon **drained capers.** Makes 1½ cups.
PER TABLESPOON: 84 calories, .25 gram protein, .10 gram carbohydrate, 9 grams total fat, 11 milligrams cholesterol, 12 milligrams sodium.

MUSTARD VINAIGRETTE. Stir together ½ cup **olive oil** or salad oil, ¼ cup **white wine vinegar,** 2 tablespoons chopped **parsley,** 1 clove **garlic** (pressed or minced), 1 tablespoon **Dijon mustard,** and ⅛ teaspoon **pepper.** Makes 1 cup.
PER TABLESPOON: 62 calories, .02 gram protein, .37 gram carbohydrate, 7 grams total fat, 0 milligram cholesterol, 29 milligrams sodium.

Marinated Artichoke Hearts

PREPARATION TIME: 40 to 45 minutes
COOKING TIME: 20 to 25 minutes
STANDING TIME: At least 2 days
PER ¼ CUP: 143 calories, 1 gram protein, 5 grams carbohydrate, 14 grams total fat, 0 milligram cholesterol, 93 milligrams sodium

Tiny artichokes—called hearts or baby artichokes—sprout along the artichoke plant's stem, beneath the larger thistles. Because the fuzzy centers are so small, these little vegetables are entirely edible once you've trimmed off the coarse outer leaves.

These marinated artichoke hearts keep for weeks; they're splendid as a relish or in salads—or as a first course, brightened with chopped chives or parsley.

Makes 4 cups

4 **pounds tiny (1½- to 2-inch-diameter) artichokes**
Acidulated water (3 tablespoons vinegar or lemon juice per quart water)
1 **cup** *each* **olive oil and distilled white vinegar**
1 **carrot, peeled, ends trimmed**
1 **small onion, peeled**
1 **small stalk celery**
2 **cloves garlic**
1 **small cinnamon stick, broken in half**
5 **bay leaves**
½ **teaspoon** *each* **whole black peppercorns and salt**

Wash artichokes in cold water; drain. Break off coarse outer leaves of each artichoke down to tender yellowish inner leaves. Cut off top third of each artichoke; cut off stem end, then trim stem end carefully in the shape of a cone. You should have 4 cups trimmed hearts. As artichokes are trimmed, drop into enough acidulated water to cover; keep immersed as completely as possible by floating a pan lid or inverted plate on water.

When all artichokes have been trimmed, drain; then place artichokes in a 4- to 5-quart noncorrodible pan. Add oil, vinegar, carrot, onion, celery, garlic, cinnamon stick, bay leaves, peppercorns, and salt. Cover and bring to a boil over high heat; reduce heat and simmer until artichoke bottoms are tender when pierced, about 20 minutes.

Let stand in cooking liquid, covered, until next day. Remove and discard onion, bay leaves, and celery. Cut artichokes in half or leave very small ones whole, as desired.

Return artichokes to cooking liquid and bring to a boil. With a slotted spoon, lift artichokes from liquid; arrange in 2 wide-mouth 1-pint jars or in a bowl. To each pint, add 1 or 2 carrot slices, 1 piece cinnamon stick, and 1 clove garlic. Bring remaining cooking liquid to a boil; pour into jars to cover artichokes. Cover and refrigerate until next day (or for up to 3 weeks) before serving. The entire artichoke is edible, including the fuzzy center.

Butter-steaming for Peak Flavor

A cross between stir-frying and steaming, butter-steaming is a technique we developed to cook vegetables quickly, with maximum retention of color, flavor, and texture. It's a method that works well with a wide variety of vegetables; whatever your choices, be sure that the pieces are small and the pan hot. Cook the vegetables covered, but stir them occasionally.

Though butter-steaming is typically done in a frying pan, you can use a wok if you prefer.

> **Butter or margarine (use amount suggested for each vegetable)**
>
> **Vegetables, prepared as directed below**
>
> **Water, Homemade Chicken Broth (page 58), or canned regular-strength chicken broth (use amount suggested for each vegetable)**

Melt butter in a 10- to 12-inch frying pan over high heat, or in an electric frying pan set at high heat. Add vegetables, then add water (if used; some vegetables do not require added liquid). Stir and cover. Cook over high heat, stirring occasionally, until vegetables are tender-crisp (or until greens are just wilted) and liquid has evaporated. Season as directed for each vegetable and serve at once.

VEGETABLES FOR BUTTER-STEAMING. Prepare as directed below.

Beet greens. Follow basic directions for butter-steaming, using 2 tablespoons **butter** or margarine, 4 cups chopped **beet greens,** ¼ teaspoon **dry basil,** and 3 tablespoons **broth.** Cover and cook, stirring occasionally, for 5 to 7 minutes. Season to taste with **salt** and **pepper.** Makes 3 servings.

Bell peppers with onion. Melt 2 tablespoons **butter** or margarine in a 10- to 12-inch frying pan over medium heat. Add 1 medium-size **onion,** chopped; stir often until soft. Increase heat to high and add 3 large **green or red bell peppers,** stemmed, seeded, and sliced, and 5 tablespoons **water.** Cover and cook, stirring occasionally, for 6 minutes. Season to taste with **salt** and **pepper.** Makes 5 or 6 servings.

Broccoli. Trim and discard tough stalk ends from 1½ pounds **broccoli.** Thinly slice tender stalks; set flowerets aside. Follow basic directions for butter-steaming, using 2 tablespoons **butter** or margarine, the sliced stalks, and ¼ cup **water.** Cover and cook, stirring occasionally, for 4 minutes. Stir in broccoli flowerets and 3 more tablespoons **water.** Cover and cook for 3 more minutes, stirring frequently. Season to taste with **salt** and **pepper.** Makes 4 or 5 servings.

Dilled cabbage. Follow basic directions for butter-steaming, using 2 tablespoons **butter** or margarine, 5 cups thinly sliced **green cabbage,** ½ teaspoon **dry dill weed,** and ¼ cup **water.** Cover and cook, stirring occasionally, for 3 to 4 minutes. If desired, stir in ¼ cup **mayonnaise;** then sprinkle with additional **dry dill weed** and season to taste with **salt** and **pepper.** Makes 4 or 5 servings.

Anise carrots. Follow basic directions for butter-steaming, using 2 tablespoons **butter** or margarine, 3 cups thinly sliced peeled **carrots** (10 to 12 slender carrots), ¼ teaspoon **anise seeds,** and 3 tablespoons **water.** Cover and cook, stirring occasionally, for 5 minutes. If desired, add 3 tablespoons **whipping cream** and stir until almost all liquid has evaporated. Season to taste with **salt** and **pepper.** Makes 4 or 5 servings.

Green beans. Snap stem ends from 1 pound **green beans;** cut beans into 1-inch lengths. Follow basic directions for butter-steaming, using 2 tablespoons **butter** or margarine, the beans, and 5 tablespoons **water.** Cover and cook, stirring occasionally, for 7 minutes. Season to taste with **salt** and **pepper.** Makes 4 or 5 servings.

Mustard greens with bacon. In a 10- to 12-inch frying pan, cook 4 slices **bacon** (diced) over medium heat until crisp. Lift out bacon with a slotted spoon, drain on paper towels, and set aside. Pour off and discard all but 2 tablespoons of the drippings. Then follow basic directions for butter-steaming, using the 2 tablespoons drippings, 4 cups chopped **mustard greens** (tough stems trimmed off), and 2 tablespoons **broth.** Cover and cook, stirring occasionally, for 5 to 7 minutes. Sprinkle with bacon. Makes 4 or 5 servings.

Lettuce. Follow basic directions for butter-steaming, using 2 tablespoons **butter** or margarine and 6 cups shredded **iceberg lettuce.** Cover and cook, stirring occasionally, for 2 to 3 minutes. Season to taste with **salt** and **pepper.** Makes 4 servings.

Piquant spinach. Discard tough stems and any yellow or wilted leaves from 2 pounds **spinach.** Rinse remaining spinach leaves well, but do not pat dry. Follow basic directions for butter-steaming, using 2 tablespoons **butter** or margarine and the spinach (with water that clings to it). Cover and cook just until wilted. Remove cover and add 2 teaspoons **sugar** and 3 tablespoons **whipping cream.** Stir until almost all liquid has evaporated. Add 1 to 2 tablespoons **vinegar,** season to taste with **salt,** and sprinkle with **ground nutmeg.** Makes 5 or 6 servings.

Spinach with cream cheese sauce. Clean 2 pounds **spinach** as directed above. Follow basic directions for butter-steaming, using 1 tablespoon **butter** or margarine and the spinach (with water that clings to it). Cover and cook until just barely wilted. Remove cover and blend in 1 small package (3 oz.) **cream cheese,** diced, and ½ to ¾ teaspoon **Worcestershire;** stir until cheese is melted. Season to taste with **salt** and **pepper.** Makes 5 or 6 servings.

Summer squash. Follow basic directions for butter-steaming, using 2 tablespoons **butter** or margarine, 4 cups thinly sliced **zucchini** or crookneck squash, and 6 tablespoons **water.** Cover and cook, stirring occasionally, for 4 to 5 minutes. Remove cover and add 2 tablespoons crumbled **blue-veined cheese** or ¼ cup freshly shredded Parmesan cheese; stir until cheese is melted. Season to taste with **salt** and **pepper.** Makes 4 or 5 servings.

Swiss chard. Rinse 1 pound **Swiss chard;** thinly slice stems and chop leaves. Follow basic directions for butter-steaming, using 2 tablespoons **butter** or margarine and the sliced stems. Cover and cook, stirring occasionally, for 3 to 4 minutes. Stir in chopped leaves and cook, covered, for 3 to 4 more minutes. Season to taste with **salt** and **pepper.**

To serve as a main dish, add 4 **large eggs,** beaten, and stir until eggs are as set as you like. Makes 3 or 4 servings.

Roman Artichoke Platter

Pictured at left

PREPARATION TIME: 45 to 50 minutes
COOKING TIME: 25 to 30 minutes
COOLING TIME: At least 30 minutes
PER SERVING: 65 calories, 3 grams protein, 15 grams carbohydrate, .25 gram total fat, 0 milligram cholesterol, 102 milligrams sodium

Artichokes served bottoms up, as you typically see them in Roman restaurants, have a surprisingly different look. The artichokes are trimmed down to the completely edible inner leaves; the stems are peeled.

Eat these artichokes with knife and fork, trimming out the choke as it is exposed. Serve at room temperature in a vinaigrette dressing, as in this recipe; or serve hot, with melted butter, mayonnaise, or another sauce.

Makes 10 to 12 servings

> **10 to 12 medium-size artichokes**
> **About 1 cup Mustard Vinaigrette (page 184), Shallot Dressing (page 220), or other vinaigrette dressing**

Break off outer leaves of each artichoke down to pale green inner leaves. With a knife, slice off about the top third of remaining leaves. Peel green surface from base and stem; trim stem just to remove tip end. Wash artichokes and boil in seasoned water as directed for Boiled Artichokes (page 184); cooking time is 25 to 30 minutes.

Drain cooked artichokes thoroughly and arrange in a shallow dish; pour dressing over artichokes. Cover lightly and let stand until cooled to room temperature, turning occasionally in dressing.

To serve, stand artichokes, stems up, on a shallow rimmed platter; pour dressing over them.

Edible-pod Peas with Egg Butter

W E S T E R N   C L A S S I C

PREPARATION TIME: About 15 minutes
COOKING TIME: 3 to 5 minutes
PER SERVING: 129 calories, 4 grams protein, 6 grams carbohydrate, 10 grams total fat, 113 milligrams cholesterol, 107 milligrams sodium

Both fresh and frozen edible-pod peas are found in most Western supermarkets. You may see them sold as sugar, snow, or sugar snap peas, or as Chinese pea pods. Here, they're boiled briefly, then served with a sauce of hard-cooked eggs mashed with butter.

Makes 4 to 6 servings

> **2 hard-cooked large eggs, finely mashed**
> **¼ cup (⅛ lb.) butter or margarine, at room temperature**
> **1 tablespoon minced green onion (including top), optional**
> **Salt and pepper**
> **1 to 1½ pounds edible-pod peas, ends and strings removed**

Castroville, California claims to be the "Artichoke Capital of the World"—but Italy grows lots, too. For Roman Artichoke Platter (recipe at right), buds are trimmed and rakishly upended, drenched with vinaigrette, and served as a first course.

Blend eggs, butter, and onion (if used); season to taste with salt and pepper. Set aside.

In a 3- to 4-quart pan, bring 8 cups water to a boil over high heat. Add peas and cook, uncovered, just until peas turn bright green and are barely tender to bite. Drain immediately, arrange equally on 4 to 6 individual plates, and top each serving equally with egg butter.

Cheese-stuffed Squash Blossom Appetizers

W E S T E R N   C L A S S I C

PREPARATION TIME: About 30 minutes
COOKING TIME: 8 to 10 minutes
PER APPETIZER: 53 calories, 2 grams protein, 2 grams carbohydrate, 4 grams total fat, 33 milligrams cholesterol, 48 milligrams sodium

The bright yellow blooms of any squash—winter or summer, acorn to zucchini—are delicious to eat. They're a not-so-secret specialty of Italian cooks, who often stuff and fry them. You may be able to find the blossoms year round in fancy produce markets, but they're most plentiful in summer (if you grow zucchini, you'll have a good supply in your garden). Male blossoms stay open; female flowers, with swelling fruit at their bases, tend to be closed.

Makes 15 to 20 appetizers

> 15 to 20 squash blossoms, *each* about
>   3 inches long from base to tip
> 1 small package (3 oz.) cream cheese,
>   at room temperature
> 1 tablespoon milk
> ⅓ cup freshly grated Parmesan cheese
> ⅛ teaspoon pepper
> 1½ tablespoons canned diced green chiles
>   All-purpose flour
> 2 large eggs
>   Salad oil

Rinse blossoms with a gentle spray of cool water; shake off excess. Trim off stems completely (close to blossoms), since they may be bitter. Discard stems and set blossoms aside.

In a bowl, blend cream cheese, milk, Parmesan cheese, pepper, and chiles. Spoon about 1 teaspoon filling into each blossom; twist tip of blossom to close. Roll blossoms in flour to coat lightly; set aside.

In a small bowl, beat eggs with 1 tablespoon water.

Heat ¼ inch oil in a 10- to 12-inch frying pan over medium-high heat. With a fork, dip 1 blossom at a time into beaten egg; let drain briefly. Place in oil (do not crowd blossoms in pan) and cook, turning as needed, until golden brown. Drain on paper towels and set in a 150° oven until all blossoms are cooked. Serve hot.

Spaghetti Squash Hash Browns

PREPARATION TIME: At least 30 minutes to cool baked squash; about 10 minutes to combine with seasonings
COOKING TIME: 15 to 60 minutes to bake squash; about 6 minutes to cook each patty (3 or 4 can cook at once)
PER SERVING: 128 calories, 3 grams protein, 12 grams carbohydrate, 8 grams total fat, 20 milligrams cholesterol, 175 milligrams sodium

Spaghetti squash has been a vegetable garden curiosity for a long time, but its commercial popularity increased greatly after Sunset *presented a collection of cultivating and cooking tips in the early '70s. The flavor of the squash is deceptively rich, almost nutlike, and its golden strands make an interesting alternative to shredded potatoes for hash browns.*

Makes 6 to 8 servings

> 6 cups cooked spaghetti squash
>   (directions follow)
> ⅓ cup all-purpose flour
> ½ cup freshly shredded or grated
>   Parmesan cheese
> ¼ cup (⅛ lb.) butter or margarine
>   Salt and pepper
>   Sour cream

In a bowl, combine squash strands, flour, and cheese. Mix well, lifting squash strands with 2 forks.

In a 10- to 12-inch frying pan with a nonstick finish, melt 1 tablespoon of the butter over medium-high heat. Drop squash mixture into pan in ¼-cup portions. With a fork, quickly pat and press each portion to form an evenly thick cake about 3 inches across; leave about ½ inch between cakes.

Cook cakes until bottoms are lightly browned (lift with a spatula to check), 2 to 3 minutes. Turn cakes over; if they break apart, use fork to press back together. Cook until bottoms are lightly browned, 2 to 3 minutes. With a spatula, transfer cakes from pan to a platter, making a single layer; keep warm in a 150° oven or on a warming tray until all cakes are cooked. Add remaining 3 tablespoons butter to pan as needed.

Season hash browns to taste with salt and pepper. Serve with sour cream.

COOKED SPAGHETTI SQUASH. Pierce skin of a 4- to 5-pound **spaghetti squash** in several places with a fork.

To bake, set squash in a 9- or 10-inch-wide baking pan; bake in a 350° oven until shell gives slightly when pressed, about 1 hour.

To microwave, place squash on bottom of oven. Microwave on **HIGH (100%)**, turning squash over several times, until shell gives slightly when pressed, 15 to 20 minutes.

Let squash stand until cool to touch. Cut in half lengthwise. With a fork, lift out and discard seeds. Run fork through squash to separate strands. Scoop squash out of shell; you should have about 6 cups. If made ahead, cover and refrigerate for up to 2 days.

Colorful Grilled Vegetables

Pictured on page 178

The recent boom in the popularity of grill-cooked foods across the United States (and even into Europe) has been touted as a new phenomenon—but out West, barbecuing is nothing new. We've long savored the fresh, simple flavors of grilled foods, and we've always enjoyed cooking out of doors. Even in the '30s, extensive outdoor kitchens were typical of Western homes—and at the heart of it all was the barbecue, where steaks and chops shared company with vegetables and fruits.

Here's a handy list of vegetables you can barbecue. Some are best if blanched before grilling; they cook more evenly and quickly that way. Others work well from the raw state. Keep the vegetables moist as they cook by basting with herb-seasoned oil; or brush them with the basting sauce used on accompanying meat, poultry, or fish.

> **About 2 pounds vegetables (choices follow; use 1 or several kinds)**
>
> ⅓ **cup olive oil or salad oil (or basting sauce)**
>
> 2 **tablespoons minced fresh thyme, fresh oregano, fresh rosemary, or fresh tarragon; or 2 teaspoons dry herbs**
>
> **Salt and pepper**

Choose 1 or several vegetables and prepare as directed.

If desired, blanch vegetables. Bring about 12 cups water to a boil in a 6- to 8-quart pan. Add 1 kind of vegetable (up to 1 lb. at a time). When boil resumes, cook until vegetable is barely tender when pierced (see each choice for times). Lift out with tongs and plunge into ice water to cool quickly; lift out and drain well. Repeat as needed, blanching vegetables in sequence. (At this point, you may let cool, then cover and refrigerate for up to 24 hours.)

To grill, coat raw or blanched vegetables with oil and herbs (or with basting sauce). Place *blanched vegetables* on a grill 4 to 6 inches above a solid bed of hot coals (you should be able to hold your hand at grill level for no more than 2 to 3 seconds). Grill *raw vegetables* over medium coals (you should be able to hold your hand at grill level for 4 to 5 seconds) unless otherwise instructed. Cook, turning often and brushing with as much oil as needed to keep moist, until vegetables are hot, tender, and covered with brown streaks (see each choice for times).

Serve hot or at room temperature. If made ahead, cover and let stand at room temperature for up to 4 hours or refrigerate until next day. To reheat, place cold vegetables in a single layer in 10- by 15-inch rimmed baking pans; put in a 350° oven until hot, 7 to 10 minutes. Season to taste with salt and pepper. Allow about 2 pounds vegetables for 6 to 8 servings.

VEGETABLES FOR GRILLING. Rinse well, drain, trim, and blanch as directed.

Bell peppers (red, yellow, or green), fresh pimentos, or fresh chiles. Grill whole peppers for 8 to 10 minutes.

Broccoli. Cut off tough stalk ends; peel tender stalks. Leave bunches whole; or, if bunches are thicker than 2 inches, cut in half lengthwise. Blanch for 2 to 3 minutes. Grill for 4 to 6 minutes.

Cabbage (red or green) or radicchio. Cut cabbage into quarters lengthwise. Cut radicchio in halves. Grill over hot coals for 8 to 10 minutes.

Corn. Strip husks and silk from corn. Omit oil and herbs. Grill for 10 to 12 minutes. Squeeze lime juice over corn and sprinkle with salt.

Eggplant. Cut stem ends from slender Oriental eggplants or small regular eggplants. Cut Oriental eggplant in half lengthwise; cut regular eggplant lengthwise into 1½-inch-thick wedges. Blanch for 2 to 3 minutes; grill until very soft when pressed, 12 to 15 minutes.

Fennel. Cut off and discard woody stems and any damaged areas from large fennel heads. Cut each head vertically into 4 equal slices. Trim feathery leaves; reserve.

Grill over hot coals for about 25 minutes. To serve, sprinkle with reserved leaves (chopped); offer lemon wedges.

Leeks. Trim off root ends and dark green tops of leeks; split leeks lengthwise to within ½ inch of root ends. Wash well. Blanch for 1 to 2 minutes; grill for 4 to 6 minutes.

Mushrooms (button, shiitake, oyster). Thread button mushrooms (1- to 1½-inch caps) through stems onto slender skewers. Cut off tough stems of fresh shiitake. If using dry shiitake, soak in hot water to cover until soft, about 15 minutes. Squeeze out water; trim off stems. Grill large mushrooms whole; thread small ones on slender skewers.

Grill all mushrooms over hot coals for about 10 minutes.

Onions (green). Trim root ends and top 2 inches of green tops. Grill for 6 to 8 minutes.

Onions (red, yellow, white). Cut small unpeeled onions in half lengthwise, large peeled onions into quarters. Thread quarters through layers onto slender skewers, arranging so they will lie flat. Grill for 15 to 20 minutes.

Potatoes (russet, thin-skinned, sweet or yams). Scrub well; cut lengthwise into 1-inch wedges. Blanch for 4 to 5 minutes. Grill for 8 to 10 minutes.

Summer squash (zucchini, crookneck, pattypan). Trim off stem ends. If thicker than 1 inch, cut in half lengthwise. Blanch for 2 to 3 minutes. Grill for 8 to 10 minutes.

Tomatoes. Cut firm-ripe tomatoes in halves. Grill for 8 to 12 minutes.

Fresh corn tamales, steamed to tender morsels in their own green husks, are spiked by a little chile, a little cheese. These treasures of the Southwest and Mexico make one-bite delights to go with grilled meats. The recipe for Green Corn Tamales with Cheese & Chiles is on the facing page.

Fresh Tomatoes Jean

PREPARATION TIME: About 30 minutes

COOKING TIME: About 2 minutes

PER SERVING: 63 calories, 1 gram protein, 7 grams carbohydrate, 4 grams total fat, 10 milligrams cholesterol, 51 milligrams sodium

Less than perfectly shaped tomatoes from autumn gardens—or less flavorful winter tomatoes—are perfect candidates for these attractive spheres of seeded, herb-seasoned tomato pulp. To cut preparation time, you can form the tomato mixture into balls early in the day, then heat in butter just before serving.

Makes 6 servings

- **4 large firm-ripe tomatoes (shapes can be irregular), about 2 lbs. *total*, peeled**
- **1½ teaspoons chopped fresh marjoram or ½ teaspoon dry marjoram leaves; or 2 tablespoons chopped fresh basil or 1 teaspoon dry basil**
- **2 tablespoons butter or margarine**

Core tomatoes, cut in half crosswise, and squeeze out seeds and juice (reserve for other uses). Chop pulp finely and mix with marjoram.

Spoon 3 to 4 tablespoons of the tomato mixture at a time onto several layers of cheesecloth or a piece of muslin. Bring up ends of cloth and twist firmly to remove excess liquid, shaping tomato mixture into a compact ball. (Reserve liquid for other uses.) Unwrap ball and set on a flat surface. Repeat until all tomato is formed into balls; you should have 10 to 12 balls *total*. (At this point, you may cover lightly and refrigerate for up to 8 hours.)

Melt butter in a 10- to 12-inch frying pan over medium heat. Add tomato balls; they are fragile, so handle gently. Cook until warmed through, 1 to 2 minutes; turn gently several times. Transfer to serving plates.

Dried Tomatoes in Oil

PREPARATION TIME: About 40 minutes
DRYING TIME: 7 to 24 hours
PER ¼ CUP: 332 calories, 2 grams protein, 8 grams carbohydrate, 34 grams total fat, 0 milligram cholesterol, 564 milligrams sodium

When split, lightly salted, and dried, bland-tasting pear-shaped tomatoes become tart and intense in flavor, meaty and chewy in texture. Eat them as a snack, as you would dried apricots; or pack them in olive oil and herbs, then use in sandwiches or in any of the other ways noted below.

Though imported dried tomatoes are sun-dried (or at least labeled as such), we recommend simpler, faster drying in the oven or a dehydrator.

Makes about 6 ounces (1 pint) dried tomatoes

> **3 pounds ripe pear-shaped, Roma-type tomatoes**
>
> **2 teaspoons salt**
>
> **2 dry rosemary sprigs (*each* about 6 inches long) or 1 tablespoon dry rosemary**
>
> **About 1¼ cups olive oil**

Wash tomatoes; slice lengthwise almost completely in half. Lay tomatoes cut side up and sprinkle with salt.

To dry in a dehydrator, place tomatoes, cut side up, about 1 inch apart on a dehydrator rack. Put in a 125° dehydrator until individual tomatoes shrivel to small, flattish ovals and feel dry to the touch but are still flexible (not brittle), 17 to 23 hours.

To dry in the oven, set tomatoes, cut side up, on wire racks placed in 2 shallow 10- by 15-inch rimmed baking pans. Bake in a 200° oven until tomatoes feel and look as described for dehydrator method, 7 to 9 hours.

Pack tomatoes loosely in a 1- to 1½-pint jar with rosemary. Pour in oil to cover tomatoes (they may mold if exposed to air).

Tomatoes are good to eat right away, but to develop the flavor characteristic of Italian tomatoes, let them stand airtight at room temperature for 1½ months. (Refrigerate if you see any bubbles; they indicate fermentation. Cold oil will turn opaque.) Tomatoes keep indefinitely; use as long as oil tastes fresh.

USING DRIED TOMATOES. Use homemade or purchased dried tomatoes in oil in these combinations.

Antipasto. Lift **dried tomatoes** from oil and arrange on a platter with sliced cold Italian meats such as **dry salami** or prosciutto, **tiny cooked, shelled shrimp, olives,** and **pickled peppers.** Moisten surface with **seasoned tomato oil;** squeeze **lemon juice** over all.

Sandwich. For each serving, moisten 1 side of a **toasted French bread slice** with **seasoned tomato oil;** cover with slices of **fontina cheese.** Broil 6 inches below heat until cheese is melted, then top with several well-drained **dried tomatoes** and return to broiler just to warm. Sprinkle with chopped **parsley.**

Salad. Sliver ½ cup drained **dried tomatoes.** Mix with 4 cups torn **butter lettuce** leaves. In a 10- to 12-inch frying pan, combine ¼ cup **seasoned tomato oil** with ½ cup sliced **button mushrooms.** Stir over high heat until hot; add 2 tablespoons **vinegar** and season to taste with **pepper.** Pour mushroom mixture over lettuce; mix. Makes 4 servings.

Spread. Whirl drained **dried tomatoes** in a food processor or blender until coarsely chopped. Add **seasoned tomato oil** to moisten to a spreading consistency. Spread on **toast triangles.** Serve as an appetizer, or with soup or salad.

Tomato Cocktail Sorbet

PREPARATION TIME: 15 to 20 minutes
FREEZING TIME: At least 5 hours
PER ¼ CUP: 17 calories, .79 gram protein, 4 grams carbohydrate, .19 gram total fat, 0 milligram cholesterol, 88 milligrams sodium

Fresh tomato purée is the base for this lively vegetable cocktail sorbet. Offer it in small cups between courses at a grand meal; it's also a tasty partner for breakfast scrambled eggs and sausages. Though the sorbet requires several hours to freeze, preparation is easy—you just whirl the vegetables and seasonings in a blender.

Makes 2½ cups

> **1¾ to 2 pounds ripe tomatoes, peeled; or 2 cups canned tomato juice**
>
> **1½ teaspoons Worcestershire**
>
> **½ teaspoon *each* ground cumin and celery salt**
>
> **¼ to ½ teaspoon liquid hot pepper seasoning**
>
> **Salt and pepper**

Core tomatoes, cut in half crosswise, and gently squeeze out seeds; discard seeds or reserve for other uses.

Whirl seeded tomatoes in a blender or food processor until puréed, adding Worcestershire, cumin, celery salt, and hot pepper seasoning. Season purée to taste with salt and pepper.

Pour purée into an 8- or 9-inch-wide metal pan. Cover airtight and freeze at 0° or colder until solid, at least 5 hours; frozen purée can then be stored for up to 1 month.

To serve, let purée stand at room temperature for 15 to 20 minutes to soften slightly; then break into chunks with a heavy spoon. Whirl chunks in a food processor or beat with an electric mixer (start slowly, then beat faster as mixture softens) until a thick, icy slush forms.

You may also freeze purée in a self-refrigerated ice cream machine, following the manufacturer's directions.

Sorbet has the best texture when softly frozen—just after it is beaten into slush. At this point, it can be held in the freezer for up to 20 minutes. If stored longer, cover; before serving, let sorbet stand at room temperature until you can break it up with a spoon. If desired, you can whirl or beat sorbet again. Because sorbet melts quickly, serve it in small cups.

Garden Purées Capture Summer's Harvest

"Bursting at the seams" describes the condition of many Western vegetable gardens from late summer through autumn. As each warm day brings more vegetables to maturity, the overwhelmed gardener often wonders what to do with the excess.

We suggest you lightly cook your vegetables and purée them. In this form, they take up relatively little space in the freezer, and they'll keep well for a year. Use the purées to make dips, timbales, soups, soufflés, vegetable accompaniments, and sauces.

Beets, carrots, tomatoes, and zucchini are all quickly puréed in a food processor. You can also use a blender with tomatoes and zucchini. A food chopper is a slower alternative for the firm vegetables; the purée will be somewhat coarse.

Beet Purée

Cut off the green tops 1 inch above the crowns of about 5 pounds **beets** (about 10, 3-inch diameter); reserve greens for another use or discard. Scrub beets well. In a 6- to 8-quart pan, bring about 4 quarts **water** to a boil. Add beets and boil, covered, until tender when pierced, 20 to 60 minutes depending on size and maturity. Drain; when cool, trim stem and root flush and slip off skins. Cut beets into about 1-inch chunks. Whirl a portion at a time in a food processor until smooth, or put through a food chopper fitted with a fine or medium blade. Let cool. Use (suggestions follow) or freeze.

To freeze, spoon into ice cube trays or 1-cup freezer cartons. Place in freezer. When solid, transfer cubes to freezer bags. Makes about 2 quarts.

Carrot Purée

Peel about 5 pounds **carrots** (about 36, 8 inches long). Cut into 1- to 1½-inch pieces. In a 6- to 8-quart pan, bring 3 to 4 quarts **water** to a boil. Add carrots and cook, uncovered, until tender when pierced, 10 to 12 minutes; drain. Whirl a portion at a time in a food processor until smooth, or put through a food chopper fitted with a fine or medium blade. Let cool. Use (suggestions follow) or freeze as directed for beet purée. Makes about 2 quarts.

Tomato Purée

Wash about 5 pounds **tomatoes** (about 10, 3- to 4-inch diameter). Core toma-

Carrot and zucchini purées lend colorful contrast to sole fillets.

toes and cut in half crosswise; squeeze out seeds and discard (or save for other uses). Cut into 1- to 1½-inch chunks. Purée a portion at a time in a food processor or blender.

Pour purée into a 5- to 6-quart pan and boil, uncovered, stirring occasionally, until thick and reduced by half; as tomatoes thicken, reduce heat and stir more often. Let cool. Use (suggestions follow) or freeze as directed for beet purée. Makes about 1 quart.

Zucchini Purée

Wash about 5 pounds **zucchini** (about 12, 7 inches long). Trim off and discard stem and blossom ends. Cut zucchini into ½- to ¾-inch-thick slices.

In a 6- to 8-quart pan, bring 3 to 4 quarts **water** to boiling. Add zucchini and boil, uncovered, just until zucchini is barely tender when pierced, 5 to 7 minutes. Drain well. Purée a portion at a time in a food processor or blender. Let cool. Use (suggestions follow) or freeze as directed for beet purée. Makes about 1¾ quarts.

Vegetable Timbales

- 4 large eggs
- ½ cup whipping cream or milk
- ⅛ teaspoon *each* ground nutmeg and white pepper
- 1 cup tomato or zucchini purée; or ⅔ cup beet or carrot purée (thawed if frozen)
- Salt

Beat together eggs, cream, nutmeg, pepper, and vegetable purée until blended. Season to taste with salt. Pour mixture into 6 to 8 buttered indi-

vidual ½-cup molds set in an 11- by 17-inch roasting pan, filling molds about ⅔ full. Pour about 1 inch hot water into roasting pan.

Bake in a 375° oven until center appears firm when mold is gently shaken, 25 to 30 minutes. Lift out of water; let cool for about 5 minutes. Run a knife around edges to loosen; unmold on a serving dish. Serve hot. Makes 6 to 8 servings.

Vegetable Purée Soufflé

- ¼ cup (⅛ lb.) butter or margarine
- ¼ cup all-purpose flour
- 1 cup milk
- ¼ teaspoon dry thyme leaves or dry tarragon
- ⅛ teaspoon ground nutmeg
- 1 cup beet, carrot, tomato, or zucchini purée (thawed if frozen)
- 1 cup (4 oz.) shredded Swiss cheese
- 4 large egg yolks
- Salt
- 5 large egg whites

In a 2- to 3-quart pan, melt butter over low heat. Add flour and stir constantly until bubbles form all over; do not brown. Remove from heat and slowly stir in milk, thyme, nutmeg, and vegetable purée. Brig to a boil, stirring; add cheese and stir until melted. Remove from heat and stir in egg yolks; season to taste with salt.

In a large bowl, beat egg whites with an electric mixer on high speed until whites hold stiff, moist peaks. Stir about ¼ of the whites into the vegetable sauce, then fold in remaining whites until blended. Pour into a buttered 1½-quart soufflé dish.

Bake in center of a 375° oven until golden brown, 25 to 35 minutes. Serve immediately. Makes 3 or 4 servings.

Hot Vegetable Purée

In a 10- to 12-inch frying pan, melt 2 tablespoons **butter** or margarine over medium heat. Add 1 large **onion,** finely chopped; stir often until onion is very soft and slightly golden. Add ⅓ cup **whipping cream** and 1 cup **beet, carrot, tomato, or zucchini purée** (thawed if frozen). Boil gently, uncovered, stirring, until hot and thick. Season to taste with **salt** and **pepper.** Makes 2 or 3 servings.

Garden-fresh Anchoïade Dinner from Provence (recipe below) features crisp vegetables, ham slivers, and eggs to dip in Anchovy Sauce. Cut vegetables as you eat; even the base and hearts of artichokes are good raw.

Anchoïade Dinner from Provence

Pictured above

PREPARATION TIME: 45 to 50 minutes
PER SERVING: 247 calories, 19 grams protein, 26 grams carbohydrate, 9 grams total fat, 293 milligrams cholesterol, 687 milligrams sodium

This sophisticated version of French crudités combines fresh raw vegetables with a pungent sauce and complementary cold meat.

Makes 4 to 6 servings

    8 to 12 inner stalks of celery, with leaves
    12 to 24 radishes with tops
    10 to 12 green onions, root ends and coarse
        parts of tops trimmed off
    2 or 3 fresh green or red California
        (Anaheim) chiles
    2 or 3 large red or green bell peppers
    12 to 18 green beans
    8 to 12 pear-shaped, Roma-type tomatoes or
        small regular tomatoes (1½ to 2 lbs. *total*)
    4 to 6 small (2½- to 3-inch-diameter)
        artichokes

    Vinegar
    4 to 6 hard-cooked large eggs
    ⅓ to ½ pound cured ham (such as prosciutto
        or Westphalian ham), sliced paper-thin
    Anchovy Sauce (recipe follows)

Rinse celery, radishes, onions, chiles, peppers, beans, tomatoes, and artichokes well. Break coarse outer leaves from artichokes; trim bottoms flat and rub with vinegar. Arrange vegetables and hard-cooked eggs in a flat basket; arrange ham on a tray alongside.

Let each guest select some of each item. Cut chiles, bell peppers, and tomatoes to eat; eat just the tender base of each artichoke leaf (plus the heart, trimmed of fuzz). Dip into sauce.

ANCHOVY SAUCE. In a blender or food processor, combine 2 **hard-cooked large egg yolks,** 1 **large egg,** 1 can (2 oz.) **anchovy fillets** and their oil, 1 tablespoon chopped **shallot,** and 1 tablespoon **white wine vinegar.** Whirl until fairly smooth. With motor running, add 1 cup **olive oil** in a slow, steady stream. Pour into a small bowl. If made ahead, cover and refrigerate until next day. Makes about 1⅓ cups.
PER TABLESPOON: 106 calories, 1 gram protein, .12 gram carbohydrate, 11 grams total fat, 40 milligrams cholesterol, 26 milligrams sodium.

Celery Victor

PREPARATION TIME: 15 to 20 minutes
COOKING TIME: About 20 minutes, plus 30 minutes to cool
PER SERVING: 182 calories, 5 grams protein, 12 grams carbohydrate, 13 grams total fat, 96 milligrams cholesterol, 292 milligrams sodium

Named for the chef who created it years ago at San Francisco's St. Francis Hotel, artfully garnished Celery Victor is an especially eye-catching first course.

Makes 6 servings

> 3 **celery hearts (small celery bunches with coarse outer stalks removed), about 1 pound** *each*
> 3 **cups Homemade Chicken Broth (page 58) or canned regular-strength chicken broth**
> 2 **tablespoons white wine vinegar**
> ¼ **cup olive oil or salad oil**
> 2 **hard-cooked large eggs, chopped**
> 12 **canned anchovy fillets, drained**
> 6 **canned pimento strips, drained**
> **Salt and pepper**

Trim each celery heart to a length of about 8 inches, cutting off leafy ends of stalks. With a vegetable peeler, pare coarse strings from outer stalks of each heart. Cut each heart in half lengthwise; tie each half with cotton string at the center to hold pieces together.

Bring broth to a boil in a 12- to 14-inch frying pan. Add celery; reduce heat, cover, and simmer until tender when pierced, about 20 minutes. Lift from broth and carefully place in a shallow 9- by 13-inch dish. Mix vinegar and oil and pour over celery. Cover and refrigerate until cold, about 2 hours (or until next day); occasionally spoon dressing over celery.

Place 1 celery heart half on each salad plate; drizzle equally with dressing. Mound eggs onto hearts, dividing equally. Crisscross 2 anchovy fillets atop each serving; garnish each with 1 pimento strip. Season to taste with salt and pepper.

Spinach with Bacon & Raisins

PREPARATION TIME: 10 to 15 minutes
COOKING TIME: About 10 minutes
PER SERVING: 147 calories, 6 grams protein, 15 grams carbohydrate, 8 grams total fat, 10 milligrams cholesterol, 228 milligrams sodium

Spinach with hot bacon dressing is familiar to most of us as a salad. Here, slightly wilted spinach and crisp bacon bits gain a sweet note from plump, hot golden raisins.

Makes 4 or 5 servings

> 1½ **pounds spinach**
> 6 **slices bacon**
> ½ **cup golden raisins**
> 3 **tablespoons wine vinegar**

Discard tough stems and any yellow or wilted leaves from spinach. Wash spinach well; then place leaves, with water that clings to them, in a 4- to 5-quart pan. Set aside.

In a 10- to 12-inch frying pan, cook bacon over medium heat until crisp. Lift bacon out, drain on paper towels, and set aside. Pour off and discard all but 2 tablespoons of the drippings.

Add raisins to drippings in pan and stir over medium heat until plump and lightly browned. Add vinegar and stir over high heat until almost all vinegar has evaporated.

Meanwhile, place pan of spinach over medium-high heat; cook, covered, just until spinach is wilted and bright green, 2 to 4 minutes. Drain well and pour into a serving dish.

Pour hot dressing over spinach; crumble bacon over top.

Florentine-style Swiss Chard

PREPARATION TIME: 25 to 30 minutes
COOKING TIME: 6 to 8 minutes
PER SERVING: 65 calories, 2 grams protein, 4 grams carbohydrate, 5 grams total fat, 0 milligram cholesterol, 223 milligrams sodium

An unusual presentation distinguishes this very simple Italian dish. To make it, you enclose chopped, seasoned chard in blanched large chard leaves, making neat little dark green rolls. Drizzle with olive oil and serve at room temperature, with juicy lemon wedges to squeeze on top.

Makes 8 servings

> 2 **pounds green Swiss chard**
> 1 **tablespoon lemon juice**
> 3 **tablespoons olive oil**
> **Salt and freshly ground black pepper**
> **Lemon wedges**

Wash chard leaves well. Cut off discolored stem bases and discard, then cut off stems at base of leaves and set aside.

In a 5- to 6-quart pan, bring 12 cups water to a boil over high heat. Push chard stems down into water. Cook, uncovered, until limp, about 4 minutes. Lift out.

At once, push leaves gently down into boiling water and cook until limp, 1 to 2 minutes. Lift out carefully and drain. To preserve the best green color, immerse at once in ice water. When cool, drain.

Select 8 of the largest, most perfect leaves and set aside. Chop remaining leaves and stems together. Mix with lemon juice and 2 tablespoons of the oil; season to taste with salt and pepper.

Lay out reserved leaves; mound an equal amount of chopped chard on each. Fold each leaf to enclose filling; set seam side down on a serving dish. If made ahead, cover and refrigerate for up to 24 hours; bring to room temperature to serve.

Drizzle with remaining 1 tablespoon oil and accompany with lemon wedges.

The Best of Sunset

PASTA, GRAINS & LEGUMES

Pasta, grains, and legumes have never known as much glamour as surrounds them today. But their basic ability to comfort and nourish has remained unchanged through time.

Use these sturdy foods to build a main course, accompany an entrée, or fortify a salad. From porridge to soup, there are countless possibilities, both classic and newly invented.

Use our Homemade All-purpose Pasta as a springboard to tantalizing options inspired by Italy, Asia, and our own Southwest. Other recipes honor Western harvests of corn, rice, wild rice, barley, and assorted lentils and beans. From up-to-the-minute Green Chili with White Beans to our Fifties' Potluck Special, a home-style favorite that stretches or squeezes in quantity, you'll find Sunset's characteristic breadth of choices in this chapter.

Red bell peppers bring sweet, rich flavor and carrot-orange color to egg-tender pasta ribbons. Mix with melted butter and grated cheese; serve to start a meal or to accompany a simple entrée such as roast chicken. The recipe for Red Bell Pepper Pasta is on page 203.

Capellini with Broccoli Cream Sauce

PREPARATION TIME: About 10 minutes

COOKING TIME: 8 to 10 minutes

PER SERVING (RECIPE PREPARED WITH 1¼ CUPS CHEESE): 605 calories, 17 grams protein, 42 grams carbohydrate, 42 grams total fat, 133 milligrams cholesterol, 474 milligrams sodium

A far cry from classic tomato-sauced spaghetti, this elegant entrée celebrates a newer, richer, more subtle Italian tradition. Thin strands of capellini and cooked fresh broccoli are lightly coated with cream, then mixed with plenty of grated Parmesan.

Makes 6 to 8 servings

- 1½ pounds broccoli
- 1 package (10 oz.) dry capellini or coil vermicelli
- 6 tablespoons butter or margarine
- 2 cups whipping cream
- ¼ teaspoon ground nutmeg
  About 2 cups (about 10 oz.) freshly grated Parmesan cheese

Cut off and discard tough broccoli ends. Peel stems. Set aside a few whole flowerets for garnish; finely chop remaining broccoli. In a 5- to 6-quart pan, bring 3 quarts water to a boil over high heat. Add pasta; cook, uncovered, until tender to bite, about 3 minutes. Drain pasta, rinse with cold water, and drain again.

While water is heating, melt butter in a 12- to 14-inch frying pan over medium-high heat; add broccoli (including reserved flowerets) and ⅓ cup water. Cover and cook until broccoli is tender when pierced, about 5 minutes; set flowerets aside. Add cream and nutmeg to pan; bring to a boil, then add cooked, drained pasta. Cook, stirring, until mixture is hot and cream clings to pasta. Remove from heat. Sprinkle with 1¼ cups of the cheese; mix with 2 forks.

Put pasta onto a hot platter and top with broccoli flowerets and 3 to 4 tablespoons of the remaining cheese. Serve at once; offer extra cheese to top individual servings.

Bacon & Egg Carbonara

PREPARATION TIME: 10 to 15 minutes

COOKING TIME: 10 to 15 minutes

PER SERVING: (WITHOUT CHEESE): 680 calories, 18 grams protein, 48 grams carbohydrate, 46 grams total fat, 343 milligrams cholesterol, 372 milligrams sodium

Guests finish the preparation in this refreshing variation on classic spaghetti carbonara. For each serving, you spoon hot cooked pasta mixed with bacon and chives into warmed sour cream, then top with an egg yolk. Diners mix the ingredients together as they eat.

Makes 4 servings

- ½ pound sliced bacon, cut into 1-inch pieces
- 2 cups sour cream
- 8 ounces very thin dry pasta strands such as capellini or coil vermicelli
- ¼ cup chopped chives or green onions (including tops)
- 4 large egg yolks
- 1 cup (about 5 oz.) freshly grated Parmesan cheese

In a 10- to 12-inch frying pan, cook bacon over medium heat, stirring occasionally, until crisp and browned. Pour off and discard all but about 3 tablespoons of the drippings; keep pan with bacon warm.

While bacon is cooking, bring 7 to 8 cups water to a boil in a 4- to 5-quart pan over high heat. When water comes to a boil, spoon ½ cup of the sour cream into each of 4 wide 1½- to 2-cup soup bowls; set bowls in a 150° oven to warm while you finish the carbonara.

Add pasta to boiling water; cook, uncovered, until tender to bite, about 3 minutes. Drain, then immediately add to bacon along with chives; mix.

Put equal portions of pasta mixture atop sour cream in each warm bowl. Make a nest in center of each serving and slip in an egg yolk. Let diners mix pasta with egg and sour cream; offer cheese to sprinkle on top.

Pasta Shells with Spiced Lamb Ribs

PREPARATION TIME: About 10 minutes

COOKING TIME: About 2 hours

PER SERVING: 719 calories, 27 grams protein, 56 grams carbohydrate, 43 grams total fat, 90 milligrams cholesterol, 365 milligrams sodium

Pasta means more than spaghetti and lasagne—there's a wealth of whimsical shapes to discover and enjoy. Here, pasta "seashells" make a bed for lamb ribs simmered in cinnamon-scented tomato sauce.

Makes 3 or 4 servings

- 2 pounds lamb spareribs
- 2 tablespoons olive oil or salad oil
- 1 large onion, finely chopped
- 2 cloves garlic, minced or pressed
- 1 can (about 1 lb.) tomatoes
- ¼ cup *each* canned tomato paste and chopped parsley
- ¾ teaspoon ground cinnamon
- ½ teaspoon crushed dried hot red chiles
- 8 ounces medium-size dry pasta shells (about 3 cups)
  Freshly grated Parmesan cheese

At your meat market, have lamb ribs cut across the bones into 2- to 3-inch lengths, then cut between ribs to make small pieces.

Heat oil in a 5- to 6-quart pan over medium heat; add lamb, about half at a time, and cook until browned on all sides. Remove from pan and set aside.

Pour off and discard all but 1 tablespoon of the drippings. Add onion and garlic; cook, stirring occasionally, until onion is soft, about 5 minutes. Add tomatoes (break up with a spoon) and their liquid, tomato paste, parsley, cinnamon, chiles, and browned lamb. Stir in ¼ cup water. Reduce heat, cover, and simmer until lamb is very tender when pierced, about 1½ hours. Skim and discard fat.

About 20 minutes before lamb is done, bring 3 to 4 quarts water to a boil in a 5- to 6-quart pan over high heat. Add pasta shells. Cook, uncovered, just until tender to bite, about 10 minutes; when boil resumes, reduce heat to keep water boiling gently. Drain pasta well and place in a serving bowl. Spoon lamb and sauce over pasta. Offer cheese to sprinkle on individual servings.

Green Lasagne Donatello

PREPARATION TIME: About 1 hour to shape (by hand) and cook pasta (plus an additional 30 minutes to let dough rest); about 10 minutes to make cream sauce; about 40 minutes to make veal sauce (while shaping noodles)

BAKING TIME: About 1 hour, plus 25 to 30 minutes for lasagne to rest after baking

PER SERVING: 605 calories, 27 grams protein, 34 grams carbohydrate, 40 grams total fat, 178 milligrams cholesterol, 645 milligrams sodium

This is the traditional lasagne Bolognese, as featured at Donatello's in San Francisco. It's a subtle composition of wide sheets of homemade spinach pasta layered with a rich nutmeg-flavored cream sauce, a thick veal sauce, and two kinds of cheese.

Once baked, the lasagne needs to rest for about half an hour before serving, so portions will hold together when cut and removed from the pan (lasagne stays plenty hot).

Makes 10 servings

- 1 recipe Spinach Pasta dough (page 203)
- 1 tablespoon salad oil
  Cream Sauce (recipe follows)
  Veal Sauce (recipe follows)
- 1 cup (about 5 oz.) freshly grated Parmesan cheese
- 8 ounces mozzarella cheese, thinly sliced

Mix and knead Spinach Pasta dough as directed. Divide dough into 8 equal portions; cover with plastic wrap and let rest for 10 minutes. With a pasta machine (or by hand, on a lightly floured board), roll out each portion of dough into a ¹⁄₁₆-inch-thick (or slightly thinner) sheet.

Cut pasta sheets to make them about 2 inches longer than a shallow 3-quart casserole or 9- by 13-inch baking dish. If made ahead, lay pasta sheets between pieces of wax paper, fold loosely, and seal in a plastic bag; refrigerate until next day, or freeze for longer storage. Let frozen pasta thaw at room temperature, unwrapping it as it thaws.

To cook pasta, bring oil and 4 to 6 quarts water to a boil in a 6- to 8-quart pan. Have ready a large bowl full of ice cubes and water. Drop 1 sheet of pasta at a time into boiling water. (If pasta is on paper, peel off.) Cook 1 or 2 sheets until just tender to bite, 2 to 3 minutes.

Using slotted spoons, transfer pasta to ice water. Repeat until all pasta sheets are cooked; pasta can stand in ice water for up to 30 minutes.

To assemble lasagne, drain 1 pasta sheet at a time; pat dry with a muslin towel. Arrange pasta sheets in a single layer to cover bottom (overlapping sheets slightly in the center) and about 1 inch up sides of buttered shallow 3-quart casserole or 9- by 13-inch baking dish. Spread with 1 cup *each* Cream Sauce and Veal Sauce. Sprinkle with ⅓ cup of the Parmesan cheese. Top with a layer of pasta, more Cream Sauce and Veal Sauce, and half the mozzarella.

Add another layer of pasta, sauces, and Parmesan. Repeat, using remaining ingredients, ending with Cream Sauce and Parmesan. Using a spatula or knife, tuck edges of noodles down along sides of pan. (At this point, you may cover and refrigerate for up to 1 day.)

Bake, uncovered, in a 400° oven until lightly browned and hot through, about 50 minutes (1 hour and 5 minutes if refrigerated). Let stand for 25 to 30 minutes before cutting; lift out portions with a wide spatula.

CREAM SAUCE. In a 2- to 2½-quart pan over medium heat, melt ½ cup (¼ lb.) **butter** or margarine. Blend in ½ cup **all-purpose flour** and stir until mixture is light golden. Remove from heat and mix in 2 cups **Homemade Chicken Broth** (page 58) or 1 can (14½ oz.) regular strength chicken broth; then stir in 2 cups **half-and-half** or light cream. Return to high heat and bring to a boil, stirring. Season to taste with **ground nutmeg.** Let cool. If made ahead, cover and refrigerate for up to 2 days.

VEAL SAUCE. In a 10- to 12-inch frying pan, heat 2 tablespoons **olive oil** or salad oil and 2 tablespoons **butter** or margarine until butter is melted. Add ½ cup *each* finely chopped **onion, celery,** and **carrot.** Cook, stirring, until onion is lightly browned. Crumble in 1 pound **ground veal** and cook, stirring, until meat loses its pink color. Add 1 cup **dry white wine** and boil over medium-high heat, stirring, until wine has evaporated. Reduce heat and add 1 can (about 14 oz.) **pear-shaped tomatoes** (break up with a spoon) and their liquid, 2 tablespoons **canned tomato paste,** and ½ cup **whipping cream.** Simmer, uncovered, stirring often, until sauce is reduced to 4 cups, about 15 minutes. Let cool. If made ahead, cover and refrigerate for up to 2 days (freeze for longer storage).

Lasagne al Forno

PREPARATION TIME: About 25 minutes for lasagne; about 1 hour for meat sauce
BAKING TIME: About 20 minutes
PER SERVING (RECIPE PREPARED WITH 1 CUP PARMESAN CHEESE): 945 calories, 49 grams protein, 48 grams carbohydrate, 61 grams total fat, 195 milligrams cholesterol 835 milligrams sodium

Many years ago, a touring Sunset *editor came upon this unusual version of lasagne in Bologna, a city noted for its lavish use of cream and cheese. The lasagne isn't layered, making assembly easy.*

Makes about 8 servings

> ¼ cup (⅛ lb.) butter or margarine
>
> 1 large onion, finely chopped
>
> ¼ cup all-purpose flour
>
> 2 cups Homemade Chicken Broth (page 58) or 1 can (14½ oz.) regular-strength chicken broth
>
> 1½ cups milk
>
> ⅛ teaspoon ground nutmeg
>
> 4 cups (1 lb.) shredded fontina or tybo cheese
>
> 10 ounces dry lasagne noodles
>
> Meat Sauce (recipe follows)
>
> About 2 cups (about 10 oz.) freshly grated Parmesan cheese

Melt butter in a 5- to 6-quart pan over medium-high heat. Add onion; cook, stirring often, until soft but not browned. Blend in flour, remove from heat, and gradually stir in broth and milk. Return to high heat and cook, stirring, until boiling. Stir in nutmeg and 2 cups of the fontina cheese; remove from heat. If made ahead, cover and refrigerate until next day; reheat before using.

Bring about 4 quarts water to a boil in a 6- to 8-quart pan over high heat. Add lasagne noodles and cook, uncovered, until tender to bite, about 10 minutes. Drain well.

Mix cheese sauce with hot lasagne noodles and spread in a shallow 3-quart baking dish. With a fork, lightly mix in 1½ cups of the Meat Sauce. Cover with remaining 2 cups fontina and 1 cup of the Parmesan. (At this point, you may cover and refrigerate until next day.)

Bake, uncovered, in a 375° oven until heated through, about 20 minutes (30 minutes if refrigerated). Spoon portions of lasagne onto individual plates and top generously with remaining hot Meat Sauce. Offer additional Parmesan to sprinkle over individual servings.

MEAT SAUCE. Remove casings from about ¾ pound **mild Italian sausages** and break up meat in a 10- to 12-inch frying pan or 5- to 6-quart pan over high heat. Crumble in 1½ pounds **ground lean beef.** Then add 1 large onion, finely chopped; 2 large stalks **celery,** diced; and 2 medium-size **carrots,** finely chopped. Cook, stirring, until meat is lightly browned and juices have evaporated. Stir in 1 can (6 oz.) **tomato paste;** 2 cups **Homemade Chicken Broth** (page 58) or

1 can (14½ oz.) regular-strength chicken broth; 1½ teaspoons **dry basil;** and ½ teaspoon **dry rosemary.**

Boil rapidly, stirring as needed, until liquid has evaporated. Use hot. If made ahead; cover and refrigerate until next day (reheat before using).

Cannelloni

Pictured on facing page

PREPARATION TIME: About 1 hour to shape (by hand) and cook pasta; about 15 minutes to assemble filling and 35 minutes to cook; about 45 minutes to make cream sauce (as filling cooks); about 45 minutes to make tomato sauce (while shaping pasta)
BAKING TIME: About 15 minutes
PER SERVING: 825 calories, 48 grams protein, 35 grams carbohydrate, 54 grams total fat, 375 milligrams cholesterol, 338 milligrams sodium

A superlative cheese-drenched, meat-filled fresh noodle dish, this cannelloni came to the West from the kitchens of northern Italy. The recipe has been a Sunset *classic since its publication in 1963.*

To make our cannelloni, you'll need to prepare a meat filling, the fresh noodles in which it is enclosed, and a cream sauce using fresh tomatoes. All can be made at least a day in advance, leaving only final assembly to do at the last minute.

Makes 8 servings

> 1 recipe Rich Egg Pasta dough (page 203)
>
> 1 tablespoon olive oil
>
> ¾ pound boned, skinned chicken pieces (preferably thighs), cut into 2-inch chunks
>
> ½ pound boneless veal, cut into 2-inch chunks
>
> ½ cup (¼ lb.) butter or margarine
>
> 1 large onion, chopped
>
> 1 small clove garlic, minced or pressed
>
> 8 ounces (1 cup) ricotta cheese
>
> ½ cup freshly grated Parmesan cheese
>
> 2 large egg yolks
>
> ⅛ teaspoon ground nutmeg
>
> Salt
>
> 1½ tablespoons all-purpose flour
>
> 1 cup milk
>
> 1½ cups Homemade Chicken Broth (page 58) or canned regular-strength chicken broth
>
> 1 cup Fresh Tomato Sauce (recipe follows)
>
> About 1½ pounds teleme, fontina, or jack cheese

Mix and knead Rich Egg Pasta dough as directed. Divide dough into 4 equal portions; cover with plastic wrap and let rest for 10 minutes. On a lightly floured board, roll out each portion to make a thin sheet about 10 inches square. Cut each dough sheet into four 5-inch squares.

In a 10- to 12-inch frying pan, bring about ½ inch water to a boil over high heat. Add oil. Lay 3 or 4 noodle pieces in water. Cook until just tender to bite but not soft, about 2 minutes. With a slotted spatula, lift noodles from water; drain in a single layer on a

One of the finest of traditional Italian dishes, tender Cannelloni (recipe begins on facing page) bake under a coating of smooth, stretchy teleme cheese. Round out an exquisite West Coast menu with a crisp green salad, French bread, and a bottle of Italian wine.

muslin towel. Repeat to cook remaining noodles. If made ahead, stack drained noodles, separating with double thicknesses of wax paper; enclose in a plastic bag and refrigerate until next day.

To make filling, place chicken and veal in a 9- or 10-inch square baking pan. Set aside. Melt ¼ cup of the butter in a 10- to 12-inch frying pan over medium heat. Add onion and garlic; cook, stirring often, until soft but not browned. Spoon onion mixture over meats in baking pan; bake, uncovered, in a 350° oven until chicken is no longer pink in center (cut to test), about 30 minutes. Let cool slightly. Whirl meat and any juices in a food processor until finely ground (or put through a food chopper fitted with a fine blade). Mix in ricotta cheese, Parmesan cheese, egg yolks, and nutmeg; season to taste with salt. Cover and refrigerate until ready to use or until next day.

To make sauce, melt remaining ¼ cup butter in a 3- to 4-quart pan over medium heat. Blend in flour; stir until golden. Remove from heat and slowly blend in milk and broth. Return to heat; simmer gently, uncovered, stirring occasionally, for about 25 minutes. Add Fresh Tomato Sauce; continue to simmer gently for 15 more minutes. Use hot. If made ahead, let cool, then cover and refrigerate for up to 2 days; freeze for longer storage. Reheat before using.

To assemble cannelloni, divide filling into 16 equal portions. Mound 1 portion of the filling evenly along side of 1 noodle square; roll to enclose. Repeat to fill remaining noodle squares. Pour hot sauce into a 16- by 20-inch baking dish (or into four 8- by 10-inch baking dishes); sauce should be about ¼ inch deep. Arrange cannelloni in sauce, seam side down and at least 1 inch apart. Cut teleme cheese into 16 slices, each just slightly larger in length and width than the top of each cannelloni; place 1 cheese slice atop each cannelloni. Bake in a 425° oven until heated through, about 15 minutes.

FRESH TOMATO SAUCE. Peel, core, seed, and dice 5 medium-size ripe **tomatoes.** Set aside.

Melt 1½ tablespoons **butter** or margarine in a 3- to 4-quart pan; add 2 tablespoons chopped **shallot** (or white part only of green onion) and cook, stirring often, until soft. Add tomatoes, ½ cup **Homemade Chicken Broth** (page 58) or canned regular-strength chicken broth, and ¼ teaspoon **dry basil.** Simmer, uncovered, stirring occasionally, until reduced to 2 cups, about 40 minutes. Season to taste with **salt.**

Homemade All-purpose Pasta

When it comes to pasta, dry noodles just can't compare to fresh homemade for tenderness. You do need patience to make perfect pasta—but once you get the knack, the process moves very smoothly, particularly if you use a food processor to knead the dough and a pasta machine to roll and cut it.

For plain pasta, you need only three ingredients: eggs, flour, and water. Plenty of work space is important, even if you have a pasta machine, and an extra pair of hands can also be a big help.

Our basic recipe makes an all-purpose pasta to cut and shape as you like. For variation, you can change the flour to make whole wheat, triticale, or chewy semolina pasta; add extra egg yolks for an extra-rich and tender product; or add puréed spinach, carrot, tomato, bell peppers, or chiles for delightful variety in color and flavor.

Fresh pasta cooks very quickly, so be sure not to boil it for more than a few minutes. Drying the strands slightly before cooking helps prevent them from sticking together.

Serve your homemade pasta with butter and cheese, or dress with any of the sauces in this chapter.

All-purpose Pasta

About 2 cups all-purpose flour
Water
2 large eggs

To machine-mix and knead dough, put 2 cups flour, 3 tablespoons water, and eggs in a food processor with metal blade. Whirl until dough forms a ball, at least 30 seconds. If dough feels sticky when pinched, add 2 tablespoons more flour; process until dough forms a ball again, at least 30 more seconds. If dough is crumbly, add up to 3 tablespoons more water, a teaspoon at a time, processing after each addition. Divide dough into quarters; cover with plastic wrap and let rest for at least 10 minutes.

To hand-mix and knead dough, mound 2 cups flour in a bowl or on a board; make a well in center and add eggs. Beat eggs lightly with a fork; add 2 tablespoons water. Stir with a fork, drawing flour in from the sides and adding 1 to 4 more tablespoons water, until dough is well mixed (it will be stiff). Pat into a ball and knead on a

Tender ribbons of fresh Whole Wheat Pasta need only the lightest tossing with oil, garlic, parsley, and chiles to provide a glorious experience.

lightly floured board until dough feels smooth, about 10 minutes; add flour as required to prevent sticking, using as little as possible.

Divide dough into quarters; cover with plastic wrap and let rest for at least 10 minutes.

To roll and cut with a pasta machine, set rollers on widest opening. Flatten and lightly flour 1 portion of dough; feed dough through rollers, then fold dough into thirds lengthwise. Roll repeatedly until dough feels smooth and supple, 10 to 20 times. If dough

gets sticky, brush with flour; shake off excess.

Run dough through half-closed rollers. Reduce roller space to about 1/16 to 1/32 inch opening or narrowest setting (depending on how thick you want pasta to be) and run dough through again; if dough gets too long to handle easily, cut strip in half or into thirds. Lay rolled sheets in a single layer on wax paper on a flat surface. Let dry, uncovered, until dough has the feel and flexibility of soft leather, 5 to 10 minutes. (If dried too long, pasta will be too brittle to cut well.) Turn dough over 2 or 3 times as it dries.

Feed sheets, 1 at a time, through cutting blades of pasta machine.

If you plan to cook pasta within 2 hours, you can pile it in loose coils.

If you are making the pasta ahead, lay cut strands out straight in single layers on wax paper. Cover with wax paper; roll up, enclose in plastic bags, and seal airtight. Refrigerate for up to 2 days or freeze for up to 2 months.

To roll and cut by hand, roll 1 portion of dough at a time on a lightly floured board until as thin as possible, ⅟₁₆ to ⅟₃₂ inch thick. Use as little flour as possible. Let dough dry as directed for machine-rolled pasta. When dry, cut into ¼-inch (or narrower) strips with a sharp knife (use a ruler as a guide) or noodle cutter.

To store, follow directions for machine-rolled pasta.

To cook pasta, in a 6- to 8-quart pan, bring 4 to 6 quarts water to a boil over high heat. Drop in 1 recipe All-purpose Pasta (do not thaw, if frozen) and stir with a fork. Cook, uncovered, until just tender to bite, 1 to 3 minutes. Drain noodles well. Makes about 4 cups.

Fresh Pasta with Butter & Cheese

To 4 cups hot cooked **All-purpose Pasta** (or any of the following variations), add 4 to 6 tablespoons melted **butter** or margarine. Lift pasta with 2 forks to mix. Sprinkle with about 1 cup (about 5 oz.) freshly grated **Parmesan cheese.** Lift and mix again; serve at once, letting diners season pasta to taste with **salt** and **pepper.** Offer additional freshly grated **Parmesan cheese,** if desired.

Instead of Parmesan cheese, you may use 2 cups finely diced cream cheese or 2 cups (8 oz.) shredded smooth-melting cheese such as jack, fontina, or teleme. Sprinkle with a little minced **parsley,** if desired.

Whole Wheat or Triticale Pasta

Follow directions for **All-purpose Pasta,** but substitute 1¾ cups **whole wheat flour** (not stone-ground) or triticale flour and ¼ cup **toasted wheat germ** for the all-purpose flour. Roll dough slightly thicker than for All-purpose Pasta, no less than ⅟₁₆ inch or the third from the narrowest opening on the pasta machine. *Cooking time:* 4 to 6 minutes.

Semolina Pasta

Follow directions for **All-purpose Pasta,** but substitute 2 cups **semolina flour** for the all-purpose flour (or use any combination of semolina and all-purpose flour to make 2 cups; the more all-purpose flour used, the easier the dough will be to knead and roll). Also increase water to 3 to 8 tablespoons. After adding the first 3 tablespoons water, dough may seem sticky; process or mix well before adding more water. Let dough rest for 30 minutes before rolling and cutting. *Cooking time:* about 2 minutes.

Rich Egg Pasta

Follow directions for **All-purpose Pasta,** but substitute 3 **large egg yolks** (or 2 large egg yolks and 1 large egg) for the 2 eggs. *Cooking time:* 2 to 4 minutes.

Spinach Pasta

Cook ½ package (10-oz. size) **frozen chopped spinach** according to package directions. Let cool, then squeeze out as much liquid as possible. Mince the spinach finely; you should have ¼ cup. Then follow directions for **All-purpose Pasta,** but stir the minced spinach in with eggs and omit water. *Cooking time:* 2 to 3 minutes.

Carrot or Tomato Pasta

Follow directions for **All-purpose Pasta,** but stir in with the eggs either 3 tablespoons **canned puréed carrots** (baby food) or canned tomato paste. Omit water unless dough is crumbly— if it is crumbly, add only a few drops of water at a time until dough holds together. *Cooking time:* about 2 minutes.

Red Bell Pepper Pasta

Pictured on page 196

Place 2 pounds **red bell peppers** (about 4 large peppers) in a 9- or 10-inch square baking pan. Bake, uncovered, in a 500° oven, turning occasionally, until skins are blackened on all sides, 40 to 45 minutes. Cover pan and let peppers stand until cool. Pull off and discard pepper skins along with stems and seeds. In a blender or food processor, whirl peppers until smoothly puréed.

Follow directions for **All-purpose Pasta,** but omit 1 large egg and the water, using red bell pepper purée instead. Rolled dough takes longer to dry, about 50 minutes total. *Cooking time:* 1 to 2 minutes.

Ancho Chile Pasta

Follow directions for **Red Bell Pepper Pasta,** but use 2 pounds **fresh ancho (poblano) chiles** (about 8 large chiles) instead of bell peppers. *Cooking time:* 1 to 2 minutes.

Jalapeño Chile Pasta

Follow directions for **Red Bell Pepper Pasta,** but roast 6 or 7 **fresh jalapeño chiles** instead of bell peppers. (Or use 6 or 7 canned jalapeño chiles and omit roasting step.) Use 2 large eggs and whirl with chiles in a food processor or blender until smoothly puréed. *Cooking time:* 1 to 2 minutes.

Dried Chile Pasta

Place 2 ounces **dried California (Anaheim), New Mexico, or ancho (poblano) chiles** (about 6 chiles) in a single layer in a 9- by 13-inch baking pan. Bake, uncovered, in a 500° oven just until chiles smell toasted, about 2 minutes. Remove stems and seeds; discard. Rinse chiles and put in a bowl; add 8 cups **boiling water.** Let stand for 1 hour; drain.

In a blender or food processor, whirl 2 **large eggs** with the soaked chiles until smoothly puréed. Follow directions for **All-purpose Pasta,** using chile purée in place of water and the 2 eggs. Rolled dough takes longer to dry, about 50 minutes total. *Cooking time:* 1 to 2 minutes.

Won Ton Ravioli

PREPARATION TIME: About 30 minutes to shape ravioli; 10 to 15 minutes to assemble each filling; 10 to 15 minutes to assemble each sauce

COOKING TIME: About 5 minutes for ravioli; 10 to 15 minutes for each filling; 35 to 40 minutes for each sauce

PER SERVING WITH CHICKEN-PROSCIUTTO FILLING: 503 calories, 35 grams protein, 49 grams carbohydrate, 17 grams total fat, 222 milligrams cholesterol, 725 milligrams sodium

PER SERVING WITH SAUSAGE-SPINACH FILLING: 550 calories, 33 grams protein, 51 grams carbohydrate, 23 grams total fat, 206 milligrams cholesterol, 775 milligrams sodium

Some say that Marco Polo brought pasta to Europe when he returned from his travels through the Orient. Whether or not the story is true, Oriental noodle products and Italian fillings and sauces can make great partners—as here, where we use won ton skins as wrappers for ravioli fillings. The result? Tender ravioli that are every bit as impressive and delicious as those made the traditional way, but significantly faster to put together.

Makes about 6 servings

6 to 7 dozen thin won ton skins (about 1 lb.)
Chicken-Prosciutto Filling or Sausage-Spinach Filling (recipes follow)
1 large egg white
Tomato Cream & Mint Sauce or Mushroom-Tomato Sauce (recipes follow)
Freshly grated Parmesan cheese

Place 1 won ton skin (cover remaining skins with plastic wrap) on a board and evenly spread a rounded tablespoon of chicken or sausage filling to within about ⅜ inch of edges. Brush edges with egg white. Cover with 1 more skin and press edges well to seal. If desired, run a ripple-edged pastry wheel just inside edges to make a decorative trim. Discard trimmings. Repeat to fill remaining skins.

Place ravioli in a single layer on flour-dusted baking sheets; cover with plastic wrap. (At this point, you may refrigerate ravioli for up to 4 hours. Or freeze until firm, then package airtight in plastic bags or rigid containers.)

To cook, bring 11 to 12 cups water to a boil in each of two 5- to 6-quart pans over high heat. Add about half the fresh or frozen ravioli to each pan. Cook, uncovered, over medium heat until just tender to bite—4 to 5 minutes, 6 minutes if frozen (when boil resumes, adjust heat to keep water at a gentle simmer). With a large slotted spoon or skimmer, gently lift out ravioli (they're fragile) and drain. Layer ravioli with sauce on individual plates or a platter. Offer cheese to sprinkle on ravioli.

CHICKEN-PROSCIUTTO FILLING. Coarsely chop 6 ounces thinly sliced **prosciutto** or cooked ham. Remove bones and skin from 1 pound **chicken breast.** Cut meat into about ½-inch pieces. In a 10- to 12-inch frying pan over medium heat, combine 1 large **onion,** chopped, and 2 tablespoons **butter** or margarine; stir until onion is very soft. Add chicken; stir until no longer pink in center (cut to test), about 3 minutes. Add prosciutto. Whirl in a food processor until coarsely ground; or mince with a knife. Mix with 2 **large egg yolks,** ⅔ cup freshly grated **Parmesan cheese,** 8 ounces (1 cup) **ricotta cheese,** ⅛ to ¼ teaspoon **ground nut-**meg, and **salt** and **white pepper** to taste. If made ahead, cover and refrigerate until next day.

SAUSAGE-SPINACH FILLING. Thaw 1 package (10 oz.) **frozen chopped spinach;** squeeze out liquid. Set spinach aside. Remove casings from 6 ounces **mild Italian sausages.** Break up meat in an 8- to 10-inch frying pan. Stir over medium-low heat until browned and crumbly. Drain off fat. Mix sausage, drained spinach, 1 pound (2 cups) **ricotta cheese, 2 large egg yolks,** 1 cup (about 5 oz.) freshly grated **Parmesan cheese,** ⅛ teaspoon **pepper,** and ¾ teaspoon *each* crushed **fennel seeds** and **dry oregano leaves.** If made ahead, cover and refrigerate until next day.

TOMATO CREAM & MINT SAUCE. In a 10- to 12-inch frying pan over medium heat, combine 2 medium-size **onions** (finely chopped), 2 cloves **garlic** (pressed or minced), and 3 tablespoons **salad oil.** Stir often until onions are soft. Add 1 large can (28 oz.) and 1 can (about 14 oz.) **pear-shaped tomatoes** (break up with a spoon) and their liquid, 1½ tablespoons **dry mint,** 1½ teaspoons **dry basil,** and 1 cup **Homemade Chicken Broth** (page 58) or canned regular-strength chicken broth. Simmer, uncovered, until sauce is slightly thickened and reduced to 6 cups, about 20 minutes. Stir in ½ cup **whipping cream.** Add **salt** and **pepper** to taste. If made ahead, cover and refrigerate for up to 24 hours. Makes about 6 cups.
PER ¼ CUP: 45 calories, .72 gram protein, 3 grams carbohydrate, 3 grams total fat, 6 milligrams cholesterol, 83 milligrams sodium.

MUSHROOM-TOMATO SAUCE. In a 10- to 12-inch frying pan over medium heat, combine ½ cup chopped **shallots** or onion, 1 pound **button mushrooms** (sliced), and 3 tablespoons **butter** or margarine. Stir often until onions are lightly browned. Stir in 2 tablespoons **canned tomato paste** and 1 teaspoon **dry basil.** Add 2 cups **dry vermouth,** then stir in 2 cups **Homemade Chicken Broth** (page 58) or 1 can (14½ oz.) regular-strength chicken broth. Stir over high heat until reduced to 3 cups.

Reduce heat to low. Add 1 cup (½ lb.) **butter** or margarine and stir constantly to blend in butter as it melts. Use at once. Makes about 4 cups.
PER ¼ CUP: 150 calories, 1 gram protein, 6 grams carbohydrate, 14 grams total fat, 37 milligrams cholesterol, 159 milligrams sodium.

Potsticker Tortellini

Pictured on facing page

PREPARATION TIME: 10 to 15 minutes to assemble each filling; about 45 minutes to shape tortellini

COOKING TIME: 10 to 15 minutes for each filling; about 4 minutes for tortellini; about 5 minutes for cream sauce

PER SERVING WITH CHICKEN-PROSCIUTTO FILLING: 1048 calories, 53 grams protein, 54 grams carbohydrate, 69 grams total fat, 393 milligrams cholesterol, 1464 milligrams sodium

PER SERVING WITH SAUSAGE-SPINACH FILLING: 1095 calories, 51 grams protein, 56 grams carbohydrate, 75 grams total fat, 377 milligrams cholesterol, 1514 milligrams sodium

Tortellini made with potsticker skins? When you consider the proximity of San Francisco's Oriental and

Italian communities, such cross-cultural culinary marriages seem only natural. Labeled as gyoza (their Japanese name), potsticker skins are sold alongside the won ton skins in Asian markets and well-stocked supermarkets.

Makes about 6 servings

> **Chicken-Prosciutto Filling or Sausage-Spinach Filling (page 204)**
> **6 to 7 dozen thin potsticker (gyoza) or won ton skins (about 1 lb.)**
> **1 large egg white**
> **Cream Sauce (recipe follows)**
> **About 1½ cups (about 7½ oz.) freshly grated Parmesan cheese**
> **2 tablespoons butter or margarine**
> **Freshly grated nutmeg**

Prepare chicken or sausage filling as directed on page 204, but omit 1 egg yolk, 1 cup ricotta cheese, and ½ cup Parmesan cheese from each filling.

Place about 1 teaspoon of filling in center of 1 potsticker skin. (If using won ton skins, cut several skins at a time with a 3- to 3¼-inch-round cooky cutter; discard trimmings.) Cover remaining skins with plastic wrap. Moisten edges of circle with egg white, fold circle in half, and press together to seal. Draw ends together to overlap; moisten, then press to seal. Repeat to fill remaining skins. As skins are filled, arrange in a single layer on flour-dusted baking sheets; cover with plastic wrap. (At this point, you may refrigerate for up to 4 hours. Or freeze until firm, then package airtight in plastic bags or rigid containers.)

In each of two 5- to 6-quart pans, bring 11 to 12 cups water to a boil over high heat. Drop about half the fresh or frozen tortellini into each pan. Cook, uncovered, over medium heat until just tender to bite—4 to 5 minutes, 6 minutes if frozen (when boil resumes, adjust heat to keep water at a gentle simmer). With a slotted spoon or skimmer, gently lift out tortellini (they're fragile) and drain. Add to pan of Cream Sauce and gently turn in sauce to coat. Sprinkle with 1 cup of the cheese; add butter and mix gently until butter is melted. Offer remaining cheese and nutmeg to sprinkle on tortellini.

CREAM SAUCE. In a 12- to 14-inch frying pan over high heat, boil 3 cups **whipping cream** and ⅛ teaspoon **freshly grated or ground nutmeg** until big, shiny bubbles form all over and sauce is reduced to 2 to 2¼ cups; stir occasionally. Use hot.

Potsticker Tortellini (recipe begins on the facing page) are quickly made with purchased potsticker or won ton skins. Stuff them with your choice of chicken or sausage filling; serve with a rich, simple cream sauce and freshly grated Parmesan.

Thai Crunchy Noodles

PREPARATION TIME: About 30 minutes to soak tamarind; about 30 minutes to prepare remaining ingredients
COOKING TIME: About 30 minutes (includes time to heat oil)
PER SERVING: 554 calories, 44 grams protein, 60 grams carbohydrate, 15 grams total fat, 160 milligrams cholesterol, 1026 milligrams sodium

Rice noodles are one of many Southeast Asian foods that have gained great popularity among Westerners. In this exotic Thai specialty—an immediate favorite with a Sunset taste panel—the brittle noodles are deep-fried, then dressed with a sweet-sour sauce of pork, chicken, and shrimp.

If you've never fried rice noodles, you'll find it's a dramatic procedure. When the noodles hit hot oil, they puff almost instantly, swelling to several times their original size and turning crackling crisp. Cook the noodles a day ahead, if you like; they reheat well.

Makes 4 servings

  Salad oil
  ¼ **pound thin rice noodles (rice sticks)**
  ⅓ **cup tamarind liquid (directions follow) or lemon juice**
  ½ **cup sugar**
  ¼ **cup bean sauce (also called yellow bean sauce)**
  2 **tablespoons canned tomato paste**
  2 **tablespoons fish sauce** (*nam pla*) **or soy sauce**
  1 **small onion, finely chopped**
  4 **cloves garlic, minced or pressed**
  ½ **pound lean boneless pork (butt or leg), trimmed of fat and cut into ⅛- by ½- by 2-inch strips**
  1 **whole chicken breast (about 1 lb.), skinned, boned, and cut into ⅛- by ½- by 2-inch strips**
  ½ **pound medium-size shrimp (about 45 per lb.), shelled and deveined**
  Garnishes (suggestions follow)

In a wok or 12-inch frying pan, heat 1 inch of oil to 375°F on a deep-frying thermometer. Drop in about ⅙ of the noodles. As they puff and expand, push them down into oil; then turn entire mass over when crackling stops. Cook until all are puffy and no longer crackling, 10 to 15 seconds; remove and drain briefly on paper towels. Skim and discard any bits of noodles from oil before cooking next batch. Keep warm in a 200° oven. If made ahead, let cool, then package airtight and hold at room temperature for up to 1 day. To reheat, scatter noodles in a 10- by 15-inch rimmed baking pan; place in a 200° oven until hot, about 10 minutes.

In a bowl, stir together tamarind liquid, sugar, bean sauce, tomato paste, and fish sauce; set aside.

Heat 2 tablespoons oil in wok or frying pan over high heat. Add onion and garlic; stir for 1 minute. Add pork and stir for 3 more minutes. Add chicken and shrimp and stir until shrimp turn pink, about 3 minutes. Stir in sauce mixture; cook, stirring, until sauce boils, thickens, and turns glossy, 3 to 5 minutes. Remove from heat and let cool for 3 minutes. Using 2 forks, fold in noodles, about ¼ at a time, until all are lightly coated with sauce. Mound noodles on a platter; surround with garnishes. Serve immediately.

TAMARIND LIQUID. In a bowl, combine ⅓ cup **hot water** and 2½ tablespoons **packaged tamarind pulp** or a 4- to 5-inch-long whole tamarind pod (shell and coarse strings removed). Let stand for 30 minutes. Knead pulp from seeds; discard seeds.

GARNISHES. Arrange around finished dish (or place on a separate serving plate): ⅓ pound **bean sprouts,** coarsely chopped; 3 **green onions** (including tops), cut into thin strips; and 1 **lime,** cut into wedges.

Spätzle

PREPARATION TIME: About 5 minutes (for plain spätzle)
COOKING TIME: About 10 minutes
PER SERVING: 247 calories, 8 grams protein, 34 grams carbohydrate, 8 grams total fat, 177 milligrams cholesterol, 197 milligrams sodium

These tiny, eggy dumplings—traditional fare in Germany and other European countries—vary according to the custom of the cook. Our version involves rubbing a soft batter through a special perforated utensil called a spätzle machine, mill, or maker; a large slotted spoon works well, too. Heat or brown the cooked spätzle in butter and serve as you would rice or potatoes, or use in the simple main dishes we suggest.

Makes about 3½ cups, 4 or 5 servings

  3 **large eggs**
  ¼ **teaspoon salt**
  Water
  1¾ **cups all-purpose flour**
  2 **tablespoons butter or margarine**

In a bowl, beat eggs, salt, ½ cup water, and flour until very well blended.

Bring 3 to 3½ quarts water to a boil in a 5- to 6-quart pan over high heat. Hold a spätzle maker or a large slotted spoon several inches above boiling water. Partially fill maker or spoon with batter; force batter through holes with a wooden spoon or rubber scraper, breaking up strands as they fall into water.

As you are making spätzle, melt butter in a 10- to 12-inch frying pan over low heat. When all spätzle have returned to surface of water (stir several times), cook for 10 more seconds; then skim from water, drain, and add to butter in frying pan to keep warm. Repeat to cook remaining batter.

If made ahead, remove from heat, cover, and let stand for up to 4 hours; or cover and refrigerate for up to 4 days. To reheat, gently stir over medium-low heat until hot.

SPÄTZLE WITH LOOSE BEEF

Melt 2 tablespoons **butter** or margarine in a 10- to 12-inch frying pan over medium heat. Add 2 medium-size **onions,** chopped; cook, stirring, until lightly browned. Remove onions from pan. Add 1 pound **ground lean beef;** cook over high heat, stirring, until meat is well browned and crumbly. Return onions to pan along with 1½ cups **spätzle;** stir to heat through. Season to taste with **salt.** Offer **sour cream** to spoon over each serving; accompany with **marinated cucumbers** and sliced **tomatoes,** if desired. Makes 3 or 4 servings.

SPÄTZLE IN BROWNED BUTTER

Prepare **spätzle** as directed, but melt butter over medium-high heat and cook until lightly browned; add spätzle and brown lightly, turning frequently. If desired, sprinkle with freshly grated **Parmesan cheese,** minced parsley, or chopped chives.

SPÄTZLE SUPPER EGGS

Melt 2 tablespoons **butter** or margarine in a 10- to 12-inch frying pan over medium heat. Add 1 cup **spätzle** and cook, stirring, until just beginning to brown. Beat together 4 **large eggs** and 2 tablespoons **water;** pour over spätzle. Reduce heat to low. Cook, lifting cooked portion from pan bottom to allow uncooked eggs to flow underneath, until eggs are set to your liking. Season to taste with **salt.** Serve with **sour cream;** accompany with **sweet pickles** and buttered **dark bread,** if desired. Makes 2 servings.

Pan-browned Polenta

W E S T E R N   C L A S S I C

PREPARATION TIME: About 10 minutes
COOKING TIME: 15 to 20 minutes to boil polenta (at least 30 minutes to cool); about 10 minutes to brown
PER SERVING: 189 calories, 3 grams protein, 26 grams carbohydrate, 8 grams total fat, 0 milligram cholesterol, 4 milligrams sodium

One of many dishes dating back to antiquity, polenta was the staple food of the Roman army. The original version was made with wheat and millet, but today the dish is based on coarsely ground cornmeal. These thick slices of vegetable-flecked polenta, browned quickly in a little oil, make a good accompaniment for steak or skewered beef.

Makes 8 servings

    1 **small onion, finely chopped**

    3 **tablespoons** *each* **minced green bell pepper and drained, minced oil-packed dried tomatoes**

    3 **cloves garlic, minced or pressed**

    About ¼ cup oil from dried tomatoes; or ¼ cup olive oil

    4½ **cups Homemade Chicken Broth (page 58) or canned regular-strength chicken broth**

    1½ **cups polenta (Italian-style cornmeal) or yellow cornmeal**

In a 4- to 5-quart pan over medium heat, combine onion, bell pepper, tomatoes, garlic, and 2 tablespoons of the oil. Cook, stirring occasionally, until onion is soft, about 5 minutes. Add 3 cups of the broth; bring to a boil, uncovered, over high heat.

Meanwhile, mix polenta with remaining 1½ cups broth. Using a long-handled spoon, gradually stir

polenta mixture into boiling broth; it will thicken and spatter. Reduce heat to low and continue stirring for 5 more minutes. Remove from heat and at once spoon polenta into a 4- by 8-inch loaf pan. Let stand for 30 minutes to firm (or let cool, then cover and refrigerate for up to 3 days).

Run a knife around edges of pan and turn polenta out onto a board. Carefully cut crosswise into 8 slices; cut slices diagonally in half.

Heat 2 tablespoons oil in a 10- to 12-inch nonstick frying pan over medium heat. Add as many polenta slices as will fit without crowding. Cook, uncovered, turning as needed, until golden on each side, about 5 minutes; remove from pan and keep warm. Repeat to cook remaining polenta, adding more oil to pan as needed.

Golden Toasted Rice

W E S T E R N   C L A S S I C

PREPARATION TIME: About 45 minutes (including toasting rice)
COOKING TIME: About 20 minutes
PER SERVING: 157 calories, 4 grams protein, 27 grams carbohydrate, 3 grams total fat, 8 milligrams cholesterol, 277 milligrams sodium

In 1948, a Kitchen Cabinet contributor sent us a new way to fix an old, tried-and-true family staple—rice. You simply toast white rice in the oven until golden, then cook it in a savory broth. The result? The rice grains split, acquiring a fluffy, feathery texture—most appealing to editors, tasters, and readers alike.

Makes 6 servings

    1 **cup long-grain white rice**

    1 **to 2 tablespoons butter or margarine, melted**

    1 **can (10½ oz.) condensed consommé and ½ cup water**

    Soy sauce

    3 **or 4 green onions (including tops), finely chopped**

Pour rice into a 9- or 10-inch-wide baking pan; bake, uncovered, in a 350° oven until rice is golden, about 45 minutes. Stir occasionally.

Melt butter in a 2- to 3-quart pan over medium heat. Add rice; cook until lightly browned, stirring constantly. Add broth; bring to a boil over high heat. Reduce heat to very low; cover and cook until rice is tender to bite, about 15 minutes. Season to taste with soy; sprinkle with onions.

Saffron-crusted Rice

PREPARATION TIME: About 10 minutes
COOKING TIME: About 20 minutes to boil rice; about 1¼ hours to brown rice
PER SERVING: 204 calories, 3 grams protein, 30 grams carbohydrate, 8 grams total fat, 21 milligrams cholesterol, 80 milligrams sodium

Pulverized saffron threads add color and flavor to this Persian dish, a traditional accompaniment to beef or lamb stew. The crisp, golden rice crust is presented on one dish, the hot rice on another.

Makes 8 to 12 servings

> 2¼ **cups long-grain white rice**
> **Salt**
> 4 **teaspoons saffron threads**
> 2 **teaspoons sugar**
> ½ **cup (¼ lb.) butter or margarine**

In a 5- to 6-quart pan with a nonstick surface, bring 5 cups water to a boil. Add rice; cover and cook over medium-low heat until rice is tender to bite and liquid is absorbed, about 20 minutes. Season to taste with salt. Spoon rice out of pan and set aside. (At this point, you may let cool, then cover and let stand at room temperature until next day.)

With a mortar and pestle (or with the back of a spoon), pulverize 3 teaspoons of the saffron with 1 teaspoon of the sugar. Pour into pan used for rice and add ½ cup water and ¼ cup of the butter. Place over medium heat until butter is melted. Stir in 2 cups of the cooked rice, mixing well, then spread in an even layer over pan bottom. Mound remaining rice on top; dot with remaining ¼ cup butter.

Cover and cook over low heat until a crisp crust forms on bottom of rice, 1 to 1¼ hours (slip a spatula around edge of pan to see if crust is forming).

Spoon just the white rice from top of pan into a serving dish; keep warm. Pulverize remaining 1 teaspoon saffron with remaining 1 teaspoon sugar and mix with 2 tablespoons hot water. Mix in 1 or 2 large spoonfuls of the cooked white rice, then spoon this colored rice atop center of rice in serving dish.

With a wide spatula, gently ease rice crust free from pan bottom, keeping it intact if possible. Invert crust onto another serving dish; cut into triangles.

Rice Pilaf with Fruit & Nuts

PREPARATION TIME: About 10 minutes
COOKING TIME: About 30 minutes to boil rice; at least 1 hour to fluff rice; about 10 minutes to toast nuts and heat fruit
PER SERVING: 406 calories, 6 grams protein, 59 grams carbohydrate, 18 grams total fat, 28 milligrams cholesterol, 115 milligrams sodium

In cuisines from many regions of the world, fluffy white rice plays a subtle counterpoint to more exuberantly flavored ingredients—often including sweet, tangy fruits and crunchy nuts. A specialty of Fresno's well-fed Armenian-American community, this pilaf offers one mouthwatering

Called nasi kuning, *Indonesian Yellow Rice (recipe on facing page) makes a spicy and aromatic accompaniment for barbecued meats, such as the grilled pork shown here. Coconut and red bananas continue the tropical theme.*

example—at its best as an accompaniment to grilled lamb shish-kebabs.

Makes 12 servings

> **5 cups Homemade Chicken Broth (page 58) or canned regular-strength chicken broth**
> **½ cup (¼ lb.) butter or margarine**
> **½ teaspoon sugar**
> **2 cups long-grain white rice**
> **Salt**
> **3 tablespoons butter or margarine**
> **1 cup whole blanched almonds**
> **1 cup raisins or currants**
> **1 cup pitted dates, cut into quarters**
> **1 cup dried apricots, cut into quarters**

In a 5- to 6-quart pan, bring broth, the ½ cup butter, and sugar to a boil over high heat. Add rice; stir until mixture returns to a boil. Reduce heat, cover, and simmer for 15 minutes. Season to taste with salt. Pour into a 2½-quart casserole; cover and put into a 325° oven to fluff, at least 1 hour or up to 1½ hours.

Meanwhile, melt 1 tablespoon butter in a 10- to 12-inch frying pan over medium heat. Add almonds; cook, stirring, until golden brown. Lift from pan with a slotted spoon and drain on paper towels. Melt remaining 2 tablespoons butter in pan. Add raisins and stir until puffy, then add dates and turn in butter; finally, add apricots and stir to heat. If made ahead, set aside; stir over low heat to re-warm. Pour fruits over pilaf; sprinkle with almonds.

Indonesian Yellow Rice

Pictured on facing page

PREPARATION TIME: About 10 minutes; allow an additional hour if making coconut milk
COOKING TIME: About 40 minutes
PER SERVING: 306 calories, 5 grams protein, 50 grams carbohydrate, 9 grams total fat, 0 milligram cholesterol, 12 milligrams sodium

Once reserved for religious ceremonies, nasi kuning *is still served on special occasions in Indonesia and in the West's large Southeast Asian communities. This sweet, aromatic rice dish is good with roasts and barbecued meats. (Galangal is a root that tastes much like ginger, though it's hotter; you may find it sold in Asian markets and spice shops as* laos, *its Indonesian name.)*

Makes 8 to 10 servings

> **3 cups long-grain white rice**
> **1½ cups coconut milk (directions follow); or use canned or thawed frozen coconut milk**
> **3 cups water**
> **1 tablespoon ground turmeric**
> **1 stalk fresh or dry lemon grass (about 12 inches long), cut into 4-inch lengths; or yellow part of peel only pared from 1 lemon**
> **1 slice dry galangal, ¼ teaspoon ground laos, or 1 thin, quarter-size slice fresh ginger**
> **1 bay leaf**
> **Salt**
> **Tomato and cucumber slices**

In a 2- to 3-quart pan, combine rice, coconut milk, water, turmeric, lemon grass, galangal, and bay leaf. Bring to a boil over medium heat. Reduce heat to medium-low; cook, uncovered, until liquid is absorbed, about 10 minutes. Reduce heat to low, cover, and cook until rice is tender to bite, 15 to 20 minutes. Add salt to taste. Remove lemon grass, galangal, and bay leaf. Fluff rice with a fork, then shape into a cone on a serving plate. Garnish with tomato and cucumber.

COCONUT MILK. In a blender or food processor, combine 2 cups **dried unsweetened shredded coconut** and 2 cups **very hot water.** Whirl until mixture is a thick, pulpy mass. Line a colander with moistened cheesecloth and set in a bowl. Pour coconut mixture into colander; let drain briefly, then gather cheesecloth to form a bag and squeeze firmly to extract all remaining liquid.

Discard coconut. Use milk; or cover and refrigerate for up to 3 days. Stored milk will separate into layers of thick cream and thin milk; stir to reblend before using. Makes 1½ to 2 cups coconut milk.

A quick alternative. Mix ¾ teaspoon **imitation coconut extract** and ¾ teaspoon **sugar** with 1½ cups **whipping cream.** (This substitute does not separate into thick cream and thin milk.) Makes 1½ cups.

Thyme Rice Salad

PREPARATION TIME: About 15 minutes (starting with cooked rice)
CHILLING TIME: At least 30 minutes to crisp lettuce
PER SERVING: 353 calories, 8 grams protein, 33 grams carbohydrate, 22 grams total fat, 17 milligrams cholesterol, 178 milligrams sodium

Raisins from the Central Valley, olives from Oroville and Visalia, apples from Watsonville, and rice from the Sacramento Valley make this a very California salad.

Makes 5 or 6 servings

> **½ cup golden raisins**
> **3 cups cold cooked rice**
> **6 tablespoons olive oil**
> **2 tablespoons vinegar**
> **2 teaspoons dry thyme leaves**
> **1 medium-size red apple, cored and finely slivered**
> **1 tablespoon lemon juice**
> **¾ cup chopped pitted black ripe olives**
> **Salt**
> **1 cup (about 4 oz.) diced Swiss, Gruyère, or Samsoe cheese**
> **Butter lettuce leaves, washed and crisped**

In a bowl, mix raisins, rice, oil, vinegar, and thyme; blend well. Mix apple with lemon juice; stir lightly into salad along with olives. Season to taste with salt. If made ahead, cover and refrigerate for up to 4 hours.

To serve, mix cheese with rice, then spoon into a salad bowl lined with lettuce leaves.

Wild Rice Salad

PREPARATION TIME: About 10 minutes

COOKING TIME: About 55 minutes (plus at least 30 minutes to cool)

PER SERVING: 208 calories, 5 grams protein, 26 grams carbohydrate, 10 grams total fat, 0 milligram cholesterol, 42 milligrams sodium

A relatively new California crop, wild rice is grown in significant amounts in the Sacramento Valley. The cultivated grain tends to be larger than truly "wild" wild rice, but it's no less flavorful. Dressed with a simple vinaigrette, it makes a fine salad.

Makes 8 servings

> 1½ **cups wild rice**
>
> 3 **cups Homemade Chicken Broth (page 58) or canned regular-strength chicken broth**
>
> ⅓ **cup salad oil**
>
> 2 **tablespoons raspberry or wine vinegar**
>
> 2 **tablespoons minced shallot or onion**
>
> 2 **teaspoons Dijon mustard**
>
> ¼ **teaspoon pepper**

Rinse rice with water and drain. In a 2- to 3-quart pan, bring rice and broth to a boil. Reduce heat, cover, and simmer, stirring occasionally, until rice is tender to bite and almost all liquid is absorbed, about 50 minutes. Let cool.

In a small bowl, mix oil, vinegar, shallot, mustard, and pepper. Stir into cooled rice. If made ahead, cover and let stand at room temperature for up to 4 hours or refrigerate for up to 2 days. Serve at room temperature.

Wild Rice Waffles

PREPARATION TIME: 10 to 15 minutes

COOKING TIME: 50 minutes to cook rice; about 20 minutes to bake waffles

PER SERVING: 286 calories, 7 grams protein, 32 grams carbohydrate, 15 grams total fat, 106 milligrams cholesterol, 401 milligrams sodium

These crisp waffles offer a delicious way to stretch costly wild rice. You cook the rice in advance, then sprinkle it over the whole wheat and cornmeal batter right in the waffle iron. Serve the waffles as an elegant accompaniment to roast meats and their juices; or go a more familiar route and enjoy them at breakfast, with butter and syrup.

Makes 6 to 8 servings

> 2 **large eggs, separated**
>
> 1½ **cups milk**
>
> ½ **cup (¼ lb.) butter or margarine, melted**

> 1 **cup all-purpose flour**
>
> ⅓ **cup coarse-ground buckwheat flour; or ¼ cup all-purpose flour and 2 tablespoons whole wheat flour**
>
> ⅓ **cup whole wheat flour**
>
> ½ **cup polenta (Italian-style cornmeal) or regular cornmeal**
>
> 2 **teaspoons** *each* **sugar and baking powder**
>
> ½ **teaspoon salt**
>
> **Melted butter or margarine; or salad oil**
>
> **Cooked wild rice (directions follow)**

Beat egg yolks with milk and the ½ cup melted butter until blended.

Stir together all-purpose flour, buckwheat flour, whole wheat flour, cornmeal, sugar, baking powder, and salt. Add egg mixture and stir just to blend. Beat egg whites until they hold soft peaks; fold gently into batter.

Heat a waffle iron to medium or medium-hot. Brush grids lightly with melted butter. Ladle batter onto center of grid (for a 9-inch square iron, use 1 cup batter) and quickly spread out slightly, then sprinkle with wild rice (2 tablespoons rice for a 9-inch waffle). Close iron and bake until waffle is browned on the outside and dry in the middle (make a small crack in waffle to test), 4 to 5 minutes. Repeat to make each waffle.

Serve waffles as they are baked; or let cool on racks, then wrap airtight and refrigerate for up to 1 day. Reheat in a single layer on oven rack in a 350° oven for 3 to 4 minutes, or reheat individual waffles in a toaster.

COOKED WILD RICE. Rinse 3 tablespoons **wild rice** with water; drain. In a 3- to 4-cup pan, combine rice and 1 cup **water;** bring to a boil over high heat. Reduce heat, cover, and simmer, stirring occasionally, until rice is tender to bite, about 50 minutes. Drain; use hot or cold. If made ahead, cover and refrigerate for up to 3 days.

Barley & Pine Nut Casserole

PREPARATION TIME: About 15 minutes

BAKING TIME: About 1¼ hours

PER SERVING: 306 calories, 6 grams protein, 34 grams carbohydrate, 18 grams total fat, 31 milligrams cholesterol, 124 milligrams sodium

Westerners have a long-standing interest in cooking with nutritious whole grains and nuts. In this simple casserole (presented in our June 1969 Kitchen Cabinet), pine nuts mingle with lightly toasted barley baked in broth.

Makes 4 to 6 servings

> 6 **tablespoons butter or margarine**
>
> ¼ **to ½ cup pine nuts or slivered almonds**
>
> 1 **medium-size onion, chopped**

1 cup pearl barley, rinsed

½ cup minced parsley

¼ cup minced chives or green onions
(including tops)

¼ teaspoon pepper

4 cups Homemade Chicken Broth (page 58)
or 2 cans (14½ oz. *each*) regular-strength
chicken or beef broth

Salt

Parsley sprigs

Melt 2 tablespoons of the butter in a 10- to 12-inch frying pan over medium heat. Add pine nuts and stir until lightly toasted. Remove nuts with a slotted spoon; set aside. Add remaining 4 tablespoons butter to pan with onion and barley; cook, stirring, until barley is lightly toasted. Remove from heat; stir in pine nuts, minced parsley, chives, and pepper. Spoon into a 1½-quart casserole. (At this point, you may cover and refrigerate for up to 1 day.)

Bring broth to a boil, pour over barley mixture, and stir to blend well. Bake, uncovered, in a 375° oven until barley is tender to bite and almost all liquid is absorbed, about 1 hour and 10 minutes. Season to taste with salt; garnish with parsley sprigs.

Old-fashioned Hot Cereal

PREPARATION & COOKING TIME: 20 to 45 minutes, depending on grain
PER SERVING: 116 calories, 3 grams protein, 26 grams carbohydrate, .33 gram total fat, 0 milligram cholesterol, 1 milligram sodium

Cooked cereal can hardly be called a brand-new idea in food, but it can still be utterly current in its makeup. In typically Western style, we base our cereal on unusual grains—barley, brown rice, or bulgur—and add a handful of raisins or apricots for sweetness. Top bowlfuls of cereal with spiced butter and milk or cream for a delicious breakfast with staying power.

Makes 4 to 6 servings

2 cups water

1 cup pearl barley (rinsed), brown rice, or
bulgur (medium cracked wheat)

1 cup raisins or chopped dried apricots
(optional)

Spiced Butter (recipe follows),
brown sugar, or honey

Half-and-half, light cream, whipping
cream, or milk

In a 2- to 3-quart pan, bring water to a boil over high heat. Add grain; return to a boil. Reduce heat, cover, and simmer until grain is tender to bite, about 40 minutes (about 15 minutes for bulgur). About 10 minutes before grain is done, stir in raisins (if used).

Serve, or cover and refrigerate for up to 3 days. To reheat, spoon 1 or more portions of grain into top of a double boiler over simmering water; cover and cook until hot, about 10 minutes. Or spoon into a nonmetallic cereal bowl, cover with plastic wrap, and reheat in a microwave oven on **HIGH (100%)**, stirring once or twice, until steaming.

Sweeten cereal portions as desired with Spiced Butter, sugar, or honey; top with half-and-half.

SPICED BUTTER. Blend together ½ cup (¼ lb.) **unsalted butter** or margarine (at room temperature), 2 tablespoons **sugar**, ¼ teaspoon **ground cinnamon**, and ⅛ teaspoon **ground nutmeg**. If made ahead, cover and refrigerate for up to 1 week.
PER TABLESPOON: 114 calories, .12 gram protein, 3 grams carbohydrate, 12 grams total fat, 31 milligrams cholesterol, 2 milligrams sodium.

Sesame Wheat Pilaf

W E S T E R N   C L A S S I C

PREPARATION TIME: About 10 minutes
COOKING TIME: About 40 minutes
PER SERVING: 290 calories, 6 grams protein, 42 grams carbohydrate, 12 grams total fat, 16 milligrams cholesterol, 65 milligrams sodium

In the West, quick-cooking cracked wheat is better known as "bulgur." When prepared in a pilaf, it has a fine toasted flavor, accented here with toasted sesame seeds. If you buy bulgur in a Middle Eastern market or a health food store (or in bulk at a supermarket), you'll probably find a choice of grain sizes. Choose medium, not coarse or fine cracked wheat.

Makes 6 to 8 servings

½ cup sesame seeds

¼ cup (⅛ lb.) butter or margarine;
or ¼ cup salad oil

1 medium-size onion, chopped

1 clove garlic, minced or pressed

¼ pound small whole button mushrooms
(or large button mushrooms, sliced)

2 cups bulgur (medium cracked wheat)

3½ cups Homemade Chicken Broth (page 58);
or 3½ cups canned regular-strength
chicken or beef broth; or 2 cans (10½ oz.
each) condensed beef bouillon and
¾ cup water

1 tablespoon chopped parsley

Toast sesame seeds in a 10- to 12-inch frying pan over medium heat until golden, about 2 minutes, shaking pan frequently. Pour out of pan and set aside.

Melt butter in frying pan; add onion, garlic, and mushrooms. Cook, stirring often, until onion is golden and mushroom liquid has evaporated. Add bulgur and sesame seeds; stir until grain is coated with butter. Add broth and parsley; stir to blend and bring to a boil over high heat. Reduce heat, cover, and simmer until grain is tender to bite, about 15 minutes.

"FLOWER CHILDREN" of the 1960s were a colorful part of a social revolution that has changed many aspects of our lives—including our diets. Today, Westerners are much more appreciative of a greater variety of foods. We accept tofu as an everyday ingredient—and find whole grains, brown rice, and vegetables to be not only healthful, but delicious.

Falafels

PREPARATION TIME: About 5 minutes to mix falafels; about 20 minutes for batter to rest; about 15 minutes to make tomato salad; about 10 minutes to make dressing

COOKING TIME: About 20 minutes to fry falafels (includes time to heat oil); about 35 minutes to cook tomato salad

PER SERVING: 164 calories, 9 grams protein, 18 grams carbohydrate, 7 grams total fat, 69 milligrams cholesterol, 205 milligrams sodium

A Mediterranean favorite, falafels are simply fried balls of spicy legume flour. To make them, start with the dry mix sold in well-stocked supermarkets and Middle Eastern grocery stores. Tuck the crisp-fried falafels into pocket bread, then top with our tomato relish and garbanzo dressing and eat out of hand.

Makes 6 to 8 servings

    2 **large eggs**
    2 **cups dry falafel mix**
    ¼ **cup chopped parsley**
    1 **cup water**
      Salad oil
      Spicy Tomato Salad (recipe follows)
      Pocket breads
      Garbanzo Dressing (recipe follows)

In a bowl, lightly beat eggs. Add falafel mix and parsley; gradually stir in water, blending well. Let stand, uncovered, for 20 minutes; mixture should have the consistency of a moist unbaked meat loaf mixture.

In a 10- to 12-inch frying pan over medium heat, heat 1 inch of oil to 350°F on a deep-frying thermometer. For each falafel, use a rounded large melon ball scoopful or a rounded measuring teaspoonful of falafel mixture. Carefully drop falafels into oil, 10 to 12 at a time; cook, turning often, until golden brown, about 2 minutes. Lift from oil with a slotted spoon; let drain and cool on paper towels. If made ahead, wrap airtight and refrigerate. To recrisp, arrange in a single layer in 10- by 15-inch rimmed baking pans; bake, uncovered, in a 350° oven for about 10 minutes.

To serve, stuff falafels and Spicy Tomato Salad into pocket breads; spoon Garbanzo Dressing atop falafels and salad.

SPICY TOMATO SALAD. Heat 3 tablespoons **olive oil** in a 10- to 12-inch frying pan over medium heat. Add 1 large **onion**, chopped; cover and cook, stirring occasionally, until soft, 5 to 7 minutes.

Meanwhile, whirl 1 can (about 1 lb.) **tomatoes** and their liquid in a blender until finely chopped, then add to pan along with 1 can (6 oz.) **tomato paste.** Cook, stirring often, until reduced to 2 cups, about 25 minutes.

Remove from heat; scrape into a bowl. Mix in 2 tablespoons *each* **lemon juice** and chopped **parsley;** ¼ teaspoon **liquid hot pepper seasoning;** 1 small **green bell pepper,** stemmed, seeded, and chopped; and 3 or 4 **green onions** (including tops), thinly sliced. Season to taste with **salt.** If made ahead, cover and refrigerate for up to 3 days. Makes about 2 cups.
PER TABLESPOON: 22 calories, .46 gram protein, 2 grams carbohydrate, 1 gram total fat, 0 milligram cholesterol, 67 milligrams sodium.

GARBANZO DRESSING. In an 8- to 10-inch frying pan, toast ¼ cup **sesame seeds** over medium heat until golden, about 2 minutes, shaking pan frequently. Set aside.

Drain 1 can (about 1 lb.) **garbanzo beans,** reserving liquid. Whirl garbanzos in a blender until very smooth, adding sesame seeds, 6 tablespoons **lemon juice,** 1 tablespoon **salad oil,** and 1 clove **garlic.** Use 2 to 3 tablespoons reserved garbanzo liquid to thin dressing. Season to taste with **salt.** If made ahead, cover and refrigerate for up to 3 days. Makes about 1 cup.
PER TABLESPOON: 47 calories, 2 grams protein, 5 grams carbohydrate, 2 grams total fat, 0 milligram cholesterol, 88 milligrams sodium.

Vegetable Tabbouleh

Pictured on facing page

PREPARATION TIME: 1 hour to soak bulgur; 15 to 20 minutes to prepare salad

CHILLING TIME: At least 30 minutes to crisp lettuce

PER SERVING: 154 calories, 2 grams protein, 21 grams carbohydrate, 7 grams total fat, 0 milligram cholesterol, 7 milligrams sodium

No cooking is required for this easy bulgur salad. Simply soaked in water, the nutty-tasting grain becomes deliciously tender, yet still retains a nice chewiness. Combine the softened bulgur with crisp water chestnuts, fresh mint, and garden vegetables for a refreshing salad.

Makes 6 to 8 servings

    1 **cup bulgur (medium cracked wheat)**
    1 **can (about 8 oz.) water chestnuts, drained and chopped; or 1 cup peeled, chopped fresh water chestnuts or jicama**
    ½ **cup minced green onions (including tops)**
    ½ **cup chopped carrot**
    ⅓ **cup chopped fresh mint**
    ¼ **cup** *each* **olive oil and lemon juice**
      Salt
    2 **medium-size firm-ripe tomatoes, cored (optional)**
      Small romaine leaves, washed and crisped
      Fresh mint sprigs

In a strainer, rinse bulgur well; drain. In a bowl, combine bulgur with 1 cup cold water and let stand until soft to bite, about 1 hour. Drain off any remaining liquid.

Mix bulgur with water chestnuts, onions, carrot, chopped mint, oil, and lemon juice. Add salt to taste. If made ahead, cover and refrigerate until next day.

To serve, spoon into a wide, shallow bowl. If using tomatoes, cut into thin wedges; chop enough to make 1 to 2 tablespoons. Sprinkle chopped tomatoes over salad; surround salad with tomato wedges and lettuce. Garnish with mint sprigs.

From Middle Eastern markets and Mediterranean cooks comes Vegetable Tabbouleh (recipe on facing page)—a colorful, cool bulgur salad flavored with mint, onion, and lemon. Water chestnuts or jicama add crunch.

Curried Lentil Stew

PREPARATION TIME: About 20 minutes

COOKING TIME: 20 to 40 minutes

PER SERVING: 315 calories, 15 grams protein, 41 grams carbohydrate, 12 grams total fat, 0 milligram cholesterol, 41 milligrams sodium

Few know—unless they read Sunset *or travel to Central Asia—that* daal-bhatt *is generally cited as the national banquet of Nepal. At the heart of the menu is this savory lentil stew. Offer it with steamed rice, roast chicken and one or more spicy chutneys.*

Makes 6 to 8 servings

> 2⅓ cups lentils (1 lb.)
>
> 2 tablespoons coriander seeds
>
> 1 cup coarsely chopped shallots or red onion
>
> 6 tablespoons salad oil
>
> 5 teaspoons ground turmeric
>
> 2 tablespoons chili powder
>
> ½ cup thinly sliced chives or green onions (including tops)
>
> ⅓ cup lime juice

Salt

Fresh cilantro (coriander) sprigs

Lime wedges

Sort lentils and remove any debris. Rinse lentils, drain, and set aside.

Whirl coriander seeds in a blender until finely ground, about 2 minutes. Add shallots and ½ cup water; whirl until coarsely ground.

In a 5- to 6-quart pan over medium-high heat, combine oil and shallot mixture. Cook, stirring, until almost all liquid has evaporated, about 5 minutes. Add turmeric, chili powder, and chives; cook for 2 minutes, stirring constantly.

Stir lentils and 8 cups water into shallot mixture. Bring to a boil over high heat; reduce heat to low, cover, and simmer, stirring occasionally, until lentils are tender to bite—10 to 15 minutes for decorticated lentils, about 35 minutes for unskinned lentils. Stir in lime juice and season to taste with salt. If made ahead, let cool, then cover and refrigerate for up to 2 days. Reheat to simmering before serving.

Pour hot lentils into a bowl or tureen and garnish with cilantro sprigs. Offer lime wedges to squeeze over individual portions.

Black Bean Cassoulet

PREPARATION TIME: About 1¼ hours to assemble; about 3¼ hours to cook

BAKING TIME: About 1 hour

PER SERVING: 682 calories, 48 grams protein, 47 grams carbohydrate, 33 grams total fat, 138 milligrams cholesterol, 492 milligrams sodium

This party-size entrée is ready to serve when you are, right after assembly or later. Black beans, pork, chicken, and sausage make a hearty—and tasty—combination.

Makes 2 cassoulets, 10 to 12 servings *each*

> 3 **pounds dried black beans (about 7½ cups)**
> 6 **large onions (3 to 3½ lbs. *total*), unpeeled**
> ½ **pound bacon, chopped**
> ¼ **cup coarsely chopped fresh ginger**
> 1 **or 2 fresh jalapeño chiles, stemmed, seeded, and minced**
> 3 **tablespoons dry oregano leaves**
> 2 **tablespoons *each* dry thyme leaves and cumin seeds**
> 8 **cloves garlic, minced or pressed**
> 4 **pounds boneless pork shoulder or butt, trimmed of fat and cut into 3-inch cubes**
> **About 3½ quarts Homemade Chicken Broth (page 58) or canned regular-strength chicken broth**
> 20 **chicken thighs (6 to 7 lbs. *total*)**
> 2 **pounds mild Italian sausages**
> ½ **cup (¼ lb.) butter or margarine**
> **About 3 slices fresh bread, torn into coarse crumbs (1½ cups crumbs)**
> ½ **cup finely chopped fresh cilantro (coriander)**

Sort beans and remove any debris. Rinse beans, drain, and set aside.

Peel and coarsely chop 1 of the onions. In a 12- to 14-quart pan over medium heat, cook chopped onion and bacon, stirring often, until onion is golden, about 30 minutes. Add ginger, chile, oregano, thyme, cumin seeds, and half the garlic; cook, stirring, until garlic is soft, about 2 minutes.

Add pork, beans, and about 3 quarts of the broth (to cover meat and beans). Bring to a boil; reduce heat, cover, and simmer until pork is very tender when pierced and beans mash easily, about 2½ hours. Stir occasionally. With 2 forks, tear pork in pan into shreds.

Meanwhile, put remaining 5 unpeeled onions in a 9- or 10-inch square baking pan. Bake in a 350° oven until onions feel soft when pressed, about 1¼ hours. Let cool; peel and quarter.

At the same time, arrange chicken, skin side up, and sausages in a single layer in two 10- by 15-inch baking pans. Bake in a 350° oven (in sequence, if needed) until chicken is no longer pink at bone and

sausages are no longer pink in thickest part (cut to test), about 40 minutes; remove as cooked. Diagonally cut sausages into ⅜-inch slices.

Melt butter in a 10- to 12-inch frying pan over medium-high heat. Add remaining garlic and bread crumbs; cook, stirring, until crumbs are very light brown, about 3 minutes. Set aside.

To assemble cassoulets, divide bean mixture evenly between 2 shallow 6- to 7-quart baking dishes. Top each equally with onions, chicken, and sausage slices. (At this point, you may let cool, then cover and refrigerate cassoulet and crumb mixture separately for up to 3 days.)

Pour 1 cup broth into each cassoulet. Sprinkle with crumbs. Bake, uncovered, in a 350° oven until hot in the center, about 1 hour. Top with cilantro.

Baked Soybeans

PREPARATION TIME: At least 6 hours to soak beans; about 3 hours to cook beans; about 25 minutes to prepare casserole

BAKING TIME: About 1 hour

PER SERVING: 350 calories, 12 grams protein, 27 grams carbohydrate, 23 grams total fat, 13 milligrams cholesterol, 729 milligrams sodium

Indigenous to China and Japan, soybeans have been used since before recorded history. The nutlike flavor and tender texture of these highly nutritious legumes come as a pleasant surprise for the uninitiated. Here, the beans take on a lively dimension when baked in a sweet, spicy sauce.

Makes 6 servings

> 1½ **cups dried soybeans**
> 1 **small onion, finely chopped**
> ¼ **pound salt pork, diced**
> 3 **tablespoons molasses**
> 1 **cup catsup**
> 1½ **teaspoons *each* dry mustard and Worcestershire**
> ¼ **teaspoon pepper**
> **Salt**

Sort beans and remove any debris. Rinse and drain beans; place in a 4- to 5-quart pan (beans almost triple in volume) and add 4½ cups water. Cover and soak for at least 6 hours or until next day. Drain beans; reserve liquid for cooking. Pick over beans and discard loose, fibrous bean skins.

Return beans and soaking water to pan, adding more water if needed to cover beans. Bring to a boil over high heat; reduce heat, cover, and simmer until beans are tender to bite, about 3 hours. Stir occasionally and add more water as needed to keep beans from sticking. Drain.

In a 1½-quart casserole, combine cooked beans, onion, salt pork, molasses, catsup, mustard, Worcestershire, and pepper. Cover and bake in a 300° oven for 30 minutes. Remove lid and stir beans well. Continue to bake, uncovered, until sauce is thick, about 30 more minutes. Season to taste with salt.

A Fifties' Potluck Special

A popular dish at suburban potlucks of the '50s, this *Sunset* favorite is still sure to please. It may not win you ribbons at your next gourmet get-together, but when you need a dish to take to the school supper, cart to a weekend cabin, or serve the kids economically, dust off this tried-and-true classic.

Italian Delight Casserole

Heat oil over medium-high heat—in a 4- to 5-quart pan for 8 to 10 servings, an 8- to 10-quart pan for 16 to 20 servings, or a 12- to 16-quart pan for 24 to 30 servings. Crumble in beef and stir often until well browned. Lift meat from pan with a slotted spoon.

Add onion, garlic, and bell pepper to drippings in pan; cook, stirring often, until vegetables are soft, 10 to 20 minutes. Tilt pan; spoon out and discard excess fat. Stir in browned meat, tomato sauce, mushroom gravy, oregano, thyme, Worcestershire, and mushrooms and their liquid. Bring to a boil over high heat, stirring often; reduce heat, cover, and simmer for 10 minutes.

Cook spaghetti, uncovered, in boiling water until just tender to bite, about 8 minutes; drain. (For 1 package spaghetti, use a 4- to 5-quart pan and 7 to 8 cups water; for 2 packages, an

Remember casseroles? Whether or not you're old enough to have dined during the 1950s, our Fifties' Potluck Special dishes up the best of that era—in family to crowd-size quantity.

8- to 10-quart pan and 3½ to 4 quarts water; for 3 packages, a 12- to 16-quart pan and 5 to 6 quarts water.)

Mix cooked spaghetti with sauce and corn. Season to taste with salt and pepper; pour into a greased shallow casserole. Sprinkle cheese on top. (At this point, you may cover and refrigerate until next day.)

Bake, uncovered, in a 350° oven until cheese is melted and casserole is heated through. Cooking time is about 30 minutes for a 3-quart casserole (40 minutes if refrigerated); about 50 minutes for a 6-quart casserole (1 hour if refrigerated); 50 to 60 minutes for a 9-quart casserole (1 to 1¼ hours if refrigerated).

Multiplication Table for Italian Delight Casserole
Here's how to figure quantity according to the size of your group

	Serves 8 to 10	Serves 16 to 20	Serves 24 to 30
Salad oil	¼ cup	½ cup	¾ cup
Ground lean beef	1 pound	2 pounds	3 pounds
Onion, chopped	1 large	2 large	3 large
Garlic, minced or pressed	1 clove	2 cloves	3 cloves
Green bell pepper, stemmed, seeded, and chopped	1 large	2 large	3 large
Tomato sauce (8-oz. can)	1 can	2 cans	3 cans
Mushroom gravy (12-oz. jar)	1 jar	2 jars	3 jars
Dry oregano leaves	¼ teaspoon	½ teaspoon	¾ teaspoon
Dry thyme leaves	¼ teaspoon	½ teaspoon	¾ teaspoon
Worcestershire	1 tablespoon	2 tablespoons	3 tablespoons
Sliced mushrooms or stems and pieces (4-oz. can)	1 can	2 cans	3 cans
Dry spaghetti (8-oz. package)	1 package	2 packages	3 packages
Corn kernels (12-oz. can), drained	1 can	2 cans	3 cans
Salt and pepper	To taste	To taste	To taste
Shredded Cheddar cheese	1 cup (4 oz.)	2 cups (8 oz.)	3 cups (12 oz.)

Basque Beans

PREPARATION TIME: 25 to 30 minutes (if starting with canned or cooked beans)
COOKING TIME: About 3 hours
PER SERVING: 199 calories, 12 grams protein, 36 grams carbohydrate, 1 gram total fat, 3 milligrams cholesterol, 287 milligrams sodium

Basque shepherds began arriving in Nevada and California's Central Valley almost a century ago. Their barbecues are great gatherings, occasions for feasting on barbecued lamb, Basque sausages, beans, breads, and crisp salad.

Canned beans are perfectly acceptable in our classic Basque beans, but if you'd rather cook your own, refer to the instructions for cooked pinto beans in Black Tie Chili, facing page. Multiply the amounts in the recipe by one and one-half, using 3 pounds of pinto, pink, or red beans.

Makes 20 to 25 servings

- **1 to 2 pounds meaty ham hocks**
- **1 large onion, sliced**
- **5 large carrots, diced**
- **1 green bell pepper, stemmed, seeded, and cut into squares**
- **3 cloves garlic**
- **3 or 4 parsley sprigs**
- **2 large cans (28 oz. *each*) tomatoes**
- **2 cans (8 oz. *each*) tomato sauce**
- **2 teaspoons chili powder**
- **1 or 2 small fresh jalapeño or Fresno chiles**
- **4½ quarts cooked or 8 to 10 cans (about 1 lb. *each*) pinto, pink, or red beans**

Place ham hocks and onion in a 3- to 4-quart pan; add water to cover. Bring to a boil, then reduce heat, cover, and simmer until meat is tender when pierced, about 2 hours. Lift out ham; discard onion and broth. When ham is cool enough to handle, discard skin, bones, and fat; tear meat into bite-size chunks. Set aside.

In a food processor or blender, combine carrots, bell pepper, garlic, parsley, tomatoes and their liquid, tomato sauce, chili powder, and chile. Whirl until vegetables are finely chopped.

Pour vegetable mixture into a 6- to 8-quart pan. Bring to a boil over high heat; reduce heat and simmer, uncovered, stirring occasionally, for 20 to 25 minutes. Drain beans (reserve liquid) and stir into vegetable sauce along with ham. Simmer, uncovered, over low heat for about 30 minutes to blend flavors; stir often. If beans start to stick, stir in some of the reserved bean liquid.

Green Chili with White Beans

PREPARATION TIME: About 45 minutes (if starting with canned or cooked beans)
COOKING TIME: About 2¼ hours
PER SERVING: 397 calories, 31 grams protein, 40 grams carbohydrate, 12 grams total fat, 60 milligrams cholesterol, 1147 milligrams sodium

White beans combine with green chiles and pork for a light, flavorful variation on the standard dish of red beans with red chiles and beef. (For a big party, you might serve a pot of each type.) Use canned white beans, or cook 2 pounds of small white beans as directed for pinto beans in Black Tie Chili, facing page.

Makes 10 to 12 servings

- **2 large green bell peppers, stemmed and seeded**
- **3 tablespoons salad oil**
- **2 cups sliced green onions (including tops)**

A tongue-in-cheek black-tie bash held in Washington— to which we were invited one year—begins with this prize-winning, crowd-size Black Tie Chili (recipe on facing page). Hosts set out corn-bread and condiments; guests supplement with appetizers and desserts.

8 cloves garlic, minced or pressed

4 teaspoons ground cumin

6 cans (13 oz. *each*) tomatillos

4 cans (7 oz. *each*) diced green chiles

6 cans (15 oz. *each*) Italian white beans (cannellini), drained; or 9 cups drained cooked small white beans

3 pounds boneless pork shoulder or butt, trimmed of fat and cut into ½-inch cubes

4 teaspoons dry oregano leaves

½ teaspoon cayenne

½ cup lightly packed fresh cilantro (coriander) leaves

Thinly slice bell peppers crosswise. Heat oil in a 10- to 12-quart pan over medium-high heat; add bell peppers, onions, garlic, and cumin. Cook, stirring, until onions are soft, about 5 minutes. Mix in tomatillos (break up with a spoon) and their liquid, chiles, beans, pork, oregano, and cayenne.

Bring to a boil; then reduce heat and simmer until pork is tender when pierced, 1½ to 2 hours. For a thin chili, cook covered; for thicker chili, cook uncovered to desired consistency. Stir occasionally. (At this point, you may let cool, then cover and refrigerate for up to 3 days. Reheat before continuing.)

Reserve a few cilantro leaves; chop remaining leaves. Stir chopped cilantro into chili; garnish with reserved leaves.

Black Tie Chili

Pictured on facing page

PREPARATION TIME: About 2 hours

COOKING TIME: About 4 hours

PER SERVING: 309 calories, 36 grams protein, 15 grams carbohydrate, 12 grams total fat, 96 milligrams cholesterol, 280 milligrams sodium

Mellow dried red chiles and a variety of spices give this thick beef chili a pleasant authority. Some cooks claim the chili benefits from resting in the refrigerator for a day or two—the standing gives the flavors time to blend.

Makes 7 to 8 quarts, 20 to 30 servings

6 to 8 ounces dried red New Mexico or California (Anaheim) chiles (18 to 32 chiles)

4 cans (12 oz. *each*) or 6 cups beer

15 to 16 pounds bone-in beef chuck

About ¼ cup salad oil

8 large onions (about 4 lbs. *total*), chopped

2 heads garlic (30 to 35 cloves), minced or pressed

3 tablespoons *each* chili powder and paprika

2⅔ tablespoons ground cumin

2 tablespoons dry oregano leaves

1 tablespoon sugar

2 teaspoons ground coriander

1 teaspoon cayenne

½ teaspoon ground allspice

4 cups Homemade Chicken Broth (page 58); or 2 cans (14½ oz. *each*) regular-strength chicken broth

1 can (15 oz.) tomato sauce

¼ cup bourbon whiskey (optional)

Salt

Cooked pinto beans (directions follow)

Condiments (suggestions follow)

Rinse chiles; discard stems and seeds. Combine chiles and beer in a 4- to 5-quart pan. Bring to a boil; reduce heat, cover, and simmer, stirring occasionally, for 30 minutes. Whirl chiles and cooking liquid in a food processor or blender until smoothly puréed. With a spoon, rub purée through a fine wire strainer (or force chiles through a food mill); discard residue. Reserve purée.

Meanwhile, cut beef from bones. Trim off and discard most of fat; cut meat into ½-inch cubes.

Place a 10- to 12-quart pan over medium-high heat. Add ¼ cup oil and ¼ of the meat; cook, uncovered, stirring frequently, until meat is well browned. Lift meat from pan with a slotted spoon and set aside. Repeat to brown remaining meat, adding more oil as needed.

Add onions and garlic to pan. Cook, uncovered, over medium heat, stirring often, until onions are soft, about 20 minutes. Add chili powder, paprika, cumin, oregano, sugar, coriander, cayenne, and allspice. Cook, stirring, for 2 minutes; remove from heat.

To pan, add browned beef and any juices that have accumulated, chile purée, broth, tomato sauce, and whiskey (if used). Stir to blend ingredients, then bring to a boil over high heat. Reduce heat, cover, and simmer until beef is very tender to bite, about 2 hours. Stir occasionally; if needed, add water, ¼ cup at a time, to prevent sticking. Season to taste with salt.

Serve chili from cooking pan or a large tureen. If made ahead, let cool, then cover and refrigerate for up to 2 days. To reheat, stir frequently over medium heat until chili is hot, about 20 minutes.

Ladle chili into individual bowls to top with beans and condiments.

COOKED PINTO BEANS. Sort 2 pounds **dried pinto beans** and remove any debris. Place beans in a 5- to 6-quart pan; rinse well with several changes of water, then drain. Add 4 quarts **water** to beans, cover, and bring to a rolling boil; remove from heat and let stand for at least 1 hour or until next day.

Drain beans, discarding liquid. Add 4 quarts **water** and 2 **bay leaves.** Bring to a boil over high heat; reduce heat, cover, and simmer until beans are very tender to bite, 1 to 1½ hours. Add **salt** to taste. Drain beans and serve hot. If made ahead, refrigerate beans, covered, in cooking liquid for up to 2 days; to serve, bring to simmering, then drain. Makes 2½ to 3 quarts.

CONDIMENTS. Arrange in separate dishes: 4 to 5 cups (1 to 1¼ lbs.) shredded **Cheddar cheese,** 4 to 6 cups **sour cream,** and 2 cups (about 24) sliced **green onions** (including tops).

The Best of Sunset

SAUCES, DRESSINGS & PRESERVES

Sauces and dressings, pickles and chutneys add the final flavor accent to many foods. Any green salad tastes better with a touch of vinaigrette; a spoonful of tangy relish takes steak or chicken or fish from plain to sublime.

This chapter presents some of Sunset's favorite finishing touches, chosen from a collection spanning over 50 years. Some are regional classics—home-cured olives, Guacamole, Pomegranate Jelly. Our own creativity brings you Garlic or Shallot Jelly and beautiful sun-dried jams. And as always, you'll find recipes with international flavor— Dijon-style Mustard, Italian Gravy, and bright, fresh salsas from Mexico and South America.

In classic Italian pesto, basil leaves are pulverized with grated Parmesan cheese, olive oil, and fresh garlic to form a pungent green paste that tastes wonderful on everything from pasta to raw vegetables. The recipe for Basic Pesto Sauce is on page 221.

Shallot Dressing

W E S T E R N   C L A S S I C

PREPARATION TIME: About 5 minutes
PER TABLESPOON: 82 calories, .02 gram protein, .45 gram carbohydrate, 9 grams total fat, 0 milligram cholesterol, 38 milligrams sodium

Fresh, crisp green salad is an everyday event for most Westerners, with a favorite oil-and-vinegar dressing its constant companion in many households. Here is our own favorite—an all-purpose shallot-sprinkled dressing for salad greens and other vegetables.

Makes about ¾ cup

In a small bowl, whisk together 1 tablespoon **Dijon mustard,** 1 tablespoon minced **shallot** or red onion, 3 tablespoons **wine vinegar,** and ½ cup **olive oil** until blended. If made ahead, cover and refrigerate for up to 2 days; stir well before using.

Avocado Sauce Piquant

W E S T E R N   C L A S S I C

PREPARATION TIME: About 5 minutes
PER TABLESPOON: 35 calories, .22 gram protein, 4 grams carbohydrate, 2 grams total fat, 6 milligrams cholesterol, 86 milligrams sodium

This piquant taste of yesterday pleases the palate equally well today. Originally published in a Kitchen Cabinet column of the 1950s, the warm dressing is a delicious accent for halved avocados.

Makes about ⅔ cup

In a 2- to 4-cup pan, combine 2 tablespoons **butter** or margarine and 2 tablespoons *each* **catsup, Worcestershire, vinegar,** and **sugar.** Stir over low heat just until sugar is dissolved. Serve warm.

Honey-Vinegar Salad Dressing

PREPARATION TIME: About 5 minutes
PER TABLESPOON: 36 calories, .03 gram protein, 10 grams carbohydrate, 0 gram total fat, 0 milligram cholesterol, .83 milligram sodium

Hot, tart, and sweet, this light salad dressing of honey, vinegar, and crushed red chiles makes a perfect foil for fruit, fish, or crisp vegetables.

Makes ½ cup

In a 1- to 1½-quart pan, combine 1 cup **distilled white vinegar,** ¼ cup **honey,** and ¼ teaspoon **crushed dried hot red chiles.** Boil rapidly, uncovered, until reduced to ½ cup. Let cool to room temperature. If made ahead, cover and refrigerate for up to 3 days; stir well before using.

Pine Nut Salad Dressing

W E S T E R N   C L A S S I C

PREPARATION TIME: About 10 minutes
PER TABLESPOON: 59 calories, .99 gram protein, .75 gram carbohydrate, 6 grams total fat, 0 milligram cholesterol, .20 milligram sodium

Harvested in the West from piñon pines native to California, Arizona, and New Mexico, pine nuts add richness to a well-seasoned dressing for greens.

Makes 1⅔ cups

- ¾ **cup pine nuts**
- ½ **teaspoon dry tarragon**
- ¼ **teaspoon grated lemon peel**
- ⅛ **teaspoon ground nutmeg**
- ½ **cup salad oil or olive oil**
- ⅓ **cup vinegar**
-    **Salt**

Spread pine nuts in a 10- by 15-inch rimmed baking pan. Toast in a 350° oven until golden, about 6 minutes; shake pan often. Let nuts cool, then coarsely chop and combine with tarragon, lemon peel, nutmeg, oil, and vinegar. Season to taste with salt.

If made ahead, cover and refrigerate for up to 2 days; stir well before using.

Dijon-style Mustard

PREPARATION TIME: About 15 minutes
COOKING TIME: About 35 minutes
PER TEASPOON: 6 calories, .25 gram protein, .59 gram carbohydrate, .31 gram total fat, 0 milligram cholesterol, 47 milligrams sodium

As any connoisseur will tell you, Dijon mustard—named for the French city—is unexcelled in flavor. Here's how to make your own. It's quite hot when freshly made, but grows milder with age.

Makes 2 cups

- ½ **cup cold water**
- 1 **cup dry mustard**
- 1⅓ **cups** *each* **dry white wine and white wine vinegar**
- 1 **small onion, chopped**
- 3 **large cloves garlic, pressed or minced**
- 2 **bay leaves**
- 8 **whole allspice**
- 2 **teaspoons** *each* **salt and sugar**
- 1 **teaspoon dry tarragon**

In a bowl, stir together cold water and mustard. Let stand for at least 10 minutes.

Meanwhile, in a 2- to 3-quart noncorrodible pan, combine wine, vinegar, onion, garlic, bay leaves, allspice, salt, sugar, and tarragon. Bring to a boil; boil, uncovered, until reduced by half (or slightly more for a hotter mustard), 15 to 20 minutes.

Pour mixture through a fine strainer into mustard paste, pressing all juices out. Blend and cook, stirring often, in the top of a double boiler over simmering water until as thick as very heavy cream, 10 to 15 minutes (mixture thickens as it cools). Let cool. To store, cover and refrigerate for up to 2 years.

Citrus Beurre Blanc

W E S T E R N   C L A S S I C

PREPARATION TIME: About 10 minutes
COOKING TIME: 5 to 8 minutes
PER TABLESPOON: 75 calories, .19 gram protein, 2 grams carbohydrate, 8 grams total fat, 21 milligrams cholesterol, 79 milligrams sodium

A Sunset variation on classic French beurre blanc, this citrus-based sauce gilds fish with an exquisite buttery tartness. The sauce can be made ahead and kept in a hot water bath until ready to serve.

Makes about ¾ cup

> 1 tablespoon *each* lemon and lime juice
> ¼ cup *each* orange and grapefruit juice
> 3 tablespoons chopped shallots
> ½ cup (¼ lb.) butter or margarine
> ¼ teaspoon *each* finely shredded lemon, lime, orange and grapefruit peel

In a 10- to 12-inch frying pan, combine lemon, lime, orange, and grapefruit juices with shallots. Boil, uncovered, until reduced to about ⅓ cup. Reduce heat to low. Add butter in 1 chunk; stir until melted and well mixed into sauce. Stir in shredded peels.

To hold for up to 4 hours, pour into a measuring cup and set in hot tap water. Stir occasionally, replacing hot water as necessary. (Sauce will separate if reheated, so don't let it cool.) Or hold for up to 4 hours in a thermos.

Basic Pesto Sauce

Pictured on page 218

PREPARATION TIME: About 15 minutes
PER TABLESPOON: 78 calories, 3 grams protein, 1 gram carbohydrate, 7 grams total fat, 5 milligrams cholesterol, 110 milligrams sodium

The enticing aroma of tender fresh basil leaves is enough to explain the magic of pesto. Fabled as the synthesis of sunny Ligurian flavors and fragrances, it's actually just an innocent-looking, quickly produced paste of basil, Parmesan cheese, and olive oil.

Makes about 1½ cups

> 2 cups lightly packed fresh basil leaves
> 1 cup (about 5 oz.) freshly grated Parmesan cheese
> ½ to ⅔ cup olive oil
> 1 or 2 cloves garlic (optional)

In a blender or food processor, whirl basil, cheese, ½ cup of the oil, and garlic (if used) until smoothly

puréed; add more oil if needed. If made ahead, cover and refrigerate for up to 5 days; or freeze in small, easy-to-use portions.

PESTO BUTTER
Blend 3 tablespoons **Basic Pesto Sauce** with ½ cup (¼ lb.) **butter** or margarine, at room temperature. Makes ⅔ cup.

PESTO MAYONNAISE
In a food processor or blender, combine 1 **large egg,** 2 tablespoons **lemon juice,** and 1 clove **garlic.** Whirl until blended. Turn motor off and add ½ cup **Basic Pesto Sauce.** With motor running, gradually add ½ cup (¼ lb.) melted **butter** or margarine and ½ cup **salad oil** in a slow, steady stream. For sauce with a pouring or dipping consistency, serve at room temperature; for a thicker sauce, cover and refrigerate. Makes 2 cups.

PESTO DRESSING
Blend 6 tablespoons **Basic Pesto Sauce,** ⅓ cup **wine vinegar,** ⅔ cup **olive oil,** and 1 clove **garlic,** minced or pressed. Stir well before using. Makes 1⅓ cups.

Chimichurri Sauce

PREPARATION TIME: 10 to 15 minutes
PER TABLESPOON: 48 calories, .06 gram protein, .64 gram carbohydrate, 5 grams total fat, 0 milligram cholesterol, 2 milligrams sodium

Among the mouthwatering events from other cultures that Sunset has celebrated in print, Argentina's asado— a lavish barbecue meal—stands out as especially memorable. A tradition begun by gauchos on the Argentine pampas, the asado includes this distinctive sauce to accompany the grilled beef.

Makes about 4 cups

> 2 medium-size carrots, peeled
> 1 large firm-ripe tomato, cored
> 1 stalk celery
> ½ medium-size green bell pepper, stemmed and seeded
> 1 lemon, ends trimmed
> 1 clove garlic
> ½ teaspoon *each* pepper and crushed dried hot red chiles
> ¼ cup *each* red wine and vinegar
> ¾ cup *each* olive oil and salad oil; or 1½ cups salad oil
> Salt

Cut carrots, tomato, celery, bell pepper, and lemon into chunks. In a food processor, whirl vegetables and lemon chunks with garlic, a portion at a time, until very finely chopped. (Or chop very finely with a knife.)

Mix chopped vegetable mixture, pepper, chiles, wine, vinegar, and oil. Season to taste with salt. If made ahead, cover and refrigerate for up to 5 days. Stir well before using.

IN THE EARLY '40s, Westerners contributed to the war effort by curtailing travel, conserving energy, recycling everything from tin foil to magazines, and planting large victory gardens. Sunset chipped in with directions for raising your own rabbits and chickens—as well as recipes for canning or preserving homegrown crops.

Guacamole

PREPARATION TIME: About 10 minutes
PER TABLESPOON: 26 calories, .31 gram protein, 1 gram carbohydrate, 2 grams total fat, 0 milligram cholesterol, 6 milligrams sodium

One of the great sauces of the Western Hemisphere, guacamole was already popular in the New World when Columbus arrived. Though favorite seasonings vary, the mixture usually includes hot and tart flavors to balance the essential avocado's buttery smooth, mellow character. Dip it, spoon it, spread it—on tostadas, salads, fish, meat, poultry. You'll find many excuses to use it.

Makes about 1 cup

- **1 large ripe avocado**
- **1 tablespoon lime juice or lemon juice**
- **1 to 2 tablespoons finely minced onion or green onion (including top)**
- **1 tablespoon canned diced green chiles**
- **1 tablespoon minced fresh cilantro (coriander)**
- **¼ teaspoon minced canned hot chile (such as jalapeño) or a few drops liquid hot pepper seasoning**
  Salt

Pit and peel avocado; place in a bowl and mash coarsely with a fork, blending in lime juice. Mix in onion, green chiles, cilantro, and hot chile. Season to taste with salt. Serve at room temperature or chilled. If made ahead, cover and refrigerate for up to 2 days; freeze for longer storage (do not add onion until mixture is thawed for serving). Stir before serving.

Green Taco Sauce

PREPARATION TIME: About 10 minutes (about 20 minutes if using fresh tomatillos)
PER TABLESPOON: 4 calories, .15 gram protein, .73 gram carbohydrate, .05 gram total fat, 0 milligram cholesterol, 7 milligrams sodium

A familiar sight in many Western markets, tart, papery-husked tomatillos are the base for a number of Mexican sauces and salsas. This nippy version is made with fresh or canned tomatillos, cilantro, chiles, and a splash of lime juice.

Makes about 1½ cups

- **About 1½ cups chopped fresh tomatillos (husks removed); or 1 can (13 oz.) tomatillos, drained**
- **¼ cup lightly packed chopped fresh cilantro (coriander)**
- **1 clove garlic**
- **2 tablespoons chopped onion**
- **2 to 4 tablespoons canned diced green chiles**
- **1½ teaspoons lime juice**
  Salt

If using fresh tomatillos, place in a 1- to 1½-quart pan and add enough water to cover. Bring to a boil; then reduce heat, cover, and simmer until tomatillos are tender when pierced, about 10 minutes. Drain well.

In a blender or food processor, whirl tomatillos, cilantro, garlic, onion, chiles, and lime juice until smoothly puréed. Season to taste with salt. If made ahead, cover and refrigerate for up to 4 hours.

Italian Gravy

PREPARATION TIME: 35 to 40 minutes
COOKING TIME: About 3¼ hours
PER ¼ CUP: 24 calories, .64 gram protein, 3 grams carbohydrate, 1 gram total fat, 0 milligram cholesterol, 178 milligrams sodium

Contributed to Sunset over 20 years ago by a San Francisco cook of Italian heritage, this sauce enhances veal scaloppine, lasagne, spaghetti, and much more. Our recipe—for a meatless gravy and its variation made with beef—makes enough for you to stock a few jars in your refrigerator or freezer.

Makes about 10 cups

- **1 cup dried porcini mushrooms (cèpes or boletes)**
- **3 tablespoons olive oil or salad oil**
- **3 cups chopped parsley**
- **2 or 3 stalks celery, chopped**
- **1 medium-size onion, chopped**
- **2 cloves garlic, minced or pressed**
- **1 fresh rosemary sprig (about 2 inches long) or ½ teaspoon dry rosemary**
- **2 or 3 fresh thyme sprigs or ½ teaspoon dry thyme leaves**
- **5 small fresh sage leaves or ½ teaspoon dry sage leaves**
- **2 cans (about 1 lb. *each*) tomatoes**
- **4 cans (8 oz. *each*) tomato sauce**
- **1 small dried hot red chile**
  Salt

Place mushrooms in a small bowl and add enough hot water to cover. Let stand until mushrooms are soft, about 15 minutes.

Heat oil in a 5- to 6-quart pan over medium heat. Add parsley, celery, onion, garlic, rosemary, thyme, and sage. Cook, stirring often, until vegetables are soft. Add tomatoes (break up with a spoon) and their liquid, tomato sauce, and chile to vegetable mixture. Lift mushrooms from liquid; chop, then add to pan. Pour soaking liquid into pan, being careful not to add any grit from bottom of bowl. Bring to a boil; reduce heat, cover, and simmer slowly until reduced to 10 cups, about 3 hours. Season to taste with salt. If made ahead, let cool, then cover and refrigerate for up to 3 weeks (freeze for longer storage).

ITALIAN MEAT GRAVY

Follow directions for **Italian Gravy,** but brown 2 pounds **ground lean beef** in the oil before adding vegetables. Makes about 13 cups.

Fonduta (recipe below), Northern Italy's fontina cheese sauce, makes an elegant finish for sautéed chicken—especially when dotted with slivered truffles.

Fonduta

Pictured above

PREPARATION TIME: 5 to 10 minutes
COOKING TIME: 10 to 15 minutes
PER TABLESPOON: 47 calories, 3 grams protein, .44 gram carbohydrate, 4 grams total fat, 41 milligrams cholesterol, 4 milligrams sodium

Northern Italy's velvety version of Swiss fondue is impressively versatile. Spoon the elegant custard-based sauce over a variety of foods, from broccoli and poached eggs to veal and pasta; or serve it as an appetizer dip for cubes of crusty bread. Stir slivered truffles through the sauce for an extravagant touch of tradition.

Makes about 2⅓ cups

> **4 large egg yolks**
> **1 cup milk**
> **3 cups (12 oz.) finely shredded fontina cheese**
> **1 can (½ oz.) white or black truffles (optional)**

In the top of a double boiler, thoroughly mix egg yolks and milk. Place over slightly bubbling water (water should just touch the bottom of the top unit). Cook, stirring constantly with a flexible spatula, until mixture is thickened enough to coat a metal spoon with a thick, velvety layer, 7 to 8 minutes. If overcooked, the custard mixture begins to look grainy, then separates.

Immediately stir in cheese; continue to cook, stirring, until all but a few slivers of cheese are smoothly melted. Remove double boiler from heat, but leave fonduta over hot water for about 10 minutes, stirring occasionally.

If made ahead, cover and refrigerate for up to 5 days. To reheat, place desired quantity over simmering water; stir until warm enough to serve.

If using truffles, drain liquid from can into fonduta. Cut truffles into paper-thin slices; reserve a few slices and stir remainder into sauce. Use reserved slices as garnish (see serving suggestions below).

FONDUTA WITH VEGETABLES. Ladle warm **fonduta** onto **hot cooked vegetables,** such as broccoli, green beans, spinach, cauliflower, artichoke hearts or bottoms, asparagus, Italian green beans, celery, onions, leeks, or zucchini; or sautéed mushrooms, eggplant, or bell peppers. Allow 2 to 3 tablespoons fonduta for each ½ cup vegetables.

FONDUTA WITH VEAL OR CHICKEN. Prepare **veal** (chops, roasts, steaks) or **chicken** (breasts, legs, or the whole bird) by a simple method such as roasting, sautéing, or broiling. Accompany with **fonduta** to ladle over individual portions. Allow ¼ to ⅓ cup sauce for each ½ pound boneless meat.

FONDUTA WITH EGGS. Spoon warm **fonduta** over **poached eggs;** allow about 3 tablespoons sauce for each egg.

Curing Your Own Green Ripe Olives

Olive trees flourish in many gardens of California and the Southwest, often causing inky stains on paving from their spilled fruit. This same fruit, though unbelievably bitter when straight from the tree, can become a glorious home-cured delicacy.

Curing olives at home naturally interests *Sunset*. With the assistance of the Food Technology Department at U.C. Davis and the U.C. Agricultural Extension Service, we developed this process for curing green ripe olives. Follow directions carefully for safe results. *Note: Do not home can olives. If improperly handled, the fruit can cause severe food poisoning.*

Try to avoid bruising or skinning fruit as you gather it from the tree. Use a basket, a pail of water, or an old pillow case. If you can't start the curing within a day after picking, place fruit in a brine made of ¾ cup salt for each 1 gallon water. Let stand in a cool, well-ventilated place for up to 4 days.

Curing these mellow, smoothly succulent green ripe olives takes about 2 weeks. Once cured, they'll keep at room temperature or in the refrigerator for up to 6 months.

Lye-cured Green Ripe Olives

Pick olives of the 'Ascolano', 'Manzanillo', 'Mission', or 'Sevillano' varieties, choosing those that are light green, pale straw color, or rosy red. Black fruit will get too soft when cured.

Start processing the olives early in the day. The first steps take at least 12 hours and you must check the fruit's progress frequently. For every 2 gallons of olives, you will need 1 large container (at least 10 to 12 quarts), such as a stoneware crock, glass bowl, or plastic pail (do *not* use aluminum or galvanized metal); heavy-duty rubber gloves; a long-handled wooden or stainless steel spoon; household lye (from the supermarket or a drug store); and salt. To keep fruit covered in the crock, you'll need clean muslin cloths.

Sort through **olives,** discard any that are bruised, and measure fruit. Work with multiples of 1-gallon units. Also prepare a solution of 1 cup **vinegar** and 1 cup **water** in a bowl; keep it nearby to wash your skin in case of lye burn.

LYE-CURING PROCESS. Pour water into the crock, allowing 1 gallon **water** to cover each 2 gallons olives. Using the gloves to protect your hands, measure ¼ cup (2 oz.) **lye** for each gallon of water. Slowly pour lye into water, stirring continuously with the long-handled spoon until lye dissolves. The lye heats the solution; allow it to cool for 30 minutes before adding olives. *Do not put lye in before the water or taste olives at any time during the lye-curing process.*

Slowly pour in olives, being very careful not to splash lye solution. Crumple cloth down into solution on top of olives to keep them submerged. Exposure to air will cause fruit to oxidize and darken. (Commercial black ripe olives are green olives oxidized by a special process.)

Let stand, covered, where the temperature is 60° to 70°, stirring every 2 to 3 hours. After 6 hours, drain olives and set aside in another container. In the first container, prepare a fresh lye solution, using the proportions given previously. Add fruit and let stand for 6 hours.

Olives must remain in the solution until the lye has penetrated to the pit in order to remove bitterness. To check lye penetration, cut 2 or 3 olives of varying sizes in half; wear gloves. Penetrated flesh will have turned a dark yellow-green; unpenetrated flesh closer to the pit will be a lighter color. (Before you begin the curing process, you might cut open a few fresh-picked olives so you'll have a basis for comparison when you check for lye penetration.) This process takes at least 12 hours, but can take as long as 30 hours, depending on the variety, maturity, and size of the olives.

If lye penetration is not complete after 12 hours, prepare a fresh lye solution, following preceding directions. Let olives stand in solution until penetration has occurred. If convenient, stir and check every few hours, but there's no harm in letting olives stand overnight without stirring or checking.

If necessary, change lye solution again after 12 hours. As soon as most of the olives have been completely penetrated (a few of the largest ones may not be quite finished), you can proceed to the next step.

RINSING PROCESS. When lye penetration is complete, pour off lye solution and cover olives with fresh, cold water, taking care to keep the fruit submerged with a clean cloth. Cover crock and let stand for at least 6 hours or overnight. Thereafter, change the water once a day until the color of the water changes from dark red to light pink (4 to 7 days).

BRINING PROCESS. Prepare a weak brine solution, using ½ cup **table salt** for each 1 gallon **water**—you'll need 1 gallon water for each 2 gallons olives. Stir until salt is dissolved. Slowly pour fruit into brine; cover container and let stand for 12 hours (olives will float initially). Drain brine; prepare a second solution, using same proportions of salt and water. Let olives stand, covered, for 1 week. You can now eat olives. If they are too salty, remove them from brine and cover with fresh water for 30 to 60 minutes, then drain and serve.

If you do not plan to use all your olives within 3 days, replace the brine with a holding solution of 1¼ cups (1 lb.) table salt for each 1 gallon water. You can keep olives for 6 months in the refrigerator, covered; replace the holding solution after 4 months.

To store large quantities of olives at room temperature, place the fruit in a holding solution of 2¼ cups (about 1¾ lbs.) salt for each 1 gallon water. Store, covered, for up to 6 months.

To reduce saltiness before eating, soak olives overnight or longer in fresh water. Drain and serve; refrigerate leftover drained olives and use within 3 days.

If at any time olives become mushy, moldy, or malodorous, discard them promptly. Do not taste them.

Chirmol

PREPARATION TIME: 20 to 25 minutes
PER TABLESPOON: 3 calories, .10 gram protein, .61 gram carbohydrate, .01 gram total fat, 0 milligram cholesterol, 1 milligram sodium

Appreciative of the fresh, exuberant flavors of much south-of-the-border cooking, Sunset has explored and published countless Latin American specialties. In El Salvador, this bold tomato relish accompanies barbecued beef.

Makes about 2½ cups

> 4 medium-size firm-ripe tomatoes, peeled, cored, seeded, and chopped (about 2 cups)
>
> 1 medium-size onion, finely chopped
>
> ⅓ cup finely chopped green bell pepper
>
> 1 tablespoon finely chopped fresh cilantro (coriander)
>
> 1 tablespoon finely chopped fresh mint or crumbled dry mint
>
> ¼ to ½ teaspoon liquid hot pepper seasoning
>
> Garlic salt

Combine tomatoes, onion, bell pepper, cilantro, mint, and hot pepper seasoning. Season to taste with garlic salt. If made ahead, cover and refrigerate for up to 3 days.

Tomato Lemon Chutney

PREPARATION TIME: 8 to 10 minutes
COOKING TIME: About 20 minutes
PER TABLESPOON: 31 calories, .30 gram protein, 7 grams carbohydrate, .56 gram total fat, 0 milligram cholesterol, 27 milligrams sodium

A sauce for sausages, a spicy chutney, or a sophisticated catsup—pick the definition that appeals to you most. By any description, this condiment adds just the right flourish to a platter of bratwurst or kielbasa.

Makes 1¾ cups

> 1 or 2 lemons
>
> 1 can (about 1 lb.) tomatoes
>
> 1 tablespoon salad oil or olive oil
>
> 1 small dried hot red chile
>
> 1 tablespoon mustard seeds
>
> ½ teaspoon cumin seeds
>
> ¼ teaspoon ground nutmeg
>
> ½ cup *each* raisins and sugar

Grate enough lemon peel to make 2 teaspoons; set aside.

Using a sharp knife, cut peel and all white membrane from 1 lemon. In a blender, whirl lemon with tomatoes and their liquid just until blended.

In a 1½- to 2-quart pan, combine oil, chile, lemon peel, mustard seeds, cumin seeds, and nutmeg. Cook over medium-high heat, stirring, until seeds begin to pop. Add tomato mixture, raisins, and sugar.

Boil gently, uncovered, until mixture thickens to a jamlike consistency, about 20 minutes; stir often. If made ahead, let cool, then cover and refrigerate for up to 3 days; reheat before serving.

Sweet Red Bell Pepper Relish

W E S T E R N   C L A S S I C

PREPARATION TIME: 35 to 40 minutes
COOKING TIME: 50 minutes to 1 hour; about 40 minutes to fill and process jars
PER TABLESPOON: 14 calories, .14 gram protein, 3 grams carbohydrate, .05 gram total fat, 0 milligram cholesterol, 52 milligrams sodium

As green bell peppers gradually turn to red, the transformation is more than visual. Much richer in vitamin A, the mature red pepper is sweeter, mellower, and fuller in flavor. It's perfect for a bright relish to serve with barbecued or roasted meat—or to give to friends.

Makes 3½ to 4 quarts

> 3 pounds onions (about 6 large onions), cut into 1-inch chunks
>
> 6 pounds red bell peppers (about 12 large peppers), stemmed, seeded, and cut into 1-inch squares
>
> 4 cups distilled white vinegar
>
> 3 cups sugar
>
> 2 tablespoons salt
>
> 1 tablespoon mustard seeds

In a food processor, whirl onions and bell peppers, a portion at a time, until coarsely chopped. (Or put through a food chopper fitted with a medium blade.)

Put vegetables in a 6- to 8-quart pan and stir in vinegar, sugar, salt, and mustard seeds. Bring to a boil over high heat, stirring constantly. Then reduce heat to medium and boil gently, uncovered, until reduced by about a third; stir often to prevent sticking.

Ladle hot relish into 7 or 8 hot sterilized 1-pint canning jars, filling to within ¼ inch of rims. Run a narrow spatula down between relish and jar to release any air. Wipe off rims; top with scalded lids and firmly screw on bands.

Place jars, sides not touching, on a rack in a canning kettle or other deep pan half-full of hot water. Add more hot water to cover jars by 1 to 2 inches. Bring water to a simmer, then cover and simmer for 15 minutes. Lift out jars and let cool on a towel away from drafts. Test seal of each jar by pressing lid. If it stays down, seal is good. If it pops when pressed, there's no seal; store unsealed relish in the refrigerator and use within 1 month.

Nestled in a spicy sauce of currants and Madeira, Pub Onions (recipe below) lend a sweet-tart accent to grilled meats. A great favorite in England, they please Westerners, too.

Pub Onions

Pictured above

PREPARATION TIME: About 20 minutes
COOKING TIME: About 40 minutes, plus 30 minutes to cool
PER ¼ CUP: 92 calories, 1 gram protein, 17 grams carbohydrate, 3 grams total fat, 0 milligram cholesterol, 9 milligrams sodium

Steeped in a sweet-sour sauce, these tiny sautéed onions may remind travelers of relishes served in many English pubs. We found them too tasty a tidbit to leave behind. For a light lunch, serve them with cheeses, buttered toast, and a watercress salad. They also add a bold accent to curry or meats.

Makes about 4 cups

 1½ **cups Madeira or port**
 ¾ **cup vinegar**
 ½ **cup firmly packed brown sugar**
 ½ **cup currants or raisins**
 ⅛ **teaspoon cayenne**
 2 **pounds small (¾- to 1½-inch-diameter) white onions**
 3 **tablespoons salad oil**
  Salt

In a 3- to 4-quart pan, combine Madeira, vinegar, sugar, currants, and cayenne. Boil rapidly, uncovered, until reduced to 1¼ cups; set aside.

Peel onions; arrange a single layer of onions in a 12- to 14-inch frying pan (reserve extra onions to cook in sequence). Add oil. Cook over medium-high heat until lightly browned, about 7 minutes, shaking pan to turn onions. With a slotted spoon, transfer browned onions to pan with Madeira sauce. Brown remaining onions in frying pan, then add to sauce.

Bring onions and sauce to a boil. Reduce heat, cover, and simmer gently; allow 10 minutes for small onions, 15 minutes for larger ones. Onions will be slightly crisp inside. Let cool; season to taste with salt. If made ahead, cover and refrigerate for up to 4 days; serve at room temperature.

Mango-Apricot-Date Chutney

PREPARATION TIME: About 20 minutes
COOKING TIME: About 1 hour, plus about 35 minutes to fill and process jars
PER TABLESPOON: 39 calories, .25 gram protein, 10 grams carbohydrate, .03 gram total fat, 0 milligram cholesterol, 4 milligrams sodium

Sweet to tart, mild to hot, Asian chutneys combine fruits, vegetables, and spices in countless variations. Mangoes are the primary ingredient in many chutneys, including the popular Major Grey type. In this easy (and relatively inexpensive) chutney, we used dried mangoes from an Asian market—where you'll also find the preserved or pickled ginger.

Makes 6 to 7 cups

 3½ **cups water**
 ½ **pound *each* dried mangoes and dried apricots; or 1 pound dried apricots**
 ¾ **cup *each* golden raisins and currants**
 1¼ **cups pitted dates, coarsely snipped or chopped**
 1½ **cups white wine vinegar**
 1¼ **cups firmly packed brown sugar**
 1 **cup preserved ginger in syrup or pickled ginger, drained and coarsely chopped**
 1 **tablespoon mustard seeds**
 1½ **teaspoons chili powder**
  Salt

In a 5- to 6-quart pan, combine water and mangoes. Bring to a simmer, cover, and cook for 5 minutes. Add apricots and continue to simmer, covered, for 5 more minutes. (If using all apricots, simmer for only 5 minutes *total*.) Add raisins, currants, dates, vinegar, sugar, ginger, mustard seeds, and chili powder. Simmer, uncovered, stirring more frequently as mixture thickens, until most of the liquid has evaporated and chutney is thick, 45 minutes to 1 hour. Season to taste with salt.

Seal in jars and process (directions follow); or let cool, then cover and refrigerate for up to 1 month.

To process, ladle hot chutney into 6 or 7 hot sterilized ½-pint canning jars, filling to within ¼ inch of rims. Run a narrow spatula down between chutney and jar to release any air. Wipe off rims; top with scalded lids, then firmly screw on bands.

Place jars, sides not touching, on a rack in a canning kettle or other deep pan half-full of hot water. Add more hot water to cover jars by 1 to 2 inches. Bring water to a simmer, then cover and simmer for 10 minutes.

Lift out jars and let cool on a towel away from drafts. Test seal of each jar by pressing lid. If it stays down, seal is good. If it pops when pressed, there's no seal; store unsealed chutney in the refrigerator and use within 1 month.

Pickled Strawberries & Pears

PREPARATION TIME: 10 to 15 minutes, plus 30 minutes to heat and cool liquid
CHILLING TIME: At least 4 hours
PER ¼ CUP: 50 calories, .20 gram protein, 13 grams carbohydrate, .08 gram total fat, 0 milligram cholesterol, 3 milligrams sodium

Tarragon-laced and wine-soaked, this simple relish of strawberries and pears appeared in Sunset Magazine in a springtime picnic menu, as an accompaniment to cold roast pork loin and wild rice salad.

Makes about 8 cups

    2½ **cups dry white wine**
     1 **tablespoon dry tarragon or 2 tablespoons fresh tarragon**
     1 **cup sugar**
     ¼ **cup raspberry vinegar or lemon juice**
     4 **cups hulled medium-size strawberries**
     2 **cans (1 lb. *each*) Bartlett pear halves in light syrup, drained**

In a 2- to 3-quart pan, combine wine, tarragon, and sugar. Bring to a boil over high heat, stirring until sugar is dissolved. Remove from heat, add vinegar, and let cool.

Place strawberries and pears in a 2-quart jar. Pour tarragon syrup over fruit; cover and refrigerate for at least 4 hours or up to 1 day. Serve cold or at room temperature.

Young Ginger Pickles

PREPARATION TIME: About 15 minutes to assemble
CHILLING TIME: About 36 hours
PER TABLESPOON: 18 calories, .12 gram protein, 4 grams carbohydrate, .05 gram total fat, 0 milligram cholesterol, 104 milligrams sodium

Young ginger comes to market, mostly from Hawaii, between July and September. Though many Western supermarkets stock it, Asian grocers offer the most plentiful supply. The young rhizomes differ from older ones in their translucent, pink-tinged skin and relatively mild, yet penetrating flavor. Capture their youthful zest in this traditional sushi relish.

Makes 2 cups

    ½ **pound fresh young ginger, scrubbed and rinsed**
     2 **tablespoons salt**
     ¾ **cup distilled white vinegar**
     ½ **cup sugar**

Slice ginger across the grain as thinly as possible (you'll have about 1¾ cups). Mix with salt. Cover and refrigerate until next day. Rinse well and drain.

In a 1- to 2-quart pan, combine vinegar with sugar; bring to a boil, stirring. Add ginger. Return to a boil, then remove from heat and let cool. Cover and refrigerate for at least 24 hours or up to 3 weeks.

Sour-Hot Lemon Pickles

PREPARATION TIME: About 10 minutes
MICROWAVING TIME: About 20 minutes, plus at least 30 minutes to cool
PER ¼ CUP: 83 calories, 1 gram protein, 7 grams carbohydrate, 8 grams total fat, 0 milligram cholesterol, 1649 milligrams sodium

Though these Nepalese pickles are traditionally sun-cured, you can get excellent (and much faster) results by using a microwave oven. Try the spicy-hot pickles with Curried Lentil Stew (page 213).

Makes 2 cups

    1½ **tablespoons black or white mustard seeds**
        About 1 pound lemons (4 or 5 lemons)
     1 **fresh hot chile such as jalapeño (optional), stemmed, seeded, and finely chopped**
     2 **tablespoons salt**
     2 **teaspoons cayenne**
     ¼ **cup salad oil**

Toast mustard seeds in a 6- to 8-inch frying pan over medium heat just until seeds begin to pop, 2 to 5 minutes, shaking pan frequently. Set aside.

Trim ends off lemons. Cut lemons in half crosswise, then cut each half into about 1-inch wedges; pluck out obvious seeds. Place lemons in a nonmetallic 2½- to 3-quart bowl; stir in chile (if used), salt, cayenne, oil, and mustard seeds.

Cover bowl with plastic wrap. Microwave on **HIGH (100%)** until mixture is slightly thickened and lemons are easy to pierce, 16 to 20 minutes, stirring every 4 minutes. Let cool. Serve; or cover and refrigerate for up to 4 months.

Jalapeño Jelly

PREPARATION TIME: About 15 minutes
COOKING TIME: About 10 minutes, plus about 10 minutes to fill jars
PER TABLESPOON: 43 calories, .01 gram protein, 11 grams carbohydrate, 0 gram total fat, 0 milligram cholesterol, 22 milligrams sodium

Jalapeño chiles give assertive flavor to this jelly, which in turn makes an emphatically good condiment for chicken, pork, ham, or beef.

Makes about 7 cups

> **About 5 medium-size canned jalapeño chiles**
> **½ cup chopped green bell pepper**
> **¼ cup chopped red bell pepper (or additional green bell pepper)**
> **6 cups sugar**
> **2½ cups cider vinegar**
> **2 pouches (3 oz. *each*) liquid pectin**

Wearing rubber gloves, rinse jalapeño chiles; discard stem ends, any bits of blackened skin, and about half the seeds. Chop jalapeños (you should have ¼ cup). In a blender or food processor, whirl jalapeños, green bell pepper, and red bell pepper until finely ground (or put through a food chopper fitted with a fine blade). Put ground vegetables and any juice in a 5- to 6-quart pan; stir in sugar and vinegar.

Bring to a rolling boil over high heat, stirring constantly. All at once pour in liquid pectin, return to a rolling boil, and boil for 1 minute, stirring constantly. Remove from heat and skim off foam. Pour hot jelly into about 7 hot sterilized ½-pint canning jars, filling to within ¼ inch of rims. Wipe off rims; top with scalded lids, then firmly screw on bands. Let cool on a towel away from drafts, then test seal of each jar by pressing lid. If it stays down, seal is good. If it pops when pressed, there's no seal; store unsealed jelly in the refrigerator.

Garlic or Shallot Jelly

PREPARATION TIME: About 20 minutes to flavor vinegar
STANDING TIME: At least 24 hours for vinegar
COOKING TIME: About 10 minutes for jelly; about 30 minutes to fill and process jars
PER TABLESPOON: 43 calories, .04 gram protein, 11 grams carbohydrate, 0 gram total fat, 0 milligram cholesterol, 1 milligram sodium

One whiff of these jellies clues you to the bold presence of garlic or shallots. Both jellies are fragrant, tart, yet sweet—and both are excellent relishes for beef, lamb, or chicken.

Makes 7 cups

> **½ cup finely chopped garlic or shallots**
> **About 3 cups white wine vinegar**
> **2 cups water**
> **6 cups sugar**
> **2 pouches (3 oz. *each*) liquid pectin**

Combine garlic (or shallots) and 3 cups of the vinegar in a 2- to 2½-quart pan over medium heat. Simmer gently, uncovered, for 15 minutes. Remove from heat and pour into a glass jar. Cover and let stand at room temperature for 24 to 36 hours, then pour through a fine strainer into a bowl, pressing garlic or shallots with the back of a spoon to squeeze out as much liquid as possible; discard residue. Measure liquid and add vinegar if needed to make 2 cups.

In a 5- to 6-quart pan, combine flavored vinegar, water, and sugar. Bring to a rolling boil over medium-high heat. Stir in pectin and bring to a boil that cannot be stirred down. Boil, stirring constantly, for 1 minute.

Skim off foam, then spoon hot jelly into about 7 hot sterilized ½-pint canning jars, filling to within ¼ inch of rims. Wipe off rims; top with scalded lids, then firmly screw on bands. Process jars in a hot water bath, let cool, and test seals as directed for Mango-Apricot-Date Chutney (page 226).

Pomegranate Jelly

PREPARATION TIME: 35 to 40 minutes for fruit; up to 1 hour to drain juice
COOKING TIME: About 10 minutes, plus about 10 minutes to fill jars
PER TABLESPOON: 38 calories, .02 gram protein, 10 grams carbohydrate, 0 gram total fat, 0 milligram cholesterol, .29 milligram sodium

How do you get the seeds from a pomegranate without making a mess or spending the whole afternoon at the task? Sunset *offers a helpful suggestion—you work under water. Once you've removed the seeds, use their juice for this sparkling jelly.*

Makes about 6 cups

> **7 or 8 medium-size pomegranates**
> **¼ cup lemon juice**
> **1 package (2 oz.) dry pectin**
> **4½ cups sugar**

Cut crown end off each pomegranate and lightly score peel lengthwise down sides, dividing fruit into quarters. Immerse fruit in a bowl of cool water and let soak for 5 minutes. Holding fruit under water, break sections apart with your fingers and separate seeds from pulp; as you work, seeds sink to bottom and pulp and peel float. With a strainer, skim off pulp and peel; discard. Scoop up seeds and drain in a colander; let dry on paper towels.

Whirl 1½ to 2 cups pomegranate seeds at a time in a blender until liquefied. Set a colander in a bowl; line colander with moistened cheesecloth. Pour in pomegranate purée and let juice drip through cloth. To speed the process, gather edges of cloth with rubber-gloved hands and twist *slowly* (juice tends to squirt) to extract liquid. You need 3½ cups juice *total*.

In a 5- to 6-quart pan, combine pomegranate juice, lemon juice, and pectin. Bring to a rolling boil over high heat, stirring constantly. Add sugar and stir to blend; bring to a rolling boil, then boil for exactly 2 minutes. Skim off foam. Fill about 6 hot sterilized ½-pint canning jars, seal, let cool, and test seals as directed for Jalapeño Jelly (at left).

Fresh Fruit Jams

The West's cornucopia of fruits and berries has inspired many delectable uses. In this case, you dehydrate fruit purées to create splendid, fresh-tasting, naturally sweet jams. Your oven, a dehydrator, or warm sunshine does the drying. As the moisture evaporates, the purée thickens like cooked jam, but the color is more natural—and because dehydrating concentrates the fruit flavor, you need very little added sugar or honey.

Dehydrated jam, step by step

1. For each batch of jam, prepare a drying tray or pan as directed for the drying method you're using.

2. Wash unpeeled fruit, using mild soap or detergent; rinse very well and pat dry. Rinse berries in cool water; drain well on paper towels.

3. Prepare 2 cups fruit purée (directions follow). Adjust sweetness after dehydrating, since jams taste sweeter after drying.

4. Pour up to 2 cups fruit purée into prepared drying tray or pan and spread to make a layer about ⅜ inch thick. Dry as directed for each method. About once an hour, carefully scrape jam from edges with a rubber spatula; stir well, then spread evenly again.

5. Dry until jam is almost the thickness you prefer (it will be slightly thicker when cold). Jams take 2 to 4 hours in oven or dehydrator, often a little longer in the sun. Spoon jam into a container and stir in a little more sugar, honey, or lemon juice, as desired.

6. Cover and refrigerate for up to 6 days or freeze for up to 6 months. Makes about 1 cup apricot, peach, plum, or berry jam, about ½ cup melon jam.

Drying methods for jams

To dehydrate jams, use any of these three methods.

OVEN DRYING. Lay a continuous sheet of parchment paper in a 10- by 15-inch rimmed baking pan; paper should extend beyond pan rims. Or line pan with a continuous sheet of plastic wrap and secure wrap to underside of pan with tape.

Pour purée into prepared pan; put pan in oven, heated to 120° to 130° (lowest setting for most ovens). Leave oven door open several inches and check temperature with an oven thermometer.

DEHYDRATOR DRYING. If your unit has a door and removable drying trays, cover 1 tray with a continuous sheet of plastic wrap; secure wrap at each corner and on sides with tape.

If your unit has drying trays that stack over a heat source on the bottom, set a shallow-rimmed metal, plastic, or glass container on 1 tray; choose a container that's about tray size but permits air circulation all around it. Or make a container of double-thick heavy foil: turn up 1 inch on all sides and pinch together at corners to secure; each container should have an area of at least 60 square inches and should be shaped to fit dimensions of your dehydrator trays.

Use temperature recommended for drying fruit in your dehydrator, or about 130°. Be sure to preheat dehydrator.

SUN DRYING. The weather should be 85° or warmer with less than 60 percent relative humidity, and you should start early in the day.

Pour fruit purée into a 9- by 13-inch glass, metal, or plastic pan and spread evenly. Set pan on a level surface, such as a table, in full sun. Cover pan with plastic wrap, leaving open about 1 inch down 1 long side.

If purée is not sufficiently dehydrated by day's end, bring it indoors and refrigerate, covered; return to the sun the next day.

Fruit purées for jams

The quantities given below yield 2 cups of each purée. For best flavor, start with ripe, peak-season fruit.

APRICOT. Halve and pit about 1½ pounds ripe **apricots** (about 3 cups halves). In a blender or food processor, whirl until smooth. Blend in 1 tablespoon **lemon juice** and 2 to 4 tablespoons **honey** or sugar, depending on sweetness of apricots.

PEACH OR NECTARINE. Halve and pit about 4 medium-size (about 1½ lbs. *total*) peeled ripe **peaches** (or peeled or unpeeled nectarines); whirl in a blender or food processor until smooth. Blend in 1 tablespoon **lemon juice** and 2 to 4 tablespoons **sugar** or honey, depending on sweetness of fruit.

PLUM. Cut flesh away from pits of about 1¼ pounds ripe **plums** or prune plums (you should have about 3½ cups) and whirl in a blender or food processor until smooth. Blend in 2 to 4 tablespoons **sugar** or honey, depending on sweetness of plums; pour mixture into a 1½- to 2-quart pan. Bring to a simmer over medium heat, stirring occasionally. Cover and simmer for 2 minutes. Let cool slightly before pouring on prepared tray.

RASPBERRY, BOYSENBERRY, OR OLLALIEBERRY. Whirl about 3 cups **berries** in a blender or food processor until puréed, then press through a fine strainer and discard seeds. Combine purée with 1 tablespoon **lemon juice** and 4 to 6 tablespoons **sugar,** depending on sweetness of berries.

STRAWBERRY. Remove and discard stems from about 3 cups **strawberries.** Whirl berries in a blender or food processor until smooth. Blend in 1 tablespoon **lemon juice** and 2 to 4 tablespoons **sugar,** depending on sweetness of berries.

MELON. Cut peeled and seeded **cantaloupe, Persian, or honeydew melon** into chunks. In a blender or food processor, whirl enough melon to make 2 cups purée. Blend in 2 tablespoons **lemon juice** and 1 to 2 tablespoons **sugar** or honey, depending on sweetness of melon.

The Best of Sunset

BREADS

Fragrant, freshly baked bread is comforting food the world around—and an international array makes up Sunset's *list of favorites. Some are earthy and humble, like coarse, chewy Mother Loaf from Italy; some are light, tender, and showy, like Russian Kulich. Still others are rich in Western tradition. We include a full report on sourdough, the feisty leavening that made San Francisco famous. We explain how to bake crusty Pueblo bread, starting by building your own outdoor adobe oven. And we offer breads made with blue cornmeal, long used in New Mexico's cooking.*

For the kitchen artist, there's Portuguese Sweet Bread to twist and coil into golden loaves and buns; bright-eyed Spring Dove Breads; and Whimsy Bread, to shape however you please. There's plenty of novelty, too—Arab breads that puff into pockets, coffee can breads that pop their lids when it's time to bake, a spicy loaf made with green chiles. You'll find nothing ordinary in this chapter.

Basque shepherds came West to tend flocks in California, Nevada, and Idaho. In camp, they bake giant-size loaves in Dutch ovens, burying the pans in a pit—but for more predictable results, you can bake your Sheepherder's Bread (recipe on page 232) in a conventional oven.

Sheepherder's Bread

Pictured on page 230

PREPARATION TIME: About 1 hour
RISING TIME: About 2½ hours
BAKING TIME: About 50 minutes
PER SERVING: 209 calories, 5 grams protein, 37 grams carbohydrate, 4 grams total fat, 10 milligrams cholesterol, 207 milligrams sodium

As they tend their flocks in remote Western rangelands, Basque shepherds still bake big loaves of bread in Dutch ovens buried in pits. The same simple bread can also be baked in a conventional oven—with much more predictable and reliable results. To produce the unique dome shape and ring-patterned top, you'll need a 5-quart cast-iron or cast-aluminum covered Dutch oven.

Makes 1 very large loaf, 24 to 26 servings

 3 cups very hot tap water
 ½ cup (¼ lb.) butter or margarine
 ⅓ cup sugar
 2 teaspoons salt
 2 packages active dry yeast
   About 9½ cups all-purpose flour
   Salad oil

In a large bowl, combine hot water, butter, sugar, and salt. Stir until butter is melted; let cool to about 110°F. Stir in yeast and set in a warm place until bubbly, about 5 minutes.

With a heavy spoon, beat in about 5 cups of the flour to make a thick batter. Stir in about 3½ cups more flour or enough to make a stiff dough. Turn dough out onto a floured board; knead until smooth and satiny, 10 to 20 minutes, adding more flour as required to prevent sticking. Place dough in a greased bowl; turn over to grease top. Cover with plastic wrap and let rise in a warm place until doubled, about 1½ hours.

Punch dough down and knead briefly on a floured board to release air; shape into a smooth ball. With a circle of foil, cover the inside bottom of a 5-quart cast-iron or cast-aluminum Dutch oven. Grease foil, inside of Dutch oven, and underside of lid with oil.

Place dough in Dutch oven and cover with lid. Let rise in a warm place until dough pushes up lid by about ½ inch, about 1 hour (watch closely).

Bake, covered with lid, in a 375° oven for 12 minutes. Remove lid and continue to bake until loaf is golden brown, 30 to 35 more minutes. Remove from oven and turn out of pan onto a rack (you'll need a helper). Peel off foil, turn loaf upright, and let cool.

Light & Crusty French Bread

PREPARATION TIME: About 45 minutes
RISING TIME: 5½ to 6 hours (includes resting time)
BAKING TIME: 30 to 40 minutes, plus about 20 minutes to dry and crisp loaves
PER SERVING: 171 calories, 6 grams protein, 35 grams carbohydrate, .51 gram total fat, 0 milligram cholesterol, 221 milligrams sodium

After delving into the secrets of professional bakeries, we've come up with a light, crackly-crusted French bread that rivals the best bakery fare. The following tricks of the trade make such a feat achievable—but be warned, the process does take time.

Professional bakers start with an unusually soft dough, so soft that it needs support from a special canvas cradle while rising. Today, you can buy such cradles in many cookware shops.

Another secret is to let the dough rise slowly, in three stages rather than the usual two. Finally, when the loaves are in the oven, you spray them lightly with water from a mister—the type used for houseplants. This duplicates the crisping effect that a commercial oven's steam jets have on crusts.

Makes 3 regular loaves or 4 baguettes, 18 to 20 servings *total*

 2 packages active dry yeast
 2½ cups tepid water (70° to 75°F)
 2 teaspoons salt
   About 6½ cups bread flour or unbleached all-purpose flour
 ¼ cup cornmeal

In a large bowl, sprinkle yeast over water and let stand for about 5 minutes to soften. Stir in salt. Then mix in flour in 1 of the following ways.

With a heavy-duty mixer and dough hook. Add 5 cups of the flour, 1 cup at a time, beating on medium speed until smooth. Continue to beat until dough begins to pull from sides of bowl. Gradually beat in 1 to 1½ cups more flour, ¼ cup at a time, until dough begins to clean sides of bowl.

With a regular mixer and by hand. Add 4 cups of the flour, 1 cup at a time, beating on medium speed until dough begins to pull from sides of bowl, about 10 minutes. Gradually add as much more flour as your mixer can handle, beating as much as possible with mixer. Then, using a heavy spoon or your hands, gradually beat in remaining flour, ½ cup at a time.

Dough mixed by either method should be soft, but not too sticky to knead. Turn dough out onto a floured board and knead until smooth, up to 15 minutes for hand-mixed dough; add more flour as required to prevent sticking. Dough is ready when you can slap your hand against it and hold it there for 10 seconds, with dough just barely sticking to your hand.

Place dough in a well-greased bowl and turn over to grease top. Cover with plastic wrap. Let rise away from drafts at 70° to 80°F (use a room thermometer to check) until doubled, 2 to 2½ hours. Do not try to speed rising by setting dough in a warmer place; it will become sticky and hard to handle.

Punch dough down, cover, and let rise at 70° to 80°F a second time until tripled in size, about 1½ more hours. Meanwhile, assemble canvas bread cradles; use 3 for regular-size loaves, 4 for baguettes. Lightly dust inside of canvas with flour.

Punch dough down and turn out onto a floured board. Divide into 3 or 4 pieces; cover with plastic wrap and let rest for 15 minutes. For each loaf, shape 1 portion into a ball (keep others covered), then flatten into a 6-inch round. Fold round in half and flatten again. Repeat folding and flattening process 2 more times, then roll dough into a smooth 15-inch loaf; pinch seam.

Lay loaf, seam side up, in a cradle and cover with a clean cloth. Let rise at room temperature, away from drafts, until very puffy and more than doubled, 1½ to 2 hours. Meanwhile, lightly grease two 12- by 15-inch baking sheets and sprinkle each with 2 tablespoons of the cornmeal.

Turn 2 loaves out onto 1 baking sheet (seam sides should be down); quickly make 3 diagonal slashes on top of each with a razor blade (loaves will appear to deflate, but they'll puff up again as they bake). Spray with water and *immediately* place in a 450° oven. Repeat steps with remaining loaves.

Bake loaves at 450° for 9 minutes; spray with a fine mist of water 3 minutes, 6 minutes, and 9 minutes after start of baking. Reduce oven temperature to 425° and bake for 16 to 20 more minutes (*total baking time is 25 to 30 minutes*). If you have only 1 oven, stagger racks; switch positions of baking sheets halfway through baking time.

Turn oven off and leave door open for 3 minutes. Then close door and let loaves stand in oven for 15 minutes. Transfer loaves to racks and let cool.

Bread is best served freshly baked. If you wish to store, wrap and freeze loaves; then unwrap and thaw as needed. To reheat, set loaves directly on racks of a 350° oven until crusty and heated through, about 15 minutes; let cool slightly before serving.

Mother Loaf

PREPARATION TIME: About 1 hour (by hand)
RISING TIME: About 4 hours
BAKING TIME: About 50 minutes
PER SERVING: 162 calories, 5 grams protein, 33 grams carbohydrate, .48 gram total fat, 0 milligram cholesterol, 119 milligrams sodium

Though fine texture and even shape were for years considered essential characteristics of good bread, today there's a growing appreciation for more rustic, country-style loaves like this one. Affectionately called the "mother loaf" because it's so basic, it's the kind of bread that Italian farm women draw out of their stone ovens. The crust is crackly-crisp; the coarse interior is riddled with irregular holes. The hearty, resilient texture comes from using bread flour—and from plenty of beating.

Makes 1 loaf, 12 to 14 servings

  1 package active dry yeast
1¾ cups warm water (about 110°F)
  ¾ teaspoon salt
    About 4½ cups bread flour
    Cornmeal

In a large bowl, sprinkle yeast over warm water; let stand for about 5 minutes to soften. Stir in salt. Beat in flour in 1 of the following ways. If at any point mixer becomes too hot or dough climbs hook or beater, or your arm tires, let dough rest for up to 15 minutes, then continue.

With a heavy-duty mixer and dough hook. Add 4½ cups flour; mix on low speed to blend. Beat on high speed for 25 minutes.

With a regular mixer and by hand. Use 4 cups flour. Add 1½ to 1¾ cups of the flour to bowl; beat on low speed to blend, then on high speed for 25 to 30 minutes. With a heavy spoon, thoroughly beat in remaining 2¼ to 2½ cups flour, ¼ cup at a time.

By hand only. Use 4 cups flour. Add 2 cups of the flour and beat steadily with a heavy spoon for at least 30 minutes. Gradually add remaining 2 cups flour, ¼ cup at a time, beating at least 5 minutes after each addition.

At end of beating time, scrape dough down from bowl sides; cover bowl with plastic wrap. Let rise at room temperature until tripled, about 3 hours.

Meanwhile, grease a 14-inch pizza pan or 10- by 15-inch rimmed baking pan and sprinkle generously with cornmeal.

Do not punch or stir dough down. Using a bowl scraper to free dough from sides of bowl, gently ease dough out onto pan. With floured fingers, gently tuck dough edges under to shape a round loaf. Sprinkle dough with about 2 tablespoons flour; cover with a flour-dusted cloth. Let rise at room temperature until doubled and very puffy, about 1 hour. Remove cloth.

Bake in center of a 400° oven until golden brown and crusty, about 50 minutes. Transfer to a rack and let cool for at least 30 minutes. To serve, tear into chunks or cut into slices.

CRUSTY BREAD—a comfort shared by people all over the world—has always intrigued Sunset. We've sampled hearty loaves from many nations, reproduced them at home—and then offered the recipes to our readers. In 1971, we told how to construct an outdoor adobe oven for baking bread with a distinctively crackly crust.

Coffee Can Batter Bread

Pictured on facing page

PREPARATION TIME: About 35 minutes (beating with an electric mixer and by hand)
RISING TIME: About 1 hour
BAKING TIME: 45 to 60 minutes
PER SERVING: 191 calories, 5 grams protein, 35 grams carbohydrate, 3 grams total fat,
4 milligrams cholesterol, 171 milligrams sodium

Batter breads are made from very soft yeast doughs that are beaten vigorously, but not kneaded. Very popular at one time, and still fun to make, are loaves baked in 1- or 2-pound coffee cans. The can gives the loaf its distinctive shape—tall, round, and domed.

The plastic lids that come with the coffee cans prove useful at two different stages. First, they seal the batter in the can for freezing if you want to wait and bake the bread another time. Next, the lids tell you when the dough is ready to bake—they pop off! Don't be concerned if the lids pop off (from air pressure) before the dough reaches the top of the cans—just put the lids back on until the dough pushes them off.

Makes 2 small loaves or 1 large loaf, 12 to 14 servings *total*

> 1 package active dry yeast
> ½ cup warm water (about 110°F)
> ⅛ teaspoon ground ginger
> 3 tablespoons sugar
> 1½ cups milk or 1 can (12 oz.) evaporated milk
> 1 teaspoon salt
> 2 tablespoons salad oil
> About 4½ cups all-purpose flour
> Melted butter or margarine

In a large bowl, sprinkle yeast over warm water; blend in ginger and 1 tablespoon of the sugar. Let stand until bubbly, about 5 minutes. Stir in remaining 2 tablespoons sugar, milk, salt, and oil. Beat in flour in 1 of the following ways.

With a heavy-duty mixer and dough hook. Beat in 3 cups of the flour until dough begins to pull from sides of bowl; then beat in about 1½ cups more flour, ½ cup at a time, until dough almost pulls cleanly from sides of bowl.

With a regular mixer and by hand. Beat in 3 cups of the flour, 1 cup at a time. When dough is too stiff to beat with mixer, beat in about 1½ cups more flour with a heavy spoon, ½ cup at a time, until dough pulls from sides of bowl but is too soft to knead.

Divide batter in half and place 1 portion in each of 2 well-greased 1-pound coffee cans; or spoon all batter into 1 well-greased 2-pound coffee can. Cover with well-greased plastic can lids. (At this point, you may cover and freeze for up to 2 weeks.)

To continue, let covered cans stand in a warm place until batter rises and pushes off plastic lids—45 to 55 minutes for 1-pound cans, 55 to 60 minutes for a 2-pound can. *If frozen,* let batter stand in cans at room temperature until lids are pushed off—4 to 5 hours for 1-pound cans, 6 to 8 hours for a 2-pound can.

Set cans on lowest rack of a 350° oven. Bake, uncovered, until crust is very brown—about 45 minutes for 1-pound cans, about 60 minutes for a 2-pound can. Brush tops lightly with butter. Let cool in cans on a rack for about 5 minutes; then loosen loaves around edges of cans with a thin knife, slide bread from cans, and let cool in an upright position on rack. Serve warm or cool; to serve, slice crosswise.

ENGLISH MUFFIN BATTER BREAD

Follow basic directions for **Coffee Can Batter Bread,** but make these changes. Omit ginger; mix yeast with ⅔ cup **warm water** (about 110°F) and 4 teaspoons **sugar.** Let stand until puffy, about 15 minutes. Stir in 1 cup **milk** and ½ teaspoon **salt.** Using a heavy-duty mixer or a regular mixer as directed, mix in 2 cups **all-purpose flour;** beat to blend well, then add ½ teaspoon **baking soda** mixed with 1 tablespoon **water.** Continue to mix as directed, adding about 1½ cups more **all-purpose flour** or enough to make a stiff dough that is too soft to knead.

Fill 2 well-greased, cornmeal-dusted 1-pound coffee cans equally with batter. Cover cans and let batter rise as directed. Carefully remove lids and bake in a 375° oven until tops of loaves are very well browned, 25 to 30 minutes. Let cool as directed. Serve slices plain or toasted. Makes 2 loaves.

Bolillos

W E S T E R N   C L A S S I C

PREPARATION TIME: About 1 hour
RISING TIME: About 2 hours
BAKING TIME: 45 to 60 minutes
PER ROLL: 190 calories, 5 grams protein, 37 grams carbohydrate, 2 grams total fat,
4 milligrams cholesterol, 291 milligrams sodium

Bolillo describes the form of these Mexican rolls; roughly translated, the word means "spindle-shaped." To get the characteristic crisp outer crust, you brush the rolls with a cornstarch-water mixture just before baking. Bolillos are best served warm from the oven; try them as a dinner roll, or at breakfast with lots of butter and jam.

Makes 16 rolls

> 2 cups water
> 1½ tablespoons sugar
> 2 teaspoons salt
> 2 tablespoons butter or margarine
> 1 package active dry yeast
> About 6 cups all-purpose flour
> 1 teaspoon cornstarch and ½ cup water, stirred together

No kneading? Our readers couldn't believe that such a tender, springy loaf could result without it. But Coffee Can Batter Bread (recipe on facing page) needs no kneading or special shaping—two obvious reasons for its lasting popularity.

In a 1- to 2-quart pan, combine the 2 cups water, sugar, salt, and butter. Warm over low heat, stirring, to about 110°F. Pour into a large bowl; stir in yeast until dissolved. Using an electric mixer or a heavy spoon, beat in 5 cups of the flour until dough is stretchy.

Scrape dough out onto a board coated with about ½ cup more flour; knead until dough is smooth and velvety, about 10 minutes. Add more flour as required to prevent sticking. Place dough in a greased bowl and turn over to grease top. Cover with plastic wrap and let rise in a warm place until almost doubled, about 1½ hours.

Punch dough down and knead briefly on a lightly floured board to release air. Shape dough into a 16-inch roll and divide it into 16 equal pieces. Knead each piece into a smooth ball; shape each ball into an oblong by rolling it and gently pulling from center to ends until roll is about 4 inches long (center should be thicker than ends). Place rolls about 3 inches apart on greased baking sheets; you'll need 3 baking sheets, each about 12 by 15 inches.

In a standard-size oven with 2 racks, you can bake 2 sheets of rolls at a time. If you have only 1 oven, cover the third pan of shaped bolillos with plastic wrap and refrigerate for up to 30 minutes.

Cover rolls lightly with plastic wrap and let rise in a warm place until almost doubled, about 35 minutes (45 minutes if refrigerated). Remove plastic wrap.

In a 2- to 4-cup pan, bring cornstarch-water mixture to a boil, stirring. Let cool slightly, then brush evenly over rolls. With a very sharp knife or a razor blade, cut a slash about ¾ inch deep and 2 inches long on top of each roll.

Adjust oven racks so they are equally spaced in oven from top to bottom, then stagger baking sheets to get the best heat circulation. Bake rolls in a 375° oven until they are golden brown and sound hollow when tapped, 35 to 40 minutes; switch positions of baking sheets halfway through baking. If made ahead, let cool on racks, then wrap airtight and store at room temperature until next day (freeze for longer storage). To reheat, place rolls (thawed if frozen) directly on racks of a 350° oven until hot, 15 to 20 minutes.

Bread from Your Own Adobe Oven

Over the years, *Sunset* Magazine has published at least a dozen stories on baking bread in adobe ovens similar to those used by the Pueblo Indians. In 1940, we featured such an oven on our cover. An outdoor oven was our cover subject again in August, 1971—and in that issue, we also gave simple instructions for building your own primitive oven.

Our Pueblo oven makes impressive bread with a spectacular crisp crust, but it also handles other foods, such as roasts and vegetables, with ease. Operating the oven is a straightforward matter—you build a fire in it to heat walls and floor, then clean it out and cook in the declining heat.

The oven withstands rain and sun, but should you tire of it, you can break the crust with a sledgehammer and free the unmortared interior bricks and concrete blocks.

Building materials

You'll need concrete blocks (6 by 8 by 16 inches); bricks; 4-inch concrete wire; chicken wire; cement; plenty of mud (any soil type from loamy to hard clay will do); an empty 1-pound can (both ends removed); plastic sheeting to cover the oven while its mud coating cures; and exterior latex paint. To form the oven's top contour, use a 28-gallon paper barrel or drum (about 27 inches tall), split lengthwise with a hacksaw or saber saw. Buy the drum from a lumberyard or check the listings under "Barrels & Drums" in the Yellow Pages.

Finally, you'll need a 2-inch-thick wooden oven door, at least 18 inches tall and wide. Give it an arched top and be sure to add a handle.

Constructing the oven

Arrange and level 12 concrete blocks in a 32- by 48-inch rectangle. Top with 2 layers of bricks (you'll need 96 bricks). Cut a draft hole to fit a 1-pound can in top curve of bottom end of halved drum; then set cut edge of drum on a U-shaped wall of bricks stacked 3 high. (This takes 33 more bricks—three 3-layer stacks beneath end of drum, plus four 3-layer stacks supporting each side.) Shape a 3- by 4-foot piece of 4-inch concrete wire over drum, tucking the excess under drum front. Mold a 3-by 4-foot piece of chicken wire over top and back of drum; cut out wire over draft hole.

Fit an empty 1-pound can with both ends removed in draft hole, leaving 4 inches protruding outside drum. Then force blended mud through wire onto drum, making walls at least 4 inches thick. To make blended mud, mix 12 shovelfuls mud with 4 shovelfuls concrete plus enough water to make a thick, malleable paste; you need about 3 bags of cement *total*.

Set door in place. Mold a close-fitting oven opening around door; remove door when mud has firmed slightly. Smooth surface of oven by hand with a little water. Cover with wet cloths and plastic sheeting.

Let cure for 4 to 5 days, moistening cloths frequently to keep them wet. Then uncover and paint with exterior latex. (After frequent use, repaint to help conceal cracks and smoke marks.)

Heating & cleaning the oven

Begin by heating the oven with a blazing, well-fed wood fire. Let fire burn until outside of oven is hot to the touch, about 3 hours; keep wood loosely piled so draft can help fire burn vigorously.

Working quickly, scoop out wood and place in a fireproof container such as a covered barbecue. Clear oven corners with a hoe. Sweep oven out with a damp broom, then clean with a slightly damp cloth mop.

Plug draft hole with wet rags, then check the heat by setting a mercury oven thermometer (one that registers up to 700°F) in middle of oven where you can easily see it. If oven is properly heated, temperature will be near 600°F. Leave oven open to cool; depending on drafts, air temperature, and original heat of oven, it will take 30 to 40 minutes to drop to bread baking temperature of 325°F.

A warning: The oven holds intense heat, and can char a loaf or roast in very few minutes if too hot. Trust the readings of your oven thermometer; most cooks who have trouble put the food in the oven before it is cool enough.

An adobe oven dinner

To produce a meal of distinction from your adobe oven, follow this routine.

When oven temperature drops to 500°, push a 9- or 10-inch square baking pan with rack holding a 5-pound cross-rib or sirloin tip roast (with meat thermometer in thickest part) to very back of oven, but *do not* close door. Just before oven is ready for bread (about 350°), put alongside pan as many as 6 *each* medium-size russet potatoes (scrubbed) and medium-size onions in their skins.

Put in Adobe Oven Bread (recipe follows) and set door in place; bake as directed for 1 hour to 1 hour and 20 minutes *total*.

Remove baked bread to hearth to cool; reclose oven and let roast and vegetables continue cooking until meat thermometer registers 135° to 140°F, about 45 more minutes.

Slice roast, peel onions, split potatoes, break bread, and apply butter, salt, and pepper as needed. Serve with green salad and wine.

Adobe Oven Bread

1 package active dry yeast
4 teaspoons sugar
4 cups warm water (about 110°F)
1 tablespoon salt
11 to 12 cups all-purpose flour
1 large egg and ¼ cup water, beaten together

In a large bowl, sprinkle yeast and sugar over warm water; let stand for about 5 minutes to soften. With a heavy spoon, beat in salt and 10 cups of the flour, then scrape dough out onto a board coated with 1 cup more flour. Pat some of the flour over dough (it is sticky). Then knead until dough is smooth and velvety, about 10 minutes; add as little flour to board as possible (just enough to prevent sticking).

Place dough in a greased bowl and turn over to grease top. Cover with plastic wrap and let rise in a warm place until doubled, about 1¼ hours.

Punch dough down and scrape out onto a lightly floured board; knead briefly to release air. Divide dough into 2 to 8 equal pieces. Shape each piece by kneading into a smooth ball; then (if you like) form an oval or long loaf.

Place loaves well apart on floured muslin cloth on baking sheets; dust lightly with flour and cover with cloth. Let loaves rise until puffy, 30 to 40 minutes. (Refrigerate briefly if loaves are ready before oven has cooled sufficiently.)

In the declining heat of this handsome, handmade mud oven, you can bake crusty loaves that match the best you've ever tasted. The oven cooks other foods, too; instructions for an adobe oven dinner are given on the facing page.

When preheated adobe oven has cooled to about 350°, prepare to transfer loaves (1 or 2 at a time) onto a floured bread paddle: lift cloth to roll a loaf slightly onto your palm, then slip bread paddle under loaf and roll it onto the paddle. (To improvise a bread paddle, secure a steady handle to a smooth, thin board large enough to hold at least 1 loaf.)

Slash top of each loaf in several places with a very sharp knife or razor blade, then brush surface with egg mixture; take care not to let egg run onto board.

When preheated adobe oven has cooled to between 325° and 300°, slip loaves onto clean oven floor; if you can, load from front to back, since back is hottest. Work quickly. When all loaves are in oven, set door in place. Check temperature in 5 minutes; if above 400°, remove door until temperature drops to 350°, then set door in place again. After a total of 10 minutes, use a mister to spray loaves all over with water. Close door; after 10 more minutes, spray loaves with more water.

Close door and continue to bake until loaves are a rich golden brown, 40 to 60 minutes, depending on size of loaves and oven temperature. Pull out onto oven hearth to cool; serve while still slightly warm to touch or when cooled completely. Break or slice loaves. Makes 2 large or 8 small loaves.

Note: In baking bread in an adobe oven, the most critical timing comes when dough is ready to shape. A team operation works best, as loaves should be formed just before you clean oven and steps may overlap.

A good timetable is to start the fire first; make dough about 1½ hours before you expect oven to be ready to clear; shape loaves and at once clear oven to start cooling it. If loaves are ready to bake before oven has cooled, refrigerate them; if oven is ready first, close door.

Dark Rye Bread

Pictured below

PREPARATION TIME: About 1 hour
RISING TIME: About 3½ hours (includes resting time)
BAKING TIME: About 35 minutes
PER SERVING: 181 calories, 6 grams protein, 36 grams carbohydrate, 2 grams total fat, 0 milligram cholesterol, 246 milligrams sodium

This deli-style rye is a perfect sandwich bread for hearty fillings of sliced meats and cheeses. Darkly caramelized sugar and unsweetened cocoa give the loaf its deep brown color; the sturdy texture comes from dark rye flour.

A note of caution: When sugar caramelizes to this degree, it smokes; it also spatters when water is added. Be sure there's ample ventilation around your range; protect your hands with heavy potholders or oven mitts.

Makes 2 loaves, 16 to 18 servings *total*

½ **cup sugar**
¾ **cup boiling water**
3 **packages active dry yeast**
2 **cups warm water (about 110°F)**
¼ **cup unsweetened cocoa**
2 **teaspoons salt**
2 **tablespoons caraway seeds**
2 **tablespoons solid vegetable shortening, butter, or margarine, melted**
 About 3½ cups all-purpose flour
2 **cups dark rye flour**
2 **tablespoons cornmeal**

Pour sugar into a 10- to 12-inch nonstick frying pan. Place over medium-high heat. As sugar melts, shake and tilt pan to mix liquid with sugar. Continue to cook until sugar smokes and is very dark in color (but not charred and burned smelling), about 2½ minutes. Immediately add boiling water; stir until melted sugar is dissolved and liquid is reduced to ½ cup. Let cool.

In a large bowl, sprinkle yeast over warm water and let stand for 5 minutes to soften. Add cooled sugar mixture, cocoa, salt, caraway seeds, shortening, and 2 cups of the all-purpose flour. Beat until smooth. Add rye flour. Using a regular electric mixer or a heavy-duty mixer and dough hook, beat on medium speed for 4 minutes. Using a dough hook or your hands, work in 1 cup more all-purpose flour.

Sprinkle ¼ cup more all-purpose flour on a board; scrape dough out onto board, cover, and let rest for 10 minutes. Then knead until dough is elastic and just tacky to the touch, about 10 minutes, adding more flour as required to prevent sticking.

Place dough in a greased bowl; turn over to grease top. Cover with plastic wrap and let rise in a warm place until doubled, about 1 hour. Punch dough down, turn over, cover, and let rise again until doubled, about 1 more hour.

Sprinkle a 12- by 15-inch baking sheet evenly with cornmeal. Punch dough down and knead briefly on a floured board to release air. Divide in half. Shape each half into a smooth ball and flatten slightly; place loaves 3 to 4 inches apart on baking sheet. Cover lightly with plastic wrap and let rise until doubled, about 1 hour and 15 minutes. Remove plastic wrap.

Bake in a 375° oven until bread sounds hollow when tapped, about 35 minutes. Let cool on racks.

For a picnic, tasty basics include cold meats, cheeses, and dark rye bread. In our recipe (above), we pass on professional bakers' secrets to creating those incredibly good, dark deli loaves.

Whole Wheat Hearth Bread

PREPARATION TIME: About 30 minutes
RISING TIME: About 1¾ hours
BAKING TIME: About 30 minutes
PER SERVING: 146 calories, 5 grams protein, 29 grams carbohydrate, 2 grams total fat, 3 milligrams cholesterol, 75 milligrams sodium

Unlike pan breads, hearth breads are baked freeform, unconstrained by the sides and corners of a container. They're often a bit irregular in shape, but always homey and inviting. Cut into wedges or slices to serve.

Makes 2 loaves, 16 to 18 servings *total*

> **1 package active dry yeast**
> **2 cups warm water (about 110°F)**
> **2 tablespoons butter or margarine, at room temperature**
> **1 tablespoon honey**
> **½ teaspoon salt**
> **3 cups whole wheat flour**
> **About 2½ cups all-purpose flour**

In a small bowl, sprinkle yeast over ½ cup of the warm water; let stand for about 5 minutes to soften.

In a large bowl, blend butter, honey, and salt; add remaining 1½ cups warm water, yeast mixture, whole wheat flour, and 2 cups of the all-purpose flour. Stir with a heavy spoon until flour is moistened and dough holds together. Scrape out onto a floured board and knead until dough is smooth and velvety, about 10 minutes; add more flour as required to prevent sticking. Place dough in a greased bowl and turn over to grease top.

Cover dough with plastic wrap and let rise in a warm place until almost doubled, about 1 hour. Punch dough down; knead briefly on a lightly floured board to release air. Divide dough in half; shape each half into a smooth ball. Place balls well apart on a greased 12- by 15-inch baking sheet; press each with your palm until 1 inch thick. Cover lightly with plastic wrap; let rise until almost doubled, about 45 minutes. Remove plastic wrap.

Bake in a 375° oven until crust is light brown and a slender wooden skewer inserted into bread comes out clean, about 30 minutes. Let cool on racks.

Sopaipillas

W E S T E R N   C L A S S I C

PREPARATION TIME: About 40 minutes
RISING TIME: About 1 hour
DEEP-FRYING TIME: About 2 minutes per sopaipilla (several can cook at once)
PER SOPAIPILLA: 151 calories, 3 grams protein, 21 grams carbohydrate, 6 grams total fat, 4 milligrams cholesterol, 100 milligrams sodium

A springy yeast dough flecked with bits of whole wheat flour, rolled out thin and deep-fried, makes the light, tender bread pillows called sopaipillas. *Serve them hot—plain, drizzled with honey or syrup, or sprinkled with cinnamon sugar or powdered sugar. You can also split them, then stuff with savory fillings for sandwiches and appetizers, or with fruit and cream for desserts.*

Makes about 2 dozen sopaipillas

> **1 package active dry yeast**
> **¼ cup warm water (about 110°F)**
> **1½ cups milk**
> **3 tablespoons lard or solid vegetable shortening**
> **1 teaspoon salt**
> **2 tablespoons sugar**
> **1 cup whole wheat flour**
> **About 4 cups all-purpose flour**
> **Salad oil**
> **Honey (optional)**

In a large bowl, sprinkle yeast over warm water and let stand for about 5 minutes to soften.

Meanwhile, in a 1- to 2-quart pan, combine milk, lard, salt, and sugar; heat to 110°F (lard does not need to melt). Stir milk mixture into yeast mixture; add whole wheat flour and 3 cups of the all-purpose flour. Beat in 1 of the following ways.

With a heavy-duty mixer and dough hook. Beat until dough is very stretchy; then add about 1 cup more all-purpose flour, ¼ cup at a time, beating until dough pulls cleanly from sides of bowl.

With a regular mixer and by hand. Beat until dough is very stretchy; with a heavy spoon, beat in about 1 cup more all-purpose flour, ¼ cup at a time, until dough feels only slightly sticky when touched.

Scrape dough (mixed by either method) out onto a floured board. Knead until smooth and no longer sticky, adding more all-purpose flour as required.

Place dough in a greased bowl and turn over to grease top. Cover with plastic wrap and let stand at room temperature for 1 hour. Punch dough down. (At this point, you may cover and refrigerate until next day.)

Turn dough out onto a lightly floured board and knead briefly to release air. Divide dough into thirds. Roll out, a portion at a time, to a thickness of slightly less than ⅛ inch. Cut dough into 3½ by 5-inch rectangles. Place on lightly floured baking pans; cover. If you work quickly, you can let cut sopaipillas rest at room temperature for about 5 minutes; otherwise, refrigerate until all are ready to fry.

In a deep 10- to 12-inch frying pan or 3- to 4-quart pan, heat 1½ to 2 inches oil to 350°F on a deep-frying thermometer. Add 2 or 3 sopaipillas. When bread begins to puff, use a slotted spoon to gently push portion of bread where bubble is forming down into oil a few times—to help it puff evenly. Turn several times; cook just until golden brown on both sides, 1 to 2 minutes *total*. Drain on paper towels.

Serve sopaipillas as fried; or keep warm until all are fried. Eat hot sopaipillas plain or with honey.

If made ahead, let cool, then cover and refrigerate until next day (freeze for longer storage). To reheat, arrange sopaipillas (thawed if frozen) in a single layer on baking sheets and bake, uncovered, in a 300° oven just until warm, 5 to 8 minutes; turn once. Don't overheat or sopaipillas will become hard.

Peda Bread

PREPARATION TIME: About 40 minutes
RISING TIME: About 40 minutes
BAKING TIME: About 35 minutes
PER SERVING: 209 calories, 6 grams protein, 35 grams carbohydrate, 5 grams total fat, 18 milligrams cholesterol, 136 milligrams sodium

This flat, sesame-seeded bread is familiar in Western cities with sizable Armenian communities. Enjoy it warm and cut into wedges, with plenty of butter; or let cool and use as an excellent sandwich bread.

Makes 2 loaves, 16 to 18 servings *total*

> 2 packages active dry yeast
> ½ cup warm water (about 110°F)
> 1¾ cups warm milk (about 110°F)
> 2 tablespoons sugar
> 1 teaspoon salt
> About 3 tablespoons olive oil
> About 6 cups all-purpose flour
> 1 large egg yolk beaten with 1 tablespoon water
> ¼ cup sesame seeds

In a large bowl, sprinkle yeast over warm water and let stand for about 5 minutes to soften. Stir in milk, sugar, salt, and 3 tablespoons of the oil. Then mix in flour in 1 of the following ways.

With a heavy-duty mixer and dough hook. Add 3 cups of the flour; beat on medium speed for 5 minutes. Then add about 3 cups more flour; beat until dough is elastic and pulls cleanly from sides of bowl.

With a regular mixer and by hand. Add 3 cups of the flour and beat on medium speed for 5 minutes. With a heavy spoon, work in 2½ cups more flour. Spread about ½ cup more flour on a board; scrape dough out onto board. Knead until smooth and elastic, about 5 minutes, adding more flour as required to prevent sticking.

Cover dough (mixed by either method) with plastic wrap and let rest for 20 minutes. Knead on a lightly floured board to release air, then pinch off 2 small portions of dough, each about ½-cup size. Divide remaining large portion of dough in half. Knead each of these 2 portions into a smooth ball.

To make each loaf, place 1 large ball of dough on a greased 12- by 15-inch baking sheet and flatten into a round cake. Poke a hole in the center, then pull sides of hole in opposite directions to make a 4-inch-diameter hole. Flatten dough rim to make loaf 10 inches in diameter. Place 1 of the small balls of dough in center and flatten gently to fill hole. Brush lightly with oil. (At this point, you may cover loaves airtight with plastic wrap and refrigerate for 2 to 24 hours.)

Cover shaped loaves lightly with plastic wrap and let stand at room temperature for 20 minutes. (Or uncover refrigerated loaves and let stand at room temperature for 10 minutes.) Brush each loaf with egg yolk mixture, then sprinkle each with 2 tablespoons of the sesame seeds.

Bake in a 350° oven until crust is deep golden and a slender wooden skewer inserted in center of bread comes out clean, about 35 minutes. Let cool slightly on racks before cutting.

ARMENIAN immigrants clustered in California's Central Valley, where climate and geography reminded them of their home in Asia Minor. With them, they brought a wealth of delicious cooking. In 1934, Sunset editors described the how-to of re-creating an Armenian dinner from George Mardikian's Omar Khayyam Restaurant—then in Fresno, later in San Francisco. Regular reporting of other Armenian recipes has followed.

Arab Pocket Bread

PREPARATION TIME: About 1¼ hours
RISING TIME: About 2½ hours
BAKING TIME: About 6 minutes per bread (3 to 5 can bake at once)
PER POCKET BREAD: 214 calories, 6 grams protein, 44 grams carbohydrate, 1 gram total fat, 0 milligram cholesterol, 221 milligrams sodium

There are two basic tricks to making Arab breads puff up to form hollow pockets: the handling of the dough and the bake-broil cooking. You knead and shape each bread in the palm of your hand; be careful not to poke or stretch the dough rounds while they rest or when you transfer them to baking pans. If you have two ovens, set one at 475° and the other on "broil" to speed the baking.

Makes 20 pocket breads

> 1 package active dry yeast
> 1 tablespoon sugar
> 3 cups warm water (about 110°F)
> 2 teaspoons salt
> 1 tablespoon salad oil
> About 9 cups all-purpose flour

In a bowl, sprinkle yeast and sugar over warm water and let stand for about 5 minutes to soften yeast. Stir in salt and oil. Place 9 cups of the flour in a large bowl and make a well in center. Pour in about half the yeast mixture and mix with your hands until well combined. Add remaining yeast mixture, mixing and kneading until dough holds together.

Scrape dough out onto a floured board, shape into a log, and divide into 20 pieces; keep covered with plastic wrap. Flour your hands lightly. To shape each bread round, place a piece of dough in your palm. Use your other hand to pull dough out away from sides, then fold it back toward center and press in middle; work around edge, gently pressing and pulling dough until it's smooth on the palm side. Place rounds, smooth side up, on a cloth-lined tray; cover lightly with another cloth, then with a damp cloth (wrung out thoroughly). Let rise in a warm place until puffy, 1 to 1½ hours.

Place each bread on a floured board. Flatten with a rolling pin and roll out to form a round 6 inches in diameter, using 4 strokes in each direction. Shake off excess flour and place breads at least ½ inch apart on a dry cloth. Cover with another dry cloth; top with damp cloth. Cover all with plastic wrap. Let stand at room temperature until slightly puffy, about 1 hour. Meanwhile, adjust oven rack so it's 2 inches from oven bottom. Preheat oven to 475°.

Carefully transfer 3 to 5 breads to an ungreased 12- by 15-inch baking sheet, placing them about ½ inch apart. Bake until breads puff to form hollow pockets in center and bottoms are lightly browned, about 5 minutes. Immediately increase heat to broil and move baking sheet to 4 inches below heat. Broil until tops are lightly browned, about 1 minute. Slide breads off baking sheet onto a cloth (keep breads in a single layer). *Return oven to 475°* before baking next batch.

Let baked breads cool completely. If made ahead, press gently with your hand to flatten, then wrap airtight and refrigerate for up to 5 days.

Giant Upside-down Pecan Rolls

W E S T E R N   C L A S S I C

PREPARATION TIME: About 1¾ hours (includes resting time)
RISING TIME: About 3½ hours
BAKING TIME: About 35 minutes
PER ROLL: 1354 calories, 19 grams protein, 191 grams carbohydrate, 60 grams total fat, 178 milligrams cholesterol, 639 milligrams sodium

In the Pacific Northwest, particularly around Seattle, these super-size sticky buns are especially favored.

Makes 6 large rolls

⅔ cup **milk**
1¾ cups **sugar**
¾ teaspoon **salt**
¾ cup (⅜ lb.) **butter** or margarine
2 packages **active dry yeast**
½ cup **warm water** (about 110°F)
About 5½ cups **all-purpose flour**
2 large **eggs**
Brown Sugar–Nut Syrup (recipe follows)
1 tablespoon **ground cinnamon**
1 cup coarsely chopped **pecans**

In a 1- to 2-quart pan, combine milk, ¾ cup of the sugar, salt, and ½ cup of the butter (cut into small pieces). Stir over high heat until butter is melted. Let cool to about 110°F.

In a large bowl, sprinkle yeast over warm water and let stand for about 5 minutes to soften. Blend in cooled milk mixture. Add 3 cups of the flour and stir to moisten. Beat with an electric mixer on medium speed for 5 minutes. Beat in 1 whole egg and 1 egg yolk (reserve remaining white); beat in 1 cup more flour. With a heavy spoon, stir in 1 cup more flour.

Turn dough out onto a board coated with about ¼ cup flour. Knead until dough is smooth and elastic, about 10 minutes, adding more flour as required to prevent sticking. Place dough in a greased bowl; turn over to grease top. Cover with plastic wrap and let rise in a warm place until doubled, about 2 hours.

Punch dough down. Scrape out onto a lightly floured board and knead briefly to release air; let rest for 10 minutes. Meanwhile, make syrup. Then roll and stretch dough to make an 18- by 24-inch rectangle. Melt remaining ¼ cup butter; brush over dough.

Combine cinnamon and remaining 1 cup sugar; sprinkle evenly over dough, then sprinkle with pecans. Starting from an 18-inch side, roll dough up jelly roll style. Moisten edge of dough with water and pinch snugly against roll to seal. With a sharp knife, cut roll crosswise into 6 equal slices. Arrange slices, cut side up, in syrup-coated pan. Cover lightly with plastic wrap; let rise in a warm place until doubled, about 1½ hours. Remove plastic wrap.

Brush surface of rolls with reserved egg white beaten with 1 teaspoon water. Bake in a 350° oven until well browned, 30 to 35 minutes. Immediately invert onto a serving tray. Serve; or, if made ahead, let cool, wrap airtight, and freeze (let thaw wrapped). To reheat, wrap thawed rolls lightly in foil and set in a 350° oven until hot, 20 to 30 minutes.

BROWN SUGAR–NUT SYRUP. In a 1½- to 2-quart pan, combine ¼ cup (⅛ lb.) **butter** or margarine, 2 tablespoons **water,** and 1 cup firmly packed **dark brown sugar.** Bring to a boil over high heat; boil for 1 minute. Immediately pour into a 9- by 13-inch baking pan; tilt pan so syrup forms an even layer. Arrange 1 cup **pecan halves,** flat side up, on syrup.

Green Chile Bread

PREPARATION TIME: 40 to 45 minutes
RISING TIME: About 2½ hours
BAKING TIME: About 40 minutes
PER SERVING: 166 calories, 5 grams protein, 31 grams carbohydrate, 2 grams total fat, 6 milligrams cholesterol, 266 milligrams sodium

Since chiles appear in so many Western foods, it's no surprise that they sometimes show up in bread as well. This subtly green-hued loaf makes superb cheese sandwiches; toast the sliced bread to bring out the aroma and flavor of chiles.

Makes 1 loaf, 12 to 14 servings

1 can (7 oz.) **diced green chiles**
⅛ to ¼ teaspoon **cayenne** (optional)
1 package **active dry yeast**
¼ cup **warm water** (about 110°F)
½ cup **milk**
2 tablespoons **butter** or margarine
1 teaspoon **salt**
1 tablespoon **sugar**
4 to 4½ cups **all-purpose flour**

In a blender or food processor, whirl chiles until smoothly puréed; you should have ¾ cup. Taste purée; add cayenne if you want a hotter flavor.

In a large bowl, sprinkle yeast over water; let stand for about 5 minutes to soften. Meanwhile, in a 2- to 4-cup pan, heat milk and butter to 110°F (butter need not melt completely). Add to yeast along with salt, sugar, chile purée, and 1½ cups of the flour, stirring to moisten thoroughly.

Stir in 1½ cups more flour until moistened, then beat vigorously with a heavy spoon until dough forms long, stretchy strands, about 10 minutes. Scrape out onto a board coated with 1 cup more flour and knead until smooth, about 8 minutes; add more flour as required to prevent sticking. Place dough in a greased bowl; turn over to grease top.

Cover dough with plastic wrap and let rise in a warm place until doubled, about 1½ hours.

Punch dough down, turn out onto a floured board, and knead briefly to release air. Shape into a smooth loaf and place in a greased 5- by 9-inch loaf pan. Cover with plastic wrap and let rise in a warm place until dough has risen 1½ inches above pan rim, about 1 hour. Remove plastic wrap.

Bake in a 375° oven until golden brown, about 40 minutes. Turn out onto a rack to cool.

Sunset's Sourdough French Bread

W E S T E R N   C L A S S I C

PREPARATION TIME: 45 to 50 minutes
RISING TIME: About 3½ hours, plus 6 to 8 hours for starter to develop
BAKING TIME: About 35 minutes
PER SERVING: 185 calories, 5 grams protein, 38 grams carbohydrate, .50 gram total fat, .27 milligram cholesterol, 190 milligrams sodium

Using our flavor-controlled, yogurt-based starter, you can make French bread rivaling the best that San Francisco bakeries offer. You begin by mixing the starter with flour and water to make a "sponge," which must stand for at least 6 hours to develop a good sour flavor and leavening vigor (the bread uses no other yeast).

Makes 2 loaves, 22 to 24 servings *total*

- **2 cups warm water (about 110°F)**
- **1 cup sourdough starter (page 244)**
- **About 8 cups all-purpose flour**
- **2 teaspoons** *each* **salt and sugar**
- **6 tablespoons cornmeal**
- **1 teaspoon cornstarch and ½ cup water, stirred together**

In a large bowl, combine the 2 cups warm water, starter, and 4 cups of the flour; stir until smooth. Cover bowl with plastic wrap and let stand at about 85°F until very thick, bubbly, and spongy looking, 6 to 8 hours or until next day. Stir in salt, sugar, and about 3 cups more flour or enough to form a very stiff dough. Then mix in 1 of the following ways.

With a heavy-duty mixer and dough hook. Beat in about 1 cup more flour until dough pulls cleanly from sides of bowl.

By hand. Measure 1 cup more flour and spread part of it on a board. Scrape dough out onto board and knead until smooth and elastic, 10 to 12 minutes; add more flour as required to prevent sticking. Place dough in a greased bowl and turn over to grease top.

Cover dough (mixed by either method) with plastic wrap and let rise in a warm place until doubled, 1½ to 2 hours. Punch dough down and knead briefly on a lightly floured board to release air. Divide dough in half. Knead each piece gently just until smooth. (If you have only 1 oven, wrap 1 piece of dough in plastic wrap and refrigerate.)

Shape each piece of dough into a smooth log by rolling it back and forth, gently elongating loaf to about 14 inches. For each loaf, sprinkle a piece of stiff cardboard (about 7 by 18 inches) with 3 tablespoons of the cornmeal and set loaf on top.

Cover loaves lightly with plastic wrap; let rise in a warm place until puffy and almost doubled, 1 to 1½ hours. Remove plastic wrap.

Adjust oven racks to the 2 lowest positions. Place a 12- by 15-inch baking sheet on top rack as oven preheats to 400°. Just before bread is ready to bake, place a 10- by 15-inch rimmed baking pan on lowest rack and fill with about ¼ inch boiling water.

Meanwhile, in a 2- to 4-cup pan, bring cornstarch-water mixture to a boil, stirring; let cool slightly. With a razor blade or very sharp knife, cut 3 or 4 (½-inch-deep) slashes in top of each loaf. Brush loaves evenly with cornstarch mixture, making sure to moisten sides. Slip each loaf from cardboard onto baking sheet in oven.

Bake at 400° for 10 minutes; then brush each loaf evenly again with cornstarch mixture. Continue to bake until loaves are golden brown and sound hollow when tapped, 20 to 25 more minutes. Let cool on racks. (If you have only 1 oven, when you put first loaf in oven, remove second piece of dough from refrigerator and shape as above; it will take slightly longer to rise. Bake as directed.)

Colorful Vegetable Breads
Pictured on facing page

PREPARATION TIME: About 50 minutes (by hand) for 1 flavor of bread
RISING TIME: About 2¼ hours
BAKING TIME: 30 to 45 minutes
PER SERVING: See under individual vegetable purées

Using vegetable purée for part of the liquid in a simple yeast dough gives you added nutritional value, an interesting flavor, and colorful bread. The recipe makes two loaves—in one or two colors, as you choose.

Makes 2 loaves, 14 to 16 servings *total*

- **1 package active dry yeast**
- **2 tablespoons sugar**
- **¼ cup warm water (about 110°F)**
- **½ cup milk, at room temperature**
- **¼ cup (⅛ lb.) butter or margarine, at room temperature**
- **1 large egg**
- **1 teaspoon** *each* **ground nutmeg and salt**
- **Vegetable purée (choices follow)**
- **About 5½ cups all-purpose flour**

In a large bowl, sprinkle yeast and sugar over warm water; let stand until bubbly, about 5 minutes. Add milk, butter, egg, nutmeg, salt, vegetable purée of your choice, and 3 cups of the flour. (To make 2 kinds of bread, measure half the dough into another bowl. To each bowl, add a half recipe of vegetable purée, then continue as directed, adding half the flour to each bowl.) Mix in 1 of the following ways.

With a heavy-duty mixer and dough hook. Blend ingredients, then gradually beat in about 2 cups more flour to make a soft dough. Continue to beat until dough pulls cleanly from sides of bowl, adding a little flour as required.

By hand. With a heavy spoon, blend ingredients, then gradually mix in about 2 cups more flour to make a soft dough. Scrape dough out onto a floured board and knead until smooth and satiny, 10 to 15 minutes; work in as little flour as possible, adding only enough to prevent sticking. Place dough in a greased bowl; turn over to grease top.

Cover dough (mixed by either method) with plastic wrap and let rise in a warm place until doubled, about 1½ hours. Punch dough down; knead briefly on a lightly floured board to release air. Divide dough in half. Shape each half into a ball or oval.

Place each in center of a greased 12- by 15-inch baking sheet and flatten slightly. Dust very lightly with flour, then cover lightly with plastic wrap. Let rise in a warm place until almost doubled, about 45 minutes. Remove plastic wrap. With a razor blade or very sharp knife, make ½-inch-deep slashes on surface of loaves in an "X" or crosshatch design.

Bake in a 350° oven until loaves are golden brown on bottoms and sound hollow when tapped, 30 to 45 minutes. Let cool on racks.

BEET PURÉE. For a full recipe, make 1½ cups purée (you'll need 1½ pounds **beets**); for a half recipe, make ¾ cup purée from ¾ pound beets.

Trim beet tops. Scrub and quarter beets; steam on a rack over boiling water in a covered pan until tender when pierced, 25 to 30 minutes. Let cool; slip off skins. Purée beets in a food processor or blender.
Per Serving: 99 calories, 2 grams protein, 11 grams carbohydrate, 4 grams total fat, 26 milligrams cholesterol, 197 milligrams sodium.

CARROT PURÉE. For a full recipe, make 1½ cups purée (you'll need 1½ pounds **carrots**); for a half recipe, make ¾ cup purée from ¾ pound carrots.

Peel carrots; cut into 2-inch pieces. Steam on a rack over boiling water in a covered pan until tender when pierced, 15 to 20 minutes. Purée carrots in a food processor or blender.
Per Serving: 103 calories, 2 grams protein, 15 grams carbohydrate, 4 grams total fat, 26 milligrams cholesterol, 190 milligrams sodium.

POTATO PURÉE. For a full recipe, use 1 pound **russet potatoes;** measure 1¼ cups when mashed and mix in ¼ cup **milk.** For a half recipe, use ½ pound potatoes and 2 tablespoons milk to make ⅔ cup.

Peel potatoes and cut into 2-inch pieces. Steam on a rack over boiling water in a covered pan until tender when pierced, about 20 minutes. Let cool, then smoothly mash (not in a food processor).
Per Serving: 109 calories, 3 grams protein, 16 grams carbohydrate, 4 grams total fat, 27 milligrams cholesterol, 180 milligrams sodium.

SPINACH PURÉE. For a full recipe, make 1½ cups purée (from 3 pounds **spinach**); add 1½ teaspoons **dry oregano leaves.** For a half recipe, use 1½ pounds spinach and ¾ teaspoon oregano for ¾ cup purée.

Discard spinach stems and any yellow or wilted leaves; wash remaining leaves well and drain briefly. Place leaves in a 12- to 14-inch frying pan over medium heat. Cover; cook just until wilted, about 3 minutes, stirring often. When cool, squeeze very dry. Purée spinach in a food processor or blender.
Per Serving: 101 calories, 4 grams protein, 13 grams carbohydrate, 4 grams total fat, 26 milligrams cholesterol, 225 milligrams sodium.

TOMATO PURÉE. For a full recipe, stir together 1 can (12 oz.) **tomato paste** and 1½ teaspoons **Italian herb seasoning.** For a half recipe, use 1 can (6 oz.) tomato paste and ¾ teaspoon Italian herb seasoning.
Per Serving: 105 calories, 3 grams protein, 15 grams carbohydrate, 4 grams total fat, 26 milligrams cholesterol, 346 milligrams sodium.

Brilliantly tinted by fresh vegetable purées, Colorful Vegetable Breads (the recipe begins on the facing page) offer a bonus of nutrition as well as distinctive flavors. Take your pick from five purées: beet, carrot, potato, spinach, or tomato.

All About Sourdough

For generations, sourdough has mystified cooks and aroused their curiosity. Some credit its invention to a prospector who mixed up a bowl of pancake batter, let it sit for a few days while he was away from camp—and then returned to find a bubbling mixture that smelled decidedly sour, but made the best hotcakes he'd ever tasted.

Regardless of the origin, Westerners took a liking to the unique flavor of sourdough, and a good starter became a treasure to nurture and share. In fact, sourdough breads were so popular among frontiersmen that these rough and ready explorers acquired the nickname "sourdough."

Sourdough starter '73

Sunset has been working with sourdough for years. Our first sourdough story ran in 1933; since then, we've published more than 25 articles on the subject. And in 1973, we came up with the definitive starter recipe.

Making sourdough starter was originally something of a hit or miss affair—you mixed milk and flour and let it ferment, hoping to capture yeast and bacteria from the air that would produce a good sour flavor and aroma. The results weren't predictable, though; there was no guarantee that your starter wouldn't have a peculiar taste or an odd aroma (and produce breads with the same problems).

In 1973, working with food technologists at the University of California at Davis, our home economists developed an excellent, dependable starter based on yogurt, milk, and flour. If you follow our directions carefully, you should get a good, active starter—and marvelous breads and rolls—every time.

Start with a 1½-quart glass, pottery, rigid plastic, or stainless steel container. Rinse with hot water for several minutes, then wipe dry.

Heat 1 cup **nonfat, low-fat, or whole milk** to 90° to 100°F (nonfat milk gives the most tang, whole milk the least). Remove from heat and stir in 3 tablespoons freshly opened **low-fat or regular plain yogurt** (low-fat gives the tangiest flavor). Pour milk into the warm container, cover tightly, and let stand in a warm place where the temperature is between 80° and 100°F.

Above 110°F, bacteria may be killed—the mixture may smell sour, but won't get bubbly. Below 70°F, the bacteria don't grow well.

Good places to set the starter include the tops of water heaters or built-in refrigerators, or other partially enclosed areas where heat collects.

If you have an electric oven, you can adjust 1 rack so top of container will be 2 to 2½ inches under oven light. Turn oven to lowest setting and leave on just until air inside feels slightly warmer than room temperature; turn oven off. Place container directly in front of (but not touching) light. Close door and turn light on (or prop door open just enough to keep light on). If the room is cold, remove container and repeat oven warming technique occasionally.

After 18 to 24 hours, starter should be about the consistency of yogurt; a curd will form and mixture won't flow readily when container is slightly tilted. If some clear liquid rises to top of mixture during this time, simply stir it back in. However, if liquid is light pink in color, milk is beginning to break down; discard starter and begin again.

After a curd has formed, gradually stir 1 cup **all-purpose flour** into starter until smoothly blended. Cover tightly and let stand in a warm place (80° to 100°F is ideal) until mixture is full of bubbles and has a good sour smell; this takes 2 to 5 days.

During this time, if clear liquid forms, stir it back into the starter. But if liquid turns pink, spoon out and discard all but ¼ cup of starter, then blend in a mixture of 1 cup *each* lukewarm milk (90° to 100°F) and all-purpose flour. Cover tightly and let stand again in a warm place until bubbly and sour smelling. Use; or cover and store in refrigerator.

This procedure yields about 1½ cups starter. To maintain your supply, each time you use part of your starter, replenish it with equal amounts of lukewarm milk (90° to 100°F) and all-purpose flour. (For example, if you use ½ cup starter, blend in a mixture of ½ cup lukewarm milk and ½ cup all-purpose flour.) Cover and let stand in a warm place until mixture is bubbly again, several hours or until next day. Then cover and refrigerate until the next use. For consistent flavor, continue adding the same type of milk you

Heat milk to 90° to 100°F on a thermometer. Remove from heat and stir in 3 tablespoons plain yogurt.

Let mixture stand, tightly covered, in a warm place for 18 to 24 hours or until a curd forms.

Gradually stir 1 cup all-purpose flour into milk mixture; then cover and let stand in a warm place until bubbly, 2 to 5 days.

Finished starter is bubbly and spongy looking; it has a good sour aroma.

originally used. Before using your starter, always let it warm to room temperature; this takes 4 to 6 hours. If you want to bake in the morning, leave the starter out the night before.

If you bake regularly, starter should stay lively and active; if you don't, it's best to discard about half the starter and replenish it with milk and all-purpose flour about every 2 weeks. Or freeze your freshly fed starter for 1½ to 2 months. The fermenting action is considerably slowed during freezing, so you'll need to let starter thaw at room temperature, then put it in a warm place until bubbly, about 24 hours.

Sour Rye French Bread

PREPARATION TIME: 45 to 50 minutes
RISING TIME: About 3½ hours, plus 6 to 8 hours for starter to develop
BAKING TIME: About 35 minutes
PER SERVING: 175 calories, 5 grams protein, 37 grams carbohydrate, .54 gram total fat, .23 milligram cholesterol, 193 milligrams sodium

The same steps used to make Sunset's *Sourdough French Bread (page 242) produce these tangy sourdough rye loaves. Because the bread is made with rye flour, it has a denser texture than our plain sourdough bread.*

Like all doughs made with sourdough starter and no yeast, this one has a slightly different feel from regular yeast doughs: it's just a trifle sticky to the touch. When you knead it, though, add as little flour as possible, to keep the dough (and the baked loaf) moist, light, and springy.

Makes 2 loaves, 26 to 28 servings *total*

> 2 cups warm water (about 110°F)
> 1 cup sourdough starter (page 244)
>   About 7½ cups all-purpose flour
> 2 cups rye flour
> 2 tablespoons light molasses
> 2 teaspoons salt
> 1 tablespoon caraway seeds
> 1 teaspoon baking soda
> 6 tablespoons cornmeal
> 1 teaspoon cornstarch and ½ cup water, stirred together

In a large bowl, stir together the 2 cups warm water, starter, and 4 cups of the all-purpose flour. Cover bowl with plastic wrap and let stand at about 85°F until very thick, bubbly, and spongy looking, 6 to 8 hours or until next day.

Stir in rye flour, molasses, salt, caraway seeds, baking soda, and about 1½ cups more all-purpose flour or enough to form a stiff dough. Then mix in 1 of the following ways.

With a heavy-duty mixer and dough hook. Beat in about 2 cups more all-purpose flour until dough pulls cleanly from sides of bowl.

By hand. Measure 2 cups more all-purpose flour and spread some of it on a board. Turn dough out onto board and knead with well-floured hands until smooth, about 15 minutes. Add more flour as required to prevent sticking. Place dough in a greased bowl and turn over to grease top.

Cover dough (mixed by either method) with plastic wrap and let rise in a warm place until doubled, 2 to 2½ hours.

Following directions for *Sunset's* Sourdough French Bread (page 242), punch dough down, shape, place on cornmeal-dusted cardboard, proof, glaze with cornstarch-water mixture, and slash tops of loaves. Bake as directed for *Sunset's* Sourdough French Bread until richly browned, 30 to 35 minutes *total.* Let cool on racks.

Orange-Honey Sourdough Rolls

PREPARATION TIME: 35 to 40 minutes
RISING TIME: About 2¼ hours
BAKING TIME: About 35 minutes
PER ROLL: 302 calories, 5 grams protein, 45 grams carbohydrate, 11 grams total fat, 26 milligrams cholesterol, 180 milligrams sodium

Luscious pinwheels flavored with honey and filled with butter, brown sugar, orange peel, and almonds add a glamorous dimension to baking with sourdough.

To speed up preparation time, yeast is often added to doughs using sourdough starter. The flavor of the starter isn't as apparent in the baked product, since the dough doesn't go through the sponge stage—but the bread still has a special, mildly tangy character.

Makes 15 rolls

> 1 package active dry yeast
> ¼ cup warm water (about 110°F)
> ½ cup milk
> ½ cup sourdough starter (page 244)
> ¼ cup (⅛ lb.) butter or margarine, melted
> ¼ cup honey
> ½ teaspoon salt
>   About 3¼ cups all-purpose flour
>   Orange-Nut Filling (recipe follows)

In a large bowl, sprinkle yeast over warm water and let stand for about 5 minutes to soften. Stir in milk, starter, butter, honey, and salt. Gradually mix in 3 cups of the flour; dough will be sticky. Cover with plastic wrap and let rise in a warm place until doubled, about 1½ hours.

Beat dough to expel air, then scrape out onto a lightly floured board and knead until smooth, about 5 minutes, adding more flour, a little at a time, as required to prevent sticking. Roll dough out into a 12- by 15-inch rectangle; spread filling evenly over dough. Starting with a long side, roll up jelly roll fashion. Cut roll crosswise into 15 about 1-inch-thick slices and arrange, cut side up, in a heavily buttered 9- by 13-inch baking pan. Cover lightly with plastic wrap and let rise in a warm place until almost doubled, about 45 minutes. Remove plastic wrap.

Bake in a 350° oven until browned on top, about 35 minutes. Transfer rolls to a serving board; quickly scrape out any syrup in pan and spread over rolls. Serve warm. Or let cool, then cover and store at room temperature until next day (freeze for longer storage). To reheat, place rolls (thawed if frozen) in a baking pan, cover loosely with foil, and set in a 350° oven until hot, about 20 minutes.

ORANGE-NUT FILLING. Beat together ½ cup (¼ lb.) **butter** or margarine (at room temperature); ½ cup firmly packed **brown sugar;** 1 tablespoon grated **orange peel;** and ¼ cup **honey.** Stir in ½ cup *each* **all-purpose flour** and sliced **almonds,** then add 1 teaspoon **orange extract.**

With their bright raisin eyes and almond beaks, *Spring Dove Breads* (recipe at right) make a sensation at brunch. To shape each dove, you just knot a rope of dough for the body, then tuck in a teardrop-shaped piece for the head.

Spring Dove Breads

Pictured at left

PREPARATION TIME: About 1 hour
RISING TIME: About 2¼ hours
BAKING TIME: About 15 minutes
PER ROLL: 306 calories, 7 grams protein, 39 grams carbohydrate, 14 grams total fat, 120 milligrams cholesterol, 191 milligrams sodium

Create these beguiling dove-shaped rolls from a tender, easy-to-work yeast dough lightly flavored with cardamom and rich with butter and eggs. Seedless raisins make each dove's eyes; a whole almond forms the beak.

Makes 1 dozen rolls

- ½ cup (¼ lb.) butter or margarine
- 6 tablespoons whipping cream
- ⅓ cup sugar
- ½ teaspoon salt
- ½ teaspoon ground cardamom or nutmeg
- 1 package active dry yeast
- ¼ cup warm water (about 110°F)
- 3 large eggs
  About 4 cups all-purpose flour
- 24 raisins
- 12 whole blanched almonds
- 1 large egg yolk beaten with 1 tablespoon water

In a 1- to 2-quart pan, melt butter; remove from heat and stir in cream, sugar, salt, and cardamom. Let cool to lukewarm.

Meanwhile, in a large bowl, sprinkle yeast over warm water; let stand for about 5 minutes to soften. Add cooled butter mixture, eggs, and 2 cups of the flour. Mix in 1 of the following ways.

With a heavy-duty mixer and dough hook. Beat until well blended, then beat on medium speed for 2 minutes. Gradually beat in about 1⅔ cups more flour to make a stiff dough. Then beat until dough pulls cleanly from bowl sides, adding about ⅓ cup more flour as required.

With a regular mixer and by hand. Beat until well blended, then beat on medium speed for 2 minutes. With a heavy spoon, gradually mix in about 1⅔ cups more flour to make a stiff dough. Scrape dough out onto a board coated with some of remaining ⅓ cup flour; knead until smooth and slightly elastic, about 10 minutes, adding more flour as required to prevent sticking. Place dough in a greased bowl and turn over to grease top.

Cover dough (mixed by either method) with plastic wrap and let rise in a warm place until doubled, about 1½ hours.

Punch dough down and knead briefly on a lightly floured board to release air. Divide into 12 equal portions. Pinch off a ¾-inch ball of dough from each portion and set aside (these will be dove heads).

Roll 1 large portion of dough into a 9-inch-long tapering rope that measures about ½ inch in diameter at 1 end and 1 inch in diameter at other end. Tie an overhand knot at thin end of dough rope to make dove body. For dove tails, make several slashes in wide ends of rope to resemble feathers. Repeat with the remaining 11 large portions of dough, placing bodies of doves at least 2 inches apart on greased 12- by 15-inch baking sheets.

Now go back and shape reserved balls of dough for dove heads, forming them into smooth teardrops. Settle narrow ends of heads into cavities of dough knots; press down lightly to secure. Make small slashes on each side of heads and insert raisins for eyes. At front of each head, make a small slash and insert wide end of almond for beak. Cover doves lightly with plastic wrap and let rise in a warm place until puffy, about 45 minutes. Remove plastic wrap.

Before baking, push raisins and almonds back into heads to secure. Brush rolls all over with egg yolk mixture. Bake in a 375° oven until golden, 12 to 15 minutes. Serve hot, or let cool completely on racks, wrap airtight, and freeze. To reheat, thaw wrapped rolls at room temperature. Place on a 12- by 15-inch baking sheet, cover with foil, and heat in a 375° oven until hot throughout, about 10 minutes.

Kulich

PREPARATION TIME: About 1½ hours (by hand)
RISING TIME: About 4 hours, plus 30 minutes for sponge to develop
BAKING TIME: About 1 hour
PER SERVING: 267 calories, 5 grams protein, 32 grams carbohydrate, 13 grams total fat, 165 milligrams cholesterol, 74 milligrams sodium

At Easter, the West's Russian bakeries always offer kulich, a tall, cylindrical sweet yeast loaf capped with white icing—or with a starched linen kerchief or lace paper doily. You can duplicate this festive bread in your own kitchen, but be prepared to spend time on it—to achieve the desired light, springy texture, you must beat the rich, soft dough for 30 to 45 minutes with a dough hook or your hands.

Makes 2 loaves, 16 to 18 servings *total*

- ½ **cup milk**
- 1 **cup (½ lb.) unsalted butter, at room temperature**
- 3½ **cups all-purpose flour**
- 1 **large egg**
- 1 **package active dry yeast**
- 1 **cup sugar**
- ¼ **cup warm water (about 110°F)**
- ½ **teaspoon salt**
- 8 **large egg yolks**
- 1 **vanilla bean (6 to 8 inches long)**
- 1 **tablespoon vodka or brandy**
- 1/32 **teaspoon ground saffron (optional)**
- ¼ **cup finely chopped candied orange peel**
  Lemon Glaze (recipe follows)
  Small rosebuds (fresh or candies)

In a 1- to 1½-quart pan, combine ¼ cup of the milk and 2 tablespoons of the butter. Bring to a boil, stirring. At once, dump in ¼ cup of the flour; remove from heat and stir vigorously until mixture is smooth and pulls away from pan sides. Add egg and beat until thoroughly blended. Let cool to lukewarm.

In a bowl, sprinkle yeast and 1 teaspoon of the sugar over warm water; let stand for about 5 minutes to soften yeast. Stir yeast mixture into cooked mixture in pan. Cover and let stand in a warm place until doubled and very foamy, about 30 minutes.

In a large bowl, beat remaining butter with salt and remaining sugar until blended, then beat in egg yolks, a few at a time. Split vanilla bean lengthwise with a sharp knife; scrape out black seeds and add seeds to butter mixture. (Place vanilla bean in a jar of sugar to make vanilla-flavored sugar.)

Stir vodka and saffron (if used) into butter mixture, then stir in yeast mixture. Mix in remaining 3¼ cups flour, adding remaining ¼ cup milk at intervals. Add orange peel. Dough will be very soft. Beat in 1 of the following ways.

With a heavy-duty mixer and dough hook. Beat on medium speed until dough begins to pull fairly cleanly from sides of bowl, about 30 minutes.

By hand. Lightly oil or butter your hands; then rapidly pull handfuls of dough from bowl (a big bowl is easier to handle) and forcefully throw dough back in; continue until dough lifts as a whole lump when pulled from bowl, cleaning the bowl fairly well as it comes up. Mixing by hand takes about 45 minutes.

Cover dough (mixed by either method) with plastic wrap and let rise in a warm place until almost doubled, 2 to 2½ hours (dough is slow to rise).

Line bottoms of two 46-ounce juice cans with rounds of baking parchment. Then line sides of each can with parchment, extending it about 2 inches above can rim; secure with a paper clip. (If parchment is not available, use wax paper; butter heavily and dust with flour.)

Beat dough to expel air, then divide into 2 equal portions and scrape 1 portion into each parchment-lined can.

Cover with plastic wrap and let rise in a warm place until almost doubled (dough should be within 1½ inches of top rim of can), about 1½ hours. Remove plastic wrap.

Set cans upright on lowest rack of a 325° oven. Bake for 15 minutes, then reduce heat to 300° and continue to bake until a slender wooden skewer inserted into breads comes out clean, about 45 more minutes.

Let breads cool in cans for 10 minutes, then remove from cans and parchment. Lay loaves horizontally and cradle them in folded towels to preserve their rounded shape; set on racks and let cool.

When loaves are cool, stand on end. To store, wrap airtight and freeze; let thaw unwrapped.

Just before serving, spoon Lemon Glaze over tops of loaves, letting it drizzle down sides. Decorate with rosebuds, setting them in glaze while it's still soft. Slice loaves crosswise to serve.

LEMON GLAZE. Smoothly blend 1 cup **powdered sugar** with 1 tablespoon **lemon juice** and 1½ teaspoons **water.**

Whimsy Bread

PREPARATION TIME: About 1 hour
RISING TIME: About 2 hours
BAKING TIME: About 30 minutes
PER SERVING: 270 calories, 7 grams protein, 35 grams carbohydrate, 11 grams total fat, 127 milligrams cholesterol, 187 milligrams sodium

A teddy bear for a new baby, a mermaid for a fisherman? Let your fancies roam when you personalize a great big loaf of bread for family or friends. To make the biggest loaf possible, you need an extra-big baking sheet—easily improvised by overlapping two large baking sheets and wrapping them in foil. Once you have your baking sheet assembled, draw a paper pattern that fits the sheet, keeping the outline bold and the details simple. Use your pattern as a guide for shaping the loaf, keeping in mind that the dough will swell and spread as it proofs and bakes.

Makes 1 large loaf, 12 to 16 servings

>   1 package active dry yeast
>   ¼ cup warm water (about 110°F)
>   ¾ cup (⅜ lb.) butter or margarine, at room
>   temperature
>   ½ cup sugar
>   ⅓ cup milk
>   ½ teaspoon salt
>   6 large eggs
>   About 4¾ cups all-purpose flour

In a large bowl, sprinkle yeast over warm water and let stand for about 5 minutes to soften. Add butter, sugar, milk, salt, and 5 of the eggs. Then beat in flour in 1 of the following ways.

With a heavy-duty mixer and dough hook. Add 4¾ cups of the flour and beat on medium speed until dough pulls from bowl sides, about 10 minutes.

With a regular mixer and by hand. Add 2 cups of the flour and beat on medium speed for 10 minutes. Mix in 1 cup more flour with mixer on low speed or with a heavy spoon. With a heavy spoon, stir in 1¾ cups more flour, moistening thoroughly (do not knead).

Cover dough (mixed by either method) with plastic wrap and let rise in a warm place until dough is almost doubled, about 1½ hours. Beat to expel air, then turn out onto a lightly floured board.

If you used a dough hook, shape dough into a smooth ball. *If you prepared dough without a dough hook,* knead dough until smooth and velvety, about 10 minutes, adding as little flour as possible.

Overlap two 12- by 15-inch rimless baking sheets; adjust overlap so combined sheets cover within 1 inch of the full width or depth of your oven. Cover with a sheet of foil; butter foil.

Divide dough into proportions to fit presketched design. Remember to save a small piece to make decorative details.

For a solid area, shape dough into a ball and place smooth side up, then pat or roll out to achieve desired dimension and form (make no thicker than about an inch, or bread may crack as it bakes). The dough expands as it bakes, so make the shape skinnier than you want the baked figure to be.

Butt pieces of dough against main shape if they are to be joined to it, such as head and tail of mermaid, feet and comb of chicken. Leave at least 2 inches of space between sections you don't want joined together or touching each other, such as mermaid arms and curve of tail, teddy bear limbs.

For attached decoration such as eyes, bust, or bellybuttons, make teardrop-shaped pieces and set into holes punched in dough. Attach larger decorations such as a chicken's wing by pushing an edge into the base; pinch lightly to hold.

To create surface detail such as mermaid eyes or scales, or to separate areas such as fingers, snip dough with kitchen scissors.

To make strands for arms, legs, or hair, roll pieces of dough between your palms.

Cover shaped dough lightly with plastic wrap and let rise in a warm place until puffy, about 30 minutes. Remove plastic wrap. Beat together remaining egg and 1 tablespoon water; brush over dough.

Bake in a 350° oven until richly browned, about 30 minutes. Let cool on baking sheet for about 10 minutes, as bread is quite fragile while hot. Slip a spatula under bread to free; slide gently onto rack to cool (or onto a tray if you plan to serve warm).

To store, wrap cooled loaf airtight and freeze. To reheat, let thaw uncovered, then place on a 12- by 15-inch baking sheet. Set in a 325° oven until hot, about 20 minutes.

Monkey Bread

W E S T E R N   C L A S S I C

PREPARATION TIME: About 40 minutes
RISING TIME: About 1½ hours
BAKING TIME: About 30 minutes
PER SERVING: 231 calories, 5 grams protein, 33 grams carbohydrate, 9 grams total fat, 24 milligrams cholesterol, 180 milligrams sodium

Though monkey bread has been around for a long time— it was very popular at luncheons in the '50s—the origin of the name remains obscure. Regardless of this little mystery, the tender bread is always popular for its shape and flavor. To make it, you layer buttered diamonds of dough in a ring mold, then bake. To serve, just invert the loaf onto a serving plate and pull off leaves of prebuttered bread.

Makes 1 loaf, 10 to 12 servings

>   1½ packages active dry yeast
>   1 cup warm milk (110°F)
>   ¼ cup sugar
>   ½ teaspoon salt
>   ½ cup (¼ lb.) butter or margarine, melted
>   About 3½ cups all-purpose flour
>   Melted butter or margarine

In a large bowl, sprinkle yeast over milk and let stand for about 5 minutes to soften. Mix in sugar, salt, the ½ cup butter, and 3½ cups of the flour. Beat with a heavy spoon until well blended and stretchy; then cover with plastic wrap and let rise in a warm place until almost doubled, about 1 hour.

Punch down dough and knead briefly on a lightly floured board to release air. Roll out to a thickness of about ¼ inch. Cut rolled-out dough into diamond-shaped pieces about 2½ inches long. Dip each piece in melted butter; arrange pieces in overlapping layers in a buttered 9-inch ring mold or tube pan. Cover with plastic wrap and let rise in a warm place until almost doubled, about 30 minutes. Remove plastic wrap.

Bake in a 400° oven until golden brown, about 30 minutes. To serve, turn hot bread out of mold onto a plate; pull apart to eat.

Portuguese Sweet Bread

W E S T E R N   C L A S S I C

PREPARATION TIME: About 1¼ hours
RISING TIME: About 1¾ hours (includes resting time)
BAKING TIME: 20 to 40 minutes, depending on shape
PER BUN: 370 calories, 9 grams protein, 60 grams carbohydrate, 10 grams total fat, 112 milligrams cholesterol, 300 milligrams sodium

Hawaiians quickly adopted traditional Portuguese pão doce when it was introduced by immigrants to the Islands in the late 1800s. The springy, slightly sweet bread is most commonly seen in plain round loaves, sometimes with a hole in the center. But the dough can also be shaped into coils or braids for handsome golden loaves or buns.

Makes 2 loaves or 1 dozen buns

⅔ **cup water**
¼ **cup instant mashed potato mix**
⅔ **cup sugar**
¼ **cup instant nonfat dry milk**
½ **cup (¼ lb.) butter or margarine, cut into pieces**
2 **packages active dry yeast**
⅓ **cup warm water (about 110°F)**
About 5½ **cups all-purpose flour**
4 **large eggs**
1 **teaspoon salt**
½ **teaspoon vanilla**
¼ **teaspoon lemon extract**
Sugar (optional)

In a 1- to 2-quart pan, bring the ⅔ cup water to a boil. Stir in potato mix and immediately remove from heat. Stir in the ⅔ cup sugar, dry milk, and butter. Let cool to 110°F (butter need not melt completely).

Meanwhile, in a large bowl, sprinkle yeast over warm water and let stand for about 5 minutes to soften. Stir in cooled potato mixture. Add 2 cups of the flour and beat with a heavy spoon until blended. Stir in 3 of the eggs, salt, vanilla, and lemon extract until smoothly blended. Then beat in 1½ cups more flour.

Mix in 1 to 1½ cups more flour or enough to make a stiff dough. Scrape dough out onto a floured board and knead until smooth and satiny, 10 to 20 minutes, adding as little flour as possible to prevent sticking. Place dough in a greased bowl; turn over to grease top. Cover with plastic wrap and let rise in a warm place until doubled, about 1 hour.

Punch dough down and knead briefly on a lightly floured board to release air. Let dough rest for 10 minutes; then shape in 1 of the following ways.

For coiled loaves, divide dough in half. Roll each portion into a 30-inch-long rope. For each loaf, coil a rope into a greased 9-inch pie pan, starting at outside edge and ending in center; twist rope slightly as you lay it in pan.

For coiled buns, divide dough into 12 equal portions. Roll each into a 12-inch-long rope. On greased 12- by 15-inch baking sheets, coil each rope into a round bun, starting at outside edge and ending in center; twist rope slightly as you coil it. Make buns 2½ to 3 inches in diameter and space them at least 2 inches apart.

For braided loaves, divide dough into 6 equal portions. Roll each into a 14-inch-long rope. For each loaf, arrange 3 ropes side by side on a greased 12- by 15-inch baking sheet. Pinch together at top and loosely braid; pinch ends together and tuck underneath.

For round loaves, divide dough in half. Shape each half into a smooth ball; place each in a greased 9-inch pie pan. Gently flatten each into an 8-inch-diameter round.

Cover shaped dough lightly with plastic wrap and let rise in a warm place until almost doubled—35 to 45 minutes for loaves, 20 to 30 minutes for buns. Remove plastic wrap. Lightly beat remaining egg and brush over dough; sprinkle with sugar, if desired.

Bake in a 350° oven until browned—25 to 30 minutes for loaves, 20 to 25 minutes for buns. Let cool on racks. Serve warm or at room temperature. To store, wrap cooled bread airtight and freeze. To reheat, let thaw unwrapped; then place on a 12- by 15-inch baking sheet, cover loosely with foil, and set in a 350° oven until warm—10 to 15 minutes for buns, 25 to 30 minutes for loaves.

PORTUGUESE EASTER BREAD
Prepare dough and shape into coiled buns as directed for **Portuguese Sweet Bread,** but shape buns so there's a little space open at the center of each. Into center of each bun, push 1 **hard-cooked egg** (shells may be colored, if you like); egg should touch the baking sheet. Let buns rise as directed; brush proofed dough (but not egg shells) with beaten egg, then sprinkle with sugar or tiny, multicolored round cake decorating candies. Bake as directed.

RUSSIANS came to the Northwest in search of furs, and settled as far south as California. Later, many Russians who fled the Revolution of 1917 settled in San Francisco—where bakeries along Clement Street offered tall golden loaves of kulich and pyramids of sweet white paskha cheese at Eastertime.

Blue Corn Tortillas

PREPARATION TIME: 25 to 30 minutes
COOKING TIME: About 1½ minutes per tortilla
PER TORTILLA: 84 calories, 2 grams protein, 18 grams carbohydrate, .27 gram total fat, 0 milligram cholesterol, 45 milligrams sodium

A part of New Mexico's cookery since ancient times, blue cornmeal is finally increasing in availability elsewhere in the West. Mixed with water, the coarsely ground meal—harina para tortillas—makes much firmer and less flexible tortillas than does yellow tortilla flour. Eat blue tortillas warm, since they become very hard when cool; serve them with butter, or stuff with a taco filling. Any leftover tortillas can be used to make blue corn chips—brittle, crisp, and a very popular snack in Santa Fe.

Makes 1 dozen tortillas

> **2 cups blue cornmeal for tortillas**
> **¼ teaspoon salt**
> **1 cup warm water**

Cut 24 pieces of wax paper, each about 6 inches square. Set aside.

In a bowl, mix cornmeal, salt, and warm water until meal is moistened. Cover bowl with plastic wrap and let dough stand for at least 2 minutes; keep covered at all times to prevent drying.

Divide dough into 12 equal portions and quickly roll each between your hands to form a ball; flatten slightly and return each to covered bowl.

To shape with a tortilla press, cover bottom half of press with 1 square of wax paper and set 1 dough piece on paper. Lay another piece of wax paper on dough; close press tightly.

To shape with a rolling pin, place 1 piece of dough between 2 squares of wax paper; flatten slightly with your hand. Lightly run a rolling pin over dough several times. Flip dough and paper over and continue to roll out until you have a ragged 6-inch circle.

Carefully peel off top piece of paper; lay it gently back on tortilla and turn papers and tortillas over. Gently peel off paper that is now on top.

To make a perfectly shaped tortilla, you can cut dough into a 5- to 6-inch round; use the end of a 2-pound coffee can as a cutter. Let tortilla stand, uncovered, for 1 to 2 minutes to dry slightly.

As you are shaping the first tortilla, place a cast-iron or other heavy 10- to 12-inch frying pan or griddle over medium-high heat (or use an electric frying pan or griddle set at medium-high or 375°). When pan is hot, lift tortilla, supporting it with paper, and turn over into pan. At once, peel off paper. Cook tortilla until surface looks dry and bottom is flecked with brown, about 30 seconds. With a wide spatula, flip tortilla over and continue to cook for about 1 more minute; put on a plate, cover with foil, and keep warm.

While 1 tortilla is cooking, shape another; cook it as you shape the next. Stack tortillas as baked and keep covered.

Serve warm; upon cooling, tortillas become hard and brittle. Any cold leftover tortillas may be stored airtight in the refrigerator for up to 5 days; use for Blue Corn Chips (recipe follows).

BLUE CORN CHIPS

Stack warm or cold **Blue Corn Tortillas,** then cut stack into 4 to 6 wedges. Pour about ½ inch **salad oil** into a 10- to 12-inch frying pan over medium-high heat. When oil is hot, add tortilla wedges to fill pan in a single layer. Cook and stir just until crisp, about 30 seconds. Lift from oil with a slotted spoon and drain on paper towels. Repeat until all are cooked.

Serve chips to dip in **red or green chile salsa** as an appetizer or snack. If made ahead, store airtight at room temperature for up to 5 days.

Blue Corn Muffins

PREPARATION TIME: 10 to 15 minutes
BAKING TIME: About 20 minutes
PER MUFFIN: 149 calories, 4 grams protein, 20 grams carbohydrate, 6 grams total fat, 59 milligrams cholesterol, 260 milligrams sodium

The parched-corn flavor of blue cornmeal gives muffins an interesting earthy character. You'll find blue cornmeal in many Western specialty food and health food stores; for these muffins, you can use either coarse-ground meal (harina para tortillas) or the more finely ground type labeled harina para atole (atole *is a cooked, sweetened gruel).*

Makes 1 dozen muffins

> **1 cup all-purpose flour**
> **1 cup blue cornmeal for tortillas or for atole**
> **2 tablespoons sugar**
> **1 tablespoon baking powder**
> **½ teaspoon salt**
> **2 large eggs**
> **1 cup milk**
> **¼ cup (⅛ lb.) butter or margarine, melted**
> **Butter and honey**

In a bowl, stir together flour, cornmeal, sugar, baking powder, and salt. In another bowl, beat eggs, milk, and the ¼ cup butter until blended. Pour liquids into dry mixture; stir just to moisten. Grease twelve 2½-inch muffin cups (or line with paper baking cups); spoon in batter. Bake in a 400° oven until tops of muffins are browned and a slender wooden pick inserted in centers comes out clean, 18 to 20 minutes. Serve hot with butter and honey.

If made ahead, let cool on racks; then wrap airtight and hold at room temperature until next day (freeze for longer storage). To reheat, arrange muffins (thawed if frozen) on a baking sheet; place in a 350° oven until warm, about 10 minutes.

Say "good morning" with hot, wholesome Ready-bake Bran Muffins (recipe below). Fruited and cake-tender, they're easy to make from a batter that you can refrigerate for several weeks.

Ready-bake Bran Muffins

Pictured above

PREPARATION TIME: 20 to 25 minutes (includes cooling time for cereal)
BAKING TIME: About 20 minutes
PER MUFFIN: 143 calories, 3 grams protein, 26 grams carbohydrate, 4 grams total fat, 19 milligrams cholesterol, 223 milligrams sodium

Freshly baked bran muffins for busy-morning breakfasts are a luxury easily achieved. These wholesome, almost cakelike muffins are made from a fruit-dotted batter that keeps in the refrigerator for several weeks. Bake the muffins at your convenience, a few at a time—or even one at a time, following our microwave instructions.

Makes 2 to 2½ dozen muffins

   3 cups whole bran cereal
   1 cup boiling water
   2 large eggs, lightly beaten
   2 cups buttermilk
   ½ cup salad oil
   1 cup raisins, currants, chopped pitted
      dates, or chopped pitted prunes
   2½ teaspoons baking soda
   ½ teaspoon salt
   1 cup sugar
   2½ cups all-purpose flour

In a large bowl, mix bran cereal with boiling water, stirring to moisten evenly. Let cool. Add eggs, butter-milk, oil, and raisins; blend well. Stir together baking soda, salt, sugar, and flour, then stir into bran mixture.

Bake muffins as soon as batter is mixed; or refrigerate batter in a tightly covered container for up to 2 weeks, baking muffins at your convenience. Stir batter to distribute fruit before using.

Spoon batter into greased 2½-inch muffin cups, filling ⅔ to ¾ full. Bake in a 425° oven until tops spring back when lightly touched, about 20 minutes. Serve hot.

MICROWAVE READY-BAKE BRAN MUFFINS
Prepare batter as directed for **Ready-bake Bran Muffins.** To bake each muffin, nest 2 paper baking cups, one inside the other; invert doubled cup and wrap a strip of tape around middle of outside cup. Turn doubled cup right side up and spoon in ¼ cup batter. Microwave on **HIGH (100%)** for 45 to 60 seconds; rotate muffin after 20 to 30 seconds if it seems to be baking unevenly. When done, muffin will look dry on top and spring back when lightly touched; it may feel moist, but it shouldn't be sticky. If necessary, microwave further, in 5- to 10-second increments. Let stand for 30 to 60 seconds before eating.

Fresh Corn Madeleines

PREPARATION TIME: 25 to 30 minutes
BAKING TIME: 10 to 25 minutes
PER MADELEINE: 52 calories, 1 gram protein, 7 grams carbohydrate, 2 grams total fat, 13 milligrams cholesterol, 89 milligrams sodium

Tender corn kernels are a pleasing foil for the crunch of Italian-style coarse cornmeal (polenta) or regular cornmeal. For muffins with a fancy shape, bake the batter in madeleine pans.

Makes 2 to 3 dozen madeleines

> About ⅓ cup butter or margarine
> 1 small onion, minced
> 1 cup all-purpose flour
> About 1 cup polenta (Italian-style cornmeal) or yellow cornmeal
> 1 tablespoon baking powder
> ½ teaspoon salt
> 1 large egg
> 1 cup milk
> 1 cup fresh corn kernels (or frozen corn kernels, thawed)

Melt ⅓ cup of the butter in a 10- to 12-inch frying pan over medium-high heat. Add onion and cook, stirring occasionally, until soft, about 5 minutes. Set aside.

In a bowl, stir together flour, 1 cup of the polenta, baking powder, and salt. In another bowl, whisk egg and milk until blended. Stir onion mixture, milk mixture, and corn into flour mixture just until blended.

Butter madeleine pans (1½- to 2-tablespoon size) or petite (1½-inch-diameter) muffin pans. Sprinkle pans with polenta; shake out excess. Spoon batter into pans, filling to rims.

Bake in a 350° oven until firm to touch—about 10 minutes for 1½-tablespoon-size madeleines, 15 minutes for 2-tablespoon-size, 25 minutes for muffins. Let cool slightly, then invert pans to remove cornbreads, easing free with a narrow spatula if necessary. Serve hot or at room temperature.

If made ahead, let cool, wrap airtight, and hold at room temperature until next day (freeze for longer storage). To reheat, lay muffins (thawed if frozen) side by side in a 10- by 15-inch rimmed baking pan and place in a 300° oven until warm, 10 to 15 minutes.

Wheat Germ Zucchini Bread

W E S T E R N   C L A S S I C

PREPARATION TIME: About 20 minutes
BAKING TIME: About 1 hour
PER SERVING: 345 calories, 5 grams protein, 40 grams carbohydrate, 19 grams total fat, 46 milligrams cholesterol, 243 milligrams sodium

For Western gardeners and cooks, zucchini is both a blessing and a bane. It's easy to grow and delicious to eat; but because the vines are so prolific, it's a constant challenge to keep thinking of new ways to cook the squash, serve it, and—especially as the season wears on—disguise it. This long-time favorite bread has earned perhaps the ultimate compliment from many who've tasted it: "You'd never know there's zucchini in it!"

Makes 2 loaves, 16 to 18 servings *total*

> 2½ cups all-purpose flour
> ½ cup toasted wheat germ
> 2 teaspoons baking soda
> 1 teaspoon salt
> ½ teaspoon baking powder
> 1 cup finely chopped walnuts
> 3 large eggs
> 1 cup salad oil
> 1 cup *each* granulated sugar and firmly packed brown sugar
> 1 tablespoon maple flavoring
> 2 cups coarsely shredded zucchini (about 4 medium-size zucchini)
> ⅓ cup sesame seeds

Combine flour, wheat germ, baking soda, salt, baking powder, and walnuts. Set aside.

In a large bowl, beat eggs with an electric mixer until blended. Add oil, sugars, and maple flavoring; continue to beat until mixture is thick and foamy. Add flour mixture and stir just until blended. Stir in zucchini.

Divide batter equally between 2 greased, flour-dusted 5- by 9-inch loaf pans. Sprinkle sesame seeds evenly over batter. Bake in a 350° oven until a slender wooden pick inserted in centers of loaves comes out clean, about 1 hour. Let cool in pans for 10 minutes; turn out of pans onto racks and let cool completely. To store, wrap airtight; hold at room temperature for up to 4 days or freeze for up to 1 month.

Crisp Heart Waffles

PREPARATION TIME: 10 to 15 minutes
COOKING TIME: About 4 minutes per waffle
PER WAFFLE: 157 calories, 2 grams protein, 16 grams carbohydrate, 9 grams total fat, 33 milligrams cholesterol, 106 milligrams sodium

The cream-based batter for these crisp waffles literally explodes in the iron, then holds its fragile form with the aid of baking powder. For the prettiest-looking waffles, we suggest baking the batter in a special Scandinavian heart-shaped iron (available in cookware shops), but you can also use a standard waffle iron.

Makes 8 to 10 waffles

> 1¼ cups all-purpose flour
> ¾ cup water
> 1¼ cups whipping cream
> 2 tablespoons sugar
> 1½ teaspoons vanilla
> 2¼ teaspoons baking powder

PROLIFIC and easy to grow in Western gardens, zucchini has led the pack as the most called-for ingredient in Sunset recipes. We've been inundated with readers' ideas for using zucchini raw, cooked, or preserved—and for serving it in soups, salads, casseroles, breads, and cakes. One reader even successfully disguised the squash as fruit in a cobbler.

In a bowl, beat together flour and water until smooth. Stir in ¼ cup of the cream, sugar, vanilla, and baking powder. Beat remaining 1 cup cream until it holds stiff peaks, then fold into batter; let stand for 10 minutes.

Place a heart-shaped waffle iron over medium-low heat, turning it over until water dripped inside sizzles (or heat an electric waffle iron to medium-low or 325°).

Open iron and spoon about ⅓ cup batter into iron (or use amount recommended for other shaped grids). Close iron; if using a nonelectric iron, squeeze handles gently, then turn iron over about every 30 seconds until waffle is golden brown, about 4 minutes. Open iron often to check doneness.

Transfer waffles to a rack as cooked. Serve warm. If made ahead, let cool completely; then package airtight. To reheat, arrange waffles in a single layer on baking sheets and place in a 350° oven until hot and crisp, about 5 minutes.

Twice-baked Ginger Toast

PREPARATION TIME: About 20 minutes
BAKING TIME: About 55 minutes, plus 10 minutes to cool between the two bakings
PER PIECE: 151 calories, 3 grams protein, 20 grams carbohydrate, 7 grams total fat, 40 milligrams cholesterol, 91 milligrams sodium

A nice change from regular breakfast toast, this slightly sweet bread is baked in a flat loaf, then sliced and toasted in the oven. Twice-baked Italian Cookies (page 258) are made the same way, from much the same dough; both cookies and toast are great to dunk in coffee.

Makes 1½ dozen pieces

    ¾ cup sugar
    ⅔ cup coarsely chopped almonds
    ⅓ cup butter or margarine, melted
    2 tablespoons water
    1½ tablespoons minced crystallized ginger
    4 teaspoons anise seeds
    1 teaspoon vanilla
    2 large eggs
    1⅔ cups all-purpose flour
    2 teaspoons baking powder

In a bowl, mix sugar, almonds, butter, water, ginger, anise seeds, vanilla, and eggs; beat to blend. Mix flour with baking powder; stir thoroughly into sugar mixture. Scoop dough out into center of a greased 10- by 15-inch rimmed baking pan. With a rubber spatula, shape dough to make a rectangular log about 1¼ inches thick, 3 inches wide, and 15 inches long. Bake in a 350° oven until golden brown, about 35 minutes.

Remove loaf from oven; let cool slightly. Cut loaf diagonally into long slices, ½ to ¾ inch thick. Tip slices over onto cut sides and arrange slightly apart in pan. Return to oven and bake until toasted a deep gold, about 20 more minutes. Let cool on racks. If made ahead, store airtight at room temperature for up to 1 week (freeze for longer storage).

Finnish Rieska

PREPARATION TIME: 5 to 10 minutes
BAKING TIME: About 12 minutes
PER SERVING: 130 calories, 3 grams protein, 17 grams carbohydrate, 6 grams total fat, 17 milligrams cholesterol, 192 milligrams sodium

This sturdy flatbread goes together and bakes in just minutes. It's best served warm; tear it into chunks and spread with butter, or cut into wedges and use as a base for open-faced sandwiches.

Makes 8 or 9 servings

    All-purpose flour
    2 cups rye flour
    ¼ teaspoon salt
    2 teaspoons *each* sugar and baking powder
    1 cup half-and-half or light cream
    2 tablespoons butter or margarine, melted

Generously grease a 12- by 15-inch baking sheet, then dust it with all-purpose flour. Invert a 12-inch plate on center of sheet. Trace around plate with a wooden skewer; lift off plate.

In a bowl, combine rye flour, salt, sugar, and baking powder. Add half-and-half and butter and stir with a fork just until flour is evenly moistened. Gather dough into a ball; place in center of circle on baking sheet. Dust hands with all-purpose flour, then press dough out to edge of circle, forming an even layer. Prick surface all over with a fork. Bake in a 450° oven until lightly browned, 10 to 12 minutes. Serve warm.

Giant Bread Sticks

PREPARATION TIME: 5 to 10 minutes
BROILING TIME: About 5 minutes
PER BREAD STICK: 269 calories, 5 grams protein, 32 grams carbohydrate, 13 grams total fat, 33 milligrams cholesterol, 447 milligrams sodium

When we entertain at Sunset, we often serve these whimsical-looking, oversized bread sticks as an accompaniment to a casual meal. They're especially quick to fix, since you start with purchased baguettes.

Makes 8 bread sticks

    ½ cup (¼ lb.) butter or margarine, melted
    ½ cup minced green onions (including tops)
    ¼ teaspoon dry thyme leaves
    2 cloves garlic, minced
    2 baguettes (½ lb. *each*), cut lengthwise into quarters

Stir together butter, onions, thyme, and garlic. Brush over cut sides of bread quarters. Lay bread pieces buttered side up in a 10- by 15-inch rimmed baking pan. Broil about 4 inches below heat until golden, about 5 minutes. Serve warm or cool.

The Best of Sunset

DESSERTS

Bringing both dinner parties and cook books to a happy ending, dessert is designed for pure, sweet indulgence. Unlike more substantial dishes on the menu, its primary purpose is to delight the palate. Of course, you'll often elect simply to offer perfectly ripe fruit or a wedge of cheese, with port or one of the West's elegant dessert wines for sipping. But sometimes you'll want to go further and whip up a fantasy from these pages.

Many of our desserts are showpieces for glorious Western fruits and nuts. If you'd like to taste the truth of this, sample Nut Mosaic Tart, Chocolate-striped Oranges, Pear Pepper Pie ... the list goes on. And while we've provided a wealth of sophisticated sweets, no desserts chapter would be complete without a few treats for the young and young at heart—like Cooky Cones to top with Frozen Fruit Yogurt, Tofulato, or Gelato. Turn the page for more classics and sweet surprises.

This gracefully curved, miniature basket is actually a
hand-molded cooky. Ice cream and bright fruit complete
its delicious design. To craft your own, turn to page 256
and follow the recipe for Fruit-filled Cooky Baskets.

Cooky Cones

PREPARATION TIME: About 10 minutes
BAKING TIME: 1½ to 2 minutes per cone
PER SMALL CONE: 129 calories, 2 grams protein, 13 grams carbohydrate, 8 grams total fat, 64 milligrams cholesterol, 80 milligrams sodium

As handmade cones began to appear in a few West Coast ice cream parlors, Sunset also produced a version that was not only handmade, but easily homemade. We used a regular waffle iron's smooth griddle surface—the reverse side of the waffle grid on some types of irons (the grid itself makes the cooky cones too thick). An 8- or 9-inch round or square iron produces either small or large cones; a rectangular iron limits cone size according to its griddle width.

To shape the cones, use purchased metal cream horn forms (available in stores selling gourmet cookware). Or fashion your own forms: make a lightweight cardboard cone about 7 inches long with a 2½-inch top opening, or wrap a purchased pointed sugar cone with foil. Cookies cool quickly, so you need only one or two forms.

Makes about 1½ dozen small cones,
about 9 large cones

> 3 large eggs
> ⅔ cup sugar
> ⅔ cup (⅓ lb.) butter or margarine, melted
> 2 teaspoons vanilla
> 1 teaspoon almond extract
> 1 cup all-purpose flour

In a bowl, beat together eggs, sugar, butter, vanilla, and almond extract until blended. Add flour; stir until batter is smooth. Place flat griddle plates on electric waffle iron and preheat to medium-hot.

For each 5-inch cone (maximum size for most rectangular griddles), use 1½ tablespoons of the batter; for a 7- to 8-inch cone, use 3 to 4 tablespoons. Pour batter onto center of hot griddle (lightly grease griddle for the first few cookies, if needed); close tightly to flatten. Let bake until golden brown (over-browned cookies are more likely to crack), 1½ to 2 minutes.

Quickly lift off cooky with a fork or spatula and place on a flat surface. Immediately wrap around cone form. Hold firmly at tip to make a sharp point. (If your fingers are sensitive to heat, wear trim-fitting clean cotton gloves.) Let cooky cool, seam side down, on a rack until firm, about 2 minutes. Remove cone form to use again.

If made ahead, carefully stack cones and store airtight in a rigid container at room temperature for up to 1 week (freeze for longer storage).

KOEKJE, *which means "little cake" in Dutch, probably inspired the name of our own cookies—those popular little cakes enjoyed not just in the West, but across the U.S.A. Cookies bring out a special creative zeal in cooks. And Sunset, in dozens of years, has published many dozens of mouth-watering examples. Made of every good thing from oatmeal to white chocolate, hazelnuts and anise seeds, our cookies have fed the young-at-heart of all ages at every kind of occasion. Not long ago, we published a proud collection,* **Sunset Books'** **Cookies.**

Fruit-filled Cooky Baskets

Pictured on page 254

PREPARATION TIME: About 15 minutes
BAKING TIME: About 12 minutes per cooky (several can bake at once)
PER COOKY BASKET: 228 calories, 2 grams protein, 25 grams carbohydrate, 14 grams total fat, 22 milligrams cholesterol, 94 milligrams sodium

You can shape these confection-like cookies into delightful dessert baskets while they're still warm and flexible from the oven. The trick is in the timing. If the cookies are too hot, they'll stretch and tear; if too cold, they'll be brittle and impossible to shape. Check the warm cookies' texture by loosening one edge from the baking sheet. If you find you've waited too long, simply return the cookies to the oven; they'll quickly soften again.

Makes 4 to 6 cooky baskets

> ¼ cup (⅛ lb.) butter or margarine
> ¼ cup *each* firmly packed brown sugar and light corn syrup
> 3½ tablespoons all-purpose flour
> ½ cup finely chopped nuts
> 1 teaspoon vanilla
> Vanilla or nut ice cream
> 1½ to 2 cups fruit, cut into bite-size pieces if necessary

Melt butter in a 1- to 2-quart pan over low heat. Add sugar and corn syrup. Bring to a boil over high heat, stirring constantly; remove from heat and stir in flour and nuts until blended. Stir in vanilla.

Grease and flour-dust 12- by 15-inch or 14- by 17-inch baking sheets (they must be flat, not warped). Place 2 to 3 tablespoons of the batter on baking sheet; if there's room, place another 2- to 3-tablespoon portion of batter 8 inches away from first portion and at least 4 inches from side of sheet. (Depending on baking sheet size and cooky size, you can bake only 1 or 2 cookies at a time.) If batter has cooled and does not flow easily, evenly press or spread it out to a 3- to 4-inch circle. Bake in a 325° oven until a rich golden brown all over, about 12 minutes. (You can bake on 2 baking sheets at a time, staggering them in oven and changing positions halfway to ensure even browning.) Let cookies cool on baking sheet on a rack until slightly firm, about 1 minute.

When cooky edges are just firm enough to lift, loosen edges from sheet with a wide spatula, then slide spatula under entire cooky to remove. Lift cooky—it should still be hot and flexible (somewhat stretchy), but firm enough to move without pulling apart. Turn cooky over and drape over a glass that measures about 2 inches across the bottom. With your hand, gently cup cooky around the base; make bottom flat and flare cooky out at sides. If cooky becomes too firm to shape, return to oven for a few minutes, until pliable. Let shaped cooky cool until firm, about 2 minutes. Gently remove from glass. Repeat, using remaining batter; grease and reflour baking sheets each time.

If made ahead, store baskets airtight in rigid containers at room temperature for up to 1 week (freeze for longer storage). To serve, place a small scoop of ice cream in each basket and top with fruit. Serve immediately.

White Chocolate Chip Cookies

PREPARATION TIME: About 25 minutes
BAKING TIME: 12 to 14 minutes
PER COOKY: 162 calories, 2 grams protein, 20 grams carbohydrate, 8 grams total fat, 27 milligrams cholesterol, 125 milligrams sodium

What could be better than a chocolate chip cooky? To some ways of thinking, this white chocolate chip version is a delectable improvement on tradition. The cookies are made almost palm-size; a basketful is an impressive offering for party or potluck.

Makes about 2½ dozen cookies

> 1 cup (½ lb.) butter or margarine, at room temperature
> 1½ cups sugar
> 2 teaspoons baking soda
> 1 large egg
> 1 cup plus 2 tablespoons all-purpose flour
> 2 cups quick-cooking rolled oats
> 6 ounces white chocolate, coarsely chopped (1¼ cups)

In a large bowl, beat butter, sugar, and baking soda with an electric mixer until creamy; beat in egg. Gradually add flour and oats, blending thoroughly. Stir in chocolate.

Roll 2-tablespoon portions of dough into balls and place 4 inches apart on greased 12- by 15-inch baking sheets. Bake in a 350° oven until light golden brown, 12 to 14 minutes. Let cool on baking sheets until firm to the touch, then transfer to racks and let cool completely. If made ahead, store airtight at room temperature for up to 3 days (freeze for longer storage).

Piñon Fingers

PREPARATION TIME: About 40 minutes
BAKING TIME: 25 to 30 minutes
PER COOKY: 60 calories, .86 gram protein, 7 grams carbohydrate, 4 grams total fat, 7 milligrams cholesterol, 26 milligrams sodium

"Melt-in-the-mouth" describes the texture of these delicate morsels from the Southwest. They're much like the rich cookies known as Mexican wedding cakes. You'll get delicious results using imported shelled pine nuts—but in New Mexico, nuts from native piñon pines give the cookies local character.

Makes 5 to 6 dozen cookies

> 1 cup (½ lb.) butter or margarine, at room temperature
> 2¼ cups powdered sugar
> 2 teaspoons vanilla
> 2 cups all-purpose flour
> 1 cup pine nuts

In a bowl, beat butter, ¼ cup of the sugar, and vanilla until creamy. Stir in flour and pine nuts until well mixed. Pinch off about 2-tablespoon portions of dough; on a lightly floured board, roll each portion into a rope about ½ inch thick. Cut rope into 2-inch lengths.

Place pieces of dough side by side, about 1 inch apart, on ungreased 12- by 15-inch baking sheets. Bake in a 275° oven until edges are tinged light golden brown, 25 to 30 minutes. Switch positions of baking sheets halfway through baking.

While cookies are still warm and on baking sheets, evenly sift remaining 2 cups sugar over them; let cool. If made ahead, store airtight at room temperature for up to 1 week (freeze for longer storage).

Black Pepper Cookies

PREPARATION TIME: About 30 minutes
BAKING TIME: 20 to 25 minutes
PER COOKY: 85 calories, .59 gram protein, 12 grams carbohydrate, 4 grams total fat, 10 milligrams cholesterol, 57 milligrams sodium

Sunset *readers come to expect the unexpected from us—and these black-peppered, hot-sweet cookies are certainly out of the ordinary. Treats for adult palates, they grow hotter as you nibble; offer juicy pears and port to temper the spicy bite.*

Makes about 2 dozen cookies

> 1 cup all-purpose flour
> 1 teaspoon baking powder
> 1 cup sugar
> 1 to 1½ teaspoons whole black peppercorns, coarsely crushed
> ½ cup (¼ lb.) butter or margarine
> Whole black peppercorns

In a food processor (or a bowl), combine flour, baking powder, ¾ cup of the sugar, and crushed peppercorns. Whirl (or mix with a fork) until blended.

In a 1- to 2-quart pan, stir butter over medium heat until browned (stir through white foam to check). Add to flour mixture; whirl until dough forms a compact ball, about 1½ minutes. Or stir in butter with a fork, then work dough with your hands to form a smooth-textured ball.

Pinch off 1-inch pieces of dough and roll into balls. Arrange balls, slightly apart, on an ungreased 12- by 15-inch baking sheet. Dip the bottom of a glass into remaining ¼ cup sugar and press each ball gently to ½-inch thickness. Press a peppercorn into center of each cooky.

Bake on lowest rack of a 300° oven until browned on bottom, 20 to 25 minutes. Transfer cookies to a rack and let cool completely. If made ahead, store airtight at room temperature for up to 3 days (freeze for longer storage).

Pecan Graham Crisps

PREPARATION TIME: About 15 minutes
BAKING TIME: 8 to 10 minutes, plus 10 minutes to cool and cut
PER COOKY: 97 calories, .51 gram protein, 9 grams carbohydrate, 7 grams total fat, 10 milligrams cholesterol, 53 milligrams sodium

Variations on dressed-up graham crackers have appeared in Sunset *every few years for decades. In this 1986 recipe, the crackers are topped with caramel, pecans, and chocolate for an extra-sweet snack.*

Makes 4 dozen cookies

> 12 **graham crackers (***each* **about 2½ by 4¾ inches)**
> 1 **cup (½ lb.) butter or margarine**
> 1¼ **cups firmly packed brown sugar**
> 1 **cup chopped pecans or walnuts**
> 1 **teaspoon vanilla**
> 1 **cup chopped semisweet or milk chocolate, or semisweet chocolate chips (6 oz.)**

Fit crackers side by side in a single layer in a 10- by 15-inch rimmed baking pan. In a 2- to 3-quart pan, melt butter over medium heat. Stir in sugar and pecans; bring to a boil, stirring often. Continue to boil until candy thermometer registers 238°F, about 2 minutes. Remove from heat, stir in vanilla, and pour over crackers; spread to cover completely.

Bake in a 375° oven to crisp crackers (topping should not darken), 8 to 10 minutes. Remove from oven and at once sprinkle with chocolate. Let stand for about 10 minutes; if desired, spread melted chocolate over topping. Cut into 24 squares, then cut each square in half diagonally; let cool.

Koggetjes

PREPARATION TIME: About 25 minutes (mix dough while caramel cools)
BAKING TIME: 12 to 15 minutes
PER COOKY: 72 calories, .49 gram protein, 9 grams carbohydrate, 4 grams total fat, 10 milligrams cholesterol, 46 milligrams sodium

In bringing home the best of Europe, Sunset *editors could not overlook the many tempting versions of Dutch* koekje—*or "little cake." Here's a crunchy Dutch drop cooky dotted with bits of caramelized sugar.*

Makes about 3 dozen cookies

> ¾ **cup (⅜ lb.) butter or margarine, at room temperature**
> ½ **cup sugar**
> ½ **teaspoon vanilla**
> 1¼ **cups all-purpose flour**
> ½ **teaspoon baking powder**
> 2 **tablespoons water**
> **Caramelized Sugar (recipe follows)**

In a bowl, beat together butter, the ½ cup sugar, and vanilla until light and fluffy. Stir together flour and baking powder; stir into butter mixture alternately with water. Stir in crushed caramelized sugar. Drop rounded teaspoonfuls of dough about 2 inches apart onto nonstick or well-greased baking sheets. Bake in a 325° oven until edges are lightly browned, 12 to 15 minutes. Let cool on baking sheets for 1 minute, then transfer to racks and let cool completely.

CARAMELIZED SUGAR. Place an 8- to 10-inch frying pan over medium-high heat. Add ½ cup **sugar;** as sugar begins to melt, shake and tilt pan to mix liquid with sugar. Cook just until all sugar is melted and liquid is amber colored; then immediately pour melted sugar onto a 10- to 12-inch square of buttered foil. Let stand until cool and hardened. Break caramel into pieces, then whirl in a food processor until coarsely crushed.

Twice-baked Italian Cookies

W E S T E R N   C L A S S I C

PREPARATION TIME: About 35 minutes
CHILLING TIME: At least 2 hours
BAKING TIME: 35 minutes
PER COOKY: 75 calories, 2 grams protein, 9 grams carbohydrate, 3 grams total fat, 20 milligrams cholesterol, 33 milligrams sodium

Italian immigrants have settled widely in the West, bringing their own vitality to Western cuisine. These hard biscotti *are a small but enormously popular contribution; traditionally, they're served to dunk in wine or strong espresso coffee.*

Makes about 9 dozen cookies

> 2 **cups sugar**
> 1 **cup (½ lb.) butter, melted**
> ¼ **cup anise seeds**
> ¼ **cup anisette or other anise liqueur**
> 3 **tablespoons bourbon; or 2 teaspoons vanilla and 2 tablespoons water**
> 2 **cups coarsely chopped almonds or walnuts**
> 6 **large eggs**
> 5½ **cups all-purpose flour**
> 1 **tablespoon baking powder**

In a bowl, mix sugar, butter, anise seeds, liqueur, bourbon, almonds, and eggs; beat to blend. Stir together flour and baking powder; add to butter mixture and blend thoroughly. Cover and refrigerate dough until firm, 2 to 3 hours.

On a lightly floured board, shape dough with your hands to form flat loaves that are ½ inch thick, 2 inches wide, and about 17 inches long. Place no more than 2 loaves, parallel and well apart, on buttered 12- by 17-inch baking sheets. Bake in a 375° oven until golden brown, about 20 minutes.

Remove loaves from oven and let cool on baking sheets until you can touch them, then cut into ½- to ¾-inch-thick diagonal slices. Lay slices, cut side down and close together, on baking sheets. Return to oven and bake until lightly toasted, about 15 more minutes. Let cool on racks.

Tender Scotch Short-bread (recipe below) brings a buttery taste of the Highlands to tea tables as far away as the western United States. Enjoy the ginger variation, too.

Scotch Shortbread

Pictured above

PREPARATION TIME: 15 to 20 minutes

BAKING TIME: About 40 minutes

PER COOKY: 144 calories, 1 gram protein, 17 grams carbohydrate, 8 grams total fat, 21 milligrams cholesterol, 78 milligrams sodium

Also called "petticoat tail" for the fluted frill at the outer curve of each wedge-cut piece, shortbread can turn a few strawberries and a cup of tea into an epicurean event. Our version and its gingered variation are toasty, buttery, and deliciously tender.

Makes 8 to 12 cookies

1¼ **cups all-purpose flour**

3 **tablespoons cornstarch**

About ⅓ cup sugar

½ **cup (¼ lb.) butter or margarine, cut into chunks**

In a bowl, combine flour, cornstarch, ¼ cup of the sugar, and butter. With your fingers, rub mixture together until it is very crumbly and no large particles remain. Then press into a firm lump with your hands. Place dough (it is crumbly) in an 8- or 9-inch-diameter cake pan with a removable bottom and press out firmly and evenly. Impress edge of dough with the tines of a fork to make a decorative border; then prick surface evenly.

Bake in a 325° oven until pale golden brown, about 40 minutes. Remove from oven and, while warm, cut with a sharp knife into 8 to 12 wedges and sprinkle with about 1 tablespoon sugar. Let cool, then remove pan sides and transfer cookies to a serving tray or airtight container. Store at room temperature for up to 1 week (freeze for longer storage).

GINGER SHORTBREAD

Follow directions for **Scotch Shortbread,** but omit cornstarch; add ½ teaspoon **ground ginger** and 2 tablespoons minced **crystallized ginger.**

Artistry with Cookies

A cooky dough that behaves like clay in the hands of an artist, professional or otherwise, is a cooky sculpture requirement. To try out our own golden and cocoa sculpture dough, we asked Dora De Larios, a Los Angeles artist noted for her many whimsical works, to take it in hand. Her efforts confirmed that our almond paste–strengthened dough is splendidly malleable, holds its shape well, and results in eminently edible sculpture.

De Larios used techniques basic to ceramics—forming slabs, rolling ropes of varying thicknesses, and making impressions with a fork's tines, the head of a screw, and other objects. For contrasting color, she used both the golden and cocoa doughs in her creations. Children—as well as "butterfingers" of all ages—can use the same methods to turn the rich, exceptionally cooperative dough into a good-tasting artistic success.

Admire, then eat—that's the way to enjoy our rich, almond-flavored sculpture cookies.

Golden Almond Sculpture Cookies

> 1 cup (½ lb.) **butter** or **margarine,** at room temperature
>
> 1 can (8 oz.) or ¾ cup firmly packed **almond paste**
>
> ¾ cup **sugar**
>
> 1 large **egg**
>
> 3 cups **all-purpose flour**
>
> **Cocoa-Almond Sculpture Dough** (recipe follows), optional

Using an electric mixer, beat butter, almond paste, and sugar until smoothly blended. Thoroughly mix in egg. Add flour and beat until well blended.

Use both golden and cocoa doughs at room temperature; if made ahead, cover airtight and refrigerate for up to 3 days (freeze for longer storage).

Shape dough directly on a baking sheet (preferably one without sides); allow 1 to 2 inches between each cooky. For best results, the cooky's maximum thickness should not exceed ¾ inch.

Form cookies as desired, following "Hints for Shaping Dough" (at right).

Bake cookies in a 300° oven until they are darker on the bottom than the top and feel dry and firmer than raw dough when lightly pressed (while hot, cookies are still soft enough to hold an impression and are easily cut with a sharp knife). Baking time varies with thickness; allow about 20 minutes for ¼-inch-thick cookies, 30 minutes for ½-inch-thick cookies, and 35 to 40 minutes for ¾-inch-thick cookies.

Let cookies stand on baking sheets until firm and cool enough to touch (they become rigid when cooled to room temperature), then slide a spatula under cookies to be sure they are free. Lift with a wide spatula (or by hand) onto racks to cool.

If made ahead, package airtight and hold at room temperature for up to 3 days (freeze for longer storage). Makes about 3⅔ cups dough, enough to make 8 round cookies, each 4 inches in diameter and ½ inch thick.

COCOA-ALMOND SCULPTURE DOUGH

Follow directions for **Golden Almond Sculpture Cookies,** but decrease flour to 2½ cups and add ½ cup **unsweetened cocoa** with the sugar. Makes about 3¾ cups.

HINTS FOR SHAPING DOUGH

When baked, the dough retains its surface texture and shape well, but as you work, keep these points in mind:

• The thicker the cooky, the more it tends to spread and flatten out as it bakes.

• Gently molded shapes hold better than sharp edges.

• Rounded shapes (coils, noses, and so on) flatten slightly.

• Thinner areas brown more quickly than thicker ones.

• You can make designs by cutting into the dough with a blade or by pressing objects into the dough.

• To get fine strands, force bits of dough through a garlic press.

• For contrasting effects, use both golden and cocoa sculpture doughs.

Plum Picture Cake

PREPARATION TIME: 25 to 30 minutes

BAKING TIME: About 40 minutes, plus 30 minutes to cool and 30 minutes to let sugar dissolve

PER SERVING: 221 calories, 3 grams protein, 33 grams carbohydrate, 9 grams total fat, 89 milligrams cholesterol, 96 milligrams sodium

As this cake bakes, the tender, buttery batter swells up around the fruit topping, creating a golden frame for each juicy piece—hence the name "picture cake." Late-season prune plums (in markets from August through October) are exceptional in this dessert; Bartlett pears are a wonderful alternative.

Makes 10 to 12 servings

  ½ cup (¼ lb.) butter or margarine,
    at room temperature
  ½ cup granulated sugar
  3 large eggs
  ½ teaspoon vanilla
  1 cup all-purpose flour
  14 to 16 prune plums
  2 to 3 tablespoons granulated sugar
    Powdered sugar

In a small bowl, beat butter and the ½ cup granulated sugar with an electric mixer until smooth and creamy. Add eggs, 1 at a time, beating well after each addition. Stir in vanilla; then stir in flour until batter is well mixed. Spread batter evenly in a buttered, flour-dusted 11-inch tart pan with a removable bottom.

Halve and pit plums. Arrange plum halves, cut side up, over surface of batter, placing fruit close together. Sprinkle fruit evenly with the 2 to 3 tablespoons granulated sugar.

Bake in a 375° oven until center of cake feels firm when lightly pressed, about 40 minutes. Let cool in pan on a rack for at least 30 minutes; then remove pan sides and serve warm, or let cool completely and serve cold. About 30 minutes before serving, dust liberally with powdered sugar; this allows time for sugar to dissolve on fruit, making a distinct pattern on cake.

PEAR PICTURE CAKE

Prepare batter as directed for **Plum Picture Cake,** but add ¼ teaspoon **anise seeds,** ½ teaspoon **anise extract,** and 1 teaspoon grated **lemon peel.** Spread batter in pan as directed.

Omit plums; instead, halve and core 6 large **Bartlett pears.** Slice off rounded back of each pear half; cut each of these pieces in half lengthwise. Arrange pear halves on batter; fit small pear pieces in between. Sprinkle pears with 2 tablespoons **lemon juice,** ½ teaspoon **anise seeds,** and the 2 to 3 tablespoons sugar.

Bake, cool, and serve as directed for **Plum Picture Cake.**

Lemon Crunch Cake

W E S T E R N   C L A S S I C

PREPARATION TIME: About 30 minutes.

PER SERVING: 328 calories, 4 grams protein, 52 grams carbohydrate, 12 grams total fat, 155 milligrams cholesterol, 250 milligrams sodium

Years ago, candy crunch cake was a highlight of West Coast luncheon, tea, and bridge party gatherings. The contrasting textures of chewy sponge cake, soft whipped cream, and crunchy crushed candy made this dessert a mouthwatering social success—and it's still a real winner today.

Makes 14 to 16 servings

  1½ cups granulated sugar
  ⅓ cup water
  ¼ cup light corn syrup
  1 tablespoon baking soda
  ⅛ teaspoon oil of lemon
    10-inch sponge or chiffon cake,
    purchased or homemade
  2 cups whipping cream
  ¼ cup powdered sugar
  ⅛ teaspoon lemon extract

In a heavy 3- to 4-quart pan, combine granulated sugar, water, and corn syrup. Cook over medium-high heat, stirring occasionally, until syrup registers 300°F on a candy thermometer.

Remove from heat immediately; quickly stir in baking soda and oil of lemon. Stir until blended; then immediately pour foamy mixture onto a 12-inch square of buttered foil. Let cool; break into coarse crumbs with a flat-surfaced mallet or a rolling pin.

Split cake horizontally into 4 equal layers. Whip cream until stiff; blend in powdered sugar and lemon extract. Reassemble cake on a serving plate, spreading half the cream between layers. Spread remaining cream over top and sides of cake. Pat crushed candy generously over top and sides. (You'll have leftover candy; store it airtight.)

CINNAMON CRUNCH CAKE

Follow directions for **Lemon Crunch Cake,** but substitute ⅛ teaspoon **oil of cinnamon** for the oil of lemon; use ½ teaspoon **vanilla** in place of lemon extract.

COFFEE CRUNCH CAKE

Follow directions for **Lemon Crunch Cake,** but add 1 tablespoon **instant coffee powder** to syrup mixture before cooking; omit oil of lemon. Omit lemon extract; instead, flavor whipped cream with ½ teaspoon **instant coffee powder.**

Western nuts call for delicious celebration—perhaps a Kona Torte (lower right), filled with Hawaiian macadamia nuts, or a Central Valley Pistachio Cake (top left). Recipes for both appear on the facing page.

Swedish Sour Cream Apple Cake

PREPARATION TIME: About 1 hour

BAKING TIME: About 35 minutes

COOLING AND CHILLING TIME: About 3 hours

PER SERVING: 323 calories, 6 grams protein, 35 grams carbohydrate, 18 grams total fat, 173 milligrams cholesterol, 135 milligrams sodium

Credit for this grand old treat goes to the Northwest's Swedish settlers. Sour cream custard laden with sliced apples bakes in a zwieback crumb crust for a dessert that's much like cheesecake.

Makes 9 to 12 servings

>   2 tablespoons butter or margarine
>   6 cups peeled, thinly sliced Golden
>   Delicious apples
>   ⅔ cup sugar
>   1½ tablespoons *each* cornstarch and water,
>   stirred together
>   6 large eggs
>   2 cups sour cream
>   2 teaspoons vanilla
>   Zwieback Crust (recipe follows)

Melt butter in a 10- to 12-inch frying pan over medium heat; add apples and sugar. Cover and cook, stirring often, until apples just start to soften, about 10 minutes. Stir in cornstarch mixture; cook, stirring gently, until thickened. Remove from heat.

Beat together eggs, sour cream, and vanilla until smooth; combine with apple mixture. Pour into crust-lined pan.

Bake in a 325° oven until center of cheesecake looks set and jiggles only slightly when pan is gently shaken, about 35 minutes. Let cool, then cover and refrigerate until cold.

To serve, remove pan sides and cut cake into wedges.

ZWIEBACK CRUST. Finely crush 1 package (6 oz.) **zwieback;** combine crumbs with 2 tablespoons **sugar,** 1 teaspoon **ground cinnamon,** and ¼ cup (⅛ lb.) **butter** or margarine (at room temperature). Press crumb mixture evenly over bottom and about 2 inches up sides of a 9-inch cheesecake pan or cake pan with a removable bottom.

Central Valley Pistachio Cake

Pictured on facing page

W E S T E R N   C L A S S I C

PREPARATION TIME: About 30 minutes for cake (starting with shelled nuts); about 15 minutes for sauce
BAKING TIME: About 45 minutes
COOLING TIME: About 1 hour
PER SERVING: 519 calories, 12 grams protein, 39 grams carbohydrate, 37 grams total fat, 213 milligrams cholesterol, 246 milligrams sodium

Colorful relative of the mango and the cashew, the pistachio grew wild in Biblical times in the high-desert regions of the Middle East. The trees were first planted in California in the 1930s, but it wasn't until the 1970s that the large-kernel 'Kerman' variety was introduced. From the Central Valley, here's a sumptuous pistachio dessert with tangy citrus sauce.

Makes 6 to 8 servings

> 2⅓ cups shelled (4⅔ cups or 1¼ lbs.
>   in shell) natural, roasted, or roasted salted
>   pistachio nuts
> 1 cup sugar
> ⅔ cup (⅓ lb.) butter or margarine,
>   at room temperature
> 5 large eggs, separated
> ½ cup fine dry bread crumbs
>   Natural or roasted pistachios in the shell
>   Citrus Sauce (recipe follows)

Coarsely chop pistachios; set aside ⅓ cup for garnish. In a large bowl, beat ¾ cup of the sugar with butter until creamy. Add egg yolks, 1 at a time, beating well after each addition. Gradually sprinkle in bread crumbs and chopped pistachios (about 2 cups); blend well.

Beat egg whites with remaining ¼ cup sugar until whites hold stiff peaks. Stir half the whites into batter until blended. Fold in remaining whites.

Spoon batter into a greased, flour-dusted 9-inch cheesecake pan with a removable bottom. Bake in center of a 350° oven until top is golden brown and center feels set when lightly touched, 40 to 45 minutes. Let cool in pan on a rack. If made ahead, wrap airtight and store at room temperature for up to 2 days.

Run a sharp knife around edge of cake to loosen, then remove pan sides. Garnish with whole pistachios. To serve, cut into wedges. Serve with Citrus Sauce; sprinkle with reserved chopped pistachios.

CITRUS SAUCE. In a 10- to 12-inch frying pan, combine 4 **large eggs,** ½ cup **sugar,** 1 teaspoon grated **lemon peel,** and ¼ cup *each* **lemon juice, orange juice,** and **whipping cream.** Cook over medium-low heat, stirring constantly, until mixture thickly coats the back of a metal spoon, about 8 minutes. Gently rub through a fine strainer; discard residue. Serve warm or cold. If made ahead, cover and refrigerate for up to 3 days. Makes 1½ cups.
PER TABLESPOON: 38 calories, 1 gram protein, 5 grams carbohydrate, 2 grams total fat, 48 milligrams cholesterol, 13 milligrams sodium.

Kona Torte

Pictured on facing page

W E S T E R N   C L A S S I C

PREPARATION TIME: 50 to 60 minutes
BAKING TIME: About 1 hour
COOLING TIME: About 2 hours
PER SERVING: 457 calories, 5 grams protein, 39 grams carbohydrate, 33 grams total fat, 65 milligrams cholesterol, 227 milligrams sodium

It took the University of Hawaii 20 years to develop commercial macadamia varieties from plants that were originally brought from Australia in the 1880s. Even today, the nuts do not reproduce predictably, so all seedlings are grafted with cuttings from bearing adult trees. Celebrate the macadamia with this rich torte.

Makes 14 to 16 servings

> 2½ cups (12½ oz.) roasted salted
>   macadamia nuts
> 2¾ cups all-purpose flour
> 2½ cups sugar
> 1 cup (½ lb.) butter or margarine,
>   cut into chunks
> 1 large egg
> 1 cup whipping cream
> 1 large egg white, beaten until frothy
>   Roasted salted macadamia nuts (optional)
>   Whipped cream (optional)

Rub the 2½ cups macadamias in a towel to remove salt; lift nuts from towel and set aside.

In a food processor or a bowl, combine flour and ½ cup of the sugar. Add butter; whirl (or rub with your fingers) until mixture resembles fine crumbs. Add egg and whirl (or mix with a fork) until dough holds together. Pat into a ball.

Press ⅔ of the pastry over bottom and up sides of a 1½-inch-deep 9-inch-diameter cake pan with a removable bottom. Cover and refrigerate. Roll remaining pastry between 2 sheets of wax paper into a 9-inch round. Refrigerate flat.

Pour remaining 2 cups sugar into a 10- to 12-inch frying pan and place over medium-high heat. As sugar begins to melt, shake and tilt pan to mix liquid with sugar. Cook just until all sugar is melted and liquid is amber colored. Pour in cream; caramelized sugar will harden. Cook, stirring, until caramel melts and sauce is smooth. Remove from heat; stir in the 2½ cups nuts. Let cool for 10 to 20 minutes, then spoon into pastry shell.

Peel off 1 sheet of wax paper from pastry round and invert over nut-filled torte. Peel off remaining paper. If necessary fold edge of pastry under to make flush with pan rim; press with tines of a flour-dipped fork to seal. Brush top of torte lightly with beaten egg white.

Bake in a 325° oven until golden brown, about 1 hour. Let cool in pan on a rack for 10 to 20 minutes. Run a sharp knife around edge to loosen torte from pan; remove pan sides and let cool completely. Garnish with macadamias, if desired. If made ahead, store airtight at room temperature for up to 2 days. To serve, cut into thin wedges; offer whipped cream to spoon on top, if desired.

Almond Fudge Torte

PREPARATION TIME: About 25 minutes for torte; about 5 minutes for glaze

BAKING TIME: About 30 minutes

COOLING TIME: Up to 1 hour for torte; up to 4 hours to harden glaze

PER SERVING: 337 calories, 4 grams protein, 35 grams carbohydrate, 22 grams total fat, 107 milligrams cholesterol, 116 milligrams sodium

The glossy, pastry-shop look of this torte belies its simple preparation. Its fudgy texture is made even moister, richer, and chewier by the addition of almond paste.

Makes 10 servings

> 1 teaspoon instant coffee powder
> 2 tablespoons hot water
> 4 ounces semisweet chocolate, melted
> 3 large eggs, separated
> ½ cup (¼ lb.) butter or margarine, at room temperature
> ¾ cup sugar
> 2 ounces almond paste, crumbled or shredded (about ⅓ cup)
> ½ cup all-purpose flour
> Chocolate Glaze (recipe follows)

Dissolve coffee in hot water. Stir in melted chocolate. In a large bowl, beat egg whites with an electric mixer on high speed just until they hold stiff, moist peaks.

In another bowl, beat butter and sugar until creamy. Beat in almond paste until thoroughly blended. Mix in egg yolks, chocolate mixture, and flour. Fold in beaten egg whites, about ⅓ at a time, just until blended. Spread batter in a greased, cocoa-dusted 8-inch-diameter cake pan and bake in a 350° oven until lightly browned, about 30 minutes (do not overbake).

Let cool in pan on a rack for about 10 minutes, then invert from pan onto a serving dish and let cool thoroughly. Spread glaze over top and sides. Let stand until glaze is hardened—2 to 4 hours at room temperature, 10 to 15 minutes in the refrigerator.

If made ahead, cover and refrigerate for up to 2 days. Bring to room temperature before serving. Cut into small wedges to serve.

CHOCOLATE GLAZE. In the top of a double boiler, combine 4 ounces **semisweet chocolate** (coarsely chopped) and 1 tablespoon **solid vegetable shortening.** Stir over barely simmering water just until melted. Remove from heat. Let cool, stirring occasionally, until mixture thickens slightly; then use.

Persimmon Pudding

W E S T E R N   C L A S S I C

PREPARATION TIME: 35 to 40 minutes

STEAMING TIME: 2¼ to 2½ hours

PER SERVING: 497 calories, 7 grams protein, 70 grams carbohydrate, 23 grams total fat, 93 milligrams cholesterol, 406 milligrams sodium

Here's a Western variation on English steamed Christmas pudding. Puréed soft persimmons give it color and

tender texture; nuts and dried prunes add to the flavor blend. Flame the pudding with brandy and serve with "soft sauce"—a lighter, fluffier version of the traditional hard sauce.*

Makes 8 to 10 servings

> 1½ cups sugar
> 1½ cups all-purpose flour
> 1½ teaspoons ground cinnamon
> ½ teaspoon ground nutmeg
> 1 tablespoon baking soda
> 3 tablespoons hot water
> 1½ cups ripe persimmon pulp
> 2 large eggs
> 1½ cups chopped pitted prunes
> 1 cup coarsely chopped almonds, walnuts, hazelnuts, or pistachio nuts
> About ¾ cup brandy
> 2 teaspoons vanilla
> 1½ teaspoons lemon juice
> ¾ cup (⅜ lb.) butter or margarine, melted and cooled to lukewarm
> Soft Sauce (recipe follows)

Mix sugar, flour, cinnamon, and nutmeg. In a bowl, stir together baking soda and hot water, then mix in persimmon pulp and eggs; beat until blended. Add sugar mixture, prunes, almonds, ⅓ cup of the brandy, vanilla, lemon juice, and butter. Stir until evenly mixed.

Scrape batter into a buttered 9- to 10-cup pudding mold, either plain or tube-shaped; cover tightly. Place on a rack in a deep 5- to 6-quart (or larger) pan. Add 1 inch water, cover pan, and steam over medium heat until pudding feels firm when lightly pressed in center, about 2¼ hours for tube mold, 2½ hours for plain mold. Add boiling water as needed to keep about 1 inch in pan.

Uncover pudding and let stand on a rack until slightly cooled, about 15 minutes. Invert onto a dish; lift off mold.

If made ahead, let cool completely. If desired, wrap pudding in a single layer of cheesecloth and moisten evenly with 3 to 4 tablespoons of the brandy. Wrap airtight in foil and refrigerate for up to 2 weeks; freeze for longer storage (thaw wrapped). To reheat, steam foil-wrapped pudding (discard cheesecloth) on a rack over 1 inch boiling water in a covered 5- to 6-quart pan until hot, about 45 minutes.

Serve pudding hot. To flame, warm remaining 3 to 4 tablespoons brandy in a 2- to 4-cup pan until bubbly. Carefully ignite with a match (not beneath a vent, fan, or flammable items) and pour over pudding. Slice and serve with Soft Sauce.

SOFT SAUCE. Beat 2 **large egg whites** until they hold soft peaks; gradually beat in ½ cup **powdered sugar** until whites hold stiff peaks. With same beaters, whip 2 **large egg yolks** with ½ cup **powdered sugar** and ½ teaspoon **vanilla** until very thick. Fold whites and yolks together. Serve; or hold at room temperature for up to 2 hours (stir before serving). Makes about 2¼ cups.

PER TABLESPOON: 17 calories, .33 gram protein, 3 grams carbohydrate, .31 gram total fat, 15 milligrams cholesterol, 3 milligrams sodium.

Marengo Cavour

PREPARATION TIME: 50 to 55 minutes for meringue and filling
BAKING TIME: About 1½ hours
DRYING TIME: 3 to 4 hours
CHILLING TIME: At least 8 hours
PER SERVING: 389 calories, 5 grams protein, 40 grams carbohydrate, 24 grams total fat, 59 milligrams cholesterol, 63 milligrams sodium

This Italian meringue torte makes a grand dessert for a special meal. Baked to a dry crispness, the meringue layers contrast with a mocha-cream filling strewn with chunks of milk chocolate.

Makes 8 to 10 servings

    4 large egg whites (about ½ cup)
    ½ teaspoon cream of tartar
    1 cup sugar
    1 teaspoon vanilla
    1 teaspoon instant coffee powder
    ¼ cup coffee liqueur; or 2 teaspoons instant coffee powder, 2 tablespoons water, and 1 teaspoon vanilla
    2 cups whipping cream
    About 10 ounces milk chocolate, coarsely chopped (about 2 cups)

In a mixer bowl that holds at least 6 cups below the top curve of the beaters, combine egg whites and cream of tartar. Beat whites on highest speed *just* until frothy (no bottom layer of free-flowing viscous white). Beating constantly, add sugar, 1 tablespoon every minute, sprinkling it gradually over whites. When all sugar is incorporated, add vanilla and beat for 1 to 2 more minutes. Whites should hold very stiff, sharp, unbending peaks.

Grease and flour-dust 2 baking sheets (9 by 14 inches or larger); trace an 8-inch-diameter circle on each. Using a pastry bag with a plain tip (or a spoon and spatula), pipe or spread about half the meringue onto 1 baking sheet in a solid 8-inch disk of even thickness. On second baking sheet, shape remaining meringue in a solid 8-inch disk with a decorative surface of puffs and swirls.

Bake meringues in a 250° oven for 1½ hours (color should be pure white to faint amber). If you have 2 ovens, position each meringue just below center in each oven. If you have 1 oven, position meringues just above and below center, then switch their positions halfway through baking.

Turn off heat and leave meringues in closed oven for 3 to 4 hours to continue drying. Remove from oven; while baking sheets are still warm, flex them to pop meringues free, but leave disks in place to cool at room temperature. If made ahead, store cooled disks airtight at room temperature for up to 5 days.

To assemble torte, dissolve instant coffee in liqueur. Whip cream until it holds stiff peaks; fold in coffee mixture and chocolate.

Place plain meringue disk on a flat serving plate; spread whipped cream mixture evenly on disk, spreading just to edges. Place decorative meringue disk atop whipped cream. Cover and refrigerate for at least 8 hours or until next day. Cut into wedges to serve.

Italian Honey-Confection Cake

PREPARATION TIME: 50 to 55 minutes
COOKING TIME: About 40 minutes
COOLING TIME: At least 1 hour
PER SERVING: 272 calories, 3 grams protein, 51 grams carbohydrate, 8 grams total fat, 0 milligram cholesterol, 2 milligrams sodium

A delight that's long been found in San Francisco's Italian markets is panforte de Siena, *named for the city of its origin. A cross between confection and cake, the honey-sweetened treat makes good use of Western almonds.*

Makes 1 cake (2½ lbs.), 16 servings

    ½ pound (about 2 cups) whole blanched almonds
    ½ pound *each* candied orange peel and candied lemon peel, finely chopped (about 2½ cups *total*)
    ½ cup all-purpose flour
    2 teaspoons ground cinnamon
    ¼ teaspoon ground allspice
    ¾ cup *each* honey and granulated sugar
    Powdered sugar

Spread almonds in a single layer in a 10- by 15-inch rimmed baking pan. Toast in a 350° oven until golden, 8 to 10 minutes, shaking pan once or twice; let cool.

Grease and flour-dust an 8- or 9-inch-diameter cake pan with a removable bottom. Line pan bottom with cooking parchment or brown paper; butter well and set aside.

Place toasted almonds and candied peels in a large bowl. Combine flour, cinnamon, and allspice; add to nut mixture and stir until well blended. Set aside.

In a 2- to 3-quart pan, combine honey and granulated sugar. Cook, uncovered, over medium-high heat, stirring often, until mixture boils and registers 265°F on a candy thermometer. Remove from heat and pour over nut-fruit mixture; stir until mixed.

Pour mixture into prepared cake pan and press down slightly to form an even layer. Bake in a 300° oven until edges look dry, about 40 minutes. Let cool completely in pan on a rack.

Sift powdered sugar generously in a 10-inch-diameter circle in center of a sheet of wax paper. Run a sharp knife around pan sides, then invert cake onto sugar-dusted paper. Carefully remove pan bottom and parchment, cutting paper away if necessary. Generously sift powdered sugar over cake, then invert cake onto a plate. Generously dust with powdered sugar once more.

If made ahead, wrap cake airtight and store in a cool, dry place for up to 3 weeks. To serve, cut into thin wedges.

Summer Cheesecake

PREPARATION TIME: 3 to 4 days to make cheese; 25 to 30 minutes to make cake
BAKING TIME: About 50 minutes
CHILLING TIME: At least 2 hours
PER SERVING: 342 calories, 8 grams protein, 31 grams carbohydrate, 21 grams total fat, 147 milligrams cholesterol, 129 milligrams sodium

Spending time to achieve quality results has never bothered Sunset readers. To make this reader-favorite cheesecake, for example, you start by preparing your own cheese from fresh whole milk. The cheese takes 3 to 4 days to set and drain, but the resulting cake is as cool, refreshing, and delicate as any imaginable—and definitely worth the wait.

Makes 10 to 12 servings

 1½ cups finely crushed arrowroot biscuits
 6 tablespoons butter or margarine, melted
 1 recipe Fresh Summer Cheese made with milk (recipe follows)
 1 cup sugar
 2 teaspoons vanilla
 2 tablespoons lemon juice
 4 large eggs
 2 cups sour cream
  Fresh strawberries or other berries

Blend biscuits and butter; press mixture evenly over bottom and about 1 inch up sides of a 9-inch cheesecake pan or cake pan with a removable bottom.

In a bowl, combine fresh cheese, ¾ cup of the sugar, 1 teaspoon of the vanilla, and lemon juice. Beat until smooth. Beat in eggs, 1 at a time, blending well after each addition.

Pour mixture into crumb-lined pan; bake in a 325° oven for 40 minutes. Blend sour cream, remaining ¼ cup sugar, and remaining 1 teaspoon vanilla; remove cake from oven and spread sour cream mixture evenly over top. Return to oven for 10 more minutes. (If desired, you may omit the sour cream topping and simply bake cake until center appears set when pan is gently shaken, about 50 minutes.)

Let cool; then refrigerate until cold before serving. (To hold until next day, cover lightly.) Accompany with berries.

FRESH SUMMER CHEESE. Heat 8 cups **whole milk** or 1½ cups whipping cream to lukewarm (90° to 100°F) and pour into a bowl. Stir in ¼ cup freshly opened **buttermilk.** Cover and let stand at room temperature (about 70°F) until a soft curd forms, 24 to 48 hours; mixture should look like soft yogurt. Curd forms faster on hot days than on cool ones.

Line a colander with muslin; set in sink. Pour in curd; let drain for about 10 minutes. Fold cloth over curd. Set colander on a rack in a rimmed pan (for milk curd, allow 1 inch between rack and pan bottom). Cover entire unit airtight with plastic wrap. Let curd drain in refrigerator for 36 to 48 hours. Spoon from cloth to use. Makes 2 cups if made with milk, 1 cup if made with cream.

Gianduia Cheesecake

PREPARATION TIME: About 50 minutes (includes time to roast nuts)
BAKING TIME: About 50 minutes
COOLING AND CHILLING TIME: At least 2 hours
PER SERVING: 441 calories, 8 grams protein, 32 grams carbohydrate, 33 grams total fat, 114 milligrams cholesterol, 200 milligrams sodium

Italy's milk chocolate-hazelnut candy is called gianduia in honor of a legendary hero of Piedmont. This small, rich cheesecake bears the same heroic name; it's made with purchased gianduia or an easily made mixture of roasted hazelnuts and chopped milk chocolate.

Makes 6 servings

 1 large package (8 oz.) and 1 small package (3 oz.) cream cheese, at room temperature
 ¼ cup granulated sugar
 1 large egg
 1½ tablespoons whipping cream
 8 ounces milk chocolate with hazelnuts (gianduia); or roasted hazelnuts with chocolate (directions follow)
 1½ tablespoons hazelnut liqueur
  Powdered sugar
  Whipped cream

Beat cream cheese and granulated sugar until well mixed. Add egg and the 1½ tablespoons cream and beat until smoothly blended.

Coarsely chop gianduia. Place gianduia or roasted hazelnuts with chocolate in the top of double boiler; set over hot water and stir until melted. Stir melted chocolate and liqueur into cream cheese mixture.

Butter a 6-inch-diameter cake pan (at least 2 inches deep). If pan bottom is not removable, line with wax paper; butter wax paper. If pan bottom can be removed, set pan on a large sheet of foil and fold edges of foil up and slightly above rim to prevent seepage. Pour batter into pan.

Set cake pan in a slightly larger pan and place in center of a 350° oven. Pour boiling water into larger pan until it reaches about ⅔ of the way up sides of cake pan. Bake until cake appears set in center when pan is gently shaken, about 50 minutes. Let cool, then cover and refrigerate for at least 1 hour.

Run a knife around pan sides. If pan has a removable bottom, remove sides and set cake on a serving plate. If pan bottom is stationary, cover top of cake with wax paper; lay a plate on paper. Hold pan and plate together and quickly flip; lift off pan and peel paper lining from cake bottom. Lay a small serving plate on cake; holding the 2 plates together, quickly flip. Dust cake with powdered sugar; cut into wedges. Accompany with whipped cream.

ROASTED HAZELNUTS WITH CHOCOLATE. Put ⅔ cup **hazelnuts** in a 9-inch pie pan. Bake in a 350° oven until nuts are lightly browned beneath skins, about 15 minutes. Let cool slightly, then pour onto a clean towel. Fold towel to enclose; rub nuts between your hands to remove as much of skins as possible. Lift nuts from towel and whirl in a food processor or blender until a paste forms. Combine with 5 ounces chopped **milk chocolate.**

Two Pastel Pies

Pictured at right

PREPARATION TIME: About 1 hour
BAKING TIME: About 30 minutes
PER SERVING: 425 calories, 5 grams protein, 36 grams carbohydrate, 30 grams total fat, 125 milligrams cholesterol, 175 milligrams sodium

These are designer pies, created for raspberries, blackberries, strawberries, blueberries, gooseberries, or red currants. It's hard to choose just one flavor—so we suggest choosing two. The little pies are called "pastel" for their pale, luscious berry colors.

Makes 2 tarts, 4 servings each

> **About 1½ cups *each* (3 cups *total*) of 2 kinds of berries (use strawberries, raspberries, blackberries, blueberries, gooseberries, or red currants)**
>
> **4 ounces cream cheese**
>
> **½ cup powdered sugar**
>
> **½ teaspoon *each* vanilla and grated lemon peel**
>
> **2 teaspoons lemon juice**
>
> **1⅓ cups whipping cream**
>
> **2 baked Butter Pastry Shells (recipe follows)**
>
> **Granulated sugar**
>
> **Fresh mint leaves**

Hull, remove blossom ends, or stem berries as necessary. Rinse and drain. In a food processor or blender, separately whirl ¾ cup of each kind of berry until smoothly puréed. Pour each purée through a fine strainer into separate bowls, rubbing pulp to extract as much as possible; discard seeds. Cover and refrigerate.

Using an electric mixer, beat cream cheese, powdered sugar, vanilla, lemon peel, and lemon juice on high speed until smoothly blended. Scoop half the mixture into another bowl. Add 1 berry purée to each bowl; beat to blend well.

Whip cream until it holds soft peaks; add half the cream to each berry mixture and fold to blend.

To make each pie, spread ¾ cup of 1 berry mixture into a pastry shell. Set aside a few berries of the matching flavor, and lay the remainder onto berry filling (slice strawberries; sprinkle gooseberries with about 1 tablespoon granulated sugar). Top with remaining same-flavor berry mixture, swirling over fruit. Garnish with reserved berries and mint leaves. Serve, or cover lightly and refrigerate for up to 6 hours.

BUTTER PASTRY SHELLS. In a food processor or a bowl, combine 1⅓ cups **all-purpose flour** and ¼ cup **sugar.** Add ½ cup (¼ lb.) **butter** or margarine, cut into small pieces; whirl (or rub with your fingers) until fine crumbs form. Add 1 **large egg yolk;** whirl (or mix with a fork) until dough holds together. Divide dough in half. Press each portion over bottom and up sides of a 7½-inch tart pan with a removable bottom (you need 2 pans). Bake pastry shells in a 300° oven until pale gold, 25 to 30 minutes; let cool. If made ahead, cover and let stand at room temperature until next day.

Too tempting to resist, elegant Pastel Pies (recipe at left) begin with a purée of fresh berries. The decorative garnish of mint and berries tells you what flavor to expect.

Fresh Pineapple Pie

WESTERN CLASSIC

PREPARATION TIME: About 45 minutes
BAKING TIME: About 45 minutes
COOLING TIME: At least 30 minutes
PER SERVING: 446 calories, 5 grams protein, 63 grams carbohydrate, 20 grams total fat, 64 milligrams cholesterol, 151 milligrams sodium

Sunset *has made a practice of showcasing Western produce—and that includes Hawaiian fruits. Juicy fresh pineapple features regularly in our recipes; here, it fills a golden two-crust pie given to us by an Island cook.*

Makes 8 or 9 servings

> 1 small ripe pineapple (about 3 lbs.)
> Pastry for a 9-inch double-crust pie
> 1 cup sugar
> 2 tablespoons cornstarch
> 2 large eggs
> 1 teaspoon grated lime peel
> 1 tablespoon lime juice
> 1 tablespoon butter or margarine

With a sharp knife, cut top off pineapple. Also cut away peel, slicing deep enough to remove eyes; remove core. Finely chop remaining fruit; place in a colander over a bowl and let drain well (you should have 3 cups pineapple).

On a floured board, roll out half the pastry into a ⅛-inch-thick round. Fit into a 9-inch pie pan; trim excess from edges. Mix sugar and cornstarch; beat with eggs until thick and lemon colored. Stir in lime peel, lime juice, and drained pineapple.

Pour fruit mixture into pastry-lined pan. Dot filling with butter. Roll remaining pastry into a ⅛-inch-thick round; place over filling. Fold top pastry under bottom pastry. Flute edge. Slash top in a few places to allow steam to escape. Bake in a 425° oven until well browned, about 45 minutes. If pastry edges begin to brown too much, cover edge with a strip of foil. Serve warm or at room temperature.

Pear Pepper Pie

PREPARATION TIME: 45 to 50 minutes
BAKING TIME: About 1 hour
COOLING TIME: At least 30 minutes
PER SERVING: 383 calories, 5 grams protein, 61 grams carbohydrate, 14 grams total fat, 95 milligrams cholesterol, 121 milligrams sodium

Pears and pepper may seem an odd partnership—but the spice actually heightens the sweetness of the pears, while the fruit, in turn, tempers the pepper's heat.

Makes 8 or 9 servings

> ¾ cup sugar
> ¼ cup quick-cooking tapioca
> ¼ teaspoon white pepper
> 5 to 7 large firm-ripe pears such as Bosc, d'Anjou, or Comice

> Butter Pastry (recipe follows)
> 1 large egg, lightly beaten
> ¼ cup whipping cream

In a large bowl, mix sugar, tapioca, and pepper. Peel, core, and thinly slice pears to make 8 cups. Mix pears with sugar mixture; set aside.

On a floured board, roll out half the pastry into a ⅛-inch-thick round. Fit into a 9-inch pie pan; trim excess from edges. Pour in pear mixture. Roll remaining pastry into a ⅛-inch-thick round; place over pears. Fold top pastry under bottom pastry. Flute edge. Slash top in a few places to allow steam to escape; brush with egg. Bake in a 400° oven until bubbly, about 1 hour.

Cut a 3-inch hole in center of top crust; lift out pastry and slowly pour in cream, lifting pears slightly with a knife so cream seeps in. Replace pastry and let pie cool in pan on a rack. Serve warm or at room temperature.

BUTTER PASTRY. Place 2 cups **all-purpose flour** in a food processor or a bowl. Add ½ cup (¼ lb.) **butter** or margarine, cut into chunks. Whirl (or rub with your fingers) until crumbs are pea-size. Add 1 **large egg** and 4 to 5 tablespoons **cold water;** whirl (or mix with a fork) until dough holds together. Press dough into a ball.

Double Blueberry Tart

WESTERN CLASSIC

PREPARATION TIME: 35 to 40 minutes
COOLING TIME: 10 minutes for filling
PER SERVING: 552 calories, 6 grams protein, 78 grams carbohydrate, 25 grams total fat, 130 milligrams cholesterol, 245 milligrams sodium

Small scale gives this two-layer blueberry tart extra appeal. It's just the right size to serve the family or a small group of guests, with no tempting leftovers.

Makes 4 servings

> 3 to 3½ cups blueberries
> 6 tablespoons granulated sugar
> ½ teaspoon grated lemon peel
> 1 tablespoon lemon juice
> 1 baked Butter Pastry Shell (page 267)
> Powdered sugar

In a 1- to 1½-quart pan, combine 2 cups of the blueberries, granulated sugar, lemon peel, and lemon juice. Bring to a boil over high heat; stir often until berries are as thick as soft jam, 8 to 10 minutes. Let cool. If made ahead, cover and refrigerate until next day.

Remove pan sides from pastry shell; pour sauce into pastry shell and spread evenly. Neatly arrange remaining 1 to 1½ cups berries on sauce to completely cover surface. If made ahead, let tart stand at cool room temperature for up to 4 hours. To serve, generously sprinkle top of tart with powdered sugar. Cut into wedges.

Crunch-top Apple Pie

W E S T E R N   C L A S S I C

PREPARATION TIME: About 35 minutes
BAKING TIME: About 1 hour
COOLING TIME: About 30 minutes
PER SERVING: 678 calories, 7 grams protein, 74 grams carbohydrate, 41 grams total fat, 57 milligrams cholesterol, 311 milligrams sodium

Crunch-top Apple Pie and Caramel-topped Apple Pie (below) are among the recipes most requested by Sunset readers. The best description of both pies is this: they're just plain good!

Makes 8 or 9 servings

> 6 **medium-size tart apples (about 2½ lbs.** **total), peeled, cored, and sliced**
> **Unbaked 10-inch pastry shell**
> 1 **cup** *each* **sugar and graham cracker** **crumbs**
> ½ **cup** *each* **all-purpose flour and** **chopped walnuts**
> ½ **teaspoon ground cinnamon**
> ½ **cup (¼ lb.) butter or margarine, melted**
> 1 **cup whipping cream (optional)**

Arrange apples evenly in pastry shell. Mix sugar, cracker crumbs, flour, walnuts, and cinnamon; sprinkle over apples. Pour butter evenly over topping. Bake in a 350° oven until apples are tender when pierced, about 1 hour. Serve warm or at room temperature. Whip cream and offer to spoon over pie.

Caramel-topped Apple Pie

W E S T E R N   C L A S S I C

PREPARATION TIME: About 35 minutes (includes 10 minutes for sauce)
BAKING TIME: About 40 minutes
COOLING TIME: About 30 minutes
PER SERVING: 420 calories, 4 grams protein, 66 grams carbohydrate, 17 grams total fat, 2 milligrams cholesterol, 180 milligrams sodium

Make this pie with the popular cellophane-wrapped caramels sold in supermarkets—or try candy-shop or "gourmet" caramels, if you like.

Makes 8 or 9 servings

> 5½ **cups peeled, sliced tart apples** **(about 2 lbs.)**
> ¼ **cup water**
> **Unbaked 9-inch pastry shell**
> ¾ **cup** *each* **sugar and graham cracker** **crumbs**
> 1 **tablespoon all-purpose flour**
> ½ **teaspoon** *each* **ground cinnamon and** **nutmeg**
> ½ **cup chopped pecans**
> ⅓ **cup butter or margarine, melted**
> ½ **pound vanilla caramels**
> ½ **cup milk**

In an 3- to 4-quart pan, combine apples and water. Bring to a boil; boil for 1 minute, then pour into a 10-by 15-inch rimmed baking pan to cool quickly. Spoon apples into pastry shell.

Combine sugar, cracker crumbs, flour, cinnamon, nutmeg, pecans, and butter; sprinkle over apples. Bake in a 425° oven for 10 minutes. Reduce oven temperature to 350°; continue to bake until apples are tender when pierced, 20 more minutes.

Meanwhile, combine caramels and milk in the top of a double boiler. Stir over simmering water until melted and smooth. Pour caramel sauce over pie; continue to bake until caramel just begins to bubble at pie edges, about 10 more minutes. Let cool.

Raspberries with Lemon Whirligigs

PREPARATION TIME: About 25 minutes
BAKING TIME: About 25 minutes
PER SERVING: 242 calories, 3 grams protein, 42 grams carbohydrate, 7 grams total fat, 43 milligrams cholesterol, 318 milligrams sodium

Sweet, bubbly berry cobbler topped with rich biscuit pinwheels dishes up as much delight today as it did when we first published the recipe over 20 years ago.

Makes 8 servings

> ⅔ **cup sugar**
> 2 **tablespoons cornstarch**
> ⅛ **teaspoon** *each* **ground cinnamon and** **nutmeg**
> 1 **cup water**
> 3 **cups raspberries, boysenberries,** **loganberries, or blackberries**
> **Lemon Biscuit Whirligigs (recipe follows)**
> **Whipping cream**

In a 1- to 1½-quart pan, combine sugar, cornstarch, cinnamon, and nutmeg. Gradually stir in water. Bring to a rolling boil over high heat, stirring constantly. Remove from heat. Place berries in a shallow 1½-quart baking dish; pour hot sauce evenly over them. Bake, uncovered, in a 400° oven for 10 minutes.

Pat out each biscuit whirligig slightly, then arrange biscuits atop berries. Continue to bake until biscuits are golden brown, about 15 more minutes. Serve warm, with cream (whipped, if desired).

LEMON BISCUIT WHIRLIGIGS. In a bowl, stir together 1 cup **all-purpose flour,** 2 teaspoons **baking powder,** and ¼ teaspoon **salt.** Rub in 2 tablespoons **solid vegetable shortening** with your fingers until mixture is crumbly. Add 1 **large egg,** lightly beaten, and 2 tablespoons **milk,** half-and-half, or light cream; stir with a fork to moisten evenly. Pat dough into a flat cake and roll out on a lightly floured board to make a 6- by 12-inch rectangle.

Combine ¼ cup **sugar,** 2 tablespoons melted **butter** or margarine, and ¼ teaspoon grated **lemon peel;** spread over dough. Roll up dough from a long side, jelly roll style; cut crosswise into 8 equal slices.

WESTERN BERRIES start up their flavorful season in spring. Though early blueberries are shipped here from the East, most of our berry bounty comes from the Northwest or is shipped from Watsonville, California. The glittering berry parade includes strawberries, raspberries, and blackberries in spring, followed by gooseberries, currants, and later varieties of the others through the summer.

An autumn harvest of toasted almonds, hazelnuts, and macadamias goes into golden Nut Mosaic Tart (recipe below).

Nut Mosaic Tart

Pictured above

WESTERN CLASSIC

PREPARATION TIME: About 35 minutes

BAKING TIME: About 1 hour (includes time to roast nuts)

PER SERVING: 487 calories, 10 grams protein, 44 grams carbohydrate, 32 grams total fat, 123 milligrams cholesterol, 142 milligrams sodium

Autumn signals the West's great nut harvest—walnuts from California, Oregon, and Washington; almonds and pistachios from California; hazelnuts from Oregon; pecans from Arizona; and macadamias from Hawaii. This showy tart makes the most of their naturally rich flavors.

Makes 10 to 12 servings

3 cups whole or half nuts (almonds, walnuts, hazelnuts, macadamias, pistachios, or pecans)

1 recipe Butter Pastry Shell dough (page 267)

3 large eggs

1 cup honey

½ teaspoon grated orange peel

1 teaspoon vanilla

¼ cup (⅛ lb.) butter or margarine, melted

Whipped cream (optional)

Place nuts (if unroasted) in a 10- by 15-inch rimmed baking pan and bake in a 350° oven until lightly toasted beneath skins (break nuts open to check, if necessary), 8 to 15 minutes. Let cool. Press pastry dough evenly over bottom and up sides of an 11-inch tart pan with a removable bottom.

In a bowl, combine eggs, honey, orange peel, vanilla, and butter; beat until well blended. Stir in toasted nuts. Pour into pastry-lined pan. Bake on lowest rack of a 350° oven until top is golden brown all over, about 40 minutes. Let cool in pan on a rack.

To serve, remove pan sides. Cut into wedges; offer whipped cream to top each serving, if desired.

(If you shell your own nuts, count on getting about these amounts from 1 pound nuts in the shell: almonds—2 cups whole, halves, or chopped; walnuts—2 cups whole or halves, 1 to 1¾ cups chopped; hazelnuts—1⅓ to 1½ cups whole, halves, or chopped; macadamias—1 to 1¼ cups whole, halves, or chopped; pistachios—1¾ to 2 cups whole, halves, or chopped; pecans—2 to 2¼ cups whole or halves, 2 cups chopped.)

Apricot Almond Tart

W E S T E R N   C L A S S I C

PREPARATION TIME: 35 to 40 minutes (includes time to cook and cool filling)
BAKING TIME: 25 to 35 minutes
PER SERVING: 502 calories, 6 grams protein, 61 grams carbohydrate, 28 grams total fat, 98 milligrams cholesterol, 132 milligrams sodium

California's almonds and dried apricots join forces in an attractive pastry with a sweet-tart filling and crunchy topping. A small-scale dessert for a small party, it's perfect for four diners.

Makes 4 servings

- ½ cup *each* moist-pack dried apricots and water
- ½ cup sugar
- ½ cup *each* sliced almonds and whipping cream
- 1 baked Butter Pastry Shell (page 267)

In a 3- to 4-cup pan, simmer apricots, water, and 2 tablespoons of the sugar over low heat, covered, until apricots are soft and liquid is absorbed, 15 to 20 minutes. Stir often. Uncover; let cool for at least 10 minutes or until next day.

In a 1- to 1½-quart pan, combine remaining 6 tablespoons sugar, almonds, and cream. Bring to a boil, stirring; boil until sauce forms large, shiny bubbles as it cooks.

Spoon apricots into pastry shell; pour hot sauce over fruit. Bake in a 350° oven until nuts are golden, 25 to 35 minutes. Let cool. If made ahead, let stand at cool room temperature for up to 4 hours. To serve, remove pan sides; cut tart into wedges.

Rhubarb Yorkshire

PREPARATION TIME: 10 to 15 minutes
BAKING TIME: About 25 minutes
PER SERVING: 404 calories, 5 grams protein, 51 grams carbohydrate, 21 grams total fat, 144 milligrams cholesterol, 414 milligrams sodium

Yorkshire pudding makes a great showcase for the pink hothouse rhubarb of early spring, as well as the later, greener garden-grown stalks. Serve this hot dessert in bowls; offer thick brown sugar syrup and cold whipping cream to pour over each serving.

Makes 4 to 6 servings

- ¼ cup (⅛ lb.) butter or margarine
- 2 large eggs
- ¾ cup all-purpose flour
- ¼ teaspoon salt
- ¾ cup milk
- ½ pound rhubarb, cut into ¾-inch pieces
- ⅓ cup butter or margarine
  About 1 cup firmly packed brown sugar
  Whipping cream

Place the ¼ cup butter in a 1-quart soufflé or deep baking dish. Set in a 425° oven until butter is melted and bubbly.

Meanwhile, in a blender or food processor, whirl eggs, flour, and salt until smooth. Add milk; whirl until smooth. Pour batter into bubbling butter; drop rhubarb into center of batter. Bake until edges of crust are dark brown, about 25 minutes.

When pudding is nearly done, melt the ⅓ cup butter in a 1- to 2-quart pan; stir in sugar and cook, stirring, until sugar is dissolved and mixture is a thick syrup.

Spoon hot pudding into bowls; offer hot brown sugar sauce and cream to top individual servings.

Angel Pie

W E S T E R N   C L A S S I C

PREPARATION TIME: 20 to 25 minutes
COOKING TIME: About 40 minutes to bake meringue; 10 to 15 minutes to make sauce
CHILLING TIME: About 2 hours for sauce; at least 2 hours for assembled pie
PER SERVING: 273 calories, 4 grams protein, 39 grams carbohydrate, 12 grams total fat, 170 milligrams cholesterol, 46 milligrams sodium

A tart lemon sauce crowns the meringue base of this perennially popular dessert, which first appeared in Sunset Magazine in 1929. Various versions have graced our pages at least a dozen times in the years since.

Makes 6 to 8 servings

- 4 large eggs, separated
- ½ teaspoon cream of tartar
- 1½ cups sugar
  Grated peel of 2 lemons
- 3 tablespoons lemon juice
- 1 cup whipping cream

In a large bowl, beat egg whites with an electric mixer on high speed until frothy. Sprinkle in cream of tartar; continue to beat until whites hold soft peaks. Gradually add 1 cup of the sugar, 2 tablespoons at a time, beating until meringue is glossy and holds very stiff peaks.

With the back of a tablespoon, spread meringue in a well-greased 9-inch pie pan, pushing it high on pan sides so it resembles a pie shell. Bake in a 300° oven until meringue is firm and dry but not browned, about 40 minutes. Let cool in pan on a rack. If made ahead, cover airtight and hold at room temperature until next day.

In the top of a double boiler, beat egg yolks, the remaining ½ cup sugar, lemon peel, and lemon juice until blended. Cook over simmering water, stirring constantly, until sauce is thick, about 10 minutes. Let cool, then cover and refrigerate until cold, about 2 hours (or until next day).

Whip cream until it holds soft peaks; fold into chilled lemon sauce. Spoon mixture into meringue shell. To mellow flavors, refrigerate for at least 2 hours or up to 8 hours before cutting.

White Chocolate Baskets

PREPARATION AND COOKING TIME: About 50 minutes for baskets; about 15 minutes for mousse; about 10 minutes for cranberries

CHILLING TIME: About 1 hour for baskets; about 1 hour for mousse; about 30 minutes for cranberries

PER SERVING: 308 calories, 4 grams protein, 34 grams carbohydrate, 17 grams total fat, 24 milligrams cholesterol, 59 milligrams sodium

FITNESS is a way of life for many today. With their appreciation of salads, seafood, and fresh, beautiful fruits and vegetables, Westerners have had a head start in the well-being race. But there's always room for the occasional indulgence, too—frozen tofulato or chocolate gelato; light Salzburger Nockerln or dense caramel-macadamia torte; trendy White Chocolate Baskets or traditional (but extra-special) Summer Cheesecake.

Not that it makes a shred of difference to its sublime appeal, but white chocolate technically isn't chocolate. Though made with cocoa butter from cocoa beans, it lacks the definitive chocolate liquor that flavors dark chocolate. Painted into muffin cups, then chilled, white chocolate makes crisp, sweet baskets to fill with a snowy mousse. Garnish with poached cranberries and strands of orange peel for a stylish holiday dessert.

Makes 8 servings

> 6 ounces white chocolate, coarsely chopped (about 1¼ cups)
> White Chocolate Mousse (recipe follows)
> Poached Cranberries (recipe follows)
> Thin strands of orange peel

Place chocolate in the top of a double boiler. Place over simmering water and stir just until chocolate is melted. Remove from hot water.

Meanwhile, grease 8 muffin cups (2½-inch diameter) with solid vegetable shortening. Line each cup with a 5-inch square of plastic wrap (shortening helps hold it in place). Do not trim off excess plastic. Place 1 tablespoon melted chocolate in bottom of each cup. With a small brush, paint chocolate up cup sides. Refrigerate until firm, about 1 hour (or cover and refrigerate for up to 1 week). Lift from cups and carefully peel off plastic; avoid touching chocolate.

Fill each chocolate basket with an equal amount of cold White Chocolate Mousse and top with ⅛ of the cranberries (and some of the cranberry poaching liquid, if desired). Garnish with a few strands of orange peel. To eat, scoop out mousse, then crack chocolate basket into bite-size pieces.

WHITE CHOCOLATE MOUSSE. Place 6 ounces **white chocolate,** coarsely chopped (about 1¼ cups) in the top of a double boiler. Place over simmering water; stir chocolate until melted. In a small bowl, beat 3 **large egg whites** with an electric mixer on high speed until foamy. Beating constantly, sprinkle in 1 tablespoon **sugar;** beat until stiff. Fold in hot melted chocolate until blended. In another small bowl, whip ½ cup **whipping cream** until it holds stiff peaks. Add cream to egg white mixture, folding to blend. Cover and refrigerate until cold, at least 1 hour (or until next day).

POACHED CRANBERRIES. In a 1- to 1½-quart pan, combine ½ teaspoon grated **orange peel,** ¼ cup **orange juice,** 2 tablespoons **sugar,** and ¾ cup **cranberries.** Simmer, uncovered, until cranberries pop, about 5 minutes. Let cool, then cover and refrigerate until cold, about 30 minutes (or until next day).

Spirited Chocolate Fondue

PREPARATION TIME: About 10 minutes for fondue; about 15 minutes for dippers

COOKING TIME: About 10 minutes

PER SERVING: 303 calories, 4 grams protein, 24 grams carbohydrate, 25 grams total fat, 27 milligrams cholesterol, 9 milligrams sodium

Who can say no to chocolate—especially in a rich fondue with fresh and dried fruit, nuts, and cookies as dippers?

Makes 2⅓ cups, about 10 servings

> 1 pound bittersweet, semisweet, or milk chocolate (or a mixture of all 3), chopped
> 1 cup whipping cream
> ¼ cup orange liqueur or brandy
> 5 to 6 cups dippers (suggestions follow)

Combine chocolate and cream in the top of a double boiler. Place over simmering water and stir just until chocolate is melted, about 10 minutes. (Or use a chafing dish set over hot water.) Stir in liqueur.

Serve from a chafing dish set over hot water. Offer dippers of your choice to dunk into fondue.

DIPPERS. You'll need 5 to 6 cups dippers *total.* Choose seasonal **fresh fruits,** such as strawberries or cherries with stems, chunks of fresh coconut or pineapple, kiwi slices, or orange segments; whole or half **nuts; dried fruits,** such as apricots, peaches, pears, or dates; and **butter cookies.**

Persian Baklava

PREPARATION TIME: 35 to 40 minutes for pastry; about 10 minutes for syrup

BAKING TIME: 50 to 60 minutes

COOLING TIME: At least 2 hours

PER PIECE: 278 calories, 4 grams protein, 30 grams carbohydrate, 17 grams total fat, 25 milligrams cholesterol, 3 milligrams sodium

In parts of the West where Middle Eastern immigrants have settled, exotic pastries like baklava are apt to show up in local bakeries. Here's how to make your own—with purchased fila, domestic almonds and pistachios, and a fragrant rose water syrup.

Makes about 40 pieces

> 4 cups very finely chopped blanched almonds
> 2 cups sugar
> 2 teaspoons ground cardamom
> 2 cups (1 lb.) unsalted butter, melted
> 1 package (1 lb.) fila pastry, thawed if frozen
> Rose Water Syrup (recipe follows)
> About ½ cup coarsely chopped pistachio nuts (optional)

Combine almonds, sugar, and cardamom. Generously brush the bottom of a 9- by 13-inch baking pan with some of the butter. Carefully fold 3 fila sheets to fit pan; place in pan 1 at a time, brushing each layer with a little of the butter. Sprinkle about ⅓ cup of the almond mixture over top sheet of fila. Fold 1 more fila sheet to fit pan; brush with butter and sprinkle evenly with ⅓ cup more almond mixture.

Add more layers, using 1 folded sheet of fila, a generous brushing of butter, and about ⅓ cup of the almond mixture for each, until nut mixture is used up. Fold remaining sheets of fila to fit pan and place on top, brushing each layer with butter before adding the next.

With a very sharp knife, carefully cut diagonally across pan to make 2½-inch diamond shapes, cutting all the way to bottom of pan. Pour any remaining butter evenly over the top. Bake in a 300° oven until lightly browned, 50 minutes to 1 hour.

Pour Rose Water Syrup evenly over top of hot pastry; decorate each piece with a few pistachio pieces, if you wish. Let cool before serving. If made ahead, cover and refrigerate for up to 1 week.

ROSE WATER SYRUP. Bring 2 cups **sugar** and 1 cup **water** to a gentle boil in a 1½-quart pan. Boil gently, uncovered, until syrup registers 230° to 234°F on a candy thermometer. Stir in 2 tablespoons **rose water.** Keep warm until ready to pour over baklava.

Chongos Zamoranos

PREPARATION TIME: About 1½ hours for chongos; 7 to 8 minutes for syrup
COOKING TIME: At least 6 hours
PER SERVING: 433 calories, 11 grams protein, 75 grams carbohydrate, 11 grams total fat, 46 milligrams cholesterol, 297 milligrams sodium

Tender, sweet lumps with a cheeselike consistency and a subtle caramel flavor, chongos are a specialty of Zamora, Mexico, a city famous for its desserts.

Makes 5 or 6 servings

    8 **cups whole milk**
    4 **rennet tablets, finely crushed**
  ¼ **cup cold water**
1¾ **cups sugar**
    1 **tablespoon vanilla**
    2 **cinnamon sticks (***each* **about 3 inches long), broken into smaller lengths**
    2 **cups water or chongos liquid**

In a 4- to 5-quart pan, heat milk to 110°F. Mix rennet with cold water, ¾ cup of the sugar, and vanilla; stir thoroughly into milk in pan. Let stand at room temperature until set, about 1 hour. Using a sharp knife, divide surface into 1- to 2-inch squares (smaller pieces make firmer chongos; larger pieces are softer in texture), cutting straight down through mixture to pan bottom. Set pan over lowest heat and cook, uncovered, for 6 hours; mixture should never get hot enough to cause motion in pan, since this will break up chongos. *Do not stir.* After 6 hours, the chongos should be white and as firm as warm cream cheese.

In a 3- to 4-quart pan, combine cinnamon sticks and remaining 1 cup sugar with 2 cups water. (Or use 2 cups chongos liquid: drain or siphon out liquid, disturbing chongos as little as possible, then pour

liquid through a cloth to remove scraps. If needed, add water to make 2 cups liquid.) Bring to a boil; boil for 5 minutes. Using a slotted spoon, gently transfer chongos to hot syrup. Let stand until lukewarm before serving, or refrigerate until cold. To store, cover and refrigerate for up to 2 weeks. To serve, spoon several chongos and some of the syrup into each bowl.

Electric frying pan method. Heat milk in frying pan to 110°F. Turn off pan heat and flavor milk as directed. Let stand at room temperature until set, then cut as directed, also running knife around edge of pan. Turn on heat at lowest setting. Cook, uncovered, for 6 hours. Or cook the lumps overnight (up to 10 hours); they'll be firmer and less moist.

Gently spoon chongos into hot prepared syrup.

Salzburger Nockerln

PREPARATION TIME: 10 to 15 minutes
BAKING TIME: 7 to 10 minutes
PER SERVING: 126 calories, 4 grams protein, 12 grams carbohydrate, 7 grams total fat, 188 milligrams cholesterol, 66 milligrams sodium

This airy delight offers a heavenly combination of flavors and textures: hot, sweet, soufflé-like puffs of egg, slightly browned butter, melting bits of chocolate, cool whipped cream. The dessert goes together quickly, with ingredients you're likely to have on hand.

Makes 4 to 6 servings

    4 **large eggs, separated**
  ¼ **cup sugar**
    4 **teaspoons all-purpose flour**
    1 to 2 **tablespoons butter or margarine**
    1 to 2 **ounces semisweet chocolate, grated**
    Whipped cream (optional)

In a large bowl, beat egg whites with an electric mixer on high speed until they hold stiff peaks. Gradually add sugar, beating constantly; continue to beat until whites hold very stiff peaks. Set whites aside.

Place egg yolks in a small bowl. Using the same beaters, beat yolks on high speed until very light colored and slightly thickened. Gradually beat in flour. Fold yolks into whites, blending evenly (don't worry if a few streaks of whites remain).

While you are folding together yolks and whites, melt butter in a shallow 7- by 11-inch baking pan over medium heat until bubbly. Spoon mounds of egg mixture into pan; then bake in a 350° oven until top is tinged with brown, 7 to 10 minutes. Serve immediately; sprinkle chocolate over each portion and top with whipped cream, if desired.

RUM & APRICOT NOCKERLN

Follow directions for **Salzburger Nockerln,** but add 2 tablespoons **rum** to egg yolks as you beat. While nockerln are baking, combine 2 tablespoons **apricot jam** and 1½ tablespoons **rum** in a 1- to 2-cup pan; stir over low heat until melted and hot. Pour hot sauce over baked nockerln; serve at once with **chocolate** and, if desired, **whipped cream.**

Russian Cream

PREPARATION TIME: 15 to 20 minutes
CHILLING TIME: At least 4 hours
PER SERVING: 257 calories, 3 grams protein, 22 grams carbohydrate, 18 grams total fat, 52 milligrams cholesterol, 34 milligrams sodium

Snowy white and smooth as velvet, this dessert is named for its flavor resemblance to paskha *(page 177), Russia's homemade cheese. If made with whipping cream, it tastes richer and more mellow; made with half-and-half, it has a tangier flavor. Either version is a cool, refreshing spread to enjoy with whole strawberries and crisp cookies or crackers.*

Makes 8 servings

 ¾ cup sugar
 1 envelope unflavored gelatin
 ½ cup water
 1 cup whipping cream, half-and-half, or light cream
 1½ cups sour cream
 1 teaspoon vanilla
 Strawberries
 Crisp vanilla or lemon-flavored cookies (optional)

In a 2- to 4-cup pan, blend sugar and gelatin. Stir in water; let stand for about 5 minutes to soften gelatin. Then bring to a rolling boil over high heat, stirring constantly. Remove from heat and stir in whipping cream. In a bowl, mix sour cream with vanilla, then gradually whisk in hot sugar mixture.

To make individual desserts, pour cream equally into 8 small serving dishes or 8 (½-cup) metal molds. Or pour mixture into a 4-cup metal mold. Cover and refrigerate until set, at least 4 hours or until next day.

Serve cream in bowls, or unmold onto a serving plate or individual plates. To unmold, dip container up to rim in hot-to-touch tap water until edges of cream just begin to liquefy; it takes only a few seconds. Quickly dry mold and invert it onto a serving dish (or dishes). The cream will slowly slip free; if it's stubborn, return it briefly to hot water bath. If you unmold dessert before serving time, return it to refrigerator until surface has firmed, then cover lightly.

Accompany cream with strawberries and cookies, if desired. Eat with a spoon, or mound cream onto cookies and top each bite with a berry.

Zabaglione

PREPARATION TIME: About 5 minutes
COOKING TIME: About 5 minutes
PER SERVING: 86 calories, 3 grams protein, 6 grams carbohydrate, 6 grams total fat, 272 milligrams cholesterol, 9 milligrams sodium

Nothing dramatizes dinner quite like the showy performance of whisking zabaglione right at the table, in its own pan, over a hot, denatured alcohol flame. Simply pour the frothy result into stemmed glasses, then serve. The dessert can be made with a number of different wines; you can also use anisette, if you like.

Makes 6 to 8 servings

 8 large egg yolks
 3 to 4 tablespoons sugar
 ½ cup dry Sauterne, Sauternes (sweet), dry Semillon, Malvasia Bianca, Marsala, Madeira, or sweet Muscatel

In a round-bottomed pan or in the top of a double boiler, beat together egg yolks, 3 tablespoons of the sugar, and wine. Place pan over direct heat; set double boiler over simmering water. Beat mixture with a whisk until it briefly holds a slight peak when whisk is withdrawn, about 5 minutes.

Taste; if desired, whisk in 1 tablespoon more sugar. Pour into stemmed glasses; serve at once.

ANISETTE ZABAGLIONE
Follow directions for **Zabaglione,** using dry Sauterne or dry Semillon. Add 2 teaspoons **anisette** or other anise liqueur and ¼ teaspoon grated **lemon peel** along with the wine.

SHERRY ZABAGLIONE
Follow directions for **Zabaglione,** using dry Sauterne or dry Semillon; add 1 tablespoon **sherry.**

ZABAGLIONE WITH CREAM
Prepare **Zabaglione** or either of the variations above. To serve, spoon a little cold **sweetened whipped cream** into the bottom of each stemmed glass; fill glasses with hot zabaglione.

Chocolate-striped Oranges

PREPARATION TIME: 15 to 20 minutes
PER SERVING: 250 calories, 2 grams protein, 28 grams carbohydrate, 17 grams total fat, 2 milligrams cholesterol, 10 milligrams sodium

Winter is prime time for big, beautiful navel oranges. And here they earn their stripes as a first-class dessert. Partially coated in dark chocolate, orange segments are then drizzled with white—making an ideal refreshment for those torn between virtue and indulgence.

Makes 6 to 8 servings

 2 large navel oranges
 8 ounces semisweet chocolate, chopped
 About 2 tablespoons solid vegetable shortening
 3 ounces white chocolate (or white pastel coating), coarsely chopped

Carefully peel oranges and separate into segments without breaking membrane. Pull off all loose pith and white fibers.

In the top of a narrow double boiler over water just below simmering, combine semisweet chocolate and 1 teaspoon of the shortening. When chocolate begins to soften, stir until smooth. Remove from heat but keep over hot water.

Tilt pan to make deepest pool of chocolate possible. Dip 1 end of each orange segment into chocolate, coating half the segment. Set segments upright, spaced well apart, on a tray lined with wax paper. Refrigerate just to firm chocolate, about 10 minutes. Save remaining chocolate for other uses.

Wash and dry top of double boiler; add white chocolate and ½ teaspoon of the shortening. Set over water just below simmering; when chocolate softens, stir until smooth. If needed, stir in up to 1½ tablespoons shortening to achieve drizzling consistency. Remove from heat but keep over hot water.

Hold each orange segment by uncoated end over white chocolate; dip fork tines into white chocolate, then drizzle in a quick, steady motion over dark chocolate to make thin stripes. Return segments to tray.

Refrigerate just to firm; serve, or cover loosely with plastic wrap and refrigerate for up to 4 hours.

Plums in Port

WESTERN CLASSIC

PREPARATION TIME: 5 to 10 minutes
COOKING TIME: About 10 minutes
CHILLING TIME: At least 1 hour
PER SERVING: 213 calories, 2 grams protein, 56 grams carbohydrate, .58 gram total fat, 0 milligram cholesterol, 3 milligrams sodium

One of the treasures of late summer and autumn is the Western purple prune plum. The raw fruit is blue-purple in color, with yellow flesh that's sweet—almost bland— in flavor. But with cooking, the skin turns red; the flesh turns succulent and pleasantly tart. Here, the little plums blend beautifully with port in a sumptuous offering for brunch or dinner.

Makes 6 to 8 servings

> 1 (½-inch-thick) slice cut from center of 1 medium-size orange
> 6 whole cloves
> 4 cups prune plums, *each* slashed on 1 side to pit
> 1 cup port
> ½ cup sugar
> 1 cinnamon stick (3 to 4 inches long), broken into smaller pieces
> Sour cream (optional)

Cut orange slice into quarters; stud pieces with cloves. In a 3- to 4-quart pan, combine orange pieces, plums, port, sugar, and cinnamon stick. Bring to a boil; then reduce heat and simmer, uncovered, until fruit just begins to soften, about 10 minutes. (Time varies with size and ripeness of fruit.) Let cool; remove cinnamon stick and refrigerate plums until cold (flavor becomes richer after 1 or 2 days in the refrigerator). Serve fruit with juices; top with sour cream, if desired.

Wine & Berry Compote

Pictured below

WESTERN CLASSIC

PREPARATION TIME: 15 to 20 minutes
PER SERVING: 271 calories, 2 grams protein, 44 grams carbohydrate, 11 grams total fat, 38 milligrams cholesterol, 53 milligrams sodium

Next best to eating berries warm from the vine may be to dress them up in an old-fashioned compote. Drench them in wine syrup, then spoon over ice cream.

Makes 6 to 8 servings

> 1 to 1½ pounds (4 to 6 cups) mixed berries (strawberries, raspberries, blackberries, blueberries, gooseberries, or red currants)
> 1 cup *each* dry red wine and water
> ¾ cup sugar
> 6 tablespoons lemon juice
> 1 vanilla bean (6 to 7 inches long), split lengthwise; or 1 teaspoon vanilla
> 1½ to 2 pints vanilla ice cream
> Fresh mint sprigs

Hull, remove blossom ends, or stem berries as necessary. Rinse and drain.

In a 4- to 5-quart pan, combine wine, water, sugar, lemon juice, and vanilla bean. Bring to a boil over high heat, stirring until sugar is dissolved; boil, uncovered, until reduced to 1¼ cups (if using vanilla, add at this point).

Remove vanilla bean and scrape seeds into syrup. (Rinse bean, let dry, and save to reuse.) If syrup is made ahead, let cool, then cover and refrigerate for up to 3 weeks. To continue, reheat to a simmer.

Gently stir berries into hot syrup; set aside to cool slightly.

For each serving, place 1 large scoop ice cream in a dessert bowl or rimmed plate. Spoon fruit and syrup around ice cream. Garnish with mint.

Savor the flavors of a Western summer with our sumptuous Wine & Berry Compote (recipe above).

Fresh Raspberry Curd

PREPARATION TIME: About 10 minutes

COOKING TIME: About 10 minutes

CHILLING TIME: About 45 minutes

PER TABLESPOON: 42 calories, .81 gram protein, 2 grams carbohydrate, 4 grams total fat, 42 milligrams cholesterol, 38 milligrams sodium

Intrigued by the sweet-tart lemon curd that Britons spread on biscuits at tea time, Sunset experimented with raspberries and created this similarly smooth and spreadable delight. An elegant tart filling, it also improves poached pears, pineapple slices, toasted English muffins for breakfast, or warm scones for tea.

Makes about 2 cups

> **About 1 cup raspberries**
> 2 **tablespoons lemon juice**
> ½ **cup (¼ lb.) butter or margarine**
> 3 **tablespoons sugar**
> 4 **large eggs**
> **Several drops red food coloring (optional)**

In a food processor or blender, whirl raspberries with lemon juice until puréed. Pour into a fine strainer set over a measuring cup. Stir with a spoon to force pulp through strainer; discard seeds. You need ½ cup raspberry purée.

In a 2- to 3-quart pan over medium heat, melt butter; add raspberry purée, sugar, and eggs. Reduce heat to low and stir constantly with a flexible spatula until sauce is thickened and smooth, about 10 minutes. For a deeper hue, stir in food coloring, a few drops at a time, until mixture is the shade desired. Let cool, then cover and refrigerate until thickened, about 1 hour (or for up to 1 week).

Frozen Fruit Yogurt

PREPARATION TIME: About 1 hour

FREEZING TIME: 20 to 30 minutes

PER ½-CUP SERVING OF APRICOT-ORANGE YOGURT: 110 calories, 4 grams protein, 21 grams carbohydrate, 1 gram total fat, 29 milligrams cholesterol, 64 milligrams sodium

With fewer calories than ice cream, smooth and tangy frozen yogurt has won a widespread following in the West. Freshly homemade (in an electric or hand-crank ice cream freezer) and laced with summer fruits, Sunset's frozen yogurt is sure to win you over, too, whether you bother to count calories or not.

Makes 1 gallon

> **Sweetened fruit mixture (suggestions follow)**
> 3 **large eggs, separated**
> ¼ **teaspoon cream of tartar**
> ¼ **cup sugar**
> 8 **cups homemade thick yogurt (page 175) or purchased plain yogurt**

Working with ingredients listed under fruit flavor of your choice, combine fruit and sugar (plus honey, if used) in a 3- to 4-quart pan. Bring to a boil, stirring, over high heat. Reduce heat to medium and cook, stirring constantly, until fruit softens and partially disintegrates—1 to 4 minutes, depending on ripeness of fruit. Break up any large pieces with a fork. Remove from heat and stir in citrus juices, spices, and flavorings listed under each flavor version.

Lightly beat egg yolks; stir in about ½ cup of the hot fruit mixture. Then stir yolk mixture back into fruit mixture; let cool to room temperature.

In a large bowl, beat egg whites and cream of tartar with an electric mixer on high speed until whites hold soft peaks. Gradually add the ¼ cup sugar and continue to beat until whites hold stiff peaks.

Spoon yogurt into a 6- to 8-quart bowl; use a wire whisk if necessary to smooth out any lumps. Fold fruit mixture into yogurt until well blended. Add half the egg whites and stir to blend well. Fold in remaining whites.

Pour mixture into 1-gallon container of an ice- and salt-cooled ice cream maker. Use 1 part salt to 4 parts ice; freeze until crank is hard to turn or until machine shuts off. (Or use a self-refrigerated ice cream maker; if freezer container is too small to hold all the yogurt mixture, freeze it in batches, keeping unfrozen yogurt mixture in the refrigerator. Transfer frozen yogurt to freezer as prepared; cover.)

Serve yogurt softly frozen (remove dasher). Or, to firm and mellow yogurt, cover container with plastic wrap, then with lid; repack with 1 part salt to 4 parts ice, cover with several heavy cloths, and let stand for 1 to 2 hours. (Or place covered self-refrigerated container in freezer for 1 to 2 hours.) Serve or store in freezer; for best flavor and texture, use within 3 weeks.

SWEETENED FRUIT MIXTURES. Any of the following will flavor a full recipe of frozen yogurt.

Apricot-orange. Use 4 cups thinly sliced unpeeled ripe **apricots,** 2 cups **sugar,** 2 tablespoons **lemon juice,** ½ cup **orange juice,** 1 teaspoon grated **orange peel,** and 4 teaspoons **vanilla.**

Banana-honey. Measure 4 cups thinly sliced ripe **bananas,** then coarsely mash them. Also use 1¼ cups **sugar,** ¾ cup **honey,** 3 tablespoons **lemon juice,** and 2 tablespoons **vanilla.**

Blackberry. Use 4 cups lightly packed **blackberries** (fresh or thawed unsweetened frozen), 2 cups **sugar,** and 4 teaspoons *each* **lemon juice** and **vanilla.**

Blueberry. Use 4 cups **blueberries** (fresh or thawed unsweetened frozen), 1¾ cups **sugar,** 2 tablespoons **lemon juice,** and 1 tablespoon **vanilla.**

Papaya. Coarsely mash enough peeled and seeded **papayas** to make 2½ cups purée (about 3 medium-size papayas). Also use 2 cups **sugar,** 2 teaspoons **vanilla,** and ¼ cup **lime juice.**

Peach. Use 4 cups sliced peeled **peaches,** 2 cups firmly packed **brown sugar,** 3 tablespoons **lemon juice,** 2 tablespoons **vanilla,** and ¾ teaspoon *each* **ground nutmeg** and **ground cinnamon.**

Raspberry. Use 4 cups **raspberries** (fresh or thawed unsweetened frozen), 2 cups **sugar,** and 4 teaspoons *each* **lemon juice** and **vanilla.**

Tofu + Gelato = Tofulato

What happens when Japanese tofu meets Italy's gelato? Suddenly, tofulato tops everyone's cone. Combining the best of both parents, the delectable frozen dessert is at once low-fat, creamy, and intensely flavored. You can adjust its richness according to the dairy ingredient you choose (options are given below). For example, ½ cup of vanilla tofulato made with buttermilk has about 109 calories; with whole milk, the same portion has about 122 calories; and with whipping cream, about 222 calories (plus the creamiest texture).

Once it's out of the freezer, tofulato melts quickly; add gelatin, if you like, to keep it firmer longer.

Vanilla Tofulato

1 envelope unflavored gelatin (optional)

⅓ cup water (optional)

⅔ cup sugar

1 package (1 lb.) soft tofu, drained (2 cups)

1½ cups buttermilk, plain yogurt, whole milk, or whipping cream

⅓ cup whipping cream

2 teaspoons vanilla

Additional flavoring (suggestions follow), optional

If using gelatin, sprinkle over water in a 1- to 2-cup pan and let stand for 5 minutes to soften. Add sugar; stir over medium heat until gelatin is completely dissolved.

In a food processor or blender, whirl gelatin-sugar mixture (or just sugar, if not using gelatin) and tofu until smooth. Stir mixture into buttermilk, adding the ⅓ cup whipping cream, vanilla, and, if desired, additional flavoring. Pour into 1-quart or larger container of a self-refrigerated or ice- and salt-cooled ice cream maker (use 1 part salt to 6 parts ice). Crank or process according to manufacturer's directions until tofulato is softly frozen and hard to mix, then serve (remove dasher).

Or, to firm and mellow tofulato, cover and freeze for 1 to 2 hours. Or cover ice- and salt-cooled container with plastic wrap, then with lid; re-

It's simply a cool way to sweeten summer.

pack with 1 part salt to 4 parts ice, cover with several heavy cloths, and let stand for 1 to 2 hours. Serve, or store in freezer; for best flavor and texture, use within 3 weeks.

To make hard-frozen tofulato easier to scoop, let it soften at room temperature (about 30 minutes for a full batch). Makes about 1 quart.

ADDITIONAL FLAVORING. Vanilla tofulato can be flavored in many ways. Choose from the following. Variations made without dairy ingredients yield only 2½ to 3 cups.

Nondairy Vanilla Tofulato. Prepare **Vanilla Tofulato**, but omit all dairy ingredients.

Banana Tofulato. Prepare **Vanilla Tofulato**, using buttermilk or yogurt and the ⅓ cup whipping cream. Add ⅓ cup mashed ripe **banana**.

Ginger or Ginger-Banana Tofulato. Prepare **Vanilla Tofulato**, using buttermilk or yogurt and the ⅓ cup whipping cream. Add ⅓ cup chopped **crystallized ginger** (plus ⅓ cup mashed ripe **banana** for ginger-banana flavor).

Carob Tofulato. Melt ½ cup chopped **carob** over lowest heat in a 6- to 8-inch frying pan, stirring constantly. Prepare **Vanilla Tofulato**, using milk and the ⅓ cup whipping cream (or omit dairy products); whirl in melted carob.

Chilly Chile Tofulato. Beat ½ cup **red, green, or yellow jalapeño jelly** until smooth and whirl in as flavoring for **Vanilla Tofulato;** make with buttermilk or yogurt and the ⅓ cup whipping cream.

Hazelnut Praline Tofulato. Combine 1 cup **sugar and ½ cup hazelnuts** in a 10- to 12-inch frying pan. Cook over medium-high heat, stirring, until sugar melts and turns pale golden; sugar will firm at first, then melt with continued heat.

Pour hot melted sugar mixture onto a well-buttered piece of foil (about 12 by 15 inches). Let cool until hard, at least 30 minutes. Pull praline off foil. Break into chunks about 2 inches square and put into a food processor; or make chunks about 1 inch square and put into a blender. Whirl until praline pieces are about the size of rock salt.

Prepare **Vanilla Tofulato,** using milk and the ⅓ cup whipping cream (or omit dairy products); add praline pieces.

Fresh Berry Tofulato. Purée 1½ cups **berries** (strawberries, raspberries, ollalieberries, boysenberries, or blueberries) with 3 tablespoons **sugar;** if desired, rub purée through a fine strainer and discard seeds.

In a 2- to 3-quart pan, bring purée to a boil. Reduce heat to maintain a gentle boil and cook, uncovered, until fruit is reduced to ½ cup, about 20 minutes, stirring often. Stir in 2 teaspoons **lemon juice.**

Prepare **Vanilla Tofulato,** using buttermilk or yogurt and the ⅓ cup whipping cream; add berry purée.

Malt or Malt-Banana Tofulato. Prepare **Vanilla Tofulato,** using milk and the ⅓ cup whipping cream (if making malt-banana, you can omit the dairy products); whirl in ½ cup **unflavored malted milk powder** (plus ⅓ cup mashed ripe **banana** for malt-banana flavor).

Chocolate Malt Tofulato. Melt 1 cup **semisweet chocolate chips** or chopped semisweet chocolate (6 oz.) in a 6- to 8-inch frying pan over very low heat, stirring constantly.

Prepare **Malt or Malt-Banana Tofulato** (above), with or without dairy products, and whirl in melted chocolate.

Fresh Berry Ice

Pictured below

PREPARATION TIME: 5 to 10 minutes

FREEZING TIME: At least 4 hours

PER ½-CUP SERVING OF STRAWBERRY ICE: 82 calories, .52 gram protein, 20 grams carbohydrate, .32 gram total fat, 0 milligram cholesterol, 1 milligram sodium

Easier to make since the advent of food processors, fresh fruit ices offer festivity without many calories. Try our berry ice, then experiment with other fruit flavors.

Makes about 3½ cups strawberry ice, 3 cups raspberry ice

>   **4 cups hulled strawberries or raspberries**
>   **½ cup water**
>   **1 tablespoon lemon juice**
>   **About ½ cup sugar**

In a food processor or blender, whirl berries until smoothly puréed. Rub through a fine strainer; discard seeds. In blender, combine berry purée, water, and lemon juice; sweeten to taste with sugar. Whirl until sugar is dissolved, about 5 seconds, then pour into a shallow metal pan, cover, and freeze until solid.

Remove ice from freezer and break into chunks with a heavy spoon. In a food processor, whirl about ⅓ of the ice at a time, using on-off bursts at first to break up ice. Then process continuously until you have a velvety slush. (Or place all ice in a large bowl and continue to smash into small pieces with a heavy spoon. Then beat with an electric mixer until smooth, beating slowly at first, then gradually increasing mixer speed.) Pour into a bowl, cover, and freeze for at least 1 hour (or for up to 3 weeks; after 3 weeks, flavor and texture begin to deteriorate).

Or pour unfrozen mixture into a self-refrigerated ice cream maker; freeze according to manufacturer's directions until softly frozen.

Let ice soften at room temperature for about 10 minutes before scooping out portions; serve in clear glasses for the prettiest presentation.

Long popular in Europe, intensely flavored strawberry, pineapple, and papaya ices bring hot summer days to a cool and sophisticated close. The recipe for fruit ices begins on this page.

PINEAPPLE ICE

Peel and core 1 medium-size ripe **pineapple** (about 4 lbs.), then cut into chunks. In a food processor or blender, whirl half the chunks at a time until puréed; you should have 4 cups *total*. Pour purée into a bowl and stir in 1 cup **water** and 2 tablespoons **lemon juice;** sweeten to taste with about ⅓ cup **sugar.** Freeze and serve as directed for **Fresh Berry Ice.** Makes about 5 cups.

PAPAYA ICE

Peel 2 medium-size ripe **papayas** (about 1 lb. *each*). Cut in half, remove seeds, and cut into chunks. In a food processor or blender, whirl papaya until puréed; you should have 2 cups. Add 3 tablespoons **lime or lemon juice** and ½ cup **water,** then sweeten to taste with about ¼ cup **sugar** or honey. Whirl until sugar is dissolved, then freeze and serve as directed for **Fresh Berry Ice.** Makes about 3 cups.

LEMON ICE

Use a vegetable peeler to remove the colored outer part of peel from 1 small **lemon;** cut into ½-inch pieces. In a food processor or blender, whirl peel with 1 cup **sugar** until finely chopped. Add 1 cup **very hot water** and whirl for about 10 seconds to dissolve sugar. Add 3 cups **cold water** and ⅔ cup **lemon juice.** Whirl to blend, then freeze and serve as directed for **Fresh Berry Ice.** Makes about 5 cups.

Gelato (Italian Ice Cream)

PREPARATION TIME: About 1½ hours
FREEZING TIME: 20 to 30 minutes
PER ½-CUP SERVING OF VANILLA GELATO: 121 calories, 5 grams protein, 16 grams carbohydrate, 5 grams total fat, 145 milligrams cholesterol, 34 milligrams sodium

What's the difference between Italy's gelato and American ice cream? While many ice creams are judged by their degree of richness, gelato—made with a lighter milk custard base—is ranked by its intensity of flavor. Other than that, though, both frozen desserts are made in the same way.

Makes about 1½ quarts

   3 cups milk
   ¾ cup sugar
   **½ vanilla bean (2- to 3-inch piece);
     or 1 teaspoon vanilla**
   **3 thin strips lemon peel (colored outer part
     only),** *each* **about 2 inches long**
   **6 large egg yolks
   Flavorings (choices follow)**

In a 3- to 4-quart pan, combine milk, sugar, vanilla bean (if using vanilla, add later, as directed), and lemon peel. Stir over medium heat just until sugar is dissolved.

Place egg yolks in a bowl. Gradually whisk in 1 cup of the warm milk mixture; then pour egg mixture into pan, stirring. Continue to cook, stirring with a flexible spatula, until liquid coats the back of a metal spoon in a thin, even, smooth layer; this takes about 10 minutes (do not scald or custard will curdle).

Pour mixture through a fine strainer into a large bowl; discard lemon peel. Rinse vanilla bean, let dry, and reserve for other uses. If you did not use vanilla bean, add vanilla at this point.

Let gelato base cool to room temperature before using; or cover and refrigerate for up to 3 days.

In a large bowl, smoothly stir 1 cup of the gelato base into the hazelnut, almond, chocolate, or banana flavoring (vanilla is incorporated as the gelato base is prepared; see following). Then gradually stir in remaining gelato base.

Pour into container of a self-refrigerated or ice- and salt-cooled ice cream maker (use 1 part salt to 8 parts ice). Process or crank according to manufacturer's directions until gelato is softly frozen and hard to mix, then serve (remove dasher).

Or, to firm and mellow gelato, cover and freeze for 1 to 2 hours. Or cover ice- and salt-cooled container with plastic wrap, then with lid; repack with 1 part salt to 4 parts ice, cover with several heavy cloths, and let stand for 1 to 2 hours. Serve or store in freezer; for best flavor and texture, use within 1 month.

To make hard-frozen gelato easier to scoop, let it soften slightly at room temperature (about 10 minutes for a full batch).

FLAVORINGS. Vanilla flavor is added as you cook the gelato base. Chocolate and banana flavorings must be used at once, so be sure to make and cool the gelato base *before* you prepare these flavorings.

Almond. Spread 1 cup sliced **almonds** in a 9- or 10-inch-wide baking pan. Toast in a 350° oven until golden, about 8 minutes; shake pan occasionally. Whirl nuts in a food processor or blender along with ¼ cup crushed **almond macaroons** until mixture forms a smooth paste. If made ahead, cover and refrigerate for up to 1 week; bring to room temperature to use.

Banana. Smoothly mash or purée 3 medium-size ripe bananas with 3 tablespoons lemon juice. Use at once.

Chocolate. With a fork, stir ½ cup **strong hot coffee** into about 2¼ cups grated or finely chopped **semisweet chocolate** and 1 cup (3 oz.) **unsweetened cocoa** until chocolate is melted. Use at once.

Hazelnut. Spread 1½ cups whole **hazelnuts** or large pieces in a 10- by 15-inch rimmed baking pan. Bake in a 350° oven until nuts are lightly browned beneath skins, about 15 minutes. Let cool slightly, then pour onto a clean towel. Fold towel to enclose and rub nuts between your hands to remove as much of skins as possible. Lift nuts from towel and place in a food processor or blender. Whirl until nuts form a smooth paste. If made ahead, cover and refrigerate for up to 1 week; bring to room temperature to use.

Vanilla. Use 2 whole **vanilla beans** (*each* about 6 inches long) in gelato base instead of ½ bean; split beans lengthwise and, with a knife, scrape seeds from pod. Add seeds and pod to milk as directed. (To substitute vanilla extract, omit vanilla bean and add 1 tablespoon vanilla after straining instead of 1 teaspoon.) Makes about 1 quart.

Index of Western Classics

Recipes You Can Make in 45 Minutes or Less

General Index